PIMLICO

61

SCOTLAND

Michael Lynch, who was born in Aberdeen and is a graduate of the Universities of Aberdeen and London, has taught in the University of Wales and is now Senior Lecturer in the Department of Scottish History at the University of Edinburgh. He has published books on Edinburgh and the Reformation, Mary, Queen of Scots, and Scottish burghs in both the medieval and early modern periods, as well as articles on a range of topics from intellectual to economic history. He is past editor of the ecclesiastical history journal, *The Innes Review*, and literary editor of the Scottish History Society.

SCOTLAND

A New History

MICHAEL LYNCH

PIMLICO

To Brigid, James and Deobrah

PIMLICO
20 Vauxhall Bridge Road, London SW1V 2SA

London Melbourne Sydney Auckland Johannesburg
and agencies throughout the world

First published by Century Ltd 1991
Pimlico edition, published with revisions, 1992
Reprinted 1992, 1993, 1994 (twice), 1995 (twice), 1996,
1997 (twice), 1998

Filmset by SX Composing Ltd, Rayleigh, Essex
Printed and bound in Great Britain by
Mackays of Chatham PLC, Chatham, Kent

ISBN 0-7126-9893-0

CONTENTS

ILLUSTRATIONS

Sources of Illustrations

Maps

*These maps are reproduced from *An Historical Atlas of Scotland c.400-c.1600*,
edited by Peter McNeill and Ranald Nicholson, with the permission of the
Trustees of the Conference of Scottish Medievalists.

Acknowledgements

In a book which has taken so long as this has to write my debts are many. My particular thanks go to Owen Dudley Edwards, whose idea it first was, and to Euan Cameron of Century, who as editor has been a model of tact and the art of gentle persuasion throughout. The publishers are to be warmly thanked for agreeing that the first full-length one-volume history of Scotland to appear for over twenty years should have full reference notes, to reflect the work which has appeared since then. I am most grateful to Duncan McAra, whose contribution as an editorial consultant has been invaluable. My thanks also go to the staff of Edinburgh University Library and of the National Library of Scotland, who have been both courteous and efficient in their dealings with a demanding reader. I owe an especial debt to the staff of the Computer Services Department of Edinburgh University for their work in translation of disks of the text and to Ray Harris for his drawing of four of the maps. I also have pleasure in acknowledging with thanks the permission of the Trustees of the Conference of Scottish Medievalists to reproduce three of the maps.

In the time which I have spent teaching and studying Scottish history at Edinburgh University, I have benefited immeasurably from the help, advice and scholarship of my colleagues, both within the Department of Scottish History and beyond. Professor Geoffrey Barrow and Dr John Durkan have both been inexhaustible providers of answers to a barrage of queries, always given with their matchless grace and good humour. Dr John Bannerman, Dr David Brown, Dr Richard Finlay, Dr Julian Goodare, Dr Norman Macdougall and John Simpson have all been unfailingly generous with their time and have read substantial parts of the text. Errors of fact or interpretation which remain are indelibly my own. Dr Frank Bardgett, Dr James Brown, Charles Burnett, Dr Helen Dingwall, Dr Mark Loughlin, Professor Alasdair MacDonald, Dr Maureen Meikle, Dr Pat Torrie, Dr Michael Yellowlees and Dr Allan White OP will all recognise where they have influenced this book and I am glad to acknowledge a special debt to them. Mrs Doris Williamson has played a vital role in protecting a harassed author from his own inefficiencies; without her consistent help this book would not have been written.

Thanks are due to Margaret Moore and Martin Hilland, who provided a haven for me to think about medieval Scotland. A last, great debt is to my wife, Maureen, and my children, who have had to endure a long journey through the many centuries of Scottish history. It has kept me from them too often and too long. The dedication of the book is a token repayment.

MICHAEL LYNCH

Preface

The potential contents of a book which tries to cover the history of a nation are vast. The basic approach of this book is chronological, but individual chapters have been set aside to deal adequately with topics such as the Columban mission, the medieval Church and the Highlands in the time of the Clearances. Also, the first chapter in each of the five parts of the book attempts an overview of some aspects of the period with which it deals: in Part I the physical evidence is used to explore some of the enigmas of the period; in Part II the different layers of medieval society are examined; in Part III the combined effects of the price rise, the secularisation of kirklands and the growth of Edinburgh in the century of the Reformation are assessed; in Part IV a seventeenth-century renaissance and the rise of a new, self-confident 'middling sort' of lairds and professions is suggested as the backdrop to a century of revolution, war and Union; and in Part V the confusing shifts in how Scots thought of themselves in the period between Culloden and the end of the Victorian age is a prelude to analysis of the rapid changes which overtook Scottish society in the age of the Industrial Revolution, the rise of the cities and the new politics after the Reform Acts. In these and other chapters, sub-headings have been used to suggest the approach taken as well as the subject matter. The extensive reference notes are intended both as an aid to study and as a guide to further literature on the subject.

Conventions and Abbreviations

All sums of money are in £ Scots unless otherwise stated; a merk was two-thirds of a £. With dates the year is deemed to have begun on 1 January. Names have generally been modernised. In the Notes, the place of publication of books has been given at their first citation, unless it was Edinburgh. Thereafter, short references are given, usually giving textbooks as *Scotland*. The following abbreviations have been used in the notes; they follow the guidelines laid down in the 'List of Abbreviated Titles of the Printed Sources of Scottish History to 1560', *SHR* xlii (1963), which is an invaluable bibliography in itself.

APS	*The Acts of the Parliaments of Scotland*, eds. T. Thomson and C. Innes (1814-75)
Atlas	P.G.B. McNeill and R. Nicholson (eds.), *An Historical Atlas of Scotland, c.400-c.1600* (St Andrews, 1974)
Atlas II	P.G.B. McNeill (ed.), *An Atlas of Scottish History to 1707* (1993)
BUK	*Acts and Proceedings of the General Assembly of the Kirk of Scotland*, ed. T. Thomson (Bann. Club, 1839-45)
Exch. Rolls	*The Exchequer Rolls of Scotland*, eds. J. Stuart *et al.* (1878-1908)
HMC	Historical Manuscripts Commission

IR	*The Innes Review*
PSAS	*Procs. of the Society of Antiquaries of Scotland*
RSCHS	*Records of Scottish Church History Society*
SESH	*Scottish Economic and Social History*
SHR	*Scottish Historical Review*
SHS	Scottish History Society
SRS	Scottish Record Society
STS	Scottish Text Society

Note to the Pimlico Edition

In this edition, the opportunity has been taken to make various corrections and amplifications, often in response to points made by colleagues, readers and reviewers. My thanks go to all of them. A more extensive Bibliography has also been added.

April 1992

INTRODUCTION

Albanaich! The war-cry of the men of Alba, heard in battle against Viking invaders in 903, was repeated over two centuries later at the Battle of the Standard. There David I, King of Scots, led an extraordinary army made up of all the peoples of his kingdom – including French, Anglo-Norman and Fleming settlers, Cumbrians and Galwegians as well as Scots. It was testimony to two facts: before there was a kingdom, in the sense of a consolidated territory, there was a people and an intensely felt pride in being Scots; and this was an emotion which was shared by the 'new' Scots, who fought for David I in 1138, as well as by the descendants of the Scots of Dalriada who had given their name to the kingdom.

We arra peepull! is the strange, defiant cry heard from some of Scotland's football terraces in the late twentieth century. But which people? A foreign visitor might well feel confused. Unlike England, which has two national anthems, both products of mid-eighteenth century xenophobia, or Wales which has one, written in Welsh as part of a nationalist revival in the nineteenth century, Scotland has none – although that may be changing. The adoption by such a conservative Scottish institution as the Scottish Rugby Union, of 'Flower of Scotland' was a striking gesture to popular sentiment – or sentimentality. The emergence of this modern song, which was far less popular when it was first written because it was then closely associated with the Scottish National Party, is testimony to the gap which tends to exist within Scottish patriotism between culture and politics.

In lieu of an anthem, this visitor would see that Scotland has not one national flag but two – the red and yellow of the lion rampant and the blue and white of the saltire. They illustrate neatly the double thread which for centuries ran side by side through Scottish history. The Scots were held together both by their long line of Kings and by the Church. When the Scots defended Stirling Castle against an English invader in 1304, they did so – even though they did not have a king – for the 'Lion', the symbol of Scottish kingship. In 1385, an act of parliament enjoined every man in the Scottish army to wear a cross of St Andrew, symbolic of the fact that the independence of kingdom and people was intertwined with that of the Church. By the seventeenth century, however, these two defenders of Scottish nationhood – King and Kirk – had begun to travel in different directions. James VI, who claimed to be 107th in a line of Kings of Scots, tried, after he succeeded to the throne of England in 1603, to become a British king – and failed. A new, Protestant Church Militant came to represent not only Scottish independence but the preservation of the 'auld estate' – despite the fact that it also threatened revolution.

On other football terraces, the same visitor might see different flags, including a saltire, blended with two other flags to create a flag symbolising a British union. That flag, the Union Jack, however, is used on terraces such as Ibrox Park, Glasgow, home of Rangers, to demonstrate the group solidarity of one section of Scottish society, which fused an immigrant Irish Protestant community with a native Covenanting tradition, rather than its embrace of a union of the kingdoms and peoples of the British Isles. The flag of Union is a highly misleading piece of historical evidence, for the compelling unity of the Scots behind it belonged not to the century after the Union of Crowns in 1603 when it was first devised, nor to the century after the Union of Parliaments in 1707; it was part of the rapturous embrace made by Scots, not of Britain, but of a British Empire, which opened up in the 1780s and disappeared after 1945.

On another terracing in Glasgow, the display of an Irish flag is symbolic of the massive influx of Catholic Irish immigrants, despite the facts that it was past its peak over a century ago and soccer was for a long time after 1892 regarded by the Irish themselves as an 'unIrish' game. These 'new' Scots of the nineteenth century, who accounted for probably a third of the population of Glasgow in the 1840s, were only one of a series of groups of immigrants who have made up the Scottish people over its history. The Scots of Dalriada, who came from Antrim in the sixth century, the Norsemen who settled in the Northern and Western Isles in the ninth and tenth centuries, and the Normans and Flemings who arrived in the twelfth century all integrated into existing society rather than conquering it. In 903, the crozier of Columba, patron saint of Dalriada, was carried into battle, evidence of the process by which the culture of a pan-Celtic people which stretched across the Irish Sea – the Scots of Dalriada – had linked up with that of another, the Picts, who had long controlled much of the mainland of present-day Scotland north of the formidable natural barrier of the Firth of Forth. In 1314, Robert Bruce, descendant of a Norman settler family, took not only the saltire, the symbolic cross of St Andrew, to the battlefield of Bannockburn, but the *Brecbennach* of Columba as well; he led both a feudal host and a 'common army of Scotland', which traced its loyalties to Kings of Scots back to a period long before feudalism. The different peoples of Scotland – who variously spoke French, Scots and Gaelic – were united by their differences. It is a fine judgement as to whether the same could be said about present-day Scottish society.

Before the battle of Flodden in 1513, a Gaelic bard urged 'Gael' and 'Gall', Highlander and Lowlander, to unite against the Saxon English. For centuries, more things had linked Highlands and Lowlands than set them apart. There was little difference in the medieval period between 'clan' society and the rest of Scotland, where the social fabric was bound together by kinship. After acquiring lands in the Highlands, Norman settler families – not least the Stewarts – had become naturalised rather than importing foreign ways. Nobles, the Church and Kings were all part of a hybrid society. By 1400 a double-edged relationship between Highlands and Lowlands had begun to emerge as well as a 'Highland line'. A sense of separateness grew up, more strongly felt in the Lowlands, between the 'wild Scots', a pan-Celtic people whose language and culture linked them to Gaelic-speaking peoples on the other side of the Irish Sea, and the 'domestic' Scots of the Lowlands. Gaelic, which had formerly been 'Scottish speech', was overtaken by a brand of English, which had been called 'Teutonic speech' and now became known as 'Scots'. It fast became the language of the court and government and Lowland society. The Reformation hastened the process by which Gaels became a race apart, 'uncivilised', 'troublesome' and 'ungodly', but the troubles of the period between 1637 and 1746 – the crisis of the three kingdoms – showed the Highlands to be prominent in their support for the Stewarts, if on their own ambiguous terms. After a period following the last, very Highland Jacobite rising, which ended at Culloden in 1746, the Highlands were embraced in the nineteenth century by a British monarchy and Scottish Lowland society which were both in search of a cultural identity; tartan and bagpipes, stigmata of a defeated Gaelic culture, became new symbols of a wider Scottishness. Scotland was conjoined again.

Scottish history and the historians

More Scottish history has been written since 1960 than in any generation before it. Although Scotland, until the introduction of the Standard Grade syllabus in 1990, was one of the few countries in Europe where a nation's own history was not a compulsory part of the history curriculum in its schools, a resurgence of interest in its past took place in the 1970s, partly the result of the prospect of a Scottish Assembly. That revival has not only survived the happenings of 1979, when devolution was approved in a Referendum of the Scottish people but not by the majority demanded, but increased. Local history, encouraged by the formation in 1982 of an umbrella organisation, the Scottish Local History Forum, is flourishing. Popular history, seen at its best in the works of distinguished and avowedly populist historians such as Ian Grimble and John Prebble, is booming. The work of a generation of academic historians has led one American observer to write of a second Enlightenment. Since the appearance of the last full, single-volume history of Scotland, in 1970,[1] the output of academic work – in articles, sets of essays and PhDs as well as in books – has been enormous. Two of the best results have been an eight-volume series spanning twenty centuries and a three-volume series focusing on Scottish society since 1760.[2]

These are different kinds of history, and their practitioners tend to operate in separate worlds. The sheer volume and pace of academic work threatens to open up a gulf separating it from the other circles of Scottish history. This book is an attempt to help close some of that gap. As a one-volume history of a nation, it also has an impossible task to perform. At the risk of over-simplification, it tries to stress the over-arching continuities which give coherence to that story rather than the seeming watersheds in it – which can stem both from popular history's pursuit of 'great Scots' and academic history's natural instinct to periodise and pidgeon-hole. At stake is the real history of Scotland, ever under threat from calculated manipulation by one of its own main industries – tourism.

'Who controls the past controls the future; who controls the present controls the past,' wrote George Orwell in *Nineteen Eighty-Four*. Historians have been for centuries the guardians of the national past. King-lists devised in the twelfth and thirteenth centuries still govern our perception of kings of the ninth century: some histories of Scotland begin with Kenneth mac Alpin (843-58), for no better reason than that he was described by later medieval chroniclers as the first 'King of Scots', which he was not. The deliberate renumbering of monarchs did not begin after 1603, nor has Elizabeth II been the first to be given the wrong numeral. The numbering of kings only from Kenneth onwards means that Constantine, the second Scottish king of that name, has ever since become Constantine I (862-77). Jenny Geddes, symbol of the revolution of a whole people against an anglicising king, was an invention of the nineteenth century, which was in search of historic defenders of the independence of Scotland's Kirk; she was alive in 1637, when the stool was hurled in the High Kirk of St Giles to spark off a revolt against Charles I, but there is no evidence that she threw it.

Such icons in the national memory usually should tell more about those who forged them than historic reality – if the act of creative writing is detected. The laying down of a line of kings was the work of official chroniclers, anxious to stress the continuity of kingship amidst a period marked by new, alien influences – David I had been brought up in England; his grandsons who succeeded him, Malcolm IV and William the Lion, were half-French. All needed to be portrayed as Celtic kings as well as feudal monarchs. Jenny Geddes was pressed into service along with John Knox and Andrew Melville as part of the battle between different strands of presbyterianism, each claiming to represent the authentic tradition of the Reformation and the Covenants. The fact that Adam Smith and John Buchan have been erected in the present age as spiritual forerunners of modern Conservatism, while a better candidate, Henry Dundas, remains largely unclaimed as the father of the Tory party,[3] is only a recent example of the habit of the present to recycle the past to suit its own needs. At times, however, it is necessary to unravel contemporary and later myth-making. Rob Roy MacGregor, a convenient symbol of tartanry for the modern tourist industry, was a kind of national hero when he died in 1734, almost a century before he was romanticised by Walter Scott. The fame of this cattle dealer turned cattle thief reveals much about the cultural vacuum into which Scottish society had fallen after 1707. No longer held together by the religious nationalism of Kirk and Covenant, but not 'North British' either, Scotland was a society in search of its own identity and so almost any hero would do.

Scotland's history is bestrewn with great heroes and heroines. It is fashionable for historians – and especially some modern historians – to despise them, and to get on with the serious business of telling the history of the Scottish people. Much of the best writing in the past generation has been taken up with showing that 'less happened, and less dramatically, than was once thought'.[4] The 'age of cotton' brought not only the new environment of the cotton mill in the 1790s but spirited resistance to it amongst the skilled sections of the workforce, who managed to delay its full implementation for forty years. The social cost of industrialisation is now far better known. The dramatic history of Highland Clearances now needs to be set against the less dramatic, but no less important story of the earlier, drawn-out and half-hidden history of a clearance of sub-tenants from Lowland farms over the course of the eighteenth century. The continuities of history – which usually include the experience of ordinary people – can now be better set against the process of change, which, for some, is what history is all about.

An odd by-product of the more intensive working of the eighteenth and nineteenth centuries – when records exist which allow that fuller story to be told – has been to reinforce the older notion of a sharp break in Scotland's history. It is usually found somewhere in the later seventeenth century or in the eighteenth. Its precise location varies – school textbooks are prone to begin the history of 'Modern Scotland' c.1750, just before the onset of those twin horses of the apocalypse, the Agricultural and Industrial Revolutions. Some intellectual historians, accepting the propaganda of historians of the new 'enlightened' 1750s, the 'historical age' of David Hume, are prone to date it from the Enlightenment and the discovery of 'modern' ideas. The pursuit of great thinkers has often the effect of shifting concentration towards the dramatic impact they made and away from the storehouse of existing ideas on which they drew. Other historians have found the roots of the Enlightenment in Restoration society after 1660; they are also, it is argued here, to be found in a renaissance of letters which stretched across the whole of the seventeenth century. Economic historians would give different answers – perhaps now more often favouring 1660 rather than 1740 or 1780. A few still cling to the old favourite – the turning-point of 1707 – although the more sophisticated now argue that it was a watershed with a delayed-action fuse: a curious historical device. The view of a sharp break in the eighteenth century is shared even by dedicated Marxist historians, the most distinguished of whom has seen post-Union society as emerging from 'feudal and theological squalor'.[5] But theology did not disappear after 1707. The evangelicals in the Kirk were more numerous than the 'Moderates' in the age of the Enlightenment and religion was still the most important force in Scottish politics in the second half of the nineteenth century. Old habits die very hard in Scotland. The search for a 'modern' age is a deception practised on the facts of history. Few Scottish historians would look to 1600, the point where a recent history of modern Ireland began.[6] There is, however, much to be said for 1600 – or 1603 – as a better starting-point.

Less important than the arbitrary dating of a watershed in Scotland's history is the realisation that in every century in Scottish history until the nineteenth, the forces of continuity outweighed those of change. There was 'Improvement' in the twelfth century as well as the eighteenth; the changes in the twelfth, which altered the map of settlement on the land for six centuries, deserve equal attention. The 'Agricultural Revolution' succeeded most quickly, in areas such as Lothian, where there were no revolutionary changes; here there was a long period stretching back a century or more before the 1780s in which land was enclosed, co-tenancies phased out and crop yields increased by various means. The first phase of the 'Industrial Revolution', which turned Glasgow into a fast-growing textile town, was quite distinct from the second, after 1840: the period before 1840 was the age of domestic industry and the weaving shed as well as of the cotton mill; it was the period after 1840 which saw the unrestricted emergence of the factory, and only that after 1870 which witnessed the appearance of a new skilled workforce, different in structure from before.

A national history needs its heroes, and Scotland is not short of them. The cult of personality – of John Knox, Mary, Queen of Scots, and all that – has had the same effect of chopping Scotland's history into a series of dramatic turning-points, often bestrewn with a good deal of blood or melodrama. The idea that the most important turning-point of all was the Reformation of 1560 – or perhaps the fall of Mary in the revolution of 1567 – is both an important truth and a half-truth. The Reformation came as a shattering change, with the mass, Latin, auricular confession, and much else abolished officially, virtually overnight in 1560. The process of converting Scotland to Protestantism took much longer, and it succeeded most readily where it changed least. The need for symbols – Catholic Queen and Protestant reformer – of a bitter confrontation whose effects still reverberate should not become a vehicle for thinking that the change was inevitable. The success of the Reformation was, in one sense, the result of the sheer hard work of the first two generations of the

Protestant ministry. In another sense, its success depended on the caprice of history; Mary's position was not irrevocable in 1561, when she returned to Scotland, nor was it so even after she was deposed in 1567. Stewart monarchs, such as James II, had a habit of making political come-backs. Scottish monarchs, such as David II and James I, had been held in English prisons before but had returned to resume their rule. Mary was unusual because she did neither.

The high drama of Mary's reign is only one example of where historians have been led into the trap of explaining the history of events before they happened. Rationalisation of the tangled events of 1561-7 as the story of a 'tragic queen' – or alternatively that of a tragic-comic incompetent – lends a spurious inevitability to the outcome. An alternative reading of the reign might stress that Mary's position was never more promising than in 1566, the year of the Riccio murder. If that interpretation is right, it suggests that even in the most heavily trampled ground of Scottish history historians need to read events forwards as contemporaries saw and reacted to them, rather than backwards from the point the ultimate result is known. If Mary's fall in 1567 was both sudden and *unexpected*, the bitter civil war which followed it is more easily explained. It also explains why propagandists of the new regime, suddenly swept to power, needed to rewrite history – the Casket Letters and George Buchanan's monumental *History of Scotland*, published in 1582, the most influential work ever written in Scottish history, were the result. They are with us still.

It was the unforeseen element in the revolution of 1567 which provoked the painful period of adjustment which followed it. The same could be said of the Union of 1707. The debate over the causes and consequences of the Union of 1707 has been skewed by a focus on its 'inevitability'. The political jobbery which was needed to ease the passage of the Treaty is well known, although the activities of some of the chief actors remain mysterious. So fundamental has the Union become to the expectations of Scottish society since 1707 that it has only recently been that the economic case – for Scotland's 'inevitable' gravitation into the commercial revolution generated by its large, southern neighbour – has been challenged. The highly unusual nature of that union – which did not include, what in the mid-sixteenth century had seemed to be the vital element, a common religion – is too easily forgotten. Union was a speculative investment, not a certainty. Although it prepared the way for a Hanoverian succession, the actual settlement of 1714, when George I came to the throne, was a revolutionary one, which threw the Union into jeopardy. A Union settlement took another forty years. A genuinely British state, with a place reserved within it for a Scottish nation, did not mature until a century after Culloden.

Scotland and England – and Greater Britain
The thread which connects much of Scotland's history between 1296 and 1560 was war with England. Cultural and social links, which brought waves of Anglo-Norman settlers to Scotland in the twelfth and thirteenth centuries gave way to an unusual kind of conflict, called by one contemporary chronicler a 'general war between England and Scotland'. Edward I paraded the spoils of his earlier conquest of Wales in his progress through Scotland in 1296; he tried to run Scotland as a puppet kingdom, and then as a colonial 'terre', as he had both Ireland and Wales.

The effect of this attempt to erect an English empire throughout the British Isles was to sharpen a sense of Scottish nationhood, galvanise the Scottish Kirk into a church militant and force its 'multinational' nobility to decide where their first loyalties lay.

In the 1540s, largely because of the weakness of the English succession, a second attempt to draw Scotland into an English empire saw a revival of Edward I's suzerainty claims, massive investment by Henry VIII and his successor in a chain of forts across the Border and up the east coast and, in 1547, the largest English army ever to invade Scotland. But Henry also offered more than old-style conquest. A marriage alliance, a wider concord which would be the first stage on a road to a British union and a Protestant amity were all part of the 'Rough Wooing'. Some Scottish minds had already begun to drift in a few of these directions, most notably that of the distinguished academic John Mair, in his *History of Greater Britain* (1521). In 1560, too, the Scottish Protestant Lords offered not only a godly amity between the two nations but a joint Protestant mission to Elizabeth I's other island – Ireland. It came to nothing, but it illustrated that even in the sixteenth century Scots and English meant different things when they talked of union.

James VI inherited the English throne in 1603 and talked incessantly of a 'perfect union', which would unite the two nations into a greater whole. No union before or since had been so determinedly even-handed, but it lacked two essential ingredients – a cohesive establishment and symbols of unity on which a new patriotism could draw. There was no 'British' nobility in the seventeenth century, as there had – in a sense – been in the thirteenth, and no sense of 'Britishness'. The War of the Three Kingdoms which overtook James's son in the 1640s was largely about various efforts to frustrate the creation of a British Stuart state. The Covenanters thought in pan-British terms, to a far greater extent than their allies in the English House of Commons. In the Solemn League and Covenant, agreed with the English parliament in 1643, the Scots cited the 'example of the best reformed churches', but the English wanted their relationship to be 'according to the Word of God'.

The 1650s revealed God to be English and Cromwell as God's supreme Englishman. The Cromwellian Union was an incorporating one, more complete than James's had ever been, but it was not a British union. The Commonwealth regime could not bring itself to use the term 'Britain' because of its associations with the Stuarts. It was, officially, the 'Commonwealth of England, Scotland and Ireland'. Here was the first explicit formulation of an English empire, dedicated to the 'civilising' of hostile native societies in the Americas and throughout the British Isles. The War of the Three Kingdoms had resulted in the shutters coming down to protect English identity. The next century was, at bottom, about the consolidation of an English empire. It was a campaign which began at Dunbar in 1650 and ended at Culloden.[7]

After 1707, Scotland was admitted to the largest free trade zone of the eighteenth century, but it was not given full membership of this very English empire. Dedicated unionists recast themselves as North Britons, whereas the English, buoyed into new heights of xenophobia by a century of imperial wars, hardly used the term 'British' at all. It was only after the collapse of the centrepiece of this second English empire in 1776, with the revolt of the American colonies, and the unexpected opening up of a different empire, in India, after 1784 that Scots gained full admission to the wider benefits of Union. This new, British Empire became the credo for a wider patriotism, made attractive to the Scottish landed classes by its plentiful supply of jobs for their sons, in the British army and the Indian civil service. By 1860, much of Scotland's new complex of heavy industry was tied to the Empire, making Glasgow a thoroughly imperial city. Meanwhile, a new sentimental identity had emerged, offering a born-again sense of Scottishness in the form of tartan and a sanitised Highland culture. With Queen Victoria, Scotland had found a monarch who epitomised its dual identity – as a re-awakened Caledonia which was part, not of Britain, but of a Greater Britain extending to the far corners of the globe. Its combined force was compelling and helps explain why Scotland, alone of the three 'Celtic' nations in the British Isles, failed to develop a significant nationalist movement in the nineteenth century.

The new political nationalism which emerged in the late 1920s and 1930s did not cut loose for the most part from the ties of Empire or succumb to crude xenophobia. Some, especially in the Scottish National League, formed in 1920, cultivated either an anti-imperial stance or a pan-Celtic axis, but they were in the minority. Few nationalists outside the sparse ranks of the Scottish National League could, like C.M. Grieve (Hugh MacDiarmid), sum up their politics as simply as he did when, in his Who's Who entry, he gave 'anglophobia' as his hobby. The mainstream of opinion in the National Party of Scotland, founded in 1928, saw self-government as a means of preserving the Empire rather than breaking it up. Andrew Dewar Gibb, who between 1936 and 1940 was Chairman of the Scottish National Party, which had resulted from a merger of the NPS and the Scottish Party in 1934, saw Scotland and England as the two 'mother nations' of the Empire, occupying a unique position as its 'defenders and begetters'.[8] Until the Empire broke up, after the Second World War, most shades of Scottish political opinion worked within an imperial world of some kind. Most twentieth-century ideas of Scottish self-government were tied until 1945 in some way to the notion of a Greater Britain.

It was with the emergence of a lesser Britain, shorn of its imperial assets, which transformed the nature of unionism and left Scotland with a starker choice. It raised not only the question of self-government but that of a post-Union Britain. The so-called 'West Lothian' question (the right of Scots MPs to debate essentially non-Scottish matters in a post-devolution Westminster parliament) was, for the Labour government in power in 1979, less important than the 'East Surrey' question – the prospect of a permanent Conservative majority in the House of Commons if the number of Scottish members were to be reduced. The balance of power within the British state was the hidden question at issue in the Referendum of 1979, and the reason why the vote on a Scottish Assembly had the unique attachment added to it, requiring not only a majority of those who voted but a percentage (40 per cent) of all those who might vote.

Scotland within Europe

Within Scotland itself, where nationality for almost two centuries has been expressed in dual terms, the creation by the Scottish National Party in the late 1980s of a new formula, of 'independence in Europe', should not have occasioned surprise. The prospect of a greater Europe, in 1992 and after, may offer an alternative to the break-up of Britain. It is much the same journey as that earlier one from Home Rule to 'Home Rule all round'. It also re-establishes one of the most important threads of continuity in Scottish history. Throughout the Middle Ages and beyond, Scottish soldiers, students, scholars and traders had tramped the roads of Europe and left their mark. Scotland's main medieval staple port, through which most of its exports were funnelled, was successively based at Bruges, Middelburg and Veere, all on the Scheldt estuary, which gave river access to the Rhineland as well as to the Low Countries. The *Schottendyk* at Bruges was one of many canals or streets which make it likely that there were colonies of Scottish merchants established in Flemish and Dutch towns in the early Middle Ages. They complemented the Red and White Halls, of Flemish and German merchants, based in Scotland's main medieval port of Berwick; those thrived until their members perished along with many of the burgh's other inhabitants in the sack of Berwick by Edward I in 1296. In the seventeenth century there were 'English churches', in reality made up largely of Scots, in Amsterdam and Rotterdam. Scots traded with the eastern Baltic from at least the thirteenth century onwards and by the seventeenth they had begun to settle in large numbers in Poland; William Lithgow, who visited it in 1616 and claimed that 30,000 Scottish families had settled there, saw it as 'mother and nurse of the youth and younglings of Scotland, clothing, feeding and enriching them'. By the seventeenth century, Scots, especially from east-coast ports such as Arbroath and Montrose, had begun to settle also in the western Baltic. They have left their mark in Swedish towns such as Gothenburg: the firm of D. Carnegie & Co. was founded in 1803 and that of William Gibson & Sons in 1848; and the Chalmers Technological University was opened in 1829 with funds from the estate of another Scots émigré, William Chalmers. The Low Countries and the Baltic were the destinations for Scotland's first waves of emigrants.[9]

In 1633, as part of the elaborate celebrations organised to welcome Charles I to his capital, a tableau was erected in the High Street of Edinburgh, a huge timber-framed Parnassus depicting Scotland's 'ancient worthies for learning'.[10] Two aspects of the scholars lionised by their fellow Scots were striking. It was a notable tribute paid by what was by then a very presbyterian nation to men who were mostly clergy of the pre-Reformation Church; learning was a bridge across the troubled waters of the Reformation. Most of those scholars – Duns Scotus, Hector Boece, Gavin Douglas, William Elphinstone, John Mair (or Major) and George Buchanan – had either studied or pursued their careers on the Continent. Ambitious young Scots clergy went in a steady stream to the Universities of Cologne and Louvain in the fifteenth and early sixteenth centuries to take second degrees; characteristically they accounted for more than one in ten of the *pauperes*, asking to be relieved of their fees, at both.[11] Scotland's main intellectual stimulus lay in universities such as these. From them flowed the ideas which gave Scotland both its Reformation and the Catholic reform movement which tried to counter it in the 1540s and 1550s: Patrick Hamilton, the first Protestant martyr, had studied at Luther's Wittenberg; John Hamilton, Archbishop of St Andrews, drew his inspiration from orthodox reform at Cologne. The journeys of Scots to the great centres of European learning was a trend which remained unbroken after 1560. Many stayed, a notable sixteenth-century 'brain drain'. More returned home, as propagandists for the culture of France, the Low Countries, Germany or Scandinavia. Andrew Melville attended the Universities of Paris and Poitiers before going on to the Academy in Calvin's Geneva; by the time he was invited home in 1574 to take up the Principalship of

Glasgow University his reputation as a teacher had already spread throughout Europe. By 1600 Scots were going to Heidelberg or the Huguenot *académies* rather than Paris or Geneva. By 1625 large numbers of both theology and law students were beginning to travel to the Netherlands, and especially to Leiden.[12] The 'Erasmus' exchange scheme, set up in the 1980s to encourage students in Continental and British universities to spend a year abroad, has re-established a very old pattern; students at King's College, Aberdeen, had a year of study abroad, at Louvain, in the early sixteenth century. The rationale behind Bishop Elphinstone's foundation of a university college at Aberdeen is also worth remembering – it was *pro patria*. The pursuit of the intellect has long been a very Scottish obsession; it was also, for the Scots, a very European phenomenon.

Part I
EARLY SCOTLAND

THE LAND AND ITS PEOPLE BEFORE AD 400

THE RECORDS OF MUCH OF EARLY SCOTTISH HISTORY ARE NOT WRITTEN. THEY LIE rather in the standing stones, the brochs and forts which guarded most of its western and northern coastline, and the very sites of royal or ecclesiastical centres, or in the terrain itself. There is little written between Adomnán's *Life* of Columba composed in the seventh century and Tacitus' account of Agricola's last Roman campaign, which provides us with the first recorded battle in Scottish history, at Mons Graupius in the early autumn of AD 83. That account of the relentless pursuit made by the Roman governor of Britain across the Forth and Tay of native tribes led by a chieftain called Calgacus ('the swordsman'), eventually inflicting huge casualties of 10,000 dead against Roman losses of 360, bears the unmistakable ring of the excesses of military memoirs.[1] More than a dozen possible sites have been suggested for the location of Mons Graupius, including the Pass of Grange near Keith and Durno, under the lee of Bennachie near Inverurie in eastern Aberdeenshire. The most plausible is perhaps a site south of the Mounth, where the Bernie Water flows below Knock Hill near Monboddo, in the Mearns, a district which in the tenth century was known as 'the Swordland'. The importance of the battle is as elusive as its location. Although the tribesmen suffered heavy casualties, it is clear from Tacitus' own account that most escaped into the safety of the nearby hills to fight another day.[2]

Forts, duns and brochs

The physical evidence provides a tantalising glimpse of what lay further back in Scotland's past. It is clear that a huge site such as Traprain Law, near Dunbar in East Lothian, represented a native hill fort which must have flourished during the period of intermittent Roman occupation of the area to the south of the Forth between AD 78 and 215. Here, on a site 784 feet high which overlooked much of Lothian, there was, it is likely, a settlement which had a much older provenance, dating back perhaps to the beginning of the first millennium BC. In complete contrast, at Newstead where Dere Street crossed the River Tweed near Melrose, was Trimontium, the military equivalent of a new town, a recently rediscovered archaeological site which is now thought to have been not a temporary fort but a Roman supply camp and industrial centre, making and repairing iron weapons, armour and tools, fashioning small objects in bronze and lead, roof tiles and pottery vessels. Different again was the fort at Inveresk, near Musselburgh, built early in the Antonine period, probably about AD 140, atop a steep slope surrounded on three sides by a river, but with a thriving and substantial civilian settlement (*vicus*) outside it, on its eastern side. The different kinds of Roman sites suggest a sophisticated system of communications and services for commercial operations as well as careful surveying of the military problems posed by the terrain of northern Britain.[3]

The fort at Inveresk looked towards the dramatic Din Eidyn, the volcanic rock on which Edinburgh Castle now stands, barely five miles to the west; this was the centre of the Gododdin court of the North British king, Mynyddog, c.600. In the period of the first Roman invasions it lay within the territory of the Votadini, precursors of the Gododdin, but recent archaeology has traced human settlement on it some 1,000 years before that. Despite its apparent strategic importance, which would be capitalised upon by kings of Scots and English invaders alike from the thirteenth century onwards, there is no evidence that the Romans ever occupied it. Greater and potentially more important than all of these in the early centuries AD was the enigmatic Tap o' Noth, near Rhynie in Strathbogie. Here, on the summit of a hill over 1,800 feet high, lay a fort of some fifty acres in area, with clear evidence of at least 200 timber roundhouses, making it four times the size of any other fort in the north-east.[4] Its origins are likely to go back at least as far as those of Traprain Law or Din Eidyn, but its precise status remains a mystery. If a physical site is a guide to the politics of the tribes whom the Romans encountered, this may have been one of their key gathering points and Agricola's expedition of AD 83, even if it reached Strathspey, came no nearer than ten or fifteen miles of it.

If the huge natural fortified symbol of Tap o' Noth represents the political grouping or confederation of the tribes north of the Forth/Clyde line – probably in reaction against the Roman threat – the different chains of place-names, standing stones, or smaller forts and brochs may be taken as a measure of the extent of their influence or territory. The 'quaking ground of place-names'[5] trembles nowhere so alarmingly as in the tracing of Pictish influence, for the 300 or more 'pet' or 'pit' names which can be traced are likely to refer only to good arable or pastoral land. Their distribution would limit Pictish influence to the eastern coast from the Black Isle to the line of the Firth of Forth, infiltrating inland and westwards for only a way along the straths of the Spey, Dee, Don, Tay and Earn. The distribution of Pictish monuments is more complicated for they are divided conventionally into three classes, but their overall distribution pattern is much the same as that for 'pit' names.[6]

For contemporaries, however, the most recognisable points of location were fortified places. The Ulster Chronicle in its account of the century after 638 refers to no fewer than twenty-four forts or strongholds, with perhaps ten more which are unidentifiable, stretching in an arc around the coastline from Dunadd in Kintyre and Dun Ollaig near Oban in the west, to Dun Foither (Dunnottar) near Stonehaven and Etin (Edinburgh) in the east. Also in the east as far north as the southern side of the Moray Firth and in the south-west are to be found the traces of timber-laced or vitrified forts; such are Craig Phadraig near Inverness, Burghead further east along the Moray Firth or Dundurn further south in Strathearn. Some seventy of these strongholds are vitrified forts, where fire has at some time spread along the network of wooden beams fusing the rest of the dry-stone walling into a vitrified mass. Some of these hill-forts have been dated to almost the beginning of the first millennium BC (c.800 BC), but carbon dating of the wall at Burghead suggests it was built about AD 400 and the novel technique of driving iron nails more than seven inches long into the oaken cross beams links it to Dundurn. Abandoned in the ninth or tenth centuries or consumed in later medieval fortifications, the importance of these forts is easy to forget; but their period of occupation – for 500

4

years after the building of the wall in the case of Burghead – compares well with the strength or viability of most of Scotland's medieval castles. They testify to the political strength of a warrior people otherwise almost unknown to written record.

In the west and north, the commonest forms of fortification were not the hill-forts or vitrified forts seen mostly in the Lowlands and the east but the dun and broch, both stone-built structures of a modest size dating from late in the first millennium BC; over 500 broch sites have been identified along the Atlantic coast. These thick-walled and sometimes double-walled structures, often with towers between forty and fifty feet in height, which were built to defend a homestead rather than a natural promontory or the court of a king or chieftain, flourished in the first century AD, the age of Agricola, but had a much shorter useful life than other forms of fortification. Their interpretation is the subject of fierce debate: for some archaeologists, the broch is as cherished an emblem of the distinctiveness or insularity of the culture it represents as are the images of Pictish art to some historians of the Picts. To some Irish historians, both the broch and the vitrified fort point to a common link with wider Celtic culture, in Ireland and elsewhere: the broch is a cousin of the Irish stone cashel or Iron Age stone forts in the north-west of Spain; the timber-laced fort is to be found in pre-Roman Gaul.[7]

The point is unresolvable but fundamental: all three kinds of fortifications stretch back well beyond the point in 297 when a Roman historian attached the longest-surviving nickname, *Picti* (or 'painted people'), to one set of the native tribes in the British Isles. Brochs apart, they suggest not only a long continuity in the material culture of the tribes who built and occupied them over a period of up to 1,600 years but also an essential if loose cultural unity amongst the various tribes first identified by Ptolemy in the second century AD and other observers after him as inhabiting the bulk of the mainland of modern-day Scotland north of the Forth/Clyde line. And they hint, if darkly, at a common Celtic heritage which underpinned these mysterious peoples. Later, more sophisticated forts, sometimes built on a hierarchical plan around an enclosure, such as Dunadd or the inland fort at Dundurn at the head of Loch Earn in Perthshire, suggest the emergence by about AD 600 of viable overkings who could demand tribute from a loose grouping of tribes.[8]

Early peoples

The terrain of Scotland is the final piece of material evidence to guide us and it is, if anything, the most important. The first map of Scotland was drawn by Ptolemy in his *Geography* of the second century AD, but it is based on second-hand knowledge of material of a century earlier. The next, compiled no less than eleven centuries later, was part of a manuscript drawn up by a monk of St Albans, Matthew Paris. It is likely that the origin of the first was prepared from the battle plan of an invading army trying to enforce authority on elusive and stubborn native peoples; the second was based probably on reports brought back by travelling monks, but it may have been used later by Edward I, who followed a similar route to that of Agricola in his conquest of the north in 1296.[9] Edward crossed the Forth at Stirling before marching north and east towards the fertile plain of Angus and that of Aberdeenshire beyond the formidable natural barrier of the Mounth, before swinging north-west into Strathspey. In Paris's imagination, the bridge at Stirling

1 ▣ Antonine Wall
2 ▣ Hadrian's Wall

CORNAVII
SMERTAE
LUGI
OCEANUS DUECALEDONIUS
CARNONACAE
DECANTAE
VARAR AESTUARIUM
TAEZALI
CREONES
CALEDONII
VACOMAGI
CERONES
VENICONES
1
EPIDII
DAMNONII
VOTADINI
SELGOVAE
2
NOVANTAE
BRIGANTES

Map 1 Early Scotland, after Ptolemy

across the dangerous, tidal waters of the 'sea of Scotland' was the sole link between Scotland north and south of the Forth. He exaggerated only slightly. Stirling was the first point at which the river might be crossed but it was also in the neck of a narrow isthmus of land bridging difficult marshland which was drained only in the eighteenth century. The Forth and its boggy shores separated the halves of the country as surely in 1250 as for the Romans almost twelve centuries earlier.

Beyond it, north of the Forth, according to Ptolemy, lay ten tribes. Their names, such as the *Venicones* placed by him in Fife, the *Cornovii* in Caithness, or the *Creones* somewhere between Loch Linnhe and Loch Carron in the west, are relatively unimportant. More significant is the contrast between the tribal patterns north and south of the Forth/Clyde line, which looks as if it was regarded by contemporaries as a natural frontier. The seven tribes south of it controlled seemingly more consolidated territorial tracts than the ten northern tribes which were wedged into comparatively short spans of coastline, but Ptolemy is silent as to how far their authority extended into the vast heartland of the Highlands. The *Novantae* controlled Galloway and much of the south-west; they were separated and insulated from the *Damnonii*, who held a large area in Clydesdale, by the natural barrier of the Carrick hills; and the *Votadini*, based probably at Traprain Law, controlled most of Lothian and modern Berwickshire and Northumberland. Most of these tribal territories were dictated by the facts of geography. South of the natural barrier of the Forth, the breaks in the terrain ran south to north – a basic, inconvenient physical fact which would perplex and lure to the Forth successive invaders from the Romans in the first and second centuries AD to the Northumbrian kings in the sixth and seventh centuries and Henry VIII of England in the sixteenth. Those breaks in the terrain were few and help explain the make-up of these early tribes: the territory of the *Votadini* was divided from that of the *Selgovae* in Liddesdale and Teviotdale and their control of the southern uplands in turn ended at the valley of the Nith, beyond which lay the *Novantae*.

Ptolemy's knowledge of geography and politics north of the Forth was much sketchier, as was that of successive Roman military commanders; neither Roman legions nor intelligence were able to pursue the northern tribes far up the glens and straths which ran east and west. If there was a barbarian heartland, the Romans never found it. The clues left by various later Roman commentators are well known but confusing. For Tacitus, the whole of the mainland from the Forth to the 'northern sea' was 'Caledonia' and Ptolemy not only placed the *Caledonii* both east and west of the Highland massif but also named the Atlantic coast as the Caledonian Ocean. The territory invaded by a large Roman task force, numbering perhaps 40,000 men under the command of the Emperor Septimius Severus in AD 209, was still called Caledonia. In AD 297, in the first reference to 'Picts', complaints were made of attacks on the Roman fortified frontier by 'Picti and Scoti' (or Irish). And Gildas, a monk born in Strathclyde but resident in Wales for much of his life, who wrote c.540 of the Roman evacuation of Britain a century earlier in what was the first 'British' history, made much the same distinction about 'the foul hordes of Scots and Picts', who 'were to some extent different in their customs but were in perfect accord in their greed for bloodshed'. A description made in 310 of 'the woods and marshes of the *Caledones* and other Picts' suggests that the Caledonians were seen, at least by their enemies, as one of the Pictish peoples.

A number of references from the second half of the fourth century onwards suggest a division of the Picts into two peoples. In 368, Ammianus Marcellinus distinguished the *Dicalydones* (obviously a derivative of the word *Caledonii*) from the *Verturiones*, whose name suggests a connection with the later emergence of the Pictish kingdom of Fortriu, located in Strathearn and Menteith between the head waters of the Forth and Tay. This division seems to accord with the analysis of Dio Cassius made in AD 197 between the *Maeatae*, who 'dwelt next to the cross wall that divides the island in half' (which must mean the Antonine Wall built fifty years earlier across the Forth/Clyde isthmus), and the Caledonians, who lived 'beyond them'. The details are self-contradictory, as many intelligence reports often are, but they point to two sets of conclusions. From an early point, the Pictish tribes seem to have been united not in one confederacy but two, and the division between them probably followed the line of that great natural obstacle of the Mounth, stretching eastwards and thickening from Stonehaven. In contrast, their enemies, whether Roman or (later) British, saw a broader threat – of Pictish and Irish peoples acting in concert.

The implications of geography are important. The terrain north of the natural frontier of the Forth/Clyde line was conducive to the development of a large number of separate tribes. In early Ireland, the limits of the tribal chieftain or *rí* and his *tuath* or petty kingdom were based not on distance but on difficulty of communication. The result in Ireland was tens of minor tribes, each with its own king and also, to some extent, its own distinctive customs and law. The surprise is surely not that Ptolemy detected ten northern tribes in Caledonia but that he did not trace more. The emergence of two loose confederations of tribes by the end of the second century AD – probably in part a reaction against a common Roman enemy – suggests a need to guard against an over-deterministic view of Scotland's geography. Minor physical barriers could become stepping stones between tribes; the links between individual members of the confederations surely suggests a great amount of migration and contact by sea. Equally, it is probable that the two Pictish confederations fitted the lines imposed by the two greatest geographical barriers of all, the Forth and the Mounth. Any authority, whether native king or invading army, had difficulty in imposing its will across the vast territory between the Forth and the Northern Isles. The sea, always in early history a conduit for mutual contact and influence rather than a barrier, is as likely to have linked the different Pictish peoples of Caledonia with Ireland as with themselves.

Roman 'conquest', occupation and withdrawal

Successive Roman attempts to cope with the difficulties of Caledonia's geography are instructive. The three major sets of campaigns, beginning with Agricola's in AD 79-83, reveal a series of shifts in strategy. Between 79 and 80 he established a chain of forts in the valley between the Forth and the Clyde, which was already recognised as a potential frontier line. After his campaign of 83 into the far north-east, his successor, whose name is unknown, extended the chain of roads and forts south of but parallel to the diagonal line of the Highlands, extending deep into Strathmore. The hub of this northern complex was Inchtuthil, a fort for a full legion of some fifty-three acres, on the Tay.[10] Within a year, however, Inchtuthil was abandoned and the Roman army fell back to a natural line of defence, the River Earn. The strategy of using advance forts as fire-breaks, to dampen native insurrections, was abandoned in AD 87 in favour of the quite different device of the construction of a permanent barrier to separate what were probably client peoples from the more hostile tribes beyond. This was the rationale behind Hadrian's Wall, a seemingly formidable barrier of stone and turf twenty feet high and ten feet deep, built some thirty years later in 118. Yet this, the most obvious monument to the Roman presence north of the Humber, was laid up as near-obsolete within twenty years. The same strategy was adjusted to produce a wall further north on a more natural frontier line, between the Forth and Clyde: the Antonine Wall, built of turf on a base of sandstone boulders in 142-3, stretched for thirty-seven miles rather than eighty and had eighteen forts rather than one at every mile. This time more emphasis was placed on forts built beyond the wall to protect its flanks, like that at Duntocher at its western end and Bertha at its eastern edge, which lay as far north as the Earn. Again within a short space, between 155 and 161, the entire system was in turn abandoned, reoccupied and refurbished, and abandoned again as part of a strategic withdrawal to a re-equipped Hadrian's Wall. The Roman occupation of the south-eastern part of Caledonia beyond the Forth had lasted only five years.[11]

Until AD 207 the only active signs in a new policy of containment by a chastened army of occupation were modest attempts made to patrol the potentially hostile territory between the southern wall and the Cheviots. The ambitious and expensive campaign conducted by Emperor Septimius Severus in 209 resulted in treaties with the native tribes and gave him the title of 'conqueror of Britain' but no conquest of Britain was more short-lived than this. Shortly after 211, when Severus died at York, an ambitious new fort at Carpow, near Newburgh on the southern side of the Tay – which was, it has been argued, a new Inchtuthil – was abandoned.[12] The first attempt to create a pale between Hadrian's Wall and the Antonine Wall was more or less at an end, in the face of what was the opposition of perhaps the first confederation of Pictish peoples south of the Mounth. After 215 a few forts were maintained north of Hadrian's Wall and the valleys beyond it were patrolled. A punitive expedition somewhere to the north of Hadrian's Wall was led by Emperor Constantius Chlorus in 306, but Rome was clearly on the defensive throughout the third and fourth centuries, relying on a combination of the strategies of a permanent barrier and a pale, now minimally patrolled. By 367 there are accounts of Hadrian's Wall being overrun. Two years later the forts to the north of it were abandoned, as was the Wall itself c.400. In the face of increasing seaborne attacks by both Picts and Irish on the Roman southern province, Hadrian's Wall by the mid-fourth century had become expensive to maintain and obsolete.

The reasons for the Romans' failure to conquer the north have been the subject of fierce debate. But the case for the defence and the rival, Pictish case for the success of the tribes in throwing off the yoke of Rome are usually directed at the non-conquest of the north rather than the Romans' failure to guard the pale they tried to create between the walls. It seems plausible that revised priorities, which demanded that troops be sent to the Danube in AD 83, may have been what brought to an end the Agricolan experiment. And it may be that the withdrawal after the death of Severus stemmed from a failure of will rather than a lack of military capability.[13] Both explanations may miss the essential point. It had not been the animosity of the northern tribes which had defeated Roman strategy so much as the facts of geography, both north and south of the Antonine Wall. Southern governments as late as the reign of Elizabeth I would strive in vain to contain or stem the natural currents of trade, culture and aggression which united a highland zone inconveniently traversing a largely artificial frontier line. The Scottish 'Borders' were the immediate neighbours of England's northern highlands, which posed their own problem of order for central authority. And to underscore the fact that governments seldom learn from history, one exasperated Elizabethan border official in the 1580s suggested a new Roman wall, to keep out the Scots.

The effects of the uneven waves of Roman occupation between AD 79 and 215 are difficult to measure. Most Roman forts were probably quickly overgrown and forgotten, but some parts of their road system were still in use ten centuries later: Robert I in 1314 waited at Stirling for the progress of the English army of Edward II up Dere Street. Roman finds from non-Roman sites beyond the Antonine Wall, whether of the first or second century, are sparse and, north of the Mounth or north and west of the Great Glen, rare. Further south, Roman imprints are heavier but concentrated in certain areas: finds stray only rarely away from the upper part of the Firth of Clyde, the line of established roads such as Dere Street or the western route, which linked Carlisle with Cadder, near the western edge of the Antonine Wall. The impact of Roman withdrawal was obviously greater from the more regularly occupied zone south of the Forth, but its effect may have been more lasting on the local economy than on tribal politics. If the elaborate communications network between the two walls, with three cross-routes running east/west between the two main roads which connected the walls, had encouraged extensive civilian settlement, as at Cadder and Inveresk, it is difficult to imagine that these centres of trade or industry survived the withdrawal of the army.[14] Not only Roman camps and forts were deserted; within fifty years the site of Traprain Law was abandoned by their client tribe, the *Votadini*. At Inchtuthil, the Roman legion left behind it almost one million unused nails, carefully hidden below the floor of a workshop. At Traprain Law the *Votadini* buried a silver hoard, which probably represented some of their income as Roman clients. By contrast, less spectacular finds of both native and imported metalwork in Berwickshire, Roxburghshire and Kirkcudbrightshire, all in the immediate shadow of Hadrian's Wall, hint at a lasting legacy in the pattern of rural settlement and farming rather than a traumatic break about 400. Overseas trade may well have disappeared for centuries, but the finds of bridle, harness, ploughshares, sickles and other implements suggest a legacy of working habits and labour skills less easily displaced or forgotten.[15]

More difficult still to assess is the legacy of Roman Christianity. If Ninian's mission to an already Christianised south-west centred on Whithorn can be dated to the second half of the fifth century, a strong element of continuity must have existed there, made more tangible by the fact (for such are few and far between) that he trained in Gaul, perhaps before AD 450.[16] Sea routes to Gaul and other parts of the Continent from the south-west may have survived, though there is little by way of evidence to show what passed along them. Between the Roman evacuation and Adomnán's *Life* of Columba, which sketches a brief glimpse of a cohesive people ruled over by typical Dark Age kings in the late sixth century, there is very little evidence on which to draw. The *Novantae* of Galloway are the most mysterious of the many early peoples of Scotland.[17] The enigmatic Ninian is one of the few markers in an otherwise barren historical landscape. The historical understanding of early Scotland suffers greatly, it has been said, from the 'immense distortion' caused by this gap in the evidence between the end of the second century and the sixth.[18] The best solution to the problem is a simple one: it is the leap in the mind rather than the hope of new, unexpected archaeological finds which will bring us closest to Dark Age Scotland.

THE MAKING OF THE KINGDOM OF FORTRIU

T HE HISTORY OF THE PICTS CAN BE LIKENED TO A MYSTERY STORY WITH FEW CLUES and no satisfactory ending. There is no firm explanation either of their origins before the third century AD or their disappearance in the mid-ninth century. Yet that period of over five centuries, too easily cast off as part of the 'Dark Ages', is crucial to any understanding of the mature medieval Scottish kingdom which would evolve after it. The period has, with justice, been called 'an age of migrations',[1] when the different tribal peoples – Picts, Scots, Angles, Britons and Scandinavians – who inhabited the mainland of modern-day Scotland moved, fought, displaced and intermarried with each other. Yet the effort to plot these movements, either on a map or in the mind, is liable to produce too sharply etched a picture of coup and counter-coup, forced marches and counter-marches, and pitched battles with decisive results.

Whatever the Picts were, they are likely, as were other peoples either in post-Roman western Europe or in contemporary Ireland, to have been an amalgam of tribes, headed by a warrior aristocracy which was by nature mobile. Their culture was the culture of that warrior élite rather than of the people as a whole. Inevitably the historian's eye is attracted towards any core of 'facts', however suspect, to explain this mysterious people. Much of their history, as a result, has been written by deduction, either from the point where they first emerge in the annals of chroniclers, such as Bede writing of the sixth century in his *Ecclesiastical History* compiled in the 720s, or where they disappear from history, in a conveniently neat palace coup conducted by the Dalriadic king, Kenneth mac Alpin in the 840s. But Bede was writing as the official spokesman of both the Northumbrian Church and royal house. His account was drawn up partly to justify the increasing influence of his own church in Pictland over the previous twenty years and perhaps also he was writing at the point where, with Pictish envoys coming to the Abbey of Jarrow to discuss Roman customs such as the dating of Easter, it was convenient for the reign of Nechtan, King of the Picts, to develop its origin legends. It found them not in the reign of Bridei, son of Maelchon and contemporary of Columba who died *c.* 586, but twenty-eight kings and 943 years earlier in the legendary figure of Cruithne.[2] For Bede himself, Ninian, operating from Whithorn sometime in the fifth century, was a more convenient apostle of the Picts than Columba, working from Iona in the next century.

Alternatively, it is tempting to turn to the notion, which was much embellished from the late tenth century onwards, of a hostile take-over of the kingship by Kenneth mac Alpin in 840, followed a few years later by a wholesale and still more mysterious destruction of the Pictish nobility. What is undoubtedly mysterious is the extraordinary disappearance of the culture of the Pictish people within the course of the first two or three generations of mac Alpin kings. The intriguing history of a *gens* who dominated much of modern-day Scotland for five centuries or more should not be consumed by the story of an obscure intrigue that seemingly produced a genocide, of Pictish customs, law and culture.

The twentieth century has seen produced a number of versions of a case for the defence. Pictish art, Pictish studies and even Pictish politics are in vogue. The 1300th anniversary of the battle at Nechtansmere, celebrated in 1985 by a gathering at its site of Dunnichen Moss in Angus, saw it being hailed as the most decisive battle in Scottish history. Not the least of the many ironies of Scottish history may be that this most celebrated of all Pictish victories was won by a king of Picts whose father was a Dumbarton Briton; it has even been suggested that his opponent, Ecgfrith, King of Northumbria, was a rival external candidate.[3] Defenders of the Picts have often conflicted on the detail, at times with that peculiar acrimoniousness which often marks out scholarly debate of the indeterminate. Most make common cause, however, in their stress on the distinctiveness of Pictish art, culture or customs.

The best evidence is the standing stones of the Picts, which are sprinkled over the whole of the mainland of present-day Scotland from the Cromarty Firth to the Firth of Forth as well as in the Northern Isles and northern parts of the Western Isles.[4] But how distinctive were these products of this enigmatic set of peoples? The inspiration of these Pictish artists is deeply controversial: similarities between Pictish animal art and animal evangelist symbols in products of Celtic art such as the Book of Durrow have brought argument and counter-argument as to which was the inspiration of the other.[5] The directions in which cultural influence flowed is debatable; the broad common heritage of Irish, Northumbrian and Pictish art, whether pre-Christian or Christian, can more readily be agreed. Pictland was not a self-contained enclave. There must have been regular links, flowing in both directions, between Pictland, Ireland and Northumbria. In each case, it may be permissible to think of a common culture stretching across the Irish Sea as well as north and south of Forth, even if each area had its own highly distinctive variants.[6]

The haunting images of Pictish art and the intricate details of matrilinear succession, again often argued to be unique in the whole of Europe, have often been devised as answers to a very difficult historical problem – as a unique Pictish solution to the 'problem of the Picts'. Archaeologists in turn debate the aptness of terminology: whether 'Pictish' is appropriate to certain cultural patterns regardless of date or only to a specific historical period, between AD 300 and 850. The underlying uncertainty in this debate can be detected by the currency of a relatively new phrase 'proto-Pictish'. The overall effect has been an odd one: the Picts have become a curiosity rather than a major force in the telling of Scottish history. Their distinctiveness, argued so formidably by Pictish historians, has become the explanation for their disappearance from history. The case mounted on behalf of the Pictish 'world we have lost' has had a peculiar effect: as much as the efforts of those historians of medieval kingship looking for its roots and finding them in the mac Alpin dynasty, it has served to lose or obscure the real history of the Picts and their kings.

Scottish history before 1000, as a result, has come to be focused in the work of some recent historians on the question of the 'making of the kingdom', the complex process by which a cluster of different peoples – Britons and even some Scandinavians as well as Picts and Scots – came in the ninth and tenth centuries to owe common allegiance to a single king, 'of Scots'.[7] The question is a legitimate one to ask of a process which was all the more noteworthy because both Ireland and southern England in the ninth century were still made up of a patchwork of fragmented and warring kingdoms. But the same question, in the case of Scotland, may also usefully be asked of the 'Dark Age' which came before the making of a mac Alpin dynasty of kings, for many of the forces which are often thought to have produced this new dynasty in the ninth century had been at work for three centuries or more. Before beginning to think of Scottish history as a series of watersheds, with the making of the mac Alpin kingdom in and after the 840s as one of the most vital, it may be as well to consider an alternative – of the making of a Pictish kingdom before it.

Origins of the Picts

The first mention of the Picts was made by a Roman observer in AD 297. The name itself, even if it simply meant 'painted people', was less a nickname than a *nom de guerre*, like that given by the Romans to the 'Franks', inhabitants of northern Gaul.[8] Its occurrence at that point, when the main periods of both Roman invasion and occupation of a southern pale were already over, may suggest that the name implied a new power grouping in the north rather than indicating a tribe newly arrived from elsewhere. A hundred years before the name *Picti* appeared, the eleven or twelve northern tribes which Ptolemy had earlier described were already being subsumed into two great peoples, the *Caledonii* and the *Maeatae*, bound together in an alliance against the Romans. The *Maeatae*, explained Dio Cassius, *c.*310, 'live close to the wall that divides the island into two parts' but the *Caledonii* are 'beyond them'. His dividing line between Roman and hostile territory would have been the Antonine Wall and the likely border between these two cognate peoples was the natural barrier of the Mounth. From this point until the sixth century, it is noticeable that there are consistently said to be two main groups of peoples north of the Forth/Clyde line: in 310 there is a reference to the '*Caledones* and other Picts'; by 368 Ammianus Marcellinus describes the *Dicalydones* (obviously related to the *Caledones*) and the *Verturiones*; and Bede, in dealing with the sixth century, distinguishes clearly between 'northern Picts', a pagan people first touched by Columba in his mission up the Great Glen, and the 'southern Picts' who, he asserted, had been converted to Christianity much earlier by Ninian.

It is at this point that interpretation either becomes simpler or collapses into complex confusion under the weight of competing and changing tribal names. For *Caledonii* had also been one of the names of the dozen tribes described by Ptolemy in the second century AD. And what is to be made of the survey, the *De Situ Albanie*, which dates probably from the twelfth century, and some Pictish king lists which describe seven provinces of Pictland: four south of the Mounth and three to the north of it?[9] Attached, as ever in the history of the Picts, is a legend, of the seven sons of Cruithne who each ruled a province, and each in his turn was overlord of an under-king. The divisions are more significant than the legend, which can be safely ascribed to the ingenuity of anonymous genealogists. South of the Mounth were the 'provinces' of Circenn (Angus and the Mearns), Fotla (Atholl), Fortriu (Strathearn and Menteith) and Fib (Fife). To the north were areas which are more difficult to draw with any precision: Ce covered Mar and Buchan, Fidach can be equated with

Moray and Ross, but Cait probably extended beyond modern Caithness into south-east Sutherland.[10]

These sources are impressionistic surveys made at a later date, with the advantage of hindsight. It is highly unlikely that these provinces all materialised at the same time, as part of a federal kingdom. There are significant gaps between the first mention of these provinces: Circenn appeared before 600 and Fortriu in 664, and these names may conceal much older divisions, perhaps even older than the Pictish kingdom itself. Fortriu was a later form of *Verturiones*. By contrast, neighbouring Fotla, which is first mentioned only in 739 as *Athfotla* ('new Ireland'), does suggest a newly recognised migrant tribe acquiring a territory. If there was a consolidation of a Pictish kingdom between the sixth and ninth centuries, it is unlikely to have taken the form of the amalgamation of neat territorial divisions, with a clear relationship between king and peoples.

Pictish kings

Three points of reference may help in this search for the nature of the Pictish kingdom. The rediscovery of the Picts as a Celtic people has encouraged closer comparison with practices in contemporary Ireland.[11] Oddly, however, there has been little attempt to place the Picts in the context in which Roman observers must have seen them, of other hostile barbarian tribes on the mainland of western Europe such as the Franks or Goths. The first benchmark rests, however, in Scotland itself. Recent research in Scottish medieval kingship has taught us not to think in terms of its consolidation as the story of the steadily growing power of kings who ruled and to whom subjects automatically rendered obedience. Power was highly devolved, even as late as the sixteenth century; kings may have been formidable and ruthless men, but they relied on the power of their great nobles to extend their writ into the far-flung corners of the realm. Pictish kingship should not be judged by impossible standards which few if any kings before James VI would have been likely to have met. Medieval kingship was highly personalised and informal. Pictish kingship was certainly no more than these things and probably a good deal less; early kings cannot be expected to have been administrators or autocrats. They were warlords, whose authority was expressed and acknowledged largely in the receiving of tribute, and of whom were expected military successes and the acquisition of prestige goods, by war, plunder or treaty.

Yet these Pictish warlords had, in some respects, more power than the medieval kings who followed them. It is clear from the one account that exists outlining the social and military structure of early warrior society, the Dalriadic *History of the Men of Scotland*, or *Senchus fer nAlban*, that a surprisingly comprehensive fiscal system underpinned the rationale of that society: each of the districts within the kingdom of Dalriada was assessed in terms of the number of its houses. Each house, it seems likely, was treated as a unit on which rent or tribute was payable, to nobles or kings. In addition, military service was also due and it is likely that a far higher proportion of society was mobilised for war before 1000 than after. It is also not surprising to find that in a terrain where most communication was by sea it was called 'galley service'. The *Senchus* was, in part, a muster list for a war fleet.[12]

Such details are not available for the Pictish kingdoms but it would be surprising if similar arrangements had not existed there too. For it is certain that Pictish kings had a large navy.[13] Pictish ships had been able to harry the Romans south of Hadrian's Wall in the third century. Pictish kings were able, at least until the eighth century, to dominate the Northern Isles; it seems likely that they did so from a chain of naval bases sited, like Burghead, on natural promontories along the Moray Firth. The *Annals of Tigernach* record that in 729 no fewer than 150 Pictish ships were wrecked off a headland called Ross Cuissini. The size of these ships was probably akin to the typical Dalriadic warship, which was a boat of ten benches, twenty oars and a crew of twenty-two, a good deal smaller than the Norse longship which might have as many as sixty oars.[14] The considerable evidence of a sizeable Pictish war fleet suggests a well-developed knowledge of shipbuilding, high navigational skills and a familiarity with the whole of Scotland's coastline which may not have been emulated again before the sixteenth century.[15]

The second point to bear in mind relates to barbarian peoples in the rest of western Europe. Most of these *gentes*, such as the Alams, Vandals, Ostrogoths or Visigoths, were not separate peoples but aggregations of diverse elements grouped around a common core who gave their name to the group as a whole. The transition which took place between the second and sixth centuries north of the Forth/Clyde line from a dozen tribes to two, who may also have taken on one of the old tribal names, was typical of a process of mobilisation of tribes taking place throughout much of western Europe following the collapse of imperial power in the fifth century. It is possible, as for example with the Vandals and the Alams, to find regular cases of kings described as being 'of' one people but king of another, or other cases where they are described as kings of different peoples at different times.[16]

Such examples parallel and demythologise the many, often-quoted examples of Pictish kings who had fathers who were 'of' different kingdoms, whether of Dalriada, the Dumbarton-based kingdom of Strathclyde or elsewhere. It suggests an alternative to the notion that Pictish kings were chosen, almost uniquely, through a system of matrilinear succession.[17] If the custom of the Picts was that royal succession was not confined to the kindred of their own *gens*, they were in common company with other barbarian peoples of Europe.[18] The point which should not be lost sight of is that by the sixth century, if not before, the northern tribes had all come to be known as Picts. That achievement was a notable one, to be compared with the acceptance at much the same time of the name of the Franks as a collective title for all the tribes of northern Gaul. The mature kingdom of the Picts stretched from Caithness to the Forth; it conceded to the Norse only the Northern Isles and the northern tip of the mainland; and its southern frontier, despite successive incursions of Britons from Strathclyde, Angles from Northumbria and Scots from Dalriada, remained relatively stable from the fifth century until the ninth.

The strengths and weaknesses of the Pictish dynasty of kings are not to be measured by later practices, such as the virtually automatic succession of father by first son, which suited very different times. In the shifting circumstances where large numbers of tribes were drawn together in loose confederations or 'nations', a rotating or oscillating system of royal succession which usually avoided the uncertainties of minorities was only sensible. Here the practice of Irish kingship and the role of the *derbfine* (or kindred) have much to tell us.[19] Succession was usually confined to the two most powerful segments of a dynasty. Power within one or other of the main segments was the usual arbiter of succession rather than complicated formulas of custom or law. Kings survived by being strong; they succeeded by representing the strongest of the segments of the royal family.

Kings and kingship: the example of Dalriada

But what was a king? In Ireland, there were three types of king. The *rí* or *rí túaithe* was king of a tribe or petty kingdom; the *ruirí* or 'great king' was, as well as being a tribal king, the overlord of a number of other tribes and tribal kings. And above all of these was the *rí ruirech*, 'king of overkings'.[20] Until the tenth or eleventh centuries, it is likely that counterparts of each of these grades of kings existed in Scotland. It may be easier to grasp the analogy in an account of the kings of a smaller kingdom, that of Dalriada. The Scots of Dalriada, who had begun to migrate to south-west Argyll from modern-day Antrim sometime before their king, Fergus Mór, arrived *c.*500, were never a single *gens*, although all for long owed allegiance to him and his successors. From the beginning, the Dalriadic Scots were divided into three or more tribes, each with its *rí* and its own territory: the Cenél nÓengusa ('kindred of Óengus') occupied the island of Islay; the Cenél Loairn ('kindred of Loarn') held Colonsay as well as present-day Lorne and the northern frontier against the Picts; and the Cenél nGabráin ('kindred of Gabran'), who held the overlordship of the Scots, occupied Kintyre and the territories and islands fringing on the territory of the Britons of Strathclyde, modern-day Cowal, Bute and Arran. The relative importance of each of the three tribes is confirmed by the survey in the *Senchus* outlining the manpower each could produce: Cenél nGabráin had 560 houses or clients and could muster some 800 men; both Cenél Loairn and Cenél nÓengusa, which had 420 and 430 houses, could probably raise 600 men apiece.[21]

As the most strategically placed as well as having the greatest available manpower, the Cenél nGabráin enjoyed undisputed status as *ruirí* of the Scots of Dalriada throughout the sixth century and for much of the seventh. Their status could not have been other than greatly enhanced when Aedán mac Gabráin, great-grandson of Fergus Mór, was ordained as overking of Dalriada in 573 by Columba, himself son of a royal house, on the explicit instructions, it was said, of an angel from Heaven; the novel overlaying of Christian imagery on the much older rite of inauguration of kings must have conveyed a potent extra symbolism. True to type, Aedán set out to prove himself a great warlord: the poem known as *Berchan's Prophecy* claims that he fought the Picts for thirteen years without a break. It is known that he waged an apparently successful campaign as far away as Orkney; his warriors certainly penetrated eastwards along the valley of the Forth, drawn no doubt by the crumbling power of the Gododdin kings based on Edinburgh's castle rock. But his ambitious expeditions led to defeats inflicted by the Picts somewhere in Angus and the Mearns and by the Angles of Northumbria in 603 at Degsastán, which has never been satisfactorily identified but was certainly somewhere within Northumbrian territory.

A series of further defeats, in Ireland as well as Pictland, inflicted on Aedán's grandson, Domnall Brec, who was killed in battle with Owain, King of Strathclyde, at Strathcarron in 642, not only ended a period of Dalriadic expansionism but also promoted the kingdom of Strathclyde as the major alternative seat of power in northern Britain. It was almost certainly a direct result of the military failures of successive kings of Cenél nGabráin that their hold on the overkingship of Dalriada

Map 2 *The Scots of Dalriada*

began to slip. By the end of the seventh century they were being challenged within their own territory by the emergence in Cowal of a new tribe, the Cenél Comgaill, and they had already been displaced as overkings of Dalriada by the Cenél Loairn.[22]

Why did the Cenél Loairn suddenly emerge in the later seventh century as a more potent force in Dalriada and slip back less than a hundred years later? The route to power in early Scotland, as with many barbarian peoples elsewhere, is rarely to be found in the conventional working terms of medieval or early modern historians: consolidation, expansion, hegemony. The Cenél Loairn do not seem to have succeeded to the overkingship of Dalriada as a result of a greater consolidation of their power within their own heartland. On the contrary, the *Senchus* shows that the Cenél Loairn, spread out over the rugged country of northern Argyll, had only the same total fighting strength as the tighter-knit Cenél nÓengusa based on Islay. The picture of the dynasty of Cenél Loairn in the early eighth century, under attack on three fronts, was typical of early kingship, in Dalriada and elsewhere in northern Britain. There were also internal feuds, which resulted in Selbach, King of Dalriada, having to lay waste to Dunollie, a stronghold of one of the Cenél Loairn septs, in 701. The overkingship was disputed by the Cenél nGabráin, who briefly gained the upper hand after a naval victory over Selbach somewhere in Dalriadic waters in 719; it was the first recorded sea battle in the history of Britain. Most seriously of all, they faced the brunt of a sustained period of aggression waged by Óengus, King of Picts, which culminated in the 'smiting of Dalriada' in 741. The result, it is likely, was the eclipse of Cenél Loairn ambitions. Yet it would be another segment of this divided royal house which, barely a century later, would capture control of Pictland in the person of Kenneth mac Alpin. The chequered history of Dalriadic kings suggests some need for refinement of the historian's conventional tools used to describe the mechanics of kingly power and the displacement of one ruling house by another.

The consolidation of the kingdom of Fortriu

The locus of power in the Pictish kingdom is hard to locate. Not surprisingly, in a confederation of tribes that was looser and covered a far greater area than the Scots of Dalriada, power shifted both at the level of the many *túatha* and in the location of the overking. Separated amongst themselves by the barrier of the Mounth, it is likely that there may long have been two overkings, corresponding to the two sets of Pictish peoples, north and south of it. Yet there are also hints from the sixth century or even before that one was senior. Where might he have been located? In the fourth century, the seat of Pictish power seems to have lain in Strathearn and Menteith; the survey in the *De Situ Albanie* gave premier place to Circenn, in Angus and the Mearns, but at an undisclosed date; by the late sixth century, when Columba visited King Bridei at his court near Inverness, the focus of Pictish power seems to have lain in the north. Bridei was certainly overlord of the Pictish people to the north of the Mounth, but it may be that the notion of a high kingship can be traced to this period.[23] A hundred years later in 685, when Bridei mac Bile defeated Northumbrian invaders at Dunnichen Moss in Angus, there is no doubt that he was acknowledged as high king of all the Picts. By then, however, the centre of the Pictish royal power had moved decisively southwards, to Fortriu, where it would remain.

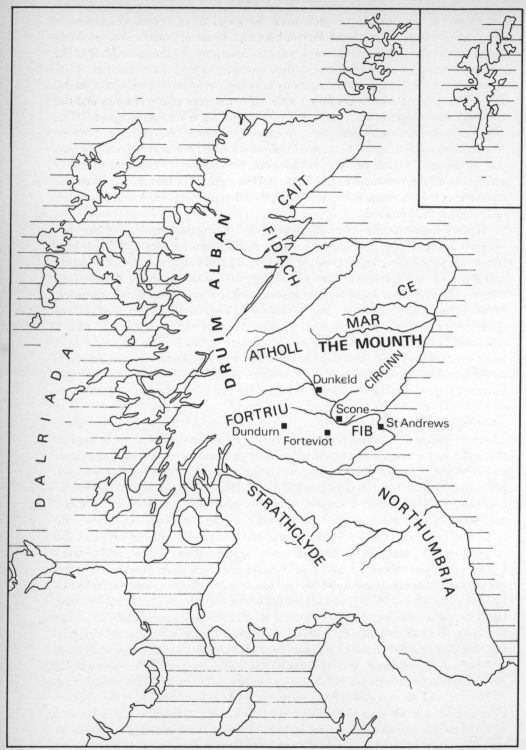

Map 3 *Provinces and territories in early Scotland*

Viewed in retrospect, the growth of the kingdom of Fortriu conveniently summarises the development of Pictish kingship. Kings of Fortriu were probably originally tribal *rí*, whose power was limited to Strathearn; by the second half of the seventh century, it is likely that they were also acknowledged as overkings of the Picts south of the Mounth. Half a century later they were also high kings of all the Picts. The nomenclature is confusing if the three different grades of kings and the three different usages of the phrase 'King of Fortriu' are not borne in mind.[24] The position, however, was clear to contemporary chroniclers, whether Irish or Northumbrian. Bede certainly viewed Pictland as a single political entity in his own day, in the early eighth century; he describes the kingdom of Nechtan in 710 as embracing all the provinces of the Picts. And the writers of *Irish Annals* often use the name of Fortriu as synonymous with the Pictish nation as a whole from the reign of Bridei (d. 693) onwards.

It is not surprising that it was shortly after this, during the long reign of Nechtan between 706 and 724, that the genealogists probably got to work on Pictish king lists and polished the origin legends of their royal patron. The contrast of Dalriada and Pictland is informative: Dalriadic kings were middle-ranking kings of an increasingly fissiparous set of peoples located within a small but difficult territory. Pictish kings would come to be described as *reges Pictorum*, high kings of a far-flung collection of peoples; their new-found status was all the more notable in such a widespread territory. The achievement of the kings of Fortriu in the eighth and ninth centuries was one of the most notable in Scottish history, but its nature is easily mistaken if overlaid with the conventional vocabulary of later, medieval kingship: their success was not to consolidate but to confederate.

The making of a kingdom

The early history of Scotland is seen conventionally as the story of progress towards the 'making of a kingdom', with the decisive steps being taken in the ninth, tenth and eleventh centuries. But the story was longer than this and it was a two-stage process. The first stage had begun by the end of the third century with the confederation of a number of loosely related tribes under a common name; by the sixth century they were grouped under two overkings and by c.700 under one overking. The second stage, which belongs largely to the ninth century, was the consolidation of these peoples during a number of key, lengthy reigns which remain amongst the most obscure in the whole of Scottish history. Later chroniclers of the twelfth and thirteenth centuries would focus their attention on the reign of Kenneth mac Alpin (843-58) as marking the end of centuries of Pictish rule and the beginning of a new dynasty. Yet it makes much more sense to think of a crucial century and a half in which fluctuation and consolidation in the Pictish kingdom went hand in hand. What was happening was what historians of a later period might call a clash of continuity and change; such clashes should not be reserved for seemingly decisive reigns, such as those of David I or James VI – or Kenneth mac Alpin.[25] It is likely that such a clash marked the whole period between the reign of Constantine, son of Fergus (789-820) and Constantine II (900-43). Viewed in this way, the decisive ninth century turns less on the single, fairly brief reign of Kenneth mac Alpin. Perhaps, rather, we should think of a 'long' ninth century belonging to a trio of kings called Constantine.[26]

The mechanics of these processes were complicated and thinking of them in modern terms, of power bloc politics, brings confusion and contradiction to the problem rather than light. It can be argued that the reign of Óengus I, who emerged in 729 as victor in a power struggle after the retiral of Nechtan, marked the beginning of a Pictish take-over of Dalriada;[27] in 736 he himself captured the fortress of Dunadd in the territory of Cenél nGabráin and his brother, Talorcán, routed a Dalriadan army a few miles away, at Loch Awe. Yet, even if Óengus won by conquest the overlordship of Dalriada in 741, by 750 he is said in the *Annals of Ulster* to have lost it, perhaps because of the intervention of Teudubr, King of Strathclyde. By 768 it was a Dalriadic king, Áed Find, who was invading the Pictish heartland of Fortriu, though with what result is unknown.

The crucial eighth and ninth centuries need to be viewed as a three-dimensional picture. There was recurrent jostling for power on the frontiers of neighbouring kingdoms; except where natural physical barriers reinforced them, frontiers were not fixed and in such circumstances migration across them was as natural an instinct as cattle raiding. There was calculated destabilisation of one kingdom by another or the creation of satellite states. But the status of such client kingdoms might range from the simple paying of tribute to outright overlordship. And there was also considerable cultural cross-fertilisation between peoples, whether produced by intermarriage, changing dedications of saints, or the efforts of holy men.

The result is a confusing one, not to be explained adequately by a history of coup and counter-coup. The King of Picts whom the Dalriadic king, Áed Find, fought in 768 was called Ciniod or Kenneth, son of Dérile; but that was a Gaelic name, as was that of the Pictish king, Óengus son of Fergus, who had devastated Dalriada in the 730s. Both Ciniod and Óengus I almost certainly had at least some blood of the Scots of Dalriada in their veins. The evidence for a successful Pictish assault on Dalriada in the mid-eighth century and for a Dalriadic take-over of Pictland in the mid-ninth century can be assembled, but it is more useful to think of two kingdoms coming more closely together in a process which was often acrimonious and on several occasions hostile. These were the quarrels of an extended family, and all the more bad-tempered as a result.

The century before the 840s saw these important processes at work. They depended, however, on a new set of political circumstances, most important of which was the sharp decline in the influence of the kingdom of Northumbria. For some, that decline can be seen to have begun as a direct result of the defeat of the Northumbrians at Nechtansmere, which put to an end the short-lived career of Bishop Trumwine and the see of Abercorn, to which he had been appointed only four years before, in 681. Yet set-piece battles, if such Nechtansmere was, seldom mark great turning-points. The reign of Nechtan, which began barely thirty years later, had seen the revival of Northumbrian pressure, spearheaded by issues involving the Pictish Church. But Northumbrian violence was as much a weapon as the gentler overtures of Bede and his abbey of Monkwearmouth and Jarrow; the Picts had been heavily defeated by the Northumbrians on the plain of Manaw, probably somewhere in West Lothian, in 711. The period of the writing of Bede's *Ecclesiastical History* was, however, a high-water mark of Northumbrian power. The end of Nechtan's reign coincided with the beginning of a century or more of steady decline of Northumbrian influence, not only north of the Forth but also in Lothian and the south-east. That steady but obscure slippage in Northumbrian control over its northern frontier was stemmed briefly by Anglian incursions, supported by the Picts, into Strathclyde in 750 and 756 resulting in the adding of the plain of Cyil (or Kyle) and the winning of tribute from the King of Strathclyde in 756. It is difficult, however, to trace Northumbrian influence between that point and the fall of York in the face of Danish attack in 866.

If the eighth century saw the withering of the influence of Pictland's southern neighbour, it may also have seen a new, closer relationship with another, the British kingdom of Strathclyde. For, as we have seen, the Pictish king victorious at Nechtansmere was Bridei mac Bile, who may have had a father who was a Strathclyde Briton. Nechtan, King of Picts between c.600 and 630, may also perhaps have been, it has been argued, a former King of Strathclyde called Neithon before he became overking of the Picts.[28] The power of kings, whether of the Picts or of other peoples, depended as much on their relationships with their neighbours as on the internal strength of their rule. Status and others' perceptions of it were the key to the authority of early kings. The essential contrast between the two periods, of Northumbrian and British influence, is that much is known and perhaps too much made of the first – both by Pictish historians eager to make Nechtansmere the great turning-point it never was and by devotees of Bede who may give the reign of Nechtan a greater centrality than it deserves – and too little is known of the second.[29] The story of the increasing merging of the Scots of Dalriada and the Picts thus, of necessity, has to be told without reference to the impact made on their relations by their mutually closest neighbour, the kingdom of Strathclyde. Here was not a marriage of two peoples, but a *ménage à trois*, by its nature more complicated and volatile. We can only guess at its intricacies.

There were two sets of processes at work in relations between Dalriada and Pictland. One had been going on for centuries, the Celticisation of parts of the far-flung kingdom of the Picts. A Celtic aristocracy has been detected amongst the Caledonians as early as the first or second centuries; these were a warrior élite who must have held in subjugation a native, non-Celtic peasantry.[30] The name of the minor kingdom of Gowrie, if it can be associated with Gabráin, father of Aedán, is an indicator in the sixth century of Dalriadic influence in a part of the kingdom of the Picts well to the east of Fortriu. And both a son and two great-grandsons of Aedán may have become kings of Picts in the late sixth century. These points may all be contentious in themselves, but the emergence of the kingdom of Atholl ('new Ireland') by 739 clearly indicates the presence over a long period of time of new settlers from the west. With Celticisation came intermarriage. There was nothing new about intermarriage between Scots and Picts in the ninth century, nor was it unique. There had, it is likely, long been a similar pattern of intermarriage between Picts and Britons. Two seventh-century Pictish kings – Bridei and Nechtan – were probably linked, as we have seen, to the kingdom of Strathclyde.

The second, parallel process was an almost inevitable consequence of the first: intermarriage between one major dynasty and another or even between the families of minor kings brought about a steady widening of the *derbfine*. It also increased the likelihood of family squabbles which might lead to tension or violence, either on the frontier or at court. The political purpose of kings of the Picts was clear enough, for by the seventh century they had largely achieved by these means a modus vivendi with their three main neighbours. It is not surprising that by early in the ninth century examples begin to proliferate of kings of Picts who held or had held other kingdoms. More significantly, in the two sons of Fergus, Constantine and Óengus II who ruled between 789 and 820 and between 820 and 834, are to be found the first examples of simultaneous dual kingship of Picts and Scots. Constantine, King of Picts since 789, also became King of Dalriada in 811. His brother, Óengus, who seems to have succeeded him on his death in 820, left as his successor his son, Eóganán, who succeeded to both kingdoms after a short interval during which the two kingships were not combined. Significantly, both Constantine and Óengus were described in the *Annals of Ulster* at their deaths as 'King of Fortriu'. And in 839 Eóganán met his death leading the 'men of Fortriu' in battle against the Norsemen. Although Skene in his *Celtic Scotland* argued that the end of the house of Fortriu came in 889, with the death of Giric, who had succeeded the two sons of Kenneth mac Alpin, the date 839 is a more significant one.[31] In 877, when Eochaid, a grandson of Kenneth, disputed the succession, the struggle for the kingship was, as it had often been before, a family quarrel, between the immediate heirs of Kenneth and his brother, Donald I. *Plus ça change, plus c'est la même chose.*

The difference between the two periods before and after the mid-ninth century lay not so much in the impact made by a new kind of king, in the person of Kenneth mac Alpin, but in the after-effects of the shattering defeat in 839 when not only Eóganán fell, but also his brother, Bran, 'and others almost without number'.[32] Amongst them, almost certainly, were other prominent members of the *derbfine*. That defeat ranks amongst the most significant in Scottish history, far more serious than that at Flodden, for here as well as a culling of the major families of the kingdom was effected a decisive shift in the pattern of succession. It was, as we shall see, not quite the beginning of a new dynasty, that of the mac Alpin kings, but it was the effective end of the dynasty of Fortriu, which had ruled with increasing authority since the reign of Bridei, son of Bile, who had been the first to be called 'King of Fortriu' at his death in 692.

The long line of kings of Fortriu deserves a greater place in the process of the making of the Scottish kingdom. By 729 they had clearly been acknowledged as overkings of all the Picts. They left behind them a distinctive and close relationship between King and Church which would lay the foundations for the sons of Malcolm and Margaret in the early twelfth century. They also, probably early in the eighth century, had constructed a mythology of their own past. Frankish kings at about the same date had invented for themselves a Trojan origin;[33] Pictish kings were presented with an equally satisfying Irish one, in the figure of Cruithne, who ruled for no less than fifty years as a 'merciful judge'. By the end of the eighth century, they had also found, in the figure of Constantine, a renewed mythology of kingship which exactly paralleled the revival elsewhere in western Europe in the second half of the eighth century of the idea of a reborn Christian Roman empire of Constantine under a new, more prestigious kind of king.[34] The same process in Gaul would eventually produce a new-style King of Franks, Charles the Great or Charlemagne. In the Pictish kingdom, it produced a series of kings called Constantine, each more closely attached to the Church which cultivated him than the last. The cult of Constantine neatly complemented the cult of St Peter which had been promoted at the Pictish court since the reign of Nechtan, earlier in the same century.[35] Pictish kingship and the Pictish Church, both in a state of slow but profound change in the eighth and ninth centuries, were nourished by each other. It is no accident that the office of 'chief bishop of Fortriu' emerged by 865, in the reign of Constantine I.

But the Constantine who succeeded as King of Picts in 789 was a son of Fergus and elder brother of an Óengus, both obviously Gaelic names. That deliberate choice of names, Constantine and Óengus, made for prospective Pictish kings is as good an example as any, not only of the integrated nature of Pictish society, but also of the wider vision and ambition of the house of Fortriu. A balance was in process of being struck between old and new, between a revived native culture with disparate roots and the importation of a consciously novel western European cult of kingship. Much the same balance between old and new would be struck again, three centuries later, in the reign of David I. The clash of continuity and change lay at the heart of the history of Pictish kingship, fully a century before the reign of Kenneth mac Alpin. By the reign of the first Constantine (789-820),[36] the process of confederation had brought the peoples of the north to the point where the process of political consolidation might begin. The *gentes* of Picts and Scots had been coming together for a century or more into one people, even if it was, inevitably, a loose confederation. The next stage was for *regnum* and *gens* to come together.[37]

3

APOSTLES OF THE SCOTS, PICTS AND BRITONS

THE SEARCH FOR SCOTLAND'S HISTORY IS ALMOST INDISTINGUISHABLE FROM THE quest for Scotland's faith. Yet both are often obscured by wishful thinking, not only of modern-day seekers after their spiritual roots, but also of medieval chroniclers and later Protestant historians. Turn to the modern Greater Glasgow telephone directory and you will find there one of the most puzzling paradoxes of Scottish history. In a country which for the last 400 years has been riven by religious sectarianism, both the Roman Catholic faith and most shades of the reformed tradition share considerable numbers of churches dedicated to Columba or *Colum Cille* (dove of the church). With the possible exception of Queen Margaret, Scotland's only royal saint, no other figure in Scotland's religious past commands such widespread ecumenical agreement. There are many ironies about this, not least that almost invariably it is the Protestant churches which tend to prefer the Latin form, Columba, or that it was the Roman Catholic Church in the west of Scotland, desperately trying to cope with a flood of often unchurched Irish in the nineteenth century, which was prone to see itself as a new Irish missionary church, distinctly different from the Catholic Church in the rest of Scotland, resulting in a much higher proportion of its parish churches dedicated to *Colum Cille* than elsewhere. The real historical figures of Ninian, Columba, Kentigern and other 'apostles' of early Scotland need to be disentangled from their various cults, of both the Dark Ages and the medieval period. The myth of the Culdees as defenders of the Celtic Church against Roman influences, presbyterians some hundreds of years before their time, was first invented, as has been so much else in Scottish history, by George Buchanan, Moderator of the General Assembly of the Protestant Church shortly after the Reformation of 1560 and author of a history of Scotland first published in 1582 which repeated and embellished the story of the legendary kings of Scotland stretching some eight centuries into pre-history.

Amidst the misunderstandings and half-truths, there remains in the notion of Iona as the spiritual home of Scottish Christianity an important truth. It is likely that that was its status from the seventh century until at least the tenth, although the cult of Iona as a holy island of kings was embellished by later chroniclers and compilers of king-lists. Most though perhaps not all of the mac Alpin kings were probably buried there up to and including Donald II Ban, who died in 900. Its position thereafter was increasingly ambiguous. Constantine II (900-43) chose to retire as a monk to St Andrews and was buried there in 952. Iona retained its status, but had already begun to lose its influence, its role perhaps not unlike that of Geneva, an honoured grandparent of Protestant Scotland after the first flush of the generations of John Knox and Andrew Melville was past. Kings of Scots, such as Malcolm (d.954) and Indulf (d.962), were buried there again in the second half of the tenth century and emblems of Columba served as bringers of victory in that century as surely as they had in his own lifetime, but by then the real centre of ecclesiastical power had shifted eastwards, to Dunkeld and St Andrews. The last King of Scots to be buried on Iona was Donald III Ban (1093-7).[1]

Saints and saints' cults

Saints are not born, they are created. More powerful in death than in life, they become, once acclaimed, the servant of future generations of the servants of Christ. Ninian, Columba, Adomnán (the most important but not the first of Columba's hagiographers), and Kentigern, probably the four best-known early Scottish saints, all became subjects of a cult within a few decades of their deaths, but they were all also later recast, often as late as the twelfth or thirteenth centuries, as born-again saints to fit new fashions of hagiography or the demands of contemporary ecclesiastical politics. Our information about them and other early apostles of Scotland is entangled with the assumptions and motives of many generations of biographers and hagiographers. Medieval Scottish chroniclers were intent on tracing the long genealogy of present kings to demonstrate their status. Medieval chroniclers of the early Church were concerned with subsuming the long, difficult and doubtless uneven story of the progress of Christianity into a cult of the personality of a few holy men, at the expense of the trials of successive generations of missionaries whose role remains obscure and unsung.

Unpicking the story of Scottish Christianity is as much a task of stripping off the layers of camouflage put in place by hagiographers as it is a search for clues beyond the few hard facts that exist. Much turns on the interpretation of laconic, sometimes one-line pronouncements which have often been made the headlines of the story of early Christianity. Bede wrote of Ninian only in an aside to his fuller story of Columba's mission to convert the northern Picts: 'the southern Picts who live on this side of the mountains had, it is said, long ago given up the error of idolatry and received the true faith through the preaching of the Word by that reverend and saintly man, Bishop Nynia'. But who said this? Bede may have been the first of many historians to conflate Ninian and the Ninianic mission, a saint and his cult. More laconic still is the 'letter' sent by Patrick to Coroticus, King of Strathclyde, criticising him for invading Ireland and enslaving some of Patrick's own converts with his war band of 'mercenaries, heathen Scots and apostate Picts'.[2] If Patrick was so scathing because this was an act of treachery rather than another act of violence, the spiritual treachery of recent converts who by the 470s had deserted the faith, who had converted these 'Picts' but Ninian? But if this was so, it may show how fragile conversion was in the first Christian centuries, even by a charismatic leader such as Ninian. Early evangelisation, which depended so much on a conversion of the senses rather than the intellect, on the magic of miracles and prophecies rather than the preaching of the faith, could be countered by a greater magician or by the failure of its own magic, when crops failed, women turned barren or battles were lost. There was no tidal wave of Christianity sweeping across a hostile and difficult terrain, nor should we expect one.

Bede, by contrast, saw Columba not only as 'apostle of the Picts' beyond the mountains of the Mounth but also as the key link with the church of his own day: his 'monasteries placed within the boundaries of both peoples [Picts and Scots] are down to the present time held in great honour by them both'.[3] The historic abbot, the cult of *Colum Cille* and the expanding *paruchia* or monastic family of Iona are

27

not distinguished from each other. It would have been surprising if they had been for since the time of Columba the work of some seven generations of abbots, who were literally his 'heirs' (which is the meaning of the usual Irish word for abbot, *comarba*), had been to advance the reputation of a growing and eternal spiritual family, of monks and monasteries. Yet how did Columba, a kinsman of an Irish royal family, whose efforts in his own lifetime were narrowly concentrated along the western seaboard of Scotland, from Loch Awe in the south to Skye in the north, and who was thus a saint not even of Dalriada but of the Cenél Loairn whose territory this mostly was, come to be acknowledged as a saint of the confederation of peoples which would come to be encompassed in the kingdom of the Scots?

The story of the consolidation of Christianity under the mac Alpin kings is almost as mysterious as that of its beginnings. When Giric succeeded c. 878 a note in a much later Latin king list says that he 'was the first to give liberty to the Scottish Church, which was in servitude up to that time after the custom and fashion of the Picts'. This may mean that the rights of lay proprietors were abolished, in acute anticipation of the settlement of the tithe on parish churches in the reign of David I, some 250 years later, or it may simply mean that a Church, like a people in a time of the assimilation of cultures, laws and customs, *expected* to have its privileges acknowledged and confirmed by kings. In 906, Constantine II and his bishop Cellach climbed the 'hill of Faith' near Scone to proclaim that 'the rights in churches and gospels should be kept in conformity with [the customs of] the Scots'. The secular equivalent of the pronouncements of Giric and Constantine may have been the promulgation of the mysterious *leges Kenneth Macalpinae*, another guarantee of continuity with the past rather than a harbinger of change.[4] But this can only be speculation, as is so much else. In a sense, the first 500 years of the story of Scottish Christianity begin and end with a conundrum.

Ninian, a first apostle?

Hardest of all to determine is where the story should begin, for, like St Patrick, neither Ninian nor Columba can properly be thought of as a missionary in the modern sense of the term: all three almost certainly went to places where Christianity in some form already existed. Patrick and Ninian were not pioneers but bishops and it would have been unusual for a bishop even in the fifth century to be sent to work and die in a place beyond the known frontier if a community of Christians did not already exist there. Columba came, a century or so later in 563, not as a missionary but as a pilgrim; the role he cast for himself was that of the archetypal Irish pilgrim, the ascetic penitent. Ninian and Patrick were both Britons. Patrick, it has been argued, was born c.410, probably near Carlisle where he was educated, rather than as some have suggested further north in Strathclyde, and returned there about 445 before being sent as a bishop to Ireland c.460.[5]

The dates and nature of Ninian's career are much more a matter of speculation. Modern reviews of early saints conventionally ask for a date of birth: here is a saint for whom it would be difficult even to give the right century with any confidence. Bede does not say that Ninian was the founder or first bishop of St Martin's Church at Whithorn, the celebrated *Candida Casa* ('white house'), and the only clue to his precise period of operation is in an eighth-century work, the *Miracula Nyniae Episcopi*, which mentions a contemporary minor king called Tudwal. That king has been variously identified with both Man and the Dumbarton Britons, but even estimates of the period of the Strathclyde king vary from 450 to 570.[6] If, as seems more likely, Ninian belongs to the same century as Patrick, it is possible that the origin of this already established Christian colony in Galloway may point to a direct sea link with Gaul, where Ninian had trained, as well as to the more obvious encroachment across the Roman frontier of Hadrian's Wall of Romano-British Christianity. By 500 the seat of the diocese seems to have shifted to Kirkmadrine, in the Rhinns of Galloway some twenty-five miles to the west, where inscribed stones commemorate two 'holy and outstanding bishops', Viventius and Mavorius.

The purpose of this see is obscure: Ninian's mission, according to Bede, was to the southern Picts, but Kirkmadrine was so far west as to look more like a mission to the Irish. The shift of location and perhaps of focus is an odd commentary on Ninian's mission. Where did he make contact with the southern Picts? Some historians have seen him as far north as Fife or even Angus, both across the formidable barrier of the 'sea of Scotland'. Others have speculated that Pictish occupation south of the natural frontier of the Forth/Clyde line in the fifth century is a more plausible explanation than long-distance expeditions by Ninian to the north of it. The most likely area where contact was made, apart perhaps from possible scattered Pictish enclaves further east in Lothian, was in the frontier triangle bounded by present-day Edinburgh, Stirling and Glasgow, which would for long mark the uncertain and shifting boundaries between the kingdoms of the Picts, Strathclyde Britons and Bernicia. This was the frontier land competed for by Picts and Britons in the fifth and sixth centuries and which the Angles would win and lose in the course of the seventh. Saints, Ninian included, were to kings weapons of war rather than bringers of peace. Here too are significant numbers of *Eccles-* place-names suggesting early churches and dedications.[7] It would not be surprising if, for one reason or another, already by 540 a legend had grown up of Ninian consecrating a cemetery at St Ninians near Stirling, the linchpin of the three frontiers.

But what of the evidence of a mission by Ninian further north, beyond the Forth and even beyond the Tay into Angus? The specific evidence of dedications to Ninian and the general pattern of finds of long cist cemeteries to the north of the Forth both argue for his influence there, and especially in Fife,[8] but there was also a vogue in the twelfth century of dedications to Ninian which can lay false trails. With Ninian, perhaps more than with any other of Scotland's saints, the work of the man and the work of the cult are difficult to separate. The inhabitants of east Fife were, at least according to Bede, still pagan when Cuthbert, an Anglian monk from Melrose, was driven ashore in a storm in the mid-seventh century. If Christianity spread north from Whithorn through the river valleys of the Nith and Clyde, as well as consolidating in the easier terrain of the Tweed basin to the east, it must have taken the work of successive generations of Ninian's missionaries as well as his own lifetime. As in Ireland, the mission probably moved at the pace of the conversion of ruling families. By c.600 it had spread eighty miles to the north, allowing Kentigern to be established as the first bishop of the Dumbarton kingdom of Strathclyde; his seat, probably at Govan rather than Glasgow, marked the northernmost extent of the Ninianic mission some 150 years after his death.

Kentigern may himself give the lie to over-rigid notions of the missionary frontier; he may have been born in what was the territory of the Gododdin, perhaps near Culross on the northern shore of the Forth. If so, he crossed the frontier to pursue his career as a holy man. But little of this is apparent in 'official' accounts of him. The firmest fact known about this celebrated but enigmatic figure, the rogue amongst the communion of Scottish saints, is the date of his death, c.612. Some historians have even speculated that he is a composite figure, groomed if not born in the imagination of his hagiographers. Most that is known comes from a twelfth-century *Life* of Kentigern written by Jocelyn, a monk of Furness. Some have thought that this drew on an older *Life*, though estimates of how old that was range from the early seventh century to c.1000. Whatever its age, its results can be seen reproduced in Jocelyn's later *Life*, an unlikely picture of a Briton transformed into a saint of the Celtic Church, whose holiness is attested by a string of miracles, all the asceticism and more of a *Colum Cille*, and encounters with other Celtic saints. Like kings, religious centres as they gathered in prestige needed a foundation legend and it may be that the first attempt to provide one came within a century or so of Kentigern's death. If this is so, it is intriguing that Glasgow, so close to the seat of the kings of Strathclyde, by c.700 may have wanted a Gaelic saint rather than a British one.[9]

Heirs of Ninian

It was the seventh century which would also see the first revival of the cult of Ninian, but in the east rather than the west, for much of it was the product of a quite different mission – that of the neo-Northumbrian Church. No doubt anxious to find or invent its spiritual roots and to placate local opinion, it gave to the first and third Anglian bishops of Whithorn, which it took over as a diocese in 710, the names of *Pechthelm* and *Pechtwine*, 'leader of the Picts' and 'friend of the Picts': personal names, as important to holy men as to early kings, allowed the *arrivistes* of the Northumbrian Church to claim that they were true successors of Ninian.

The considerable interchange between the Churches of Northumbria and southern Pictland from the 680s onwards was probably also significant in giving birth to a burgeoning cult of Ninian there. The medieval Church would, from the twelfth century to the very eve of the sixteenth, forge and reforge holy alliances of Celtic and continental European saints in a tradition which links Jocelyn of Furness writing in the 1180s to the famous *Breviary* of Bishop Elphinstone of Aberdeen, compiled in 1506. The Pictish Church had done much the same fully 500 years before Jocelyn; by the time of the reign of Nechtan (706-24) the native cult of Ninian was being used to prepare the way for a new cult of St Peter, the symbol of its Roman party. Dedications to Ninian stood beside others to St Peter, especially in Angus and the Mearns and in Mar and Buchan. For almost eight centuries, until the time of the *Aberdeen Breviary*, churches at Restenneth and at Rosemarkie in Ross were linked with a legendary mission of a St Boniface as an apostle of Peter. Such churches were 'built after the Roman manner', in stone. But things are not always what they seem. For Boniface shared the saint's day of Curetán, an Irish bishop and abbot and colleague of Adomnán, abbot of Iona a century after Columba.[10] It may be that Curetán had been made to take on a Roman guise as Boniface: Celtic abbot became Roman saint.

The point is a speculation, but it may illustrate that the Pictish Church had to cope with – as well as be able to exploit – the customs and saints of not one tradition but three: a Romano-British tradition which went back to Ninian, a new Roman cult of Peter, and the powerful, fast-growing reputation of Columba's Iona. By the eighth century a new, still more exotic addition would be added to the communion of saints of the Pictish Church – Andrew, the Apostle. A legend was cultivated that St Rule was told by an angel to take the relics of St Andrew to Scotland and they along with the relics of Columba would become the twin emblems of a Church of the Scots which would emerge out of the Church of the Picts. Much is often made of the clash which, as we shall see, would surface at the Synod of Whitby in 664 in the shape of a dispute between Iona and Wilfrid, Bishop of the Northumbrian Church, over the dating of Easter and the tonsure. But these were minor matters when compared with what bound Iona, the Northumbrian Church and Rome together – bishops, the sacraments, the Latin liturgy and the mass. The clash at Whitby was of rival *paruchiae*, rather than competing cultures, Roman and Celtic. It takes a great deal of wishful thinking to turn the tension between the Celtic and Roman strains of seventh- and eighth-century Scottish Christianity into a Reformation struggle nine centuries before its time.[11]

Columba, Adomnán and the Ionan paruchia

For both Ninian in the fifth century and Wilfrid and Bede in the seventh- and eighth-century Northumbrian Church, the terrain of Scotland was the main arbiter of their thinking. They sought to claim as their own the natural breaks of valleys which mostly ran south and north to the barrier of the Forth and to find ways to hurdle that natural frontier. For Columba and his successors as abbots of Iona the geography of Scotland was quite different. Their natural routes of communication were by sea, across to Ireland and along the west coast of the Scottish mainland. The natural barrier for them was the Highland massif, which they called *Druim Alban*, 'the spine of Britain'. The dove of the church and his followers did not make their first push due east as the crow flies, across the massif before reaching the easier ground of the straths of the Tay and the Earn, but north-east through the huge fault of the Great Glen towards Inverness and south-east towards Lothian and Berwickshire. What is important to realise about that route is that when it *was* taken, by kings of Dalriada when they became kings of Picts in the ninth century, the Dalriadic church – of Iona – followed, but in a new guise. Columba's relics were split up: some went east to Dunkeld in 849, the rest went to Ireland. Two new *paruchiae* of Dunkeld and Kells were formed, with Dunkeld as the senior. The cult of Columba went with these kings, but not all of the monks themselves. The shape of the Church which resulted is difficult to pin down precisely: it was not quite a Celtic Church for a Pictish people, nor was it wholly a Roman Church for Pictish kings who had begun to emerge as kings of Scots. It was both of these things and more and therein lay its distinctive strength.

Columba came to Scotland in 563, but he probably went first to the unidentified island of *Hinba* and may not have settled on Iona until the early 570s. He made one expedition, and perhaps more, up the Great Glen to the court of Bridei, King of the northern Picts. But none of Columba's hagiographers claimed that he converted Bridei or significant numbers of his people. This was not a mission to preach the gospel but an expedition to impress a pagan king, by tribute and magic. The first account of Columba, the *Amra*, a vernacular poem written probably within a few years of his death in 597, recounted how a serpent had killed a man who had tried to avoid listening to the word of God; when Columba 'made the sign of the cross with his staff over the man's chest, he immediately arose'. By the time of the second account, the *Liber de virtutibus sancti Columbae*, written by one of Columba's successors as Abbot of Iona sometime in the 660s, the man had acquired a name – that of Maelchú, son of Bridei himself.

By then Iona had become a missionary church, preaching amongst the northern Picts in the name of the blessed Columba. But in Columba's own lifetime the efforts of Iona were confined largely to the territory of the Cenél Loairn, which must have been at least partly Christianised before he came to it. The first contact of this kinsman of the Irish royal family of Uí Néill after 563 was Conall mac Comgaill, King of Dalriada. By ordaining Conall's successor, Aedán mac Gabráin, Columba became at once the client and protector of the kings of Dalriada. Far from being an apostle of the Picts, as Bede claimed, Columba was the official apostle of the Dalriadic Scots. Beyond the quite narrow confines of the territory of Cenél Loairn, what may have been more significant than his contacts with the pagan King of Picts was his friendship with the King of the Dumbarton Britons, Rhydderch, who may have been a Christian. The routes to both the north-east and to the south-east were already mapped out in the lifetime of Columba, but these twin missions began only after his death.

The natural axis of the Ionan Church in Columba's lifetime was the Irish Sea. The *Amra* already acclaimed him as the 'protector of a hundred churches'. Where they were is difficult to say, at least in Ireland: many church dedications to him are to be found in the lands of the northern Uí Néill but none is explicitly mentioned in the annals before the seventh century. The important foundation of the monastery of Durrow in the southern Uí Néill lands may, however, have taken place in the last years of his life.[12] In Dalriada, Columba must have overseen the foundations on the mysterious islands of *Hinba* and *Elen*, at *Cell Diuni* to the south on the shores of Loch Awe, and at *Campus Lunge*, somewhere on Tiree to the north, as well as considerable activity on Skye. These were the beginnings of the Columban *paruchia*, a vast family chain of monasteries which within little more than a century of his death would stretch from the shores of the Moray Firth to the north of Ireland and as far south as Kells, founded in 807. Yet if only the skeleton of this *paruchia* was in place before 600, there can be no doubt that Columba was acknowledged within his own lifetime as both the vital head of this monastic family and as the confidante and protector of kings on both sides of the Irish Sea. A year after his ordination of Aedán as King of Dalriada, Columba was at the Convention of Druim Cett in 575 establishing an alliance of kings across the water and fostering a future high king of the Uí Néill. The key to the advancement of the Columban *paruchia* was the patronage of kings, both in Ireland and Dalriada.

Iona was the vital umbilical cord which linked the different parts of this monastic empire. Small though the island was, it acted as a base camp housing what were probably sizeable numbers of monks. There they lived in individual cells made of turf or stone. One historian has speculated that the ten-acre site of the vallum would have accommodated at least twenty monks,[13] but it is known that sixty-eight were massacred on the island in a Viking raid of 806. Both the early *Amra* and the later *Life* written by Adomnán suggest a community of 150 or more. Not all these were monks: the community was naturally divided into teachers, student deacons, workers and the active ministry. Most almost certainly came from Ireland, which was both Iona's strength and its eventual weakness. The great plague in Ireland of 664 probably did more than the Synod of Whitby in the same year to weaken its mission. When the Viking raids began – and Iona was attacked three times between 795 and 806 – the natural instinct of most of the community was to withdraw to the safety of Ireland, and especially to the new foundation at Kells. To some Irish historians, this has signalled the beginning of the displacement of Iona by Kells as the natural centre of the Columban world,[14] but the seniority of Dunkeld suggests that it was Iona's main heir.

Columba was an abbot and a pilgrim. Iona fitted both roles to perfection. This busy transit camp of the Columban *paruchia* became in Adomnán's *Life*, written *c.*690 at what must have been the peak of its activity, a 'small and remote island of the Britannic ocean'; Iona was recast as the backdrop for his picture of a simple holy man, giving it a timelessness and universality which rings deep chords even to this day. Prophet, apostle and pilgrim – his vision of Columba is a compelling one, which was designed to elevate its subject amongst the saints not just of the Irish Church but of western Christendom as a whole.[15]

Adomnán's *Life* was in itself an exercise in piety, but it was also a skilfully disguised political tract for its times. It was written only twenty-five years after the Synod of Whitby, where not only the leadership of Iona had been challenged by one of its own converts, the infant Church of Northumbria which had begun on Lindisfarne in the 630s under the guidance of Aidan, but the very reputation of Columba had been called into question. The issues of the dating of Easter and the tonsure camouflaged what was in essence a dispute over jurisdiction, one made more complicated by the secular politics of the court of Oswiu, King of Northumbria. This was *not* simply a clash between a Celtic and a Roman Church. In the course of the seventh century these issues would create tensions in the Churches of England, Pictland and Ireland. Iona was out of step with most of the Irish Church which had accepted these changes in 630. Like the Irish Church, that in Northumbria was of at least two minds: the dispute at Whitby in 664 was the first instalment of what by the 670s would crystallise as a struggle within it between Lindisfarne and Ripon, whose newly dedicated church and building programme marked the favour shown to it by the Anglian court.[16] By invoking the authority of St Peter as superior, Wilfrid, a monk of Lindisfarne but also future bishop at Ripon and the spokesman for the Roman party in the Northumbrian Church, in 664 had called in question the cult of Columba.

The tract of the Ionan abbots, Ségéne and his nephew Cumméne, was the first blast of the trumpet against Wilfrid; Adomnán's *Life* was the second, more subtly tuned one. At once selective with the facts and concerned only with the essential truth of *Colum Cille*, it took its subject out of the sphere of ecclesiastical politics into which he had been dragged by Wilfrid in 664. The most notable achievement of the expanding Columban Church – the founding of Lindisfarne in 635 – went unmentioned; little or nothing was said of the power and prestige of the Ionan *paruchia*. This was the life of a simple man of God whose simplicity mattered above all else. It has been the picture of Columba which has predominated ever since.

This compelling vision of *Colum Cille* was made at the expense of other members of the Columban Church, both in his lifetime and after, and also of other missionaries who did not belong to the Ionan *paruchia*. There are many heroes of the Celtic Church as a whole whose efforts have remained largely unsung. Two other Irish monks, Comgall of Bangor and Brendán of Clonfert, who both visited Columba on Iona, probably founded monasteries on Tiree, only twenty miles to the north-west of Iona and an alternative natural staging post for a monastic-based mission. Brendán, better known as the navigator of the North Atlantic, may also have founded a monastery on the Garvellach Islands in the Firth of Lorne, now remote but then another potential offshore base for a mission to the territory of the Cenél Loairn. Another monk of Bangor and contemporary, Moluag, made as his base the much larger island of Lismore further up the same Firth of Lorne. It was best located of all for a mission to the Cenél Loairn, a fact reflected in its choice as the seat of bishops of Argyll in the twelfth century.

The most explicit rivalry in the late sixth century lay between Columba's Iona and Donnán, who was based on the island of Eigg, between Iona and Skye and adjacent to the territory of northern frontier between the Cenél Gabráin and the Picts. Eigg, which had a community of no less than 150 in 617, became the focal point of a rival Celtic *paruchia* spreading over much of north-western Pictland. Dedications to Donnán range from Caithness and eastern Sutherland on the far north-eastern mainland to the Outer Isles of South Uist and Lewis in the far west; from Kildonan or Cille Donnain on the mainland in the north of Wester Ross beside Little Loch Broom to the islands of Kishorn and Eilean Donan, strategically placed in Loch Carron and Loch Alsh on the northern approaches to Skye from the mainland. The frontier between the churches of Columba and Donnán lay on Skye itself, where there may have been outright competition. Columba died the death of a white martyr, collapsing 'weary with age' before the altar of his church on Iona; Donnán and his community on Eigg died as red martyrs, massacred reputedly after a celebration of the mass in 617. The community on Eigg was revived early in the eighth century, for a list of holy men associated with it survives in the *Annals of Ulster*, but their names are their only witness. It almost certainly had disappeared before the end of that century when confronted by a renewed threat of violence, this time from the Vikings. The inheritor of Donnán's mission to the north-west was probably another monk from Bangor, Máelrubai, rather than a revived community on Eigg. The impact of Máelrubai's foundation in 673 at Applecross, on the mainland of Wester Ross directly looking over to the heart of Skye, extended across the north-west from Skye to Dingwall in the footsteps of Donnán and perhaps beyond.[17]

Although Columba, as has been seen, was the inspirer of a mission rather than a missionary himself, it may be that his expedition to the court of the northern Pictish king, Bridei, was in part to secure permission for a north-eastern mission to the Picts. If that is so, it is unlikely that much came of this mission before c.650. Geography and a rash of Christian standing stones, of both Class II and III, may combine to suggest that Rosemarkie, a natural terminus at the end of the Great Glen situated on the Black Isle on the northern shore of the Moray Firth, may have been a forward base for this post-Columban mission. Rosemarkie is associated with the shadowy figure of its bishop, Curetán, who would later be reclaimed by the Roman party in the Pictish church as St Boniface. The spread of Ionan influence further east, into Aberdeenshire, is more enigmatic still. The work of the real foot soldiers of the post-Columban Church remains an unwritten chapter in its history; it may be glimpsed, occasionally, in dedications to what seem to be strictly local saints, such as St Ternan or St Machar near Aberdeen who do not figure in the *Martyrology* of Óengus, the 'who's who' of saints of the Irish Church. And the frontier between the Ionan mission, which by the last quarter of the seventh century must have received some official recognition by both the Pictish Church and Pictish kings, and a rival mission pushing northwards from Fortriu is uncharted territory. By then, however, the most important figure in the mission was Adomnán himself, who was probably a regular visitor to Pictland.

The abbacy of Adomnán was the high point of the Columban mission to the Picts. Dedications to him are far more widespread than to any other figure in the Ionan mission save for Columba himself. They extend from west to east across the face of modern-day Scotland, from the peninsula of Kintyre in south-west Argyll to the furthest tip of the north-eastern mainland in Aberdeenshire. The bulk of them lie in Pictland itself, from the Ythan estuary, near Ellon in Aberdeenshire, to the shores of the Forth.[18] The real apostle to the Picts was not Columba but Adomnán, the prime mover of the cult of *Colum Cille*. The commentary of Bede, written within twenty years of his death, is silent testimony to the success of this, the most self-effacing of all Scottish saints. Adomnán's impact may also be measured, and perhaps more reliably, by his contact with kings and the aristocracy, not only of Ireland and Dalriada, but of Pictland and Northumberland as well. Columba had been influential at the Convention of Druim Cett in 575; the best measure of the widespread respect in which Adomnán was held is the Synod of Birr (in Co. Offaly) of 697 where his 'Law of the Innocents' was promulgated. This Law, which gave protection to women, children and the clergy against the brutalities of Dark Age warfare, would be ratified by the kings of the Picts and the Dalriadic Scots, and perhaps also by the King of Strathclyde, as well as by a long list of kings in Ireland. It is singular testimony to the widespread common Celtic (and now Christianised) culture extending from Ireland across Dalriada and Pictland to Lindisfarne and it marks the peak of the pan-Celtic influence of the Ionan *paruchia*.

The widespread acceptance of Adomnán's Law showed the Church acting in concert with kings. Sainthood was itself the reflection of the patronage of secular kings: it was, in a sense, the honours list of Irish and other kings. Adomnán was an abbot of Iona but also, like Columba, a kinsman of the Irish dynasty of Cenél Conaill. In the eighty-two years which separated Columba's death and Adomnán's elevation in 679, all but one of Columba's successors had come from his own kindred. But Adomnán, who was probably over fifty and had not been a monk of Iona before his elevation, was more than this. He was of a different line in the Cenél Conaill family than Columba and his previous successors, and was directly related to the northern ruling dynasty. His period as abbot (679-704) saw Iona linked more closely than ever to this Irish royal house, as well as better connected to reopen negotiations with Northumbria.[19] Adomnán, as a result, would within a few decades of his death achieve saintly status. As early as 727, his relics had begun to be transported across the Ionan *paruchia* in a portable shrine. Both Columba and Adomnán can also lay claim to a status something like that of a royal saint.

The official adoption of a cult of Adomnán, marked by the conservation of his relics, directly copied the pattern of the original cult of Columba. The famous

Brecbennach of Columba, a house-shaped portable shrine for his relics, which later somehow became associated with Monymusk in Aberdeenshire, became the most visible and potent symbol of the post-Columban Church. The Monymusk reliquary and other emblems of Columba would be carried into battle not only by kings of Dalriada but also by later kings of Scots. His crozier or *bachall* would accompany the armies of Constantine II which defeated Ivar II and his Vikings somewhere in Fortriu in 903 and Ragnall, Norse King of York, at the Tyne in 918. The *Brecbennach* would even be carried before the army of Robert Bruce at Bannockburn in 1314. But in 1314 the Scots went not with one patron saint but two, for they also carried with them the banner of St Andrew. This cult of twin national saints had begun five centuries before Bannockburn, amidst the complicated politics, both secular and ecclesiastical, of the kingdom of the Picts.

Kings, holy men and a 'national' church

The first duties of holy men were as the magicians and clerks of kings rather than acting as their conscience. Magic was demonstrated at the inauguration of a king or at his victory in battle; Aedán mac Gabráin prospered after he was ordained by Columba as King of Dalriada in 574 but his grandson Domnall Brecc met with a series of catastrophes ending in his death in 642 because, it was said, he had breached the promise made by his own kindred to remain faithful to Iona and the Irish family of Cenél Conaill. It is no coincidence that the appearance of origins legends of a line of kings, as perhaps in the reign of Nechtan (706-24), coincided with the emergence of an active clergy around the king. Clerics brought to the person of kings a heightened sense of the old ways, as the bringer of benefits and victories, before they promulgated a new view of kingship. Yet that came too.

The literate clergy were a mandarin class which forged a role for itself as the advocates and interpreters of high kingship. Columba and Adomnán concerned themselves with overkings, of Dalriada and of Picts, who were worthy of Christian record, like kings of Judah and Israel. The merging of different peoples under an overking of Picts in the eighth and ninth centuries was accompanied by the cultivation of different traditions of saints as well as the compilation of genealogies of kings by the learned orders. In the course of the eighth century, the Church of the Picts in turn adopted a cult of Peter, probably in the reign of Nechtan, and a cult of Andrew, perhaps in the next important reign, of Óengus (729-61). Both of these long reigns and especially that of Constantine (789-820) saw, it is likely, a flowering of officially sponsored ecclesiastical art of various kinds. It is not surprising that Pictish kings should begin to see themselves as God-given patrons of the Church after the fashion of the Roman Christian Emperor Constantine. The adoption by Pictish kings of the cult of Constantine (with no less than four kings so called between 789 and 997) mirrors its growing popularity after c.750 in western Europe, where the majesty of kingship and its nearness to God became increasingly intertwined, especially with the reign of Charlemagne.[20]

The most striking religious image sponsored by a Pictish king is the St Andrews tomb shrine, which (in similar vein to that at Meigle showing Daniel in the lions' den) depicts David holding open the jaws of a lion. It has similarities, too, with motifs in the *Book of Kells*, which was begun probably on Iona in the late eighth century.[21] The purpose of this stone-built shrine or sarcophagus, nearly six feet in length with elaborately carved panels and corner posts, which was found by workmen digging in the precincts of the later Cathedral in 1833, is unclear; perhaps it was to hold the relics of a saint, such as Andrew or Regulus, the legendary carrier of Andrew's bones to Scotland. There is also a crucial difference between it and the *Brecbennach*.[22] Columba's shrine in this form was portable, designed to be carried throughout the Ionan *paruchia*. The bewildering journeys of Columba's relics back and forward across the Irish Sea from their base on Iona in the seventh and eighth centuries were part of a saint's progress among the faithful. The St Andrews sarcophagus, in contrast, suggests a Church based firmly in an established royal centre rather than a missionary one. It hints at a Church of kings of Picts and Scots rather than a pan-Celtic one.

The cult of Columba was, however, still too powerful to be cast aside by these kings. Iona itself had been abandoned in 807 in the face of the Viking threat; most monks went probably to Ireland and only a token community was left behind. In the 840s the emblems of Columba were split, going west or east to the safer parts of the old Ionan *paruchia*. What is now known as the *Book of Kells* went from Iona to the new monastery at Kells; the fragmentary psalter known as the *Battler* also went to Ireland. The *Brecbennach* went east, as did Columba's crozier. His relics themselves were divided up in 849 to what in effect were now almost separate daughter churches, although Dunkeld could lay claim to seniority. In Ireland, the centre of Columba's *paruchia* shifted first to Kells and, in the mid-twelfth century, to Derry. In Scotland, the cult of Columba followed Kenneth mac Alpin eastwards to the royal and religious centre which he established at Dunkeld.

What Kenneth was doing was no more than a continuation of a process begun by previous kings of Picts. The two religious centres of the emerging kingdom of the Scots were at Dunkeld and St Andrews, carefully dedicated to different traditions of saints. It was a distinctively Scottish solution to a Scottish problem. In the ninth century Gaelic-named kings of Picts still chose to be buried in the sacred place of Iona. On the other hand, it had been a Pictish king with the very Gaelic name of Óengus who had founded a church at Kilrimont dedicated to a new, exotic saint, thereby creating a royal centre which would, as St Andrews, shortly become the focal point of the Church of the mac Alpin dynasty.[23] The very nature of ninth- and tenth-century kingship was composite; so was its Church.

Not surprisingly, the dual imagery of this Church – of Picts and Scots – was also reflected in its organisation. Traces of something like a regional episcopate can perhaps be deduced in parts of the kingdom of the Picts, such as Dunkeld, Brechin and St Andrews as early as the eighth century. But it is no coincidence that the boundaries of these three dioceses were confused and overlapped for they had sprung up around new religious centres. South of the Forth, diocesan boundaries may have been clearer because they corresponded more closely to the secular divisions of the old kingdoms of Strathclyde and Northumbria and were not further complicated by survivals of Columban monasteries. In an organisational sense there may have been by 1000 two churches of the kingdom of the Scots, north and south of the natural barrier of the Forth. But in each there had been a common heritage of Ionan, Pictish and Northumbrian influences; the difference lay in their different proportions.

It is also too easy to say that episcopacy was on the advance and monasticism was on the retreat. The revival in the Irish Church in the eighth century of the cult of asceticism, a return to the purity of the Columban-type pilgrim, was also felt in Pictland. In the next two centuries, new communities of *Céli Dé* (servants of God) were established, but they were no longer confined to minor centres such as Loch Leven; they were now also attached to major royal and religious centres such as Kilrimont and Dunkeld. The Culdees, as they are usually called, are the symbol of a Celtic revival in a post-Columban Church, which had survived the dismemberment of the Ionan *paruchia*. Its bishops, whose authority and jurisdiction were gradually being extended, are a reminder that the links of this Church with Rome were being strengthened at one and the same time.[24]

This was a Church within which 'Roman' bishops and 'Irish' abbots were partners rather than rivals, and sometimes combined in the figure of the same cleric. By 865 the annals refer to an abbot of the new or revived centre of Dunkeld who had a Gaelic name, Tuathal son of Artgus, but who was also 'chief bishop of Fortriu'. By 906, it is thought, Constantine II had a bishop who may have been based in St Andrews, called Cellach, and it would be to a monastery there rather than on Iona that this king retired in 943. Cellach and Constantine, however, made their announcement in 906 at Scone and it seems obvious that the authority of these two bishops extended far beyond the narrow bounds either of St Andrews or the old tribal kingdom of Fortriu. The first appearance of a bishop who was denoted by the specific name of his diocese came only in the reign of Alexander I, with Turgot, who was referred to in 1108 as 'Bishop of the Church of St Andrew of Scotland'. And the saying attributed to Giric (878-89), who gave 'freedom to the Scottish Church' was probably not written until about the same period.

The first explicit recognition of a national 'Scottish Church' came in a papal bull of 1174, which acknowledged its status as a 'special daughter' of Rome. There are, however, many examples in the later tenth and the eleventh centuries of bishops of Kilrimont who were called either 'Bishop of the Scots' or 'High Bishop of Scotland'. Their status was probably akin to that in the Irish Church of bishops resident at Armagh.[25] By then, well before the better-known efforts of Queen Margaret and her sons between 1070 and 1153, the firm foundations of a distinctive, national Church had been laid. A close link between Church and King, the merger of two cults of national saints and a new vision of the duties of Christian kings had all existed since the eighth century. Yet each of these developments had in turn come from the varied experiences of the different early kingdoms which made up the later composite kingdom of the Scots. The ninth- and tenth-century Church lay at ease with its past. In this, the church of a confederate people, Roman and Celtic traditions, abbot and bishop co-existed, as did the cults of Columba and Andrew, Adomnán and Ninian.

4

THE MAC ALPIN KINGS AND ALBA

BETWEEN 850 AND 1050 *REGNUM* AND *GENS* BEGAN TO COME TOGETHER, WITH far-reaching results for the shape of Scottish history.[1] In this period, a federal Pictish kingdom evolved, by accident as much as by design, into Alba, a kingdom expressed in terms of a territory as well as of a group of peoples; kings of Picts became kings of Scots, a new but significant collective name for what was still a collection of separate peoples. The centre of this kingdom still lay in Fortriu, at Scone, but the acquisition of Lothian, south of the 'sea of Scotland', and the loss of the Northern Isles and part of the west to the Norsemen in the ninth century, followed in the tenth by the steady incursion southwards of Norwegian earls of Orkney from their bridgehead in Caithness, provoked a vital shift in its internal balance.

For five centuries after this, the kingdom would not begin and end at a natural geographical barrier, from the Pentland Firth to the Forth/Clyde line. It would traverse that 'inland sea' of the Forth and, by 1018, although its frontier line in the north would remain a hazy one, the beginnings of the notion of a southern frontier line at the River Tweed had begun to emerge.[2] This, as much as the better-known twelfth century – which brought the novel force of feudalism to bear on the structure and customs of society – was an age that saw a profound clash between continuity and change. Kings consolidated their power but localities also developed a stronger sense of their own identity; kings of Scots emerged, but so did the mormaers (or 'great stewards') in a number of regions, and especially in Moray. These kings of Scots of the tenth and early eleventh centuries may often have had less power there than kings of Picts in the eighth or early ninth century. A surprising number of kings would meet violent deaths in the north between 900 and 1058.

What is often seen as the 'making of the kingdom' of the Scots[3] was a rearrangement of the basic facts of geography as well as of the balance of power between greater and lesser kings. The upshot, at least in terms of geography, was a rather different kingdom, and much of the dual character of Scottish kingship would result: for kings themselves as much as their vital fortress at Stirling, which guarded the first fordable point on the Forth, would be the 'brooch' which held Scotland together.[4] Medieval kings of Scots would lend unity to a people habitually described in royal charters as 'French, English and Scots'; in the case of the charter of King William to Robert de Brus, granting the huge lands of Annandale in the south-west c.1174, the scribe thought it prudent to add 'and Galwegians'. Yet these vital two centuries form a curiously enigmatic period, which begins and ends with two of the most celebrated but least-known of kings, Kenneth mac Alpin (c.843-58) and Macbeth (1040-57).

Reign of Kenneth mac Alpin

The seizure of the Pictish kingdom by Kenneth mac Alpin sometime between 839 and 844 is a curiously loose concept to hold as central a place as it usually does in Scottish history. The origins of this Dalriadic king who probably came from a previously obscure branch of the Cenél Gabráin are uncertain.[5] He was not the first king of Picts to rise without trace, but he differed from them in at least one important respect: here was not a Dalriadic newcomer to Forteviot[6] but a latecomer from the Gaelic west to a place which had seen many similar royal migrants before him. Why then did he have such difficulty in being acknowledged as king? Like Robert Bruce four and a half centuries later, Kenneth seems to have been on probation for at least the first half of his reign. Within a century of his death in 858, the notion of some sort of illicit coup had materialised. By the eleventh and twelfth centuries it was believed that Kenneth had achieved power by force or fraud. Variants of a common story began to appear about 1100; in Berchan's Prophecy the purge of the native Pictish nobility was accomplished in a single act of treachery – at perhaps the first, but certainly not the last 'black dinner' in Scottish history. Extra colour was given to the story in the later account of Giraldus Cambrensis, who told of a banquet at which traps were set under benches for the unsuspecting Pictish nobles.

Irrespective of how this 'destruction' of the Picts was achieved – and the sources which allege it differ as to whether it took place at Scone or Forteviot – many later chroniclers and compilers of king-lists thought that Kenneth's reign did mark a new departure in the practice of kingship and, with obvious hindsight, that it also represented the beginning of a new dynasty of kings. This interest seems to have been at its keenest in the reign of William the Lion (1165-1214): the list of kings in the Poppleton compilation, a late twelfth-century description of Scotia, calls Kenneth 'primus rex Scottorum'; and his successors were only then given a regnal order which has acquired a permanence ever since. And in the Irish Synchronisms, dating from the eleventh century, he was acknowledged as 'the first king from among the Gaels that assumed the kingdom of Scone'. Kenneth was not, however, the first to hold both kingships simultaneously, nor was he the first to come via the route of Dalriada, of which he was king from 840, to Pictavia, to which he succeeded sometime after 842. He and his next three successors – in turn his brother Donald, and his two sons Constantine and Aéd – were all called 'King of Picts' when their deaths were recorded in the near-contemporary Annals of Ulster. Nor was Kenneth the first king of Picts to give to his first two sons Roman and Gaelic names, in this case Constantine and Aéd. So Constantine (862-77), a King of Picts rather than 'King of Scots', still enjoys the chroniclers' title of Constantine I even though he was the second king of Picts of that name; historical 'faction' successfully passes for historical fact. Viewed in terms of a change of usage, it is the reign of Constantine's son, Donald II (889-900), which marks a turning-point. The Scottish Chronicle in the Poppleton manuscript, despite its stress on Kenneth as first in a long line of kings of Scots, still uses the form 'Pictavia' until Donald II's reign, when it begins to use 'Albania'. It was Donald, a grandson of Kenneth, who was the first of the mac Alpin kings to be called rí Alban ('King of Alba') in the Annals of Ulster.

What, if anything, marked out the reign of Kenneth mac Alpin from those which went before it? The Scottish Chronicle recorded, though in vague terms, that he invaded Lothian or 'Saxonia' fully six times; it also described how the Britons raided as far east as Dunblane and the Danes as far north as Dunkeld. Clearly Kenneth did not bring a new peace in his time. Even though the bulk of his attention seems to have focused on his southern frontier, there are indications, too, that he experienced trouble in the north. It was only after his reign, according to a note in the Latin king-list of Dalriada, that the *regnum* of the Scots was transferred to the land of the Picts, centred at Forteviot.[7] His own authority, it has been suggested, was acknowledged at most only in the four Pictish provinces south of the Mounth: in Fortriu itself, and in Fife, Atholl and Circenn.[8] Although he was claimed to be King of all the Picts, his sphere of influence was no greater than that of most kings of Picts in the century before him, and considerably less than that of Constantine (789-820) or Óengus (820-34), whose reigns marked the golden age of the Pictish kingdom of Fortriu and perhaps also the peak of Dalriadic migration eastward.[9] The three provinces north of the Mounth – Ce (Mar and Buchan), Fidach (Moray and Ross), and Cait (Caithness and south-east Sutherland) – may have been drifting out of the hands of the kingdom of Fortriu in the reign of Kenneth as part of an internal family struggle involving rivals from the Cenél Loairn. Though perhaps not yet damaging to Fortriu authority, it was the beginning of a process which would severely test mac Alpin kings in the century after 950. Here was, it seems, an ambitious and ruthless warlord, but not an overly successful one. Nor does he cut a very convincing figure as a national hero, even of legend, in the traditional role of defender of his people. It has plausibly been suggested that both Kenneth's rise to power in Dalriada in the 830s and his difficult consolidation of his authority in the Pictish kingdom after 842 rested on an alliance forged between him and Gothfrith, a king of the Hebrides, whose Norse name suggests that he, like Somerled after him, probably had mixed Scandinavian and Celtic ancestry.[10]

Yet power lies as much in the eye of the subject as in the grip of a king, and nowhere more so than in early Scotland; as an early Gaelic law tract said, 'the people make the king'.[11] It has been suggested that Kenneth's reign may have seen a revival of the claim to high kingship first made in the sixth century.[12] Certainly it saw a number of gestures made which may have lent an new aura to Pictish kingship. In 849 the relics of Columba, patron saint of Dalriada but also saint-in-waiting of the Pictish Church, were moved eastward to Dunkeld. It is unclear whether Kenneth founded a new religious centre there or merely completed the work of Constantine begun half a century earlier, but the activity centred on Dunkeld probably marked an increase in the king's influence in Atholl. In the Irish Synchronisms, Kenneth is said to have been the first to possess, not the kingdom of Scots, but the kingdom of Scone and it is in his reign that Scone, which may have been the base of the kingdom of Fortriu and perhaps also the place of inauguration of its kings,[13] seems to have been deliberately cultivated anew as a holy royal centre. The foundations of the eternal- triangle which supported Scottish kingship throughout much of the medieval period were now laid, but none of them, it is likely, belongs to the reign of the first of the mac Alpin kings. St Andrews, the spiritual home of the kingdom, had acquired a new status at least a century earlier when it had been assigned a biblical saint; Dunkeld, whose venerated Celtic saint would act as a counterbalance to the cult of Andrew, had been first developed as a religious shrine by Constantine; but Scone, scene of a significant battle in Pictish history in 728, described as a 'royal monastery' in 906 and built next to a 'hill of Faith', would become the hub of the mac Alpin dynasty.[14]

What was new about the reign of Kenneth and his successor Donald may have been a careful cultivation of the old. Scone and Dunkeld, existing centres of royal and ecclesiastical authority, were given enhanced status. It would not have been a surprising posture for a usurper to take. There is one further clue to this, one of the most mysterious of all reigns in Scottish history. A thirteenth-century source refers to the 'laws of mac Alpin'.[15] What this body of laws contained is unknown. If they existed, their content would have been less important than the act of their promulgation: the notions of a true king and a civilised people would both have been embraced by the 'laws of mac Alpin'.[16] It would have been another gesture, but such gestures were important in early kingship. Another symbolic token, which cannot be proved with any certainty, would have been, as some have suggested, the bringing to Scone of the Stone of Destiny. That inauguration stone would have fitted well into the established rites of inauguration, which marked the marriage of the king to the land and the people he ruled; the proclamation of a law code in the king's name would have renewed the marriage.[17] As with Columba, so with Kenneth: the man and the cult need to be separated.

Dynastic consolidation and political crises, 858-1034

The mac Alpin dynasty ruled, in the male line (with one exception), until 1034 and the death of Malcolm II.[18] Yet direct patrilineal succession was not established in that period.[19] Without exception grandsons and cousins (or occasionally, as in 858 and 877, brothers) succeeded rather than sons, although the long reigns of Constantine II (900-43), Kenneth II (971-95) and Malcolm II (1005-34) somewhat obscure the usual rotation between different segments of the royal kindred. Also, of the fourteen kings between the death of Kenneth in 858 and 1034, no fewer than five reigned for five years or less and a further four survived less than ten. To them should be added the sizeable number of royal sons-in-waiting who died by violence, whether at the hands of foreign invaders or, more often, of members of their own kindred (such as Olaf, son of Indulf, killed by his rival from the other segment of the royal family, or Kenneth, son of Malcolm in 977). The average length of reign was twelve years, testimony not only to the violent hazards still attached to kingship but also to the fact that many may well have succeeded only when well into middle age. Part of the novelty of the long reign of Malcolm II may have been that it induced confusion within the system of segmentary selection and produced not one but two mature candidates – Duncan and Macbeth.[20] Novel, too, at least in this period, was the fact that Duncan must have been a young man, quite unlike the role later cast for him in Shakespeare's play Macbeth. This was the dynasty which, it may fairly be claimed, oversaw the vital consolidation of the kingdom of the Scots but it – a family which had failed twice in the male line in the course of a century and a half – was not a particularly stable vehicle in control of the process.

The second half of the tenth century, lying between the end of the long reign of Constantine II in 943 and the accession of Malcolm II in 1005, saw recurrent disputes over the succession and reversionary interests which often ended in attempted coups. The only reign of any length within that period was that of Kenneth II but it is likely to have been just as marked by unrest throughout much of its length as was its end, which came when Kenneth was killed, according to the *Annals of Ulster*, by 'the treachery' of his own subjects. His death was only one of many manifestations of a long-standing feud between the two main segments of the mac Alpin dynasty which had begun before his reign and went on for more than half a century beyond it. During his short reign of four years, Dubh ('the black') son of Malcolm I (962-6) was challenged twice by his rival and eventual successor Culen (966-71), first unsuccessfully somewhere in Atholl and then at Forres 'by the treacherous nation of Moray'. The phrase was significant, at least to the thirteenth-century chronicler who devised it, for it suggested that this was more than simply a palace struggle; the north had become the centre of a reversionary interest.[21]

It is tempting to call the resulting see-sawing struggle between rival segments a mid-mac Alpin crisis, an equivalent of the mid-Stewart crisis of the second half of the sixteenth century. There were, however, three vital differences: the Stewart crisis, though real enough, saw only once a rival claimant to the throne for although it may have been a dispute about royal power it was not about sovereignty itself, as this may have been. The Stewart succession, whatever else the faults of the family, did not falter and in itself provoke instability. Nor was the mac Alpin crisis neatly contained within a fifty-year period for, despite the stabilising effects of the long reign of Malcolm II, it resurfaced in the 1030s and was put to rest only with the death of both Macbeth and his stepson Lulach in 1057-8.[22]

Friction between rival segments had for centuries spotted the history of both Irish and Pictish kingship, for such was almost a built-in fault of the system of tanistry.[23] The recurrent crisis which lasted for almost exactly a century after the death of Indulf in 962 was of a more serious dimension: the period might well be thought of as the wars of the Scottish succession. It was also a civil war: the long reign of Malcolm II began in 1005 only after 'a battle among the men of Alba themselves', as the *Annals of Ulster* put it, which resulted in the death of Kenneth III, son of Dubh. It is difficult to be sure of what provoked this intermittent civil war: part of the explanation must lie in the fact that the successive killings of Dubh in 966 and Culen in 971 produced not two rival royal segments but three. The position of a mac Alpin *tánaise* (literally, the 'expected one') became suddenly far more insecure.

Kings of Scots and their neighbours in the eighth and ninth centuries

The near-breakdown in the succession is likely to have been fuelled by the complicated political triangle which still involved kings of Picts and Scots with the Dumbarton kings of Strathclyde. In the course of the later eighth century, Strathclyde had become a client kingdom of the mac Alpin kings based at Scone, but by the 970s it may have posed a serious challenge, for one of Kenneth's first actions was to mount a punitive expedition against the Strathclyde Britons.[24] The Britons were not easily subdued, for a part of Kenneth's force came to grief when it was caught in boggy ground, probably near Abercorn, on the Forth.

The problem of Strathclyde became increasingly linked with another, potentially more dangerous external threat – that of Northumbria, which was taken over by the Danes in 866. The rise of a Viking kingdom based in York was the steady accompaniment against which the story of the mac Alpin dynasty had to be played out. A clue to the seriousness with which tenth-century mac Alpin kings took the new Northumbrian threat lies, again, in the names they chose for their sons – who were not their immediate successors but kings-in-waiting with the *rígdamna*. Kenneth mac Alpin, like kings of Picts before him, had deliberately chosen alternate Roman and Gaelic names for his first two sons: the cult of Pictish kingship and the cultivation of his own Gaelic past stood side by side in the figures of Constantine and Aéd. Yet by the early tenth century, Constantine II chose a Scandinavian name for his son Indulf, who eventually succeeded in 954; Indulf in his turn gave a Scandinavian name to one of his sons, Olaf.

The Scandinavian threat was real. Eóganán, son of Óengus, had been slaughtered along with 'others almost without number' by Norsemen in 839, precipitating a crisis in the succession. Constantine I had died along with a 'great multitude' in battle against the Danes in 877 when, it was said, 'the earth burst open under the men of Alba'.[25] Defeat at the hands of hostile invaders again provoked an internal crisis: Constantine was succeeded by his brother Aéd who lasted less than a year until he was, according to the *Annals of Ulster*, ousted by his own people. The death of the last of Kenneth mac Alpin's sons left the succession in a state of confusion, which was seemingly patched up only by the expedient of a joint kingship, shared between one of the conspirators, Aéd's first cousin Giric, and one of Kenneth's grandsons, Eochaid, a son of the King of the Britons. The Strathclyde dynasty had itself good reason to be wary of Scandinavian aggression, for Al Cluith, its capital on Dumbarton rock, had fallen after a four-month siege in 870 and large numbers of captives had been ferried to Dublin in a huge fleet of 200 longships. The early years of the long reign of Constantine II were also fraught with danger: in 903 Norsemen plundered Dunkeld 'and the whole of Alba' but were trapped in Strathearn in the following year by the 'men of Fortriu' who rallied behind the 'Battle Victory', or crozier of Columba. In 918 the same emblem led the Scots into battle at Corbridge against a potentially more serious enemy, a large force of Danes led by Ragnall, King of York.[26]

The Scandinavian threat dominated the first three-quarters of a century of the mac Alpin dynasty, but it was not a united front and that could be exploited. Just as Kenneth mac Alpin may have allied himself with a Viking king of the Hebrides against his rivals in Dalriada in the 830s, and as Constantine I (862-77) almost certainly connived at the Norse siege of Dumbarton in 870, so their successors were at times also able to play off Norwegian Dublin against Danish York. The risks were considerable, for it was as likely that they might be caught up in squabbles between Dublin and York, and such seems to have been the fate of Constantine in 877. The means of self-preservation were predictable for a dynasty which was still insecure, if surprising to those fed on a diet of a story of unrelenting hostility between Scandinavians and the other peoples of the Scottish mainland. One of Kenneth's daughters was married to a Norse king of Dublin sometime in the reign of his second son, Constantine I. The precedent for appeasement by marriage was established well before the reign of Constantine II, but he was the shrewdest practitioner of it: this Gaelic king, who shared with his uncle and predecessor the name of the first Christian emperor and would end his days in a house of *Céli Dé* at St Andrews, did not scruple to marry his daughter off to a heathen King of Dublin, Olaf III.[27]

The battle fought in Strathearn in 903 marked the last of the Scandinavian invasions of the mac Alpin realm. But the safety of the realm from external threat and the stability of the dynasty was in jeopardy for fully another century. Just as the threat from Danish kings of York receded, kings of Scots (for such they were all called from Donald II (889-900) onwards) were involved in a dangerous tussle for control of Northumbria between Dublin and the kingdom of Wessex after Sitric, a Dublin nominee, died in 927.[28] Constantine, faced with the prospect of having a West Saxon aggressor on his southern border rather than a Danish one, became involved in a dangerous game of propping up a Danish buffer state. The policy was complicated by revived internal fissures within the York kingdom, which put at risk its control over Northumbria. The next invasion of Constantine's kingdom came in 934 in the shape of a determined effort by Athelstan, King of both Wessex and York, to forestall a renewed triple alliance between the Scots, their largely client kingdom of Strathclyde, and Dublin – an alliance that had perhaps been marked by the marriage of Constantine's daughter to Olaf of Dublin. This was probably a more damaging expedition than any of the extended Viking raids that had been inflicted on the Scottish kingdom over the previous century. A combined army and fleet 'laid waste' to the east coast as far north as Dunnottar, the gateway to the Mounth; and Athelstan's navy menaced the coast as far north as Caithness.[29] It seems likely that Athelstan met with little organised resistance for he returned 'without any great victory', but the scene was set for one of the most decisive battles in Scottish history, the defeat suffered by Constantine and his allies at Brunanburh, somewhere near the Humber, in 937.

It is easy enough to appreciate why Brunanburh should hold a central place in the history of Wessex, for Saxon chroniclers boasted that 'no slaughter has ever been greater in this island' and the *Annals of Ulster* acknowledged that the victory guaranteed Athelstan a place as 'summit of the nobility of the western world'. Its effects on 'the hoary warrior' Constantine, whose army was put to flight leaving one of his sons dead on the battlefield, and on his kingdom were less dramatic but no less important.[30] Scotland had been brought to a crossroads by the ambitions of mac Alpin kings, but in 937 retreated from it. The prospect of a 'greater Scotland', encompassing the Northumbrian province of Bernicia as a buffer state and extending to the Tyne/Solway gap, receded. A more viable Scottish realm resulted, but more by accident than design.

The battle of Brunanburh had probably left Strathclyde even more vulnerable than the kingdom of the Scots. In 945 Athelstan's successor, Edmund, 'laid waste the land of the Cumbrians' but, according to the *Anglo-Saxon Chronicle*, he then 'granted it all to Malcolm, King of Scots', who had succeeded when Constantine retreated into the holy life in 943.[31] This recognition by Wessex of the overlordship long exercised by kings of Scots over Strathclyde clarified the ambiguities in the treaty concluded between Constantine and Edward the Elder of Wessex in 920, which had seemed incidentally to grant the Scots an interest in Strathclyde in return for non-interference in the affairs of York.[32] The confusion into which the York kingdom fell between the assassination of Edmund in 946 and the arrival of a new, ruthless claimant in the formidable shape of the Norwegian king, Eirik Bloodaxe in 947, twice installed and twice removed in the space of the next five years, brought to a head another crisis in the intricate quadrille performed around the vulnerable York kingdom by kings of Scots, Wessex, and two sets of rival Scandinavian interests.

Between 948 and 952 Eirik Bloodaxe had brooded in exile on Orkney. His presence there could only have reinforced the insecurity felt by Malcolm I at the prospect of being encircled by hostile Norwegian interests, based not only in York but also in Caithness and the Northern Isles. It is no coincidence that Malcolm was the first of the mac Alpin kings to attempt to expand his authority north of the Spey. His success was modest: one victory somewhere in Moray against Cellach, who was probably mormaer of that province. His successors were no more effective.

It may be doubted whether Malcolm himself was killed in Moray rather than by the men of the Mearns in 954, but his son Dubh was certainly overthrown in the hostile territory across the Mounth in Moray in 966. Kenneth II in turn failed to make any impression against Sigurd, the Norwegian Earl of Orkney or to contest his annexation of Caithness; by 989 Sigurd the Stout seems to have extended his control further south, into Moray.[33] Neither Kenneth III (997-1005) nor Malcolm II (1005-34) possessed the means or authority in the north to check this powerful Earl of Orkney. Malcolm acknowledged as much by agreeing to an arranged marriage to Sigurd c.1008. It is unclear from the source – the *Orkneyinga Saga*, at once verbose and sparing with the facts – whether the bride was the daughter of Malcolm himself or of Malcolm, son of Máelbrigte and mormaer of Moray; this saga of the earls of Orkney might well not have bothered to discriminate between a 'king of Scots' and a provincial king of Moray.[34] At least in this case the prospective husband was a recent convert to Christianity. By the time of Sigurd's death, at Clontarf in 1014, the boundary between the earls of Orkney and kings of Scots lay at the Moray Firth or perhaps even further south.

Although the mac Alpin kings made little or no headway in the north in the tenth century, much of their survival depended on the progress they made in expanding and consolidating their southern frontier. The degree of control which these kings exercised over Lothian from the reign of Giric (878-89) is difficult to assess with any precision and even its chronology is uncertain. Maps give a clarity and a permanence that does not belong to a territory which was both a frontier zone and a disputed outpost of York. The extension of Scottish rule ebbed and flowed rather than edged forward. The extent of the authority of Scottish kings in the late ninth and early tenth centuries is unclear: Lothian up to the line of the Tweed or even to the Lammermuir Hills is *terra incognita*.[35] By 927 and the onset of the new interest taken by Wessex in York, the Scots' influence had been forced into retreat, though how far is uncertain. Presumably it had receded beyond Edinburgh, which again fell into Scottish hands during the reign of Indulf (954-62).

The early years of the reign of Malcolm II, which witnessed a renewal by him of raids into Northumbria, including a siege of Durham, must indicate that sometime in the intervening period there had been both an expansion and contraction of the southern frontier. Both the invasion by Malcolm I, who had reached as far south as the Tees in 949, and the two extended raids by Kenneth II in the 970s, one as far south as Stainmore, were probably parts of a renewed attempt to lay claim not simply to Lothian and the Merse (Berwickshire) but to Bernicia, stretching from the Forth to the Tees. Only the first of these two issues – control of Lothian and the Merse and overlordship, nominal or otherwise, of Bernicia – was settled in this period. Edgar, King of Wessex, had conceded the fact of the virtual Scottish occupation of Lothian in 973 and Malcolm II's victory in 1018 at Carham, immediately to the south of Tweed, had merely turned occupation into annexation. Yet 1018, so often fastened upon as marking the firm delineation of a southern frontier along the line of the Tweed, could not have seemed so decisive or final a victory at the time. Rather than settling the Lothian question, it raised again the unresolved issue of Bernicia. Carham solved nothing, but it promised this now ambitious dynasty much. Those greater ambitions never materialised, but they were nonetheless a sign of a new confidence amongst mac Alpin kings, born of a novel sense of security on their southern frontier.

The achievement of the mac Alpin dynasty was a considerable but curiously ambiguous one. Malcolm II was hailed by Irish annals as 'King of Alba, the honour of all the west of Europe'.[36] Yet his death marked a genuine crisis in the succession, after kingship passed to his daughter's son, Duncan. The dispute which ensued and threatened the whole mac Alpin line was complex and it is likely some of the key details of the two claimants are unknown. Like Duncan, Macbeth had a claim through a female line, via his wife, Gruoch. More significant to each was probably their descent in the male line, by which Macbeth was linked to the Cenél Loairn. If a dynasty is to be judged by the heirs it leaves, the mac Alpin legacy in the 1030s was an awkward variant of the parable of the talents. That the kingdom survived intact what was in effect a twenty-five-year war of the mac Alpin succession was a fluke rather than a testimony to the strength of the dynasty.

The mac Alpin dynasty: success and failure

The gains and losses of the period 839-1034 were finely balanced: the annexation of Lothian and the virtual control long exercised over at least part of the sprawling kingdom of Strathclyde was set against the conceding of much of the west to the Vikings and the inability of kings of Scots to check, still less to undo, the expansion southwards to the Moray Firth of the Norwegian earls of Orkney. The deciding element in the balance sheet might well be the north. The huge province of Moray, which stretched from the Mounth to Ross and from the west coast overlooking Skye to the Spey or perhaps even further east, has, however, perhaps the most hidden history of all of Scotland's regions. It is difficult to be confident of assessments of how much power or lack of power the mac Alpin kings of Scots had in Moray. The use by the Orkneyinga Saga of the term 'King of the Scots' to describe rulers of Moray in the tenth and eleventh centuries partly confuses the issue but also indicates how contemporaries other than kings of Scots and their chroniclers viewed them. Some of the Irish annals, too, refer to them as 'kings'.[37] Usually they are referred to in Scottish sources as mormaers.

The term mormaer was first used to describe one of the leading magnates fighting alongside Constantine II in the battle of Corbridge in 918. The first firm identification with a region was in 938, when the death of a mormaer of Angus was recorded. Three mormaers are named in 976. It is clear, by the early eleventh century at least, that the mormaers of Moray were not nominees of kings of Scots but inherited the title. It may also be that, just as the system of alternating succession was receding in the line of mac Alpin kings of Scots, it was still accepted practice amongst the mormaers of Moray. The function of the mormaer was a military one, the leader of the 'army' of his province. Yet effective power lay with him rather than with the king in Scone, to whom he owed allegiance. To borrow the language of later medieval Scottish kingship, it is likely that kings of Scots depended on the local power of the mormaers to extend an authority they would not otherwise have had into the far-flung parts of their kingdom. And, in the case of Moray, the largest and the most northerly of the mormaerdoms, allegiance must have been nominal.[38]

Kings based in Scone never seem to have been in a position to use Moray as a dower kingdom. The issue was complicated by two factors. Part of the reason for the confusion in nomenclature – with the rulers of Moray being called jarls or kings by Norwegian sources, kings by Irish chroniclers, and mormaers by later Scottish sources – may have been the claim which they made to descent from an alternative Dalriadic kindred, the Cenél Loairn rather than the Cenél Gabráin. This rival line may have had new life and status breathed into it by genealogists in the tenth century. By then, however, the mac Alpin dynasty, stemming from the Cenél Gabráin, may have spoken with two voices on the tribute owed to them in the north. From the time of Kenneth mac Alpin and his son Constantine I, the dynasty had recurrently involved itself in the affairs of Moray, with disastrous results. Three of its kings had been killed in the north or on its doorstep, in 900, 954 and 995.[39] Duncan I would be the next, killed in the north in 1040 by Macbeth, a rival who had greater power there.

The problem of Moray thus raises in acute terms the more general problem of the nature of Scottish kingship. It has even been suggested that Scotland by the late tenth or eleventh centuries saw a bipartite system, reminiscent of the situation before 650 when there were two kings of Picts, north and south of the Mounth.[40] Were the descendants of Kenneth mac Alpin dynasty kings only south of the Dee? The answer may lie again in the subtleties of the gradations of kingship. The overriding achievement of the mac Alpin dynasty was that its members were accepted, within a generation or so of the troubled reign of Kenneth, as undisputed high kings, a development significant enough to attract a new name to the territory from which they claimed allegiance: Alba or Scotia.

What was probably happening in the localities is likely to have been the same process as seen in Ireland, but in a much accelerated form, of the recasting of kings as underkings, and eventually as territorial lords. The rank of toiseach reappeared significantly in Ireland at much the same time as the mormaer, which can be seen in Buchan in the Book of Deer, to indicate that this is the old tribal rí by another name.[41] The mac Alpin kings were emerging as overkings at the expense of lesser ranks of kings. In most cases, the achievement of this dynasty was to oversee the reshuffling of a three-fold system of kingship into a two-fold relationship of king and subjects, a process revealed partly by the use of new names for the ruirí, such as the Gaelic (but non-Irish) term mormaer or comes (earl) in its Latin form.

In their own demesne, these new lords probably had as much if not more power in the eleventh century than before. Later kings of Scots, such as Alexander II or III, would insist on referring to powerful provincial rulers as 'Lord of the Isles' or 'Lord of Galloway', whereas in reality they were kings in all but the name allowed them. The consolidation of the mac Alpin dynasty was achieved, but only at the expense of a lesson which future kings of Scots would take carefully to heart: that a kingdom which so naturally divided into three different parts, to the north and south of the Mounth and beyond the Forth, was held together more securely by treating its distinctive parts differently. The characteristic balance of power which would last throughout the medieval period – between kings of Scots and their great lords in their various localities – was in the process of being struck.

Kings of Scots, their peoples and Alba

That process was greatly assisted by an important change in the notion of what the people and the land were. The early tenth century is the date of the composition of the *Senchus fer n Alban*, which recast a new origin legend, not simply for the mac Alpin kings but also for their people, who are seen as 'men of Alba' rather than of Dalriada. The subjects of Constantine II went into battle against the Vikings in 918 with the cry of *Albanaich!* It would be difficult to contend that Constantine had more power than the greatest of Pictish kings, his namesake of a century earlier, but the basis of his power rested on a new identification of the *regnum* and the *gens*. Added to this was the significance of the word Alba itself. Before 900 it had been synonymous with the whole of Britain; after 900 it became increasingly identified with the land over which the kings of Scots ruled and in which their people lived. By 1034, when Malcolm at his death was hailed as 'King of Scotia' or 'Scotland', the process was virtually complete.[42] A compelling image of a trinity of king, people and land had been coined; it would last for centuries.

The makers of this new identity for king and people are unknown. But it is very likely that they were drawn from the learned orders or the clergy of the dual Church of Picts and Scots, whose status depended on that of the king. The literate clergy had already shown themselves to be the interpreters of high kingship. They concerned themselves with overkings, like the 'kings of Dalriada' or the *reges Pictorum*, latter-day counterparts of Old Testament kings. It was they who must have developed the cults of St Peter and Constantine which had marked the eighth and early ninth centuries. Cultural achievements of the mac Alpin dynasty are curiously absent; no great ornamental sculpture or manuscripts comparable to the *Book of Kells* survive from this period. Yet the new image cast for the mac Alpin dynasty and its realm between 840 and 1050 must largely have been the creation of a written culture. In contrast, lesser kings, now recast by the scribes as mormaers or earls, would have to wait until the sixteenth century for their own written histories. What continued, in many of the far-flung parts of the realm, was a traditional oral culture which continued to sing praises of the warlord and chief of the kindred. 'Kings of Scots', by contrast, drew their authority not only from the genealogy of their kindred but also from a cultivation by the learned orders of the twin notions of 'the Scottish people' and the territory of Alba or Scotia. *Regnum* and *gens* had come together, but the result was more than the sum of the parts.

Yet in the 1030s much of this achievement was at risk. The succession of Duncan in 1034 did not, it seems, gain wide acceptance. It is debatable whether Macbeth had a better claim. What the claim of Macbeth does, however, is to illustrate the weaknesses of mac Alpin rule. The disaffection of Macbeth may have originated in the death of his wife's nephew, who was one of the many victims of Malcolm II, one of the most ruthless of the kings of Scots and dubbed the 'aggressor'.[43] In a sense, the dispute was a revival of the long feud between the descendants of Dubh and Kenneth II.[44] Duncan's own credibility as a candidate must partly have turned on his grooming in the dower kingdom of Cumbria. But his interest in Cumbria may have provoked ambitions in Northumbria and his ill-advised attack on Durham in 1039. Again, failure outside the kingdom may have helped trigger resistance within it.

Duncan's attempt in the following year to impose his authority in the north brought about his downfall: he was defeated and killed near Elgin. His death was the fourth of a series of unsuccessful attempts by kings of Scots to impose their will on Moray. The alliance forged between Macbeth and Thorfinn, Earl of Orkney, resulted probably from Duncan's efforts to reclaim Caithness; and a second defeat, at the hands of Thorfinn, who pursued the defeated Duncan as far south as Fife, may have triggered Macbeth's coup.[45] Duncan's conspicuous failure as a military leader may also help explain the impression that the new King of Scots, whose power base lay far to the north of Scone, enjoyed a long, unwonted period of harmony with his subjects.

Macbeth reigned for seventeen years (1040-57). The first attempt to oust him, which predictably came from Duncan's father Crínán, secular Abbot of Dunkeld, did not materialise until 1045 and ended with Crínán's decisive defeat and death. The beginnings of external interference by Earl Siward of Northumbria, who was connected to the house of Crínán, came in 1046. Macbeth, however, was confident enough to leave his kingdom to travel to Rome in 1050 and there, it was said, he 'scattered money like seed'. A second expedition by Siward in 1054 met with partial success. Malcolm, son of Duncan, was installed, but only apparently in Strathclyde and Lothian; Macbeth retreated northwards to his heartland. The details of the final decisive confrontation, between Macbeth and Malcolm at Lumphanan north of the Mounth in 1057, are scanty. Macbeth was killed but the war of the mac Alpin succession was not yet over. His stepson, Lulach, also son of a mormaer of Moray, took his place, until he too was killed seven months later in Strathbogie. The reasons for the success of Malcolm's two-stage coup, after seventeen years of rule by Macbeth, are elusive but they may be connected with the death of Thorfinn, Macbeth's powerful ally, if it is the case (and the mathematics are problematic) that he died in 1057.[46] As with so much of Malcolm III's long reign (1058-93), hard facts are elusive. Macbeth's own reputation is elusive too, but it would have been strange for a simple usurper to be buried, as he was, in that graveyard of Scottish kings before and after him, on Iona. 1057 or 1058 are too easily seen as a turning-point for Scotland and its kings. If the accession of Malcolm marked anything, it was the end of the crisis of the mac Alpin succession. The consolidation of the kingdom had survived the self-induced crisis of the dynasty.

Part II
MEDIEVAL SCOTLAND

5

Peoples of the Kingdom

IN 1138, AT THE BATTLE OF THE STANDARD, DAVID I (1124-53) LED A DIVERSE ARMY made up of 'Normans, Germans, English, Northumbrians and Cumbrians, men of Teviotdale and Lothian, Galwegians, and Scots'. It was, to the English they confronted, an astonishing assembly of the diverse peoples who comprised the kingdom of the Scots. David, who in his time at the court of Henry I of England (1100-35) had 'rubbed off all the tarnish of Scottish barbarity', led an army which 'bellowed the war-cry of their fathers', heard against the Viking Ivar in 903 and at Corbridge in 918, *Albanaich, Albanaich!*[1] The different *gentes* which comprised this army – new settlers such as the French, Anglo-Normans and Flemings, as well as natives such as the men of Moray who were close to the king's own line and the men of Lorn in the third rank – also made up the kingdom of the Scots. David and his successors, of the line of Canmore or macMalcolm, managed to be at once both Celtic and feudal kings. By the end of the twelfth century, the notion of a territorial kingdom, stretching to the north and south of the 'Scottish sea' of the Forth and embracing both Scotia and Lothian, was also widely accepted. Yet the tradition of submission to a king of Scots did not begin with the Canmore dynasty; it was already more than two centuries old.[2]

Their kingdom was regulated by a complex patchwork combining a typically western European feudal framework with Celtic custom, which can be traced in many of its details to Irish law tracts of the seventh or eighth centuries.[3] The result was what has been called a 'hybrid kingdom',[4] and one of its marks was the emergence of a composite common law of Scotland by the twelfth century. The conjunction of old and new marked every aspect of life in twelfth-century Scotland. The king's army was a mixture of feudal knights, products of the typical western European system of knight service, and a 'common army' of infantry and bowmen, which had for centuries acknowledged 'forinsec' or 'Scottish service' to the king. At Bannockburn in 1314 they still comprised the bulk of Robert I's army. The king's revenue was raised through a combination of the new land assessments of feudal tenure – knights' fees – and the older obligations such as *cain*. The difficulty lies in terminology, for phrases such as 'Scottish service' or 'the custom in that country' (in this case Argyll) were the invention of the king's clerks. The older, established nexus of law, custom and kingship had no convenient name – nor has to this day. Yet by 1100 Gaelic law and custom had reached almost every part of what we now know as Scotland, including Lothian in the south-east. The new feudalism of the twelfth century came into contact not with a receding Celtic culture but with a still expanding one.[5]

A series of obscure clues – early cultivated terraces revealed by place-names or aerial photography – suggests a pattern of intensive land clearance in the later Dark Ages. It is unlikely that the 400-year development of Pictish kingship was not paralleled in patterns of changing human settlement and farming. There are oblique indications, which would make sense in terms of the political consolidation of Scotland's early peoples, of a downhill movement of settlement from land above the 600-700 feet barrier; these also imply an extension of agriculture from pastoral into arable.[6] It is tempting to enter the hazardous terrain of place-names and explore the significance of the 300 or so places which can be shown to carry the Pictish word *pett-* or *pit-* (like Pitcaple or Pitfour) or the even commoner incidence of place-names with the later Gaelic element *baile* (such as Balgreen or Baldinnie),[7] but it is sufficient to note that these and a number of other place-name elements all suggest farming. There are considerable difficulties in dating such evidence, but three general patterns seem likely: there was fairly intensive land clearance, which in some cases (such as that of Bloak Moss in Ayrshire) might be dated from as early as the fifth century; there was extensive early clearance of forests; and a marked development of arable farming is suggested by the emergence of a fiscal system which, with its emphasis on units of land which could easily be subdivided such as the *davoch*, *carucate* or ploughgate, and *arachor*, had an eye on the amount of ground which could be ploughed as well as on the number of animals which could be reared.[8]

It is likely, too, that in more fertile regions such as Lothian and the Merse the pace of clearance was quickening by the tenth and eleventh centuries. In Berwickshire, the grant by Edgar (1097-1107) of Old Cambus, which already had a mill, must have been of largely arable ground although it contained within its bounds place-names with a Scandinavian element such as *-dale* (valley) and *-law* (hill), which are more precisely dateable to the tenth century once Scandinavian influence had impressed itself into northern English speech; here was land which must have been converted to arable within the previous century or so.[9] The pattern and rhythms of farming were probably much the same in 1300 as in 1000 or even 800. The underlying feature is of the continuity of settlement. Prime sites, like the Upper Tweeddale valley, had probably been staked out many centuries before 1100. Feudal settlement enlarged townships, filled in waste (which can mean moss, moor or wood), and extended the arable infield; but, especially in fertile areas like Lothian, these were usually not self-contained blocks of land but scattered strips, sometimes miles apart. Like earlier Viking settlers in Orkney, the evidence is not that the incomers pushed natives off the good land but rather that they tended to take up land which had hitherto lain uncultivated. The emphasis on arable land would also suggest that the population increase which marked the twelfth and thirteenth centuries had already begun before 1100. The exact population of Scotland in 1100, 1200 or 1300 can only be guessed at; two recent estimates for its level about 1300 have ranged from half a million to one million.[10] The precise level is, however, less important than the undoubted fact that it was increasing.

The greatest difference between farming in 800 and in 1200 was probably not in the balance between pastoral and arable, which was progressively extended over centuries, but in the mix of different kinds of animals reared: at Buckquoy in Orkney in the ninth and tenth centuries, cattle accounted for 50 per cent of the food supply, sheep for 30 per cent and pigs for 20 per cent.[11] By the twelfth century and certainly by the thirteenth, farming for cash and hence for the wool, fleece or hide rather than the carcass had resulted in a marked shift towards the rearing of sheep. By the fourteenth or fifteenth century, this is quantifiable: a fairly typical

Lothian laird in 1424 had 2,618 sheep and 248 cattle.[12] Everywhere in Scotland, both north and south of the Forth, it is likely that farming was mixed, although the balance varied. The need to keep flocks of animals for food and, increasingly after 1100, for cash, suggests a basic similarity in the shape of farming which to an extent overrode regional differences imposed by geography. It also strongly suggests a continuity over the centuries, linking the Scotland of the 'Dark Ages' with the feudal kingdom of the Scots rather than a sharp break and a new beginning sometime after 1100.

There were new departures. The twelfth and thirteenth centuries would see the appearance of a Scottish coinage, unknown before the reign of David I, and by the 1280s some forty million silver pennies are likely to have been in circulation;[13] the founding of king's or royal burghs, given extensive privileges to trade both within the kingdom and outside it; and the granting of vast tracts of land to religious houses of orders such as the Cistercians, Benedictines and Tironensians which gave a new impetus to patterns of farming of the land. Yet it would be a mistake to think of eleventh-century society as a primitive, sluggish, but moveable object which met the irresistible forces of stronger and more centralising kingship, new towns and church reform. With each of these developments, there was not a hostile take-over but some sort of new *modus vivendi*. The essential dynamics were threefold: an older society, still expanding and evolving, which must have seen extensive settlement, especially in the tenth and eleventh centuries; a new feudal system which accelerated existing patterns of change and intensified rather than transformed how Scots worked the land; and the twelfth-century general European economic boom which encouraged cultivation, trade and population increase. It was the interaction of these three elements, varying from region to region and even from place to place, which redrew the face of early medieval Scotland, but the outline of an earlier society was still clearly visible.

Lords and men

The feudal system was a method of landholding and assessment of land, by which a fief or estate was granted by the superior and his heirs to be held by a vassal and his heirs; it carried with it and guaranteed a hierarchy of rank by which lordship was exercised and homage was paid between two 'free' persons; and it gave to the king a uniform military structure, based on the armoured knight and his retinue.[14] Lordship was thus as much about power, which depended on people of various sorts, as it was about land. Lordship, it has been said, 'implied castles, halls, mills, villages or ferm touns, and indeed churches and chapels too'.[15] The mixture of old and new which so strikingly characterised the emergence of a feudal kingdom also marked its peoples. The nobility were a mixture of new Anglo-French or Flemish adventurers and an established Celtic aristocracy, such as the great mormaers of Fife or Strathearn whose power in their own accustomed territories continued unimpaired, although recast in a new terminology of 'earls'. By 1200 the process of intermarriage and assimilation between new and old nobility was already well under way. The dependants of the new aristocratic settlers, granted land in return for the obligation of knight service according to the classical pattern of military feudalism, seem to have settled beside an older, parallel class of middle- and lesser-ranking lords rather than displacing them; both were forerunners of lairds of later medieval Scotland.

The status before and after 1100 of other occupiers of the land – the bulk of the ordinary people of Scotland – is far less certain, but it is likely that most were already tied to their lord in some fashion, being liable to pay tribute of one kind or another, whether *cain* (originally reckoned in cattle but later payable in grain or cheese as well), *conveth* (originally a duty of free quarter or hospitality) or a food-rent. The recasting of a Celtic fiscal system which had already been based on land, though focused on the family unit or household and tempered by the ethos of the kindred, to one based on land measurement tied to feudal lordship was less drastic than might be imagined; many of the old features and even their names remained well into the medieval period, grafted on to the new.[16] By 1200 a class of husbandmen was beginning to appear, some of whom held land which had been split up or sub-infeudated in strict feudal terms 'of' a greater or lesser lord. But most husbandmen (who may have farmed up to thirty acres in the twelfth century) and cottars (who worked only five to ten acres) by then probably did not hold land in feudal terms, in return for a fixed fee, but more likely leased it for a money rent, usually on a yearly basis.

The twelfth and thirteenth centuries saw a dual process: the importation of a feudal model of landholding and its naturalisation as a practical, working system. The pattern of feudal settlement as a result varied from one region to another, but still more so within each locality; the already heavily settled, fertile area of east Berwickshire, for example, resembled a patchwork quilt of different working arrangements. The same centuries also saw the development of a cash economy, which was connected only indirectly to the new feudal kingship and which had as great an impact on the fabric of rural life as feudalism; surplus grain, produce and livestock might be sold in a local market, and rents were increasingly paid in cash rather than in kind. The land itself did not see a massive colonisation and extension of settlement after 1100. It was already extensively settled by 1100, shown in the striking fact that the majority of rural place-names can be traced to the period before 1250.[17] Yet over the course of the twelfth and thirteenth centuries it would be more intensively settled and farmed than ever before.

At the apex of the feudal pyramid were the great lords. In the later twelfth century there was none greater than the younger brother of William I (1165-1214), David, Earl of Huntingdon, who was granted the huge lordship of Garioch in Aberdeenshire about 1180. Garioch was typical in the sense that it was an area which had already been substantially improved in recent times, both before and after 1100. The name itself (literally 'place of roughness') suggests that the lordship originally had been restricted to the hilly country east of Oyne which bordered on the Grampian Highlands, but that there had been an eastward and downhill drift of settlement, probably starting well before 1100, along the line of the valley of the River Urie to the point where it eventually met the River Don at Inverurie. It was Inverurie which became the *caput* of Garioch once David had acquired it; a castle was established there by 1199 and it was already a royal burgh by 1195.[18] The locale and pre-feudal development of Garioch, already incorporating a mix of hilly pasture and a lower-lying grain-growing district, were both very typical; more unusual was its size (100 square miles in extent), its neat geographical rationality, and the clear-cut nature of its symbols of feudal lordship, the motte-and-bailey castle and the castle burgh, both at Inverurie.

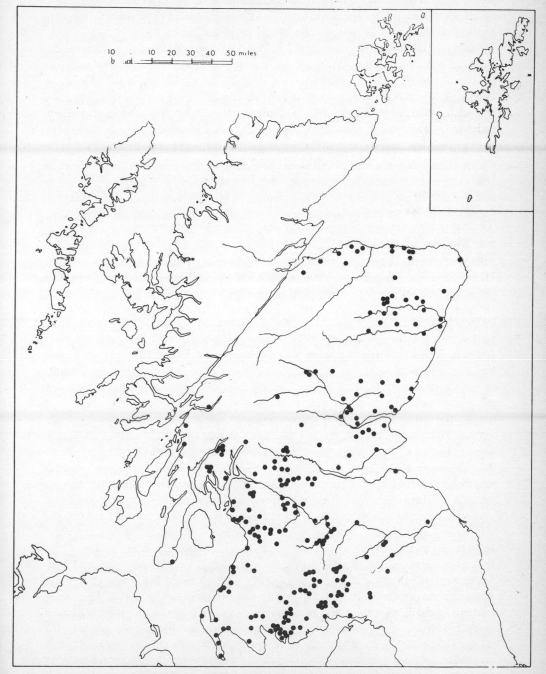

Map 4 Motte-and-bailey castles in twelfth-century Scotland

David, like his grandfather, a more famous David, Earl of Huntingdon (who became David I in 1124), was a member of an Anglo-Scottish aristocracy who brought Anglo-Norman and Flemish clients and retainers from his English to his Scottish estates to act as stewards and constables. In this he was typical of the flood of 'Norman' families recruited by successive kings of the twelfth century from David I onwards – such as Avenel, de Soules, Melville or Somerville. Some, like the family of de Brus (coming from the village of Brix near Cherbourg), were indeed Norman but most were drawn from a concoction of English, Breton, French, Picard or Flemish and their chief attribute was their obscurity. Amongst them, it is worth noting, was Walter, the third son of a steward of the lords of Dol in Brittany; arriving in 1136, he would serve as Steward to three twelfth-century kings of Scots and found a family of Stewart which by 1200 had established a great lordship based largely in Renfrew, Ayrshire, Bute and Cowal. By 1300 the Stewart family had become one of the most powerful of the west Highland chiefs. Although many of these lords retained estates or interests in England, France or the Low Countries, only the greatest (including members of the royal house) tried to run their various estates as a single concern. For some the tug of loyalties would not be settled until well into the Wars of Independence, but for most there were already by the 1150s signs that their first loyalty lay with the King of Scots.[19]

The details of royal patronage of this new foreign aristocracy are to be found in charters for knight service, such as the massive grant of the lands of Annandale in 1124 to Robert de Brus for ten knights or the grants in 1161 to the Steward of lands in Renfrewshire for five.[20] Its extent and initial purpose are perhaps most easily grasped by a glance at a map of the motte-and-bailey castles founded in the twelfth century. These primitive earthen mounds, often encircled by a dry ditch and topped by a wooden tower, bespattered the hostile and difficult country in the south-west; the fact that there were sixty-two in Dumfriesshire and Kirkcudbrightshire and a further forty-five in Ayrshire corresponds to the fact that the bulk of David I's grants were south of the Forth but it demonstrates far more graphically how hazardous life could be for these foreign colonists on the frontier of the king's authority.[21] By 1250, a new phase was opening in the king's relations with his far-flung localities; the motte was giving way to the castle, built professionally of stone and lime, and an altogether more formidable construction.

The locus in the second phase of feudal colonisation, from the 1160s onwards, was, by contrast, to the north of the Forth and the proportion of Flemish colonists favoured by Malcolm IV (1153-65) and William I (1165-1214) was much greater. Royal concerns focused especially on the troubled territory of Moray, which had revolted against David I in 1130. The death of Angus, mormaer of Moray, in that revolt had given the crown an unusual opportunity to remodel this vast earldom, but it chose a careful, staged process of encirclement; the chief vehicle of this strategy was a Flemish family called Freskin which had probably belonged to the first wave of Flemish settlers planted by David I in West Lothian and in Clydesdale. Within three generations of its first grants in the Laich of Moray, this alien family had gone native, taking in the process the surname de Moravia.[22] This story, in three episodes spread over a century and a half, of the settlement, promotion and naturalisation of a family of colonists could be taken as an archetype of the Anglo-Norman era. The period was, in one sense, about the consolidation of kingship and the growing unity of the realm. In another, it was about the re-creation of regionalised structures of aristocratic power. The new regional magnates – the earls – were as powerful and as localist as the Celtic mormaers before them.

Many of the new earls were indeed old mormaers under a new guise. The mormaers of Fife were probably the most senior noble family in Scotland before and after 1100; they claimed the privilege of the enthronement of Malcolm III in 1058 and of Alexander III in 1249. Duncan I (c.1133-54), created Earl of Fife in 1136, was the first native Scot to have his existing territory and lordship regranted in feudal terms. He and his son, Duncan II (1154-1204), were the most prominent of the Celtic aristocracy who turned 'feudal' in the twelfth century, as shown by the frequency and the prominence of their names among the witnesses on royal charters, but they were otherwise typical of a class of Celtic great lords like the earls of Lennox or Strathearn.[23] In the first two vital feudal centuries, two seemingly contradictory processes were going on at the same time. Ancient native lords were happily assuming the full panoply of new-style military feudalism; but the newcomers, whether French, Flemish or Anglo-Norman, were also rapidly being absorbed by native society, which of course varied in its racial make-up. As late as the fifteenth century earls of Lennox were also known as mormaers.

It may be useful to remember the different experiences of feudalism in Wales and Ireland. In the case of Wales, Norman lords took over ancient jurisdictions and territories but 'preserved or adopted or mangled them as occasion required'.[24] This was how feudal colonisation should have worked and it may well have done so in Lothian and in many parts of eastern Scotland north of the Forth. In Ireland, by contrast, a gap had begun to open up by the middle of the thirteenth century between the foreign colonists who retained lands and interests on both sides of the Irish Sea and those who were settlers proper;[25] the latter, who would in course of time come to be known by a revealing confusion of names including the Old English and the English-Irish, often became more Gaelicised than the Gaels themselves, thereby blurring distinctions between colonial loyalties and native power. Scotland's equivalent of the Irish Sea was the still formidable barrier of the Forth, but a different, linguistic frontier was beginning to supplant it by the fourteenth century – the so-called 'Highland line', increasingly separating Gaelic culture from that of the rest of Scotland. Although some great noble families (most notably the Campbells) bridged that linguistic divide, most lords in Celtic Scotland, whether descended from settlers of the twelfth and thirteenth centuries or from older native kindred, chose to consolidate their sense of separateness. The feudal adventurers, far from creating a homogeneous noble class, picked their separate, highly localised paths through the history of medieval Scotland – and nothing is more significant for its history.

The forebears of the lairds of later medieval Scotland were also an amalgam of lesser Celtic lords like thanes (a Latin translation of the Gaelic *toisech*, the lowest of the three layers of Celtic *rí*) and the upper ranks of the retinue of newly created feudal knights. Recruits of both Scottish kings and their great lords, these foreign vassals were drawn fairly evenly from Normans, Bretons and Flemings in the first wave of feudalism between the 1120s and 1150s. Some were specialist royal servants – armourers, falconers, even cooks or brewers. Others, especially those who migrated with a lord, were often stewards or chamberlains, the essential managers of a noble estate and household. Some of the most favoured were created minor tenants-in-chief of the king, owing the service of a knight or a military sergeand and thus becoming junior members of the *bons gens* or *nobiles viri*, but most had a parcel of their lord's land with perhaps one or two touns in it sub-infeudated to them and were delegated powers as his vassals.[26] In time these powers would crystallise in the barony, which had its own mill, parish church and court to deal with both law and order and civil matters, such as tenants' and boundary disputes. By the fifteenth century, when the pattern of lordship was becoming more complex, baronies were split up, amalgamated and increasing in number; but the essential link between the lord and his affinity remained, although now cast in the new terms of a written bond of manrent by which protection was offered in exchange for homage.[27] By then the explicit link with military feudalism had been extinct for more than a century, which has induced some historians to think of a 'bastard feudalism' in which money had replaced military service, but the other two key attributes of feudalism remained – the link between lord and land and between lord and men.

The noble incomers and their dependants did not bring with them their own peasantry and tenantry. The feudal settlement of Scotland was not a plantation, still less a conquest. It is likely that the greatest continuity between the tenth and eleventh centuries and the early medieval period lay in the people who lived on and worked the land. The reigns of David I and his two grandsons probably brought little difference to the pattern of their working lives: as late as 1200 it seems likely that the bulk of the peasantry, as before 1100, enjoyed few if any legal freedoms. Most were tied in some way to the land they worked, but freedom was still an abstract and largely meaningless concept (as were the later terms used in burghs 'free' and 'unfree') in a society where lineage and kindred were the determinants of its workings. The new lords – whether secular or ecclesiastical, earls and knights, or monasteries and abbeys – inherited a system in which *nativi*, already thirled to their lord by blood or place of birth, were expected to perform labour services on their estates, often as *neyfs* or serfs. It is unlikely that the *neyfs* were a standardised underclass, everywhere bound to their lord in the same practical terms, and by the fourteenth century they would quietly disappear from documentary record. The explanation of their disappearance lies in the changes already taking place in the twelfth century if not before towards a cash economy, in which food-rents were replaced, in whole or in part, for money rents. By then surpluses of grain, crops or produce were regularly turned into cash at a local market.[28]

By the early thirteenth century two broad bands of peasantry in Lowland Scotland were beginning to take shape: husbandmen, conventionally called bondmen by the reign of Alexander III, and cottars.[29] Rent rolls surviving from the fourteenth century show that husbandmen had land leased to them approximately seven times the acreage worked by cottars, but the variation at the extremes might be as much as fifty times. By then, with less available labour after the fall in population triggered by the successive epidemics of plague from 1349 onwards, holdings were probably a good deal larger than a century earlier; in Dalkeith in 1377 most husbandmen were farming about fifty acres whereas cottars, who were often sub-tenants of the husbandmen, worked between five and ten. With holdings as small as this, many cottars probably also worked part-time for money wages to supplement their income; until about 1250 perhaps on the prestige projects of building mottes which demanded a large supply of low-cost, unskilled labour, but more usually on the land of a neighbouring husbandman or on the demesne of their own or a neighbouring lord.

Both groups lived very similar lives, their crops confined to oats, barley and some rye, and housed in small huts made crudely of clay, turf, wattle and wood which, clustered together, made up a rural township or toun. A toun might hold one, two or three husbandmen as the major tenants, and anything between half a dozen and two dozen sub-tenants.[30] Yet both husbandmen and cottars were increasingly likely to hold their land on the same terms – a short lease, of no more than five years but as often as not of only one. In 1305 the 'poor husbandmen of the King in Scotland' petitioned Edward I of England to redress the precariousness of their tenure 'so that they shall no longer hold their land, as hitherto, from one year to the next'.[31] In practice what this meant was that rents were renegotiated annually, according to the yield of the last harvest. Tied in other ways – obliged to take grain to the lord's mill and subject to his barony court – both husbandmen and cottars were in practice still as dependent on their lord as before. Although not freeholders and thus not a part of the formal feudal system, it was husbandmen, still obliged after 1100 as before to render service to the 'common army', who must have made up the bulk of Scottish armies throughout the medieval period.

The hub of rural life everywhere in Scotland was the toun, but there were many variants. South of the Forth and especially in the fertile ground of Lothian, townships were likely to be larger, a parish church was usually at its centre and the lord's hall or castle would not be far away. North of the Forth, by contrast, settlement might be much more dispersed, the touns smaller and the church remote from other human settlement.[32] Although documentary evidence cannot prove its existence in the twelfth or thirteenth centuries, it is likely that the more precise distinction of property rights brought about by written charters encouraged a sharper division of land use, into infield (which was intensively cropped and manured) and outfield (where a third to a half of the ground was cropped in any one year, the rest being left as pasture).[33] The steady pressure of a growing population in the twelfth and thirteenth centuries resulted in more intensive use of the land: this could take a number of forms, including the cultivation of waste and marginal sites, the splitting up of existing townships and the formation of new ones. The visible traces of these processes are still there, in the place-names 'Easter' or 'Wester', 'Nether' or 'Upper', or lie half-hidden behind personal names given to the new holdings. By the fifteenth century when it first explicitly appears in written record (but perhaps as early as the twelfth), the pattern of farming in many townships had conformed to the system of 'runrig', in which rigs or strips of land were circulated systematically, year by year, amongst the tenants and sub-tenants of a toun.[34] It was a pattern of farming which lasted until the eighteenth century.

The land itself and the problems and opportunities it brought with it was the major determinant of life throughout the medieval period and beyond; it was also the greatest force for continuity. In 1100 most habitable land, both north and south of the Forth, was already settled, and in a far more even pattern than today. By 1500 comparatively little new land had been settled and it would be the sudden upward surge in population in the sixteenth century that would bring about a new impetus to break into highly marginal land; but in the medieval period the existing land was being worked as never before. Arable farming would meet the needs of a growing population, but it was sheep and cattle which provided the basis for Scotland's overseas trade – with the Low Countries, the Baltic and France – from the twelfth century until the sixteenth and what prosperity it had.

Towns, traders and craftsmen

Towns, by contrast, were almost a wholly new feature of twelfth-century Scotland. There must have been both local markets and possibly also temporary fairs before this. The size of hillfort settlements, such as those at Eildon Hill and Traprain Law, in the Dark Age period and the acceleration of cultivation and rural settlement patterns in the eleventh century make the existence of 'proto-towns' possible.[35] A few of the burghs created in the twelfth century, especially those which (like the Canongate beside Edinburgh) were associated with a new religious house, were wholly new towns built on green-field sites, but most of the places at which burghs (such as Perth and Stirling) developed were at obvious crossing points of rivers or conveniently sited at river mouths or estuaries (like Aberdeen, Berwick and Inverkeithing) and had old names associated with them.

The term 'burgh' was a legal one, which gave a set of privileges to a community of burgesses, including the right of trade and freedom from toll throughout the kingdom. Burgh charters, together with the *Leges Burgorum*, a manual of detailed practices relating to almost every aspect of urban life, trade and industry taken almost verbatim from the customs of the English town of Newcastle-upon-Tyne, were part of a calculated policy of innovation first practised by David I and continued by his two grandsons. About fifteen burghs can trace their foundation to David's reign, including Dunfermline, Edinburgh, Perth and Stirling, but the two most important for much of the early medieval period – Berwick and Roxburgh – are described as burghs before 1124.[36] By 1200, Perth was ranked second behind Berwick, their position both dependent on a flourishing cloth industry and a busy trade in the export of wool overseas, mostly to Flanders. The third vital factor – after trade and industry – in the growth of towns was the presence of the court, either as (in the case of Perth and Stirling particularly) a place of frequent resort of the king's household or as a base for a royal mint. Berwick, Roxburgh and Edinburgh each had a mint established by 1153, but by 1250 there were mints in no fewer than sixteen burghs, extending from Ayr and Berwick to Inverness.[37]

Towns are easier to trace and describe than townspeople. Even their names are elusive or, once found, enigmatic. Eighty-two burgesses of Berwick were recorded in a list of 1291 and scrutiny of a variety of documents for early thirteenth-century Perth yields about a hundred names.[38] The earliest town-dwellers, it seems likely, were a mixture of native Scots and the same range of immigrants as typified rural settlement in twelfth-century Lowland Scotland. In towns, however, the proportion of foreign incomers would have been much larger and the presence of Flemings, who brought with them the skills of cloth-making, particularly conspicuous. Foreign merchants, factors and skippers would have been common too. Berwick, Scotland's largest town, was a foreign trading colony; the Red Hall and the White Hall, both in the town's Seagate, were the bases for Flemish and German merchants by the end of the thirteenth century.[39] Most of the ships which carried Scotland's exports were foreign-owned and crewed; two-thirds of the ships carrying Scottish goods and wrecked on the English coast in the fourteenth century were Flemish.[40]

Towns were distinguished from the countryside which surrounded them by the privileges which their burgesses enjoyed and by the specialised nature of their economy and industry. The names of the earliest town-dwellers, where they are available, were often simple occupational ones such as 'le Pestour' (pistor, baker), Leiper (basketmaker) and Slater, or place-names indicating place of origin, like the twelfth-century Glaswegians John de Govan, Ralph of Haddington and Robert of Mithyngby (Miningsby in Lincolnshire).[41] They underline the narrow range of occupations in Scottish medieval towns and the wide-ranging origins of their inhabitants. Urban industry was still limited and rudimentary, tied almost entirely to animal-based products; much of it was based in the household, in a backyard rather than in a specialist workshop. Its mainstays were wool and leather. Wool spawned a range of specialist occupations, such as fulling, waulking and weaving, but in the larger towns the complicated process was controlled, to their considerable profit, by the dyers who supervised the production of a range of cloth from rough, lost-cost material for peasant consumption to finer, dyed cloths for the nobility. Leather was an even more complex and much longer industrial process involving tanners and souters, but it too seems to have been controlled by one group, the skinners; it provided much of the necessities of life, including shoes, saddles, armour and cooking utensils.[42]

The cloth and leather industries underline an important fact about medieval urban life: towns were set apart from the countryside by their privileges, but town and country fed on each other for materials, labour and capital. The long industrial processes associated with cloth and leather stretched like tentacles into the countryside. The export of wool and hides – the mainstays of Scotland's overseas trade until the sixteenth society – meant, however, that the countryside was also linked to the town by the umbilical cords of trade, coin and exchange. Towns were dangerous places, prone to warfare, disease and fire – there were seven towns including Aberdeen, Montrose, Perth and Stirling which each suffered a serious fire, according to Walter Bower, in 1244 alone. Their populations needed regular human replenishment, which could come only from the countryside.

The most obvious sign of the close connection which tied landowner and burgh merchant together was the presence in many burghs of properties or warehouses belonging to religious orders, who were the single largest wool producers. The largest flock of sheep of any of the religious houses was probably that of Melrose Abbey, which numbered 15,000 in the 1370s. The information drawn from the handbook of an Italian merchant, Francesco Pegolotti, for earlier in that century suggests that the eight main Cistercian houses had a combined flock of well over 40,000 sheep.[43] This was the main reason that by the end of the thirteenth century no fewer than fifteen religious houses, ranging from nearby Coldstream and Melrose to distant Arbroath and Kinloss, held property in the premier port of Berwick. Exporters of wool, importers of grain and consumers of urban skills, the monasteries were a vital component in the development of towns.[44] The monastic presence in the major ports, combined with the typical siting of friaries on the edge of towns, gave a highly distinctive character to urban life there.

The general conditions of life and diet in towns were probably little different from those in the small rural townships. The size of towns is to be measured usually in hundreds rather than thousands. Berwick is unlikely to have had much more than 6,000 or 7,000 inhabitants in the thirteenth century. Most town-dwellers probably lived in crudely constructed one-storey dwellings built of post and wattle walls, often covered in daub or clay for insulation, and thatched with straw, rushes or heather; most lasted little more than twenty-five years. Few houses would have been of two storeys, although some may have had a cellar below and, by the fourteenth century, a solar above. Fewer still would have have been built in stone before 1500; they were unusual enough to have been merited special mention in charters. Few towns spilled outside their original town plan as their economies developed and populations increased – Perth was the only known example of a burgh to develop suburbs before the sixteenth century. A process called repletion, not dissimilar to the infilling of congested rural settlement patterns, took place; the original burgage plots, strips of a standard width, were developed into their backlands. A short walk along a close from the merchant's house typically sited on the market frontage to the workshop or yard at the back of the rig was a progress through the ordered hierarchy of a medieval burgh; it would have begun with the most privileged of the burgesses who by the thirteenth century were organising themselves into an exclusive guild, past the ordinary burgesses who might be master craftsmen or small traders, to the unrecorded majority of 'unfree' made up of journeymen, day labourers and, it is likely, a large number of widowed or single women.[45]

The symbols of the burgh were the market cross, the tolbooth and the parish church, each in its way a token of the role of the community of the burgh. It was to the community that privileges were granted by the king and the burgh community remained in being, largely unaltered, from the twelfth century to the brink of the seventeenth. The twelfth-century Burgh Laws, carefully copied out by an Inverness burgess as late as the 1560s, and the thirteenth-century Statutes of the Guild of Berwick, transcribed for the Dunfermline guildry in the fifteenth century, linked burghs and burgesses in 1200 and 1600 and gave a far greater uniformity to Scottish burghs than their English counterparts.[46] Yet the homogeneous nature of burgh law and institutions needs to be set against the diversity of Scottish towns, each of which had its own distinctive range of industry and trade. There was no such thing as a 'typical' medieval town. The boom years of the later twelfth and thirteenth centuries brought prosperity, especially to the cloth centres of Berwick and Perth. The sharp contraction of overseas trade with the onset of the Wars of Independence, combined with the loss of Berwick to the English in 1333, brought an increasing struggle amongst the other burghs for their share of a much reduced volume of exports. Life in most towns, as a result, was a good deal harder and more unpredictable in the fourteenth and fifteenth centuries than it had been in the previous two centuries.

Highlands and 'clans'

Before the fourteenth century contemporaries did not think of a division between Highland and Lowland society. There was no 'Highland line' and the main physical divisions were still the Forth, the Mounth and druim Alban (the spine of Britain); these did not correspond to the Highland line when it emerged but cut across it, separating western from central and Grampian Highlands. A more significant

64

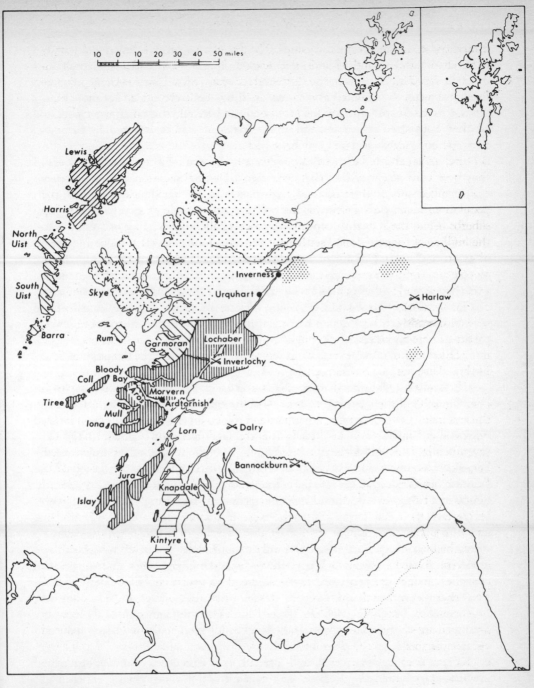

10 0 10 20 30 40 50 miles

Lewis

Harris

North
Uist

South
Uist

Skye

Barra

Rum

Coll

Tiree

Mull

Iona

Jura

Islay

Bloody
Bay

Garmoran

Morvern

Ardtornish

Lorn

Knapdale

Kintyre

Lochaber

Inverlochy

Dalry

Bannockburn

Inverness

Urquhart

Harlaw

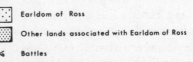

Map 5 Lordship of the Isles, 1284-1493

distinction could be made between the far north-west beyond Ardnamurchan and the rest of the Highlands. There were no monasteries in the north-west, in contrast to the medieval foundations in Argyll which were undergoing extensive refurbishment in the fifteenth century; parish kirks were spread far more thinly across its landscape. The small Isles, the Outer Isles and the north-west mainland lacked both the hall-houses and stone castles which proliferated in mainland Kintyre and Argyll, and on Lismore or Mull.[47]

All of the Highlands lacked burghs, but there were both fairs and licensed markets – seventeen in all by 1550.[48] Important medieval burghs such as Inverness, Elgin or Perth were situated on the fringes of the Highlands; the extent of their impact is unknown because so few of their early charters have survived. The volume of the export trade in hides from Inverness and the huge number of animal bones revealed in archaeological excavations in Perth, of deer as well as cattle and sheep, suggest a close link operated between town and Highland countryside. In the sixteenth century, for which more evidence is available, it is clear that the traffic was two-way: Perth's metalworkers had customers for their agricultural implements as far away as Inverness-shire.[49] Moray, Easter Ross, the Lennox, much of the Grampian and central Highlands and Argyll were all well within range of Lowland influence of various kinds.

The structure of rural settlement was much the same in the Highlands as it was in the Lowlands, although the balance, because of the poor quality of the soil, was more firmly tilted towards pastoral farming. Most of the peasantry, as in the Lowlands, held their land as tenants or sub-tenants on a short lease, although in places there might be greater expectation in the Highlands that land might be held of kinsmen; in Kintyre in 1541 two-thirds of lands leased by the crown to a Mackay were sub-let to other Mackays.[50] Nor had the Highlands escaped the impact of the Anglo-Norman era: successive waves of feudal settlers infiltrated the society of the eastern Highlands from the late twelfth century until the very end of the thirteenth. Parallel to this, as elsewhere, ran the recasting of existing custom and power structures in feudal terms. Even the west Highlands did not escape: the first surviving charter for knight service, granting land east of Loch Awe to Gillascop macGilchrist, dates from 1240. The only variant along the western seaboard was that the service was usually for a galley of so many oars rather than a mounted knight.[51] In almost every respect, the difference between Highlands and Lowlands was of degree rather than kind: both were aristocratic societies, organised for war, held together largely through the force of kin. Their differences have been neatly summed up: 'Highland society was based on kinship modified by feudalism, Lowland society on feudalism tempered by kinship.'[52]

There was, however, no single pattern of interaction between kinship and feudalism in the Highlands. Both were dynamic and flexible systems, which might interact differently in the various parts of the Highlands or when the power structure of a locality had to be re-formed. This might happen with the natural process of families dying out in the male line or with the periodic interference by the crown, displacing one family and replacing it with another. There was also, at times, a deliberate policy by the crown of balancing a nexus of feudal power against one based on kin. One example lay in thirteenth-century Moray, held for the crown after the revolt of 1215 by a seemingly unholy alliance of a Celtic MacTaggart made

Earl of Ross and the originally Flemish family of Freskin who had taken the name de Moravia (Murray) and were now made Earls of Sutherland.[53]

An even more important example for the history of the Highlands in the thirteenth century rests in the main and various sub-plots explaining the position of their two most powerful families and the political alliance between them. One was a family of incomers – the Comyns, who first gained a foothold in Moray by simultaneous elevation to an earldom and marriage to a Buchan heiress c.1210. The other was the Macdougalls, the senior of a number of lines tracing descent from the immensely powerful Somerled (d.1164), who was both *Rí Innse Gall* ('King of the Hebrides') and *regulus* (lord) of Argyll. The power of the Comyns in the Highlands depended on the range of their holdings stretching from Lochaber to Badenoch as well as on the lands the family held elsewhere in Scotland, including the earldom of Buchan; the widely acknowledged authority of the Macdougalls, whose lands were concentrated mostly in mainland Argyll, rested largely on their lineage. One is an example of lightly naturalised feudalism; the other of flexible Celtic kinship. Both were enemies of Robert Bruce, and each was destroyed by him after 1307.

The year 1307 was as important a turning-point in Highland history as the eclipse of the Lordship of the Isles in 1493. The Comyns and Macdougalls, who had been closely linked to the Balliols, were replaced by families connected to Bruce – the earls of Ross, the Campbells, MacDonalds, Macruaries and the Randolph earls of Moray – who were both smaller and differently configured.[54] The most prominent of the Celtic elements were the Campbells and the MacDonalds, one claiming links with the Britons of Strathclyde, the other descent from Somerled. Over the next 150 years, the Campbells would become the most feudal of Celtic kindreds, basing their expansion on feudal charters, the newly created sheriffdom of Argyll and an aggressive adoption of Lowland ways; the MacDonalds, in contrast, fostered a renewed, self-conscious pan-Celtic Gaeldom. A new balance resulted from the Bruce/Balliol civil war. For most of the fourteenth and fifteenth centuries the MacDonald Lordship of the Isles was a force for peace rather than a destabilising influence: its principal place of residence, at Finlaggan on Islay, was described by one chronicler as a 'mansion' rather than a fortified castle; it became a builder of abbeys and chapels and the chief patron of a renaissance of Gaelic culture and art.[55]

How violent was Highland society? By the sixteenth century – known in Gaelic poetry as the 'century of the forays' – it was notorious for its feuds, endemic lawlessness and barbarism. Yet the 'Highland problem' was largely the view of central government which had alternately ignored and exacerbated tensions in the Highlands for much of the fourteenth and fifteenth centuries. Two Lowland perceptions of the Highlands emerged in the fourteenth century and began to merge: a new concern with a problem of lawlessness began to form in both parliament and king's council after 1369; and chroniclers, beginning with Fordun in the 1380s, began to distinguish between Highland and Lowland culture, dress, and customs, but focusing above all on language:

The manners and customs of the Scots vary with the diversity of their speech. For two languages are spoken amongst them, the Scottish [Gaelic] and the Teutonic [English]; the latter of which is the language of those who occupy the seaboard and plains, while the race of Scottish speech inhabits the Highlands and outlying islands. The people of the coast are of domestic and

67

civilised habits . . . The Highlanders and people of the islands, on the other hand, are a savage and untamed race, rude and independent.[56]
Much the same views, stressing the differences between the two cultures, were repeated by almost every chronicler between Fordun and John Mair (or Major) writing in the 1520s.

By 1350 Gaelic was on the retreat, and between the Forth and the Moray Firth it was probably confined to upland parishes. Yet the occurrence of two sets of place-names, in Gaelic and Scots, in many parishes in the foothills of the Grampians indicates a bilingual population and a flexible linguistic frontier. The third language of medieval Scotland, Latin, which was still the main medium of the royal administration, continued to act as a bridge between the two cultures. It was the Lowland perception of Gaelic rather than the extent of its usage which was changing: by 1450 Lowlanders were calling it *Erse* rather than *Scotice*. They termed their own speech 'Inglis'; by 1500 they called it 'Scottis'.[57] The effect was to make synonymous in the Lowland mind the Highlands and the *Gaidhealtachd*. Gaeldom, by contrast, held to a view which it had held since the twelfth or thirteenth centuries, of acknowledging a pan-Celtic Gaeldom stretching across the North Channel to Ireland as well as an allegiance both to the King of Scots and to Scotland. It found vivid form in a Gaelic poem written on the eve of Flodden in 1513, portraying the battle between James IV and Henry VIII's England as a clash between two cultures:

> Meet it is to rise against Saxons . . . ere they have taken our country from us.
> Let us not yield up our native country. . . . Let us after the pattern of the Gael
> of *Banbha* [Ireland] watch over our fatherland . . . Fight roughly. Like the
> Irish Gael, we will have no English Pale . . . Drive the Saxons westward over
> the high sea, that Scotland may suffer no division.[58]

A poem which fed on the myths of Irish history and which, like much Irish verse, separated *Gael* from *Gall*, Highlander from Lowlander, is nevertheless the most remarkable example of Scottish patriotism between the Declaration of Arbroath and the seventeenth century. In both its view of Scotland and of itself, Highland society felt little had changed.

The new concern with Highland lawlessness which marked the last decades of the fourteenth century was linked inextricably to the activities of the Wolf of Badenoch. With the help of 'wild, wikkid hielandmen' he burned down Elgin Cathedral in 1390; his sons were the organisers of a massive cateran raid into Angus in 1392; and the ritual battle on the North Inch of Perth in 1396 between two sets of thirty-strong bands of Highlanders armed with swords, axes and bows and arrows, which became a *cause célèbre* for fifteenth-century chroniclers, was between two clans from Moray. Yet this *diabolus ex machina*, promoter of caterans and organiser of various protection rackets, was not a native Highland chief but a member of the royal house of Stewart. Alexander Stewart, the third son of Robert II (1371-90), first intervened in the politics of Moray in 1370. His rise to power over the next two decades and his struggle with the existing earls is a classic story, of both the disastrous interference of the centre in the affairs of a locality and of a division within the royal house, but it is not a tale of endemic Highland violence as such. Feuds, cattle raids, caterans and much else were all used by the Wolf of Badenoch in his war of attrition, but if there is a moral to the story it is of the lengths to which the Stewart family trait of ruthlessness could go. Repeatedly – in the Wolf's twenty-year reign of violence in the north and in James IV's attempted eclipse of the Lordship of the Isles in 1493 – it was the crown or the royal house which disrupted Highland society.[59]

The fight on the North Inch of Perth was described by Wyntoun, writing less than thirty years later, as between two 'clans', and the word was used with increasing frequency over the next two centuries to stigmatise a Highland problem of law and order. Yet violence was confined mostly to the eastern Highlands – the scene of the Wolf's operations – and the frontier zone between Highlands and Lowlands. It is difficult to see that society in the Highlands was any more or less violent than in the Lowlands in the fifteenth and sixteenth centuries. Kinship underpinned local society and the bond of manrent extended it to 'friends or allyers' who were not of the kindred; the blood-feud both afflicted the local community and regulated it throughout Scotland. The word is taken from *clann*, whose literal meaning in Gaelic is 'children', but various ideas became entangled with it which were strictly no part of it.

The nineteenth- and twentieth-century cult of the Highlands – of clan tartans, clan maps and clan societies – have all tended to obscure what a clan was. Few clans had a compact block of territory, either in the medieval period or later; 'clan maps' at best indicate where surnames occurred, but not a clan territory. In the fifteenth or sixteenth centuries, as earlier, not all members of a 'clan' were necessarily related to each other by blood; the charter chest of the Campbells of Glenorchy, for example, was stuffed with bonds of manrent, which artificially extended those to whom the chief offered protection; they in turn offered him their allegiance as his 'native men'. It is as misleading to think of these dependants as 'septs' of Glenorchy – a word which did not appear before the seventeenth century – as it is to think of them as Campbells.[60] In most cases, kinship and a common surname obtained only to the inner circle of the chief's family or to cadet branches of it. The notion that all members of a clan were descended from a common and distant ancestor is a nonsense. With a very few important exceptions, including the Campbells and the descendants of Somerled (such as Macdougalls, MacDonalds and Macruaries), most clans have their documented origins, at best, in the medieval period. In a number of cases, such as the Grants who were first called a clan in 1538, ancient lineage rests on fake genealogies.[61] Clan society was fluid and eclectic. Clan Donald embraced various vassal kindreds such as the MacLeods and MacLeans as well as the actual descendants of Donald. It was bound together by marriage as well as by genealogy, and, above all else, by a strong, shared *sense* of kinship.

Between the ninth and fourteenth centuries Highland society had experienced a long, complex process of absorbing different waves of settlers. Different clans reflected the various stages of this process: the MacLeods were of Norse descent, and the Macdougalls and MacDonalds (both descended from Somerled whose very name underlines the point) were of mixed Gaelic and Scandinavian extraction; the Chisholms, Frasers, Sinclairs and the various branches of the Stewarts (of Appin, Grandtully and others) were originally of Anglo-Norman extraction.[62] Highland society was as eclectic as in any other part of Scotland. As in Lowland society, the size and structure of the kindred could vary widely – from the confederate clan like Clan Chattan (which embraced, with varying degrees of closeness, the

Farquharsons, McCombies, MacGilvrays, Macbeans and Macqueens) to small family groups, which often voluntarily put themselves within the protective ambit of a greater chief.[63] There was no such thing as a typical clan, still less was there a 'clan system'.[64]

War, plague, slump and recovery: the fourteenth and fifteenth centuries

The century after 1296 brought war between England and Scotland and scorched-earth tactics practised by both sides, a sharp fall in overseas trade, frequent incidence of famine and a series of plague epidemics. The 150 years before 1296 had seen recurrent trouble in both the west and south-west, but war had been avoided. The expansion of trade, the growth of a cash economy, the intensive concentration of rural settlement and a steady increase in the population were all aspects of the consolidation of a feudal but hybrid kingdom. The precise levels of overseas trade are unknown before the 1360s except for isolated customs returns of 1327-33 and 1341-3, but it is clear that the 'urban revival'[65] of the twelfth and thirteenth centuries gave way to urban crisis and retrenchment which lasted for much of the fourteenth and fifteenth centuries. In the 1370s and 1380s, there was a recovery in the export of wool and hides to levels of the late 1320s, and the last decade of the reign of James I (1406-37) saw customs revenue reach 60 per cent of the levels of a century earlier, but the period was otherwise indelibly marked by a long-term decline in trade.

This was followed by a certain expansion, still uneven, fluctuating and confined to parts of the urban economy, in the last quarter of the fifteenth century when there was some increase in trade with France and the Baltic. Yet the change in the nature of the economy was immense and it clearly sets Scotland of the late fourteenth and fifteenth centuries apart from the booming wool and cloth-based economy of the period of the Canmore kings. Wool exports in the 1480s were running at less than a quarter of the level of the 1320s and those of hides at less than half.[66] The sharpness of the economic crisis caused by the Wars of Independence can, in the absence of customs records, only be guessed at but national assessments for land in the 1360s had fallen from a thirteenth-century level of £45,575 to £23,826, a drop of 48 per cent.[67]

The new economy of the later fourteenth and fifteenth centuries – for such it was despite its continuing reliance on wool, hides and skins as its main exports – had profound effects on urban life. The focus of trade narrowed in the fourteenth century: fewer foreign merchants visited Scotland and the bulk of exports was sent to a new staple port of Bruges in Flanders. The trade in cloth, except for cheap, rough-woven material sent to the Baltic ports, contracted sharply; hides and untreated wool were sent to Bruges, which provided a range of manufactured goods and better-quality finished cloth. Scotland as a result conformed far more closely to the typical shape of a modern third-world economy after 1300 than it had before. There were structural changes as well within the Scottish urban economy. The long slump coincided, after the loss of Berwick, with the increasing grip taken by Edinburgh – the only major town with a port between the Tweed and the Forth – of more and more sectors of the export trade. By the 1320s it had 21 per cent of the trade in wool, 32 per cent by the 1370s and 71 per cent by the late 1450s. Former wool towns, such as Perth, Inverness and Stirling, were forced to diversify into other areas, usually leather.[68]

By the mid-fifteenth century, however, the battleground amongst the Scottish burghs shifted from wool to the trade in hides and skins. In the 1440s, the 'four great towns of Scotland' (Edinburgh, Aberdeen, Dundee and Perth) held 52 per cent of the export trade in hides and a batch of five medium-sized towns (Ayr, Inverness, Kirkcudbright, Linlithgow and Stirling) held 40 per cent. By the 1470s the market in hides had been transformed: the share of the middle-ranking towns had dropped by fully a half whereas Edinburgh's had increased by over 40 per cent. Ayr and Stirling were able to weather the slump, but in Inverness, Kirkcudbright and Linlithgow the trade collapsed.[69] The effect of the sharp decline of the export sector of the leather trade, which was so central to medieval urban industry, must have produced either urban crisis or outright decay.

Outside Edinburgh and to a lesser extent the three other major regional centres, it is likely that life in many towns was marked by the sight of falling levels of population, abandoned workshops and a new relationship between town and country. The modest growth areas in the later fifteenth-century economy lay in salt and fisheries, which benefited small ports such as Crail in the Firth of Forth and Dumbarton on the Clyde. There were, too, the beginnings of a search for new overseas markets, helped by the abandonment of the Bruges staple in 1477 and its eventual settling at Veere in Zeeland, a more convenient and less restrictive distribution centre. Later some burghs, like Inverness, would stage a recovery through the export of salmon, but the structure of the town must by then have been distinctly different from the fourteenth century when it had been based on its trade in wool and hides. The later medieval burgh, still governed by the *Burgh Laws* of the twelfth century and the *Statutes of the Guild* of the thirteenth, survived almost completely intact; but it was, though still small, likely to be a very different working town.

The steep fall in overseas trade affected rural society – the producers of the wool, skins and hides which made up the vast bulk of exports – no less seriously. Pastoral farming must have contracted sharply. Yet these were long-term economic movements, softened by occasional recovery until the 1370s, and their seriousness, at least in the eyes of contemporaries, depended on how they interacted with other factors. There were far fewer complaints made by the chroniclers of a decay of trade than of famine. The *Chronicle of Holyrood* complained of 'a very great famine, and pestilence among animals' in 1154, and the *Chronicle of Lanercost* mentioned 'a great corruption of the air and inundation of rain' causing a wholesale failure of the harvest in 1256.[70] These seem to have been only occasional disasters, less serious than the succession of poor harvests which afflicted both Scotland and much of northern Europe in the early fourteenth century. There was widespread famine in 1315-16 and in the later 1330s. It is impossible to say whether this amounted to a subsistence crisis which brought about either a check or a stop to a long period of population increase, for this crisis was shortly overtaken by another – the Black Death.

The first serious outbreak of plague was in 1349, when it was promptly labelled 'the foul death of England' where it had struck a year before. Another epidemic came in 1361-2, although it probably affected only southern Scotland, and there were further outbreaks, confined mostly to the burghs, in 1379, 1392, 1401-3, 1430-2, 1439 and 1455. According to Fordun, 'nearly a third of mankind' died in 1349. This estimate was confirmed by Wyntoun, who, however, cast some doubt on his own credibility by asserting that one in three also died in 1362. The death toll was huge, if unquantifiable. With well over a half of the population living to the north of the Tay, it seems unlikely that Scotland would have been as badly hit as England, where the first epidemic did kill one in three people. Even so, the outbreak of 1349 was almost certainly the worst in Scotland's history, far surpassing the epidemic of 1645 which claimed one in five of the urban population.[71]

The effects of the fourteenth-century plague bring us to another turning-point in Scotland's history. The two or three centuries before it had seen a rising population and increased levels of cultivation. The drastic fall in the population, of perhaps one in five or six, had a series of repercussions. The next rise in the population would not begin before 1450 and much of it belonged to the 'long sixteenth century' between 1500 and 1640.[72] A further burst of land clearance, an increase in the number of rural townships and the splitting up of existing touns had to wait for the same period. The 100 or 150 years after 1350 saw, in sharp contrast, a shortage of labour and a shift in the relationship between lord and tenant in the latter's favour, which must have resulted in falling rents and larger holdings for husbandmen and cottars. Less pressure on food supplies would have brought both lower prices and fewer shortages of crops and grain, at least for those whose income held up.[73] The contraction of the pastoral economy must also have provoked a shift in the diet of most Scots, who became more reliant on oats and barley and less on meat. In the towns, the drop in trade brought about a shift in the balance of economic fortunes away from the merchants towards craftsmen, and it is noticeable that the half-century after 1475 was the period when crafts in the larger burghs gained incorporated status as guilds, acquired their own altars in the burgh church and began to demand political representation. The twelfth and thirteenth centuries had been the period of the lord and the cloth merchant. The late fourteenth and fifteenth centuries were the era of the husbandman and the urban craftsman. The different pressures of the sixteenth century would see the rise of feuars, lairds and lawyers. Each was a symbol of the changing, impersonal forces that governed Scottish society.[74]

Until the fourteenth century, the Scottish currency had remained fairly stable. The fall in trade and an accumulating balance of payments crisis resulted in a 35 per cent reduction in the weight of coins by the 1360s. Further devaluation followed in the 1390s, mirroring the sharp drop in trade after 1380. By 1400 the £ Scots contained only three-tenths of the silver it had had in 1296, and by 1470 less than 15 per cent. As a result, the £ Scots fell sharply against the English £ sterling, from an exchange rate of 3:4 in 1373 to 1:3 in 1451.[75] After that, the rate stabilised, until the next exchange crisis, which began in the 1570s. The inevitable result, familiar to the twentieth century but alien to the medieval consumer, was price inflation. 'All things are dearer than in times past', complained the Abbot of Dunfermline in 1309. The late medieval Scottish economy – characterised by falling exports, a balance of payments deficit and rising prices – conforms closely to the picture of many economies of the later twentieth century.

There is a tendency amongst some modern historians to write off medieval

Scotland as a poor country, with a primitive economy. A certain Whig-like economic determinism has often crept into interpretations of the 'unimproved' state of agriculture before the later seventeenth century. A basic lack of law and order, so it is sometimes argued, prevented any breakthrough into the political stability which was a necessary precondition of economic growth.[76] Yet the discovery of farming an estate for profit was not unique to the period between 1650 and 1750. The amount of medieval pastoral farming, as recent research has indicated, has been exaggerated; there was an important arable sector in the medieval rural economy that was worked intensively in the period up to 1300.

Such views stem from a vision of a single medieval period, spanning four centuries or more. In terms of trade, population and the patterns of both urban life and the cultivation of the land, it is far more appropriate to think of an early and a later medieval Scotland, separated by the new pressures and circumstances of the fourteenth century. The real dividing line came not in 1100 or 1124 but somewhere between 1296 and 1350. Before 1300, Scotland's wool trade made it one of the leading producers in Europe after England. It is difficult to think of a country which could finance cathedrals such as St Andrews or Glasgow or abbeys such as Dunfermline or Dryburgh, lay out elaborate town plans such as those of Crail or St Andrews, and begin major royal castles at Edinburgh and Stirling as poor. The extent and continuity of arable farming, in which foundations laid in the twelfth century or earlier provided a framework still recognisable in the seventeenth or eighteenth, suggests that period as the first age of Improvement. Early medieval Scotland can claim to be a dynamic society enjoying, by contemporary standards, a modest but real prosperity. Later medieval Scotland was, by contrast, a society afflicted by a series of severe problems, both natural and man-made; its population was smaller and its standard of living worse for most of its people.

6

THE MACMALCOLM DYNASTY

THE REIGN OF MALCOLM III (1058-93) WAS THE THIRD AND LONGEST OF THREE long reigns which dominated the eleventh century. Yet, like those immediately before it, Malcolm's reign began in obscure circumstances and ended amidst confusion. Unlike many of the reigns which would follow it, there do not seem to have been risings orchestrated by rival claimants to contend with but pacification of the realm was its leitmotiv rather than stability and peace. Malcolm, son of Duncan I, had gained power only with the help of Earl Siward of Northumbria and the struggle took almost four years to complete. The death of Macbeth in 1057 had resulted in the succession not of Malcolm but of Macbeth's stepson Lulach. The few details available about the episode could fit the theory that the rival claimants of 1057-8 – Malcolm and Lulach – were fellow conspirators who fell out, as well as they do the more usual explanation of a two-stage coup by Malcolm, completed only when Lulach was killed in an ambush at Essie in Strathbogie in March 1058. A month later Malcolm was inaugurated at Scone. Whichever theory is true, it remains the case that Malcolm had much to do to establish his credibility as King of Scots; the four-year crisis which he and Siward had inflicted on the country in 1054 after some fourteen years of seemingly stable rule by Macbeth made the initial task all the harder. The description of the twenty-seven-year-old new king as Canmore (better translated from the Gaelic *ceann mor* as Chief rather than great head) was probably part of a reconstruction of the image of kingship.

Nothing affected Malcolm Canmore's reign more than the deaths of his two most powerful neighbours. Siward had died in 1055 and the unpopularity in Northumbria of his replacement, the Wessex warlord Tostig, resulted in outright revolt and his flight in 1065. By 1066 he would be a suitor at Malcolm's court, canvassing for military aid to recover his earldom. An unstable Northumbria offered the new King of Scots a useful opportunity – as it had early in previous reigns in 972 and 1006 – to repay the support of those who had brought him to power as well as to buy that of the uncommitted. It was this instability in the north of England, both before the Norman invasion of 1066 that brought William I 'the Conqueror' (1066-87) to power as well as after it, that made Malcolm seem a greater threat to Northumbria than any King of Scots before him.[1] It would be the main factor in his relations with his southern neighbour throughout his reign. Malcolm would stage five major raids or invasions into Northumbria – in 1061, 1070, 1079, 1091 and 1093 – would successively be either wooed or forced into submission in 1072, 1080 and 1092, and ultimately would be caught there in a trap of his own devising in 1093. It would largely be the threat to the north, only half-conquered by the new Norman kings, William I and his sons William Rufus (1087-1100) and Henry I (1100-35), which induced no fewer than five political marriages involving the Scottish royal house with the rival Norman and Old English houses between 1069 and 1113. Anglo-Scottish relations were the making and breaking of Malcolm Canmore.

For much of the previous century, however, the main danger to kings of Scots had come from Scandinavian pressure, felt most acutely in the north. The death of the powerful Earl of Orkney, Thorfinn, gave Malcolm the chance to marry his widow, Ingibjorg.[2] It was a doubly astute match: a marriage to the widow of an ally of Macbeth not only neutralised external pressure on the north but also the potential for internal dissent within Moray; but Ingibjorg was also a descendant through the female line of Malcolm II and the marriage in effect bought out the risk of future collateral claimants.[3] Both an unwonted strategic status in the politics of the British Isles and dynastic stability would have seemed assured for Malcolm in the 1060s.

Ingibjorg died probably sometime before 1069, by which time she had given birth to two sons, Duncan and Donald.[4] Never one to squander an opportunity, Malcolm had by 1070 insisted on marrying Margaret, the sister of Edgar the Atheling ('prince'), who had fled to Scotland after the Norman forces of William I had taken control of northern England. The marriage would produce two daughters and six sons, three of whom would rule successively as kings of Scots. It would also result in a fierce family squabble over the succession after 1093. In the shorter term, it gave a fresh edge to Malcolm's territorial ambitions, both in Cumbria and Northumbria – whether as ally of Edgar or simply as a warrior king intent on uniting his diverse peoples in aggression.

In 1070 he launched his second invasion, via Cumberland, across Stainmore and into Teesdale, carefully circling rather than pushing directly into Northumbria. There were two unusual features of this expedition and both may indicate that Malcolm in 1061 had already secured a hold on Cumbria – the most mysterious of all areas in early medieval Scottish history. It was the only Scottish invasion in the eleventh or twelfth centuries to originate in the west and his army was mainly composed of men of Galloway.[5] Whatever its intentions, the invasion of 1070 ended in confusion before the walls of Durham with much of the booty lost. Retaliation came in 1072 when Willliam entered Lothian and crossed the Forth into Fife at the head of a large army, with a fleet in support. This campaign – the first full-scale invasion of Scotland by a well-organised English army – also ended inconsequentially. At Abernethy on the River Tay, some 250 miles away from his base at York and frustrated by Malcolm's Fabian tactics, William settled for an assurance from Malcolm who 'made peace . . . and gave hostages and was his man'.[6] For William (and for subsequent English chroniclers over the next six centuries) the act may have been a formal act of homage of a vassal, but for Malcolm it was an empty gesture which, despite the fact that one of the hostages was his eldest son Duncan, could be discarded when opportunity next presented itself – which it did in 1079, with Norman authority in the north in a state of collapse. Again, in 1080, a Scots expedition provoked an English counter-strike, this time led by William's son Robert Curthose, which failed to lure Malcolm into battle. At Falkirk the terms reached at Abernethy were renewed, more hostages were arranged and a border as far south as Stainmore and the Tyne was agreed – a frontier also confirmed by the rapid building by Robert on his march south of a fortress on the Tyne, the 'New Castle', some eighty miles south of the Tweed. It was the high-water mark of Malcolm's ambitions to re-establish the old Dark Age kingdom stretching from the Forth, if not to the Humber, at least to the Tyne.[7]

The fourth of Malcolm's expeditions, in 1091, was probably the most extended, beginning in May, centring on a siege of Durham and lasting much of the summer. Although Norman retaliation again ground to its familiar halt in Lothian and a further renewal of the terms of Abernethy of 1072, the balance of power on the frontier was tilted decisively by the building of a formidable castle at Carlisle, supported by what amounted to a Norman military colony in Cumberland.[8] This was not a defensive castle such as that at Newcastle but an aggressive instrument of policy of William Rufus, aimed at the soft underbelly of Malcolm's southern frontier in the west. The Norman conquest of the north-west may have had an element now lost to history, for Malcolm's reaction was not a retaliatory raid but a belated request for an audience with William Rufus at Gloucester. Whether it was a deliberate snub by William, who refused to see the King of Scots when he arrived, or the reneging by William on some part of the agreement of 1091 relating to Cumberland that provoked Malcolm into his fifth and least calculated expedition, launched into Northumbria in mid-November of 1093, is impossible to say. Both Malcolm and Edward, his eldest son by Margaret, were killed near Alnwick in an ambush. Margaret, stricken with grief, died four days later.

The legacy of Malcolm and Margaret

The conventional view of Malcolm's reign rests heavily on the influence wrought on the king by his second wife. With Margaret, the subject of the first 'official' biography of a Scottish monarch which was written by her confessor Turgot, the difficulty is to separate cult – indeed two cults – from contemporary reality. Shortly after her arrival a small Romanesque church was built at Dunfermline, the royal residence where she and Malcolm were married, and three Benedictine monks were sent at her request from the great mother house at Canterbury to form the nucleus of a Benedictine priory. It was a modest but nonetheless important first step, though in a direction which was not followed to any extent in Scotland. The beginnings of the huge, austere building (which still survives) are to be traced to its refoundation in 1128 in the reign of her youngest son, David. Yet the expansion of European monasticism, which so distinguished twelfth-century Scotland, drew not on the Benedictine impulse but on other religious orders – most notably the Augustinians or the Cistercians and Tironensians, both reformed Benedictine orders. The *Life* written by Turgot some twenty years after her death, touches on Dunfermline only briefly, as one of the many venues illustrating the faith and works of a deeply pious woman. Dedicated since her childhood – spent in recently converted Hungary – to 'a life of soberness' and meditation 'day and night upon the law of the Lord', her personal devotions found outlets in a renewed royal cult of St Andrew and in the patronage of eremitic monks of Loch Leven as well as in Dunfermline. Turgot describes how she supported twenty-four poor people all year round, ministered daily to nine abandoned young orphans and washed the feet of six of the poor during the seasons of Lent and Advent and had 300 more fed in the royal hall before herself.[9]

The impact of a queen who knew no Gaelic, unlike her bilingual husband, must have been muted beyond the immediate circles of the royal court. The reforms with which Turgot credits Margaret – establishing more regular observation of the Lenten fast, the discouragement of celebration of the mass with 'I know not what barbarous rite' and prohibitions on marriage within forbidden degrees such as a stepmother or a deceased brother's wife – all brought Scotland into closer line with established practice elsewhere in the Church Universal, but other, probably more important issues such as clerical celibacy and observance of a strict rule in monastic communities were left untouched. There can be little doubt, however, of the depth of the mark which Margaret left on her children. A firm believer in the axiom of not sparing the rod, her real legacy lay in the conspicuous piety of her sons. Yet their accession – the line of 'Margaretsons' as one modern historian has suggested mischievously[10] – was as notable a fluke of history as any other in Scottish history. To acclaim the queenship of Margaret as a fundamental turning-point in the history of Scotland is to risk reading history backwards from 1250 – which was what the royal house of macMalcolm intended when Margaret, now canonised as a saint, was formally reburied in Dunfermline in a great set-piece occasion which followed the inauguration of Alexander III.

Viewed in more conventional terms, the long reign of Malcolm III is puzzling in many respects, as is the confusion which marked its end. A civil war, it is sometimes said, lifts the veil which covers the usually hidden secrets of society. The prolonged crisis which followed the death of Malcolm III is an instructive period. The king was succeeded, not by his eldest surviving son (Duncan), but by his brother Donald Ban III (1093-7), who was the choice of the leading magnates and, according to one chronicler, also 'drove out all the English who were with King Malcolm before'.[11] Clearly some kind of reaction against the English influence and culture of the court which had marked the years of Margaret's period as Queen had set in, and it is likely that her sons – four of them (Edward, Edgar, Edmund and Ethelred) given names of her own royal house of Wessex – had to flee into exile.

The division was not a straightforward one, of Celt against English. The first rival to Donald III was Duncan, the son of Malcolm III and Ingibjorg, who had been one of the earliest of the hostages held at the English court to secure his father's good behaviour. This naturalised macMalcolm, a convenient instrument of William Rufus's determination to close what would later be called the 'postern gate' in the north, was willing to swear fealty to a Norman king to secure an invasion force of French and English to unseat his uncle, which he did in May 1094.[12] Before the end of 1094, however, Duncan II was dead. He was a set of paradoxes – a Celt by birth who spent his long years as a hostage being trained as a Norman knight, whose seal represented him on horseback wearing the conical Norman helmet, yet buried like kings of Scots before him (except for his father) on Iona. He was the victim of an alliance forged between Donald Ban, who had been brought up in the Celtic environment of the Western Isles, and Edmund, the third son of Margaret and an emblem of the alien influences at the royal court in the 1170s and 1180s.[13] The reign of Donald III, with Edmund perhaps installed as *designatus* (successor) to the sixty-year-old king, lasted a further three years. In 1097 a second army was sent north by William Rufus, this time with Edgar, Margaret's third son, as pretender. It is likely, from the evidence of a charter granted by him to the Priory of Durham in August 1095, that Edgar had some control over at least the valley of the Tweed by then. Although installed as king 'in fealty to King William' in 1097 and acknowledged by Constantine of the kin of MacDuff, the most important of the native Scottish families who would play a role in royal inaugurations of the twelfth and thirteenth centuries, Edgar (1097-1107) did not feel secure until Donald Ban was captured in 1099. Donald ended his years a blind and hapless captive but still of sufficient stature to be buried on Iona; Edmund, in disgrace, spent the rest of his days as a Cluniac monk.[14]

In one sense, the 1090s marked a severe crisis of the macMalcolm succession. It was resolved only by a combination of the most predictable twist in the dangerous game of power politics which Malcolm had been playing throughout much of his reign – the descent of Scotland into a client state of England – and the least likely of dynastic scenarios – the succession, one after another, of Malcolm's three youngest sons by Margaret.[15] In another sense, each episode in the complex wranglings between 1093 and 1099 represented some effort to reconcile the clash of the two cultures which permeated the royal house and its court. Duncan II had been accepted only 'on condition that he should never again introduce English or French into the land'. Edgar made no such promise. Yet even he, described as being 'like in all things' to Edward the Confessor (who was his mother's great uncle) and often taken as the very model of a Scoto-Norman king, was careful to establish his main residence not in Lothian but in Scotia, at Invergowrie on Tay.[16]

There are dangers, too, in the pursuit of history as the cult of personality. The differences between Malcolm and Margaret are sometimes taken as a convenient symbol of the clash between 'a man who held back time by his own existence' and a woman who consciously instigated changes 'of fundamental, far-reaching significance'.[17] It is too easy to describe the reign as a struggle between yesterday's man and tomorrow's woman. Only a long elapse of time and a calculated rewriting of history in the thirteenth century, when Margaret was elevated to a new stature, gave history to the 'progressives'. Similarly, the history of late eleventh- and twelfth-century Scotland cannot be told as a one-way traffic of the 'Normanisation' of native institutions, law and culture. Influences moved in both directions.[18] Two dynamic cultures, Celtic and Anglo-Norman, were becoming increasingly intermingled (and therefore more difficult to distinguish) during an age of rapid change. It is, in a sense, the story of the ninth century repeated, with different actors: Scottish society, like kingship itself, was a crucible. Each reign in the 150 years which separated the reigns of Edgar and Alexander III represented a different attempt to strike a balance between old and new.[19]

The balance struck in the reigns of Edgar (1097-1107) and Alexander (1107-24) differed from each other. Edgar had learned from his mother the importance of the trappings of kingship and seems to have had a taste for the flamboyant gesture: his seal bore his effigy with the inscription *Imago Edgari Scottorum Basilei*, an affectation used by William the Conqueror but not by any King of Scots before or after. He owned an exotic beast – whether it was a camel or an elephant it is hard to say. His was the reign when the sealed writ or brieve, written in Latin, made its first appearance in Scotland; the chief propagandists of kingship were its clerks for each charter, addressed to the king's subjects 'Scots and English', bore the royal seal of an enthroned king with sword and sceptre in his hands – a mixture of Anglo-Saxon and Norman practice. This seems to have been the extent of foreign influence. Otherwise his ten-year reign appears to have been marked by masterly inactivity. The see of St Andrews, vacant since 1093, remained unfilled and no religious houses were founded except for a grant of lands to the monks of Durham which would in time produce a second Benedictine priory, at Coldingham. The fact that a reign which began with a coup backed by a foreign army and saw no risings and 'no tyranny, no harshness against his people' testifies to the success of a conservative policy. Stability, however, had its price: a peaceful frontier in the west was bought by a treaty with Magnus Bareleg, King of Norway, which ceded the Western Isles including Iona.[20]

The obituary notices for Alexander, by contrast, emphasised a king who was 'strong' or 'fierce' rather than just, and who worked *laboriosissime* – which suggests both effort and difficulty – to consolidate his position.[21] Like Edgar, Alexander depended on an English king and probably paid homage to Henry I (1100-35), and the ties were strengthened further by his marriage to Henry's illegitimate daughter, Sybil. Yet this reign was marked by a certain nervousness, shown both by a castle-building programme and in Alexander's reluctance to grant his younger brother David the same jurisdiction in southern Scotland as he had himself enjoyed in the reign of Edgar. It was in his encouragement of monastic orders that Alexander's reign stood out. The bringing of Augustinian canons from Nostel in Yorkshire to found a priory at Scone c.1115 marked the beginning of the long connection between the Augustinian order and the royal house and the onset of a planned colonisation of the religious orders of western Christendom in Scotland. Further plans seem to have existed for foundations at St Andrews and Dunkeld – significantly both old royal centres – as well as at Inchcolm and Loch Tay. The bishopric of St Andrews was filled as early as 1107 and unsuccessful attempts were made to free it from the jurisdiction of York. As much as the new royal castles at Stirling, Alexander's ecclesiastical policy signalled a consolidation of his kingship in Scotia. The calculated balance of old and new, which would so indelibly mark the reign of his brother David after him, was already in operation before 1124.

David fitz Malcolm and David macMalcolm

David, youngest son of Malcolm and Margaret, would have been the son least exposed to his mother's influence for he was probably only about nine when both his parents died.[22] The whole of his adolescence was spent at the English court and after his sister's marriage to Henry I in 1100 he became a member of the royal household, witnessing royal acts as 'David, the Queen's brother'. As late as the 1130s, David was still, to English chroniclers, the epitome of Norman knighthood, which was why his expedition into England in 1138 at the head of an 'incredible army' of semi-barbarous peoples was so shocking to them.[23] Even after the death of Edgar, it would have seemed unlikely that he would succeed to the Scottish throne for Alexander, unlike Edgar, had married and was still in his thirties. In 1114 David married a widow some years older than himself, a ward of the King, securing for himself the extensive earldoms of Huntingdon and Northampton. It was the marriage of a favoured client rather than of an heir apparent, for Maud was already about forty and could not have been relied on to produce children.[24]

David has been called one of Henry I's 'new men', his dependants and colonisers of the north.[25] It was at Henry's insistence that David was granted land and power in southern Scotland by 1113. It was there, as Henry's virtual viceroy in the north, that well before 1124 the characteristic, overlapping layers of Anglo-Norman settlement which would mark his reign as King of Scots were already being planted:

a mixed group of Anglo-Norman adventurers settled in Northumbria, which had seen the last of its native rebellions a generation before, but in the more difficult west country of Cumbria a much tighter-knit band of knights, drawn mostly from Lower Normandy and Brittany, was deployed; and at Selkirk an outpost of the austere monks of Tiron was established in 1113.[26] The balance between the two Davids – David fitz Malcolm, client and marcher lord of Henry I of England, and David macMalcolm, younger brother of the King of Scots enjoying something like the customary jurisdiction in Lothian which both his father and his brother Alexander had held before him – was as yet firmly tilted towards the feudal.

In 1124 David (1124-53) succeeded on the death of Alexander I. The most unexpected aspect of his reign was probably its length. Already in middle age and older than both his elder brothers when they had come to the throne, few could have expected David to have reigned for almost three decades or to have governed with a vigour which lasted until his final days. The seal of a charter made to Kelso Abbey by his successor in 1159 shows a grey-haired, long-bearded patriarchal figure, yet it unmistakably represents a king who still holds a sword, the traditional symbol of kingly power, upright in his right hand and an orb, a novel emblem of the sacred nature of kingship, firmly grasped in his left. Much of the imagery on the Kelso seal was innovative, copied from Capetian kings of France, and kingship itself, it has been said, moved 'into a new epoch' in David's reign.[27]

David was the first King of Scots to strike his own coinage and it was in his reign that the spread of the motte, symbol and reality of centralised authority of a more developed kind, began. By the end of his reign the foundations of a new type of sheriffdom, based largely on a model already founded by Norman kings of England, had been laid. The first surviving charter of the reign, made probably in 1124 and perhaps even at the time of the inauguration ceremony itself, was a grant of the huge lands of Annandale on the south-western frontier to the Norman family, de Brus; all but one of the witnesses to it were also Norman knights. As new agents of a traditional policy recruited at the personal invitation of David, families such as the Bruces, Stewarts and Morvilles (to give their names a familiar spelling), often in origin obscure under-tenants of David's English estates or even landless knights, were in a real sense the king's own *probi homines* ('worthy men'). It was the age of the *arriviste*.

The two most novel aspects of the 'Davidian revolution'[28] were the royal burghs and the new religious orders. Towns or some form of urban settlements must have existed before 1100 but at least a dozen or perhaps as many as sixteen were given the status of a king's burgh in the reign; they included Berwick, Perth and Aberdeen, focal points for the surge in overseas trade which marked the twelfth century throughout much of western Europe.[29] In 1124 there had been monasteries only at Dunfermline, Scone and Selkirk. In 1128 the Benedictine foundation at Dunfermline was elevated from a priory to an abbey and work on the nave of the present abbey church, so reminiscent of Durham Cathedral, probably began. Further Augustinian houses were founded beside Edinburgh (at Holyrood), near Stirling (at Cambuskenneth) and at Jedburgh and St Andrews, all, like Scone, established royal centres. The patterns laid down in the time of Margaret and Alexander I were extended and fulfilled.

It was David's own patronage of three other, recently founded orders which best indicated the distinctive patronage given by the royal house to Scottish monasticism. The first abbey of the order of Tiron had been founded in northern France in 1109, only four years before the establishment of its house at Selkirk; by 1153, by which time this original house had been moved to Kelso beside the important royal centre of Roxburgh, another house had been founded at Lesmahagow, near Glasgow, and five more would follow before 1286. Two other reformed Benedictine orders – the Cistercians and Premonstratensians – also brought the new spiritual vitality of a stricter and purified Augustinianism. The white canons, first founded at Prémontré in north-eastern France in 1119, were granted a foundation at Dryburgh in 1150, and five more houses would follow by the 1220s. The most generous grants, however, were made to the white monks of the Cistercian order, founded at Cîteaux in Burgundy in 1098; Melrose was the first, founded as a daughter house of Rievaulx in Yorkshire (itself only four years old) in 1136 and Dundrennan, which has been described as the outstanding Scottish example of the all-embracing austerity of Cistercian architecture, followed some six years later. By the end of the reign four of the eleven eventual Cistercian houses had been established.[30]

Both the speed and extent of the transformation taking place in David's reign, in either its economic or its ecclesiastical forms, can be exaggerated. It is likely that the pace of the surge in overseas trade quickened more dramatically in the early thirteenth century rather than early in the twelfth. The appearance of the 'new' or 'great' customs on wool exports, which tied the revenue accruing to the crown more closely to the level of trading activity than the old 'custom and cain', came as late as the 1270s. The full impact of new ecclesiastical institutions arrived, it needs to be remembered, not with their foundation but their physical completion and even modest-sized religious houses took decades rather than years to build. Few if any of the large foundations of David's reign could have been completed in their final physical form before his death. The Church of St Mary of Melrose was dedicated in 1146, ten building seasons after an advance party of monks and laybrothers arrived, but it is unlikely that the nave and cloister were completed before 1160. When the Abbot of Rievaulx, head of the Cistercian order, visited his daughter house at Dundrennan in 1165, twenty-three years after its foundation, he was housed 'in a small dwelling [where] . . . no part of the roof, not even the space of a couple of feet, was free from the penetration of the rain'.[31] No religious house, either, was founded north of the Forth in the reign. David's notable patronage of religious orders was confined largely to the part of the kingdom which he had effectively controlled since 1113, as brother of Alexander I. Like the Anglo-Norman penetration of society, the story of the spread of a 'new' economy and new religious orders is one which lasts for a century or more and owes as much to general European trends as it does to any one king, however charismatic.[32]

A more extensive and perhaps more immediate impact on the kingdom as a whole was made by the development of a parish system. In 1100 it is likely that there were many local churches and that their number had increased markedly over the previous century as local landowners erected them on their estates. By 1200 Scotland was well on its way to completing the network of some 1,100 parishes which eventually covered much of the country. Built in stone, most parish kirks were largely the work, as a thirteenth-century church statute decreed, of the parishioners themselves.[33] Often deliberately placed at a distance from any existing shrine, chapel or hermitage dedicated to an early saint, the parish kirks of twelfth-century Scotland were the most widespread sign of a new departure for the Church.

Yet the development of a national system of parishes was not a creation out of nothing; it was rather the most obvious aspect in David's reign of a shift from existing but piecemeal developments into a systematic effort of royal policy. The law or 'assize' of David I which made compulsory the exaction of the teind (or tithe) from all who lived in the area served by a parish church was the vital, practical legal step and it rightly gives to David the accolade of founder of a system of parishes which remained virtually unchanged until the nineteenth century. Grants of lands in feudal terms often coincided, in David's reign and after, with the effective creation of new parishes. In Moray, the spread of a parish system was one of the instruments of the feudal colonisation of a troublesome province. Yet in other parts of Scotia the new parishes seem often to have been fitted into old boundaries. The huge diocese of St Andrews which stretched both north and south of the Forth shows that the emergence of a parish system was not a tidal wave carrying all before it: in Lothian and the Merse there are indeed many examples, such as the parish kirk at Ednam, of 'feudal churches' linked to new Anglo-Norman proprietors; but in Fife and especially north of the Tay in Angus and the Mearns, where the erection of parish churches generally predated feudal settlement, there was a closer correspondence between existing sites or places linked to saints' dedications and the new kirks.[34]

The same shifting balance between Celtic survival and the new Church of the twelfth century lay behind the development – or reconfiguration – of dioceses. By 1155, there were ten dioceses. Of these, only three – Moray, Ross and Caithness – were creations of the twelfth century, all significantly in the troubled north, the outlying province given special attention by David I and his successors. The remainder were all survivals of different kinds: Whithorn corresponded to the old lordship of Galloway and was little different from the see established by the Northumbrian Church in the seventh century; Glasgow, the see of St Mungo, stretched as far south as had the old kingdom of Strathclyde; and the bewildering complexity of the boundaries of the others, with detached portions speckling the map, is testimony to their origins as *paruchiae* of mother churches of a Celtic type. The lands and parishes of the diocese of Dunkeld spotted the map from Argyll to Berwickshire. Neither the diocesan system nor the bishops who ran it in the twelfth century were so very different from the sees and churchmen of the eleventh. There were bishops with Norman names in David's Scotland, but there was no dramatic, sudden swamping of the secular clergy with outsiders, as happened in William I's England.[35]

As in the Church, the 'feudalisation' of society was piecemeal and variable, a working compromise rather than a feudal formula. It was only in some parts of Scotland south of the Forth that the characteristic Norman establishment of castle, town and monastery at or near the caput of a feudal honour took place. Nine sheriffdoms seem to have been established by 1153, five of them in Scotia, but only three had a castle attached.[36] Of the sixteen likely burgh foundations of the reign, six were north of the Forth, but the bulk of them were on or near the east coast, positioned for access to the lucrative North Sea trade routes rather than placed for effect as a symbol of feudal power.[37] The different layers of the wider process of feudalisation – of not only the knight's fee and homage or the development of the sheriffdom but also grants to religious houses and the burgh charter – were all at work in David's reign, but they did not always coincide. Much of the work begun in David's remarkable reign needed at least another fifty years and the next two reigns to consolidate. The model followed by David I was not that of William the Conqueror, whose whole reign has been described as a period of experimentation, but of his own patron and mentor Henry I, who pursued a more subtle balance of power, through the adroit use of marriages, enfeoffments and patronage of offices in both church and state which favoured old families as well as new.[38] In Henry I's England, as in David's Scotland, the policy of Norman settlement was at its most radical on the frontier between the two kingdoms. But there was a vital difference: in England this was consolidation and conciliation after three decades of conquest politics; in Scotland it was a cautious first step in only one part of the kingdom. The only area where a 'conquest' took place in David's Scotland was in Moray, after the defeat in 1130 of a rising led by Angus, grandson of Lulach.

The balance of old and new was not only to do with the skilful manipulation of men and resources; it was at root about the nature of kingly power. Three hundred years later, James I would bemoan the grants of a king he saw as 'a sair [costly] sanct for the crown'. But a revitalised Church was not seen in the same way in the twelfth century as it would be in the fifteenth: far from it being a drain on the limited resources of the crown, it was a vital instrument of royal policy. New monasteries helped to anchor new families and strengthen their hold on their estates. Bishops and monks were the frontiersmen of twelfth-century Scotland, helping to advance royal authority in regions of uncertain allegiance. Yet the seats of David I's bishops were almost all in long-established ecclesiastical centres. The sword and orb which the enthroned David held in the Kelso Abbey seal were symbolic of a new royal authority, which, as the English chronicler Orderic Vitalis claimed, exalted him above his predecessors. This was also, however, the very sword of his ancestors used at his inauguration and symbolic of the fact that the accepted means of securing the royal line was by paying respect to the existing norms of kingmaking. David, it was reported, was chary of some of the old rites of inauguration in 1124; but by the 1150s he was willing to turn to MacDuff, Earl of Fife and accepted leader of the old native nobility, to secure the acceptance of his young successor as *rex designatus*.[39] In one sense, the Annandale charter granted in the first year of David's reign symbolised the feudalisation of the southern part of the kingdom of David fitz Malcolm; in another, it demonstrated the obsession of David macMalcolm, like his father before him, with the recovery of Cumbria. The expedition into the north of England in 1138 brought together the two faces of David I: it was at once a repayment of fealty owed to Maud, the deposed daughter of his liege lord Henry I, and a consolidation of his recent acquisition of Cumbria, the forward base of a King of Scots whose ambitions to create a huge pale north of the Tees belonged as much to the tenth or eleventh centuries as to the twelfth. The longer the reign went on, the more it might be claimed that David had become a Celtic king.

Kingship consolidated:
The reigns of Malcolm IV and William the Lion

Why might this have been so? David, it rightly has been claimed, was a legend in his own lifetime.[40] But the makers of the legend were his own clerks or (mostly English) chroniclers. Few living legends are wholly popular with their own contemporaries. By normal measures of history, a King who led what was one of the largest Scottish armies ever to invade England to shattering defeat at the Battle of the Standard in 1138 or who had to contend with four risings – in 1124, 1130, 1134 and 1151 – and whose death provoked a fifth, in 1153-4, met with only mixed success. Most of these revolts were not only provincial rebellions but were linked to a disputed succession – a spectre which haunted the macMalcolm dynasty until at least the 1210s.

The turning-point of the twelfth century, which left both a minor to succeed and fatally flawed David's legacy of a southern empire, was the death in 1152 of Henry, the only one of David's children to survive into adulthood. As a result, David, like Henry I of England, left an uncertain succession – despite his efforts in the last months of his life to have his elder grandson, the eleven-year-old Malcolm, acknowledged as his heir. David in a sense left not one minor but two, for the heir to the strategically important earldom of Northumbria which Henry had held was Malcolm's younger brother, William. Although Cumbria had remained in Scots hands after 1138, the reality was that David's southern pale was a product of the multifold but temporary crisis of the Anglo-Norman monarchy in the 1130s rather than a feat of arms. By 1157 it was gone and the border was settled on the line of Solway and Tweed. The almost inevitable loss of the earldom of Northumbria only four years after David's death left a bitter legacy which kings of Scots still strove to recoup more than half a century later. It was not until the reign of Alexander II that Anglo-Scottish relations were fully restored to an even keel or that serious internal challenges to the house of macMalcolm came to an end.

The short reign of Malcolm IV (1153-65) and the very long reign of his brother William I (1165-1214) – the longest before that of James VI – saw the same paradoxical mixture as before, of a consolidation of both kingdom and dynasty set against revolts of the provinces and a disputed succession. It was in Malcolm's reign that the phrases 'kingdom of Scots' or 'kingdom of Scotland' were first used by the king's scribes in charters. The process of the emergence of a single kingdom out of a single kingship was beginning to gather momentum.[41] Yet it would not be until the late 1170s that a start was made to the long and difficult process of subduing the north and the winning of the west began in a serious vein only in the 1240s. William I was the first King of Scots to tackle disorder in Moray or Ross but his intermittent successes there were consolidated only in the reign of his son. Despite the efforts of Alexander II, the first of the macMalcolm dynasty to try to bring either the western mainland or the Isles into the control of the Scottish crown, it was not until the 1260s that much progress was made.

Each reign between 1153 and 1249 had within it a prolonged difficulty over the succession. Malcolm IV, the 'Maiden', never married and left no heirs.[42] William I, although he had produced a string of bastards by the 1170s, did not marry until 1186, at the age of forty-three; and no legitimate male heir would appear until the birth of Alexander in 1198. There was a further prolonged period of uncertainty in the reign of Alexander II (1214-49). Although he married Joan, daughter of King John of England in 1221, the marriage had produced no heirs by the time she died in 1238, and it was only in 1241 – twenty-seven years into the reign – that an heir was produced by his second wife, Marie de Coucy. This was Alexander III (1249-86), who succeeded as a minor eight years later. He was the first macMalcolm king since his namesake Alexander I to show a sense of urgency as to one of the basic functions of kingship – he married Margaret, a daughter of Henry III of England, at the age of ten. The supreme irony of the dynastic crisis of 1286 and the succession of a four-year-old infant granddaughter was that it came in the first reign since 1152 which had seemed to escape early from the spectre of a failed succession. A daughter had been born in 1261, a first son in 1264 and another in 1271. It would take the deaths of all three within three years after 1281 to make Margaret, Maid of Norway, the sole legitimate successor in the macMalcolm line.

The twelfth and thirteenth centuries are sometimes seen as marking the 'triumph of primogeniture'.[43] From the death of Edgar in 1107, primogeniture operated throughout the macMalcolm line, despite minors in 1153, 1214 and 1249 and a female minor in 1286. Yet this is to compress history with a vengeance. What marked out the macMalcolm dynasty from the later royal house of Stewart was the number of times it was challenged. The crisis of the 1090s left two possible lines of claimants. One was the macWilliams, descendants of William, son of Duncan II.[44] The origins of the other – the macHeths – are obscure but their threat was nonetheless real, especially in the reign of William I. The accession of Malcolm IV in 1153 is the first firm evidence of primogeniture in operation, but the singular progress round the country made by the new young heir to the throne in 1152, accompanied by the Earl of Buchan, looks rather like an election campaign. William I tried and failed in 1195 to persuade his nobles to accept one of his two daughters as his heir. The fact that he had his son Alexander recognised twice as his heir – in 1201 and again on his deathbed in 1214 despite the fact that by then Alexander was sixteen – testifies to a lingering nervousness about the principle of primogeniture. It was not until 1249, when a boy less than eight years old succeeded his father, that the practice was secure.

Uncertainties over the succession probably contributed to much of the unrest in the reigns of Malcolm IV and William I. Malcolm's reign began with a prolonged rising in the west in November 1153 – led by the immensely powerful 'Lord' or rí of Argyll, Somerled – which was connected with the claims of Malcolm macHeth, who had married a sister of Somerled and may have traced descent from Alexander I. David I had faced a northern revolt in 1130; Malcolm IV was threatened with the prospect of a combined rising of the north and west. The reign ended shortly after another rising by Somerled, who brought a fleet up the Clyde as far as Renfrew in 1164. In the meantime, Malcolm had been forced to cede Cumberland and Westmorland to Henry II of England (1154-89) in 1157 and this may have increased his difficulties in nearby Galloway, which would be a thorn in the side of macMalcolm kings until the 1230s. In 1160, shortly after he returned from a military campaign in Aquitaine, where he had been called by his liege lord Henry II, Malcolm was confronted with what would appear to have been an orchestrated protest rather than a revolt by six of his earls, who besieged him in his own Castle of Perth. The attempted coup – if such it was – was resisted by Malcolm, who embarked on three successive punitive expeditions into Galloway.

This episode and the reign itself have been called a 'crucial turning-point' in the history of both the macMalcolm dynasty and the Norman settlement.[45] Yet the episode is obscure and the identity of only one of the six earls – Ferteth of Strathearn – is known. By 1164, it is true, Somerled had been killed and the first episode in the long subjugation of Galloway completed with the deposing of Fergus, the so-called 'King of Galloway', who ended his days as a canon in the Augustinian house at Holyrood. Marriage alliances involving two of Malcolm's sisters had been concluded in 1161 and 1162 with Brittany and Holland. Yet each rebellion during the reign seems to have been linked to an uncertain succession.[46] In terms of royal authority, Galloway, although temporarily subdued during the reign, had been added to Moray as another dark corner of the land. The legacy left by Malcom IV to his brother William was a distinctly mixed one.

William, who was dubbed 'the Lion' only after his death, succeeded at the age of twenty-two. His reign saw sheriffdoms rationalised and extended over much of the non-Highland part of the kingdom (save for the north-east) and a formidable network of royal castles established, most notably in Ayrshire, Berwickshire and Dumfriesshire, and, to the north of the Forth, in Perthshire, Moray and Ross.[47] There was a phased but deliberate policy of the extension of royal control into the provinces by means of the promotion of a number of key families through sizeable grants of estates to the point where they equalled the native earls in all but rank.[48] These, families like the Stewarts, Morvilles and Bruces, and not least the king's own brother David who was given the extensive lordship of Garioch in Aberdeenshire, were the instruments of a new and aggressive plantation of agents of the royal will in areas such as Renfrewshire, Cunningham, Lauderdale and Annandale in the south-west and in Moray in the north. Yet the west remained virtual *terra incognita* and feudalisation was far from being applied wholesale elsewhere. The grant of Garioch was made possible by some weakening of the position of the earls of Mar, while two other old earldoms, Atholl and Buchan, escaped this second phase of feudalisation almost untouched.[49] Although there can be no doubt that William, by temperament, was the most Anglo-Norman of the macMalcolm kings, his kingdom was still a highly composite one.

As with David I, the obligation of fealty to an English king gave way to the lure of lost territory in Northumbria, which provoked a rash expedition into the north of England in 1174. Unlike David, William did not escape unscathed. Captured at Alnwick and humiliated by being led with his feet tied beneath his horse in ritual procession into Northampton, he was then thrown into the dungeon of the Castle of Falaise in Normandy. The Treaty of Falaise (1174), by which William vowed homage to Henry II 'for Scotland and for all his other lands', was the end of a road first embarked on at Abernethy in 1072 – the gradual but steady elaboration of what may have begun as a mere form of homage in the marches and by degrees developed into the binding obligation expected of a liegeman.[50] Although the terms of the treaty were abrogated in 1189 by a formal quit-claim made by Richard I, 'the Lionheart' (1189-99), the claim of suzerainty of English kings over Scotland would be renewed repeatedly over the next four centuries. Edward I in the 1290s, Edward III during the third phase of the Wars of Independence in the 1330s, Edward IV in the 1480s and Henry VIII in both 1512-13 and in the 'Rough Wooing' of the 1540s each revived the claim. It appeared even in the pamphlet warfare which preceded the Union of 1707. Although the quit-claim (which cost 10,000 merks) seemed a bargain at the time, it did not settle the dispute and Scotland ultimately paid a high price for the ambition of the most aggressive of its macMalcolm kings.

The embarrassment of the king's capture at Alnwick was the signal for the first revolt of his reign, in Galloway. It took three years for Nithsdale to be reoccupied and it was probably then that the royal castle at Dumfries was constructed. The problem of the south-west lingered on until 1186, when William was again at Dumfries. In 1179 the first attempt to subdue the north took place: a royal army with the King and his brother David at its head marched into the frontier land of Easter Ross, and established two new castles there. This, it is likely, was an expedition which aimed at the containment of the southward expansion of the influence of the earls of Orkney from Caithness into Ross. The next northern rising, in 1181, was potentially a far more serious threat, for it involved a macWilliam claim to the throne. It took seven years to quell, temporarily wrenched Ross out of control of the King of Scots and threatened disorder as far south as Gowrie. By 1187 the pretender, Donald, was dead and William was able to reclaim Inverness, but it took a further ten years for the northern frontier again to be pushed northwards into Ross.

The 1180s marked a prolonged and severe crisis, which saw two theatres of provincial revolt. Both were almost certainly protests against feudal colonisation as well as a threat to the dynasty itself. The crisis was weathered but the twin problems in the north remained. The potential for disruption by Harold Maddadson, Earl of both Caithness and Orkney, provoked royal expeditions to the north in 1197 and 1202 to neutralise this threat. Disaffection with the macMalcolm line persisted, breaking out in further macWilliam rebellions in Ross in 1211 and shortly after William's death in December 1214. No king of Scots before him had as formidable an apparatus of military power as William the Lion, but few kings needed it more.

Thirteenth-century kingship and the Kingdom of Scotland
By June 1215 the rising in the north which greeted the succession of the sixteen-year-old Alexander II (1214-49) had been quashed, significantly by a native lord, Farquhar macTaggart. By October the new King, as intent on the recovery of the lost territories in Northumbria as Malcolm III or David I before him, was besieging the Castle of Norham. In January 1216 King John staged a punitive raid into Lothian, burning the towns of Berwick, Roxburgh, Dunbar and Haddington, to force the 'fox cub' back into 'his lair'. Within weeks Alexander retaliated, in a tit-for-tat raid into Cumbria.

The first thirteen months of the reign had seen three themes which would persist throughout it and much of the next reign as well. Alexander II was able to draw upon support from a far wider range of his nobility than had his father. The tendency which one English chronicler had detected in Malcolm IV and William the Lion (whose mother was a Warenne) that they 'profess themselves to be rather Frenchmen, both in race and in manners, language and culture' was checked.[51] Alexander II restored a more even balance between the two faces of Scottish kingship and in the difficult early years of his son's minority in the 1250s there was a conscious fostering of Gaelic culture and Celtic saints as part of a campaign to heighten a sense of national identity. By then Scotia had come to embrace the whole of the kingdom, south as well as north of the Forth and the term *regnum Scotiae* (kingdom of Scotland), which had featured in royal documents since the reign of Malcolm IV, had found real political meaning. The native earls, many by now hybrids themselves through intermarriage, were far more prominent at the court of Alexander II than at that of William the Lion. A new balance of power amongst the greater nobility was being forged, which also, inevitably, included a balance being struck between crown and magnates.[52]

The year 1215 had seen the last great rising in the north. But if it had shown that one key to the pacification of the kingdom was a wider involvement of the nobility and baronage, the subduing of Galloway in the 1230s and the expeditions into the west – beginning in 1221-2, continuing throughout the 1240s and resuming in the 1260s – showed that the other lay in a more stable relationship with England. Between 1215 and 1217 Alexander staged five incursions into England, but these were the final macMalcolm gestures to recover its lost territories in Northumbria and Cumbria rather than the harbingers of a renewed hostility against England's Angevin kings. The restoration of the 'Honour' (or earldom) of Huntingdon, which accompanied the marriage of Alexander to Joan, sister of Henry III (1216-72) in 1221, eased Anglo-Scottish relations without reimposing the stricter demands of homage and fealty which had straitjacketed the relationship in the 1170s and 1180s. By 1237 the new sense of realism had induced Alexander to forego all claims to territory in the English north, and the line of the border between the Tweed and Solway was in effect agreed.[53]

In 1174, William the Lion had needed the agreement of his liege lord Henry II of England before he launched an assault on Galloway. In 1234, Alexander II, a much freer agent of his own destiny, moved quickly to take advantage of the death of Alan, Lord of Galloway, who had left no legitimate male heir. The instruments of the royal will in Galloway were both, significantly, already trusted agents in the north and they came from different strains of the hybrid nobility of the thirteenth century. It was Farquhar macTaggart, a native lord who was now Earl of Ross, who led the royal army into Galloway, and Walter Comyn, Earl of Menteith and a member of the first Anglo-Norman family to secure an earldom, who policed the province after 1235.

In the west, the spearhead of kings of Scots since at least the 1140s had been another Norman family, the Stewarts. Although 'official' chronicles portray the actions of Somerled, Lord of the Isles, in 1164 as those of a rebel against his sovereign, he would have seen himself as a victim of Stewart aggression. It was not until after 1244, when relations with England were again in a settled state, that Alexander II turned seriously to his western frontier. He first used the tactics of trying to buy out the interest of King Hakon IV of Norway, who enjoyed suzerainty over both Man and the Western Isles. When diplomacy and bribery failed, force took their place. In 1249, the year of his death, Alexander II assembled a fleet and army to penetrate the Firth of Lorn and northern Argyll. He died on the Isle of Kerrera, across the bay from present-day Oban, with Argyll but not the Isles under a new royal control. The foundation for further expansion westward was laid, but it took place only after his son, Alexander III, came of age in 1260. It was then that the Stewarts (who had gained the earldom of Menteith by marriage in 1261 on the death of Earl Walter) were again on the move, pushing the effective frontier of the kingdom out from the Ayrshire coastline across the Firth of Clyde into Kintyre and Knapdale.

The new eight-year-old king, Alexander III (1249-86), the first boy to succeed for almost a century, was quickly put through a rite of inauguration, which combined tradition – being held in the open air and involving the solemn recitation in Gaelic of the new king's long genealogy back to the eponymous Scota, daughter of Pharaoh – and hints of a new-style coronation.[54] Minors had succeeded in recent times, in 1153 and 1214, but neither had involved a minority that would last ten years. For many historians, the 1250s saw the first of many minorities which would mark the next 300 years of Scottish history as essentially being a struggle between overmighty nobles and the crown. The faction-fighting of the 1250s also had, in some interpretations, the added ingredient of English interference, which split the nobles into 'native' and 'pro-English' factions.[55] Most views of a reign which lasted for thirty-six years – the second longest of the twelfth and thirteenth centuries – have either dwelt on the minority with which it began or been conditioned by the crisis of the 1290s which followed. The familiar story of a king unleashed after a strife-torn minority has in much historical writing become the standard plot of later reigns, including almost all the Stewart kings from James I onwards. The status of both Alexander III and his kingdom has, however, also had to bear the weight of a 'golden age', which was brought to a close by the prolonged crisis inflicted upon Scotland by the Wars of Independence.

Neither notion now seems to have much foundation. Apart from the years 1257-8, the minority was marked more by a deliberate closing of ranks amongst the greater nobility than a self-interested struggle for power. The pre-eminent position of the Comyns amongst the nobility and baronage was widely accepted. If there was a disruptive interest at work during the minority, it was not of an overmighty family, like the Comyns, but of a lesser family bent on self-advancement, the Durwards, who sought English support to make good the influence it lacked amongst the Scottish nobility. The infamous 'kidnapping' of the king by the Comyns at Kinross in 1257 was not a pre-emptive strike for power but a rather cack-handed attempt to redress a novel imbalance of power which threatened the cohesion of the aristocratic establishment. By 1258, the Durwards had agreed, like the rest of the nobility, to a compromise in which their own interests were subservient to those of the King who was fast approaching his age of majority.

The stability of the majority of Alexander III was not an antidote to the factionalism of the minority; it was a product of the consensus built up during it. There was no royalist counter-revolution after 1260 and no need for one. The Comyns, as they had been in the last years of Alexander II's reign and during most of the 1250s, remained the most important noble family in the kingdom, an essential instrument of royal power in both the north and the south-west. The Stewarts, for more than a century the crown's chief agents in the west, continued to combine ruthless self-interest and loyal service in pastures new, in Cowal and Kintyre. Far from taming the magnates, Alexander III relied on them to a greater extent than any king of Scots before him.[56]

Unlike David I, Alexander III did not become a legend in his own lifetime. He first became a paragon of princely power and his reign a 'golden age', it has been pointed out, almost a century after his death in the chronicle of John of Fordun, written in the 1380s. By the 1440s, the age of Walter Bower's *Scotichronicon*, the prose had become more purple and patriotic: Alexander III had become an ideal king and his reign a lost golden age.[57] The truth is probably more modest: the reign was a period of relative peace and of moderate but growing prosperity. Overseas exports were increasing although they remained narrowly based in wool and hides. Existing burghs were expanding their economies, though they still remained very modest in size. The amount of coin in circulation was steadily growing in the second half of the century, but there was no dramatic increase of the money supply.[58] The hallmarks of the reign were stability and consensus rather than a dramatic new order or prosperity.

The most significant development in the reign had been the completion of his father's expedition to the Isles. It was in the 1260s that the Hebrides were finally incorporated into the kingdom. To many Scots and to most historians of Scotland, this has had an aura of both inevitability and justice about it. The battle of Largs (1263), when Hakon IV was repulsed by the forces of Alexander III, has almost the status of a Stirling Bridge or Bannockburn in Scottish history, still annually re-enacted to impress itself on the Ayrshire consciousness, if not the national. Yet there can be little doubt that the King of Scots and his agents were the aggressors, both before and after Largs. In *Hakon's Saga*, Alexander II is portrayed as a king who died because he attacked the sacred territory of Columba. In 1262 the Earl of Ross laid waste to part of Skye and it was against a background of atrocity stories of the burning of churches and slaughter of women and children that Hakon assembled his fleet in mid-1263. The scale of the battle itself is a matter of considerable dispute. There can be no doubt that Hakon's force was repulsed, but the likelihood that only a fraction of his 120-strong fleet of ships was involved made the outcome of the battle less conclusive than many accounts portray it.

The real turning-point was probably the death of Hakon two months later, while wintering in Kirkwall. It was a crisis of confidence in Norwegian kingship rather than a renewed offensive launched by Alexander III in Caithness, Skye and other parts of the Western Isles in 1264 which brought Hakon's successor, Magnus the Law-mender, to the negotiating table.[59] The Treaty of Perth (1266) was the result. Although it involved the payment of a lump sum of 4,000 merks and an annuity of 100 merks (which continued to be paid into the fourteenth century), the Treaty did not involve homage or fealty. It was, in a real sense, an international peace treaty, a *finalis concordia*, which was sought as much by the Norwegians (who had been the initiators of peace talks) as by the Scots. In it, a firm boundary was fixed between the Northern Isles (which remained in Norwegian hands) and the Western Isles or 'Sudreys' and Man, which passed to the Scots. It thereby fixed the northern and western frontier of the kingdom as surely as the Treaty of York had fixed the southern border in 1237.[60] And the marriage of Alexander's only daughter, Margaret, to Magnus's successor King Eric in 1281 provided Scotland with an escape route from the crisis of the succession which burst upon it on 19 March 1286, when the King fell to his death while riding at night near Kinghorn in Fife. Or so it then seemed.

The thirteenth century in perspective

The twelfth and thirteenth centuries saw a clash of many cultures, too many to sum up as a single set of competing interests, Anglo-Norman versus Celtic. The position of kings of Scots was consolidated by a widening of the feudal settlement first begun in the reign of David I and a sharpening sense of a territorial kingdom already evident by the reign of Malcolm IV, but the independence of this realm was also under threat from the claims of Angevin kings which were also expressed in feudal terms.[61] Each of these macMalcolm kings practised some version of hybrid kingship, drawing on the different assets and loyalties which Celtic and feudal kingship offered them, but the balance was a shifting one. No king tipped the balance more decisively towards feudal kingship than William the Lion, who gloried in the aura of French knightly culture, but increasing involvement in the west from the 1220s onwards made necessary a reappraisal of the Celtic face of Scottish kingship. It is hardly surprising that the reign of Alexander III, the first King of Scots to mount a successful offensive against a significant section of his own Gaelic subjects, should see a renewed interest in Gaeldom.[62]

Important allies of the macMalcolm kings were, of course, the descendants of the Anglo-Norman, French and Fleming settlers first invited by David I. The role of the native nobility, the old mormaers, was no less important. Three notable examples help to illustrate the political and cultural cross-currents at work in the twelfth and thirteenth centuries. The macDuff earls of Buchan, themselves related to the royal house of the eleventh century, were the emblems of the continuing survival and influence of a native aristocracy in the next century. They fell prey, not to royal aggression or to Norman ambition, but to the usual curse of noble houses, a lack of male heirs.

David, Lord of Garioch and Earl of Huntingdon, brother of William the Lion, was symbolic of the great new lords planted by that king and his son in the far-flung provinces of the kingdom and was also the most striking case of magnates who held estates in both Scotland and England. The mixed loyalties of a noble such as Earl David, 'a man of great power in both England and Scotland', or of a family such as the Balliols who held estates extending from Picardy and through seventeen English counties to Scotland, complicated both the growing sense of national identity which marked late twelfth- and thirteenth-century Scotland and its relations with its southern neighbour.[63] Variously interpreted as infiltrators in Scottish society and as a force for reconciliation in Anglo-Scottish relations, these vast international networks of aristocratic interests were, however, by the last quarter of the thirteenth century already beginning to be severed. National shutters were beginning to come down before the Wars of Independence tested these loyalties to breaking point. Old Anglo-Norman families were fast becoming – in other parts of the British Isles as well as in Scotland – part of a territorial rather than an international nobility.[64]

The spectacular rise of the Comyns is a paradigm of thirteenth-century Scotland – an increasingly hybrid noble family as one of the main supports of a still hybrid kingship. In origin an Anglo-Norman family and one of the instruments of royal colonisation in the north early in the century, their rise to real influence is traceable to the marriage made with the daughter of the last Celtic Earl of Buchan about 1212. A web of marriage alliances with noble families old and new combined with continuing royal patronage in both Church and state to make them the pillars of the aristocratic establishment in the reign of Alexander III. Royal favour gave Comyns bishoprics, national office (such as justiciarship of Scotia), and local offices such as sheriffships.[65] The success stories of Alexander III's Scotland were the nobles who exploited the twin assets of local connection and royal patronage. The more hybrid a noble family, the more influence it was likely to have in a society which was still an amalgamation of peoples.

The resurgence of a territorial nobility in the thirteenth century had an important political price. Already well developed was the central paradox of power in later medieval Scotland: the authority of kings depended on local nobles to supply the power in the regions which they themselves lacked. Alexander III, the last king of the macMalcolm line, was in one sense far more powerful than the first, Malcolm Canmore: the status of the monarchy had never been higher, primogeniture had been fully accepted and the notion of a territorial kingdom was already a century old. Yet in another important sense the effective authority of kings of Scots, as it became more explicit, also became more obviously constrained, for it was now also visibly contingent on a nexus of noble power in the regions. The tight feudal reins which had bound nobles to their liege lord in the reigns of the twelfth century were already loosening in those of the thirteenth. Feudal kingship gained strength from a new unity of national purpose, which would later be acknowledged in explicit terms as the 'community of the realm'. But it was also circumscribed by the emergence – or reappearance – of the regional magnate. The outline script for much of the political history of the fourteenth and fifteenth centuries was already sketched.

7

THE MEDIEVAL CHURCH

O N 19 JUNE 1250, THE BODY OF QUEEN MARGARET, WIFE OF MALCOLM CANMORE, was moved from its resting place in Dunfermline Abbey to a new shrine nearer the great altar. After almost five years of petitions to Rome, Margaret had been canonised as Scotland's first (and only) royal saint. Although he did not live to see it, the ceremony was a notable triumph for Alexander II, in whose reign the Scottish Church had reached its mature form. The cleric who had organised the campaign was David Bernham, royal client, confidante and Bishop of St Andrews (1239-53). The inauguration of Alexander's eleven-year-old son five days after his father's death in July 1249, which came close to a formal rite of anointing and coronation, Margaret's canonisation two months later and her investiture in the following year were all testimony to a coming of age not only of the macMalcolm dynasty but also of the Scottish Church and of the relationship between Church and state.[1]

Church and nation

Bernham bore the old title of *episcopus Scottorum* (Bishop of the Scots), which had been in use since at least the mid-eleventh century and perhaps the mid-tenth. Churchmen had played a role in the inauguration of kings of Scots since Columba had taken part in the ceremonial installation of Aedán mac Gabráin in 574. The notion of a 'Scottish Church' had first been given voice in the reign of Giric (878-89) although the *ecclesia Scoticana* had been given new status in 1192 when Pope Celestine III (1191-8) in a bull *Cum universi* declared that all the Scottish sees except Galloway (which was under the jurisdiction of York) should enjoy the status of 'special daughter' of Rome, immediately subject to the papacy rather than to Canterbury, Durham or York.[2] Yet popes had been (and would be until the 1320s) consistently reluctant to grant to kings of Scots the full rites of anointing and coronation. They were also unwilling to grant metropolitan status to St Andrews, which by the twelfth century was the acknowledged centre of the Scottish Church, despite petitions in the reigns of David I and Malcolm IV. It was no accident that the reign of William the Lion saw both a revival of the legends of the origins of kings of Scots and a further elaboration of the cult of St Andrew. Visible evidence of the heightened dependence of the macMalcolm dynasty and the Church on each other were the *Pictish Chronicle*, which was copied during the reign with its tracing of the common origin of Scots, Picts and Britons to Scota, daughter of the Pharaoh, and the beginnings of the building of a new cathedral at St Andrews in the 1160s, at 320 feet in length and 168 feet across its transepts far larger than any other church in the realm. The intertwined identity of King, Church and people – originating in the children of Israel, linked ever since the time of Columba by a royal priesthood, and now given alternative form in a second national saint – was near-complete.

The story of the emergence of Andrew as a second or an alternative national symbol is a mysterious one, which has various possible starting-points, like the story of the emergence of a nation which it mirrors. There can be little doubt, however, that it was given fresh elaborations in the course of the twelfth century. At the defeat of the Viking Ivar in Strathearn in 903, the staff of Columba, dubbed *Cath Buaid* ('Battle Victory'), had guaranteed success, and his status as 'apostle' of the 'men of Scotland' was unchallenged at the time of the battle of Corbridge (918). It is possible, however, that a cult of St Andrew had emerged as early as the reign of Constantine, King of Picts, between 789 and 820.[3] By the middle half of the tenth century, more than a century before Queen Margaret instituted the celebrated free transport across the Forth at Queensferry for pilgrims to St Andrews, there is ample evidence that the shrine of St Andrew at what was still called Kilrimont was already a popular pilgrimage centre, whose fame had spread throughout Scotland and further afield. Another King Constantine, son of Áed, retired to the monastic life there in 952; his son, Indulf, died there in 965, as did an Irish prince called Áed, 'in pilgrimage' in 965. By the eleventh century, that older place-name was being superseded by the name of the Apostle himself.[4]

Although St Andrew was to become the patron saint of the macMalcolm dynasty – just as Columba had been that of the mac Alpin line before it – the substitution was never total. Queen Margaret enjoyed a reputation long after her death as the rebuilder of Iona as well as the patron of pilgrims of the Apostle. Donald Ban, brother of Malcolm Canmore, was the last Scots King to be buried on Iona but the usual burial place for kings of Scots from 1107 onwards was at Dunfermline rather than St Andrews. Thus the identification of Columba with the Celtic church and St Andrew with the new practices of western Christendom introduced in their various forms in the twelfth century was never absolute. It was significant that the establishment of a second route for pilgrims to St Andrews across the Forth, between North Berwick and Ardross, known as the Earl's Ferry, was the work of the premier native noble of the mid-twelfth century, Duncan, Earl of Fife.[5] As in secular politics, a balance between old and new was struck within the Church – in piety and its saints as much as in its organisation. It was a hybrid Church for a hybrid people.

Just as the staff of Columba had allowed a mixed army of Picts and Scots to fight together in 918 as *Albanaich* against a common enemy, so the authority of the Apostle was gradually cultivated: by the time of William Fraser, Bishop of St Andrews (1279-97), the legend insisted on the suzerainty of the Apostle over all the peoples of Scotland, 'the Picts, Scots, Danes and Norwegians'. By 1279 the seal of the Bishop of St Andrews bore the image of St Andrew crucified, and in 1286 it also appeared on the seal of the Guardians of the Kingdom, accompanied by the legend, 'Andrew be leader of the compatriot Scots'. By 1318, when St Andrews Cathedral was consecrated in a service of national thanksgiving 'for the notable victory granted to the Scottish people by blessed Andrew, protector of the realm' four years earlier at Bannockburn, the identification of saint and nation was complete.

In the Declaration of Arbroath of 1320, the identity of the Scottish nation was taken one stage further, to embrace the present and past activities of 'princes and people'. The reputation of Bruce as well as the status of the Scots was proven by the touchstone of 'our patron and protector', Andrew. This was a document written for the eyes of the Pope, but at home both the Church and kings of Scots were aware of

10 0 10 20 30 40 50 miles

(Birsay)
Kirkwall
ORKNEY

Shetland

TRONDHEIM
(NIDAROS)

(Halkirk?)

CAITHNESS

Dornoch

ROSS   (Kinneddar) (Spynie)
Fortrose   Elgin (Birnie)

              (Mortlach?)

MORAY

                    ABERDEEN   Aberdeen

ARGYLL

Lismore   DUNKELD   Brechin
              Dunkeld   ST. ANDREWS
                                  with
                               BRECHIN

SODOR   DUNBLANE   St. Andrews
              Dunblane

                        Lothian

              Glasgow

           Glasgow
              GLASGOW

                    Teviotdale

                                    YORK

           GALLOWAY

ARMAGH   Whithorn

                          | GLASGOW | Province |
                          | GLASGOW | Diocese |
                          | Glasgow | Archdeaconry |
                          | Glasgow | Cathedral City |
                          | (Birnie) | Earlier Cathedrals |
                          | ///// | Diocese of St. Andrews with Brechin |

Peel

Map 6 Dioceses of the medieval Church

their identities as shepherd and leader of what was still acknowledged to be a confederation of peoples. Robert Bruce, a Gaelic-speaking Celtic king as well as a feudal ruler descended from an Anglo-Norman family, had taken both symbols of the Scottish Church, the *Brecbennach* of Columba and the cross of Andrew in the form of the saltire flag, to the field of Bannockburn.[6]

The twelfth century, which was, in terms of building and the introduction of new religious orders, the most dynamic century in the history of the pre-Reformation Church, also saw the introduction of many new biblical and continental saints. Nowhere was the change more obvious than in the king's newly founded burghs, where the new parish kirks were dedicated to such as St Mary (at Berwick, Dundee, Glasgow and Haddington), St Nicholas (Aberdeen, Lanark and Renfrew) or St Giles (Edinburgh and Elgin). Elsewhere dedications were more mixed, encouraged by the number of native saints' lives written or rewritten in the twelfth century. In rural parish kirks, Andrew, brother of Peter, had to compete with St Kentigern, St Ninian, St Machar and St Serf. Local cults of Celtic or other early saints were as much a part of the early medieval church as the veneration of Andrew as a national saint.[7]

Although the fourteenth century seems to have seen a slackening of interest in such local or early saints, they experienced a marked revival from the second quarter of the fifteenth century onwards. This was the age of Walter Bower, whose *Scotichronicon* matched an anti-English patriotism with the revival of a cult of native saints. Bower, an Augustinian Abbot of Inchcolm, turned his island abbey into a devotional centre dedicated to Columba. James Haldenstone, another Augustinian prior (of St Andrews) of the same period, was an early campaigner for the canonisation of St Duthac of Tain as well as a restorer of the cathedral church dedicated to the Apostle. Bishop William Lauder of Glasgow at the same time, in 1420, was petitioning the Pope for permission to move the feretory of St Mungo to a more prominent place in his cathedral church.

The revival of interest in lesser saints, such as St Thenew at Glasgow, St Triduana at Restalrig near Edinburgh and St Ebba at Coldingham later in the same century, all marked the opening up of new archives of the historical memories of a nation. This movement reached its climax in what has been called a national liturgy, the *Aberdeen Breviary* assembled by Bishop William Elphinstone of Aberdeen – one of the earliest surviving Scottish printed books, produced in Edinburgh by Walter Chepman and Andrew Myllar in 1510. In it are to be found more than seventy native saints, all assigned feast days and each a history lesson in itself. Yet Elphinstone's liturgy, which was intended to supplant the English Sarum use, was far more than a narrow propaganda tract for its times; it included most of the major new devotions current in Europe, such as St Mary *ad Nives*.[8] In this it summed up the new fashion in the later fifteenth century for continental devotions centring on the Passion of Christ, such as the Five Wounds and the Most Holy Name of Jesus. Many of these, like the Holy Blood (still to be seen in the Fetternear Banner, which belonged to the Edinburgh merchant guild) were imported direct from Flanders. The history of Scottish worship, like much of the history of medieval Scotland, was a blend of two sets of influences – nationalist and continental.[9]

The clergy

The composite identity of the Scottish Church in the twelfth and thirteenth centuries mirrored the shifting, hybrid character of both the macMalcolm dynasty and the nobility. It also masked the clash of continuity and change going on within the Church itself, especially amongst the secular clergy. Bernham was the first native-born Bishop of St Andrews since Fothad, who had died in 1093, the same year as Malcolm and Margaret.[10] Since 1093 there had been an unbroken line of distinguished Anglo-Norman bishops, of whom the greatest were Robert (1124-59), an Augustinian canon of Scone who had supervised the enlargement of St Rule's as a cathedral and priory church and had perhaps also planned the creation of a new cathedral before his death, and William Malvoisin (1202-38), who had brought the reorganisation of the huge diocese to a conclusion. Native Scots were a rarity amongst the twelfth-century episcopate, which was largely Anglo-French in origin.

In the twelfth and early thirteenth centuries Scottish cathedrals had naturally turned to their English counterparts to provide a model for their organisation and constitutions: Moray, perhaps prompted by the example of its first effective bishop, Richard of Lincoln (1187-1203), looked to Lincoln Cathedral for its constitutions in 1212; Glasgow, however, had already adopted those of Salisbury, and Dunkeld followed suit in the 1250s. The influence of English diocesan reform on St Andrews did not come to a sudden end in 1238, for Bernham had been a member of Malvoisin's household and had modelled the development of a small group of professional administrators to run his diocese on the work of Robert Grosseteste, Bishop of Lincoln. The Sarum use in worship, as a result, had gained widespread, if not complete acceptance by then.[11] By 1250 a new breed of churchmen had emerged. Bishops were increasingly likely either to be royal servants or the kin or clients of noble families; the favour of Alexander III and the tentacles of Comyn patronage extended far into the benefice structure of the late thirteenth-century secular Church. The ecclesia Scoticana, as a result, was staffed largely by Scots by the reign of Alexander III.[12]

The new reformed religious orders established in the course of the twelfth century – Augustinians, Cistercians and Premonstratensians – were all French in origin but had been introduced via daughter houses already set up in England.[13] Only the Tironensians amongst the first generation of monastic incomers came directly from the mother house in France – at Tiron near Chartres. Whether the parentage was direct or indirect, there is an important truth in the saying that every Scottish monastery was 'a little bit of France'.[14] Like Tironensian abbots, heads of Cistercian houses were obliged to attend the regular meetings of all abbots of the order, at Cîteaux in Burgundy. In turn, it was the duty of abbots of mother houses in all orders to inspect daughter houses every year. The monastic world knew no frontiers, although few orders were as systematic in their contacts as the Cistercians, which by 1273 had no fewer than eleven houses ranging from Melrose in the Borders to Saddell in Argyll and Kinloss in Moray, each with at least thirteen monks and ten or more lay-brothers. Often granted large tracts of uncultivated land ideal for sheep farming, the Cistercians accounted for four of the fifteen religious houses which had warehouses in Scotland's premier port of Berwick in the thirteenth century; their organisation, which controlled perhaps as much as 5 per cent of the Scottish wool clip, allowed them to act as a virtual trading consortium.[15]

The involvement of the Augustinian canons with society took a different form. Not an enclosed order like Cluniacs, Tironensians or the thirteenth-century arrivals, the Valliscaulian monks, the primary mission of the Augustinians was to go out into the world of the laity, usually serving the parish churches which were appropriated to their house. They also had a strong eremitical character, which suited their take-over and reform of a number of old *Céli Dé* communities. These were often situated in remote sites, like Inchcolm in the Firth of Forth, St Serf's Inch on Loch Leven or Inchmahome on the Lake of Menteith – a name invented only in the nineteenth century. If the Tironensians were the proprietary order of David I, it was the Augustinians who had succeeded to this mantle before the end of the twelfth century, based in or near royal centres such as Holyrood near Edinburgh, Cambuskenneth across the Forth from Stirling and at St Andrews itself. No order was as close to the royal house between 1200 and 1450.[16]

The introduction, again as a result of royal patronage, of two mendicant orders – the Dominicans (Black Friars) and Franciscans (Grey Friars) – in the reign of Alexander II was a further sign of the vitality of the Scottish medieval Church. Each was brought to Scotland within two decades of its foundation as an order. By the end of the century there were already a dozen Dominican houses and six Franciscan, mostly sited on the edge of burghs, where they might practise their work of preaching, teaching and charity. Other friars – notably the Carmelites (White Friars) and the Trinitarians (Red Friars) – followed. These orders conformed to the pattern already becoming apparent in other branches of the thirteenth-century Church; they were consciously international in outlook but staffed for the most part by local men. The 1250s saw the beginning of a campaign for the establishment of a separate Franciscan province, which had a chequered history until its final establishment in 1483. The Dominicans, although nominally part of the English province until 1481, showed from an early date strong devolutionist tendencies. In 1289 a papal indulgence acknowledged the growing sense of nationalism amongst the religious by forbidding the appointment of foreigners as heads of any religious houses in Scotland.[17]

The thirteenth century brought changes, too, for many of the ordinary secular clergy, and not all of them were welcome. By 1300 more than 60 per cent of parish kirks had their teinds (tithes) appropriated, in whole or in part, to another ecclesiastical foundation – usually a religious house or cathedral chapter. By the sixteenth century, the figure would rise to 85 per cent. Already by 1250 part of the price of magnificent buildings such as the abbeys of Kelso or Dryburgh or the new cathedral churches and growing diocesan administration of sees like St Andrews and Glasgow was becoming apparent: instead of beneficed parish priests, many parishes were beginning to be served by vicars. This was almost certainly not as yet as damaging as it would be on the eve of the Reformation, by which time much of the ordinary business of the Church was carried out by curates, with the holder of the benefice absentee. Yet the process had already begun by which the 'foot soldiers' of the later medieval Church would be chaplains of various sorts, underpaid, lacking in job security and forever on the move. It is as well to remember that within most great ecclesiastics – ranging from William Wishart, a Bishop of Glasgow in the late thirteenth century who is alleged to have amassed twenty-two rectories and prebends by the time of his election, to the celebrated Bishop Elphinstone who employed a race of Elphinstones in his Aberdeen diocese in the late fifteenth century – there lurked either a pluralist or a nepotist, and that behind them was a transient and poorly paid workforce.

The descent of the parish clergy into real poverty belonged to the late fourteenth and the fifteenth centuries. In the thirteenth century, vicars-pensioner (who were paid only a fixed pension rather than a share of the teinds of the parish) were allowed ten merks and chaplains £5. By the fourteenth century such vicars were supposed to be paid a minimum of £10 but often were not. The intention of the church authorities, it is likely, was to keep the income of the parish clergy on a par with that of freeholders or husbandmen, the backbone of rural society who, if they had an income of £10, were required by parliament to be armed and horsed for military service. Their status was not unlike that of seventeenth-century ministers of the reformed Church, whose income matched that of the lairds, feuars and greater tenant farmers in their congregations. But increasingly the income of the parish clergy fell in real terms as price inflation gripped late medieval Scotland. Long before the Church was faced by a spiritual crisis, it was confronted by an economic one.[18]

The shortcomings of the medieval Church were slow to emerge and reponsibility for them is difficult to assign with any precision. Nepotism was the natural reflection of a society in which kinship counted for so much. Pluralism was endemic to an ecclesiastical system which in the twelfth and thirteenth centuries had sunk so many of its assets, in manpower as well as in stone and finance, into centres of excellence, whether in the form of the cloister or cathedral chapter. Prestigious building schemes amidst poverty were not unique to the medieval period. The dramatic beauty of Elgin Cathedral deserved its description as 'the ornament of the realm, the glory of the kingdom, the delight of foreigners'. There can also be little doubt that such bishops were concerned above all else with the bringing of the teachings of Christ to ordinary members of society; the thirteenth-century statutes of the Scottish Church are filled with a concern to administer the sacraments and teach the faith that would not be out of place in the sixteenth century or the twentieth. The parish clergy were enjoined to celebrate the sacraments 'with devout solemnity in the Catholic faith according to the precise form handed down by the holy fathers and the holy Scriptures' and parishioners were in their turn to be urged 'to explain that same faith to their children and to teach them to keep the Christian faith'.[19] Such indications as there are show that the vast bulk of them did perform their duties with an admirable reverence. There can be little doubt, however, that there was a drastic loss of status of the clergy in minor orders, linked to their falling income, in the fifteenth and early sixteenth centuries. Responsibility for this rests primarily with a hierarchy who failed to divert enough resources into the ordinary parish system, but it also belongs to the lay patrons who employed chaplains on minimum wages in collegiate churches, hospitals or other lay foundations. The laity expected more to be done for the salvation of their souls, but were unwilling or unable to pay as much for it as before.

Crown and papacy

In 1301 the immensely learned canon lawyer Master Baldred Bisset advised the Pope that the Scots had been converted to Christianity some 400 years before the English and that no fewer than thirty-six kings had ruled over the Scots while the English languished in paganism. In 1565 the Bishop of Dunblane, on a mission to raise a papal subsidy to aid a Catholic restoration under Mary, Queen of Scots, gave Pope Pius V much the same history lecture. For 1,364 years, ever since the pontificate of Victor I, he argued, a long and unbroken line of kings of Scots had protected the Church and defended the faith on behalf of the papacy.[20] At least 400 years of this history were apocryphal, as was Pope Victor, but there was an essential truth amidst these durable historical myths. The papacy and the Scottish crown had long enjoyed a special relationship, and the emergence of a Scottish Church had owed as much to successive kings of Scots as they had relied on it to underpin their own authority. The *Cum universi* bull of Pope Celestine III, which in 1192 had established all the Scottish sees except Galloway as the 'special daughter' of Rome, was reissued twice within the following thirty years, by Innocent III and Honorius III. In the process, Rome cast off the grand strategy of Pope Gregory the Great which had divided the whole of Britain into two provinces, controlled by bishops based in London and York. The twelfth century had also seen successive petitions sent to Rome by Scottish kings from Alexander I onwards as part of their resistance of claims to jurisdiction over the Scottish Church made by both Canterbury and York. It had been the encouragement given by the same kings to religious orders such as the Augustinians, with mother houses in England, and the appointment of a wave of Anglo-Norman bishops which had done much to encourage an English connection.

Papal recognition of the Scottish Church did not extend to the granting of metropolitan status to it. The anomaly of a national church, specifically under papal protection but lacking a metropolitan – which lasted until the erection of St Andrews into an archbishopric in 1472 – had two effects. It encouraged an unusually close liaison between Scotland and the papal court and representatives of both the Scottish Church and crown grew adept in the complex arts of lobbying in Rome; but it also resulted in a close interest expressed by Scottish kings in church appointments. The development after 1225 of a national provincial council of the Scottish Church, headed by a Conservator rather than an archbishop, had the effect of accelerating both tendencies. The council seems to have been ready to accept papal pressure for the centralisation of authority within the Church, usually in the form of either demands for papal taxation or the implementation of statutes for reform of the life and conduct of the clergy already enacted elsewhere.[21] It also seems on occasion to have been used by both Alexander II and III as a channel of royal interest in ecclesiastical affairs. By the 1260s what would later come to be called the 'Conservator of the Privileges of the Scottish Church' had emerged, an office rotating amongst the bishops which exerted virtual archiepiscopal functions on behalf of the council. It is likely that these provincial councils developed a higher notion of their powers than Rome may have allowed, as well as an undoubted sense of group solidarity amongst the hierarchy which would be given practical effect in pleading the Scottish cause at Rome and elsewhere during the Wars of Independence.

It was a fairly new breed of university-educated churchmen who were the moving forces in defining and refining the relationships between and within Church and state in thirteenth-century Scotland. A succession of talented churchmen –

Robert Kenleith, Abbot of Dunfermline, Bishop Gamelin of St Andrews (1255-71) and his successor, William Wishart (1273-9) – were chancellors of the realm in the second half of the century and the royal clerks who issued a growing stream of official documents and charters emphasising the notion of a *regnum Scotiae* (kingdom of Scotland) were benefice holders, sustained by the Church rather than the crown. The Church not only provided a long tradition of loyal service to the crown, it did so without payment. It was hardly surprising that the ideas of a territorial kingdom and an *ecclesia Scoticana* reached maturity together, in the reign of Alexander III.[22]

The Wars of Independence tested many loyalties, but the Scottish bishops for the most part held to a common and fairly consistent view which was unusual amongst other groups in Scottish society. It may seem surprising that churchmen proved to be those most willing to turn a blind eye to the sacrilegious murder of John Comyn by Robert Bruce in the Greyfriars' Kirk in Dumfries in February 1306, but they had more to lose than most from English hegemony. It was the cause which they backed rather than the man, who until at least 1314 was as much on trial amongst the clergy as in other sections of the political community. Their nationalism was both informed and self-interested; it stemmed from two centuries and more of intermittent claims of various parts of the English Church to jurisdiction over them. The close-knit ties of kin and clientage which bound together the middle ranks of most dioceses meant that few broke ranks. Not many, however, were as outspoken as the bishops of Glasgow and Moray who likened resistance against Edward I to a Crusade against the infidel.[23]

The shift of the papal court from Rome to Avignon after 1309 encouraged a trend which had already begun with the Anglo-Scottish wars: in the thirteenth century many Scottish students had gone to Oxford or Cambridge, but in the fourteenth they preferred the universities of Paris, Orleans, Louvain or Cologne. A new cosmopolitan nationalism affected the leading Scottish clergy as a result. The increasing control exerted by the Avignon papacy over appointments to bishoprics and to other benefices had a number of important consequences: it fuelled contests over benefices, encouraged ambitious young Scots to court patrons at Avignon, raised costs and reduced the income enjoyed by new benefice-holders.[24] The results reverberated through the clerical system: the increased costs were passed on; more parish kirks had their revenues appropriated; the vicar with a 'perpetual vicarage', enjoying some share in the teinds, might find himself a vicar-pensioner, with a fixed stipend in a period of rising prices and a falling pound, forced to resort to other devices to scrape a living. The combined effect of a country struggling to recover from the impact of a century of intermittent warfare, the slump in trade after a brief recovery in the 1370s and the new costs of papal provision to benefices did not impoverish the whole Scottish Church, but it did drastically accentuate the gap between appropriators and appropriated.

The Great Schism (1378-1417) which followed, with rival popes in Avignon and Rome, initially increased the links between Scotland and France. The support of the English Church for the Italian Urban VI resulted in a number of attempts to provide Englishmen to Scottish bishoprics and a renewed animus between the two churches: the Avignon candidate for the see of Galloway, the Scottish Franciscan Thomas Rossy, even challenged an outspoken schismatic, the Bishop of Norwich, to single armed combat – he declined. The steadfast loyalty of the Scottish Church to the Avignon popes had a number of important consequences. Clement VII (1378-94) appointed Bishop Walter Wardlaw of Glasgow, who had invested several years at Avignon, a cardinal in 1383 – the first Scot to be given the red hat. From being a promoter of Scottish interests at Avignon, Wardlaw for the last few years of his life became patronage-broker and party whip of the Avignon interest in Scotland. The see of Galloway finally broke its long but increasingly fragile link with York and became a full member of the *ecclesia Scoticana*. A long, complex dispute over the bishopric of Orkney, extending over the islands of Orkney and Shetland which were still under the control of kings of Norway, produced the first appointment, in 1384, of a Scot to the see; Robert Sinclair was the first in an unbroken line of Scots bishops. In the west, the diocese of Sodor, which extended from the Isle of Man to the northernmost of the Western Isles, was split in two during the Schism; the Roman loyalist Bishop of Sodor retained control only of the part of the diocese under English control and the Avignon candidate provided in 1382 became, in effect, the first Bishop of the Isles.[25]

Further benefits stemmed from the long pontificate of Clement's successor, Pedro de Luna or Benedict XIII (1394-1417), during which Scotland was the only kingdom in Europe to remain single-mindedly loyal to the Avignon papacy. The most notable was the founding of Scotland's first university. The exclusion of Benedict XIII from France in 1408 and his exile at Peniscola in Aragon had resulted in the return to Scotland of a number of masters who had formerly taught in French universities. By 1412 they had founded a school at St Andrews which was granted a charter of incorporation by Henry Wardlaw, Bishop of St Andrews. A year later, Benedict granted the necessary six bulls of protection and privilege according it university status and the right to confer degrees.

There was little trace in Scotland of the popular and virulent criticism of the papacy so obvious in many other parts of Europe as insults were traded between rival popes and a war of appointments was waged. The Schism, nevertheless, had raised fundamental questions about the nature of papal authority, not least the role of general councils. It was, ironically, the infant University of St Andrews, whose arms included a crescent moon in commemoration of Pedro de Luna, which was the first institution in Scotland to challenge his authority. Its Faculty of Arts resolved in August 1418 that obedience should be withdrawn from Pedro de Luna 'once called Benedict' and transferred to Pope Martin V, who had been elected in 1417 as a result of the new consensus in western Christendom reached at the Council of Constance. It announced its decision at a general council of the three estates which met at Perth three months later. It was the first and probably the last time that the decision of a university faculty changed the course of Scottish history. The Great Schism was over.[26]

The effects of the Great Schism were, however, long lasting. The liberal patronage of the Avignon popes, anxious to sustain support in Scotland for their cause, had encouraged inflated expectations amongst both churchmen and laity; these were deflated by the restored Martin V, who was anxious to reassert his accustomed rights to papal provision and full common services. Martin's election inevitably produced a renewed scramble to have benefices confirmed or challengers bought off. This was the background to the sharp friction after 1424 between a restored Scottish King anxious to make his mark and a Pope determined to defend his authority against councils. The attempts of James I's parliaments to restrict petitions by prohibiting churchmen from going abroad without permission of the King and to restrict the outward flow of money to the *Curia* by outlawing the practice of 'barratry' were countered by the papacy, which twice threatened to deprive James's chancellor, John Cameron, Bishop of Glasgow, for promoting legislation against the Holy See. The exchanges grew more acrimonious during the pontificate of Pope Eugenius IV (1431-47), who condemned the Scottish bishops as 'Pilates rather than prelates', but there were signs by 1437, on the eve of James's assassination, that a compromise might be reached.[27] Yet the tussle between crown and papacy, once begun, was hard to disengage from. Every king from James I to James V would complain about the exactions which emanated from Rome, probe the technicalities of the ecclesiastical appointments system and seek to exploit its loopholes. Parliament, once given a taste of a new secular authority over the Church, would act still more aggressively; it, more than Stewart kings, was the advocate of the rights, both accustomed and novel, of the crown over the Church.

There was a further consequence of the Great Schism. It revealed that a generation gap had opened up within the Scottish Church: most of the existing hierarchy was personally committed to Benedict XIII and distinctly out of sympathy with a new generation of churchmen, encouraged into conciliar ideas by their attendance at the reforming Council of Basle (1431-48) which sought to curb papal powers in these areas. After another rival Pope had been elected by the Council to produce the Little Schism (1439-49), the disputes over conciliarism in the Scottish Church threatened to become entangled in the factional politics of James II's minority.[28]

The reign of James III saw a series of tangled disputes between the crown and the papacy, involving various aspects of papal provision. Caught haplessly in the crossfire was Patrick Graham, promoted in 1465 at the age of thirty to the bishopric of St Andrews more through his connections than his talents. In need of further papal largesse to pay the debts still outstanding for his various bulls of provision, Graham was an all too willing agent of the papal will and was rewarded in 1472 with appointment as the first Archbishop of St Andrews. The sudden, unexpected appearance of a Scottish metropolitan in the unlikely form of Patrick Graham, who was also granted legatine powers, brought about a far more serious crisis in relations with the papacy than in the 1420s. His deprivation in 1478, a discredited and somewhat pathetic figure, was a major, if distasteful victory for the crown. His replacement by William Scheves (1478-97), a royal placeman noted for his competence as an administrator rather than his scholarship or reputation as a pastor, was as cynical an appointment in a Church which was brimming with talent as that of Graham by Sixtus IV had been.[29]

The reality of the situation in which both James III and popes found themselves in the 1470s and 1480s was that neither could afford to risk losing control over the Church. The recasting of royal authority in the fifteenth century brought about an increasing dependence of the crown on a class of skilled administrators and jurists, amongst whom William Elphinstone, trained in both canon and civil law at Paris and Orleans and chancellor under James III, was *primus inter pares*. That, together with the increasing reliance of the crown on revenue from the Church in a period when most of its other sources of income were faltering, inevitably tempted James III into a greater reliance on the heads of monastic houses in the royal administration and more efforts to control their appointments.[30]

Ultimately the contest between the Scottish crown and the papacy was an unequal one. James III's claims were part of a much longer-term campaign by the crown, made urgent by its relentless fear of insolvency and the need to reform royal household government. Although a reign of a secular king marks only a short time in the politics of the Holy See, where history is measured in centuries rather than mere decades, it is often the case that papal policy fluctuates; a forceful pope is frequently followed by a conciliator. So it was in 1485, when Sixtus was succeeded by Innocent VIII. Within a year a golden rose, the traditional mark of papal favour, had arrived and in 1487 a face-saving compromise was arranged. The Indult (privilege) of that year did not bind the Pope to accept the King's 'humble supplications' regarding provision to benefices, but it accepted that the crown should enjoy the revenues of all major benefices and abbacies for eight months after they fell vacant – two months longer than even the parliament of 1485 had dared to claim. The right of nomination by the crown was not conceded, but the door was left firmly ajar for future kings and parliaments to exploit. In 1526, during the minority of James V, parliament asserted the crown's right to nominate rather than recommend, and in 1535 the Pope, with the spectre of another Henry VIII in prospect, conceded the *ius nominandi* and extended the period of delay in making appointments to a full twelve months. The Church, though still a 'special daughter' of Rome, had a new and demanding foster parent.[31]

Schools, schoolmen and lawyers

In 1633, a centrepiece of the formal entry of Charles I into Edinburgh was a 'mountain dressed for Parnassus', constructed outside the Tron Church in the High Street, with the Muses and 'ancient Worthies of Scotland'.[32] The parade of honoured Scots – Duns Scotus, Bishop Elphinstone, Hector Boece, John Mair (or Major), Gavin Douglas, David Lindsay and George Buchanan – is striking testimony to the primacy of place given to learning in the Scots' sense of their past as well as to the continuity of scholarship and literature which linked late medieval and early modern Scotland across the seeming fissure of the Reformation of 1560. All except Lindsay and Buchanan, it is worth noting, were churchmen. The arrival of the printing press, first set up in Scotland in 1507, makes it easier to trace the continuing influence of some leading figures on the Scottish intellect: the works of Gavin Douglas, together with those of other prominent literary figures and churchmen of the late medieval period such as John Barbour, author of *The Brus*, or the vernacular poets of the reign of James IV, William Dunbar and and Robert Henryson, were the best-selling literary works of the long reign of James VI (1567-1625).[33] The impact of other medieval schoolmen, scholars, historians and poets, though far less easy to detect, is likely to have been no less real.

There were no Scottish universities before the founding of St Andrews in 1412. The next century would see a college (St Salvator's) erected at St Andrews in 1450 to teach theology and philosophy, a College of the Arts founded at Glasgow in 1451, and the setting up at Aberdeen in 1495 of the College of St Mary in the Nativity (or King's College) which in its second foundation of 1505 ambitiously proposed four faculties. Further colleges shortly followed at St Andrews: St Leonard's, erected in 1513 as a 'college of poor clerks' based on the austere model of the College of Montaigu in Paris, was fuelled by Augustinian piety; St Mary's, first mooted in 1525, given formal foundation in 1538 and reorganised in 1554, would become the centre of the movement for internal reform of the Church in the late 1540s and 1550s. All these foundations were the acts of bishops, who placed them at the centre of their dioceses, and were clerically endowed; St Salvator's and King's College were in essence collegiate churches of an academic kind.

The impact of what amounted to a national programme for higher learning – Elphinstone said his university was for the 'glory of the fatherland' – was both wider and narrower than it may first seem. It had long been university graduates who filled most of the ranks of the higher clergy and they also staffed the burgeoning departments of the royal administration under Stewart kings. Yet the curriculum of the new universities, despite ambitious plans, remained narrowly concentrated in faculties of Arts. The study of theology was patchy, and that of medicine or law negligible. The numbers of graduates were still modest – not many more than ten a year graduated from the new University of St Andrews before 1450, perhaps thirty came out of it and Glasgow in the later part of the century – but the total annual crop of graduates of all the universities was not likely to have been more than a hundred in the 1540s. The bulk of them were still churchmen; St Leonard's, like the others, saw itself as a 'holy college'. The most talented or ambitious of them who wished to pursue their studies further, usually by specialisation in those passports to ecclesiastical preferment – canon and civil law – continued to go abroad, to the great universities of western Europe, as Scots had done for centuries. Bishop William Turnbull, founder of Glasgow University, had gone to Louvain and Paris and Bishop Elphinstone had studied law at Paris and Orleans.[34]

Before 1412 Scottish students had gone abroad for both their first and subsequent degrees. Only a few are traceable before c.1340. It is known that more than thirty Scots studied at the great legal centre of Bologna between 1265 and 1294, and larger numbers probably went to both Oxford and Paris. It was the fourteenth century, however, which set in train two patterns which would have a lasting impact on Scottish society. By then, with the papacy established at Avignon, France had become the obvious mecca for Scottish churchmen and students. Both the Italian and English universities fell from favour. Although the 'auld alliance' between Scotland and France can notionally be traced to the treaty with Philip IV of 1295, the French connection laid down firm roots in the century after 1350 and no group did more to encourage the flowering of its multifold aspects than the clergy, who trained, studied, petitioned and lobbied at Paris, Orleans and Avignon. By the second quarter of the fifteenth century, encouraged by the foundation of Louvain University and the continuing importance of Bruges as a staple port, a strong Flemish cultural connection had rooted too. This was also the period which saw the rise of the university men as a class with its own distinctive traits – a small intellectual élite of clerics and lawyers with an influence vastly outweighing its numbers, looking to the Continent rather than England.[35]

Many university men made their mark elsewhere because they – like the most celebrated philosopher of his age, John or Duns Scotus, who probably came from Duns in Berwickshire and died in 1308 – chose to follow a career furth of Scotland, in his case at Oxford and Paris. Not the least of the achievements of the fifteenth and early sixteenth centuries was that the new university foundations went a long way towards reversing the academic brain drain: Lawrence of Lindores, another philosopher of distinction and the dominant figure in the Arts Faculty of St Andrews in the mid-fifteenth century, had first established his reputation at the new University of Louvain; Hector Boece, lured home by Elphinstone from the College of Montaigu to become the first Principal of Aberdeen University, was a close friend of the great Erasmus and a devotee of the new learning; and John Mair, who had gained a European-wide reputation while at Paris, returned to become Provost of St Salvator's College in 1534.

Far less is known of the other two sectors of the medieval education system – the grammar schools and the variety of 'little', song and vernacular schools. Duns Scotus had gone to a grammar school at Haddington and it seems likely that the upsurge in university education reflected a parallel increase in the number of grammar schools, which were based mostly in towns. Many were associated with cathedrals or with collegiate churches of different kinds, which were sharply increasing in number from the 1380s onwards. Some religious houses, too, had monastic schools which opened their doors, like the Cistercian abbey at Kinloss, to a wider intake of boys. Some friaries had their own 'lector' in theology or arts, and the Dominican house at Ayr had a tutor in grammar in 1420. By the time of the Education Act passed by parliament in 1496, which encouraged the attainment by the sons of barons and freeholders of 'perfyte latyn', it seems likely that the growing demands of the state for administrators and lawyers may have been threatening to outstrip supply. The rivalry between Church and state was, as yet, still a friendly one in this area. The course of the sixteenth century would see the increasingly heavy hand of state intervention in both the grammar schools and the universities, but the curriculum taught in these schools remained much the same as it had been in 1500 or 1400.

There were many other kinds of schools in medieval Scotland, although they were not necessarily parish schools. The most easy to trace are the song schools attached to both cathedral and collegiate churches, reflecting the reviving interest in the fifteenth century in church music. There were also reading or 'English' schools, situated in rural areas as well as towns and intended to give only a rudimentary education, probably mostly to boys. There were probably also some small schools designed for girls, sometimes run by women or by nuns, often described as sewing schools. It is likely that many lairds ran private schools for their children and perhaps also those of their kin or tenants – as was long the practice in Gaelic society. The schoolmasters in most of these rudimentary schools were usually chaplains of various kinds – of religious foundations, hospitals or private chaplains of lairds – eager to supplement a meagre income by taking on extra work. The effect of the Protestant Reformation was felt most keenly in this area of schooling. The generations after 1560, however, saw the consolidation rather than the establishment of an elementary national system of education; in many cases, schools were refounded or recast rather than created as new foundations.[36]

Most of the leading figures in the later medieval Church had had a legal education. Although difficult to trace with any certainty, it is likely that the foundations of the many attempts to codify the law which can be seen in the second half of the sixteenth century were laid in the previous century. The first of many commissions to overhaul the fourteenth-century law text *Regiam Majestatem* was set up by parliament in 1425, and further ones were established in 1469 and 1473. The drawn-out but steady emergence of a central civil law court, the Court of Session – which eventually came to fruition in 1532 when the College of Justice was set up with fifteen paid judges or Senators – had been going on for more than a century. Their forerunners were the many fifteenth-century jurists on the king's council. By the end of the reign of James IV (1488-1513), the body known as the Lords of the Council in Civil Causes was emerging as a 'recognisable appeal court'.[37]

The mixed composition of this body – eight ecclesiastics and nine laymen – was symptomatic of its times. In many areas – in relief of the poor, provision for education, patronage of new ecclesiastical corporations and chaplaincies, and not least in the law – the expertise and long experience of churchmen remained vital, but the laity was making increased demands and exercising a new level of patronage and control. To cast the point in a different way, the Church in 1500 was still deeply responsive to the many and growing expectations which society had of it. Most of the many aspects of the flowering of late medieval Scotland drew on it. It was ironic that the bulk of these extra demands, which made Church and state as well as clergy and society more intertwined than ever, had to be financed through the system of appropriation of the teinds of parish kirks. Although as yet hardly faced with a serious challenge from heresy, the parish system was bleeding from a thousand cuts, either self-inflicted or caused by the new demands made of it by society.

The flowering of late medieval Scotland

The later fifteenth century was an age of paradoxes. It saw the crown more in control of appointments to benefices than ever before, but it also witnessed a chorus of criticisms of the papacy in parliament and elsewhere, especially in the 1490s. The creation of a second archbishopric, of Glasgow, in 1492 had provoked parliament into protests about the 'unestimable dampnage to the realme' inflicted by the costs of rival prelates pursuing actions at Rome against each other. Yet it was a rivalry which was largely of the crown's own making for James IV had been the primary supporter of the claims of Glasgow to make good the debt he owed to its bishop, Robert Blacader, for his support in the crisis of 1488. The new archbishopric, which was assigned jurisdiction over the bishoprics of Argyll, Dunblane, Dunkeld and Galloway, was exempted from that of St Andrews. The result was that Scotland had a primate who had seen removed from him almost half of his province. The feud convinced James IV that Scheves's successor at St Andrews had to be a more compliant agent of the royal will. And so there followed, after Scheves's death in 1497, first the King's brother and after him the King's eleven-year-old, illegitimate, but highly talented son as metropolitan.[38]

It was an age of a great spiritual awakening, even though the Church was enmeshed in economic crisis. This quickening of spiritual life had many facets, and not all of them pointed in the same direction. The mass was meant to be, as the chronicler Walter Bower had explained earlier in the same century, for 'the salvation of the living and the redemption of the dead'. The primary function of the score or more of collegiate churches founded during the fifteenth century was the saying of votive masses for the dead, in order to shorten their time in purgatory.

This was, however, a deeply felt need which affected all orders of society. Two of these foundations – Restalrig and Holy Trinity, Edinburgh – were the work of the crown. A few – St Giles' in Edinburgh being the outstanding example – were burgh parish churches awarded collegiate status as the result of substantial rebuilding and lengthy petitioning, and more would follow in the sixteenth century, including St Mary's in Haddington and the Holy Rude at Stirling; there the guilds of the burgh would be expected to finance a chaplain serving an altar dedicated to a particular saint as a mark of their new incorporated status. Most collegiate kirks, however, were the tangible results of the patronage of nobles or barons; such were Kilmaurs, founded in 1403 by the local Cunningham family before it acquired an earldom, or Crichton, founded in 1449 by Lord Crichton, chancellor of James II. Roslin, the most celebrated of these churches, was typical for the fact that its foundation in 1446 was but the prelude to a century of investment, but unique in its elaborate architecture and sometimes fantastic internal decoration, such as its carving of the dance of death and the enigmatic 'Prentice Pillar'. Yet the existing chapel was only the first stage of plans for a much larger building which were cut short by the Reformation. Most of these foundations were conventional expressions of piety in an age of austerity. St Giles', in the largest burgh in the realm, had an establishment of about twenty clergy in 1466, but more typical was Kilmaurs in rural Ayrshire which had six chaplainries in 1413, each costing somewhere between £5 and £10 a year.[39]

Can the wave of collegiate foundations be taken as a sign that the mass had come to be 'above all else a mass for the dead'?[40] That would be to take a narrow view of the trends of late medieval piety. The votive mass for the dead needs to be placed beside the appeal of two other sets of devotions. A new popularity of the rosary, in itself part of a series of devotions dedicated to the Virgin Mary, spread across northern Europe and reached Scotland, like so much else in the period, via Flanders: the exquisite Arbuthnot Book of Hours, composed for the parish church of Arbuthnot by its own vicar, Sir James Sibbald, about 1480, shows an image of 'Sancta Maria in sole' surrounded by a five-decade rosary of red beads and pink roses. Books of hours were usually the precious private psalters of the rich (and especially of noblewomen), but the rosary itself was a set of devotions popular in all sections of society: both James III and IV had expensive sets of beads of gold made for them; the Fetternear Banner, the elaborate tapestry made for the Holy Blood Confraternity of the Edinburgh merchant guild about 1520, also featured a rosary; and cheap, illicit rosaries were being sold at Turriff fair in Banffshire in 1579. The cult of the Virgin Mary, which has long been a particular feature of Scottish Roman Catholicism, can be traced to the fifteenth century.[41]

The other important devotion of the period was the Passion: 'Devoit remembrance of the passion is better than our Lady and all the sanctis prayit for him', claimed one late fifteenth-century work. It is no coincidence that the three opening pieces in the most important surviving manuscript collection of pre-Reformation Scottish devotional verse are all penitential works on the Passion: the *Tabill of Confessioun* of the court poet and chaplain, William Dunbar; the *Contemplacioun of Synnaris* of the Observant Franciscan William of Touris, probably a member of the family of Touris of Inverleith near Edinburgh; and the *Passioun of Crist* of Walter Kennedy, a graduate of Glasgow.[42] But the cult of the Passion was not a Protestant devotion before its time, although it would – unlike Marian devotions – later be adapted for Protestant use. The *Contemplacioun* was written specifically for James IV, probably as part of his annual retreat at Eastertide when, girded with an iron belt, he would seek expiation for his involvement in the death of his father in the revolt of 1488.[43] These devotional poems, however, were part of a wider spiritual movement, also exemplified by the cults of the Holy Blood and the Five Wounds of Christ, which also originated in the Low Countries. The preparation through the long season of Lent for what was probably for most ordinary men and women an annual celebration of communion at Easter depended on populist representations of the Passion. The Passion plays performed in a number of burghs in the later fifteenth century, the paintings depicting the Crucifixion and Last Judgement on church walls (such as those which survive from the kirk of Fowlis Easter in Angus) and the private ritual of the rosary were all versions of the same obsession – with the salvation of souls of the living.

William of Touris, author of the *Contemplacioun*, is a useful paradigm of his age. Probably the product of a family of lairds, he belonged to the Observants, a new, breakaway branch of the mendicant Franciscan friars, which had the reformist centre of Cologne as its mother province in northern Europe. Only one major monastic foundation – the Charterhouse at Perth (1429) – had occurred since 1300, but within fifty years of their introduction to Scotland by Mary of Gueldres c.1455 no fewer than nine Observant Franciscan houses were set up. With friaries at royal centres such as Edinburgh, Perth, St Andrews and Stirling, the Observants became the favourite religious order of the house of Stewart. Mary of Gueldres founded at least four of the houses and her grandson, James IV, described himself as their 'son and defender'. Based in all three university centres as well as in the major burghs, situated beside the massive building programme going on at Stirling Castle from the reign of James IV onwards, and also enjoying links with important noble families such as the Oliphants and Setons, their position suggests that they were the most important stimulus of the age. Here was an order which kept faith with its ideal of an apostolate of work carried out while living a life of spartan simplicity, and its brethren kept in close touch with all three estates of the realm, linking learning, the royal court, and both aristocratic and urban patronage.[44]

The Observant Franciscans were only one of many channels through which the cultural and religious influences of Flanders, the Rhineland and France flowed into Scotland. Ecclesiastical architecture, seen most obviously in the collegiate churches, saints, devotional cults, the new sophistication in church music and the continuing influence of studies at the universities of Louvain, Cologne and Paris all testify to the importance of the connections with France and the Low Countries. The Church, of all the institutions in Scottish society, still did most to nurture Scotland's links with continental Europe.

The varied career of a secular cleric, Alexander Galloway, rector of the parish of Kinkell near Inverurie in Aberdeenshire, conveniently sums up many of the different strands which were set in train in the period by reforming bishops such as William Elphinstone. One of the first graduates in canon law from Elphinstone's new University of Aberdeen, he became a notary, a canon of the Cathedral of St Machar in Old Aberdeen and would rise to become Official of the diocese and a long-serving Rector of the University. This was, however, no faceless diocesan administrator or closeted academic. Galloway had probably been involved in the collection of local saints' cults for the *Aberdeen Breviary* and, as commissioner of works for the diocese, he gave physical reality to the veneration of such saints in the building of a number of sacrament houses. The impact of the University quickly began to show itself in the quality of education of the parish clergy of the diocese. The University also had connections with the local house of Dominican friars, who taught theology. The important place occupied in the diocese by the Observant Franciscans, who had settled in Aberdeen in 1469, was marked by Galloway's design of the outstanding structure of the Greyfriars' Kirk. Cathedral, university and religious orders were also intertwined with society. Two examples suffice: Galloway designed a bridge over the River Dee and the leper house, St Anne's Hospital, just outside New Aberdeen. Galloway is an exemplar not only of the highly talented group of clerics gathered together by Bishop Elphinstone but also of the many links which bound together Church and local society.[45]

Alexander Galloway was also the designer of the splendid heraldic ceiling of the nave of St Machar's, completed *c*.1520, a breathtaking representation of late medieval Christendom. In three separate rows of heraldic shields – the Pope and the Scottish Church, the princes and lords of Christendom headed by the Emperor Charles V, and the leaders of the community of the realm of Scotland with the King of Scots foremost – are portrayed the orders of Christendom. And in each, Aberdeen has its place – as a diocese and bishop's university, as the ecclesiastical burgh of Old Aberdeen, and as the king's burgh of New Aberdeen.[46] The image is theatrical, but it underpins two important realities. Local church and local society – Old and New Aberdeen, respectively ecclesiastical and secular foundations – were both integral parts of the community of the realm. And the Scottish Church was inseparable from the Scottish nation. A new Scottish identity – in state as well as Church – had been forged by the reign of James IV. Sometimes aggressively chauvinistic, not least because the King himself became one of the chief expressions of it, it was also in other dimensions both cosmopolitan and self-confidently nationalist. Fittingly, the ultimate symbol of royal authority, the Sword of State (which can still be viewed amongst the royal jewels on display in the Crown Room at Edinburgh Castle), was a Blessed Sword given to James IV in 1507 by that symbol of the Church militant, the warrior Pope, Julius II.[47]

8

THE WARS OF SCOTLAND

THE 'WAR OF INDEPENDENCE' RIGHTLY HOLDS A CENTRAL PLACE, BOTH IN THE history of Scotland and the making of the Scottish national psyche. Here is a case where history is not merely a record of past events but a regenerator of itself. The most celebrated document in Scottish history, the Declaration of Arbroath (1320), was addressed to a Pope to persuade him to lift the sentence of excommunication from a Scottish king, but it thereafter lapsed into obscurity until it was rediscovered in the seventeenth century. It has been only in the nineteenth and twentieth centuries that it has acquired the status of a surrogate Scottish constitution.[1] The simplicity of its language has much to do with the Declaration's timeless appeal: in the course of little more than 1,200 words it managed to condense a mythology of the nation's past, provide a compelling vision of the relationship of kings of Scots and the Scottish people, and summarise the history of the present struggle as one in which the issue was 'for liberty alone that we fight and contend for, which no honest man will lose but with his life'. The document skilfully obscured the fact that there were not one but numerous strands to the struggle, as well as different sets of competing principles: the issue of liberty was for most of the political nation tied up either with feudal right and overlordship or, after 1306, the moral legitimacy of one King of Scots against another.

The terminology of the period is often inadequate to deal with the complexity of the conflict. The phrase, the 'Great Cause' (signifying the prolonged debate over the succession between 1290 and 1292), is an invention of the eighteenth century, and the 'War of Independence', which is more modern still, would hardly have been comprehensible to contemporaries. The attempt to add analytical refinement by writing of 'Wars of Independence' – suggesting a civil war between Bruces and Balliols as well as different phases of the intermittent struggle with Edward I, II and III – is hardly more than a generation old. All such terms are, at best, half-truths. If the 'Hundred Years' War' (which in fact lasted 116 years) had not already been appropriated to describe the long struggle between England and France (1337-1453), it might have served as well as a catch-phrase: it would have better conveyed the bitterness and increasing cost in terms of human lives and physical destruction of the fundamental fact of Scottish history in the long century between 1296 and 1424 – war with England. To the English, these were the 'wars of Scotland'.

They were both more than and less than a war of independence. A strong sense of national identity already existed, which was why William Wallace was able, in the words of the *Book of Pluscarden*, to emerge in 1297 as 'a true champion of the kingdom for the independence of its people'.[2] In the course of the century and a half before the death of Alexander III in 1286, the macMalcolm line of kings, who traced their lineage to Kenneth mac Alpin and in turn to the Cenél nGabráin, had gradually established their own status and extended their authority over a realm which had come to have a clear territorial definition. Their achievement in forging a notion of the 'kingdom of Scotland' was also that of their chief partners: a composite but small, close-knit aristocracy and the Scottish Church which, unlike churches in Ireland or Wales in the same period that were under siege from English cultural domination, by 1250 had come to acquire a distinct sense of its own national identity.[3] During the long, increasingly bitter but intermittent wars with England, the position of kingship and the ideas of the role of the constituent elements of the kingdom – the 'community of the realm' – were repeatedly scrutinised and recapitulated, but in an ever more coherent and explicit form. Kings were tested, as never before, in their dual roles as warlord and good lord of their subjects. The peoples of the kingdom – from magnates to freeholders, husbandmen or burgesses – were for the first time dragged on to the national stage for a prolonged period.

This was also, as an English chronicler recognised as early as 1296, 'a general war between England and Scotland'.[4] English society was organised on a war footing as never before. The English dominions in Gascony, Ireland and Wales provided much of the manpower for the invasions of Scotland. The English army raised for the Falkirk campaign in 1298 was larger (except for the force gathered for the siege of Calais in 1346-7) than any other before the seventeenth century. Although Edward I might carefully explain his claims to dominion over Ireland, Wales and Scotland in strict terms of feudal right, a strong streak of populist chauvinism was the inevitable accompaniment of successive English campaigns in the so-called outlying 'lands' of the British Isles.[5] A mythology of English civilisation, which would survive as a potent vehicle of policy for centuries, was first bred as part of the successive wars of conquest – of Ireland after 1169, of Wales between 1240 and 1295, and of Scotland after 1296. The removal of the Stone of Destiny from Scone, along with the most treasured relic in Scotland, the Black Rood of Saint Margaret, which was taken as 'a sign of the resignation and conquest of the kingdom',[6] was no isolated incident. In 1284 the conquest of Wales had been marked by the removal of both the legendary crown of King Arthur and the most precious relic in Wales, a fragment of the True Cross. It was no accident that Edward took these emblems of a conquered people to Scotland on his campaign of 1296. And it was significant, too, that it was a London mob which prevented a return of the symbols of Scottish national identity as part of the peace of 1328. They remained in Westminster Abbey, physically attached to the shrine of Edward the Confessor, the 'proprietal saint' of the English monarchy.[7] These were wars of ideology as well as of conquest. They were the recruiting sergeants of a new, aggressive nationalism – in England as much as in Scotland.

The mythology of the war was as important as the course of it. By 1301 the struggle had taken the form of a war of words. Between then and 1329 at least half a dozen manifestos of the patriotic cause were composed, of which the Declaration of Arbroath is the most celebrated: they were, however, mostly composed not for a Scottish audience but for the papal court or royal courts of Europe, especially that of France. Nonetheless, there emerged from the war with England in its various forms a patriot king, a new national saint given explicit recognition in 1318 when St Andrews Cathedral was reconsecrated, and a popular martyr in the form of William Wallace: King, Church and people each had its new touchstone of nationality. Between the 1360s and 1450, a new, 'official' national history was written, beginning with Fordun and Barbour's *Brus* and culminating in the *Scotichronicon* of Walter Bower; it drew on the wars as the crucible of the Scottish nation. A populist version followed later in the fifteenth century, with Blind Harry's *The Wallace*, a hostile commentary on the pro-English drift of James III's policy as well as a secular martyrology. More than ever, present and future policy depended on an official view of the past, recent as well as distant: Robert I 'another Joshua or Maccabeus', in the words of the Declaration of 1320, became 'good King Robert', a worthy successor of the 113 kings that had gone before him.

The 1290s brought for Edward I (1272-1307) a Plantagenet action to hold on to possessions in Gascony and a war for the British Isles. The crisis in Scotland was part of what was, for Edward, a general crisis of English power: the waging of the war in Scotland was complicated by a revolt in Gascony in 1294, which by 1295-6 had intensified into a confrontation with Philip IV of France whose overtures to the Scots threatened a hostile encirclement of England; the rising of Llywelyn ap Gruffudd in 1294-5 in Wales, whose conquest had seemingly been secured in 1284, stretched English resources to new limits. The similarity of Edward's cause in Wales and Scotland, both based on a strict view of feudal right, lent an extreme nervousness to English strategy, which surfaced when things were going badly wrong. It took little imagination to make Wallace another Llywelyn.[8] The rise of Robert Bruce after 1306 seemed to bring a new threat to the conquest of Wales as well as in Scotland: panic greeted a rumour from an informer in Scotland in 1307, as Edward I lay dying, that 'preachers' involved with the cause of Robert Bruce had discovered another prophecy of Merlin, that 'after the death of *le Roy Covetous* the people of Scotland and the Britons [the Welsh] shall league together'. The three-year Irish adventure of Edward Bruce, Robert's brother, after the shattering defeat of an English army at Bannockburn (1314) struck at the soft underbelly of English power, but it also threatened by 1317 to involve an invasion of Wales as well. The response of the Welsh envisaged not only an ejection of the English but also 'a Britain in future shared by the Britons and the Scots'. The brutal reality of Edward's conquest raised the spectre of a pan-Celtic international; it never materialised in full form, but it was a consistent fear of English policy-makers.[9]

The wars produced traitors and collaborators as well as resolute patriots, defeatists and turncoats as well as resistance fighters. The chequered responses of Scots were not surprising. There were three reasons for them. Many magnates, and not least the crown itself, suffered from a series of conflicting loyalties. Some nobles – not only Anglo-Norman families by descent but native lords as well – owed fealty to English kings for their lands held in England. A few, including the Balliol family which still held land in France, or the young Earl of Carrick, Robert Bruce, whose family had recently acquired lands in Ireland, were vassals of the English king in more than one of his dominions. Part of the shifting responses of some of the Scottish nobility can be explained as a confused reaction to the extension by Edward I of the scope of the feudal rights owed to him. This took place, however, over a fifteen-year period, from the settlement of the Great Cause in 1292 until Edward's death. Few leading figures held to a fixed position throughout this period, which was marked by a restless quest for a coherent Scottish policy on Edward's part: the notion of overlordship of Scotland did not entirely sit easily with the aggrandisement of his feudal rights over individual vassals; both were overtaken by a policy of outright conquest, which by 1304 began to give way to one of conciliation. The competing issues were, as a result, a good deal more complicated in 1304 than they had been in 1296: a settlement was offered in 1305 which was more accommodating than that in 1296. After 1306 a war of English conquest became enmeshed in a Scottish civil war, between the families of Bruce and Balliol, which gave extra uncertainty to the motives of many Scots and added further bitterness to its course.

The kingless kingdom

The dynastic crisis posed by the accidental death of Alexander III in March 1286 was not unique. The curse of royal dynasties and noble families all over Europe was a failure in the male line. Alexander's younger son, David, had died in 1281 and his heir, the Lord Alexander, died after a long illness in January 1284. In 1286 his sole surviving descendant was his infant granddaughter, Margaret, the 'Maid of Norway'. She was the product of the marriage contracted between Alexander's daughter, Margaret, and the fourteen-year-old Eric II in 1281 as part of the reconciliation between the two kingdoms set in motion by the Treaty of Perth of 1266. The vacuum in authority was filled by six representatives of the political community, the 'Guardians', elected at a 'parliament' which met at Scone forty days after the tragedy. They comprised the Bishops of St Andrews and Glasgow, two earls and two barons; together they represented the major political factions (the Bruces and the Comyn/Balliol connection), the different social components of the political community, and Scotland both north and south of the Forth. The emergence in the harsh light of a potential political crisis between 1286 and 1290 of the 'community of the realm' as a practical, working arrangement, ruling a kingdom in the name of the recognised sovereign should not be seen either as surprising, given the gathering maturity of the kingdom over the previous two centuries, or as unique to Scotland. Although there were rumours in 1286 of a further outbreak of the intermittent feud between the Bruces and Balliols, it was a cautious conservatism rather than a breakdown into civil war which marked the politics of this curious period – a minority without a minor, for the Maid was still in Norway. The situation in 1286 had been further complicated by the possible prospect of a posthumous heir being born to Alexander's French widow, Yolande, daughter of the Count of Dreux, whom he had married five months before his death.[10] Until about November 1286, the Guardians had to make contingency for two possible heirs. It was in the summer of that year that Edward I was first approached, by the Guardians, for his advice.

The result of these approaches and the fruit of the government by the Guardians was the Treaty of Birgham (1290), which set out the terms for a future dynastic union through the marriage of Margaret of Norway and Edward I's son.[11] The union envisaged by the Guardians was not a take-over but a carefully crafted vision of two kingdoms linked by marriage but ruled separately and distinctly. There was no 'Rough Wooing', as in the 1540s.[12] The Treaty is a reminder that what happened in 1290 was as unexpected as the sudden death of Alexander III. It took a second dynastic catastrophe – a failure in the female line – to plunge Scotland into crisis. In September 1290, the Maid set sail from Norway; she died shortly after her ship reached Orkney. The expectations of both Edward I and the Guardians were confounded. An interregnum with a disputed succession took the place of a minority.

There was not a single direct and legitimate survivor of the past three generations of kings of Scots. There were thirteen claimants or 'Competitors' in all, many of them both remote and foreign. Only four, all descendants of Henry, son of David I, had a serious claim: John Hastings of Abergavenny; Florence V, Count of Holland; John Balliol, Lord of Galloway, whose sister had married into the Comyn family but who was himself a good example of the 'aristocrat international', with holdings in northern France and England; and Robert Bruce, Lord of Annandale, grandfather of the future Robert I, who had been, as a former governor of Carlisle, hardly less involved in English politics than Balliol.[13] The invitation to Edward I to intervene in the Great Cause probably came from the Guardians.[14] The case, in essence, once the proposition was dismissed that the realm of Scotland might be partitioned, like a feudal lordship, amongst various claimants, was fairly simple: Bruce had the claim of nearness of degree, whereas Balliol could claim seniority of line. Tellingly Balliol's submission was among the shortest and it was no surprise to the community of the realm that the adjudication, when it was made at the end of 1292, was in his favour.

The real significance lay not in the judgement but in the way it had been made. The proceedings had taken eighteen months since Edward and the Guardians first assembled at Norham, on the English side of the River Tweed, in May 1291. They began with the assertion by Edward — which he gave the Scots a mere three weeks to disprove – that he acted as overlord of Scotland. There had since been four lengthy adjournments, interspersed with ever-increasing demands from Edward for further recognition of his feudal rights. A panel of 104 arbiters had been set up – forty each for Balliol and Bruce and only twenty-four drawn from Edward's own council. The rightness of the eventual judgement in favour of Balliol was reflected in the fact that twenty-nine of Bruce's own auditors voted against him. But it was as significant that almost throughout Edward consulted the English auditors first.[15] By 1310, the propaganda of the Bruce cause would assert that 'the faithful people' of Scotland 'always believed' that Bruce the Competitor had the rightful claim. By then, however, there were many more casualties than the truth. It was more significant in 1291-2 that the game was played according to the rules laid down by Edward I, and that he became, in effect, the sole judge of both fact and law. The price paid by Balliol at the end of the legal process was a renewed act of homage to his liege lord, but that left open a number of potential feudal obligations which would demand precise formulation in the future.

Little is known of the governance of King John (1292-6), who was inaugurated on St Andrew's Day (30 November) 1292. To stigmatise it as the 'reign of Toom Tabard' or 'the Empty Jacket' is as stark an example of the reading of history backwards as any other in Scottish history. The nickname was applied not by John's subjects during his reign but later, taking its cue from the ritual humiliation inflicted by Edward on Balliol at Montrose Castle in July 1296, when he was 'stripped of his royal trappings' in a ceremony involving the physical removal of tabard, hood and knightly girdle which was usually performed on a knight found guilty of treason rather than on a king.[16] In February 1293, just over two months after his inauguration, the first of four parliaments held in 1293-4 met. From a few tantalising clues as to their proceedings, it is clear that these parliaments had wide-ranging business before them: there is evidence that petitions were invited for the redress of wrongs in 1293; one case survives of crown land being reclaimed; and there was a plan to erect three new sheriffdoms in the west, following the example of the forward policy of Alexander II and III. The dispensation of justice on an unusual scale, the re-establishment of the authority of the King and consultation with the political community in parliament as well as council all seem to have been features of the reign.[17]

If the parliaments of King John's reign underlined the continuing role of the community of the realm, with authority successfully passed from the four surviving Guardians acting in the name of the kingdom to a King acting on behalf of the community, two events which took place within a month of the new King's enthronement made clear that the drawn-out process of the Great Cause had let loose a barrack-room feudal lawyer in the shape of Edward I. The granting of the sasine of the kingdom to Balliol had been qualified by an attachment typical of Edward: 'saving our right and that of our heirs when we shall wish to speak thereupon'.[18] In December 1292, King John did homage to Edward at Newcastle. Such a ceremony was only to be expected in the light of Edward's demands made of the Guardians in 1291 that his overlordship be recognised before he adjudicated in the matter of the succession. In theory, it implied protection by the lord as well as submission by the vassal; in practice, Edward made more of his rights than his obligations.

The first of a series of legal appeals made to Edward took place within a week of the enthronement. A dispute, which showed signs of being deliberately advanced as a test case, involved Roger Bartholomew, a burgess of Berwick, and it brought sharply into focus the clash of jurisdictions and understanding. The Scots cited the terms of the Treaty of Birgham of 1290, in which Edward had promised to preserve the laws and customs of Scotland; Edward stood on the acknowledgement of his overlordship made in 1291. In his use of justice as a vehicle for the assertion of lordship, Edward was doing no more than he had already done in Wales or had had done to him by Philip IV of France over appeals from Gascony. But Scotland was a kingdom rather than a 'land' and it seems clear that King John was under considerable pressure from the community of the realm. In the well-known case of MacDuff, brother of the late Earl of Fife, who in November 1293 appealed against a judgement of imprisonment made on him in Balliol's court, John refused to respond in Edward's court because he was 'king of the realm of Scotland and dare not make answer at the suit of MacDuff, nor in anything touching his kingdom, without the advice of the people of his realm'.[19] One English chronicler commented that John was 'a lamb among wolves'; a Scot would have been more likely to see him as shepherd of a flock which had shown itself capable of directing itself and was determined to hold to the same path. Edward's reaction, sentencing Balliol for contempt and ordering him to forfeit the castles of Edinburgh, Roxburgh and Stirling – as much symbols of royal power as sword or sceptre – brought Anglo-Scottish relations to the brink.[20]

The first 'war of Scotland' (1296-1304)

It was the international crisis which engulfed Edward in 1293-4 that brought about the actual breach. War with France coincided with the outbreak of a rising in Wales led by Madog ap Llywelyn in September 1294. The Welsh revolt had partly been provoked by Edward's demands for military support. A similar summons, framed in terms of personal service, had been sent in June 1294 to the King of Scots, ten of his earls and sixteen barons. Although some Scottish nobles (such as John Comyn) had fought for kings of England in the conquest of Wales only thirty years before, overseas service had not been demanded on such a scale before, nor of a King of Scots since 1159. This may have provoked the decision made at a parliament held at Stirling in July 1295 to put the direction of affairs into the hands of a council of twelve, made up equally of bishops, earls and barons. Balliol was still king, but in effect a form of Guardianship had been restored.[21]

It was the reluctance of the Scots to become involved in the English war effort which drove them into an alliance with France, which was agreed in October 1295. The contrast could hardly have been starker. England gave Scotland the status of a client state; France offered an alliance of two independent kingdoms guaranteeing each other military assistance and a future marriage between King John's son Edward and the niece of Philip IV. Edward demanded the feudal rights due to him by his vassals. The French asked that the treaty be ratified by the community of the realm, including even the 'communities of the towns'. Instead of Edward's Scottish vassals taking ship for France, a national call to arms, involving both the 'common army' and the feudal host, resulted in an invasion force being assembled at the time-honoured mustering point of Caddonlee near Selkirk in March 1296.

The war was an uneven contest from many points of view. For the Scottish leaders, it was a conflict between equals, in which the chivalrous conventions of warfare were scrupulously observed; the starving English garrison of Stirling Castle was allowed to return home safely after it was captured by the Scots in 1299. For Edward, it was an act of rebellion by treacherous subjects; the Scots garrison commanded by Sir William Oliphant which surrendered the same castle to Edward in 1304 suffered the ritual humiliation of lowly traitors, of being paraded with ropes around their necks, and escaped hanging and disembowelling only after repeated appeals made to Edward. When the commander of Caerlaverock Castle, a nephew of the leading Scots magnate, James the Stewart, was captured in 1300, his noble birth did not prevent him suffering the same ignominious treatment as the Welsh 'rebel', David ap Gruffyd, whose head was stuck on a pike for his part in the war of 1282-3.[22] The treatment of William Wallace after his capture in 1304, which ended in the grisly, ritual horror of hanging, disembowelling, beheading and quartering, differed from the rough justice meted out to many since 1297 only in that it was preceded by a show trial at Westminster. For Edward, the 'war of Scotland' was a police action; to the Scots it was a war of conquest.

The starkest contrast between the two sides lay in manpower, resources and technology. The English army assembled in the spring of 1296 numbered 4,000 cavalry and some 25,000 infantry and it included battle-hardened veterans from the Welsh wars. The Scottish army, by contrast, was an inexperienced force which had not seen action since the battle of Largs (1263); it had a lower proportion of cavalry to infantry and had as yet only a few specialist troops such as crossbowmen.[23] The campaign of 1296 was fought by the Scots as a conventional feudal war, centred on sieges and pitched battles in which opposing cavalry forces confronted each other in open field. The Scots opened hostilities predictably, with a token one-day siege of

Carlisle. Simultaneously, the English army, which had assembled at Newcastle, assaulted the town of Berwick, which was still Scotland's premier wool centre and port. The siege lasted only a few hours; the sack which followed its capture took three days. Most of the male inhabitants of the burgh were slaughtered, along with a colony of thirty Flemish merchants in the 'Red Hall'. At the one set-piece battle in the campaign, provoked by an attempt to relieve the castle at Dunbar (27 April), the Scots host was quickly scattered by the superior weight of numbers of the English cavalry, a large number of distinguished prisoners were taken for ransom and heavy losses were sustained amongst the unprotected foot soldiers. After a seventeen-day campaign, the feudal war of 1296 was virtually at an end. The castles of Roxburgh, Edinburgh and Stirling quickly fell and by July King John and his closest advisers, who had sued for peace and were taken prisoner at Montrose, were incarcerated in the Tower of London.

The precise constitutional position remained in doubt for some time after 1296. The realm of Scotland was not annexed as Wales had been in 1284. Edward did not adopt the style of either King or Lord of Scotland and the formal price of conquest was not fully spelt out until 1305. The first extended rationale of the English position came only with the propaganda war with the Scots conducted at the papal court. It followed familiar lines. In 1301, Edward claimed in a letter to Pope Boniface VIII to 'be in possession of that realm, by right of full dominion', making feudally subject both 'John [Balliol] and our subjects, the people of Scotland'. By 1305 Scotland, like Ireland or Wales, had become a 'lordship' or 'land' (*terre*) rather than a kingdom.[24]

There was in 1296, however, little doubt of the practical consequences of English victory. King John was literally stripped of his status. The Stone of Destiny, the regalia and many of the records of the Scottish crown were removed south, along with the precious relic of Scotland's only royal saint. The Great Seal was broken up and the contempt of the conqueror was tellingly revealed by Edward's own words: 'A man does good business when he rids himself of a turd'.[25] The extended campaign made by Edward in the space of four months between May and August 1296 became a triumphant progress, during which he, in the words of a contemporary diarist, 'conquered and serched the kingdom', receiving oaths of fealty from his Scottish subjects – a process completed in a parliament held at Berwick on 28 August and formally recorded with over 1,500 names set down in the 'Ragman Roll'.[26] There was hardly a line to be drawn between the homage expected of vassals and the obedience demanded of subjects. A *junta* of English officers was set up to conduct the government of Scotland; an exchequer was established at Berwick on the Westminster model. Scotland had become a virtual colony.[27]

The invincibility of Edwardian power, however, was an illusion. It had taken three wars spread over the space of more than two decades to complete the conquest of Wales, and England was not then also faced with a hugely expensive war on two fronts. By 1297 the war with France was beginning to go badly, there were protests at home about the mounting burden of taxation and already some resistance by the earls to military service. This was the background against which a series of disturbances in Scotland broke out in the early part of 1297. By May of that year, Edward's regime acknowledged that there were 'conspiracies in very many parts of the land'. It was the beginning of a rising that came to be national in character and has usually, at least in the popular mind, been uniquely associated with the otherwise obscure figure of William Wallace, the son of a Clydesdale laird. Wallace's first act, the murder of an English sheriff at Lanark, was a replica of the trigger for the Welsh revolt of 1284, and the Scottish rising of 1297 shared much the same blend of popular protest against the excesses of foreign rule and a deeply conservative attachment to the old order. Its aim was the restoration of the *kingdom* and Wallace never wavered from his allegiance to King John, the vital symbol of independence.[28]

Although details of the multifold origins of the revolt of 1297 have long been known to historians,[29] the idea persists that Wallace led a *jacquerie* of landless peasants. Large numbers of the nobility, it is true, still languished in English prisons or had been rendered *hors de combat*. Contemporary English chroniclers, however, were firm in their suspicions. The real leaders of the revolt, two of them declared, were the ex-Guardians, Robert Wishart, Bishop of Glasgow, and James the Stewart, who was Wallace's lord. They were joined shortly after by MacDuff, son of an Earl of Fife, and Bruce, the young Earl of Carrick. The first outbreaks had taken place in the north rather than in Wallace's territory. The decisive move, which had turned a series of local stirs already threatening to fizzle out in July into a co-ordinated rising, was the linking up of opposition in Moray with a rising in the shires to the east of the Spey and in the important burgh of Aberdeen. The leader of the northern rising was Andrew Murray, the son and heir of a leading baron. Together, Murray and Wallace were acknowledged as 'commanders of the army of the kingdom of Scotland, and the community of that realm' (as they were styled in a letter sent to the prominent trading towns of Lübeck and Hamburg in October 1297).[30] Their respective roles in the revolt have been obscured by the fact that Murray died in November 1297, probably of wounds sustained at the battle of Stirling Bridge two months earlier (11 September). It was the first and the last pitched battle which Wallace won. Neither a general nor a guerrilla by instinct, Wallace nonetheless deserves to be remembered as an unflinching patriot and a charismatic warlord. That was why the community entrusted him with sole Guardianship of the realm in the spring of 1298.

Wallace's victory at Stirling Bridge, inflicted upon an English army led by Earl Warenne, Edward I's lieutenant in Scotland, came as a profound shock to English opinion. In retrospect, it marked a turning-point in the wars. After it, Wallace consolidated his position as a military leader by beginning the harrying of the northern English shires – a tactic which Robert Bruce would use repeatedly in the years after 1309. Because of it, English tactics began to change, putting more emphasis on crossbowmen than mounted knights. It was a military revolution which would take some forty years to complete but its seeds were sown in the next campaign, of 1298. At the battle of Falkirk (22 July) most of the heavy losses inflicted on the Scots, who were drawn up in four or five massive hedgehog-like schiltroms of some 1,500 spearmen each, came from the arrows of the specialist archers from Wales and Guienne in France rather than the lances of the cavalry.[31] Falkirk was the last pitched battle fought until 1314. The Scots switched to hit-and-run tactics and it was not until the 1330s that English thinking produced the solution of the mounted archer or hobelar, which would bring them victory at Crécy (1346) and other battles in the Hundred Years' War against the French. Although

119

the investment by the English in garrisoning castles after 1298 was considerable – Edinburgh Castle alone had 325 men including sixty-four cavalry in 1300 – it was never enough to do much more than hold a pale south of the Forth.

The failure of the English occupation can also be seen as the failure of the Edwardian regime itself. Although the worst of Edward's problems, both at home and in France, were over by 1298, in Scotland there had been no policy of 'thorough' to consolidate the military victory of 1296. Berwick was remodelled as a *bastide*, but otherwise there was no attempt made to colonise English settlers in Scottish towns. There was no serious effort in Scotland, as there had been in Ireland, to introduce English taxes to make the occupation pay for itself. There was no massive castle-building programme, as in Wales: three were planned but never built, and English military occupation was for the most part confined to castles south of the Forth, even after 1298. English clerics were early provided to Scottish benefices, but few managed to enjoy the fruits of their new livings; the attempt to anglicise the Scottish Church from within only made its hierarchy the more determined spokesmen for the patriotic cause. There was no mass forfeiture of the Scottish nobility, even after the English victory at Falkirk; a plantation remained a project in the minds of English chroniclers. As the course of the war ebbed and flowed, English policy found itself trapped between irreconcilable strategies: forfeiture of lands in Scotland was a necessary device to compensate the English earls and captains who remained mostly unpaid for their part in the Scottish campaigns; but a lasting reconciliation of disaffected Scottish nobles could be achieved only by a generous regrant of their lands. At the root of the difficulties of the English regime lay a clash between conquest and conciliation; hardly any of the various dilemmas it posed had been resolved by the time of Edward's death in 1307.[32]

The Edwardian conquest had already begun to crumble through its own internal contradictions. By 1305, it seemed, English policy seemed to have tilted decisively towards conciliation: the terms of the Ordinance for the government of Scotland which emerged after the fall of Stirling Castle in July 1304 were more generous than those of 1296. Although the chief officers in the government were to be English, Scots notables (including three ex-Guardians) were given a voice in the king's council in Scotland, and most of the local offices such as sheriffs and constables went to Scots. The balance between retaining the calculated loyalty of Scottish nobles, whose 'hearts if not their bodies were always with their own people', and mollifying his own barons, who had presented Edward with a demand for compensation in lieu of wages on the day after Stirling Castle fell in 1304, had been tilting towards the Scots since 1304. It was swung decisively in the opposite direction in 1306. One of the most effective recruiting sergeants for the Bruce cause was a renewed policy of conquest, involving the threat of mass confiscation of lands, the massacre of prisoners and the burning of the houses and property of 'traitors'.[33]

Conquest, resistance and the making of a patriot king (1306-28)

In the years following the defeat at Falkirk, a grim military stalemate had been played out. A massive English expeditionary army, with over 25,000 foot and including 11,000 Welsh, had been raised for the campaign of 1298. Further campaigns followed in every year except 1299, 1302 and 1305, but these were expensive shows of strength rather than an effective instrument for policing the country. In 1304 Edward refused to accept the surrender of Stirling Castle until a huge siege apparatus called the *Warwolf*, which had taken 445 workmen to construct, was given a day to demonstrate its destructive capability on the walls. It was the high point of English triumphalism. Already there were indications that smaller, more mobile units, such as had been used against the Welsh in 1294-5, were needed to counter the guerrilla tactics of the Scots. The unpopularity of the largely unprofitable Scottish war amongst the king's nobles had had the effect of reducing the number of mounted horse available. In 1300 fifty knights and thirty bannerets (light cavalry commanders) had campaigned in Scotland; by 1306 their respective numbers had fallen to thirty-six and seventeen. There was a basic paradox about the last years of Edward I's military effort: the larger the mailed fist, the less tightly it held Scotland in its grasp.[34]

These same years saw a sustained diplomatic campaign by the Scots, concentrated on the French court and the *Curia*. Its first notable success was the papal letter *Scimus fili* of Boniface VIII, which adopted much of the Scottish case against Edward's actions done, it declared, 'without regard for what was fitting'. The release of Balliol, still 'called king of Scotland' according to the letter, into custody of the Pope followed a month later in July 1299. The diplomatic pressure intensified in 1301, with a delegation to the *Curia* led by the canon lawyer, Master Baldred Bisset. One of its results was Bisset's own treatise or *processus*, which set out a historical justification for the ancient right of Scotland to freedom from domination. The reworking of a national history, which would achieve its most elegant form in the Declaration of Arbroath, had begun.[35] Just as the Scots had begun to gain advantage in the war of words, other circumstances outwith their control intervened. The twin props of the Scottish cause – the French alliance of 1295 and the support given by the papacy from 1299 onwards – both collapsed. A severe defeat inflicted on the French at Courtrai in July 1302 led to the conclusion in May 1303 of a separate Anglo-French peace from which the Scots were excluded. Boniface VIII, who, by the autumn of 1302, was already beginning to take a more critical view of the role of the Scottish bishops in the war, died in 1303; none of the next three of his successors proved as amenable to the Scottish cause.

The governing of the kingdom had meantime continued in the hands of various sets of Guardians. The effect of defeat at Falkirk had been to undermine Wallace's status as Guardian and he demitted office shortly after the battle. Four further changes in the composition of the Guardians took place between 1298 and 1302.[36] The leadership of the Scottish government was prey to all the familiar feuds, jealousies and petty disputes to which councils of regency are often subject, but there was, however, no break in the continuity of their rule and each regime acted unequivocally in the name of King John. The effect of the propaganda campaign which reached its full flow between 1299 and 1304 must have been to increase the authority of the absent king, and the appointment of Sir John de Soules as sole Guardian sometime early in 1301 made this explicit. Balliol was by this time resident in his own estates in Picardy and Soules seems to have been regarded by him as his lieutenant or *locum tenens* in the realm. The period of the Soules Guardianship, though obscure in many respects, laid a number of the foundations for eventual victory. Soules himself is the most conspicuous of many unsung heroes of the Wars of Independence: the younger son of an important family, related by marriage to the Comyns but also a friendly neighbour of Bruce in Annandale, he was able to act as an effective substitute for the increasingly controversial Comyn leadership of the national cause. His very success, in sustaining the cause of Balliol without allowing it to be taken over by a Comyn faction, may have been the critical factor which forced Robert Bruce's hand in 1302. He was, significantly, the only major magnate to go over to Edward in the period.

The behaviour of Robert Bruce in early 1302 and that of his family since 1286 has often been subjected to deeply critical scrutiny. There were, however, few leading figures amongst the nobility who practised an unswerving attachment, in public as well as private, to the cause of independence throughout the long, tangled period of the first and second wars of Scotland. Those that did – like Wallace and Soules – tended to be younger sons or lesser landowners with less to lose. Even that devoted patriot, the Bishop of Glasgow, swore fealty to the English king – in his case no less than six times by 1306. The two families with most to gain or lose were the Bruces and Comyns, and each followed its distinctive path of loyalty according to its own lights. Historians differ particularly sharply in their assessments of how ambitious the Bruces were. Bids for the throne, it has been suggested, were made by Robert Bruce the Competitor in 1286 as well as in 1290, by his son in 1296 after the battle of Dunbar, and by his grandson the Earl of Carrick in 1297.[37] Thus the threat of civil war, legal submissions in the Great Cause which latterly went so far as to suggest partition of the kingdom, the patronage of Edward I, and patriotic support for the revolt of 1297 were all part of the experience of the three generations of Bruces before Robert's submission at the time of the truce of 1302. The history of Scotland is littered with the ambitions of great noble families; Bruce's crime in 1306 was venial by comparison with others both before and after. In more general terms, it should occasion neither surprise nor particular opprobrium that duty to family might at times be put before that to the nation. Contemporaries would only have expected it to be thus.

Bruce and Comyn had quarrelled before. A council meeting at Peebles in August 1299 had degenerated into a brawl between their supporters. It needed the strong, independent figure of William Lamberton, Bishop of St Andrews, to act as a balance when they were both elected Guardians in 1299. It is impossible to be sure of the precise motives which impelled Bruce to murder Comyn before the high altar of the Greyfriars' Church in Dumfries on 10 February 1306. Embroidered accounts, both contemporary and later, variously suggest that both Bruce and Comyn had been discovered conspiring with the English against the other.[38] More significant was the double-effect of the murder. Within five weeks, Bruce had been enthroned at the traditional place of Scone, with the Bishop of St Andrews and the Countess of Buchan (as a representative of the Clan MacDuff) both performing their traditional roles in the ceremony. The date was 25 March, the feast of the Annunciation. A pontifical high mass was celebrated two days later, on Palm Sunday, which allowed parallels to be drawn between Bruce's journey into his kingdom and Christ's entry into Jerusalem.[39] The new king needed all the propaganda he could muster.

In retrospect, the years between 1306 and 1314 saw two parallel courses set in train: a claimant in a quest for support and respectability and a patriotic cause in search of an effective leader. The moral dilemma which prevented many Scots throwing in their lot with Bruce should not be under-estimated. Ever since 1297, the patriotic cause had been unflinchingly attached to the kingship of John Balliol. The recreation of a heroic past by skilled literary craftsmen such as Baldred Bisset had been firmly wrapped around the figure of King John, which made jettisoning him all the more agonising. For many, the dilemma posed by a usurper who tried to aggregate to himself the patriotic cause was more clear-cut than that between independence and a foreign king demanding his feudal rights of homage. The civil war between Bruce and Balliol polarised Scottish opinion in a way which the first 'war of Scotland' seldom had. The fealty required by Edward I and II had built-in ambiguities, which allowed many to make oaths of homage with private reservations. The loyalty demanded by King Robert was absolute.

Things went badly for Bruce in the summer of 1306, with successive heavy defeats at the hands of an English army and John of Lorne, a kinsman of the Comyns. He was fortunate that the death of Edward I in July 1307 and the subsequent domestic crisis which engulfed his successor Edward II (1307-27) prevented another major English campaign until 1310. Bruce, who had been forced to flee in the winter of 1306-7, ended up, not on Islay as he probably intended, but on Rathlin Island off the coast of Ulster and he perhaps also visited the Irish mainland as well.[40] His time was not entirely taken up, as popular legend has had it, with watching spiders. He had been given a vital breathing-space and he used it to plan how to prosecute the Scottish civil war. Such wars are not for the faint-hearted and no one could accuse Bruce of a lack of resolve in his vendetta against the Balliol/Comyn connection and its supporters. In the spring and summer of 1308, Robert Bruce pursued a relentless war of attrition in Buchan, and his brother Edward waged an even savager campaign in Galloway. By the second half of 1309, the turning-point in the first phase of the civil war had been reached. A number of major nobles, including the Lord of Argyll, had fled to England; others, such as the Earl of Ross, had submitted.

By March 1309, Bruce was confident enough to hold his first parliament, which met at St Andrews. It was at this point that the appropriation of the propaganda of the patriotic cause assembled between 1298 and 1304 began, aided probably by some of the same skilled clerical draftsmen. The Declaration of the Clergy was a party manifesto for the Bruce cause: it claimed that the tribulations inflicted on the people of Scotland since 1296 were 'for lack of a captain and a faithful leader' and asserted, dubiously, that King Robert had already restored the kingdom by his sword. It also contained black propaganda; the claim was made for the first time that Balliol had been imposed on the Scots by force of English arms over the head of the rightful claimant, Bruce's grandfather. For most ordinary Scots, however, what counted was probably neither moral scruples nor propaganda but military success.[41]

The turn of the tide against England can be dated variously. It is safe to assume that a momentum was gathering after 1309, when the English occupying force was hemmed into the triangle marked by Berwick, Edinburgh and Stirling, and the north of England was harried by raids to the point of exhaustion. The contemporary *Life of Edward II* is filled with stories of how 'Robert Bruce ravaged Northumbria burning vills and towns, driving off their cattle and compelling many to pay tribute'.[42] By March 1314, the castles of Linlithgow, Edinburgh and Roxburgh had fallen to the Scots. But to some English observers the ambush staged by Bruce at Glentrool in April 1307, three months before Edward I's death, was proof enough of the fatal weakness of the English occupying army, a lack of mobility. One Scot on the English side then went so far as to suggest that Bruce had already 'destroyed King Edward's power both among the English and the Scots'; after Edward's death, he predicted with more accuracy, 'many say openly victory will go to Bruce'.[43] Edward II inherited debts of £200,000 and a nobility which was already weary of the costly burdens of service in Scotland; but he was also heir to a mythology of Edwardian conquest and a popular animus against the Scots, fuelled since 1296 by tales of atrocities, which inevitably cast him in the role of a second hammer of the Scots.[44]

The battle of Bannockburn (23-24 June 1314) was the most unlikely of outcomes in the story of the second 'war of Scotland'. Tactically, it was for Bruce a battle which was both out of character and highly risky; some of his commanders were still advising him to withdraw after the initial skirmishes of the first day had taken place. No pitched battle had been fought since Loudon Hill in 1307, and the Scottish tactic of relying on massive schiltroms was ominously reminiscent of the defeat at Falkirk. Since his return to Scotland in the spring of 1308 Bruce had consistently kept to guerrilla tactics, known to contemporaries as 'secret warfare'. Edward had refused to call a parliament in 1314 to secure approval for his campaign, which was prompted by the need to relieve Stirling Castle, but it was by then more a status symbol than a vital strategic stronghold. His army, although almost as large as any of those of his father in terms of infantry, with some 15,000-20,000 men, had fewer archers than at Falkirk and only about 2,000 mounted men – the result of the reluctance of a number of earls to do more than send a token representation. They were confronted by a Scots force of some 8,000 men, with perhaps only about 500 of them mounted.[45] The odds were still heavily in the English favour and by all the conventional rules of warfare an English victory was not only likely but almost inevitable. Poor discipline, overconfidence, drunkenness (especially amongst the Welsh contingents), and disputes amongst leading knights were all straws grasped by English commentators to explain the shattering defeat. 'O famous race unconquered through the ages, why do you, who used to conquer knights, flee from mere footmen?', demanded one.[46] The key, however, was probably the ground which the Scots had carefully chosen – a factor not easily repeated in the future. The narrowness of the front and the boggy soil both prevented an effective deployment of the English cavalry. And the gorge of the Bannock Burn, which cut off a safe retreat, turned what might have been a minor but embarrassing reverse into a humiliation of English arms unparalleled since the loss of Normandy over a century before.

Bannockburn has been called one of the few decisive battles in Scottish history.[47] Edward lost his shield, privy seal, court poet (who was obliged to compose victory verses for the Scots), and much of his credibility. The carnage was not as great as it might have been; it was at its heaviest amongst the mounted knights, whose horses were helplessly caught in the mud and steepness of the ground beside the Bannock Burn, and slightest amongst the more experienced contingents of infantry, such as the Welsh who retreated in good order across the hundred miles of difficult terrain which separated them from the border at Carlisle. The booty plundered on the battlefield and from the huge baggage train, which had reputedly stretched for sixty miles, was immense, estimated at £200,000, and it was supplemented by lucrative ransoms. But the spoils of war did not bring an end to the second 'war of Scotland', which dragged on until peace was agreed in 1328. Nor did Bannockburn erase the prospect of a future conquest. While it took Edward II until 1319 to assemble another invasion force, his successor, Edward III, after initial difficulties, showed himself to be made of sterner stuff. The aftermath of 1314 was a stalemate: the Scots were still fighting a defensive war; the English were unable to check incursions into their northern counties or to launch an effective invasion of Scotland. In the 1330s, that stalemate would be broken. A new form of warfare, fought by different military tactics, and a new form of conquest – a puppet administration headed by Balliol's son, Edward, and a dismemberment of the kingdom – would take shape.

A good deal of the slow build-up of resources which prepared the path to Bannockburn had flowed along a supply line from Ireland. From 1309, England had lost control of the northern part of the Irish Sea. Bruce had recaptured the Isle of Man in 1313. The opening up of a second front in 1315 could have come as little surprise to Edward II, although some commentators expected it to be in Wales rather than Ireland. The motives which lay behind the Irish expedition, which began in May 1315 and lasted until Edward Bruce's death in October 1318, have been vigorously debated by historians. For some, the adventure was a means to buy off an ambitious younger brother, who had more than his due share of the family traits of ambition and calculated aggression; the initiative to extend an invitation to Edward to accept the high kingship of Ireland probably did not come from the native Irish.[48] The expedition took place only after the question of the Scottish succession had been settled. Although Edward went to Ireland as heir-presumptive – over the head of Robert's daughter Marjorie – the expectation must have been that Robert's second wife, Elizabeth de Burgh, who had recently been released after eight years as a hostage in England, would bear him an heir, as indeed she did in 1324, when a son, David, was born. The fact that Robert Bruce sent not only his brother and his most experienced general, Thomas Randolph, to Ireland but also reinforced the expedition himself for five months in the early part of 1317 suggests a complex of motives. Ireland presented a second front, a tying-up of men and resources which had been an important factor in the English war effort to date, a potential stepping stone to Wales, and a means of preventing a potentially disastrous family quarrel. The least which can be said of Edward Bruce's adventure is that it brought Scotland a three-year respite from further English invasion.

The major factor in English thinking after 1314 remained the effect of the repeated Scottish raids into northern England. Famine in 1316 was combined with despoliation. The inhabitants, it was rumoured, were forced to live off the flesh of dogs and horses. Biblical parallels about the pestilence inflicted by God on 'poor England' were commonplace.[49] The Scottish war remained the issue of confidence gnawing at the credibility of Edward's administration. Edward responded in the only way he knew how, but the massive armies raised in 1319 and 1322 were pale imitations of the blitzkrieg launched by his father. In 1296 Berwick had lasted only a few hours; in 1319 it held out, largely due to quarrels amongst the English magnates. In 1322 Edward, at last freed from most of the political difficulties which had beset him since 1307, led an army of 22,000 men up the east coast as far as Leith, but he had no clear strategy except the vain hope of luring the Scots into a pitched battle. The campaign lasted three weeks and achieved nothing, and with most of the army disbanded, Edward was almost captured by a retaliatory expedition launched by Bruce via Carlisle.[50]

The Scots could afford to take the diplomatic initiative and a thirteen-year truce was arranged at Bishopthorpe in May 1323. The eventual peace concluded at Edinburgh in March 1328, and ratified (unusually) by an English parliament at Northampton in May 1329, seemed to lay the foundations for a long-term *rapprochement* in Anglo-Scottish relations. The Scots paid £20,000 as reparations for the twenty years of damage which they had inflicted on the north of England; they received at last an acknowledgement of the independence of Scotland, 'separate in all things from the kingdom of England'; and the peace was cemented by a dynastic marriage between Bruce's son and heir, the four-year-old David, and Joan, the seven-year-old sister of Edward III. By July 1328 they were married, at Berwick. By early June 1329, however, Bruce was dead, after an illness which had lasted the better part of two years. His death would demonstrate the extent to which the winning of the second 'war of Scotland' and the consolidation of the kingdom had been his own personal achievement. With a minor on the throne, Scotland was again quickly prey to a renewed civil war, a northern English nobility thirsting for revenge, and an ambitious English king.

Reconstruction: the reign of Robert I

The greatest significance of the victory at Bannockburn had been the status which it gave to Robert Bruce as champion of the Scottish people in war. But the rehabilitation of Bruce as king was a much longer process, which was not complete by 1314. It was under way by 1308, when the first surviving acts of his government were issued.[51] Its chief agents were the anonymous clerics who staffed the 'king's chapel' or writing-office, which came to be based at the Abbey of Arbroath, and the talented members of the Church hierarchy who had long supported the patriotic cause. Chief among them were Lamberton, Bishop of St Andrews (1297-1328), whose reorganisation of his diocese after a decade of disruption coincided with Bruce's reconstruction of the kingdom. The close working relationship between state and Church was epitomised by the simultaneous meetings of parliament and councils of the Scottish Church in 1321 and 1325.[52] The head of the Bruce administration was the chancellor, a Tironensian monk, Bernard, Abbot of Arbroath (better known, mistakenly, as Bernard of Linton).[53] Quickly, a remarkable spate of charters and letters patent, surpassing the annual output achieved in the reign of Alexander III, flowed from the writing-office under his supervision; there was no more effective way to demonstrate the continuity of kingship than the written charter, issued in the name of Robert, *rex Scottorum*. From it, too, probably came the Declaration of Arbroath; it is more likely that it was composed by one of Bernard's clerks rather than by the chancellor himself. Another possible author was the canon lawyer, royal clerk and papal chaplain, Master Alexander Kinninmonth, later Bishop of Aberdeen, who was the bearer of the Declaration to the Pope in Avignon.[54] That mission failed in its primary purpose of persuading the Pope to lift the sentence of excommunication from Bruce, but Kinninmonth in 1329 successfully convinced the Pope to permit the anointing of

Scottish kings at their enthronement.[55] It was the final step in the restitution of the image and authority of the King of Scots in the person of Robert I.

Bruce's title to the throne was first recognised by the papacy in 1324. His position had been acknowledged by the more pragmatically minded Philip IV of France as early as July 1308, but Philip's death in 1314 and the three brief reigns which followed it delayed the stabilising effects which a renewed alliance with France might otherwise have had. The importance of the Treaty of Corbeil (1326), which restored the pact of 1295, lay in the future, in the 1330s and 1340s. A full restoration of amicable relations with Norway, and a securing of Scotland's frontier in the north and west, came much sooner, in 1312. The English had never managed to effect a complete blockade of Scotland's main trade routes to the Low Countries and the Baltic, and, although the evidence is slight, it is likely that by the early 1320s much of the northern trade had been resumed, despite the permanent loss of colonies of Flemish and German merchants who had formerly been based in Berwick.[56]

With the revival of trade came a closer relationship between the king and his royal burghs. The closer involvement of the burgesses in the affairs of the kingdom can be traced to 1296, when, at French insistence, the seals of six burghs had been attached to the Treaty of Paris. Although the 'coming of the burgesses to parliament' is sometimes dated to the Cambuskenneth assembly of 1326 or to 1357, when they were formally made a separate, third estate, representatives of the burghs had probably been in attendance at the parliament which approved the French treaty in 1296 and they were consulted at the time of a parliament in April 1312 about taxes and military service.[57] War taxation, the strategic importance of the east-coast ports and feu-ferm charters (granted to Aberdeen in 1318 and Edinburgh in 1328)[58] all point to a growing importance of the role played by the burghs in the community of the realm which would continue throughout the rest of the century.

The reign saw not only the careful re-establishment of the accustomed rights of the crown but a calculated recasting of a number of aspects of feudal kingship.[59] Legislation, especially the corpus of laws promulgated by the Scone parliament of December 1318, was a reworking of the old interspersed with the new. The collection of laws known as *Regiam Majestatem*, which dates from the same period and would remain the main compendium of Scots law for over three centuries, contained a number of recent English influences but stressed the association of Scots law with that epitome of Scottish kingship, David I. Not for the first time, change was cast in the clothes of continuity.[60] The success of the device can be judged by the number of references in later centuries to the laws and custom of 'good King Robert'. King and people were linked through the bond of law and custom as well as by the sanction of the Church and the mythology of a new national history.

The experience of the wars with England had underlined the need for a change in military tactics and technology. The armoured knight was no longer the ultimate battlefield weapon which he had been in the twelfth century. It had been the concentrated firepower of crossbowmen which had wreaked havoc at Falkirk. Much military service, as a result, was converted into archer service when the lands involved were small or being regrouped. The armoured knight was not declared redundant, but he occupied a lesser place in the Scottish army of the fourteenth and fifteenth centuries.[61]

The confusions of a civil war inevitably brought about spoils for the loyal supporters of Robert Bruce and a measure of retribution for the backers of the Balliol/Comyn cause.[62] There was no planned, blanket act of attainder, either in 1306 or later, but neither was there any mass restoration of the disinherited, despite opportunities afforded in the peace of 1323 and in 1328. Bruce was too careful to risk alienating the great earls by an over-hasty application of the stick of forfeiture. At times it was natural death rather than royal action which broke up estates; a third of the forty-two leading noble families failed in the male line between 1320 and 1350.[63] The reward of the king's most loyal servants was one of the natural processes of medieval kingship and the rise of men such as Thomas Randolph, created Earl of Moray in 1312, was part of it. Also a part of the natural order of things was the strengthening of the landed holdings of members of the royal house itself, and the Bruce/Stewart connection would emerge from the war in far greater control of the west than before. The causes of it are more complicated than a royal vendetta, but the fact is simple enough: there was a major redistribution of land and power during the reign. A major part of the consolidation of the kingdom stemmed from the unusually large amount of patronage available to Bruce.

By 1314 minds had to be made up. There was no room left to sit on either fence, between holdings in England and Scotland or between the rival factions in the civil war. About a dozen magnates suffered forfeiture. The bulk of these lands were granted out again, a demonstration of the prudent conservatism of a King whose position was still vulnerable; but they went largely to a score of his most loyal supporters. The names of Comyn, Balliol and Soules did not disappear altogether but there was no room left for them at the top of the feudal hierarchy. In their place were Randolphs, Douglases, Murrays, Stewarts – and Bruces. The middle ranks of the baronage echoed as never before to names such as Hay, Keith and Seton. Both the nature and extent of royal power and the personnel of the nobles who sustained it in their own territories had been transformed.[64]

Civil war renewed: David Bruce and Edward Balliol

The Scots had deliberately chosen the day of the coronation of Edward III (1327-77) in February 1327 to launch a surprise raid on Norham, the site of Edward I's preliminary hearing of the Great Cause in 1291. The retaliatory expedition into Scotland in the following summer had been an ignominious shambles, outflanked by the usual Scottish tactic of a diversionary raid. But the pursuit of the Scottish raiders also turned into a fiasco. The English camp at Stanhope Park in Weardale had been raided by the Scots during the night and the young King almost captured. Edward III's first taste of Anglo-Scottish warfare had forced this 'mere boy' of fifteen to 'burst into tears', according to Sir Thomas Grey, as he retreated towards York. The 'final peace' of 1328 had been a further blow to the esteem of this impetuous and highly talented King, who established a reputation by his mid-twenties as an ideal knight, with a reckless disregard for his personal safety.[65] The determination of a young King intent on restoring his reputation coincided with an obsession at the English court about the danger posed to English security by the restored Franco-Scottish alliance; the treaty of 1295 was frequently cited at Edward's court in the early 1330s as an attempt at the 'wholesale disherison and destruction' of the English nation.[66] By early 1332 the tangled history of the first two 'wars of Scotland' was

128

being used to justify a third, which would finally settle the Scottish 'problem'.

Despite large-scale deployment of English troops in the north, there was no official opening of hostilities until the middle of 1333. Initially, the Edwardian government, as yet without the huge resources needed for a full-blooded conquest, settled on a policy of 'cold war', in which Edward was content, as the Earl of Moray put it, to let 'le pellot aler' (the ball roll).[67] Edward Balliol, son of King John, had been given a safe conduct to travel anywhere in Edward's dominions as early as 1330; he was the chief instrument of an unofficial policy of destabilising the Scottish kingdom. His natural allies were the 'disinherited', a mixed but powerful lobby of both English and Scottish nobles anxious to reclaim their estates in Scotland which had been forfeited by Robert Bruce and ignored in the peace of 1328. By late 1331, Balliol was in England and it may have been that piece of news which galvanised the Scottish government into arranging a full-scale coronation for the young King David at Scone in late November. The second Bruce/Balliol civil war began in August 1332, with the landing of a private expeditionary force of the disinherited at Kinghorn in Fife. On the 12th, at Dupplin near Perth, it routed a vastly superior force led by the Earl of Mar, who had been made regent after Moray's death the month before. On 24 September, Balliol was enthroned at Scone, with the Earl of Fife taking his traditional role as king-maker. At Roxburgh, in December, Balliol renewed his homage to the English king and entered into an arrangement by which most of southern Scotland was annexed to the crown of England 'in all time coming'.[68]

Although a daring night raid made on Balliol's camp at Moffat a few days later forced him to flee for his safety to Carlisle, the pressure on the Bruce government increased in the following year, when Edward made the war with Scotland official. Berwick was besieged, and some of the tactics used were reminiscent of the worst excesses of his grandfather. Hostages from the town were systematically executed in full sight of its walls at a rate of two a day to force its surrender. A Scottish army sent to relieve Berwick suffered a disastrous defeat at Halidon Hill (19 July 1333), two miles to the north-west of the town. Five earls fell and enough footmen to kindle rumours that the Scottish wars were at an end.[69] The situation in 1333 could hardly have been more serious. A puppet regime of Edward Balliol was set up, based first at Berwick and latterly at Perth. Two shattering military defeats, both achieved by the new tactic of men-at-arms and archers fighting on foot and subjecting the Scots to a hail of concentrated firepower, had all but erased the effects of the long campaigns of Robert Bruce. The kingdom had been dismembered. David Bruce and his young Queen fled to Dumbarton Castle, and by May 1334 were in exile in France. Balliol ruled north of the Forth and the disinherited were reinherited. The English king had resumed claims of suzerainty and was once again lobbying the Curia, seeking to place an English cleric in the vacant see of St Andrews. South of the Forth, a ruthless campaign of forfeiture of freeholders was taking place in Lothian together with the calculated burning of crops and houses and the carrying off of chattels. This was total war of conquistadores, involving deliberate plunder on a huge scale, such as had been practised in Ireland in the early 1200s or would be used in France later in the fourteenth century. It went far beyond the policy of Edward I, who had intended that conquest in Scotland would be followed by a new order. Edward III was in process of creating a wasteland rather than a pale.[70]

The turning-point in the second civil war came on St Andrew's Day (30 November) 1335, at Culblean near Ballater on Deeside, when one of Balliol's leading supporters, David of Strathbogie, was defeated and killed by Andrew Murray, Guardian of David II's kingdom. It deserves a better-known place in Scottish history, as does Murray, the son of Wallace's compatriot in the revolt of 1297. During the course of the next two years, Murray, by reverting to the guerrilla tactics of Robert Bruce, steadily recovered most of the kingdom. By mid-1337, the disinherited had been forced back into a triangle of land in the south-west. Edward could no longer rely on a Balliol administration to hold the north for him, or even on a Scottish civil war to supplement a war of conquest. His devastation of the fertile plain of Lothian meant that his expenditure on garrisons and castles was five times as great as his income from Scotland.[71] Although a massive expeditionary force was assembled in 1335 and there were campaigns in every year up to 1338, his attention was increasingly being diverted towards France. There were invasion scares even before war with France broke out in 1337. By 1338, Edward had settled for a defensive strategy, content to secure the north against Scottish attack. By 1342 the English held only the two strongpoints of Lochmaben and Berwick.

The third 'war of Scotland' was not over, but it had entered a new phase. In 1341 David II, now aged seventeen, returned from France to begin his personal reign. The Bruce cause was finally almost secure. David was tied, however, to two, near-incompatible ends: the French alliance, which had helped pull Scotland through the traumas of the 1330s, was a barrier to the establishment of peace with England; and David, like his father before him, felt insecure until the renewed English claims to suzerainty were abandoned and he, rather than Balliol, was recognised by Edward as king. He tried to square this circle by the same means as had Robert Bruce: full-scale raids into England were launched in 1342, 1345 and 1346. It was, ironically, the heavy defeat of David's army caught at Neville's Cross near Durham (17 October 1346) which not only brought hostilities to an end but secured recognition for his kingship.

David, badly wounded by an arrow wound in the head, was captured along with a number of his leading nobles. As after Halidon, much of southern Scotland was quickly overrun by the English army and Edward Balliol reached Glasgow with an expeditionary force. The pretender, however, failed once again to find enough support amongst native Scots to make his cause worth supporting. The prospect of a lucrative ransom for David Bruce, provided he was recognised as rightful King of Scots, increasingly held more appeal for Edward III than the bottomless expenditure involved in financing a Balliol candidature. Balliol was cast adrift, to sink or swim by himself. He held out for a time in his homeland of the south-west but in 1356 eventually resigned all claims to the Scottish crown. The civil war ended with a whimper.

The third 'war of Scotland' dragged on into the 1350s. The ravaging of southern Scotland went on; Lothian was devastated in February 1356, in what came to be known as the 'Burnt Candlemas'. The repeated harrying of the marches and the vacuum in local lordship which it produced had the effect of destabilising frontier society. The 'border problem' of lawlessness and 'broken men' who flouted the authority of both central governments was largely a product of the wars of the fourteenth century; it would persist for two centuries or more. Familiar English claims – of overlordship and the possession of Scottish royal castles – were matched by a steady recovery by the Scots of the territory lost in 1346. Eventually, in October 1357, terms in the Treaty of Berwick were agreed for the ransom of David. The terms were heavy and would cast something of a shadow over David's second personal reign. The Treaty did little to settle either relations between Scotland and England or the new issues thrown up by sixty years of intermittent warfare. It brought about a truce which lasted for over twenty years, but it produced little break in the 'cold war' which was the real and lasting legacy of the Wars of Independence.[72]

9

THE MAKING OF THE STEWART DYNASTY

By 1357, WHEN DAVID II (1329-71) RETURNED TO SCOTLAND AFTER ELEVEN YEARS as a captive in England, the civil war between Bruces and Balliols, which had lasted for half a century, was finally at an end. The next century would see a period of consolidation, for the nation as much as for the crown. By 1460 a new royal dynasty, the Stewarts, who traced their claim from the marriage of Robert Bruce's eldest daughter Marjorie to Walter the Steward, had established itself; but it was probably not until the fourth of those reigns that the dynasty was fully established. The settlement of the realm after the long wars with England was achieved more quickly. By 1384, when Teviotdale was recovered, the Scots had regained almost all the land occupied by Edward III in the 1330s during the third phase of the Wars of Independence. The old frontier line was re-established, and would not seriously be challenged in the fifteenth century. Warfare could be a carrier of disease as well as an instrument of death and it is likely that far more perished from what Scots called the 'foul death of England' than fell at the hands of English soldiery. The effects of the recurrent outbreaks of the plague between 1349 and 1455 were mixed. Labour replaced land as a scarce resource; a sharp drop in population and an acute shortage of labour was matched, it is likely, by falling rents, larger holdings and what the chronicler Bower noted as 'an abundance of provisions in the kingdom'.[1] Overseas trade made something of a recovery in the 1370s and 1380s, when wool and leather exports reached again the levels of the late 1320s; but by the first decade of the fifteenth century they had fallen sharply, to less than 40 per cent of the average realised during the reign of Robert II.[2] A falling pound and a sharp drop in the revenue of the crown were two of the results. Despite appearances, of a society still headed by a small, close-knit nobility and feudal kings, Scotland in this period underwent a hidden transformation which affected all ranks of its peoples.

A new community of the realm
Was the stage set for a long and bitter struggle between a nobility motivated only by self-interest and kings anxious to establish law and order as well as their own authority? The over-mighty subject still casts a long shadow over the history of later medieval Scotland in most popular accounts of the period. In its place, more recently, there has emerged a different, but equally theatrical image – of talented, tough-minded, and often ruthless kings, such as David II, James I or II – who made up for the powers which they lacked by a personal magnetism or a calculated ruthlessness, which allowed them to get away with forfeiture of estates, show trials or even murder, as in the case of James II.[3] Yet both partners in this danse macabre were subjected to pressures beyond their control. The 1320s had seen a transformation of the nobility, set off by the conflicting loyalties engendered by the Bruce-Balliol conflict. By the 1370s natural forces had eliminated a quarter of the nobility of the 1350s through failure in the male line. Each generation between then

and 1450 saw at least one noble family in seven fail to produce a direct male heir. The Douglases who confronted James II in the 1450s were amongst the few survivors of the greater nobility of the mid-fourteenth century; the starkness of the confrontation was largely the result of a vacuum in a reign which began with only three major earls in possession.[4]

By the 1420s the crown had a very different shape from that in the reigns of Robert II and III, when the Stewarts had acted like any other ambitious noble family, stockpiling lands and power by grant, forfeiture and marriage. The main instrument of power of Robert II had been his twenty-one children: no less than twelve earldoms were distributed amongst his sons by the end of the reign; and his seven legitimate daughters all married into major native families.[5] James I had fewer such assets to use in his lifetime, and he was confronted by the sharp drop in revenue from customs, which had been the mainstay of the income of both David II and Robert II. If there was a struggle between crown and nobility, it took place against a background of bewildering change for both.

The fourteenth century had been scarred by a war of attrition with England, interspersed by periods of uneasy truce. The first half of the fifteenth century initially saw a closer working relationship with France, but set-piece confrontations on the Anglo-Scottish frontier were rare. Disengagement from the Hundred Years' War and a new independent streak in Scottish foreign policy marked the years after 1424, but the prospect of the recapture of Berwick or Roxburgh enticed James I in 1436 and his son in the second half of the 1450s into raids and sieges. After some twenty years of often uneasy peace following David's return in 1357, warfare had spluttered into life in the 1380s and 1390s in the same pattern as had marked the late 1330s and the 1340s – a stalemate, marked by Scottish raids and occasional, major English expeditions. The last major English campaign of the fourteenth century into Scotland had taken place in 1385, when Richard II (1377-99) led an army of 14,000 men as far as Edinburgh; the Scots replied by harrying the English West March with impunity and in 1388 launched a large-scale raid, which defeated an English army at Otterburn. In 1402 another major raid reached Newcastle, but ended in disaster: at Homildon Hill, near Wooler, the Scots were outmanoeuvred and the 'flower of chivalry of the whole realm' killed or captured and held to ransom. These two episodes, both resulting in the renewal of a truce, typified the pattern of the fourteenth-century war with England. Each was a turning-point: England's attempt to create a pale in southern Scotland gave way by the 1380s to better-organised defence of its own northern counties; after the losses sustained at Homildon Hill the Scots abandoned the strategy, used since the days of Robert Bruce, of the extended raid into the English north. It was a war which neither side had been able to win, but it had important results.[6]

For the Scots, the legacy of the long war was the emergence of a coherent political community, held together by common interests, a loose alliance with France and a freshly renewed national identity. The continuance of a 'cold war' with England which occasionally erupted into hostilities fuelled a widely accepted sense of a national past; the 1360s were the years when Barbour's *Brus* was written. Barbour's work glorified the role of a King of Scots as warlord and saviour of his people. But like the Declaration of Arbroath, which had stressed 'the due consent and assent of us all', it also celebrated the role of the noble houses which had been prominent in the struggle against England. Twice the war produced the same dilemma as in the 1290s, a kingless kingdom, and in neither period was there a collapse of government. During the eleven-year captivity of David II, parliaments had been held regularly in the name of the absent King. In 1357, in the first parliament held after the King's return, the widening nature of the political community had been acknowledged in the explicit recognition of 'three estates' (or *tres communitates*). During most of the eighteen years after 1406 when James I was held a prisoner in England a general council met each year. As elsewhere in Europe, frequent meetings of Estates were symbolic of a national cohesion.[7]

Kings had much to gain from this process, but had also on occasion to accept blunt criticism or outright rebuffs. Each king between David II and James II was subjected to the critical scrutiny of the political community. There were also revolts of nobles in 1363, 1411, 1437, 1452 and 1455. In reigns where it is often difficult to piece together a coherent narrative of events from the scattered comments of chroniclers, such outbreaks may take on a misleading centrality. The making of the Stewart dynasty was far less scarred by revolts than the drawn-out process in the twelfth and early thirteenth centuries by which the line of macMalcolm kings had been established. Many of the risings against David I and his heirs had been threats to the dynasty itself, but there is no indication (with the possible exception of the successful plot against James I in 1437) that sovereignty was at stake. These were, it is likely, political demonstrations, aimed at royal policy or the king's favourites rather than the king himself. The assassination of James I, organised by insiders placed within the royal household rather than dissidents outside the court, was a notable exception to the working partnership between kings and nobles which characterised much of late medieval Scottish history. It was a marriage which was often stormy, but few nobles chose to operate outside its bounds.

The century after 1357 saw a hard-won new sense of stature for the crown, a major shift in the make-up of its revenues and a series of complicated dynastic accidents. The failure of the Bruce line, despite two marriages entered into by David II and a third planned shortly before his death, resulted in a wholesale revision of expectations. The 1360s had seen the rise to prominence of the Drummonds, the kin of David's second queen, and it is likely that the noble revolt of 1363 was a protest vote against that prospect. By 1370 David, still without heirs, unceremoniously divorced Margaret Drummond and the Stewarts were back in favour. The death of the King a year later set the seal on an unexpected Stewart restoration. Robert II (1371-90) was fifty-five when he succeeded and had been heir-presumptive to the throne for almost the whole of his life.[8] His son, Robert III (1390-1406), was fifty-three when he came to the throne, by which time he already had a twelve-year-old heir. It was not, however, the eldest son, David, Earl of Carrick and Duke of Rothesay, who succeeded but his next surviving son, James, born only in 1394.[9] The first two Stewart kings were mature and practised politicians. The third, by a double fluke of history, was both a minor and, for the first eighteen years of his reign, a captive in England. From 1406 until 1420 Scotland, as a result, was governed by another son of Robert II – Robert, Earl of Fife and 1st Duke of Albany, another heir-presumptive and elder statesman whose active career stretched back to the 1380s. Albany's successor as governor after his death in 1420 was his son, Murdoch, who was then also heir-presumptive.

The relationship between kings and the community of the realm altered in this period, largely as a reflection of the changes which both royal and noble power were undergoing. Historians have often pointed to the reign of James I as marking the route to the future, in laying down foundations of royal power and policy which his successors would follow. The real watershed which occurred in that reign lay in the different structure of the dynastic politics of the house of Stewart. Twenty-nine of the years between 1346 and 1424, when James I returned to claim his throne, saw government in the hands of an heir-presumptive. Each reign between that of James II and Mary, Queen of Scots, began with a minor on the throne; the period between 1437 and 1561 saw fifty-eighty years of minorities. Only one of these minorities, that of James V, would see a Stewart heir-presumptive make his mark in politics, but each would experience the influence of a talented, tough-minded, foreign dowager queen. Until the 1420s the Stewarts were the single most important family network amongst the nobility. After the 1420s the royal house stood at a greater distance from its noble subjects. Four of the six daughters of James I married abroad, as would all future Stewart kings themselves. By the 1450s the political community, which was itself undergoing profound changes with the rise to prominence of a new, largely honorific class of titled nobles, the 'lords of parliament', was explicitly encouraging the king to 'live of his own' financially. Kings and nobles still rubbed shoulders in the intimate atmosphere of the Scottish court, which, with no fixed capital until the reign of James III, was still permanently on the move, but a new distance had opened up between them. The balance of power implicit within what is sometimes called *laissez-faire* kingship[10] was a tricky one to sustain; it involved the right of the political community to comment on a king's performance as well as its expectation that he should not exceed the proper bounds of either his income or his authority. The very model of *laissez-faire* kingship was James II, but only in the last five years of his reign. Few Stewart kings before or after him managed to hold the balance for long. Perhaps, in their very different ways, the exceptions were Robert II and James IV.

The two reigns of David II

When David II returned to Scotland in 1357, after eleven years as a captive in England, he was thirty-three but had spent only ten of the twenty-six years of his reign in his own kingdom. Exile in France during the harrying of southern Scotland by Edward III in the 1330s had, after a brief five-year personal reign, been followed by imprisonment in England, mostly in the Tower of London, following his capture at the battle of Neville's Cross in 1346. There were two reigns of David II and they seem distinctly different in character. The years after 1341 yield little evidence of a young king in a hurry. Formal acts and charters were not issued with any regularity and there seems little to distinguish the conduct of government from the years before 1341, which, with Robert the Steward at the helm, had also been marked by only occasional parliaments, justice ayres and exchequer audits.[11] Already there may have been signs, less of troublesome magnates than an inability on the part of an inexperienced king to keep a range of noble interests in balance; the seeds of resentment amongst both Douglases and Stewarts were already being sown. The chroniclers wrote of the liking of a pleasure-seeking adolescent for jousting, dancing and gaming, and only William the Lion and James IV seem to have rivalled him as a participator in the 'knichtly game'. Otherwise this was one of the most anonymous reigns in Scottish history.

Medieval kings ruled through the force of their personality. Judgements of individual reigns, as a result, are often the result of putting kings on the psychiatrist's couch. This is not an exact science. The impressions that can be gained of David's second personal reign are fuller but conflicting, as have been the judgement of historians on him. The older picture of a worthless incompetent, attracted to a procession of domineering women which was encouraged by the moralising censures of pro-Stewart chroniclers such as Bower, has been replaced by a cooler assessment, based on analysis of the growing activity of the King's administration, of a tough-minded, energetic ruler – a model for later Stewart kings such as James I or II. During the 1360s there is evidence to show a more rigorous and regular attention given to the king's government. Exchequer audits were made each January at Perth, and between 1365 and 1369 in the presence of the King; the first surviving example of the King's signet belongs to 1359 and the 1360s saw the appearance of the office of King's secretary. Routine business was transacted mostly in Edinburgh, which was coming to be the most regular seat of government; Edinburgh Castle, where extensive rebuilding was begun, was the most common place from which royal documents were issued. Set-piece events, such as parliaments or financial audits, took place at Scone or nearby Perth. The most striking achievement was the rise in royal income, which in the last exchequer audit of the reign resulted in receipts of £15,359, a fourfold increase since 1328.[12]

David had returned burdened with a ransom of 100,000 merks, payable at the rate of 10,000 merks a year. Within two years customs duties on exports had been trebled and a new assessment devised for levying direct taxation. Although such taxation was unusual, it is unlikely that the ransom cast a dark shadow over the rest of the reign. While it is true that falling rents would have put pressure on landowners, the notion of the revolt of 1363 as a protest of taxpayers seems strained. Still more far-fetched is the idea that David was prepared to trade more favourable terms for repayment of the ransom in return for conceding succession to his throne to either Edward III or one of his sons, if he were to remain childless. The negotiations which took place at Westminster in November 1363 in the presence of both kings revealed again the suzerainty card which Edward III, like his father and grandfather before him, occasionally played as the price of future 'good peace and concord' between the two kingdoms. The fact that in March 1364 David took the Westminster memoranda to a parliament at Scone, which promptly rejected them, shows that he had learned one of the key lessons of the history of the Wars of Independence. The political community was, from the first in 1357, regularly consulted over the many aspects of Anglo-Scottish relations which resulted from the aftermath of the King's captivity. In the second half of the 1360s, a series of embassies were dispatched, the ransom was twice renegotiated and truces rearranged, all in close consultation with councils or parliaments.[13] Both the restoration of the crown's finances and the avowal of the kingdom's independence were done by king and political community working in tandem.

A king is often best judged by the legacy he leaves to his successors. Here again the impression is a mixed one. James I in the 1420s would not so much institute new laws and procedures as have parliament re-enact old ones, often from the reign of

David II. On the other hand, the 'financial triumph'[14] of David II, based largely on the shifting sands of the export trade, was not a secure legacy. Robert II enjoyed even larger windfall profits from customs for a time but it was the misfortune of Robert III that he faced in the 1390s the combined spectre of a continuing slippage in the level of rents and a sudden drop in the volume of overseas trade. The years of war, the carnage at Neville's Cross and the lengthy captivity of many nobles took their toll: in 1357 David had not inherited a stable structure of magnatial power. The demands of the ransom for more than twenty noble hostages exacerbated this. During fourteen years of vigorous personal rule, a series of magnates were imprisoned, forced into exile or submission but the fate of the hostages had largely been ignored. As a result, the structure of noble power was still in a state of flux in 1371.

After his return in 1357, David rewarded the three magnates who had done most to run the realm during his captivity; the Steward, William Douglas and the Earl of March were all granted earldoms. Yet these were the three nobles at the heart of the rebellion of 1363. The timing of the protest, against 'evil counsel', gives the clearest indication of its target. The King's first wife, Joan, who had been in England since 1357, had died in August 1362. A marriage to Margaret Drummond, widow of Sir John Logie, was in prospect. The fact that the submission of the chief rebel, Robert the Steward, was enacted before the royal counsellors whom he had planned to oust and that it took place at Inchmurdoch in Fife, the scene of the recent marriage ceremony, was doubly symbolic. Robert remained heir-presumptive, but against a gathering chorus of Drummonds at court. The marriage of his eldest son to Annabel Drummond, the Queen's niece, may have implied the recognition of an alternative heir-presumptive, now made Earl of Carrick, who significantly named his first son David.[15] In the absence of a far-flung Bruce family network, the King promoted a substitute royal house, of Drummonds.

In 1369, however, the wheels of patronage were suddenly thrown into reverse when the Queen, still childless, fell out of favour. She took ship to France, to lobby the *Curia* at Avignon to overturn the sentence of divorce. Already, a third royal bride, Agnes Dunbar, was in prospect. The most telling charge against David II is not that he was a sexual libertine. It is rather that he failed to recognise that some of his liaisons had serious political repercussions. The murder of his mistress, Katherine Mortimer, on the lonely road to Soutra in 1360 was a warning shot of protest against the absence of good lordship; it was ignored. The prolonged absence of his first Queen, who was in England for fully five years before her death, skewed relations with England as well as casting a cloud of unknowing over the succession. The rise and fall of the Drummonds in six short years was highly unsettling. The prolonged ambiguity of the position of the Steward was compounded when he was again restored to luke-warm favour after 1369. In early 1371, with David still only forty-six and his heir eight years older, Scotland was poised on the brink of another royal marriage and the likelihood of a further shift in the tactics of ending the dangerous isolation of the royal house of Bruce. Agnes Dunbar was granted a pension of 1,000 merks for her trousseau. A few days later, on 22 February 1371, David died unexpectedly.[16] In a reign where the unexpected had repeatedly happened, what in 1369 had seemed the least likely of scenarios had materialised: 'yesterday's man', the Steward, whose active career stretched back to the battle of Halidon Hill in 1334, succeeded to the throne.

The rule of the first Stewarts: Robert II and III (1371-1406)

On the day after his coronation at Scone on 27 March 1371, Robert II named his eldest son, John, Earl of Carrick, as his successor. The central feature of the house of Bruce had, since 1318, been the weakness of the male line. The Stewarts, by contrast, had been prodigious in the production of male heirs. The revision of expectations involved in a Stewart line was illustrated by the highly elaborate act of succession approved by parliament in 1373. The entail prescribed the crown successively being passed, in the event of the failure of a male line, to the male heirs of Robert's four other surviving, legitimate sons. The Stewarts, who had gained the crown through a female, went to elaborate lengths to assure a male succession.[17] There were other important consequences of the enthronement of the head of what amounted to a family consortium, whose extensive lands still lay concentrated in the west and south-west. By 1377, seven of the sixteen current earldoms were in the family's control, and by the mid-1390s no fewer than twelve. The seven daughters of Robert II, by his two marriages, played their part; they added a total of eleven sons-in-law to the Stewart nexus, including the MacDonald Lord of the Isles and the earls of Douglas and March. This was part of a broader pattern of which the Stewarts were the prime exemplars: more and more power was being concentrated in the hands of fewer and fewer noble families.[18] It is hardly the conventional picture of a rapacious nobility out of control. It would be the invasion of the north and the Highlands by the Stewarts, however, which would become the most explosive ingredient in politics between 1390 and 1420.

The fact that less is known about Robert II and III than any other late medieval kings has not deterred historians from making snap judgements of them: they have both been dismissed as 'pathetically weak personalities' and their reigns characterised, in turn, as nineteen years of senility and sixteen of infirmity.[19] Robert II, it is true, when he died was older than any other known reigning king of Scots, but the description of him by Froissart as having 'red bleared eyes, of the colour of sandalwood, which clearly showed he was . . . a man who would rather remain at home than march to the field' was made when he was seventy, fifteen years into his reign and *after* the coup of 1384 which removed him from effective power.[20] The years between 1371 and 1384 showed little break in continuity with the reign before it. Robert II was able to avoid being dragged into the Hundred Years' War and continued to renew truces with England until 1383. There was no sudden collapse of royal finances or breakdown of government; there was still a healthy surplus of £1,800 in 1374 from an income of over £14,000. These were years which the chronicler Bower from the standpoint of the 1440s saw as marked by 'tranquility, prosperity and peace'.[21]

For some, reading history backwards from the 1450s and the struggle between the Douglases and James II, the acquisition by Archibald the Grim in 1372 of the lands of Wigtown, the power base of the 'Black' Douglases and one of the bones of contention in 1452, was symptomatic of the weak rule of Robert II. It was, however, another feature of the careful conservatism which marked the reign. It had been David II who had encouraged the growth of a Douglas network on the western border as part of the consolidation of the marches after three-quarters of a century of warfare. The fostering of strong local lordship – of the Kers in Roxburghshire, the Humes in Berwickshire and the Douglases in Galloway – was one of the unsung achievements of late fourteenth-century kingship.[22] David II, who in some respects can be portrayed as a 'strong', interventionist king, was also an exponent of *laissez-faire* monarchy, who was for the most part content to leave both Douglases in the south and Stewarts in the west to their own devices. Half of his charters were issued in the central Lowlands and a further third in the area between the Tay and the Mounth.[23] Robert II followed a path laid down before 1371, both by David II and by himself, as Guardian of the kingdom between 1346 and 1357.

If there was a relaxation of government, it is likely that it came only after 1384. The introduction of Robert II's eldest son, Carrick, into government in 1381 was a sensible and time-honoured means of using the heir-presumptive to ensure continuity. The circumstances which lay behind the decision to appoint Carrick as lieutenant of the kingdom for 'certain causes' three years later are uncertain: the suggestion that there had been a palace coup is as plausible as the more usual explanation of the King's senility.[24] The underlying reason in either event was, it is likely, the favour shown by Robert to his third son, Alexander, Earl of Buchan, the notorious 'Wolf of Badenoch', who was severely criticised in the general council of 1385. It may be no coincidence that the first example of the new stigmatisation of the Highlands and Highlanders as 'a savage and untamed race, rude and independent, given to rapine . . . and exceedingly cruel' came in the chronicle of John of Fordun, completed in the 1380s.[25] If the intention was a renewed even-handedness in justice, the appointment went disastrously wrong, but for a reason that could hardly have been foreseen. In 1388 Carrick was virtually incapacitated by a kick from a horse.

It may be doubtful whether or not Robert II was a 'lame-duck' king by 1384, but Carrick was certainly a lame-duck Guardian. His injury left the initiative with his younger brother, the Earl of Fife. The circumstances of the incapacity of an heir-presumptive and the fact that his heir was still under age were so unusual that Fife's appointment as Guardian in 1388 was strictly circumscribed; the door was left open for Carrick's recovery and Fife was held accountable for his actions to an annual meeting of the political community in parliament or general council. With evidence of Fife intervening to settle disputes in Moray in 1389, there is little to show that the reign of Robert II, who died on 19 April 1390, ended in confusion or collapse. The fact that the most outrageous of the Wolf of Badenoch's acts in the north – the burning of the burgh of Forres and the sack of Elgin Cathedral in May and June of 1390 – came in the interval between the death of Robert II and the enthronement of his successor in the following August may be significant. It may indicate a problem in the succession, posed by Fife, which provoked violent reaction in the north. It also strongly suggests the removal of a still significant moral force rather than the end of a long chapter of increasingly senile kingship.

The initial years of the reign of Robert III do not suggest a total collapse of government. There was still evidently a prospect that the King, who had chosen to take the name Robert rather than his own of John which would have reopened the thorny question of the status of the reign of John Balliol, might recover from his infirmity and it is possible that he did – he was able to conduct a siege of Dumbarton in 1400. Robert's injury certainly had not interfered with his genes: one of his two bastard sons was born probably in 1390, and two legitimate sons and four daughters had followed by 1406.[26] Although the King was already fifty-three, the succession seemed secure with an heir, already aged twelve, and a second surviving legitimate son, James, who was born in 1394. The rule by Fife as Guardian continued until 1392-3, still authorised by the political community and cemented by his own holdings in Fife and Menteith, centred on his private castle at Doune as well as the royal Castle of Stirling. A variety of other developments, however, were at work, including the return to favour of the Drummonds, the Queen's kin, and the steady emergence into the political arena of the King's eldest son, David, Earl of Carrick.

The 1390s were, according to various accounts in later chronicles, years of disorder and lawlessness, with a weak executive. Most outrages were limited to the north or the Highlands. The notion of a general 'Highland problem' is misleading. At least three distinct elements were involved. There had been a long-running problem of disorder in Moray and the sensational set-piece encounter of the fight to the death between two sets of 'pestiferous caterans', the Clans Chattan and Kay, on the North Inch of Perth, in the presence of Robert III, his court and invited foreign visitors in 1396 was probably part of a royal attempt to settle it. It may, as Bower noted, have had a local effect: 'for a long time the north remained quiet'.[27] But the Wolf of Badenoch until his death in 1405 remained the main cause of the growing estrangement of Highland and Lowland society: the raid of the 'savage Scots' through Angus in 1391-2 was organised by his sons.

Separate from the problem of a royal Stewart turned Gaelic chieftain was the growing estrangement of the Lord of the Isles, whose relations with the crown had been reasonably satisfactory as a result of the marriage of Robert II's daughter Margaret to John MacDonald in 1350. John's death in 1388, however, was the signal for an acrimonious dispute between his widow and his sons over her jointure of Kintyre. The result was a dispute between the Lordship and the crown which lasted for two generations, linked up with the two other elements of Highland unrest, in Badenoch and Moray, and provoked various, mostly fruitless government expeditions to the north and west between 1389 and 1431.[28] Ironically, James I, whose forces were heavily defeated at Inverlochy in 1431, had less success in bringing the Lord of the Isles to heel than Fife, who extracted submissions in both 1398 and 1412. The disaffection of successive Lords of the Isles was the signal for the erection of a new frontier marking the boundary of royal influence in the north and west; royal government was on the retreat and Highland society was in process of being typecast as an alien culture. As is the case in later reigns, the inability of Stewart kings from James I to VI to tackle the 'Highland problem' furnishes an alternative commentary on the nature of royal power.[29]

By 1398 the King's eldest son, David, now twenty, had made his entry into politics. The presence of an adult brother was a relatively rare complication in late medieval Scottish kingship – the next to be affected was James III. The phenomenon of a second reversionary interest in the form of an adult male heir made the reign of Robert III unique; it was a situation which would have tested any king, still less an invalid. The elevation of both as the first Scottish dukes in 1398 did not ease the tension between them. In 1399, amidst criticism of the growing 'misgovernance of the realm', Fife, now Duke of Albany, lost ground to the heir-presumptive, now Duke of Rothesay, who was made lieutenant of the kingdom. Rothesay's authority, however, was even more hedged about with qualifications by a council-general than Fife's had been; he was limited to a fixed three-year term of office, which was renewable only by a designated special council. Despite appearances to the contrary, the way the political community dealt with the unusual dynastic problems posed by Robert III's reign suggests a mature and independent-minded third force in politics, carefully monitoring the behaviour of a weak king and rival scions of the royal house.

In January 1402, at the end of a vigorous but unpopular term, Rothesay was arrested by his rival and imprisoned in Albany's own castle of Falkland. Within two months he was dead. The subsequent official inquiry, as such bodies tend to do, exonerated Albany of blame, maintaining that Rothesay had died 'through the divine dispensation and not otherwise'. If the Albany Isle, erected in the Church of St Giles in Edinburgh early in the fifteenth century, was a public token of penance – similar to the iron belt worn by James IV in Lent for his part in the death of his father in 1488 – Albany otherwise wore his guilt lightly. Another prominent opponent, Malcolm Drummond, died in prison in 1402, in circumstances suspiciously similar to those of his nephew, Rothesay. Albany was restored as lieutenant-general, but the situation was very different from that in his previous term. The King's heir, James, was only eight. The Queen had died in 1401, as had shortly beforehand two of Rothesay's staunchest supporters, the Bishop of St Andrews and the Earl of Douglas, whose daughter he had married after jilting two others. The death of Malcolm Drummond had blocked the prospect of a resurgent Drummond faction. In contrast to the later 1390s, Albany in 1402 stood unchallenged.

Robert III had two last cards to play. From Rothesay Castle, where he lived in semi-exile in Bute, he began to refashion the traditional Stewart lands in Renfrew, Cunningham, Kyle and Carrick into an extensive private regality for the young Prince. And in 1406, he made arrangements for James to be sent to France, ostensibly for his education, but more probably for his safety. The travel plans went wrong almost from the first. The young Prince was forced to wait for a month in the unfriendly habitat of the Bass Rock in winter. A Danzig vessel, bound out of Leith with a cargo of hides and wool, was his unlikely passage to France. It was, however, boarded by English pirates off Flamborough Head on 14 March 1406. Within three weeks, Robert III was dead and his uncrowned heir was a captive in the Tower of London. His most lasting legacy was his own devastating epitaph: 'Here lies the worst of kings and the most wretched of men in the whole realm.'

The evidence of such quotations, however convenient, is never the whole truth. It is not enough to cast aside the problems of the reign of Robert III as those stemming from a weak king, especially if the reigns of the two Roberts are bracketed together as years of 'misgovernance of the realm'. There is no evidence of a crisis in government before the mid-1380s. *Laissez-faire* kingship, often described as the norm for which late medieval kings strove, was conducted in the practised hands of Robert II. The growth of a formidable family nexus of Stewart power was the main feature of both reigns, but it does not seem to have excited the opprobrium which accompanied the rise of the Drummonds in the 1360s. If there was a turning-point in government it came in 1390, or perhaps in 1384.

Many of the problems of Robert III's reign stemmed from the simple fact that the customs, the mainstay of crown finances during the previous two reigns, were in a steep decline which would be arrested only in the 1530s; in the first decade of the fifteenth century income was a half of the average in the 1380s. The factiousness so apparent during the reign was a direct product of a highly unusual struggle between rival segments of the royal house. The 'Highland problem' had a number of distinct components. The disorder caused by 'caterans' may actually have receded in some areas, such as Moray, in the later part of the reign. Its most intractable features were the freelance activities of Stewarts in Badenoch and the growing disaffection of the Lords of the Isles after a period of harmony during the reign of Robert II; these problems were made worse by the fact that by 1400 they were beginning to become entangled with each other. 'Strong' kingship, such as would be provided by James I after 1424, was no guarantee of success, and the weakness of royal rule before 1406 can be exaggerated: the Wolf of Badenoch had been forced to appear before Robert III's council to answer for his raid on Elgin and a royal army led by Albany had extracted a submission from the Lord of the Isles in 1398.

The Albany governorships (1406-24)

When Albany was confirmed as governor in June 1406, he was already in his mid-sixties. His position remained unchallenged until his death in 1420. The anomalous situation in which the country found itself – a kingless kingdom whose king was not yet crowned – was resolved partly by a council-general which quickly decided that James should nevertheless be styled 'our king'. This was the first of regular meetings of the political community, always at Perth, throughout the whole period of James's captivity. The fact that Albany took to issuing royal charters in his own name, dated in terms of the years of his governorship, was not in itself indicative of any sinister assumption of vice-regal powers; it reflected the simple fact that James had not been crowned.[30]

James remained in captivity for eighteen years. It is difficult to be sure how hard Albany tried to have him released. By 1412 the young King's patience was beginning to wear thin and in a flurry of letters sent to eighteen Scottish notables he accused the governor of making haste slowly. There are many examples in Scottish history of exiles trying to build up a party at home to speed their return; there are few of kings doing so. The circumstances of James's eventual return strongly suggest that his pleas had made little impact; there was no ready-made royalist faction in 1424 anxious to do the King's bidding. The circumstances of his captivity were complicated by developments in England: the death of Henry IV (1399-1413) interrupted negotiations for his release which then seem to have been at an advanced stage. The reign of Henry V (1413-22), marked by domestic crisis and an aggressive policy towards France, was a far less favourable time for releasing the captive King of Scots, who was twice used by Henry in his French campaigns to compromise Scots in the service of Charles VI of France (1380-1422). The plight of the King was thrown into sharper relief after Albany's own son, Murdoch, was released by the English in 1416. Murdoch was one of the last of the hostages captured at Homildon in 1402 and had until that point more reason to be impatient than James. The masterly inactivity of Albany after 1416, when negotiations seem to have ceased altogether, throws some suspicion on his motives. James, however, learned the political lesson well. After 1424 he himself turned a blind eye to the plight of the nobles and their sons who were held to guarantee payment of his ransom.[31]

Albany's rule operated under the same difficulties as that of Robert III, compounded by the fact that the scope for 'good lordship', the vital lubricant of magnatial politics, was more limited for a regent. Against a background of steeply falling royal income, and with pensions and annuities for loyal nobles scarce, it was not surprising that Albany turned a blind eye to private raids made on the customs by nobles. The most blatant of these extortions was not as heinous as it seemed: the fees for holders of crown office were drying up too, and the Earl of Douglas usually gave a receipt to the Edinburgh 'custumars' (the collectors of export and other duties) when he staged his regular raids on the customs. By 1418 Albany was himself owed arrears in his fee as governor.[32]

Financial irregularity in the dealings of the exchequer should not be confused with lawlessness in society at large.[33] The trial and burning of an English priest, James Resby, for Wyclifite heresies in 1407 brought praise for Albany as a staunch defender of orthodoxy from chroniclers such as Wyntoun. The battle of Harlaw (1411), fought near Aberdeen between Donald, Lord of the Isles, and a royal army led by the Earl of Mar, was portrayed by chroniclers as a struggle between Highland and Lowland culture. It was also a struggle between cousins for control of northern Scotland and a protest against creeping Stewart incursions into Ross. The real stumbling-block in the way of a peaceful settlement of the north was probably not the Lord of the Isles but the agent of royal policy in the north – Alexander, Earl of Mar, the son of the notorious Wolf of Badenoch, who, until his death in 1435, also cast a blight over James I's efforts in the north.[34] Albany's policy was circumscribed by the nature of the allies he had at his disposal, but his own authority and that of the crown was secured by the submission which he himself forced from Donald at Lochgilphead in 1412. Any reign in the fourteenth or fifteenth centuries can be made to yield up spectacular crimes and Albany's regency was no exception, but the most notable, the murder of the Earl of Strathearn in 1413, was dealt with by a characteristic mixture of firmness and calculation; the murderers were promptly executed and the settlement included an attempt to find a new husband for the widow – one of his own grandsons. Later Stewart kings are praised for *laissez-faire* kingship or wise rule with an eye for self-interest. It is difficult to see why the same practices should not also be recognised in Albany, the first and the most successful of the many Stewart regents of the fifteenth and sixteenth centuries.

Albany died, aged over eighty, in 1420. He was succeeded as governor by his son, Murdoch, who was now heir-presumptive and had acted as lieutenant since his release in 1416. Murdoch, now 2nd Duke of Albany, inherited his father's problems but not his sureness of political touch. By 1422 he was already owed over £3,800 in fees and annuities by the exchequer and caught between the rival ambitions of his kinsman Mar and his eldest son, who styled himself 'the excellent prince Walter Stewart of Fife, Lennox and Menteith'. The period was not bereft of success: a commercial treaty with Holland was concluded in 1423 and in December of that year an agreement was reached at London to secure the release of the captive James I. The price was high, £40,000, to be paid in instalments of 10,000 merks to cover the 'costs and expenses' of his eighteen-year stay. Twenty-one noble hostages, measured by their estimated annual revenues, were the human surety. The greatest price, however, was to be paid by Murdoch himself.

The reign of James I

James I returned to his kingdom on 5 April 1424. He came with a new English bride, Joan Beaufort, granddaughter of John of Gaunt, and a long cultivated store of resentments, real or imagined. There are many indications that this thirty-year-old who had spent more than half of his life in captivity was a 'king unleashed'.[35] Five weeks later, even before his coronation, he arrested Murdoch's eldest son and his brother-in-law. A parliament at Perth met on 26 May, five days after his enthronement at Scone. It sat probably for four days, and reconvened at Edinburgh early in July.[36] From it resulted a novel, far-reaching 5 per cent tax on lands and goods, new export duties on a range of commodities including herring and cloth and a shoal of legislation on matters as diverse as crown lands and the government of burghs. The victims of the self-proclaimed aim 'that firm and sure peace be kept and held throughout the realm' ranged from able-bodied beggars to craft deacons, litigious clerics to footballers, who were threatened with a fine of 4d.

There was, however, no immediate orgy of retribution. Reprisals against Murdoch and his allies did not materialise until a second parliament, which met at Perth in March 1425. Eleven months is a long time in Stewart politics, suggesting that, despite the unpopularity of some aspects of Duke Murdoch's rule, the returning king probably lacked the authority to move against such an important family. Such a purge would also have damaged the war effort, for Albany's second son, John, Earl of Buchan, was commander of the large Scottish army in France. His death at the battle of Verneuil in August 1424 removed the potential embarrassment of arresting a war hero. Archibald 'the Tyneman', 4th Earl of Douglas, also fell at Verneuil. His successor, Archibald, the 5th Earl, was a man with whom James found it easier to do business, for *rapprochement* with the Douglases was a necessary first step in a campaign to isolate Albany before a trial. Even so, Murdoch and his younger son were not arrested until the ninth day of this second parliament. Their trial, which took place two months later before an assize which sat during another session of parliament, took several days; their eventual conviction was probably easier to secure after the burning of the burgh of Dumbarton by Murdoch's youngest son, James, as a protest against their arrest. Whatever scruples the nobles on the assize may have had in convicting 'giants among men of noble character',[37] they were not shared by James I, who had Murdoch, two of his sons and the eighty-year-old Lennox all summarily executed in front of Stirling Castle. The first state execution since 1320, it was an act of calculated ruthlessness which brought James three major earldoms with an annual income of over £1,000. It also probably marked the beginning of the disillusionment of the political community with its king.[38]

Two other powerful images have cast both light and shadow over the reign of the most enigmatic of all Stewart kings. This talented virtuoso, a talented musician as well as a poet and author of the *Kingis Quair*, a skilled archer and a robustly built, formidable opponent in both the joust and hand-to-hand combat, was hailed by Bower, a few years after his death, as 'our lawmaking King'. A different impression was made on Aeneas Sylvius (later Pope Pius II), who visited Scotland in 1435-6; here James was portrayed as thick-set, very fat and vindictive in nature.[39]

It was a reign which, like the King himself, had two faces. There were ten parliaments and three general councils in its thirteen years, but the flurry of legislation which had marked the years up to 1431 was not sustained after that. Many if not most of the laws enacted and procedures adopted were re-enactments of legislation and practice used by his predecessors. The burghs, the subject of the closest scrutiny in the parliaments of 1424 and 1428, were largely left to their own devices between then and 1436.[40] The Highlands, which bore the brunt of the King's attention between 1428 and 1431, saw the same pattern of a ferocious initial assault on the 'problem' and a later ignominious retreat. The royal summons for Highland chiefs to meet at Inverness in 1428 was the first example of a Stewart ploy which would be used as late as the reign of James VI – the royal kidnapping. Fifty magnates were arrested and imprisoned. The scheme backfired, for Alexander, Lord of the Isles, escaped. After two years of alternating fortunes, he inflicted a severe defeat on a royal army led by the Earl of Mar at Inverlochy in the summer of 1431. James signally failed to daunt the Isles and was forced to come to an accommodation with MacDonald power in the west.[41]

The problem of finance lay at the heart of every reign in the fifteenth century. As early as 1427 James I may have run into opposition over taxation, although as yet it may have been confined to the uses to which the tax of 1424 had been put; £26,000 had been collected for the ransom but only £12,000 used to pay it. After 1424, the law of diminishing returns quickly set in. There were, according to Bower, murmurings against a fairly modest tax of 2d in the pound levied in 1433 and increasingly James was forced to rely on the arbitrary device of 'benevolences' extracted from reluctant nobles. The sharp increase in customs duties initially yielded results: by 1428 receipts had reached £6,912, an increase of 150 per cent since 1422, but revenue by the 1430s was already tailing off. The most startling increase in the income of the crown came from crown lands, which saw a threefold rise, but that came almost entirely from the forfeiture of a total of five earldoms. In 1437, the ordinary income of the crown had still not reached the levels attained during the reigns of David II and Robert II.[42] The novelty of the reign of James I lay not in any new legislative revolution bringing to an end a 'dark age' of lawlessness but in the attempt to shift the balance between the ordinary and extraordinary income of the crown. It was a failure. As a result, James, rather than laying down a path which his successors were to follow, aroused instead that deep suspicion of taxation which would circumscribe both James II and III. James I, the first king since Alexander III to come to power untroubled by the prospect of war with England, squandered much of the opportunity given to him in 1424.

The most notable feature of the second half of the reign was a cult of honour at the court, seen most strikingly in the rebuilding of Linlithgow Castle as a palace rather than a fortified residence. It was given a powerful boost by the birth of a male heir. James, the surviving younger of twin boys, was born in 1430. The succession, which by the act of 1373 might otherwise have gone to the elderly Earl of Atholl, was assured. The King's status was further enhanced by the marriage of his eldest daughter, the twelve-year-old Margaret, to the French Dauphin in 1436. Two months later, James, an ambitious but novice military commander, suffered a humiliating reverse when an expedition to recover Roxburgh from the English had to be abandoned amidst mutual recriminations. At a general council which met in Edinburgh in October, the cauldron of smouldering resentments was brought to boiling point by the King's tactlessness, when yet another assault on baronial privileges was revealed. The protest against what was by now a thoroughly unpopular king took an unexpected form. Rather than a noble protest, such as had happened in 1363, there was a plot, conceived within the King's own household, against his life. It was organised by Atholl's grandson, Sir Robert Stewart, the chamberlain of the royal household. As such, he belonged to a scion of the royal house which may have nourished hopes of the succession based on descent from Robert II's second marriage, but it is more likely that this was an attempt to secure the governorship, which usually went to the heir-presumptive, in the resultant minority.

The details of the murder, which took place in the Dominican friary at Perth on the night of 21 February 1437, were unsavoury, though no more so than some of James's own dealings. He tried to escape via a sewer which ran below the floor of his apartment. There he was caught and stabbed to death. There were later embellishments to the story: the eight intruders increased to 300 in an account written in 1440 and the story that one of the Queen's ladies-in-waiting thrust her arm as a frail bolt through sockets of the door was an invention of the sixteenth century.[43] The resuscitation of the reputation of James I began early, when the visiting Bishop of Urbino kissed the wounds on the corpse and proclaimed the dead king a martyr for the commonwealth. The cruelty of the punishments which were meted out on the assassins, the praise of a series of pro-Stewart chroniclers and the desire of many modern historians to find strong kings to applaud should not detract from the force of the clash between James I and a political community which had gained in confidence and maturity over the previous century. The assassins, however, misjudged the mood of that community, which, while it had never given full-hearted assent to its King in the last ten years of his reign, abhorred regicide.

The reign of James II:
the reforging of the political community

The murder of James I had come with such unexpectedness that its immediate aftermath was a period of turmoil and confusion. It lasted for more than a month. The seven-year-old heir to the throne was crowned James II on 25 March 1437. The venue was Holyrood Abbey rather than Scone and he was anointed by the Bishop of Dunblane rather than of St Andrews. Although a parliament was held in Edinburgh at the time, when some of the chief conspirators were tried and executed, it may be that it was not until early May, some ten weeks after the murder when Sir Robert Graham and other plotters were executed with a ritual ferocity which was unusual in Scotland, that a settlement was achieved.[44] At stake, it is likely, was not the crown but the governorship during what was bound to be a long minority. The fact that Atholl, grandfather of one of the main conspirators, was both the main candidate to be Guardian of the kingdom and a natural suspect may have complicated the process. Although his protestations of innocence may have been true, he was a necessary sacrificial victim to the cause of the restoration of order. His death completed the eclipse of the main branches of the house of Stewart which had been under assault ever since the mass execution of the Albany family in 1424. The death in October, by natural causes, of the Earl of Angus, who had been instrumental in the arrest of the conspirators and left as his heir an eleven-year-old son, made the vacuum at the centre of power all the more striking. At the end of 1437, there were only two adult earls left in Scotland and two more were still held as hostages in England. Not only the King was a minor; so were the heirs of many of the major noble houses. The two major figures left in politics were the Queen Dowager and the 5th Earl of Douglas, head of a family which was almost the sole survivor of the great noble houses of the fourteenth century.[45]

The politics of the minority are obscure, and it is tempting to label the period as a descent into anarchy in which rival factions – Livingstons, Crichtons and Douglases – vied ruthlessly for power. The root cause of the disruption lay probably more in the natural fault in the wider body politic than the excesses of overmighty subjects which were its result. Many of the ecclesiastical hierarchy, usually the loyal servants of the crown in difficult times, were preoccupied with the conciliarist disputes going on in the Council of Basle. Even the pre-eminence of the house of Douglas was called into question between 1439 and 1443 after the death of the 5th Earl from plague. The controversial marriage of the Queen Dowager to Sir James Stewart, the 'Black Knight of Lorne', later in 1439 also threatened to recast the shape of court politics. These were further disrupted by the notorious 'Black Dinner' in November 1440, when the still under-age 6th Earl and his brother were arrested at a banquet in Edinburgh Castle and executed on trumped-up charges of treason. The successor to the Douglas empire and 7th Earl was their great-uncle, who had been created Earl of Avandale in 1437. A heavyweight in every sense, James 'the Gross' threw himself into both court and ecclesiastical politics with zest and did much to restore the status of the Black Douglases. On his death in 1443 he was succeeded by William, the 8th Earl and a young, ambitious and charismatic figure. By 1445, when the Queen Dowager died, the struggle of rival factions was already blowing itself out. The alliance of the Douglases with the Livingstons, a marriage of convenience in which there could have been little doubt as to who were the senior partners, had eclipsed the rival Crichton network.

The political community had not been entirely impotent in these difficult years. It had tried in 1439, with some success, to effect a reconciliation between the Queen Dowager and her gaolers and erstwhile allies, the Livingstons. The terms of the 'Appoyntement' between them were worked out by a general council meeting at Stirling in September 1439. Another council, meeting in August 1440, suggested that justice ayres should be held twice a year and that a progress around the country by the young King might be used as a means of discouraging disorder. And by 1444, there were clear signs of an attempt being made to enhance the status of the royal house.

Although James I had secured an important foreign marriage for his eldest daughter, Margaret, in 1426, the diplomatic offensive launched during the minority of James II was a distinct change of direction for the royal house of Stewart. All of the many daughters of Robert II and III had married native Scots. No effort was spared after 1442 to find prestigious foreign suitors for the remaining five sisters of the young King. Isabella, his second sister, married the Duke of Brittany in 1442 and two further important marriage contracts followed in 1444; the match of Mary with Wolfaert van Borsselen, heir to the Lord of Veere, further strengthened ties with the Low Countries and the betrothal of Annabella to the Count of Geneva promised to link the Stewarts with the important house of Savoy. The two remaining princesses, Eleanor and Joanna, were publicly put on the marriage

147

market in 1445, when they were sent to France. In 1447 Eleanor was betrothed to Sigismund, Duke of Austria, whom she married three years later. Joanna, who was born deaf and dumb, and her jilted sister Annabella remained on the continent for a further ten years before they returned, empty-handed, in 1458.[46]

The young King's own search for a prestigious bride, which began in 1448 and ended with his glittering marriage to Mary of Gueldres, niece of the Duke of Burgundy, at Holyrood in July 1449, set the seal on a decade which had done more than any other since the 1370s to raise the status of the new royal house in the courts of Europe. James II, as a result, enjoyed two major advantages not possessed by any of his three Stewart predecessors: he had been trained for kingship since birth and he entered the years of his mature reign with a ready-made reputation. The minority, despite its political tribulations, had reared a formidable king. It had perhaps done its work too well.

In 1449 the nineteen-year-old King, whose marriage signalled his entry into politics, cut an imposing figure. The portrait penned by a foreign visitor, Jörg von Ehingen, gives what is perhaps the first true likeness of a Scottish monarch. It shows a slim adolescent, dressed in fashionable black, with a large vermilion birthmark which completely covered one side of his face; 'James of the fiery face' became his nickname. Like his father, James enjoyed both the tourney and the hunt as well as the artistic pleasures of the court. He also had a fascination for artillery, which he had probably first seen in action as a spectator at the siege of Methven Castle in 1444. His young Burgundian Queen gave him contacts with the skilled gunsmiths of the Low Countries, and the famous cannon, Mons Meg, was a gift in 1457 from the Duke of Burgundy, for whom it had been made in 1449. Mary quickly began to make her distinctive mark as a patron of the recently founded Observant Franciscan friars, and also had a significant impact on politics. Her pleading of the cause of the bishops in parliament in January 1450 underlined the importance attached by James to securing the support of the Church. A renewed cult of monarchy, based on chivalry, artistic patronage and the support of the ecclesiastical hierarchy as much as on the crown's new firepower and aggressive stance in domestic politics, was central to the events of the 1450s.

Three times in the course of the years between 1451 and 1455 James II would confront the power of the Black Douglases. The older picture of the destruction of an overmighty subject has more recently been supplanted by the image of a ruthless king who did not scruple to land the first blow. Where opinions have differed have been on the level of risk involved. In 1455, James effectively destroyed the power base of the Douglases in the space of three months. Yet after both of his previous attempts, in 1451 and 1452, he had been forced to draw back from the prospect of a civil war and make peace, with little to show for it.[47] His motives seem to have involved a mixture of fear and greed. An unusual bond of alliance between three magnates who were scarcely natural allies – William, 8th Earl of Douglas, the Earl of Crawford and the MacDonald Lord of the Isles – was probably what lay behind the reference to 'treasonable leagues' in the settlement arrived at in 1452, but the fact that the bond has not survived has had the effect of leaving a cloud of suspicion over Douglas motives. The arrival of a well-connected foreign bride left James with an embarrassing problem of finding an annual income of £5,000 for her at a time when there was still a deficit in the comptroller's accounts.[48] An initial assault on the

Livingstons in 1449 had realised only modest returns and it was the revenues of the lucrative earldom of Wigtown which figured high in James's assaults on the Douglases. If the ransom had scarred the early years of his father's personal reign, it was Mary of Gueldres's jointure which hung like a shadow over that of James II.

The struggle between James II and the 8th Earl can be portrayed as the clash of two ambitious, headstrong young men. The Auchinleck chronicler's account of how, after almost two days of protracted wrangling at Stirling Castle in February 1452, James 'stert sodanly' towards Earl William with a knife seems in character with the aggressive stance, one hand on his dagger, drawn by von Ehingen.[49] The pack-like instincts of the King's closest associates completed the bloody work with twenty-six stab wounds. The nature of the deed, done in 'hot blood', which usually distinguished manslaughter from the more grievous crime of murder, made it easier for parliament to exonerate the King, which it did, somewhat half-heartedly, in the following June. The retaliation of the Douglases was a symbolic rather than a full-blooded act of revenge: James, the Master of Douglas and now the 9th Earl, and 600 men paraded the safe-conduct which the murdered Earl had been given through the streets of Stirling, tied to the tail of a horse. The burning of the town was almost an afterthought. Here was the ritual of *diffidatio*, by which a vassal formally renounced fealty to his lord.[50] This theatrical gesture may be the explanation for the unusual inclusion of a bond of manrent, retying the knot between liege lord and man, which was included within the settlement agreed between King and Earl at Lanark in January 1453. James had stepped back from the prospect of civil war and the Douglases still held the lands of Wigtown. A bruising draw was the result.

The Douglases did not, however, have a history of disaffection from the monarchy. They had, on the contrary, offered loyal and signal service to the crown, especially against English incursions after the grant made to them of lands in the south-west in the 1350s. Their pre-eminence in the 1440s was due more to the failure of the male line of other noble houses than a deliberate family policy of aggrandisement. They had a reputation as patrons of both the arts and the Church. *The Buke of the Howlat* was a long poem written for an entertainment organised by the Douglas Earl of Moray in the early 1450s. Earl William had himself cut a considerable dash on a pilgrimage to Rome in the Jubilee year of 1450. Conspicuous piety was matched by equally conspicuous consumption: a later history credited the Earl with a near-royal court, with ceremonial offices of carver and cup-bearer and the walls of his various halls hung with richly embroidered tapestries.[51] James, the 9th Earl, was not the untamed warlord which might be suggested by his vengeful sack of the burgh of Stirling in retaliation for the murder of Earl William. Initially intended for a career in the Church, he had been a student at Cologne and later developed a widespread reputation as the epitome of chivalry by his performance in the tournament with Burgundian knights at Stirling in 1449.

The Douglases were the prime exemplars, not of an overmighty noble class, but of the cult of chivalry and a more leisured style of living. Its symbols were the courtyard castle, steadily taking over from the cruder fortified tower house, the great hall or *aula* where nobles might themselves hold court and the carved stone armorials which reinforced status in a society where change had made many titles honorific. Its tastes lay in chivalric romances such as Barbour's and in the collegiate churches which saw a wave of foundations between 1440 and 1460.[52] The nobility were as much a part of the Renaissance as kingship itself.

The fall of the Douglases, begun in March 1455 and completed by the time of a parliament in June which forfeited them, was an awesome demonstration of the new firepower available to the monarchy. The Douglas castles at Inveravon and Abercorn were razed to the ground, and those at Douglas, Strathaven and Threave were battered into submission by the use of bombards similar in design to Mons Meg.[53] Heavy artillery, however, had also to be supplemented by the subtler arts of patronage; it seems likely that a campaign had been in progress since 1450 using grants of lands and offices to woo away from the Douglases their allies, especially in the south-west. It was probably aided by the fact that Galloway, once the Douglas heartland, since the accession of the 7th Earl after the Black Dinner of 1440, had become the soft underbelly of Douglas power, remote from its new base in Lothian and Lanarkshire.[54]

The first of the King's assaults on the Douglases, launched early in 1451, had taken advantage of Earl William's absence in Rome, but it ended in a reconciliation forged in parliaments which met in the following June and October. The second, which began with the stabbing of Earl William, was probably less well planned and was complicated by the play made by the new Earl for English support; it also ended after months of uncertainty in a two-stage settlement. The first part, a submission by the Douglases in an 'Appoyntement' made at Douglas Castle, was concluded shortly after a parliament had sat in Edinburgh; the second stage, a personal agreement between the new Earl and the King, was concluded in a bond made at Lanark five months later. The fact that James II needed only three months to destroy the Douglases in 1455 suggests that by then he enjoyed a new level of support amongst the political community, which was ready to forfeit the family soon after the opening of James's offensive.

Whatever its origins and attendant risks, there can be little doubt that 1455 was a turning-point in the history of the Stewart dynasty. A male heir, named James, had been born in 1451 and the birth of a second son, Alexander, in 1455 secured the succession further. The forfeited Black Douglas lands brought £2,000 of regular income to the crown. For the rest of the reign parliament or general council met regularly, at least once a year. In 1455 parliament, with any doubts it may earlier have harboured about the risk of civil war now set aside, took the initiative by making detailed proposals in an act of annexation of how the king should live of his own. A list of annexed lands, lordships and castles, said to be inalienable without the consent of parliament, was drawn up. A stable ordinary income, stemming from royal lands rather than customs, now seemed assured. The arbitrary forfeitures of James I and II had been approved by the political community.[55] They were part of the consolidation of the Stewart dynasty.

The crown, in its turn, made a series of conspicuous gestures of good lordship. One new earldom had already been created during the personal reign: that of Erroll in 1452. In short space between 1457 and 1458, four more were added: Argyll, Marischal, Morton and Rothes. The two unmarried sisters of the King, Annabella and Joanna, were used to secure the loyalty of two of the most critical members of the new peerage – the Gordon Earl of Huntly and James Douglas of Dalkeith, now safely detached from his kin as Earl of Morton. Lesser titles, in the form of lords of parliament, an honorific title which had first emerged in 1445, complemented the new earldoms. Seven had been created in 1452 as part of the attempt to woo support away from the Douglases, and more followed later. The dangerous vacuum amongst the nobility which had cast a shadow over both the personal reign of James I and the minority of James II was filled. The foundations of a new peerage which would dominate politics throughout the sixteenth century were laid.[56]

The new security which he enjoyed in domestic politics afforded James the chance after 1455 to cut a dash in both foreign affairs and war. Amongst the titles bestowed on his second son, born in 1455, was Lord of Man, which had been lost after the death of Alexander III. His attack on Man in 1456-7 was the first serious clash with England. The fall of the Lancastrian regime in July 1460 offered the opportunity to recover Roxburgh, another symbolic legacy of the long war with England. Within three weeks, James had laid siege to the castle, accompanied by a large contingent of his nobles. On Sunday 3 August, James was killed when one of his siege guns burst its casing. By the following Friday, Roxburgh fell. In one sense, James II had succeeded where his father had failed, for it had been the ignominious retreat from Roxburgh in 1436 which had raised to new heights the acrimony within the political community. In another sense, the fact that James II's nobles stayed on to complete the taking of Roxburgh showed the renewed resolve amongst that community. Two days later, on 10 August at Kelso Abbey, it acclaimed his heir as James III.

10

LATE MEDIEVAL KINGSHIP: JAMES III, IV AND V

J AMES II WAS ONLY SIX YEARS OLD WHEN HE SUCCEEDED IN 1437; HIS OWN SON WAS nine when the tragic accident at Roxburgh took place in 1460. The young King's education was put into the capable hands of Archibald Whitelaw, 'the perfect civil servant',[1] who earlier had also tutored at the University of Cologne the talented careerist William Elphinstone, later to become the most celebrated of all bishops of Aberdeen. It was thus that from an early age the young James III (1460-88) fell under the influence of one of the renowned class of skilled administrators and jurists whose contribution as crown servants in every reign between 1424 and 1542 lay in the recasting of royal authority.[2] It was Whitelaw, by then king's secretary, and the king's confessor, the celebrated humanist John Ireland, whose career at the Sorbonne was interrupted in 1483, who were entrusted with the education of James III's eldest son, the future James IV. The other formative influence, in each case, was a foreign queen. Mary of Gueldres, the formidable and talented widow of James II, was granted guardianship of her son by parliament in 1461 and retained it in the teeth of criticism from an excluded faction headed by James Kennedy, Bishop of St Andrews, until her death in 1463. And it was Margaret of Denmark, wife of James III, who, although estranged from her husband after 1482, was in charge of her eldest son's education until her death in 1486.

Minors, kings and royal power
The circumstances of the upbringing and education of princes were important. Every Stewart monarch between James II and James VI, as well as inheriting young, took charge of their realms while still in their teenage years. James III was seventeen when he assumed power in 1468; James IV was only fifteen when he succeeded his father and he had immediately to cope with the strains of heading an illicit regime; James V would be sixteen in 1528, when he escaped from the hands of the Douglases; Mary, Queen of Scots, would be nineteen when she returned from France in 1561, as would be James VI when he took up the reins of personal power in 1585.

Monarchs ruled, it has often been said, by the sheer force of their personality. The power of personality made up for other powers – such as a standing army, efficient tax-gathering machinery and elevated status – which they did not possess.[3] This simple fact has encouraged generations of historians to indulge in character assessments of each of the Jameses. James III has been described as being among the most gifted and also as the most unpleasant of all Stewart monarchs.[4] With James IV the differences of analysis have been at their sharpest: this pious and warlike King has been described as a 'moonstruck romantic' as well as the 'ideal medieval king'.[5] With James V, opinions have been more cautious: he has been seen as the most 'enigmatic' of Stewart kings, as well as one of the most unpopular and the 'most terrifying'.[6] Such 'psychological' analyses carry their own dangers. What seems clear is that each of these Stewart kings had a complex personality, calculated as well as impulsive in politics, pious in personal faith but also cynical in dealings with the Church and papacy. Each, too, benefited from a developing sense of the quest for an ordered community of the realm and from a growing corporate image of the Stewart dynasty, which was carefully fostered in each reign from James I onward. None flickered for a moment in his identity of the interests of realm and dynasty yet, as shall be seen, the greatest danger to the Stewarts came not from over-powerful nobles but from within, and a family all too often at war with itself.

The simple facts of minority rule have often been dwelt upon: each monarch between James I and VI succeeded as a minor and Scotland had almost exactly as many years of minority as majority rule between 1406 and 1585. Historians more recently have tended to set against the natural drawbacks of minority rule the argument that they were also often a useful corrective mechanism, allowing imbalances in the body politic or excesses of interference by the crown in local politics to be redressed. Minorities, it is argued, set limits on the real danger of overmighty kings rather than raised the spectre of overmighty subjects.[7] If James II had managed within the space of a few years of his majority to eclipse the most powerful noble family in the realm, what might he have done if his reign had gone to its expected full term rather than ending unexpectedly after a mere decade? James V in the last four years of a personal reign which lasted only fourteen years reduced the three most powerful magnates in Angus to near ciphers of the court; it was only his unexpected death in 1542 which restored the natural order of that local community.

Although the minorities of James III and Mary, Queen of Scots, can be made to fit the bill of restorers of equilibrium after strong-minded kings, those of both James IV and V seem highly special cases. James III had been deposed in 1488 by a rebellion and the first years of the reign of his son, who at fifteen was still a minor, had to counteract not only the excesses of James III but also the stigma attached to an illegal regime brought to power only through a coup. James V was brought to the throne in 1513 by his father's untimely death at Flodden. The twofold problem of his minority was the disagreement within the royal house between Queen Dowager and heir-presumptive and the vacuum left in the ranks of the nobility after Flodden; it was the combination of the two which gave power to the Douglases in 1524. A 'king unleashed' after 1528 was the price to be paid for the imbalances within the political community after 1513.

The three reigns between 1460 and 1542 raise fundamental questions as to the nature of royal power and its acceptance by their subjects. Yet the succession in 1488 of a seemingly deeply unpopular king by another whose charisma as a warrior and patron has been widely acknowledged may also obscure some of those questions, as may the unusual circumstances in which James V came of age in 1528. One answer, once much favoured by historians, is to think of 1488 as something of a watershed – either as a catharsis after years of political uncertainty or as the gateway to the triumph of a new monarchy.[8] It is difficult, however, to see much of a break in 1488 or after in the essential features of kingship – whether in terms of the problems it faced or the limited number of solutions available to it. The three main elements were, as in previous Stewart reigns, closely interrelated: royal income, justice, and the complex relationship of crown and church.

Throughout the fifteenth century the costs of monarchy were rising sharply but also rising were the expectations which loyal subjects had of their 'good lord'. Extensive and even-handed patronage was expected of kings; but the crown also needed to increase its income without unduly alienating its subjects. There was no simple answer to this near-intractable dilemma, which lay at the heart of late medieval kingship. Kings might risk going to parliament to seek consent for taxation but, like James III who was six times rebuffed, could not often expect a favourable response.[9] Much of the arbitrary and risky treatment of errant nobles – subjecting them to treason trials and annexing their estates – can be explained by the relentless fear of insolvency which haunted James I, II and III. Huge tracts of territory, such as those of the Boyds in 1469 and the Earldom of March in 1487, were added to the stock of crown lands. Various devices were found by increasingly resourceful crown servants to exploit the king's feudal income and rights. James I had begun the habit of treating resumptions of land as part of the royal demesne rather than granting it out again. Recognition, a technical infringement of feudal law, was pursued by the Lords of Council with a vigilance amounting to sharp practice in the reigns of James III and IV. Difficult to separate now and probably also in the minds of contemporaries was the tinkering by the crown's servants in legal processes for fiscal reasons and the increasing demand made by subjects for justice; both were the reflection of an increasingly complex world where an active market in land was matched by the rapid redrawing of the lines of feudal rights and responsibilities. Royal justice and expropriation by the crown went hand in hand. The effects of the multi-faceted pursuit of royal income were gradual and cumulative rather than dramatic, and it was not until the second half of the reign of James IV that there was a significant rise in crown income, and it came not from ordinary revenue but from other sources, not least the Church.

It is one of the ironies of history that every king from James I to V demonstrated a conspicuous but probably genuine piety. There is no particular reason to disbelieve the story of the chronicler Hector Boece that James III was prone to burst into fits of tears and prayers at the sight of an image of Christ or the Virgin; James IV wore an iron belt as penance for his part in the death of his father; and James V insisted on a closer attention to their rule by the monks of various orders.[10] But this was a double-sided piety: James IV went regularly on pilgrimage, especially to the shrine of St Ninian at Whithorn, was an active patron of the order of Observant Franciscans and especially their new house at Stirling Castle, and he fulfilled his father's plan of endowing a Chapel Royal at Stirling; but he also used the right of nomination to benefices, wrung from the papacy in 1487 after more than half a century of disputes, over 200 times.[11] The 'special daughter' of Rome had become a very demanding child.

Every king from James I to V probed and challenged the authority of the papacy; parliaments in each of these reigns enthusiastically passed anti-papal legislation. The struggle in the reign of James III had first resumed in 1466 in the form of a wrangle over grants of two religious houses made by the *Curia* to Patrick Graham, Bishop of St Andrews. By 1472, when St Andrews was erected into an archbishopric with metropolitan authority and Graham as the Pope's nominee, the dispute was much sharper. The careers of Graham, who was excommunicated and deprived by 1478, and of his successor, William Scheves, illustrate the conflicting loyalties at work in ecclesiastical politics. Graham, a worthy but far from outstanding papal nominee, fell victim to the pressure of an ambitious king. Scheves, a loyal servant of the crown as well as a highly cultured scholar, fell below the expectations of his fellow bishops and a number of them refused to recognise his authority. Caught between popes and kings, both noted for their worldliness as much as for their piety, churchmen found it difficult to reconcile the demands of a church that was at once supranational and national. The easiest solution was a compliant papacy: Paul II (1464-71) in 1469 had granted a limited indult (privilege) allowing the Bishop of St Andrews a right of confirmation in elections to religious houses in his diocese. For the whole thirteen years of his term, Sixtus IV (1471-84) resisted assertions by both the Scottish king and parliament, which by 1482 sought to extend the indult to all other dioceses. His successor Innocent VIII (1484-92) was not blessed with the same resolution and in 1487 complied.

Whether this made the Church a virtual 'department of state'[12] is another matter. A distinction has to be drawn between the two needs of the crown which the Church fulfilled. Kings had high expectations of their bishops and higher clergy, but as crown servants rather than as pastors. They were the chief source of manpower for the burgeoning and specialist needs of the royal administration, and the scramble for benefices was in large part a reflection of the desire to pay them an adequate stipend. The Church was, however, also the largest source of untapped income for the crown and, in this respect, the path laid down by the Indult of 1487 led directly to the ruthless exploitation of abbeys and other monastic houses by James V. Every device used by James V, including clerical taxation, had been prepared for him by one or other of his predecessors; the result by the end of his reign was that the Church had become not so much a department of state as a sub-department of the royal household.

The reign of James III (1460-88)

Like that of his father, the reign of James III began with a minority that lasted almost a decade. As before, the Queen Mother was appointed guardian and the period would see a shifting struggle for possession of the young King. There was, however, no collapse of royal government and no descent into chaotic factionalism. Like the 1440s, the 1460s saw important milestones on the road to the maturing status of the Stewart dynasty. Roxburgh had been retaken after James II's death and Berwick was ceded to the Scots by Lancastrian exiles in April 1461; the last symbol of the English occupation of the fourteenth century had been erased, although it would become a bone of contention in Anglo-Scottish relations throughout the 1480s. Parliament in 1462 reasserted the crown's rights, won by James II in 1459, to enjoy the fruits of dioceses when they fell vacant; the path to the important concessions wrenched from Pope Innocent VIII in the Indult of 1487 was resumed early in the reign. In 1468 a parliamentary commission took the initiative to settle 'the matter of Norway', by arranging an embassy to Denmark; the resulting marriage of James III to Margaret, the twelve-year-old daughter of Christian I of Denmark and Norway, brought to an end the 200-year-old dispute over payment of an annual tribute for the Western Isles and included a settlement on the Scottish crown of all the lands and rights of the Norwegian crown in both Orkney and Shetland until Margaret's dowry was paid in full. It never was, and by 1472 the Northern Isles would be annexed to the Scottish crown; the boundaries of the kingdom had reached their fullest extent.[13]

The first years of the minority saw a bad-tempered but largely inconsequential dispute between Mary of Gueldres and James Kennedy, Bishop of St Andrews. A 'great division' in politics was Kennedy's own description, that of an ambitious ecclesiastic who had acquired a bishopric at the age of twenty-nine and whose chequered career spanned three reigns. The quarrel was at least in part another of those Stewart family squabbles which littered the history of late medieval Scotland; Kennedy's mother had been one of the daughters of Robert III. There was little doubt that power resided with the Queen Dowager and a small circle of important nobles, many of whom, like the Earl of Argyll, had gained advancement in the last years of the previous reign. Mary's death in December 1463 gave Kennedy eighteen months as the predominant figure in the royal government until his own death in 1465, but the limitations of his position may be gauged by the fact that, unlike Mary, he made no important new appointments. Effective power continued with the magnates and the king's administration continued to run smoothly, in the practised hands of servants such as Archibald Whitelaw, royal secretary from 1462 until 1493.[14]

In July 1466, James was seized, probably while hunting, by the Boyds of Kilmarnock. The episode has the hallmark of a classic noble coup. The Boyds embarked on a campaign of self-aggrandisement, including the elevation of Lord Boyd's eldest son, Thomas, to the earldom of Arran and, even more daringly, the arrangement of a marriage between him and the King's elder sister, Mary. The marriage celebrations were the first recorded instance of James III's habitual resort to tears. Analogies between the Boyds and the Livingstons, the power-brokers of the long minority of James II, seem misplaced. James III was already fifteen by 1466 and the frantic efforts of the Boyds reflected the shortness of time at their disposal. Although the Boyds tried to extend their connections amongst the greater nobility, through a marriage between Lord Boyd's daughter, Elizabeth, and the Red Douglas Earl of Angus in 1468, they did not have the close liaison the Livingstons had enjoyed with a family of the status of the Black Douglases. They lacked the family solidarity which the Drummonds had maintained in the reign of David II. Their fall in the summer of 1469, which coincided with the King's marriage, was swift and predictable. The major beneficiary was the King himself; most of the forfeited Boyd lands were added to the royal demesne. There was otherwise little disruption in the pattern of politics and no state of confusion confronting the King when he came of age. The stage was set, as in 1449, for a young king to take over the reins of power.[15]

There was another important circumstance which vitally affected royal power when the monarch began his personal reign in 1469. James III had two surviving younger brothers, Alexander and John, then aged fourteen and about twelve, and three Stewart half-uncles. Each would complicate the politics of a reign which had some similarities to that of Robert III. James III was the only monarch between James I and VI to have to contend with the problem of an adult, legitimate brother, and he had two. John, Earl of Mar, was disposed of when he was accused of treason and died in imprisonment, in highly suspicious circumstances, in the winter of 1479-80.[16] It was no coincidence that it was the 1480s, after James III's elder brother, Alexander, Duke of Albany, became an active force in politics, that was the most unsettled decade in the fifteenth century. Although James III had already had a series of disagreements with various parliaments, the first real threat to his rule came only in 1479 – when Albany publicly disagreed with him, probably over the King's relentless quest for amity with England. Indicted by the King before parliament, arrested and subsequently a fugitive in France, Albany's response was natural enough: by 1482 and the collapse of the Anglo-Scottish alliance he returned, as a client of Edward IV of England, in the guise of Alexander IV, a claimant to the throne itself.

The crisis of 1482, induced by a major invasion of southern Scotland by Albany and his English allies, triggered a family conspiracy, which was in effect an astonishing vote of no confidence in James III. It was made all the more acute because the conspiracy also probably involved at some stage his queen, Margaret of Denmark. Seized by nobles led by his three half-uncles at Lauder Bridge, en route to fulfilment of his role as leader of a nation at war, the King ended up in ward in Edinburgh Castle; his closest advisers fared worse, hanged over the Bridge itself. As the invasion floundered into uncertainty and eventually into farce with the Castle half-heartedly besieged by the English army, the rival prospects of an Albany putsch and a palace coup stumbled over each other; here was a family in dispute not only with its head but also with itself. The English army withdrew and the King was released as part of a bargain struck amongst the various conspirators for their respective shares in the future governing of the kingdom; the arrangement fell apart almost as soon as it was made. By 1483, Albany was in disgrace, exposed in another conspiracy with England and James was free to continue virtually as before. The twin coups of 1482, whether designed as a short, sharp shock treatment of a delinquent king or as a full-blooded attempt to displace him, did neither.[17]

Within six years James III was displaced, in a coup led not by distant relations but by his own eldest son and heir, by then fifteen years old. Yet despite some similarities of circumstances – in the intervening years more unpopular 'black money' had been minted and further uncertainty over the King's policy towards the new English regime of Henry VII had been rekindled by complex marriage negotiations involving not only the widower (Margaret had died in 1486) but also his two eldest sons – there was little direct connection between the rebels of 1488 and those of 1482. In essence the roots of the revolt of 1488 lay in the conjunction of the deep-felt grievances of a small number of magnates and the qualms, real or imagined, of a son whose estrangement from his father had been heightened by the preferential treatment seemingly heaped upon his younger brother, created Duke of Ross in 1488.

Although the events of 1488 in retrospect constituted a revolution as real as that of 1567 when Queen Mary was deposed, the precise agenda of the rebels is unclear. Unless there was (as in 1567) a coup within a coup and the protesters were overtaken by regicides, it seems unlikely that the aim of the rebels was anything more than a council of regency, with the son as its figurehead and the father in protective custody. The King's aims were simple enough as, armed with the sword of Robert Bruce, he and his army marched from Edinburgh towards Stirling early in June: the way to quash the coup was to seize its figurehead, the young Prince James. Indeed it was at or near Stirling Bridge, close to the scene of Wallace's victory in 1297, that James III achieved the first and last military victory of his reign. His son escaped, however, to join forces with the rebels who had progressed northwards – ironically at the site of the battlefield of Bannockburn. The battle, which was nicknamed Sauchieburn only a century and a half later, was a curious mismatch: for once a king's army mustered fewer of the great nobles of the realm than the rebel force it faced, but it was also a struggle between the magnates of the south and south-east and a King who had concentrated his rule on Edinburgh to an unusual extent. Amongst the other parts of the political community, neutrality was both more widespread and more studied than it had been in the crisis of 1482.

Assessments of the crisis of 1488 are made more difficult by the fact that it took a quite unexpected course. The King was murdered in mysterious circumstances after the battle at Sauchieburn; the parliamentary inquiry which followed found no culprit and no explanation more convincing than that the King 'happinit to be slane'.[18] The circumstances, the venue and the murderers themselves remained unexplained, despite a reward offered of 100 merks of land, until various colourful accounts were composed by chroniclers forty to eighty years after. The narrowness of the rebel cause in 1488 may be judged by the weakness of the new regime in the next two years. Unlike his father, James IV was not crowned instantly. Although he began to issue charters on the day after his father's death, he was crowned fully fifteen days later and, significantly, it was at Scone, the ancient ceremonial place for inauguration of early kings although it had not been used for the purpose since 1424. The cult of kingship, which would indelibly mark the reign of James IV, began early.

The reign of James IV (1488-1513)

If there was a real change in the practice of kingship either in 1488 or after 1513, it lay less in policy than in the mechanics of politics. James IV may have been different only in the sense that he, more than any other of the Stewarts, learned from the mistakes of his predecessors. He had served a long royal apprenticeship. As after many revolutions, the immediate years that followed 1488 saw a quest for settlement; the price that had to be paid by 1490, after two major risings against the new regime, was the return to influence of many of those against whom the original revolt had been directed, including Scheves, Archbishop of St Andrews, and Elphinstone, Bishop of Aberdeen, as well as the Duke of Montrose. By then the new administration was already more broadly based than its predecessor.[19]

After 1495 the carefully balanced representation of the different parts of the kingdom took on a different form, being located not in the potentially troublesome forum of parliament but in the King's own council. James III had followed the fifteenth-century practice of almost annual parliaments, with twenty-one in the twenty years of his adult rule; James IV had begun his reign in much the same pattern, with nine parliaments held between 1488 and 1494, but only three were held in the seventeen years after 1496.[20] The gap was filled by the calling of occasional general councils and by an enlarged royal council – a device later to be used under the different name of a convention by James VI. It would be difficult to argue that James III ruled more arbitrarily than his son, for James IV's revocation of 1504 – which was no less than his fifth whereas his father had issued only one, in the conventional twenty-fifth year of his age – was almost as breathtaking in its sweeping nature as that more infamous revocation of Charles I in 1625. Its terms, allowing all grants or acts made 'in tymis bigane . . . hurtand his saule, his crowne or halikirk',[21] can be compared only to a government entering a second term of office with a blank cheque instead of a manifesto. James II had been allowed, literally, to get away with murder; James IV was allowed to be a law unto himself.

The conundrum of 'success' and 'failure' in the reigns of James IV and his father demonstrated that there was no necessary connection between arbitrary rule and unpopularity. There may be an analogy to make with the reigns of James VI and his son. James VI was probably also more arbitrary in his dealings with parliament and his subjects than Charles I, yet he and his historical reputation, like that of James IV, has escaped largely unscathed. The approving verdicts of history tend to go to the charismatic, and never more so than in the case of the 'glory of princely governing', as Sir David Lindsay called him.[22] It may also be, in the case of James III, not simply that the King's personality was unattractive but that with this king, who even his defenders admit preferred to be an observer rather than a participator in the business of government,[23] the King's personality had been subsumed within the collective image of his daily inner council. James III's government pursued unpopular policies – such as the attempts to issue a debased coinage between 1480 and 1482, the relentless and highly skilled pressure, through various fiscal devices such as recognition, to raise revenue from the crown's feudal rights and lands, or simply the breakdown of the King's efforts to reach alliance with England which had resulted in costly war and the ignominious loss of Berwick without a struggle in 1482 – but its presentation of policy was also faulty. In either case, the direction of the protest in 1482 could be against the so-called low-born favourites. Although the reign of James IV would see still more ruthless and systematic exploitation of the crown's feudal rights, it escaped the same opprobrium. Image and the careful packaging of policy counted for as much in late medieval as in modern politics. More than any other Stewart king, and so unlike his father, James IV was a participator. He was as careful a scrutineer of the business of government within the confines of his own household administration as his contemporary, Henry VII of England (1485-1509), but James also cultivated the public persona of a warrior king, and it is for that that he is most often remembered.

James is rightly celebrated as a builder of palaces and ships rather than of monasteries, for he sought earthly rather than heavenly glory. Yet hard-headed politics were always intertwined with such conspicuous expenditure. He contrived by 1502 to expel from the minds of his subjects the memory of the humiliations of the war of 1480-2 with England. A more aggressive stance was taken in foreign policy, turning English tactics of using collaborators such as the Lord of the Isles to destabilise Scottish politics (as they had in 1462) against them. The reception given to the pretender Perkin Warbeck as 'Prince Richard of England' in 1496, which included the offer of a daughter of the Earl of Huntly as a bride, was part of two campaigns: of military attrition against England and of the familiar Stewart diplomatic offensive to secure wider recognition for the dynasty in the courts of Europe. The campaign of 1496, which in many respects anticipated that of 1513, was a disappointment for Warbeck, whose entry into his pretended kingdom lasted less than twenty-four hours, but it gave James the chance to play the role of warrior in a war of gestures. It was Henry VII, forced by rebellion in Cornwall and domestic crisis, who was compelled to sue for peace in 1497, thereby preparing the way for the marriage of James to his daughter Margaret in 1503.[24]

The significance of the marriage and the Treaty of Perpetual Peace which accompanied it was not that they set the two countries on the road to union a hundred years later. Neither Henry VII nor James IV need be thought of as a Bismarck; the essential purposes on both sides were short-term and pragmatic. The alliance barely affected the prickly nature of their relations. What it gave to James was a unique opportunity to expand the scope of the cult of the Stewart monarchy. The calculated choice of the name of Arthur for a child born in 1509, who after his mother was then the nearest heir to the English throne, was one aspect of the new patriotism. Another was an arms race; between 1505 and 1511 the massive sum of at least £100,000 was spent on the building and equipping of a navy. Its flagship was the 'great' *Michael*, designed to carry no less than twenty-seven cannon and a crew of 300 and completed in 1511. Its size was staggering – probably between 150 and 180 feet in length and of 1,000 tons – for it needs to be borne in mind that the earlier and smaller *Margaret*, which cost perhaps only a quarter as much, was at 700 tons of the same scale as Henry VIII's *Mary Rose*, completed in 1509.[25] Each age produces its own ultimate weapons of war and the worrying aspect for Tudor diplomats was that Scotland seemed to be ahead in the naval race which had begun in 1505.

Extensive building work, especially at Stirling Castle, had begun in the reign of James III but it was the construction of a *palatium* or great hall at the castles of both Edinburgh and Stirling in the next reign which marked the climax of medieval monarchy.[26] These, along with the Chapel Royal at Stirling, which had been lavishly endowed in 1501, were the venues for a brilliant Renaissance court, inhabited by musicians such as the Augustinian canon of Scone, Robert Carver, and by poets such as the Observant Franciscan William of Touris as well as that better-known churchman, William Dunbar. Here was a court which had within it both fashionable figures such as an alchemist (the Italian, John Damian, the butt of vicious satire of the disgruntled, poorer-paid pensioner Dunbar) and traditional offices such as the King's Gaelic harpist (which went back to the eighth century). The flight of Damian from the walls of Stirling Castle – straight into a dung-heap below – was a mark of the exciting intellectual atmosphere at the court as well as a chance for Dunbar to even the score. It was a cosmopolitan court, which, like the King himself, conversed in at least six languages, ranging from French and Italian to Gaelic and including, almost certainly, Danish; it combined and restated the confluence of new European fashions and native tradition. At its heart lay the cult of honour; this allowed James to play more effectively than any king since David II the 'knightly game' of joust and tournament. It culminated in the three-day tourney at Holyrood in 1508, when he overcame opponents drawn from Denmark, England and France in defence of a 'black lady', who was probably the 'lady with the meikle lippis' of Dunbar's poem. What remains incalculable, although it was the central political purpose of the cult of honour, is the extent to which it was responsible for producing the marked unity of purpose amongst his nobility. It was, ironically, that very unity, producing what was probably the largest Scottish army ever to enter England,[27] which would underlay the scale of the carnage inflicted on the Scottish establishment in the king's last campaign of 1513.

The essential facts of the short campaign which led to the disaster at Flodden Field on 9 September 1513 are simple and generally agreed; the lessons drawn from the post-mortem are not. The opposing armies, the English led by the Earl of Surrey, were of roughly equal size, each with about 20,000 men. The initial position chosen by the Scots, on Flodden Hill, where they struck camp, was favourable; so was Branxton Hill, less than two miles to the north-west, to which the Scots hurried on hearing that the English army threatened to cut off their retreat. But the hill allowed English guns to pick off the Scots in their defended positions and made it difficult for the Scots, whose expert gunners were with the fleet, to train their pieces on the advancing English. In one sense, James IV died a victim of the same obsession with military technology as James II. Both forces at Flodden had sophisticated artillery but the English guns, lighter and more manoeuvrable than the Scottish culverins, were better suited to the conditions. The bombardment forced the Scots to move forward, down the rain-soaked hill. Once their traditional schiltrom formation, which had been used to such effect at Bannockburn, began to break up on the muddy ground – some of the Scots cast off their shoes and fought in their hose – the freshly imported, twenty-foot-long Swiss pikes used by the Scots proved no match in close-quarter fighting for the shorter English halberd.[28] The carnage was heavy, though probably not as severe as the 10,000 dead – amounting to half the Scottish army – claimed in English accounts. Among those who fell were the King, nine earls, the Archbishop of St Andrews, the Bishop of the Isles, two abbots and fourteen greater lords.[29] The scale of the Flodden death roll, however, can outweigh the significance of the battle. The brief campaign which had led James to Flodden Hill via sieges of the castles of Norham, Etal, Ford and Wark was no more ambitious than his own expedition of 1497 against Norham or James II's against Roxburgh in 1460. If this was a border raid which went tragically wrong, it had, to begin with, been more successful than many before it: in 1497 Norham had resisted the siege but in 1513 it fell within five days. Was James not simply a warlord who pushed his luck once too often?

Few, however, have been content to let the judgement of history rest there. Controversy surrounds James's wider aims in 1513. Was his renewed alliance with Louis XII of France and his consequent embroilment in the complex politics of the Holy League the mark of a king who was out of his depth or, in those damning words of one historian, the actions of a 'moonstruck romantic'? James, it is true, had shown earlier delusions of grandeur: from 1500 until his death he seems to have harboured the dream of joining or even leading a crusade against the Turks.[30] Yet to dream the impossible dream was part of both the psychological make-up and the appeal of the Stewart dynasty: James III had planned an invasion of Brittany in 1472, James V toyed with the offer made to him in 1538 of the kingship or Ireland, and James VI would convince many of his subjects that he would become leader not just of a Protestant isle but of a Calvinist Europe after 1603. The real difficulty in coming to a judgement lies not in the evidence but in ourselves: no other Scottish monarch except for Mary, Queen of Scots, has been so ruthlessly subjected to the judgement of hindsight as James IV. It takes a prophetically long view of the processes of history for James to be blamed for straying from the path of a high road towards union of the English and Scottish crowns. A sharper notion of the need for a choice between friendship with France and alliance with England would emerge later in the sixteenth century, but not before the 1520s, if not the 1540s. The debate over union with England would also begin in the 1520s, with the publication of

John Mair's *History of Greater Britain*, but by then its practical terms would be vitally changed by the continuing failure of Henry VIII to produce a male heir.

It also seems harsh to suggest that Flodden marked a breach in years of developing peace with England, cemented by the treaty of 1502.[31] There was certainly a debate within the king's council both over the nature of the English alliance and the advisability of the campaign of 1513.[32] But the more widely held view was that relations with England had been unsettled throughout the reigns of James III and IV and that the brittle alliance of 1503 was more dangerous than the state of mutual hostility which had preceded it. After the death of Henry VII's first son, Arthur, in 1502 each child born to James and Margaret was seen and used as an extra bargaining counter in a hostile game of diplomacy, not as a long-term investment in a notional future union of the crowns. It is true that James's recklessness shattered the unity which he had succeeded in generating amongst the Scottish nobility by 1513, but to a significant extent the Flodden campaign was itself the hallmark of a Scottish establishment again confident of its own national integrity and unified in aggression against England.

James V: new problems, old solutions?

Flodden, so often seen as a watershed in Anglo-Scottish relations or the end of a political era, was neither of these. Although nine of the twelve earls present were killed in the battle, the main elements of crown policy and at least three of its main agents – Elphinstone, Huntly and Hume – survived. The Church perhaps suffered more from the Flodden death roll than the state, for the loss of the Archbishop of St Andrews deprived it of an invaluable link with the crown. It is hard to believe that James V or his widow after him could have remained as semi-detached from its problems if Alexander Stewart, his half-brother, had continued as metropolitan of the Scottish Church. It is also clear that Flodden took its toll, in sons of the nobility, on a future generation of magnates, which may help explain the troubles of the 1540s more than those of the minority of James V. The squabble which ensued after Flodden was in large part another family quarrel within the house of Stewart – between Margaret, the Queen Dowager, and John, Duke of Albany (son of James III's brother Alexander and heir to the throne after the young Prince James). It had in some respects close analogies with the tussle between Mary of Gueldres and Bishop Kennedy after the death of James II. Again the personal reputation of a Queen Dowager became one of the main issues in politics but it is more difficult to exonerate Margaret than the skilled and blameless widow of James II. Margaret had a bewildering succession of liaisons. She married the 6th Earl of Angus, who was slightly younger than her, less than a year after Flodden; a long, acrimonious and very public separation led to divorce and another marriage. This was to a much younger, prettier and obscure minor lord in 1526. Her embittered opposition to the return to influence of Angus, as chancellor and guardian of the fourteen-year-old king in 1527, further complicated the politics of the minority. The marriage to Angus had invalidated the Queen's position as tutrix of her young son, and it provoked an undignified tussle at Stirling Castle in 1515, when Albany, who had been appointed Governor by the king's council, arrived to claim the child. From that point, the Queen did her best to turn the affairs of the kingdom into an unseemly family tug of war.[33]

To be set against the picture of a faction-ridden minority was both the conduct of Albany as Governor and the loyal service of magnates such as Argyll and Huntly (until the latter's death in 1524) and of churchmen such as the chancellor James Beaton, Archbishop of Glasgow until 1523 and then of St Andrews. Albany during his two periods of office (1515-17 and 1521-4) was able to exploit the strong residual loyalty to the crown and he continued to try to draw upon a representative cross-section of the nobility in the council. Factions came and went during the minority, but there was a striking continuity of loyal service to the crown throughout the second- and third-rank levels of the royal administration. The simple but key fact in Anglo-Scottish relations before and after Flodden remained much the same, despite the birth of a daughter and heir, Mary, to Henry VIII (1509-47) in 1516: the Queen and her young son were dangerously close to the English succession. It was that factor – which could point towards different conclusions in the conduct of foreign policy – more than any other that added a new dimension to the faction fighting of the minority.

Albany, who was able to renegotiate the auld alliance in the form of the Treaty of Rouen in 1521, offered pensions, security and a return to the glittering years of James IV. In 1523 a new weapon of war, in the shape of a highly sophisticated artillery blockhouse built at Dunbar whose remains can still be seen, was on offer along with a 13,000-strong French invasion force, which included 8,000 pikemen and 1,000 arquebusiers. Set against that was Henry VIII's attempt to create a pro-English party, represented after 1524 by Angus. Although it is sometimes said that the way to the future – and certainly to the English sympathisers in the wars of the 1540s – lay in the appearance of a pro-English party in Scottish politics in the mid-1520s, to contemporaries Henry VIII's tactics of disruption and destabilisation would have recalled the years of Edward IV and Henry VII. Too much can be made of the 'Flodden complex': the main reason why the Scottish nobles were reluctant to invade England in 1523 was probably the fact that the French expeditionary force had arrived only in mid-October, too late for the campaigning season. By then it was an unemployed army as large as the population of Edinburgh and consuming precious stocks of winter fuel. The relief of Scots and French was probably mutual when it left in November, after a six-week stay. What undermined the pro-French party, especially after Albany's return to France at the end of his agreed term in May 1524, was a new ambiguity in French policy. A French garrison remained in Dunbar until 1525 or 1526 but Francis I (1515-47), after his defeat at Pavia in 1525, was pursuing a peace with England. The events of 1522 and 1523 demonstrated that the Scots were reluctant to risk a repeat of Flodden, *unless* the campaign was a joint expedition. The plans laid for the 1523 campaign underline the point, well understood by Albany, that military posturing remained as important an element in foreign policy and kingship as in the reign of James IV. It also shows that Scotland was as securely tied to France in the 1520s as it had ever been.[34]

James V, when he came of age and escaped from the Douglases in 1528, was no more a 'new' monarch than his father had been. In most respects his governance built on the examples and precedents set by his predecessors. The systematic expropriation of the Church built on the concessions won by both parliament and king in the reign of James III, themselves the culmination of half a century of tension between the Scottish crown and the papacy. The series of six separate taxes levied on the clergy from 1533, which grasped the moment of papal fallibility during the crisis of Henry VIII's divorce, was no new departure; by 1513 the clergy had handed over £9,000 in taxes to James IV to pay for a crusade which never took place.[35] At least one of the pretexts of James V's early clerical taxation did materialise – the salaries of the judges and officials of the College of Justice, founded in 1532. A new Pope, Clement VII, decided, like Innocent VIII in 1487 over the Indult, to give way to royal demands for finance for the sake of the larger interest of Christendom. Royal bastards were again planted in some of the chief offices of the Church; the difference again was one of volume rather than kind. Five of the wealthiest abbeys and priories in Scotland were granted to under-age bastard sons of James V between 1534 and 1541; their combined revenues are impossible to assess with any accuracy because they bypassed normal accounting procedures but it is likely that the claim later made by the Catholic propagandist John Lesley, that they amounted to 'greitar profitt to him nor the whole revenew of the crown', was true – almost certainly they amounted to more than £40,000 per annum.[36]

It may be that some concern for the future leadership of the Kirk crossed the mind of James V while he counted his windfall profits into the large chest which accompanied him on his travels from one royal palace to another: the careful education planned for James, second eldest of his nine bastard sons, may indicate that the young Prior of St Andrews (ironically to become one of the leaders of the Protestant revolt in 1559-60) was intended for as glittering an ecclesiastical career as Alexander, the bastard son of James IV who had fallen at Flodden. But the knock-on effect of clerical taxation was traumatic for the Church: forced to raise cash quickly, it resorted to feuing its lands. The benefactions of David I, a previous Stewart king had complained, made him a 'sair (costly) sanct' for the crown; the depredations of James V, who taxed the Church into insolvency to pay for the glory of the Stewart monarchy, made him the unwitting but real architect of its collapse.

The wave of royal taxation hit not only the Church but the realm itself during the 1530s. The incidence of taxation was not entirely novel, for it recalled the 1490s when various fiscal demands had resulted in virtual annual taxation; but its scale was unprecedented, inducing a series of bad debts amongst the burghs and at least one bankruptcy, that of Aberdeen.[37] The campaign against the pretenders to the Lordship of the Isles was resumed in much the fashion set by James IV, but James V also overstepped elsewhere the conventions of ruling a highly devolved feudal kingdom. Minor lairds who held high office, such as the secretary, Thomas Erskine of Haltoun, were granted lands and influence on such a scale in Angus that both the shape and stability of the local community, previously underpinned by the combined power of Lords Gray and Glamis and the Earl of Crawford, were jeopardised by 1542.[38] There were further examples of Stewart brusqueness in treatment of troublesome nobles, but the vindictiveness demonstrated in the execution by burning at the stake of Lady Glamis (a sister of Angus) in 1537 for alleged treason was almost unprecedented.

On 1 January 1537 James married Madeleine, daughter of Francis I of France, at the Cathedral of Notre-Dame in Paris. She died in July barely two months after her arrival in Scotland and within a year James had found a new French bride and a second dowry in the shape of Mary of Guise-Lorraine. Two sons, James and Arthur, were born and died in infancy by 1541; the fact that their names exactly copied those of the first-born legitimate sons of James IV is as good an indication as any that James V's dynastic ambitions closely mirrored those of his father. The world of European politics, however, was even more treacherous in the late 1530s than a generation earlier, not least because of Henry VIII's 'Lutheran madness'.[39] Much the same unreal war between the two countries as had prevailed in the 1490s reasserted itself after 1536. Tension broke into open warfare after James failed to attend a conference with Henry arranged at York in September 1541. There was great resistance amongst his nobility, not against a token invasion of England, but to resist a threatened English incursion. That in itself is a measure of the notable lack of unity which James V had managed to sow amongst his magnates by 1542. Somewhere between 14,000 and 20,000 men were mustered, about half the number who assembled in 1513.[40] The campaign of 1542 was a tragi-comedy of errors, on both sides, and unmemorable. The end came at Solway Moss on 24 November. Few Scots were killed but many were taken prisoner; the King, still twenty miles away at Lochmaben, joined the retreat. It was as great a humiliation as any since the loss of Berwick sixty years earlier. Ever a Stewart fond of the grand gesture, James shortly after retired to his chamber at Falkland, where he died – less of an illness than a lack of will to live – on 14 December. His legacy was a one-week-old daughter, Mary.

Kingship and the political community

With three personalities as different as those of James III, IV and V, the extent of their popularity is problematic. It is difficult to prove how widespread the disaffection amongst the nobility was either in 1542 or in 1482; the slogan of evil counsellors in 1482 may have been no more than that and it is likely that it was orchestrated by members of the King's own family. If the issue was not so much exclusion from power as difficulty of access to the ear of the King, it is not surprising that it was amongst the King's relations – such as the Earls of Atholl and Buchan in 1482 and Prince James himself in 1488 – that it was most keenly felt. The reign of James III had ultimately turned on the domestic politics of the ruling house. In the next reign it was not surprising that the careful balancing of royal favour and displeasure included not only the major magnates such as the Earls of Bothwell and Angus but also members of the Stewart family itself; the veteran conspirator of 1482, John Stewart, Earl of Atholl, was sharply reminded of the dangers of intrigue by the threat of forfeiture in 1504.[41] James V cultivated an image as the 'poor man's king', but his treatment of his nobles revealed the unacceptable face of Stewart monarchy as least as clearly as had the venality of James III.

There were differences between the reigns of James V and his father. James IV had relied on a corps of great magnates, not only in their own far-flung territories but also in his council. Then the balance between centre and localities had been effected by the magnates' involvement at court and, especially, in the king's council. James V, by contrast, saw something of a return to the habits of government under his grandfather, when a corpus of talented administrators had conducted most of the regular business of the governing of the kingdom. The vital men in the royal administration were again churchmen, such as James Beaton, or highly trained laymen, usually lawyers such as the secretary, Sir Thomas Erskine of Haltoun. Their involvement in government was at least as unpopular as it had been in the early 1480s, and – at least in Angus – demonstrated a new feature of James V's reign, of partisanship at court infecting local politics. It was hardly surprising that the death of James V quickly brought about the eclipse of his secretary.[42]

It has been suggested that one measure of the success or failure of Stewart monarchs was the balance which they managed to maintain between court and country: kings, it is said, ruled so successfully precisely because they asked so little of the localities. It was *laissez-faire* kingship which both distinguished the Stewart dynasty from most other contemporary monarchies and made it a signal success story.[43] The notion of a balance between crown and magnates is, however, shorthand for a more complex situation. The rudimentary nature of royal government, whether civil or legal, can be overstated. It was able, well before the reign of James VI, to collect taxation on something amounting to a regular basis; both in the 1490s and the 1530s there were a series of taxes which were national in their extent.[44] Equally, both the stability of the local community and the power of individual nobles there can be exaggerated; as with kings, power had to be conceded to individual lords rather than automatically inherited by them. In the governance of late medieval Scotland, there were not one but two sets of balances at work and both needed to operate for a longer-term equilibrium to come into being. Against the background of the growing expertise of the royal administration and the need of the crown for ever greater revenue, magnates increasingly needed to be assured of the representative character of both the royal council and court. But within each of the localities, nobles also needed *force majeure* to prevail and enough status to persuade lesser lords to ally with them by bonds of manrent; only then would their dominance over the local community be secure.

If it is the case that the real difference between the period before and after 1460 lay not in the nature of kingship but in the changing character of the nobility,[45] at least one of these balances had been drastically altered. The politics and affinities of the localities were in process of being reforged in the second half of the fifteenth century. After the eclipse of the Black Douglases in 1452 there was no one single noble family in a position of such unrivalled power, until perhaps the Hamiltons in the 1540s. The 1450s had seen the beginnings of the rise to prominence of a series of families whose names would figure prominently throughout the sixteenth century and beyond – including the 'race of Hamiltons' who were first based in Renfrewshire but later ranged across much of central Scotland, the Campbells in the west who were elevated as earls of Argyll, and the Gordons in the north-east as earls of Huntly. Seven earldoms had been created by the crown between 1452 and 1458;[46] but neither influence at court nor power in a locality was guaranteed by royal favour in itself. Part of the confused picture of the politics of the 1460s resulted from the fact that none of these new creations had enough credibility at court as yet to mount a decisive challenge to a middle-ranking but ambitious noble family such as the Boyds, who had seized authority in 1466 through holding possession of the person of the King. Equally, these new earls were not yet in full command of their own territories: the Gordons took fully twenty years to displace the influence in the north-east of the Earl of Mar and the Campbells took more than half a century to cut a convincing figure as the head of Gaeldom in the Isles. The first point at which the twin balances might be said to have come into satisfactory operation was not until the second half of the reign of James IV.[47]

Kingship and the dark corners of the land

There is an extra dimension in which the politics of these three reigns can be cast and it throws some doubt on many generalisations about the workings of politics in this period. Strenuous efforts were made, especially by James IV and V, to control affairs in both the far north and the west and it is there that the crown was conspicuously unsuccessful. On the face of it, this was the period in which the Scottish crown finally made good its claims to both the Western and the Northern Isles and the kingdom achieved its mature form. The Lordship of the Isles, an office held by the Clan Donald which was traceable to the mid-fourteenth century but with a genealogy stretching back at least five centuries before that, was annexed to the crown in 1493; the son of James IV was named, significantly, as 'Prince of Scotland and the Isles'.[48] The comital rights to Orkney and Shetland, held by the Scottish family of Sinclair, were finally gained by the Scottish crown in 1470, a year after Christian I of Denmark had laid the islands in pledge as security for the dowry due on the marriage of his daughter to James III.[49]

Each acquisition was also a vivid illustration of the limits of royal power. The so-called Lord of the Isles was the derivative, via Latin, of the much older title *Rí Innse Gall*, meaning 'ruler' or 'king' of the Hebrides. The Sinclairs, who had acquired the earldom of Orkney in 1379, were heirs to a title which originated in the ninth century during the period of the Norwegian settlement of the Northern Isles. Both the Western and the Northern Isles were settled and highly conservative local societies, which proved extremely resistant to change and intervention by outsiders. It is worth remembering that the first surviving bond of manrent, usually taken as an emblem of the stability of the local community, was made between the Lord of the Isles and a lesser client.[50] In the case of Orkney and Shetland, the crown initially used bishops as its agents; the main Sinclair line, which already held lands in Fife, agreed to an exchange of the royal castle at Ravenscraig in Fife for its comital rights in Orkney. The result was a struggle which lasted for more than a century between rival branches of the Sinclair family, with the crown caught, usually helplessly, somewhere in between.[51] Here was a case where the crown had been strong enough to muscle its way into a territory, but its power was too remote to maintain the internal balance within the locality, which had hitherto been provided by a single dominant family.

The case of the Isles was more complex, not least because of the vast extent of the Lordship, which stretched from Islay in the south to Lewis in the north, or the number of men who owed loyalty to it. Bower's estimate of 10,000 Islesmen at the battle of Harlaw in 1411 may have been an exaggeration but not by much, for in 1545, in the last campaign of Donald Dubh, 180 galleys and 4,000 men were mustered at Islay. The Achilles' heel of Lordship lay in the earldom of Ross, to the east of its main holdings, which it had acquired in 1437. The focus of its running disputes in the 1480s and 1490s lay in the earldom: this had not been included in the restoration of 1476, when John MacDonald, the Lord, was rehabilitated for his dealings with England in the 1460s. In 1478 John was declared a lord of parliament, an inferior rank, in a process which seems to anticipate Henry VIII's later policy towards Irish Gaelic chieftains of surrender and regrant. Yet Clan Donald power in the Lordship, which rested on centuries of kinship and fealty, was barely touched by such censures of crown or parliament.

Like the royal house of Stewart, the real weakness of Clan Donald came from within: the efforts to regain Ross seem to have caused a fatal breach within the family, between John and his illegitimate son and heir, Angus Og. Yet the manpower available even to a divided Lordship should not be under-estimated: Angus razed the king's castle at Inverness to the ground and at 'Lagebraad', somewhere in Ross, in 1480 he inflicted one of only two defeats by rebels of a royal army (except for Sauchieburn itself) in the whole medieval period. After Angus's death in 1490, it was Alexander MacDonald of Lochalsh rather than John who took on the mantle of Clan Donald warlord and it seems to have been a series of raids made by him on Easter Ross which precipitated the forfeiture of the Lordship in 1493. Although John himself was reduced to the role of a prisoner in exile at the Scottish court until the end of his life, the Lordship itself survived the assaults of both the crown and its agents for a further fifty years. James IV journeyed to confront the Islesmen in person at least five times after 1493; his later parliaments of 1504, 1506 and 1509 were all largely concerned with insurrection in the west. There were six major risings in the Isles between 1494 and 1545; the fact that the most serious was the last one reiterates the failure even of that 'terrifying' king, James V, to 'daunt' the Isles. The entrenched resistance of the Lordship throughout these three reigns is a salutary reminder that the Stewart monarchy was not always *laissez-faire*; in the Isles it was at once at its most centralist and its most unsuccessful.[52]

The traditional policy of the crown for centuries had been to rely on dominant and trustworthy magnates to control the far-flung localities. The core of its difficulty in the west was to find a satisfactory substitute for Clan Donald. Both the Earls of Huntly and Argyll were repeatedly turned to as king's lieutenants in the north and each disappointed; as late as 1531 the Campbell 4th Earl of Argyll was dismissed for his failure to pacify the Isles. The tactics of the Campbell family, which were to claim for itself the role of 'headship of the Gael',[53] caused a further confusion of aims; cadet MacDonald clans and others naturally turned to them to intercede on their behalf at court. The Campbells found themselves in the familiar position of colonial governors, torn between going native and representing the values of 'civility' – they had added the Lowland-style 'p' to their name in the 1470s.[54] They found themselves trapped in the same set of pressures as the last Lord, fluctuating between their roles as agent of central government and natural spokesman of the values of the local community.

Stewart government exacerbated rather than solved the problem of the Isles; every reign between that of James III and VI faced a rebellion in the west. Royal policy fluctuated throughout the sixteenth century – as did that of the Tudor government confronted with much the same problem in Ireland – between attempts to 'civilise' Gaeldom and outright conquest. The case of the west suggests the need for caution in claims as to the 'triumph' of the Stewart monarchy.[55] Its route out of its difficulties in the west was ironic indeed: the two most overmighty subjects of the sixteenth century – the Earls of Argyll and Huntly – were creatures of its own making, as part of its risky investment in the 'daunting' of the Isles.

Part III
THE LONG
SIXTEENTH CENTURY

11

RICH AND POOR IN THE REFORMATION CENTURY

IN THE PERIOD BETWEEN 1500 AND 1650, SOMETIMES CALLED BY DEMOGRAPHIC historians the 'long sixteenth century', Scotland experienced a dramatic rise in its population, the first since the thirteenth century. The rise, which was probably of the order of 50 per cent, affected the whole of society, rural as much as urban, Highland as well as Lowland. Although the proportion of the Scottish people living in towns probably did not rise, remaining at somewhere less than one in ten, it was in the burghs that the population increase was most keenly felt. In Edinburgh the population doubled between 1550 and 1625 and tripled by 1650.[1] Yet in many, if not most other towns there was probably a much more modest rise in numbers which could be absorbed without disturbing the fabric of society. Such increases took place despite recurrent outbreaks of plague and regular, though usually localised, harvest failures. As a result, the poor would have been both more conspicuous and more vulnerable than in the fourteenth or fifteenth centuries, especially in the larger towns. Here, population increase was coupled with other pressures. Some, like the active market in land and a sharp rise in prices of the basic commodities of life, were new; others were familiar but felt much more sharply in this period, such as a drastic fall in the value of the currency and an increase in the size of the gulf which already separated rich and poor, landlords or landholders and landless.

Few contemporaries understood this complex of social and economic problems and fewer still tried seriously to alleviate them but, by the end of the sixteenth century, it would be the reformed Church which thought most about them. In the 1590s it tried to establish model parishes in the fastest-growing towns. There was no sudden increase in church building to cater for growing numbers of parishioners. First came planning; it was the Edinburgh presbytery which instituted the capital's first census in 1592. The direct result was two new churches, Greyfriars and the Tron, but it took over fifty years to build them both.[2]

It would be easy to label the combined effects of these pressures as a crisis of massive social dimensions, but that would convey an oversimplified picture of a century and a half of near-continual crisis. One of the paradoxes of the period was that by the later 1570s Scotland was staging a recovery in its export trade after a long slump which, with a brief respite in the 1370s and 1380s, had lasted since the Wars of Independence. By the 1590s Scottish overseas trade was booming and fortunes were being made by merchants and landowners alike. For them, the two symbols of the period might be said to be Gladstone's Land, a six-storey, luxury flatted tenement built c.1600 in Edinburgh's Lawnmarket, which was the hub of Edinburgh's merchant establishment, or the baronial houses of an increasingly confident landed 'middling sort', such as Fyvie in Aberdeenshire or Seton and Lethington (later renamed Lennoxlove) in East Lothian, all built more for display than defence. A French visitor, the Duc de Rohan, claimed in 1600 to be able to count more than a hundred such châteaux from the walls of Edinburgh Castle.[3] Few if any such durable monuments of the lower ranks of sixteenth-century society, urban or rural, have survived; their experience lies buried in the dry and often formidably complex statistics of mortality rates and subsistence crises, the likelihood of increasing mobility of population and evidence of a drastic fall in standards of diet.

The recovery of overseas trade

The factor which most obviously marks out the long sixteenth century from the two centuries which preceded it was the rise in exports. Much of it was not the result of either the finding of new markets or a shift into new commodities. The bulk of foreign trade still followed the familiar routes, to northern France, the Netherlands and the southern and eastern Baltic. It was only after the 1590s, when the recovery had found firm roots, that Scots merchants and skippers pushed further into the northern Baltic, towards Swedish ports such as Stockholm, or further south towards Spain. Until the later seventeenth century, the commodities in which they traded remained mostly the same as those which for centuries had formed the bulk of Scotland's exports: raw wool, partly treated skins and hides and other animal products. The range of imports increased steadily, although most still took the form of manufactured goods or luxury foodstuffs.

There were other areas of expansion or recovery. Manufactured cloth, much of it cheap, coarse and of low quality, was shipped from Dundee and other east-coast ports to make up a sizeable proportion of the packs of *Krämerwaren* which Scots pedlars hawked through the hinterland of Baltic ports.[4] They left a double legacy: many settled there in the sixteenth and seventeenth centuries and their names are still often recognisable even after being naturalised; and their cut-price wares often aroused local resentments. Salt and coal from the Forth basin were being shipped by the 1580s in increasing quantities from ports like Crail, Inverkeithing and Culross to the Netherlands. And by 1610 Edinburgh merchants were making vast profits from the export of surplus grain to the Netherlands and the Baltic; they made equally large returns from importing grain from the Baltic in times of dearth, like the lean years of the early 1620s when much of Lowland Scotland was hit by recurrent failures of the harvest.[5]

Recovery from the long slump came first in the late 1530s; the annual returns from the customs peaked at £5,820 in 1541, double the average figure for the 1460s. The effects of the 'Rough Wooing' – the seven years of English invasion, garrisoning, forced quarter and economic dislocation between 1544 and 1551 – were dramatic: by 1544-6, exports were running at only one-seventh of the levels of the last years of the reign of James V (1513-42). By 1551, they had recovered to £3,000 per annum, where they remained for the whole of the 1550s. This was a recovery equivalent to the level of the early 1530s, but not to the boom years at the end of that decade.[6]

The effects of this bitter war were not evenly felt throughout Scotland, for there was still no national economy as such but a collection of local economies, which, even in normal circumstances, often showed different patterns of health or decay. It is likely that much of the west coast, even as far south as Ayrshire or Galloway, remained largely undisturbed. Even on the east coast, which suffered the brunt of English activity, the fortunes of individual burghs varied widely. Haddington, which had managed to survive the economic squalls of the fifteenth century more or less unscathed, was badly hit by the troubles when it became for a time the English military headquarters; its once thriving cloth trade virtually disappeared and its economy took more than half a century to recover. By contrast Dundee, with an English force occupying the strategic point of Broughty Craig, two miles to the east of the burgh, for much of the 1540s, experienced a severe slump rather than collapse. By 1553 it had recovered, if not to the scale of its boom years, at least to that of the early 1530s. The military crisis of the 1540s accentuated the growing inequalities within the existing patterns of overseas trade.

Towns in growth and decay

Far more damaging than temporary political instability to most medium-sized or small towns, such as Stirling or Dunfermline, was the remorseless growth of Edinburgh. Since the first loss of Berwick in the 1330s, Edinburgh, with no serious trading rival between the English border and the Firth of Tay, had claimed an ever-larger share of the export trade. By 1500 it paid 60 per cent of all customs; by the 1590s its share had risen to 72 per cent. Within certain sectors of the export trade, its share was still greater: by the end of the century it monopolised the trade in wool, had over 80 per cent of the trade in hides and woolfells and even claimed 65 per cent of the export of coal. Increasingly the economic well-being of other east-coast towns depended on their ability to diversify into other areas not monopolised by Edinburgh.[7] Those which fared best were the small specialist ports, especially of Fife and the Firth of Forth like Dysart, Crail and Anstruther, which were able to exploit the new and growing demand for fish, salt and coal, or the other large regional centres, such as Aberdeen, Dundee and Perth, each of which remained the natural market place of its large hinterland. The recovery of Crail was spectacular, for by 1579 it was assessed at four times the tax it had been paying in 1535; only then, it is likely, was its elaborate double market street town plan, which had been laid out in the thirteenth century on the basis of its share of the then thriving fisheries, fully occupied. It was a striking feature of early modern Scotland that it had so few towns of any size; the only three, apart from Edinburgh, which could have had a population of 5,000 or more were Aberdeen, Dundee and Perth.

Of these larger towns, there seems to have been no one, simple recipe for economic survival or prosperity. There was no such thing as a typical sixteenth-century burgh: towns were as varied in their structure then as now. Aberdeen, which had never been a highly developed industrial centre like Perth but was the natural exit point for the produce of a vast hinterland, survived the fall in its trade in wool by a greater reliance on the lucrative trade in salmon and the export of plaiding made in the network of small towns around it, such as Alford or Inverurie. Dundee, as it lost more of its trade in skins and hides as the sixteenth century went on, increasingly relied on textile production, but here the work probably took place within its own walls; Aberdeen, in contrast, seems to have relied on a system of putting-out to weavers and spinners in its rural hinterland. Perth, far more a manufacturing centre than any of the others, though one with little interest in textiles, saw a very sharp decline in its export trade as the River Tay began to silt up; already in the 1550s its craftsmen claimed that it was a 'dry town far from the sea'. Its survival depended more and more on its inland trade; customers for its metalworking and leather trades extended far beyond the sheriffdom, even into Inverness-shire. By 1600 Edinburgh together with its port of Leith was the undisputed entrepôt for the great bulk of Scottish trade.[8]

In Edinburgh, the concentration of royal administration and the law, especially after the formal establishment of the Court of Session in 1532, joined forces with the increasing monopoly enjoyed by its merchants of most branches of foreign trade. Aberdeen merchants were forced to base themselves in Leith for much of the year, to the dismay of the town council which saw its own harbour left as a 'dry pond'. But the social consequences of the focusing of Scotland's trade on this bustling, overcrowded centre, built on a steep, eccentric site almost a mile away from running water, are difficult for the twentieth-century mind to imagine. Its wells could supply human needs but not those of medieval industries such as tanning, which were forced to cluster along the Water of Leith to the north. A miniature army of carters, carriers and sledders was needed to convey commodities to and from its port of Leith, which was almost two miles away, and the higher Edinburgh's tenements grew the larger its force of domestic servants became. The capital (for such it had in practice been since the reign of James III) was still a small town by modern standards, but by the second half of the sixteenth century it was threatening to burst at its narrow seams. Its site comprised no more than 140 acres, of which only two-thirds were available for housing.

Although a metropolis, Edinburgh thought of itself as a single community, which was symbolised by the fact that it still met, as it had done since the foundation of the burgh more than four centuries before, as a *corpus christianum* in its one parish church, of St Giles. After the Reformation of 1560, although the Protestant reformers split this awkwardly shaped collegiate kirk into three separate churches, separated by walls, and sent one of the burgh's four quarters to worship in Trinity College, on the site of the present-day Waverley station, they still retained the notion of a single 'general kirk' of the burgh. By the 1590s, however, such was the increase in population that the presbytery instigated a census, which discovered 8,003 adults, living almost exactly equally to the north and south of the High Street. The presbytery demanded eight model parishes, each catering for 1,000 parishioners, but soon settled for four. The building of separate churches took time – Greyfriars, the church of the south-west quarter, did not open until 1620 and work on Christ's Kirk at the Tron in the south-east did not begin until 1636 and finished in 1647 – but if there was one moment which for Edinburgh marked the effective break with the medieval burgh, it was the break-up of the centuries-old single urban parish.[9]

In both Aberdeen and Glasgow it was also the sheer increase in population which forced a similar breach with the past in the same decade; in Aberdeen the burgh's two ministers settled matters by drawing lots for the newly divided St Nicholas' Church. In Dundee, by contrast, where the huge St Mary's Church continued to accommodate a population that even in the 1480s already had 4,000 adult parishioners, the watershed in its history came later, during the crisis years of the Wars of the Covenant. As in other east-coast towns, probably a fifth of its population died in the severe plague epidemic of 1645, but this natural disaster was compounded by a man-made one, in the shape of Cromwell's army, which in 1651 'stripped even to the sark' its inhabitants. At least another 2,000 were killed in forty-eight hours of non-stop pillage and murder. Yet by 1660 it is likely that most of Dundee's losses in population had been made up, by migration into the town from its hinterland and further afield; the town council even offered free burgess-ship as an inducement. The result was a huge turnover in population: at least one in three Dundonians in 1660 would have been newcomers. It is difficult to imagine so great a change in the shape of an urban population before the rapid influx of Irish into Glasgow in the 1820s.[10]

In Dundee's rival on the River Tay, Perth, the story of the period is a rather different one. Here was a town which seems to have been afflicted by recurrent social and demographic crises. The generation before the Reformation of 1560 saw a bitter struggle for power between its merchants and craftsmen; by the 1580s the crafts were taking to the courts in Edinburgh rather than to the streets to force a settlement. The town had been growing in the late fifteenth century: it was the first of the Scottish burghs to develop a suburb, to its west in the area of New Row and Mill Wynd. It was also severely affected by both plague and famine: in 1584 the kirk session made a census of the town's poor, and counted 1,175, which accounted for at least a quarter of the population. The *Chronicle of Perth* graphically describes the recurrent subsistence crises which followed between then and the ill years of the 1620s; the phrase 'great dearth' is repeated in one page out of every three. By the 1630s Perth, which had been recognised since the fourteenth century as one of the 'four great towns of Scotland', was in genteel decline: in 1639 it was ranked only eighth in a tax roll based on burgh rents, behind Glasgow, Leith and even Dumfries.[11]

In most towns the rise in population could be accommodated comfortably enough and brought only modest social tensions. The great majority of the sixty or so royal burghs still had populations of well below 3,000 people; Lanark and Peebles had less than 1,000 inhabitants in 1640 and Stranraer and Nairn only about 500. The smaller the town, the more likely it was to be little different in outlook or social structure in 1650 or even 1700 from what it had been in 1500. The frontier between the medieval burgh and what is often called the pre-industrial town was a flexible one, and most Scottish towns moved across it only in the eighteenth century.

The rise of Edinburgh

It was in Edinburgh that the pace of demographic and other change was at its greatest. There, however, the physical problems which faced the town by the reign of James VI were not simply those of catering for the pressure of more human bodies competing for limited space. As early as 1500 the council complained of the 'greitt confluence of sempill peipill' who thronged daily through Edinburgh's fourteen markets; hucksters and chapmen were drawn to this trading centre from as far away as Perth or Dumfries. Increasing numbers of animals were also herded into the town, mostly along the street called the Cowgate (first mentioned in the record in the 1320s), to be slaughtered, butchered and skinned within its precincts. Their wool, hides or skins would then be carted the two miles to the port of Leith for export. The price to pay must have been utter congestion – not so much of people but of animals, with all the dirt, noise, smell and ordure that they brought with them. In 1499, Edinburgh exported 44,325 sheepskins, 28,740 skins of other animals and 24,347 hides. By 1598 the staggering total was 196,672 sheepskins, 204,526 other skins and 36,658 hides. It was small wonder that the Cowgate, which earlier in the century had been the place of residence of such notables as Cardinal Beaton and the regent, Mary of Guise, began to be vacated by the better-off. The rise in human population and the dramatic increase in productivity of traditional animal-based industries was the central factor in the social history of Edinburgh between 1550 and 1650.[12]

By 1650 Edinburgh was a different town, though a burgess born there in 1500 would have had little difficulty in finding his bearings in 1650. The basic street plan remained much the same as a century earlier, constrained by the difficulty of the terrain sloping steeply away on either side of the volcanic ridge down which the High Street ran. A new tolbooth had been constructed inside the west end of St Giles', but the old one in front of the church remained. Parliament House had been built in the 1630s where once the graveyard of St Giles' had lain and two new churches had been built. On the south side of the High Street, the number of households had doubled between 1592 and 1635, but most, it is likely, were not the typical Edinburgh multi-storey tenement we might expect: they were still either two- or single-storey ('laich') dwellings, often with a yard at the back where a craftsman pursued his trade or animals were kept. The buildings, institutions and customs of the burgh remained much the same, but in reality they were being stretched to a new breaking point.

Expansion affected the various parts of the medieval burgh community differently and in Edinburgh by 1650 it had already begun to result in a new kind of workforce. Although the population had more than doubled since 1550, some parts of it actually declined. The numbers of weavers and waulkers halved. Workers in the textile and clothing trades, who were already amongst an under-class, fled to new suburbs, like Dean, which sprang up along the Water of Leith to escape the higher taxation in the burgh. By the 1640s Edinburgh merchant capital would seek to re-organise them in a new, more disciplined working environment, the manufactory. The best-known of these was the Newmills Cloth Manufactory set up at Haddington in the 1640s; it was a failure, as was its successor re-established fifty years later, but it pointed the way towards the future. Other groups, like those working in the various branches of the leather trade, saw a sharp fall in their income in the second half of the sixteenth century. By the seventeenth century their numbers too were falling, as the bulk of the butchering of animals began to be put out to nearby towns like Dalkeith.

The wives and widows of burgesses had traditionally been given protection in the medieval burgh. Brewing for centuries had been almost a reserved occupation for them alone; 288 female brewsters were recorded in 1530. The founding of the Society of Brewers in 1596, based on new technology and backed by Edinburgh merchant capital as well as the considerable pockets of 'Jinglin' Geordie', George Heriot, goldsmith and money-lender to the crown, probably did more than any other single act to undermine the economic status of women in this period. Protected monopolies like brewing had been an important safety net in a society with no compulsory poor rate but where one household in five was made up of single women. There had been another important hedge against the uncertainties of life in the sixteenth century. Different sources of income were offered some protection against rising prices, falling real wages and fluctuations in demand, which were especially marked in the sectors of the economy geared towards the export trade: the poorer the household, the more jobs it had.

By the mid-seventeenth century, various pressures probably combined to force a new specialisation amongst the workforce. By the end of the century, the scale of social change in the capital was dramatic: the lawyers thronging the capital's law courts had, according to their tax assessments, more accumulated wealth than all the merchants and craftsmen put together. They and the gentry who had begun to acquire town houses had new tastes to satisfy: there were eighteen schoolmasters and seven schoolmistresses, forty booksellers, printers and stationers and as many as sixty-five wigmakers recorded in the poll tax of 1691. The greatest change, however, lay in the structure of the workforce. The most common occupation, accounting for 45 per cent of those employed, was in domestic service. A miniature army 4,360 strong – and three out of every four of them women – served in the households of the legal and merchant establishments and in the town houses of the landed classes. A hundred years before Edinburgh's New Town was built, on an open site to the north, a virtual new town and a new economy was already emerging out of the structure of the old.[13]

The effects of the dramatic growth of Edinburgh were felt far beyond the limited confines of the capital. In the course of the seventeenth century a new relationship was forged between town and surrounding country. Suburbs sprang up in clusters around three sides of the town. Manufactories, such as for the making of paper and glass, sprang up as early as 1612 in new industrial zones such as Dalry.[14] The satellite towns of Musselburgh and Dalkeith grew and prospered on the basis of the textile and leather trades and the food processing which had been moved out of Edinburgh. The routing of so much of the export trade in hides, fells and skins through Edinburgh and Leith by the second half of the sixteenth century had a knock-on effect on the whole of the Forth basin. Even as early as the 1570s, Kirkcaldy had no less than twenty-eight salt-pans and Dysart a further sixteen. More salt was needed to cure what must have been an over-supply of meat brought to Edinburgh. More coal was needed to fuel the salt-pans, for up to six tons of coal were needed to produce one ton of salt. The rising economic fortunes of Fife lairds in the early seventeenth century had much to do with the new profits to be made from coal and salt. By the 1630s the Earl of Wemyss was making a *weekly* profit of 4,000 merks from his salt-pans. Doyen of them all, however, was Sir George Bruce, who by then had accumulated a miniature industrial empire of forty salt-pans.[15]

The sixteenth-century economy: change and continuity
Towns were the conduits through which trade flowed and also the focal points of Scotland's economy. The commodities customed at exporting towns provide one of the very few measurements of the volume and nature of overseas trade and the pace of economic change. Scotland was in most respects still a poor, undeveloped country, in which change was slow, uneven and highly variable. The increasing funnelling of trade through the larger ports and especially Leith tends to give a misleading impression of the development of a single Scottish economy. In reality Scotland still had not one but a chain of local economies. Few areas by 1600 were regularly any more than self-sufficient in terms of crops and grain; surplus grain by the 1590s was being shipped from Caithness to Leith for consumption there or for

export, but this was as yet unusual. Scotland was still highly dependent on its income from exports precisely because it remained a largely pastoral economy in which primary produce in the form of animals or minerals was exported to pay for the import of a range of manufactured articles.

The trade statistics derived from customs records, valuable as they are, are skewed because they reflect not the volume of trade or the exact relationship between one sector and another but the excise duties levied on different commodities by the crown; and it, as governments do, tended to put higher duties on the growth areas of the economy. In the fourteenth century, the highest duties had been on wool. In the rearrangement of customs duties made in 1597, the most heavily taxed sectors were salmon and manufactured cloth. In 1614, however, a notable document was drawn up, which can claim to be both the first accurate statement of Scotland's trade and the first official report on the economy as a whole. It took the form of a survey of 'the wairris and commodaties that ar shippit and transportted furthe of this kingdome yeirlie' between 1611 and 1614. The total value of Scotland's exports, which was calculated as a yearly average by the compiler, was £736,986. By English standards, this was puny: English exports in 1613 stood at almost £2.5m sterling, or £30m Scots. Even if Scots exports overland, which were not counted in the survey, were taken account of, it is unlikely that the total volume of exports was more than 4 per cent of England's. In another sense, this is a less than useful comparison for the vital factor lay in the balance of trade at which, in the case of Scotland, we can only guess. Part of the extreme nervousness expressed by English MPs in the debates on a union between England and Scotland in 1606-7 stemmed from a fear that both the English market and some of its overseas outlets would be swamped by cheaper Scots cloth. The English textile industry was as vulnerable to foreign competition in the seventeenth century as in the twentieth.[16]

The 1611-14 survey shows an economy in state of slow but significant transition. Just over half of its exports by sea came from the produce of the land; hides and skins alone accounted for a third of the total but raw wool, once the mainstay of the export trade, had by now shrunk to 7 per cent of it. Although it is often said that Scotland still had a 'medieval' economy until rapid changes overtook it in the last quarter of the seventeenth century, a hidden transformation of it had already taken place. By the 1670s, when the market in the Baltic for hides and skins collapsed, that sector would follow the downward path already marked out by wool. The growth areas of the economy in the seventeenth century lay in fish, coal, salt and grain. In 1614 fish, especially herring from the west-coast ports of Dumbarton and Ayr, already made up over 20 per cent of exports; this sector would expand until the 1680s, but then contract rapidly. Exports of coal, worth 3 per cent by the reckoning of 1614, when about 16,000 tons were produced a year, doubled by the 1680s but then fell away for the better part of a century. The salt trade, worth appreciably more than coal in 1614, was booming by the 1630s; losses in the Dutch and Baltic trade by the 1650s may, however, increasingly have been offset by increasing domestic consumption. After c.1610 grain, mostly barley and malt rather than wheat, was brought by ship from the north and north-east to the Forth for export in modest quantities until its overseas markets began to dry up in the 1690s.[17]

The two major growth sectors of the late seventeenth-century Scottish economy are thought to have been in linen and cattle. Their value earlier in the century is unknown: although the 1614 survey noted that much linen cloth and yarn was 'daily' carried overland into England along the drove roads, it did not quantify the trade. There are, however, a number of indications to show that overland trade through both Berwick and Carlisle was sharply increasing by 1600.[18] The amount of redirection taking place in Scotland's export trade by the first quarter of the seventeenth century has probably been underestimated. As well as a shift in the balance of commodities exported there was already a drastic change in the directions taken by foreign trade. Parts of the old economy were booming, as shown by the record levels achieved by hides and skins in their traditional markets in the Netherlands and the Baltic during the 1630s. Trade was also spreading outwards, out of the grip of the monopoly previously exercised by the staple port at Veere. Traditional commodities were still largely being sent there, but grain and coal were mostly sent direct to Rotterdam or other Dutch ports; and much of the widening range of imports was also shipped from ports other than the staple.

In overseas trade, as in other parts of the Scottish economy, we need to think in terms of an old economy and a new, operating side by side in the early seventeenth century. Edinburgh's merchants happily worked in both sectors: the basis of their income came still from the traditional patterns of exports, in skins and wool, but their greatest profits came from the new trade, in finished cloth and grain.[19] The major difference between the Scottish economy in 1614 and 1750 lay only partly in the development of the linen and cattle trades with England; just as significant was the value of re-exports. By 1750 these would account for over half of all exports; in 1614 they totalled only 5 per cent. The same figure probably also demonstrates the main difference between the English and Scottish economies in the seventeenth century. England had a 'stronger' economy and a more favourable balance of trade only if its re-exports from its colonies to the Continent are taken into account; otherwise its trade was in deficit.

As in trade, so in the rest of the economy. The seventeenth century saw a dual Scottish economy – it had a basic agricultural sector, which still produced a narrow range of staple commodities; it had a more limited arable element, but only in scattered parts of the country, such as Fife, East Lothian or Caithness, was there much food produced which was surplus to local needs. It had also a more sophisticated sector of consumption, for which most materials were still imported but some, such as soap, glass and paper, were increasingly manufactured at home. Like the merchants of the capital, some landowners operated in different sectors, arable as well as pastoral. The lairds of Fife exported salt and coal rather than skins or wool. For some landlords, over the course of the long sixteenth century there was a shift from seeing their estate primarily as a source of manpower, both for purposes of farming the land and for status, to viewing it largely as a source of profit.[20] For others, there can have been little difference between the patterns of farming or settlement on the land in 1650 from those in 1500. Rural settlement was still as scattered, even though eighty-five market centres in the shape of burghs of barony were founded between 1600 and 1660. The structure of farms was still as varied.

179

The local community

Much of the concern of historians of the sixteenth and seventeenth centuries is now with the 'localities'. Power in the Scottish state was shared between centre and localities. The links between them were intermittent and ill defined. The first bridge between them came, it has been argued, when the courts of the reformed Church set up a chain of authority, extending from the General Assembly sitting regularly in Edinburgh to the rural kirk session.[21] There is truth in all of these thoughts. Yet there was no such thing as a typical locality. Just as there was no one Scottish economy but a series of local ones, each with its own distinctive features, so the notion of the 'localities' is really a contradiction in itself.

Scotland did not have a specific 'county community', such as in contemporary England, either in structure or ethos, until the 1640s, when the demands of putting the country on a war footing gave a new cohesion to the shire. To some extent, the focus of government lay in the sheriffdom, which was overseen by a royal, but usually hereditary office. But the natural bonds which held local society together or focused its attention did not always coincide with the sheriffdom. There was no equivalent of the English quarter sessions, where Justices of the Peace might meet or local gentry vie for office. The shape of the Scottish local community was looser and more fluid. By the end of the sixteenth century royal government would seek to intrude itself into this community and to impose a new uniformity, not only of local authority but also of the contacts between it and central government. The course taken by that new interference took different forms and its success varied considerably, even in Lowland Scotland. Part of the reason for this chequered record lay in the very variability of the local community.

The sheriffdom of Ayr illustrates the point; it was almost a reproduction of Scottish society in miniature. The seat of the sheriffdom was in the larger of its two royal burghs, Ayr, which lay within the bailiery of Kyle. It had within it one of the few areas of good arable land on the south-west coast and was described in an English survey made in the 1560s as 'plenteous in corne, bestiall and fische, populous of men'. But Kyle was one of three bailieries within the sheriffdom and each had a very distinct structure, political as much as economic or social. The southernmost area was Carrick, made up of underpopulated, upland pasture. It was, according to the same survey, 'a barren country but for bestiall' and 'the people for the most part speak irische'; the area traversed the boundary between Highland and Lowland culture as well as that between an upland and lowland economy. Without any substantial burghs, it had only one major religious house, Crossraguel Abbey. That was held by the Kennedy family, which enjoyed unrivalled power within the locality. The survey counted nine Kennedy lairds of substance; they and three other 'allyers', who were of a different kin, were all linked to the Earl of Cassillis. The northernmost bailiery was Cunningham, where the politics of the locality revolved around not one major noble family but two: the Cunninghams, Earls of Glencairn, and the Montgomeries, Earls of Eglinton. The survey identified a further seven Cunningham lairds and six Montgomeries. The structure of the community was complicated still further by the presence of a lesser noble, Lord Boyd, and a number of other lairds, including the Mures, whose allegiance was flexible, as well as the representative of a major outside family, the Hamiltons, who held the Abbey of Kilwinning. In Kyle itself, at the centre of the sheriffdom, local politics was more diffuse, being shared amongst more than half a dozen families, whose status ranged from lesser noble to greater laird; prominent among them were the Stewarts of Ochiltree and the Campbells of Loudoun, who held the office of sheriffship in the 1560s. But the office of provost of the burgh of Ayr was held usually by a branch of the Hamilton family, the Hamiltons of Sanquhar.[22]

It would be possible to argue that the sheriffdom of Ayr, as the equivalent of the *pays* which was the focus of much of society in western Europe of the period, did have a certain political reality. But the course of politics, religion and changes in landholding in the sixteenth century all demonstrated the diversity of what were in effect three local communities within a larger region which had at best only a loose identity. Carrick, taking its lead from the young Earl of Cassillis until he married the daughter of the very Protestant Lord Glamis in 1566, remained largely Catholic. Cunningham's religious allegiances were as divided as its politics: the Cunninghams were early converts to Protestantism but their age-old rivals in feud, the Montgomeries, stubbornly held on to the old faith for some time after 1560. The area identified by John Knox as the stronghold of Protestantism in the south-west lay in Kyle, though outwith the town of Ayr itself. Its most consistent adherents lay amongst the various Campbells, all cadet branches of the wider Campbell kindred; here, it is worth noting, the ties that bound crossed the boundaries of the local community, whether defined as Kyle or as Ayrshire. So the spread of Protestantism in Kyle and in Cunningham followed rather different paths, largely because of the different structure of the kindred on whom it depended.

In Cunningham, both religion and politics were further complicated by the intrusion into the locality of outside families from Renfrewshire; prominent among these were the Hamiltons who extended their influence by a combination of three different means, all of which have a wider importance in sixteenth-century history. Their initial southward push into Ayrshire stemmed from the feuing of royal lands in the last years of the reign of James IV. They consolidated their position through the acquisition of Kilwinning Abbey in 1527; the Hamiltons, never slow to see trends to their own advantage, were among the first of the lay commendators. The feuing of its lands and other kirklands benefited both Hamilton power and pockets; no fewer than eighty feu charters were drawn up between 1557 and 1560 by Gavin Hamilton, Commendator of Kilwinning. But his death in 1571 and the reversion of the Abbey into the hands of the Earl of Glencairn transformed the politics of Cunningham.

Landowners and feuars

Feuing is the most complicated of the many complex processes at work in sixteenth-century Scottish society. It was a reflection of an active market in land which already existed and of the need for both the crown and pre-Reformation Church to realise its landed assets to raise cash. The effects of feuing on the shape of the local community are disputed but few other processes did as much to transform it. Feuing began with crown lands which, though authorised by an act of parliament of 1458, took little actual effect until after the act was ratified in 1504. The two short but significant bouts of feuing came between 1508-12 and 1538-42. Its immediate effect was sharply to increase the crown's revenue from its lands: in 1450 this has stood at £1,840; by 1509 annual income had increased to £9,245 and by 1542 to somewhere in the region of £15,000 per annum.[23] These sums were modest and the amount of land involved would have been insignificant had the process not been followed in the 1540s and after by the much more widespread resort of the Church, under pressure to meet the steeply growing demands of taxation made upon it by the crown, to feu a large proportion of its kirklands.

Both the overall size of the feuing movement and its precise effects are incalculable. Theoretically at stake, in the hands of the Church, was a third of the agricultural land of Scotland but feuing, like every other process in early modern Scotland, varied in its effects from one local community to another. In some places, such as Shetland where lease and rent steadily displaced udal tenure, its effects were slight. In other areas, such as Strathisla in Banff, which formed part of the estates owned by the Abbey of Kinloss, the social effects of feuing set in motion in the mid-1530s lasted for over a century and a half. There three-quarters of the new feus were agreed with the existing occupants of the land; landholders enjoyed, at an initial higher price, the benefits of an enhanced security of tenure and a new status as small proprietors.[24] The genesis of a new branch of the 'middling sort' whose rise was fundamental to the shape of sixteenth- and seventeenth-century Scottish history was born of the feu charter.

Elsewhere the effects of the feuing of kirklands were more mixed: 44 per cent of all feuars, it has been calculated, occupied the land already; perhaps a further 13 per cent, whose names are obscure enough to resist identification, might be added to the total.[25] Yet averages apply to a local community which hardly ever existed. In Ayrshire, 53 per cent of kirklands went to sitting tenants in both Kyle and Cunningham. But this is to summarise a process which went on for more than forty years. The clustering of feu charters in a short space of time would often have created an impression of a sudden alienation of tenure. In Kylesmure, the pattern of feuing before 1560 concentrated holdings in the hands of small sitting or 'kindly' tenants; but after 1560 the beneficiaries were larger lairds. Rather less of the Kilwinning charters, which usually involved larger parcels of land, went to the occupants in the breakneck sale of eighty feu charters conducted in Cunningham by Gavin Hamilton on the eve of the Reformation. In Carrick, there was much more continuity in patterns of landholding until the mid-1560s, when Crossraguel fell out of Kennedy hands and its new commendator suddenly began to feu.

It may be that feuing often confirmed possession in the hands of those who already worked the land, thereby ensuring a continuity of possession which helped hold together the basic structure of the local community. Simple calculation shows, however, that as often as not tenants had their land sold from under them, usually to lairds or nobles. Also, in at least a quarter of these cases land fell into the hands of outsiders – lawyers, burgesses or crown officials – who would usually have been absentee landlords.[26] Such nobles or lairds might well be in process of becoming *rentiers*, by feuing out smaller parcels of land which they themselves had acquired by feu; here it is difficult to believe that the new economic relationship between superior and vassal did not adversely affect the existing ties of kin and bond. The price such tenants had to pay was more likely to have been higher rents rather than eviction. As such, feuing merely mirrored the general trend towards higher rents and shorter leases. The gap between the benefits enjoyed by those who owned land and those who held it on other terms was widening sharply in the period. The

Jacobean economic miracle which brought prosperity to the landed classes was paid for by their tenants.

For those fortunate enough to join the new class of feuars, it is possible to talk in terms of a new self-confident and rising class, who would in the course of the next century begin to claim influence to match their new-found status, often within the kirk session. Only very rarely, however, did their influence extend beyond the bounds of their local community. Nonetheless, power in Scotland for magnates as much for lairds largely resided within the locality. By 1625 Scotland, still a land composed of baronies and regalities, possessed most of the characteristics of a feudal kingdom, whose political focus remained in a parliament made up of tenants-in-chief of the crown. These emblems of feudal power camouflaged a political system which had undergone a hidden transformation. History was, in one historian's notable phrase, 'slipping away from the feudal superior'.[27] The process was so gradual that it should not be exaggerated; but it was so unobtrusive that it is easy to forget its eventual, revolutionary effects.

The price rise

Feuing was a Pandora's box whose effects could scarcely have been realised by either the superior or vassal who were parties to a feu charter. There was also a joker in the same box, the effects of which began to take hold only in the 1570s. It was the price rise. Once the initial down payment (the grassum) was made, the feu, although probably higher than the old rent, was fixed; as prices rose, its real value fell. Various calculations have been made to gauge the scale of price inflation; although they disagree on the detail, they have in common the conclusion that the price rise was on a scale unparalleled before the sixteenth century and unmatched until the twentieth. General prices, it has been calculated, rose fourfold between 1550 and 1625. Between the 1530s and the 1630s, some agricultural prices, however, rose almost ninefold; barley sold in Fife rose from 16s to 140s a boll over the period. In Edinburgh, the official price of bread, which was controlled by the town council, rose eightfold between the 1530s and the end of the century.[28] Just as the real income of most wage earners in the burghs, such as labourers or journeymen, can be shown to have failed to keep pace with the price rise, so it is likely that the income of most who farmed but did not own land fell as well.

Price inflation, like the effects of war, came relatively late to sixteenth-century Scotland. When it did come, in the 1570s rather than as in England in the 1540s, it was also linked to deliberate depreciation of the coinage by the crown. It was the Regent, Morton, who first called down the silver content of the coinage, in the aftermath of the civil war which ended in 1573. Like the 'black money' of James III, the new coinage was intensely unpopular and did more than anything else to alienate Morton's former allies in the war, the merchants of Edinburgh. Depreciation hastened the fall in the value of the £ Scots: in 1456 it had been worth a third of the £ sterling; in 1560 its value had sunk to about a fifth; by 1600 it had collapsed to a mere twelfth. Price inflation, so often argued to be one of the major factors undermining English society in the sixteenth century, was in Scotland far worse in its dimensions.

The combined effects of rising exports, major shifts in the patterns of landholding, severe price inflation and a falling currency demand a careful measuring stick in their effects on the different compartments of Scottish society. The losers – those on falling money wages or the tenants liable to pay higher rents – are obvious, although the scale of their falling standard of living is more difficult to assess. There was a sharp change in diet for most ordinary townspeople and rural labourers, from one based largely on meat to one dependent on barley and oats, which would give Dr Johnson the material for his dictionary entry that the diet of the Scots and their horses was indistinguishable. There was also a sixfold increase in the price of wine over the century putting it out of the reach of most.[29]

For the beneficiaries, the winnings were mixed. For the nobles, the effects were complex indeed: in 1500 most probably enjoyed payment in kind from their lands; by 1600 and certainly by 1625 most were living on credit. An expanding economy brought new luxuries, novel opportunities and a new-found indebtedness. For merchants, there was at least as much profit to be made from money-lending as from overseas trade, whether in the new economy or the old; but, as experience would show, lending money to nobles was as hazardous as investing in sea voyages liable to shipwreck or piracy. The greatest beneficiaries, though perhaps the most unexpected, were the ministers of the new reformed Church. Despite their failure to secure the whole revenues of the old Church in or after 1560, the clergy, whose income was tied to the produce of the land, gradually began to reap the benefits of incomes that were inflation-proof. By the early seventeenth century their average income was considerably above that of the average English vicar. In the local rural community, it was the minister who usually had more disposable cash than any amongst his congregation. Enjoying extra benefits such as the free education of his children, the minister, with little on which to spend his income, often lent it at interest to members of his flock. The highly paid ministers of Edinburgh – from John Knox in the 1560s to Alexander Henderson in the 1640s – lent, by contrast, to the nobility. Both are salutary and startling lessons of the unwonted effects of the long sixteenth century.

A new community of the realm?

The greatest change which took place is the one most difficult to define – for it lay in the nation's sense of itself. Scotland by 1600 was a society in ferment. Still marked out by the recognisable landmarks of a feudal kingdom – a parliament called by James VI 'the head court of the king and his vassals', sheriffdoms, royal burghs and baronies – the channels of communication between them were in a state of flux. Buffeted by impersonal and often incomprehensible economic forces, Scots clung to the familiar – to the notion of Scotland as a commonweal,[30] or to local society as a self-contained 'country' or burgh community. The century which from the 1540s onwards experienced recurrent pressure for a union of Scotland with England also produced a new flowering of patriotic literature. The poetry of Barbour and Henryson and the plays of Sir David Lindsay were never so popular as in the last quarter of the sixteenth century and the first quarter of the seventeenth. The advent of the printing press, originally intended as a propaganda arm of King and Church, had by 1600 produced a new popular literature catering to a broadly-based 'middling sort' in society ranging from lairds to lawyers, ministers to merchants.[31]

For centuries kingship had acted as a stabiliser of Scottish society. Yet at the end of the sixteenth century what it represented was deeply unsettling. When James VI rode south to claim the throne of England in 1603 he did so born of the confidence that he was of the ninth generation of the house of Stewart to reign over Scotland and the 107th of a line of Kings of Scots stretching back into early history. The notion of a king of a greater Britain – which was always what he aspired to – calculatedly put the identity of the Scots themselves in question. The king's government before and after 1603 organised a shoal of propaganda in support of union. A new British history was officially inspired, along with fresh legends of the origins of kings of Scots. Emblems of a new British identity – flags, coins, heraldic devices – were manufactured.

Old symbols of the tenants-in-chief of a feudal kingdom – charters, noble genealogies (both real and counterfeit) and histories of great and not so great families – were dug out or commissioned to combat them. A re-awakened literature of Scottish patriotism ran counter to the anglicisation of those courtiers who stayed with James VI in London after 1603. The result of the long sixteenth century was a nation in intellectual turmoil – in search of its past as much as its future. The witch-hunt, which peaked in the 1590s, the late 1620s and in 1649 and 1661-2, was another product of this age of uncertainty. Only a fraction of the 30,000 once estimated to have fallen victim to the Scottish witch-hunt did so. Nevertheless, Scotland saw far more 'witches' burned or drowned for their alleged beliefs than religious martyrs executed for their faith. No single explanation of the motives of the witch-hunters exists: Calvinist zeal, a search for scapegoats on whom to visit the sins of society and a new violence of the state were all involved. The hapless victims, nine out of every ten being women, were the scapegoats for the vagaries of a rural society in which illness struck without warning and animals died mysteriously. Yet the witch-hunt was as much the mirror of a crisis of the intellect as it was the product of a society stricken by a harsh climate and periodic economic crises. The leading persecutors were mostly lairds and ministers, the educated and better-off.[32] It was hardly surprising that many Scots – such as John Napier of Merchiston whose invention of logarithms helped him work it out to the thirty-ninth year of the seventeenth century – took refuge in the imminent prospect of the millennium.

12

ROADS TO REFORMATION

THE REFORMATION OF 1559-60 IS SEEN AS THE FUNDAMENTAL FACT OF SCOTTISH history. It marked a decisive rejection of Rome, the Latin mass, papal jurisdiction, sacerdotalism and much else. From it can be traced a national system of parish schools, the Scottish concern with the democratic intellect, and a new sense of nationhood expressed in terms of a covenanted nation.[1] Like most revolutions, however, events were confused, allegiances often mixed or ambivalent, and the new regime which came to power drew on the personnel and inherited most of the problems of the old order it replaced. Scotland already had a substantial system of different kinds of schools, located in the houses of lairds as well as in burghs; the foundation of three university colleges between 1495 and 1544 suggests increasing provision of grammar schools. The initial problem in 1560 was not more schools but better endowment of existing ones.[2] As with the revolution of 1488, most accounts of the Reformation crisis were drawn up afterwards, as party pamphlets or moral chronicles whose purpose was often to lend a renewed sense of purpose to the difficult and confusing years when they were written. Modern historians are not usually expected to supply moral certitudes or clear-cut events; they probe and ask awkward questions of the evidence. The purpose of history for them is not didactic – as it often was in the sixteenth century when John Knox, in the preface to his *History of the Reformation*, asked the 'Christian Reader' to look for the 'simple truth . . . in this last and most corrupted age'.[3] Historical truth, in reality, tends to be confusing, ambiguous and often contradictory. There is more than one possible road to the Reformation of 1560 – that of a Protestant movement which, from slender beginnings, would in the course of two generations gain sufficient strength to stage a revolt in 1559 and of the medieval Church in process of recognising its own failings while combating the spreading virus of heresy amongst both its clergy and flock. Both roads, it shall be seen, often take divergent paths from a straight and narrow interpretation of the inevitable break-up of the Church.

The growth of Protestantism

Heresy was probably a more significant problem for the Church in the fourteenth and fifteenth centuries than the scanty records reveal. It was fuelled by the regular exposure of clerics to Wyclifite, Hussite or other unorthodox ideas during their studies abroad, usually in this period at Louvain, Cologne or Paris. This very fact bred an obsessive fear in the minds of the higher clergy of the dangers of heresy. Like the foundation of St Salvator's College in 1450, part of the reason given by Bishop Elphinstone for the need to found a university college at Aberdeen in 1495 was to counter the spread of heresy, although there seems little evidence for it in the north-east. Yet Lollardy did exist. In 1494 a number of Ayrshire lairds and tenants were summoned before the Lords of Council accused of unorthodox opinions. The fact that the names of some of them – such as Reid of Barskimming or Campbell of

Cessnock – would figure amongst supporters of the Lords of the Congregation two generations later lends some support to the view that Ayrshire 'accepted each phase of the Scottish Reformation as it came'.[4] Yet deep Protestant roots in Ayrshire were confined mostly to Kyle, the centrally placed of the three districts of the shire. Kyle acted as an incubator for Protestantism but there is little or no evidence that it acted as a platform for its spread elsewhere, for even the county town of Ayr was markedly inconsistent in its religious stance up to and into the crisis of 1559. Two other features of this outbreak of Lollardy were unusual: the reason the accused escaped with no more than a mild censure may have been that they were protected by James IV's mistress – Marion Boyd, who came from a prominent Ayrshire family.[5] Despite this, there is no trace of heretical opinions at the court before the 1530s. Also, all but one of the thirty accused were lay men or women, which may help to explain the isolated nature of the group. The subsequent history of Scotland's earliest Protestants was in large part that of dissident clerics, who accounted for ten of the twenty-one executed for their faith between 1528 and 1558.

The first Protestant martyr was not only a young and talented theologian but also a member of a prominent landed family. The burning in 1528 of Patrick Hamilton, who had studied at St Andrews and Wittenberg and taught at the new Lutheran University of Marburg, may have left as deep an impression on the psyche of the Established Church as on the still fledgeling Protestant movement; the line between speculation and unorthodoxy, especially in a university community, in the swift-moving European scene of the late 1520s was a fine one and the calculated brutality of the execution may have left its mark on many. One such was Henry Forrest, then a St Andrews student, who was in minor orders when he went to the stake in 1533. The more usual response was probably a growing uneasiness; such seems to have been the reaction of John Winram, whose conversion to Protestantism came over quarter a century later, when he helped John Knox and others compose the Protestant reform programme.[6] The martyrs in the 1530s were few – ten in all – but the exiles were many. Especially after 1536 it was the intellectuals who fled. Many went first to the court of Henry VIII, whose chief minister, Thomas Cromwell, had established a circle of Protestant clergy and academics. This was, however, usually no more than a temporary refuge. Subsequently they went abroad – often to academic careers, like Alexander Alane (or Alesius), in northern Germany or, like John MacAlpine (Maccabeus), in Scandinavia. Few returned to their native land.

The result was a serious vacuum in leadership, which took a generation to fill. One who did return from England was the charismatic preacher George Wishart, who had flirted with the radical ideas of Anabaptism while at Bristol. He was, however, the first of the reformers to draw together some of the disparate strands of Scottish Protestantism. His eighteen-month preaching mission in 1544-5 was dangerous because it was conducted 'not in secret but in the audience of many', at Montrose, Dundee, Ayr, Mauchline, Leith and Haddington, where he was arrested. His trial, in February 1546, was unusual: intended as another legal showpiece before an invited audience of nobles and clerics in the great Cathedral of St Andrews, it did not follow the stereotyped procedure of most such show trials, where persecutors and persecuted alike went through well-rehearsed positions. Wishart's eloquent appeal to scripture alone discomfited the prosecution and evoked enough sympathy among the audience for the authorities to think it prudent to clear the church for the verdict.[7] The effects of his death were mixed: it left an indelible mark on the consciousness of many would-be Protestant sympathisers but it also deprived the Protestant movement of a natural spiritual leader for over a decade – until Knox returned to Scotland for a brief mission in the winter of 1555-6.

The paradox of a religious movement which seriously lacked pastors in part explains its inchoate nature. Its beliefs are too difficult to assess in strict theological terms; resort has to be made to what literature survives, such as the *Good and Godly Ballads*, a compendium of evangelical hymns and populist ballads gathered together sometime before 1560 by James and John Wedderburn, sons of a Dundee merchant, but published in its existing form only in 1565; or to the censures of Church or parliament, such as the nine statutes passed in 1541 banning 'dispute of the holy scripture' and the desecration of statues of the saints and enjoining respect for the sacraments and the Blessed Virgin.[8] Its demands before 1558 were few and simple: preaching of the Gospel, prayers in the vernacular, communion under both kinds. Yet this almost certainly disguises a deep spiritual commitment felt among its adherents to a personal faith marked by a devout biblical Christianity, which was nourished by access to William Tyndale's edition of the New Testament in English, first printed in 1526.

These very characteristics of Scotland's early Protestants have resulted in the tendency to try to assess their strength in the period between the mid-1530s and the mid-1550s by numbers – which have in themselves been the subject of fierce debate amongst historians. The case that Protestantism had a 'firm footing' a generation before 1560 is based partly on the survival of about a hundred identifiable victims of the sudden campaign against heresy waged by Cardinal Beaton between 1538 and 1543; but it also rests partly on the conjecture that the bulk of the 1,000 'assured Scots' who collaborated with the English during the wars of the 1540s had Protestant sympathies.[9] There are various other pieces of evidence which yield up less equivocal evidence and their net result is a list of 168 accused of heresy or otherwise identified by contemporaries as Protestant sympathisers in the period up to 1546, which is the nearest ever produced to a 'who's who' of the movement. One conclusion to be drawn from it is that Protestantism appealed to a broad cross-section of society ranging from barons or lairds to urban craftsmen, such as the five inhabitants of Perth executed in 1544, although nobles as yet were few. Amongst the clergy, it affected ordinary parish priests or vicars as well as scholars, canons or friars. Another is that the precise extent of early Protestantism is probably unquantifiable for there are likely to have been many more who, under pressure from the Church authorities, apostasised and 'burnt their bills'.[10] Each repentant heretic was a minor victory for the Established Church; but each recantation also helped drive the movement underground and make it all the more difficult to extirpate completely.

In practice, what mattered was the attitude of the natural leaders of society – magnates, lairds and burgh councils. Again there are two ways to deploy the evidence of numbers. In Angus and the Mearns, one of the areas where, Knox claimed, 'the greatest fervencie appeared', all five nobles in the locality – the Earls of Crawford and Marischal and Lords Glamis, Gray and Ogilvy – had some attachment to the new religion at least for part of the 1540s. So had a close-knit circle of about thirty lairds, but they amounted to only about a tenth of the lairdly establishment in Angus. The fact that Protestantism was almost everywhere a minority movement need not be disputed – most revolts start out as such. Much more important to discern are the dynamics of the movement in the localities where it had its greatest strength – in Angus and the Mearns, Fife, and Lothian in the east and in Ayrshire in the west – and the links which it managed to forge between localities, despite the absence after 1542 of that natural breeding-ground of conspiracy and fashionable ideas, the royal court.[11] In the Mearns, the vital extra ingredient was the spiritual leadership and co-ordination provided by John Erskine of Dun, a laird who would become a formidable preacher and theologian and after 1560 a superintendent of the new reformed Church. The fact that such charismatic organisers were few and far between explains both the strength of Protestantism in certain localities and its weakness as a national movement.

Another natural incubator of radical ideas was urban society – in Germany and the Netherlands it had been in the towns where Protestantism had made its first and most dramatic advances in the 1520s. In Scotland, however, towns were smaller and located further apart in a landscape of dispersed rural settlement. The case for arguing that Protestantism was a swelling movement in the generation and a half before 1560 is at its weakest in the towns. Knox claimed that eight burghs – Ayr, Brechin, Dundee, Edinburgh, Montrose, Perth, St Andrews and Stirling – were won over to Protestantism by 1559. It is more likely that there was a sizeable Protestant presence in only two – Dundee and Perth. In Edinburgh, the number of identifiable early Protestants up to 1556 is under forty and when the town was offered a religious referendum in the summer of 1559 it had been the Protestant minority that had claimed that 'Goddis treuthe' should not be made subject to the 'voiting of men'; even as late as Easter 1561, eight months after the Reformation parliament had abolished the mass, only 1,200 – one in six adults amongst the capital's population of 12,500 – went to Knox's new Protestant communion. There were few if any large-scale, overnight conversions of urban populations, either before or as a result of the Reformation crisis of 1559-60. The atmosphere in Edinburgh and perhaps elsewhere was of an overwhelming lack of commitment to either party in the fracas of 1559-60; the resultant task of the new Protestant ministers in many if not most towns after 1560 was that of missionaries in an environment that was usually suspicious rather than outrightly friendly or hostile.[12]

Yet the small numbers of Protestants in the capital had hidden strengths. Ever since the first traces had emerged in the late 1530s, Edinburgh Protestantism had been concentrated amongst the wealthier merchants and lawyers and their wives. This was less important as a platform from which to capture the rest of the burgh establishment – even by late 1562 only one-half of the top 100 Edinburgh taxpayers were willing to offer even a token conformity to the new church of John Knox – than as a linking mechanism with Protestant opinion at the court and in the royal administration. By the mid-1550s, the house cells of Edinburgh's Protestants were beginning to be organised on a more formal footing, with readings and commentary on passages from scripture and the administration of communion in a 'privy kirk'. Their meetings were attended by crown officials such as William Maitland of Lethington, future royal secretary, and the Master of the Mint, David Forrest; both would figure prominently in the diplomacy of the Congregation in 1559-60. But there also seem to have been regular visitors from some of the localities to the privy kirk in the capital, notably Erskine of Dun. It was these contacts, extended further during the mission of Knox in 1555-6 when he visited both Angus and Kyle after a brief stay in Edinburgh, which may have produced privy kirks in both those localities under the patronage of sympathetic lairds. Yet the horizons of such patrons was limited in the first instance to their own 'country' and the setting up of some kind of ministry there. That was why the revolt of 1559-60 if it was to succeed had first to establish itself as a revolt of the provinces.[13]

There is a paradox to grasp here about the strengths of Protestantism as a movement. Only in Dundee did a burgh council unequivocally allow the spread of Protestant preaching before the onset of the crisis of 1559; a blind eye was one thing, outright defiance of the crown another and even there the preachers were advised to lie low at Easter 1559. Even in Dundee it is possible to detect other directions being taken in the 1540s and 1550s. Robert Wedderburn, brother of the Wedderburn evangelists and vicar of Dundee, wrote the *Complaynt of Scotland* in the period when the burgh was being very roughly wooed by an English army, an impassioned plea for the (orthodox) reform of Church and commonweal and a powerful restatement of Catholic nationalism.[14] Even if some Dundee guilds were diverting funds from their saints' altars into other channels of piety such as relief of the poor, the town in the 1550s was still trying to have the great parish church of St Mary's erected to collegiate status. Dundee, where the 'faithful exceeded all the rest in zeal and boldness', nevertheless did act as a fulcrum for the spread of Protestantism throughout the whole of Angus and the Mearns.[15] There was by contrast, in the case of Perth, little evidence of impact beyond its walls and no trace of a privy kirk, even though it almost certainly had a larger Protestant element amongst its population than Edinburgh. Its religious convictions seem to have been enmeshed in local politics; in 1560 the craftsmen would allege that the martyrs of 1544 were victims of a political conspiracy engineered by the merchants in retaliation for an attempted craft take-over of the town council.[16] Protestantism in Perth as a result was politically tinged, inward-looking, leaderless but sharply anticlerical – and thus ripe for John Knox, who went directly there rather than to Edinburgh when he returned to Scotland in May 1559.

As events quickened in 1556-9, what was the decisive turning-point? The first sign that Protestantism was beginning to regroup after a decade of survival as an underground Church 'under the cross', came in December 1557 with a 'common bond' in which 'the Lords and Barons professing Jesus Christ' promised to 'apply our whole power, substance and our very lives to maintain, set forward and establish the blessed Word of God'. The 'First Bond' was the first of many religious covenants in the history of Scottish Protestantism. Its language was robust but its specific aims were modest and cast so as to be acceptable to all shades of Protestant opinion: it was against sin , 'Satan and all wicked power' (even if care was taken not to identify the great Satan), and for the establishing through their own efforts of 'faithful ministers purely and truly to minister Christ's Evangel and sacraments to His people'.[17] Its aim was to induce Protestantism out of the noble and lairdly household and to restore to the movement a political dimension which it had lacked since it had become tainted by the strong-arm tactics of the English invasions of the 1540s. It was also a bond of alliance and thus an attempt, like conventional bonds of alliance, to forge a link between equals. Although Knox claimed that many added their names later, only five signatories attached their names to the First Bond; but this is hardly surprising for what was being attempted was a bond between supporters of fledgeling territorial reformations. However firm the foothold, the next step was infinitely more difficult to take. Each local reformation was grounded in a deeply conservative and inward-looking society; the very act of attempted co-ordination into a national movement of protest was the most radical – and risky – step Protestants had yet taken. It would need the coincidence, in 1558, of two further events to galvanise Protestantism into action.

The marriage of Mary, Queen of Scots, to the Dauphin Francis in April 1558 heightened the nobility's fears that the administration of Mary of Guise would become increasingly French-dominated; the 'example of Brittany', which had been annexed to the French crown in 1532 after a royal marriage, may have conditioned a number of minds. What made up many minds was the burning of an obscure, elderly Protestant schoolmaster four days later, on 28 April 1558. It was out of the ashes of Walter Myln, so Knox claimed, that there sprang 'thousands of his opinion and religion in Scotland'. It was the threat of a renewed campaign against heresy which prompted the more open protection of Protestant preachers by Protestant notables. Protestant piety and Protestant politics had begun to come together. Still the tide stubbornly refused to flow in one direction. In September 1558, what on the face of it seems to have been the most spectacular demonstration of Protestant feeling to date took place; a riot broke up the traditional annual procession through Edinburgh in celebration of its patron saint. The 'idol of Sanct Giles' was seized by the demonstrators and ritually drowned in the nearby Nor' Loch. Yet the centrepiece of the day's celebrations – and what probably made them so offensive to the burgh's Protestants – was to be the public recantation of a number of heretics.[18] It may well be that in Edinburgh and elsewhere the more open display of Protestant feeling in 1558-9 took place against the background of more effective action by the Church. Clearer battlelines than before were being drawn up; the period of an unreal peace was at an end.

The pre-Reformation Church

The establishment of the twin archbishoprics of St Andrews and Glasgow in 1472 and 1492 had proved a distinctly mixed blessing for the Church. More often rivals than partners either in internal reform of the Church or the pursuit of heresy, the two archbishops would, true to type, make different choices when confronted by the crisis of 1559-60. Beaton of Glasgow fled to France before the Reformation parliament, taking with him most of the records of his archdiocese; his subsequent role in Paris was more as the career-trained diplomat which he was than as a leader-in-exile of the Scottish Church. Hamilton of St Andrews stayed on, an isolated figure lacking effective contact with the rest of the higher clergy; the locus of his strength after 1560 lay, tellingly, not within his archdiocese but in Paisley, which was part of the extensive landed holdings of his own, largely Protestant family.

Even if there was little co-ordination amongst the higher clergy, there was from the last quarter of the fifteenth century onwards a renewed closeness between Rome and its 'special daughter'. The relationship was in part about the ordinary and almost daily stream of business – dispensations, indulgences, appointments to benefices and suchlike which from the recent exploration of the records of the Roman *Rota* and the Sacred Penitentiary seems to have continued unchecked to 1559. It was also in part a contest of power-brokers – the crown seeking another papal subsidy, whether in 1532 or in 1555; the papacy itself toying with filling the vacuum in the hierarchy created by the carnage at Flodden with Italian placemen; or the unedifying but all too frequent spectacle of rival contenders for ecclesiastical office lobbying, both in Rome and at the Scottish court. The grant of the status of legate *a latere* to Cardinal Beaton two years before his murder in 1546 did, briefly, further strengthen links with the Holy See. And both the 1540s and 1550s saw a steady stream of queries from Rome about the state of the Scottish Church and a series of papal visitors to inspect it – in 1543, 1556 and 1559. By the 1550s two sets of proposals for internal reform of the Church had materialised. One was, as we shall see, the product of efforts by the Scottish province itself, emanating from St Andrews which must have been widely recognised as a Catholic reform centre by the early 1550s. The other, drawn up by Cardinal Sermoneta in 1556, was the product of the *Curia*; but three of the five bishops whom it identified as likely agents of reform were dead by 1559. Whatever the faults of the Church, it was far from being blind to its own shortcomings.[19]

It is difficult to make easy generalisations about the condition of the pre-Reformation Church, for it was a patchwork of endemic faults and new initiatives. The health of the religious – monks, canons regular and friars – tended to vary from one order to another, and at times even from one religious house to another. The monasteries, so often criticised as being out of touch with the needs of sixteenth-century society and moribund, were dealt a telling double blow by one modern historian: as an institution, he concluded in two memorable phrases, each survived only as a 'property-owning corporation' and the 'most damning fact' about their inmates was that they 'played hardly any part in the Reformation, on either side'.[20] This may cast a novel role for monks who were not trained as shock-troops in religious controversy. They were as unfitted for Catholic evangelism as for Protestant. It was the friars, and especially the Friars Preachers (the Dominicans) who took up the weapons of evangelical preaching. They were far more formidable opponents for they took on the Protestant preachers on their own ground. And this may have been the reason why so many friaries were targeted for sacking by the Congregation in 1559.

In England, Thomas Cromwell's agents had scoured the monastic houses for spiritual corruption and sexual immorality to find pretexts for the dissolution of the monasteries in 1536. They found more than enough to fuel an accompanying Protestant propaganda campaign. Scottish monasteries, however, seem to have largely escaped the worst moral vices. They were, however, in difficulty. The greatest recent change in monastic life was the rise of commendators as heads of religious houses. The trend, which began in the early part of the century but reached its height in the twenty years before 1560, may not have scarred the religious houses as grievously as was often thought; even the most scandalous of James V's appointees – the four bastard sons provided to five monasteries between 1534 and 1541 – were all at least technically clerics. Commendation did *not* result, as most historians used to maintain, in the widespread secularisation of the monasteries for more than half the commendators were bishops. More significant was the fact that the new commendators, whether sons of nobles or products of the prolific loins of James V, were all faced with the same economic pressures which induced them to secularise monastic property to keep their houses in being. Although commendation did little to lend a new sense of urgency to the religious, it probably did not fatally wound them either.[21] There were, on the contrary, signs that traditional devotions were flourishing in many houses and the number of novices was on the increase. Young men were flowing into the monasteries in the 1550s rather than flocking out. All of this might be summed up as a modest monastic revival.[22] If there was a monastic crisis, it was one of economics rather than of spirituality; these property-owning corporations were more vulnerable than most to the continuing decline in the wool trade which, after a brief upturn in the late 1530s, crashed in the dangerous years of the 1540s. It was small wonder that they chose to feu monastic lands when confronted with huge tax demands.

The century before the Reformation was, in one sense, a period of achievement for the Church. Between 1495 and 1544 three university colleges were founded – the College of St Mary in the Nativity (better known as King's College) at Aberdeen in 1495; and in St Andrews, St Leonard's College in 1512 and St Mary's in 1544. In the century after 1450 almost 100 collegiate churches were erected; by 1500 there were twelve in Lothian alone. Two-thirds of them were rural, usually sited close to the main residence of a lay magnate or laird who looked to it as the family burial place. The collegiate church, in which votive masses were said throughout the day for the souls of the dead, clearly demonstrated the widespread appeal throughout all levels of society for this kind of devotional piety. Vast sums were expended by townspeople on the erection of burgh collegiate churches – such as St Giles' in Edinburgh and Holy Trinity in St Andrews. Within each of these churches a multitude of aisles and altars were founded – more than forty in St Giles', over thirty in Holy Trinity – each with their own saint and chaplain, with masses strictly regulated by the founder, whether an individual or a guild. The incorporation of craft guilds in the burghs, which largely took place between 1475 and 1530, accompanied the new cult of purgatory and the saints. The fabric of medieval society was never so complete as in the first half of the sixteenth century: its organic unity was located in the refurbished collegiate churches, which still housed all the community; its privileged members were given new emblems of their status in the guild altars; and the burgh's sense of ordered hierarchy was symbolised by the new Corpus Christi procession. Far from being moribund by the early sixteenth century, the burgh church probably came closest in the *ecclesia Scoticana* to meeting the growing demands of its flock.

The price of both of these sets of achievements was the same – the further bleeding of the ordinary parish system. All the new university foundations and many of the collegiate churches were financed by the system of appropriating parish teinds. By now 85 per cent of all parishes had some or all of their revenues appropriated. The system had been with the medieval Church almost since a new parish structure had emerged in the twelfth and thirteenth centuries, but it meant that the sixteenth-century quest for reform created a vicious circle. It established a cycle of poverty from which there was escape only into further abuses: parish priests, in order to augment their falling incomes, resorted to pluralism and absenteeism or to imposing unpopular charges on their parishioners. The effects, though, were not as bad as they might have been: underpaid vicars and curates, for the most part, did attend to their pastoral duties diligently and as a result there was little of the aggressive anticlericalism directed against the parish clergy which marked other parts of Europe. Nor should too direct a connection be drawn between the endemic faults of the Church such as appropriation and the incidence of Protestantism. In Ayrshire, where every one of the shire's forty-three parishes were appropriated, there was a significant Protestant presence only in Kyle; in the two other districts of Cunningham and Carrick the response was much more mixed. In the Catholic heartland of the diocese of Aberdeen, where some 95 per cent of parishes were appropriated, protests came from the cathedral clergy but not from a Protestant presence which hardly as yet existed.[23]

The economic problems of the Church – appropriation, feuing of kirklands, the disparities in income between well-endowed abbeys and the mendicant orders, between the higher clergy and the impoverished parish vicars – constituted the Gordian knot which had to be cut if either Catholic reform or Protestant Reformation was to take effect. Three provincial councils of the Scottish Church met – in 1549, 1552 and 1559 – inducing a searching but not always productive self-examination. To its credit, the Church proved increasingly willing to resort to the evangelical tools of preaching and catechising. A vernacular Catechism – named the *Hamilton Catechism* after the Archbishop of St Andrews although it was written by an English exile, Richard Marshall – was printed in 1552 and short abstracts of parts of it – including the 'Twopenny Faith' – were issued to the parish clergy in 1559. The diagnoses of these councils were so critical of the failings of the Church that some historians, additionally tempted by the fact that the authority of the Pope was never cited, have concluded that they were anti-papal and flirting with moderate Protestant reform. The counter-argument of some Catholic historians that these councils were more Catholic than the papacy itself, anticipating the decrees of Trent, seems as unconvincing.[24] The precedents were clear enough, in councils of the French province of the 1530s as much as in the (still orthodox) compromises made with a branch of the Lutherans by Catholic reformers at Cologne in the 1540s.

If so, the architect of the programme of reform by provincial councils was Cardinal Beaton, who, as Bishop of Mirepoix since 1537, had become closely familiar with the French Church, rather than his successor at St Andrews, John Hamilton, who may only have carried to fruition plans already laid before Beaton's death. If these councils had indeed threatened to cross the bounds of orthodoxy, it seems strange that the papal legate to the French Church, Cardinal Truvulzio, who also had responsibilities for oversight of the Scottish Church and must have been more vigilant than most as to signs of heresy, drew no such conclusions. The real danger to the Church lay not in a drift into unorthodoxy but in a lack of resolve. The problem of feuing was only tinkered with by provincial councils and the prospect of a redistribution of finances towards the parish clergy grasped only tentatively – a minimum stipend of £16 was recommended. The fact that the Protestant reformers set themselves a target of a minimum stipend of £40 in their *Book of Discipline* drawn up in 1560 indicates the different priorities of Protestant and Catholic reform.

The higher clergy of the pre-Reformation Church have borne the brunt of criticism – both of Catholic and Protestant historians. Singled out for special treatment by both contemporary and later Protestant historians has been the near-Satanic figure of Cardinal David Beaton, the persecutor of George Wishart; he was described by Knox as a 'bloody butcher', by George Buchanan as a 'cruel tyrant' and by the twentieth-century historian David Hay Fleming as an 'Ethiopian' libertine who fathered eight children on his mistress Marion Ogilvie.[25] Yet the contemporary Catholic propagandist John Lesley, who was determined to pin the blame for the Reformation on the failings of the bishops, was hardly less critical; and a modern Catholic scholar included Beaton in his argument that the shortcomings of the bishops were primarily the failings of those who appointed them – kings and regents.[26] Responsibility for fourteen of the deaths of Protestant martyrs can be laid at Beaton's door, but also for the many more Protestant sympathisers who recanted. Beaton's instinctive reaction was to repress rather than reform, for behind the spectre of heresy he saw a graver threat, to both the authority and the privileged status of the Church. The effect of his campaign against heresy was to drive it underground and it may have become more resilient as a result. It is difficult to see his murder by a group of Fife lairds in 1546 as a simple revenge killing, in retaliation for the execution of Wishart three months earlier. The conspirators had mixed motives and some had even been disappointed clients of his.[27] His reputation as a libertine also seems exaggerated. There were many women such as Marion Ogilvie who were waiting for the Council of Trent to make honest men of their illicit partners by permitting clerical marriage; they were not to know that Trent would ultimately disappoint them. The liaison was no more or less scandalous than the similar one, of six children, confessed to by the Bishop of Galloway when he turned Protestant in 1560.

A simple verdict on churchmen such as Beaton is not easy. The line between clerical abuse and reorganisation of the Church was a fine one, as was that between hunter of heretics and reformer. Beaton was responsible for the foundation of St Mary's College in 1544, which he intended as a check on the threat of the Protestant 'well' at nearby St Leonard's. Yet St Mary's also became the hub of the movement for internal reform of the Church. Beaton's diagnosis of the ills of the Church was that what was wrong lay not so much in policy but in its presentation. He used as his agents men from a background similar to his own – small lairds and proprietors, usually from Fife or Angus and the Mearns, often with a background in civil law. Yet his was an administration of many talents as well as many kindred or placemen. To sixteenth-century society nepotism was a natural instinct – of kinship. The reforms of that celebrated Bishop, William Elphinstone, in his diocese of Aberdeen depended on the efforts of an extensive network of his own kinsmen. Nor should pluralism or absenteeism always be condemned out of hand. Robert Reid, Bishop of Orkney, who conceived the notion of a college at Edinburgh and may be regarded as Edinburgh University's first benefactor, has been described as one of the outstanding churchmen of his century; but he was also a pluralist and a commendator, holding the Abbey of Kinloss where he fostered a humanist circle which included the distinguished Italian scholar, Giovanni Ferrerio.[28] Following the view that it is usually the hawks who make peace, the best hope of the Church was that the corrupt would carry through reform. It was not purely a pious hope: there is evidence that Archbishop Beaton of Glasgow within days of the meeting of the final provincial council at the Dominican house in Edinburgh in March 1559 was putting into effect some of its decrees. Yet within three months, the venue of the council was sacked by a Protestant mob. The Reformation crisis had overtaken the prolonged soul-searching of the clerical establishment.

The Reformations of 1560 and 1567

Scotland had not one Reformation crisis but two – in 1560, with the revolt of the Lords of the Congregation, and in 1567, with the coup which resulted in the deposing of Queen Mary. Equally important, it had two periods which might be described as a Reformation settlement: the first saw the recasting of the priorities and the politics of the Congregation in the very different circumstances which obtained once a Catholic queen returned, exactly a year after the Reformation parliament; the second took place against the background of the establishment of a Protestant state under the Earl of Moray and a bitter civil war which lasted until 1573. Opinions sharply differ on both the motivation of the rebels of 1559-60 and on the amount of support they enjoyed, but few would deny that the fate of Protestantism became intimately bound up with a range of other political issues after 1561.[29]

The Reformation crisis of 1559 was sparked off by a riot in Perth in which the town's religious houses were sacked within nine days of Knox's return to Scotland from France and Geneva on 2 May. By July the Congregation, now comprising a cross-section of society from nobles to lairds and burgesses, had 'purged' a series of towns in central Scotland, including St Andrews and Dundee, and entered the capital, where Knox was installed as its first Protestant minister on the seventh of the month. Mary of Guise was deposed as Regent in October 1559 and a provisional government established, which turned to England for military aid while still protesting its loyalty to Mary and Francis as its sovereigns. Alliance with the Elizabethan government was cemented in February 1560 by the Treaty of Berwick, an astonishing document which mentioned many things but not religion. The arrival of an English fleet in January 1560 and an army two months later proved to be the decisive factor, at least in hindsight. In July, a month after the untimely death of the Regent, the Treaty of Edinburgh was concluded between English and French commissioners, arranging the removal of all foreign troops from Scottish soil.

In outline, the course of events in 1559-60 seems straightforward and their outcome decisive. Yet serious dilemmas had confronted the Congregation in the course of the revolt and their consequences would be far-reaching. The revolt had started as a religious crusade but by the summer of 1559 had failed to find sufficient support. As its two leaders explained apologetically to William Cecil, secretary to the English privy council: 'We are sorry to be judged slow, negligent and cold in our proceedings. . . . You know, sir, how difficult it is to persuade a multitude to revolt of [against] established authority'.[30] Knox had successfully raised the 'rascal multitude', as he later called it, in a town with a long history of anticlericalism and unusually sharp social and economic tensions, but there is little evidence that there was a Protestant mob in waiting in many other burghs. A number of seemingly convinced Protestant notables had changed their minds at the first sight of the dangers of social insurrection; others had behaved ambivalently. By October 1559 the Congregation had been forced to change tack. Appeals for support were made, in increasing desperation, not only to wavering Protestants but even to staunch Catholics such as Lord Sempill to fight, if not for religion, at least for 'the liberty of this your native country'.[31] The Protestant revolt became by degrees a conservative reaction on behalf of the 'born counsellors' of the realm against undue French influence in government. The language of the covenant was gradually replaced by a more seductive image – of the commonweal. What had happened was that a national movement had found fresh acceptance when recast in conservative terms; it had fallen into accord with the tenor of the demands of the localities. The distinctively radical foreign policy of the rebels – turning for aid to the old enemy of England and offering it support in a conquest of Ireland[32] – was matched by a deeply conservative domestic policy. This paradox accurately reflected the essential paradox of the Reformation crisis of 1559-60: the Congregation could succeed only with the help of foreign troops, but it could gain acceptance in Scottish society only if it was a revolt of the provinces.

The new balance forged by the Congregation – of largely unspecified religious reform and a patriotic political platform – worked. The Earl of Huntly, Catholic chancellor of the realm, gave it token support soon after the Treaty of Berwick; so did the largely Catholic burgh of Aberdeen. The Congregation won a decisive propaganda victory in the spring and summer of 1560; the military victory was largely the work of the English army, even if it signally failed to inflict defeat on the French troops or take the strategically vital stronghold of Leith. A month after the Treaty of Edinburgh a parliament met, in defiance of its terms. Its proceedings are mysterious; its decisions, prefaced in the printed record by an extract from Matthew 24:14, are laconic – abolishing the mass, proscribing the jurisdiction of the Pope, and adopting a Protestant Confession of Faith. It was signally well attended: six bishops, twenty-one commendators, fourteen earls, nineteen lords and 101 lairds as well as some twenty-three burgh commissioners.[33] Some burghs even sent more commissioners than was strictly necessary: Aberdeen sent no less than three so as to represent all shades of opinion in the town. There can be little doubt that there was a certain amount of packing but the uniqueness of the presence of lairds at a parliament in such numbers can be exaggerated; the parliaments of 1487 and 1488 had also seen an unusual number of lairds.[34] As then, many must have felt that, with so much at stake, they could not afford not to be there.

The Congregation had intended to put a 'Book of Reformation', commissioned by it in April 1560, before the parliament. The first draft of it, largely the work of Knox, did not, however, prove acceptable and an enlarged committee of ministers – the 'six Johns' – was set up to revise it. There was much internal disagreement within the committee and numerous further revisions so the curious central fact of the Reformation of 1560 is that the Reformation parliament did not approve or even have a chance to consider a Protestant programme of reform. The eventual document, now known as the *First Book of Discipline*, was presented to a thinly attended convention of nobility and lairds – thirty turned up for it, less than a sixth of the attendance in August – which met in January 1561. The *First Book of Discipline* was not approved by the convention as such but only individually, by some though not all of those who attended. It was an impressive but untidy document, which mirrored many of the strengths and weaknesses of the Protestant movement itself. At its centre lay a powerful vision of a new godly, educated society based on a parish reformation. But the convention rejected the new Church's sweeping claim to the complete revenues of the old. In doing so it mirrored the basic division which was already opening up in Protestant ranks, between ministers and 'godly magistrates'. The implementation of a Protestant reform programme needed the active support of the 'chief pillars' of the Reformation, as Knox called the nobles. That *was* given, but only fitfully and usually on the nobility's own terms. The result was that the new reformed Church found itself in a curious kind of limbo.[35]

The progress of the reformed Church after 1560 was dramatic in some aspects, mixed in others. The most impressive achievement made before the Reformation parliament had been the setting up, mostly in towns, not only of a regular ministry but also of a body to impose ecclesiastical discipline – the kirk session. Both in Dundee and St Andrews a session was in full operation ten months *before* the Reformation parliament. And to a considerable extent the progress of the Church after 1560 also depended on a series of local reformations, each moving at its own pace and with its own distinctive problems to surmount. The best available measure of its progress is the data available for tracing the settlement of a parish ministry. The Church had about 1,080 parishes. By the end of 1561, 240 of those parishes had been filled. By 1567 they were served by about 850 clergy and by 1574 just over 1,000, although they were still heavily concentrated along the east coast, in the central Lowlands and less remote parts of the south-west and Borders. In Angus and the Mearns, a majority of parishes had acquired a resident ministry as early as 1563, but in the more remote deanery of Inverness only two of the twelve parishes had a Protestant incumbent before 1568.[36]

Raw statistics, however, can be misleading. In the diocese of Aberdeen, statistics would suggest a rapid advance of Protestantism – three-quarters of its 102 parishes had an incumbent by 1563 and all but seven by 1567; the fact that the north-east remained a Catholic stronghold for at least three generations after 1560 suggests that the presence of a minister was not enough in itself to secure widespread converts. There may have been more early penetration into the Highlands than once thought, but few of the ministers sent there could speak Gaelic. Elsewhere the Kirk talked of discipline being 'a part of our religion'; it was scarcely so in the Highlands where no kirk sessions were set up to assist ministers until well into the next century.[37] In the west the Church acknowledged that 'it ought to have a lord or secular noble over it, called . . . *magistratus civilis*', as the preface of a Gaelic translation of the Genevan *Book of Common Order* published in 1567, put it. This was Calvinism of a kind, but it had also undergone a drastic process of naturalisation for elsewhere the Kirk increasingly stressed its independence of the civil magistrate.[38] It shows a basic fact about the fundamental and slow process of evangelisation of ordinary Scots, which was largely complete in Lowland Scotland by 1625 but took much longer elsewhere. The new Kirk had to fall in with the customs of the local societies which it was infiltrating – the rules for missionaries were much the same in the sixteenth century as in the sixth.

There were difficulties, too, over the quality of the ministry. It would take the universities a generation or more to begin to meet the Kirk's demand for properly qualified ministers; throughout the 1560s and 1570s there was a shortfall, which was met by a junior form of the ministry – the reader. In 1574 over three-quarters of all parishes were served by a reader rather than a minister. Erskine of Dun, far from being congratulated by the General Assembly for settling a ministry so quickly in Angus, was criticised for admitting poorly qualified candidates as ministers rather than readers. If the old Church had been a church of curates, the new one in its first generation was largely a church of readers, who had strictly limited pastoral functions. The vast bulk of these readers were former Catholic clergy. Their motives are hard to assess with any precision. Some said the Catholic mass in private while adhering to the new Protestant rite in public. Most may have been motivated by a simple concern for the souls of their flock. They were viewed with a certain suspicion by the General Assembly and systematically vetted through the medium of the exercise. Although unable to preach and still underpaid, the readers were, nevertheless, the foot soldiers of the new Kirk. Their chief weapon in the mission to convey the rudiments of the Protestant faith to their parishioners was a simple one – Calvin's *Catechism* in its basic question and answer format.[39]

Apart from financial matters, the weakness of the new Church lay in two related areas: oversight and its role in politics. The reformers of 1560 had intended a complete overhaul of the system of oversight and a rationalisation of the untidy structure of thirteen medieval dioceses into ten districts, each with a superintendent. The neatness of the scheme was pre-empted by the conversion to Protestantism of three of the Catholic bishops, who were allowed to remain where they were, their rather anomalous position reflected in the uncertain choice of words used to describe one of them in 1562: 'Bishop of Galloway and Commendator of Towngland, owirsear there'.[40] Other anomalies crept in since the provisional government established by the Congregation appointed only five superintendents, all in the early part of 1561. Various commissioners were appointed, usually on a temporary basis, to fill the gaps in the system. The position of superintendents, who never had the sacramental functions of bishops but were cast in the role of New Testament bishops as 'watchmen' of their flock, has been a subject of bitter controversy between presbyterian and episcopalian historians. These godly bishops were, the *First Book of Discipline* said, 'a thing most expedient at this time'. In 1567, they were still described as 'neidfull members of the Kirk'. When the General Assembly in 1576 embarked on the task of a wholesale revision of the polity of the Kirk, it recognised no less than five offices exercising oversight: archbishops, bishops, superintendents, commissioners and visitors.[41] The eventual adoption of a system of presbyteries, tentatively begun in 1581, was very much a creature of its own times: it was a reaction to the political pressures of the 1570s, a recognition of the very mixed success of the system of oversight through superintendents and a tidying-up process, but it is difficult to see it as essentially being a return to first principles established in 1560. Clocks could not be turned back in sixteenth-century Scotland – in Church or state.

Superintendents were the agents of the General Assembly and subject to its authority. Yet the General Assembly itself took time to clarify its role and even its name in the fast-moving circumstances of the early 1560s. Representatives of the 'particular kirks of Scotland' met somewhere in Edinburgh in December 1560, in what is usually described as the first General Assembly. Various names were used for it, including 'Convention' and 'the Assembly' until the term, 'General Assembly' began to gain currency in 1562. Yet its role was still decidedly uncertain: it was the gathering point of Protestant 'kirks and cuntries' (territories) but increasingly it came to be dominated by the areas where Protestantism had made most early ground; it was the guarantor of the purity and independence of a Protestant Church but it was also the lobbying point of a Catholic Queen who was until 1567 its chief patron. Its role would clarify only after 1567.[42]

The new Church failed to secure its claim to the revenues of the old. It was forced to make do with a compromise settlement reached early in 1562; only a third of the income from benefices of the Catholic clergy was released and the Protestant ministers had to share even that with the crown. This was the arrangement which Knox castigated as 'two parts freely given to the Devil, and the third must be divided betwix God and the Devil'.[43] There were repeated complaints made by the General Assembly about the poverty of ministers, but what was significant is that the complaints had to be made to the crown or privy council. After the return of Queen Mary in 1561, the fortunes of the reformed Church were largely outside its own control. The most significant concession granted to it between 1560 and 1592 was the grant of the smaller benefices made in October 1566: henceforward succession to all benefices worth less than £200 a year would go to Protestant ministers. Yet the grant was made by a Catholic Queen who by then was also showing favour to Catholic clergy. The position of the Kirk – with the legislation of the Reformation parliament still unratified – was deeply uncertain throughout the personal reign of Mary, despite the advances it was making at local level. Largely reliant on royal patronage for its income, it was a state Church of a kind, but its status was even more ambiguous than that of the English Church of Henry VIII in the 1530s and 1540s.

In June 1567, only ten days after Mary's defeat at Carberry, the General Assembly met in Edinburgh. In this heady and excited atmosphere it set about the task of a second Reformation; it had to rebuild the 'ruinous house of God', root out 'superstition and idolatry' and secure a 'perpetuall ordour' for the Kirk. Aided by the staging of a Protestant coup within a coup when the Queen was deposed, it quickly established its priorities: ratification of the legislation of 1560, better provision for the existing ministry, new resources of money and manpower for the parishes, a purge of universities and schools, and a new and closer relationship with what it hoped would be a godly parliament. The 'foundation' of the Kirk, it said, had been laid in 1560, but the 'kaipstone' (coping stone) had still to be added.[44]

The Reformation of 1567 did not simply begin where that of 1560 had left off. It produced no new manifesto – the *Second Book of Discipline* was still more than a decade away – but parts of the *First Book* had already been recognised as out of date; a committee had been set up to overhaul it in 1563. The road which it took was a reaction to the experiences of the years of Mary, just as the path taken by the *Second Book* was conditioned by its conflicts with the Regent Morton in the 1570s. The Reformation of 1567 was avowedly a revolution in ways in which the Reformation of 1560, with its half-hidden compromises, was not. The Moderator of the General Assembly of 1567 was George Buchanan, who would shortly begin to draw up a justification of the revolution, and he would find it in the long line of Scottish kings supposedly censured by their nobles. There was a 'party of revolution'[45] in 1567 which was more cohesive than the loose coalition of 1560 and more determined. It had the desperation born of an act of clear rebellion – the deposing of a queen and the crowning of a pretender – whereas the rebels of 1560 had always professed loyalty to their sovereign.

The Reformation of 1567 was more avowedly Calvinist than that of 1560. Then a *Confession of Faith* had been skilfully drawn up by Knox in 1560 to embrace the different ideological strands within Scottish Protestantism, produced by two generations of varied experience in Scotland and abroad. Both the experience of co-religionists in France during the first War of Religion (1562-4) and Mary's attempts in 1565-6 to woo moderate Protestants towards her had provoked a sharper and more uncompromising Calvinism in the Church, now confronted, as it thought, by an international Catholic conspiracy intent on the destruction of Protestantism. The emergence of a new Protestant regime in the state encouraged a new radicalism in the Church. Its powers of excommunication, which in theory had rested with itself alone but had seldom been used since 1560, were put into operation more vigorously: the first record of excommunicates in Edinburgh occurs in 1569. It co-operated enthusiastically with the new Protestant state when, four years before a test act was passed by parliament, the Catholic establishment of the University of Aberdeen was purged in 1569. It approved the deal struck by the privy council with two Edinburgh merchants, licensing them to strip the lead from the north-east cathedrals of Elgin and St Machar's in Old Aberdeen. The revolutionary zeal of the hawks in the Assembly after 1567, however, was tempered by a new realism. Scruples about the efficacy of readers were set aside so as to speed up the work of reformation in the parishes; more were recruited and, ironically, many of the new recruits came from a hitherto under-tapped resource – the religious houses of the old Church.[46]

Much of the new resolve in both Church and state after 1567 was the work of the Earl of Moray, who was made Regent shortly after the infant James was crowned King. It was Moray as much as any of the ministers – including John Knox – who helped to give a Calvinist tone to the Scottish Reformation.[47] His chief ally in the Church was Buchanan and he had been instrumental in gaining for his client the post of Principal of St Leonard's College in 1566. Buchanan's contribution lay in the moulding of St Leonard's into the chief seminary of the Kirk in the generation after 1567: most of the key ministers of the 1570s and 1580s – often misleadingly labelled as 'Melvillians' – were graduates trained by him. Moray's death by an assassin's bullet in 1570 prolonged the civil war between supporters of Mary and her infant son; but it also introduced a fresh uncertainty into the relationship between Protestant Church and Protestant state.

After 1570 the King's party, in a desperate effort to revive its flagging fortunes in the civil war, raided the episcopal temporalities as a campaign fund; the Kirk was robbed of its expected inheritance. The hated 'tulchan' bishops[48] were the work of another Protestant Regent, Mar. It was his successor, Morton, who suggested after the end of the war that 'it is very requisite that in this time of repose we be careful for the good order and provision of the policy of the Kirk in things ambiguous and irresolute'.[49] By then, however, the Church refused to put its faith in regents and had begun to distance itself from the state; the process of mutual distrust which would end in open conflict between James VI and the Kirk had already begun. Yet, like the pre-Reformation Church which had so often spoken with two voices, of St Andrews and Glasgow, the reformed Church in the 1570s was caught in two minds

201

over the dilemma posed by the overlapping questions of oversight and Erastianism; the General Assembly had its hotheads but it took until 1580 to declare episcopacy unscriptural. The same dilemma would return to haunt it by 1600. The Reformation of 1567 had brought about a brief rapport between Church and state – it would be the ideal which Calvinist dissidents in 1582, 1584, 1592 and 1638 would look back to. It was the failure of the Reformation of 1567 which set Protestant Church and godly prince on their separate paths to 1638.

13

The Reign of Mary, Queen of Scots

THE REIGN OF MARY (1542-67) BEGAN WITH A LONG MINORITY AND WAR WITH England; it ended in civil war and a disputed succession. Mary, born a few days before her father's death, was not crowned until September 1543 and in the meantime was kept in the secure Castle of Stirling. Many of the problems which followed the death of Henry VIII of England (1509-47) were caused by the fact that he left a will; much of the uncertainty after the death of James V in December 1542 stemmed from the fact that he had not left a will or even instructions for a council of regency, although rumours quickly began to circulate of a will of some kind.[1] It took seven months of political manoeuvres for agreement to be reached on joint custody of the young Queen. The essential and partly incongruous elements which existed at the beginning of 1543 would operate for most of the 1540s – an infant born in December 1542 on the throne; Mary of Guise-Lorraine, a Queen Dowager with limited experience of the country who was still in process of establishing her status; Cardinal Beaton, uncompromising in his pursuit of heretics but still to establish his full authority over the Church, who, since 1541, had been foremost amongst the King's advisers in urging an aggressive posture towards England; and James, 2nd Earl of Arran, a prince of the blood whose dynastic ambition came into conflict with his rumoured religious unorthodoxy.

These circumstances were further complicated by two new arrivals from France early in 1543. One was the ambitious churchman, John Hamilton, Abbot of Paisley, who would become a close confidant of the Cardinal and act as the nagging Catholic conscience of his natural brother, Arran. The main reason that Arran was usually prepared to listen was that his legitimacy and position as heir-presumptive to the throne depended on the validity of a divorce arranged between his father and his first wife. The second wife, ironically, had been a cousin of Beaton, so that Arran was tied to his chief political rival in 1543 by the umbilical cord of kin as well as by his own ambition. The second arrival was the twenty-six-year-old Matthew Stewart, 4th Earl of Lennox; still unmarried and second in line to the throne after Arran, he was a dynastic time-bomb and one prospect, which was as alarming to Beaton as it was to Arran, was a possible marriage between him and the Queen Dowager. The third important figure to return to Scotland was another ironical product of Stewart politics; this was Angus, former husband of that earlier Queen Dowager, Margaret, and the forcible custodian of James V until his escape in 1528. After fourteen years of exile in England, Angus would play the role of the wild card in the already complicated politics of the minority.[2]

The crisis of 1543
The politics of the regency were complex because there was much more at stake than the settlement of the kingdom. Several separate political processes were in dispute and they were further complicated by becoming hopelessly entangled with

each other. A battle for internal control over the Church had been going on between Gavin Dunbar, Archbishop of Glasgow, and Beaton ever since his gaining of a cardinal's hat in 1537. Their rivalry also spilled over into secular politics in a struggle for the chancellorship, which Beaton regained late in 1543 as part of a bargain struck with Arran. His primacy as metropolitan was not established until 1544 when he was also granted the status of papal legate *a latere*, significantly 'throughout the whole realm'. Even then his attempt to have his cross of authority pointedly carried in procession into Glasgow Cathedral ended in fisticuffs between the diocesan clergy of the rival sees. Until Dunbar's death in 1547, the Church, as it had for much of the time since the elevation of Glasgow to an archbishopric in 1492, still spoke with two voices – even if both spoke to Rome. The issue after 1547 would be resolved almost by accident: with Beaton removed by assassins, the seat of St Andrews and status of legate went quickly to John Hamilton and the struggle for Glasgow between another Hamilton placeman and the eventual appointee, James Beaton (a nephew of the Cardinal), dragged on until 1551. It is striking that attempts to reform the Church from within began to gain headway only after the squabbles which had so compromised its own authority were removed. It would be St Andrews that was the centre of the movement for reform of the Scottish province, with councils in 1549, 1552 and 1559.

There was, however, another movement to reform the Church, on more radical lines. This was outside the Church in the sense that it was promoted by laymen but the exact degree of its unorthodoxy is difficult to determine. Its initial expression came in the first parliament of the minority in March 1543, when Arran was formally declared Governor of the realm; two days later an act was passed permitting the 'lieges to haif . . . baith the New Testament and the Auld in the vulgar toung'. This was not necessarily a Protestant action – there had been many editions of the Bible in the vernacular before Luther's – but, in practice, it meant the use of William Tyndale's English translation of the New Testament. Within a short time, Knox later was to claim, the Tyndale Bible was to be seen 'lying almost upon every gentlemen's table'. It is quite likely that this was so. Other reformations were marked by similar, sudden outbursts of evangelical fervour; in France in 1561 the court was hit by a wave of Protestant psalm and prayer books but that moment also quickly passed. In mid-1543 an English agent had reported that the town of Leith 'be noted all to be good Christians'; by the end of the year a visiting papal legate noted 'great changes'.[3]

There were two complications at work in 1543. The act may have represented a body of opinion which operated on both sides of the shifting line which marked the boundary between Protestant heresy and an indeterminate but nonetheless deeply felt desire for reform. Two of the competing factions of 1543 may have been in competition for the favour of this body of opinion. The act, usually thought as marking the influence of the new Governor, was also backed by a group headed by the Earls of Angus and Lennox.[4] In the course of the next few months, Arran promoted Protestant preaching in a number of burghs and provoked a Catholic backlash in at least two of them, Aberdeen and Edinburgh. His 'godly fit', as it is usually called, may have been so frenetic only because he was trying to be more Protestant than his opponents; the result was that he over-reached himself. By the end of 1543 Arran had been forced into a compromise, which restored Beaton as chancellor and re-enacted the laws against the very heretics whose activities his own policy had encouraged. The return of the Governor into the bosom of Beaton's Church was a serious check to the momentum of the growing but still inchoate Protestant movement. Without a national focus, it retired into its separate localities to regroup. The preaching tour made by George Wishart between his return to Scotland in 1543 and his imprisonment in January 1546 was to a rather different kind of movement. Arran's defection had left a 'church under the cross' rather than a group which had a clear political focus or identity – other than its connections by then with England.

The years between 1543 and 1548 saw a widespread debate within the political community about the foreign policy of the realm. Ranged against the pro-French stance of the Cardinal and the Queen Dowager in 1543 was not one grouping but two – Arran's faction and the group around Angus and Lennox, both of which adopted a pro-English stance as well as a pro-reform policy. It had been Arran who held primary responsibility for the negotiation of the two treaties of Greenwich in July 1543, a peace treaty and an agreement to contract a marriage between Prince Edward (the future Edward VI) and Mary when she was ten. Already, however, there were misgivings amongst the Estates about the safeguards built into the treaties. As in 1502, England proved reluctant to concede that Scotland could maintain its existing treaties with France; more inflammatory still were the English demands that the Queen should be sent to England for her education. The road to union was even rockier than it had been in the reign of James IV.

The 'Rough Wooing'

By the end of 1543 the treaties lay in ruins, rejected by the Scottish parliament, and Arran was forced by his reconciliation with Beaton into an exaggeratedly anti-English stance. The alternative English connection, led by Lennox and Angus, tried a fresh tack by linking itself with the disaffection felt towards the Scottish crown in the Western Isles. The 'daunting' of the Isles, begun by James IV in 1493, was still uncompleted and the most serious of the seven uprisings in support of a Clanranald Lord of the Isles came in 1545, when Donald Dubh was once again at liberty. The clans of the Lordship flocked to his standard and their representatives came in force to a restored Council of the Isles which met on Islay in July 1545 to negotiate with Henry VIII's commissioners. The Governor's forces had managed to capture Lennox's own stronghold of Glasgow in the spring of 1544 and force him into flight to England, but it is difficult to imagine how they might have coped with the 4,000 Islesmen who had rallied around the pretender to the Lordship. The frightening spectre of a conquest *from* the west receded only at the end of 1545 when Donald died, without a credible heir, of a fever in Ireland.[5]

With the death of Donald Dubh, the most spectacular of Henry VIII's strategies to destabilise the Scottish realm fell by the wayside, and English efforts were concentrated for most of the rest of the 1540s on the east coast and the eastern Borders. In May 1544 an army under the command of the Earl of Hertford staged an ambitious amphibious raid on Edinburgh; £50,000 worth of grain and two ships were seized in the port of Leith and, so an English report claimed, about 600 townsmen (which would have represented over a third of the burgh's muster roll) fell in two assaults on Edinburgh, for the loss of a mere seven Englishmen. The

Palace of Holyroodhouse and the Abbey Church were looted, as were parts of the south side of the burgh; an English map made at the time showing the army's first arrival is the first surviving, authentic view of Edinburgh. The English commander's claims were much exaggerated and, in fact, his large force of 10,000 men had completely failed to storm the Netherbow port (near to where the John Knox house still stands). Less resistance was encountered by the English army as it marched back through the Borders, burning crops and spoiling churches as it went. The 'Rough Wooing', as Sir Walter Scott would later dub it, had begun.

English policy towards Scotland involved several elements. It was based in theory on the treaties of 1543, but Henry also in 1544 revived the suzerainty claim of Edward I. It attempted to create a pro-English party at court, largely in the persons of Angus and Lennox, but it would also foster a rather different English connection in the hundreds of 'assured Scots' who were encouraged, bribed or bullied into 'taking assurance of the King of England'. Assuring involved an oath of allegiance to Henry as liege lord and with time the oath became more and more detailed; the assured were made pensioners, were paid regular wages and were even insured against losses incurred through retaliation by their neighbours or the Scottish government. It was the most organised fifth column in Scottish history. Almost all of the assured came from the areas which felt the heaviest English military pressure – Berwickshire, the eastern Borders, East Lothian, Fife and Angus. Many were forced to follow their landlord or superior into assurance.[6]

Increasingly, and especially after Hertford (now Duke of Somerset) came to power with the accession of Edward VI in 1547, Protestantism was made the litmus test of English favour. The Bible, which in England was still by law officially restricted to the aristocracy, was used as an English weapon of war. That tactic may have misfired for although there was some connection between Protestantism and pro-English feeling, the two were as yet far from being identical.[7] A Protestant and pro-English party would crystallise in 1559 but it was in embryo in the 1540s. Its best chance had come when the murderers of Cardinal Beaton had seized the Castle of St Andrews in May 1546; it slowly evaporated as the 'Castilians', with Knox now among them, were left stranded in the formidable Bishop's Castle, set on a windswept, rocky headland, for the next fourteen months. No English expeditionary force was sent to relieve them, as they had been led to expect, and the Castle fell to a French force in July 1547. The 'gentlemen' were put in a French prison; the others, Knox included, into the galleys. It would not be the last time that England expected Scottish Protestants to do their duty – and failed to back them when they did.

In the second stage of the 'Rough Wooing' after 1547, there was a much more sustained effort to create a pale by establishing a chain of sophisticated fortresses – more than twenty in all – on the main passes through the Borders and at strategic points along the east coast between Berwick and Dundee. The investment was huge – more than £1m sterling (£4.5m Scots) – and it absorbed most of the profits made from the dissolution of the chantries in 1547 and successive debasements of the English coinage in the 1540s. Haddington, only eighteen miles from Edinburgh, became the military headquarters of the English occupation force. The most serious defeat inflicted on the Scots was at Pinkie, just outside Musselburgh, in September 1547. Thousands were killed, 1,500 were taken prisoner and the remnants of the

Scottish army were chased to the gates of Edinburgh. Yet Edinburgh Castle remained intact, an awkward obstacle in the way of further English advance.

By 1548 the conflict had settled into a war of attrition in Lothian and around Dundee. The Scottish Queen was safe in Stirling Castle until she was moved, first to Dumbarton, and in July 1548 to France. With her removal, English policy had in effect defeated itself: the Scots had signed a treaty approving her marriage to the Dauphin in return for a guarantee by France of the integrity of the Scottish realm. The price of Arran's agreement was the French duchy of Châtelherault. French military tactics were markedly similar to English and a counter-chain of highly sophisticated forts, including Eyemouth, Dunbar and Inchkeith, was quickly established. The combined effect of superior French resources and fire-power, a domestic crisis occasioned by two rebellions in Cornwall and East Anglia, and a palace coup displacing Somerset in October 1549 virtually brought the war to an end. English garrisons were abandoned and peace was made, first with France in March 1550, and with the Scots in June 1551. A by-product of the peace was the final settlement of the line of the Anglo-Scottish frontier; the Debateable Lands disappeared.

The costs of the war are hard to assess with any accuracy. Trade had been badly affected: by the mid-1540s overseas exports were at a seventh of the levels which they had reached in the last years of James V's reign. By 1551 they had recovered to the more modest levels attained in the earlier 1530s, but it would take until the late 1570s for them to peak again at the levels of 1540-2. [8] There was no collapse of government, nor many signs of a general crisis of Scottish society, which had shown striking resilience in the face of seven years of garrisoning, forced quarter and calculated violence. The institution which probably suffered most serious damage was the Church: the result may well have been a 'general insecurity of churches and churchmen'.[9] Yet the effects on Protestantism were also mixed: the occupation had greatly accelerated the spread of Protestant literature, which would later be blamed by the Catholic historian, John Lesley, as the principal cause of the spread of heresy, but collaboration with the English had also helped to drive the movement underground.

If England had invested vast sums in Scotland, the French between 1548 and 1550 had invested more – probably some 2m *livres* (£1m Scots) in 1549 alone, when there had been more than 6,000 French troops in Scotland.[10] After 1550 they continued to maintain five garrisons in Scotland, with a total of about 400 men. The French investment did not end in 1550. They continued to pay pensions to a number of Scots nobles and churchmen. Others, like Huntly, were granted full French nationality. The return on the investment was already clear in 1550. It was not at the eventual marriage of Mary to the Dauphin Francis in April 1558 that the first claims were made to her right to the throne of England but eight years earlier, during the French victory celebrations at the end of the war.[11] Mary, who had been adopted into the household of Henry II as 'ma fille propre', was already recognised as the vehicle for his designs on England. That plan also, at least in the mind of Henry II, included the increasing absorption of Scotland into a greater French monarchy. The rewards for the Scots of the renewed French alliance had been great but its price was higher still.

The regency of Mary of Guise-Lorraine (1554-60)

The vehicle of this other plank of French policy was Mary of Guise, who had grown steadily in stature over the course of the 'Rough Wooing'. She had been made chief of the council of sixteen set up to 'advise' the Governor as early as 1544. By 1548 she had helped to co-ordinate the French army's siege of Haddington. In 1549 she had made a rousing speech to troops in the field before the retaking of the fortress of Inchkeith. It was she who made the arrangements for what has since been called the 'brainwashing expedition'[12] made by Scottish notables to France in 1550 to view the extravagant Renaissance triumphs mounted in Rouen and elsewhere to mark the French victory over England. By 1554, when she replaced Arran (who had been given the French duchy of Châtelherault) as regent, Mary of Guise had already gained widespread acceptance amongst the Scottish political community.

Although the regent's long-term aims were radical, her policy was also in a sense a traditional Stewart one, of the conciliation of all interests – including even the Protestant one. The last heresy trial had taken place in 1550 and it had been Châtelherault, still Governor, sitting in silence throughout, who had been tainted by it. The execution of the Protestant schoolmaster, Walter Myln, in 1558, which took place while she was in France at her daughter's wedding, was probably without her knowledge or consent. The parliament of 1555 was also designed to restore stability to the realm; it re-enacted much fifteenth-century legislation on burgh government and trade, including an act which harked back to the reign of James I, banning deacons of crafts. Yet it induced a full-blown crisis for her government. There were craft riots in a number of burghs and the Regent was forced to take the unusual step of a number of personal visits to Perth to quell disturbances there.[13] Fifteen months after it was passed, the act was nullified. The programme to extend royal government into the localities had hit a major obstacle. Further troubles arose over attempts to restore the levels of taxation imposed by both James IV and V. A new 'perpetual tax' was mooted in 1556, involving a reassessment of the old extent which for centuries had guaranteed low taxation for the landed classes. Nothing came of it but five separate taxes levied within the space of sixteen months in 1556-7 strained loyalties further. The honeymoon of Mary of Guise with her subjects was over well before the beginnings of the crisis of 1558. That crisis stemmed as much from the fears which were renewed and heightened by the marriage of Mary and the Dauphin and its attendant treaty, which contained perhaps the worst-kept secret clause in Scottish history – the grant of the crown matrimonial to Francis, allowing him to succeed in the event of Queen Mary's death. The 'example of Brittany', annexed to the French crown in 1532 as a dukedom (and ironically Francis held that title), loomed large in the minds of many in 1558.

It would be wrong to imagine that Mary of Guise's position was wholly untenable. The disturbances stirred up by John Knox in Perth in May 1559 did not spread as quickly as he had hoped. The Lords of the Congregation took five months to muster enough support before they took the step of deposing the Regent in October 1559. Their position, once they did so, quickly crumbled and they were forced to abandon Edinburgh in some disarray two weeks later. Mary's difficulties in suppressing the revolt had been greatly exaggerated by the accidental death in a jousting tournament of Henry II in July 1559. The fact that it made her daughter Queen of France as consort of the fifteen-year-old Francis II carried, for the moment, few bonuses. The flaunting of the arms of England and Ireland during the marriage celebrations, claiming that Mary was Queen of four kingdoms, inflamed English opinion and played an important psychological role in provoking their increasing entanglement in the Scottish crisis. The Regent's tactic throughout the troubles of 1559-60 was to play for time and it was probably only the emergency at the French court triggered by the attempted Huguenot coup at Amboise in March 1560 which undermined the prospect of its eventual success. Even when she lay desperately ill in Edinburgh Castle in May and June 1560, there were fears amongst the English expeditionary army – aroused by the impressive procession of great nobles who called to pay their respects – that she would manage to stage another political recovery. She died, on 11 June 1560, not as the hated tyrant portrayed by Knox,[14] but as a queen held in considerable repute.

Government by the Lords of the Congregation

The Treaty of Edinburgh, concluded between English and French commissioners on 6 July, has often been thought to mark the end of the auld alliance with France. Few at the time would have thought it so; it was not called, as in 1502, a treaty of 'perpetual peace' and the victorious Lords of the Congregation were only too aware that there were divisions of opinion amongst their English allies. Elizabeth had herself almost sabotaged the Treaty by demanding an enormous sum in reparations and the return of those emblems of England's medieval empire, Calais and Boulogne. In France, still in the throes of a severe crisis at the court and in the provinces, few in royal circles would have considered throwing away the huge investment made in Scotland during the reign of Henry II. The simple fact of sovereignty – Mary was still undisputed Queen of Scots and continued to make grants and appointments under both her great and privy seals throughout the course of 1560 and 1561 – made it inevitable that France would continue to have some interest in the affairs of Scotland; what remained was for that interest to be defined. A delegation sent to France to ask for the ratification of the legislation of the Reformation parliament met with a sharp rebuff.

The Congregation, now taking on more of the mantle of a provisional government but acutely aware of its own vulnerability, tried to operate in two spheres: the 'party of revolution'[15] repeatedly went through the familiar protestations of rebels of loyalty to an absent sovereign, but it also energetically sought to give their position more security and status, ironically through that most traditional of dynastic devices – a royal marriage. The titular head of the government was Châtelherault, still heir to the throne if the marriage treaty of 1558 was disregarded; he still styled himself 'Governor'. The regime's quest for security took the form of the offer of the hand of his son, 'young Arran', to Elizabeth. Such a marriage, so the Congregation claimed, would be the surest means of securing the 'amity' between England and Scotland. It was also the best means to hold together their own fragile coalition which already showed signs of disintegration.

Any prospects of success for this stratagem, which met a very cool reception in London, lasted for only four months after the Reformation parliament. In December 1560 Francis II died suddenly, of an ear infection, and Mary's reign as Queen Consort of France came to an abrupt end. Within a month, it was clear to the more astute diplomats amongst the Congregation, such as Maitland of

Lethington, that the likelihood of her return to Scotland was great.[16] Negotiations for an English marriage continued, with the arguments used to persuade Elizabeth – the need to bolster the 'hollow hearts of a great number' of Protestants was one of the most frequent – employed with renewed urgency, but more in hope than expectation. By March 1561, the bargaining about the details of the future personal reign had begun. Mary's half-brother, Lord James, arrived in France in April. A long letter written by him to Mary shortly after his return reveals both the complexity of the negotiations and how far the leading members of the regime had by now cast in their lot with their lawful sovereign. A climate of compromise had already begun to establish itself. On important issues, such as the appointment of foreigners to offices of state, the disposal of church lands and especially on the settlement of religion, Lord James's advice was to act with circumspection: 'Abuiff all things, madame, for the luif of God presse na matters of religion, not for any mans advise on the earth'. The price of his and others' support was her choice of a 'faythful counsale'.[17] This was good advice and Mary, in consultation with her Guise relations, would take it to heart. The alternative offer, made on behalf of the Catholic Earl of Huntly, to raise three northern shires to reduce the kingdom to obedience if she landed at Aberdeen, was rejected.

On 19 August 1561, Mary, accompanied only by a few members of her household and a minimal diplomatic presence, landed at Leith. The nature of the careful bargains struck before her return became evident just five days later: on this first Sunday Mary and her household attended mass in her private chapel at Holyrood and Lord James barred the door against Protestant protesters. This, for Knox, was the defection of one of the 'chief pillars' of the Reformation. The claim which he made in a vehement sermon preached on the following Sunday in St Giles' that one mass was more dangerous than the landing of 'ten thousand armed enemies' was, in a sense, correct: the Queen's chapel by 1563 would become the mecca for Catholics from his own Edinburgh congregation and the surrounding area. The disturbance accelerated the need for order. In a proclamation issued on the day after the riot, the privy council gave voice to the policy which would remain in place for the whole of the personal reign. Its declaration of a standstill in religion gave some security but no permanence to the nascent Protestant Church. But the proclamation had within it a double ambiguity. It lent support to the legislation of the Reformation parliament but fell well short of formal ratification; that parliament had banned the mass but it had not mentioned some of the other Catholic sacraments, which were thus not illegal. Protestantism remained insecure and Catholicism was left in something of a limbo.

The quest for settlement (1561-5)

Like the three reigns before it, that of Mary began with a quest for order. The basis of stability in any Stewart reign lay in finance. It was only to be expected that the Queen's first interest would lie in restoring the revenues of the crown after a period of financial confusion rather than in promoting the old Church or giving recognition to the new. From the beginning, Mary exhibited the same distinctive Stewart combination of personal piety and venality towards the Church as both James IV and V. She did little in 1561 or after to reverse the curious situation which made a Catholic queen the chief financial beneficiary of the break with Rome; the windfall profits that had accrued to the crown from the major benefices continued to flow into the royal household. Such revenues were all the more necessary because Mary clearly wanted to avoid a return to her mother's unpopular taxation of the 1550s; she could not risk becoming another James III, rebuffed by parliament. The only national tax raised during her reign was a very special case, for the baptism of her son and heir in 1566.

The situation was eased by her own income from her jointure as a Dowager Queen of France; this realised about £30,000 Scots a year and met virtually the whole cost of the royal household.[18] So the Scottish nobility not only had a royal court for the first time since 1542, but also one which cost it little. Even the settlement of the thorny question of the lands and revenues of the pre-Reformation Church was turned to the advantage of the crown. Representatives of the Catholic clergy offered a quarter of their revenues; in 1562 they were forced to concede a third. The income from the thirds of benefices went, however, in about equal measure to the crown as well as to Protestant ministers. It yielded £12,700 to the crown in 1562 and over £32,000 by 1565. It was a compromise that offered something to all parties: it gave tacit recognition to the reformed Church and gave control over its purse strings to the crown; and it also gave the Catholic Church some hope for the future – news of the deal was greeted with much relief in Rome.[19]

Opinions have differed most sharply on the role Mary cast for herself in 1561 – a Catholic queen content to follow neutral courses in religion and politics. Did it show sensible 'opportunism' or was it 'profoundly irresponsible'?[20] The argument is at its sharpest in two areas: religious policy and her pursuit of her claim to the English succession. Circumstances need to be remembered in both. Even if Mary had had the resources and political muscle to act out the role of a committed Catholic monarch on her return, it is difficult to see what stance she could have adopted while the Council of Trent was still in session, particularly as her own uncle, the Cardinal of Guise, until mid-1563 was leader of the opposition party there. Catholic reform was not defined until 1564.

There can be little doubt that the related questions of relations with England and a royal marriage dominated the politics of the first two years of the personal reign. Mary wanted Elizabeth to recognise her claim to the English throne. If this was an obsession,[21] it was one shared by a wide cross-section of the political community, both Protestant and Catholic. It was also a variant of the same quest for security, guaranteed by an Arran marriage, which the Congregation had attempted in 1560-1. Religious differences could be set aside in pursuit of the amity with England and the notable lack of religious tension of the years 1562-4 can largely be explained by the *realpolitik* of both Queen and privy council. Her council was dominated by the same largely Protestant coalition of nobles as had masterminded the rebellion of 1559-60 and staffed the provisional government of 1560-1. Her household, by contrast, was firmly and unambiguously Catholic. The operation of the Queen's two bodies – council and household – made a good deal of sense, as a Scottish solution to a distinctively Scottish problem. There was friction between them, but the royal court also acted as the link between the two, for it was a place where minds could meet.[22]

The most conspicuous feature of Mary's rule between 1562 and 1565 was her travels around her kingdom. She spent two-thirds of the period between August

1562 and September 1563 on progress, covering 1,200 miles. In the space of fifty-four days between July and September 1564, she covered 460 miles, visiting the north-east and Inverness for a second time. And in 1565, the year of her marriage to Darnley when, some claim, her infatuation with this young, handsome newcomer led her to neglect the business of government, the Queen again spent two-thirds of the first nine months of the year on progress.[23] In what was still a highly devolved feudal realm Mary granted a conspicuous degree of access to her subjects – even to such troublesome ones as John Knox.

It was on the first of her progresses, in August 1562, that Mary's hard-headed policy claimed its first major victim – the Earl of Huntly, the most powerful Catholic magnate in Scotland. Here the stakes were high and had little to do with religion, other than the invitation made to the Queen by the 'pope of the north-east' to attend what would have been a flagrantly illegal private mass at his chapel in Strathbogie. The Catholic mass was a privilege restricted to Mary's own household; it was not for subjects, however mighty, to offer it to the Queen. Huntly was made a rebel and hunted down; he died of apoplexy. Most of the extensive Gordon network in the north-east was forfeited. Lord James was confirmed in the earldom of Moray, a traditional sphere of Gordon interest. The risk was at least as great as any of the incursions into the localities made by James IV or V – a calculated destabilisation of a whole province – but it avoided the greater danger of a national war of religion, as had already begun to engulf France. At stake was the credibility of both the standstill policy and the pursuit of the English succession; Mary had demonstrated that she could control her Catholic subjects.

Dynastic crisis or monarchy triumphant? (1565-6)

The personal reign lasted only six years. There is a tendency to concentrate on one or other part of it. Mary's admirers tend to dwell on the achievements of the years 1561-4, when the Queen's first priorities lay in the restoration of the power, status and finances of the monarchy. These were the years, according to one historian, of an 'equivocal policy' which was a 'conspicuous political success', bringing about a unity amongst the nobility unrivalled since Flodden.[24] Her detractors, by contrast, tend to focus on the years 1565-7, and the marriage by Catholic rites to Henry Stewart, Lord Darnley (the son of Lennox), in July 1565 marks for many historians the first of a series of political disasters which would bring her rule to an end. There can be little doubt that to contemporaries the central point of the reign would have been the marriage of 1565.

Between 1561 and 1565 a chain of suitors had been suggested as suitable husbands for both queens; Mary's included the Dukes of Ferrara, Nemours and Anjou, the Kings of Denmark and Sweden, Archduke Charles of Austria (the Pope's choice), and Don Carlos of Spain (Mary's own preference for a time). No marriage negotiations for any of them, however, had gone further than the first stages. Elaborate hands of diplomatic poker were being played by both Queens, with Elizabeth persistent in her refusal to name a successor. Mary, by her demand for recognition of her claim, was interfering as much in English politics as Elizabeth was in those of Scotland. Elizabeth's offer of her own favourite Robert Dudley (quickly elevated to the earldom of Leicester) as a husband for Mary may have been her attempt to play the joker in the pack, but negotiations over a Leicester match went on for fully eighteen months before they collapsed in April 1565 – just a month before Mary's betrothal to Darnley. By then the prospect of the amity offered considerably less than it had promised in 1561; a Leicester marriage was no guarantee of recognition of Mary's claim. Even if the Darnley marriage was the product of infatuation, it also happened to make considerable political sense. It would end the isolation of Mary who had no legitimate kin at court. A Darnley marriage, by grafting the Lennox Stewart line on to the royal house of Stewart, ended this dangerous isolation at a stroke. It avoided the uncertainties of a foreign match, whether Spanish, French or English. Without abandoning the amity, the marriage offered an escape from the dead-end which seemed to be its inevitable prospect. It promised an independent monarchy, free of both England and France. Darnley, in effect, could make Mary into a patriot queen.

The marriage marked the beginning of a new exploitation of the political resources of the court. With it came a huge honours list amounting to twenty knighthoods and five earldoms – as great an inflation of honours as at any time since the reign of James II.[25] By the end of the year Thomas Randolph, the English ambassador, was complaining sourly that he could hardly turn round in the Scottish court without bumping into another new peer; and, he added, the Scots begin to 'think themselves as great as we'. As in the reign of James IV, the cult of honour was used both to reassure the nobility and to foster a new sense of patriotism. There was a flurry of celebratory verse, both in Latin and Scots. Sir Thomas Craig's *Epithalamium* was the first major work of literature printed in Scotland since 1560; and the huge collection of vernacular verse, the *Bannatyne Manuscript*, was compiled, it is now clear, not in 1568 as its editor claimed but in 1565-6, as might be expected in a collection which contained more love poetry than anything else.[26]

At the centre of this glittering Renaissance court – which deserves to take its rightful place alongside the courts of Mary's grandfather, father and son – was the Queen herself, a patron of poets and an inspirer of poetry. The literature of acclaim was extravagant, stylised and followed the conventions of the French court, on which much of it was based, but it also had tangible political effects.[27] By the end of 1565 both the pleasures and the politics of the court had begun to cast their spell, much to the disgust of Knox who railed at both the 'holy water of the court' and the 'enchantment' it created by which 'all men are bewitched'. Few shared Knox's opinion of Mary as a dangerous Jezebel, and he was criticised even in the General Assembly of the reformed Church for his implacable hostility to the Queen. Many at court may have been seduced by the heady images of a virtuoso queen.

In the hard world of politics, prospects were not bright in 1565 for Knox and other Protestant radicals. For Moray and especially for the Hamiltons they were bleak: Randolph reported 'the ruin of their house' and 'no sure hope now for the establishment of the true religion'.[28] The prospect of the Darnley match had isolated both Châtelherault and Moray – into the hapless gesture of fringe politics in Scotland, a rebellion against the crown. It was even more of a gesture than most such protests, a farce which went by the ironical name of the 'Chaseabout Raid' in which no pitched battle was fought or sought, by either side. It did, however, allow Darnley to model an expensive, new suit of armour. By the end of 1565, Moray was in exile and Châtelherault was promised a pardon, on condition that he removed himself to France. The marriage had brought about a dramatic reversal of the dynastic revolution which had brought the Hamiltons to the forefront of politics in 1560.

At first the Lennox counter-revolution had been played out in the localities – the Earl had quickly reclaimed his estates from the Hamiltons in 1564, despite a twenty-year absence in England. Its subsequent focus was at court, where it engendered a wide-ranging cult of honour. By the end of 1565, this cult was taking on an explicitly Catholic face. It was on Christmas Day, while the General Assembly was sitting in Edinburgh, that Darnley chose to return to the mass. The climax of both the cult of honour and a Catholic revival at court came at Candlemas, on 2 February 1566. Like James V before him, Darnley was invested with the Order of St Michael, the greatest order in French chivalry. The ceremony took place after a solemn high mass in Mary's chapel at Holyrood, in the presence of ambassadors from France and Savoy. After it, Darnley, never one for the understated gesture, strode up Edinburgh's High Street along with other courtiers, boasting loudly that he had returned the whole realm to the true faith. He had done a good deal less than that: some sympathetic nobles had been enticed, most had not.[29]

Five weeks later, on 9 March 1566, the Queen's Italian servant David Riccio was murdered by a band of armed intruders led by Lord Ruthven, who burst into her privy chamber at Holyrood. The Catholic demonstration at Candlemas had provoked a violent Protestant counter-demonstration. Darnley was amongst the conspirators and his dagger was pointedly left in the body. The explanation for his abrupt about-turn remains obscure: was he simply jealous of the influence of Riccio over the Queen, or was he worried about where that influence was taking Mary? One suggestion made by a contemporary, then in France, was that Riccio had persuaded Mary to rehabilitate the Hamiltons. That would have been reason enough to sink a Lennox/Stewart knife into his back. Otherwise, there were probably as many motives involved as there were conspirators. The murder took place on the eve of a parliament which was due to try a number of the Chaseabout rebels; there were rumours of summary justice being wielded through the passage of an act of oblivion; it was also to discuss 'allowing bishops and rectors the full exercise of their ancient religion', which seems to reflect an attempt to implement some of the decrees of the Council of Trent reaffirming the authority and jurisdiction of bishops. Also murdered on the same night as Riccio was a Dominican friar attached to the Queen's household, John Black. He had been one of four special preachers recently selected by the Queen, another step which seems to be in line with Tridentine decrees. Black's assailants included more than a score of prominent members of the Protestant party in the capital; their motive is clear, for the position of the party brought to power in the Edinburgh town council chamber by a violent coup in 1560 had by 1566 slipped to the point where only one member of it still held office. Both murders were the acts of desperate men.[30]

When she witnessed the assault on her servant in her own private chamber the Queen was six months' pregnant. The child, a boy, was born on 19 June 1566. The intervening months since the murder had been a curious calm after the storm. There was no collapse of royal government nor panic at court. Many, including Mary's advisers, felt that the country was on the brink of a war of religion; William Chisholm, Catholic Bishop of Dunblane, expected further Catholic blood to be spilt first. In these circumstances, it is hardly surprising that the instinctive reactions of a Stewart monarch were to effect a reconciliation. Throughout the remaining months of 1566, the traditional Stewart means of regaining political consensus – remissions, respites and adjustments in the composition of the council – went into operation. By the end of March, three weeks after the murder, the rehabilitation of the conspirators of 1565 was already under way; Moray and Argyll were both offered pardons. The detaching of the fringe Riccio conspirators came next, with waves of remissions in June and July. The final stage, of pardoning the main conspirators, was reached in December.

Many historians have interpreted the birth of a son to Mary as bringing into play a dangerous new rival, who might be used to supplant the Queen; things quickly fell apart after it. That may be so in retrospect, but at the time his birth and the carefully planned spectacle of a baptism were envisaged as accelerating two processes of reconciliation – of Mary with her disaffected nobles and of Protestants with Catholics. Major concessions were planned to both magnates and to the reformed Church, which had more to fear than most from the birth of a Catholic heir. These plans were, however, delayed and put in jeopardy by the sudden collapse of the Queen at Jedburgh in October while on progress through the Borders. Mary was seriously ill for almost three weeks; her speech from what she and many of those present thought to be her deathbed gave eloquent voice to the policy that had been forming since the Riccio murder:

> Ye knaw forsythe the be the divisioun of gouernors, prouinces and regions are trublit and molestit, and [in] contrarie be agrement and unitie stablissit, pacifeit and avancit. Quhairfor above all thyngis I requyre you to have charitie, concorde and love amongis your selfis.[31]

The speech may have made as dramatic an impact as Elizabeth's smallpox attack in 1562 had made on her own nobles. The uncertain prospect which loomed in the event of Mary's death – not only of a minor but also perhaps a disputed succession stemming from the ambiguity of Darnley's own position as a king without the crown matrimonial – may well have helped to concentrate minds on the advantages she offered while still alive.

By 20 November Mary was at Craigmillar Castle, outside Edinburgh, where she stayed for two weeks. On 10 December she travelled to Stirling, for the royal baptism. History has tended to remember her stay at Craigmillar for the alleged plans laid there for the murder of Darnley, which took place two months later. Whatever the truth of that – and the point is infinitely debatable – most of the plans laid at Craigmillar concerned the baptism. Mary's son was baptised Charles James in the Chapel Royal at Stirling Castle on 17 December 1566, according to full Catholic rites. It was also the starting point for three days of elaborate celebrations designed to convey in their various ways an image of the power and stability of the Stewart monarchy.[32]

The baptism was followed by a banquet carefully organised as a meal of domestic reconciliation: Protestant magnates who had boycotted the baptism had the honour of serving the foreign ambassadors side by side with Catholic nobles. Argyll, Protestant patron of the west, and Lord Seton, the most resolute of the Catholic lords from the south-east, each carried a white staff in his hand, the traditional emblem to mark the end of a feud. The climax of the programme came in a

Renaissance triumph, modelled on the elaborate fête staged at Bayonne in 1565 which had marked the meeting between Charles IX (1560-74) and representatives of the court of Spain. A mock fort built on the present Castle Esplanade, representing the power of the monarchy, was stormed by a series of hostile assailants threatening war and chaos, including Moors and 'wyld Hieland men'. All were repulsed, amidst a spectacular fireworks display. The young 'prince of Scotland' was then proclaimed. This was the first full-scale Renaissance fête which Scotland, and indeed Great Britain, had ever seen. It had an explicit political message to convey. This was given cogent form in a celebratory poem written by a young Protestant minister, Patrick Adamson, to mark the birth of the prince but also borrowed from Bayonne:

> Our leader has transposed Mars ablaze with civil war into peace in our time. . . . A powerful young woman, whose race was from the lofty blood of kings, controls by her rule the warlike Scots . . . The importance of kingship is eternal; it will be in the power of the Stewart family; the crown of Mary awaits her grandsons . . . The fates will grant you to extend the territory of your realm, until the Britons, having finished with war, will learn at last to unite in one kingdom.[33]

The monarchy, so it was claimed, was the focal point for all the nobility, Protestant as well as Catholic. The continuance of the house of Stewart offered the best and indeed the only chance for peace and stability, as well as for an eventual union, on Scotland's own terms, with England.

This was a much more sophisticated and wide-ranging appeal than the Catholic revival planned earlier in 1566. As well as the mass, it offered liberty of conscience to all except the radical Calvinists such as Knox; two recruiting sergeants were more likely to be effective than one. The policy of concessions included the reformed Church. The grant of the smaller benefices had been made in October 1566, at what had been the original time planned for the baptism. Other concessions, including an outright gift of £10,000 in cash, were made to the Church at the time of the baptism. Mary, who had distanced herself from displays of Catholic populist feeling in Edinburgh at Easter in both 1565 and 1566, also chose this moment to restore John Hamilton, Archbishop of St Andrews, to his jurisdiction – a necessary preliminary to any process for a divorce from Darnley. By the end of 1566 Mary was thus playing the role of patron of both churches. Her privy council was by now a fully mixed body of Protestant and Catholics and included clergy from both Churches. Although the General Assembly continued to complain bitterly of the 'open erecting of idolatry', there were increasing links between the corridors of power in the royal government and the reformed Church. This was the moment, in December 1566, chosen by Knox to take sabbatical leave in England. In foreign policy, too, there were signs of a new but typically Stewart aggressive stance. Bolstered by the links of the rehabilitated Argyll with the Irish rebel Shane O'Neill, Mary's council suggested that commissioners be sent to London to renegotiate the terms of the amity.[34]

The Stirling triumph was the glittering culmination of nine months of hard work at the business of governing. Those months suggest neither panic nor collapse but a return to the policy of the years 1561-4, but with one difference – Mary was now more of an independent force in politics. If there is an analogy to be made with an earlier example of a similar demonstration of how to deal with disaffected elements in politics, it might be with the reconciliation of the nobility after two major rebellions in 1488-9. There were extra and complicating elements in Mary's reign, but the two rebellions, in 1565 and 1566, had been less serious affairs. The amount of success which the reconcilation of 1566 had effected is hard to judge. The new directions taken in policy were thrown into jeopardy by the mysterious murder of Darnley at the Kirk o' Field just outside Edinburgh, only a month after the court returned from Stirling. One small footnote in one of the most celebrated murder mysteries in Scottish history can be disposed of. There was every reason why Mary should be elsewhere on the night of 9/10 February. The marriage celebrations which she attended that night were not those of an obscure servant but of the architect of the Stirling triumph, Bastien Pagez.

The crisis of 1567

As with the Riccio murder of the previous year, there were many with motives against Darnley. There is, however, not one murder mystery but two, which help explain both its endless fascination and the amount of speculation which has gone on ever since. The first mystery – how far the Queen was involved or at least had prior knowledge of the plot in which the house at Kirk o' Field was partly blown up and Darnley killed by strangulation – can never be settled because the evidence against Mary is almost wholly circumstantial. Her husband had been effectively isolated (he had refused to attend the baptism but had failed to gain access to any of the ambassadors), but he was also still a considerable embarrassment. Far from being content with the role of Protestant plotter, Darnley had taken on the stance of being more Catholic than Mary herself, offering advice to Rome. She may have been pregnant by August 1566, but the evidence is far from compelling. And if there was, as has been argued, a new confidence and sense of direction in the royal government, that might be an additional motive for shedding Darnley through a divorce but not for risking all by having him murdered.

A solution of the second mystery – as to who actually committed the murder – demands an identification parade of a dozen or more likely candidates. They include Morton and his Douglases, or some of his other associates in the Riccio murder such as Lindsay or the Ruthvens; an agent of the Hamiltons who, as events would prove, did not scruple to resort to political assassination; an associate of Moray, who was conveniently away from Edinburgh at the time but had lost more than most in the recent redirection of royal policy; or Bothwell himself. The speculation is endless because neither mystery can be satisfactorily solved.

Less important than who committed the deed is who contemporaries thought had done it – and here the spotlight fell largely on Bothwell. Those suspicions were heightened by the nature of the trial on 12 April 1567, for it was blatantly rigged. A week later a reasonably well-attended parliament (there were fifty-nine present) agreed to further concessions, both to the reformed Church and to individual lords including Morton, Moray and Huntly. Bothwell's position was far from being entirely lost: a bond concluded in an Edinburgh tavern realised the support of eight bishops, ten earls and eleven lords. His abduction of the Queen a week later on 24 April, whether it was a pre-emptive strike to forestall a plot by others to seize Mary or she colluded in her own capture, united the disparate elements of opposition.

Even Mary's closest Catholic advisers were divided by it and by the subsequent marriage which took place, by Protestant rite, on 15 May.

A limited defence of Bothwell's own position can be made. He had long shown an admirably independent political cast of mind and had proven ability as an administrator. Although he was a Protestant, his scepticism (which prompted English observers to brand him 'of no religion') indicated that he could be comfortable in the flexible atmosphere the Queen's policy of 1566-7 had encouraged. But whatever Mary's motives, and the desire to have a strong man at her side was probably the foremost of them, it was the degree of her dependence on him in the spring of 1567 that was dangerous. Here was another Boyd or another Earl of Douglas exercising almost total control of the monarch; but it was all the more unacceptable to the political community because this was not a minority. The marriage, preceded by a divorce arranged with cynical expedition by the Archbishop of St Andrews, compounded the miscalculation. It gave fresh impetus to a strident propaganda campaign, orchestrated by the Lennox Stewarts, one of the most publicity-conscious families of the century; the powerful image of an infant prince demanding revenge was exploited through ballads, pasquils and crude pamphlets. For some, motives were entirely opportunistic; Darnley's murder brought him friends in death he had hardly known in life. Yet there was also a genuine sense of outrage amongst many, which must have been fuelled by the imagery of kingship in which Darnley had basked in 1565-6. As in 1482 and 1488, what exposed the monarchy to real danger was a sudden exposure of an internal rift within the house of Stewart.

On 15 June 1567 the Confederate Lords, as the coalition styled themselves, confronted the Queen and Bothwell at Carberry, near Musselburgh. It hardly deserves the title of a battle, for not a shot was fired nor a blow struck. Parleys took place, urging the Queen to separate herself from her new consort, individual challenges to single combat were made, but nothing came of either for almost twelve hours. Eventually a compromise was reached: a safe conduct for Bothwell was agreed and the Queen put her trust in her nobles. Bothwell went into exile and died in a Danish prison. Mary was led from the field, already taunted by insults, and taken to Edinburgh. The Confederate Lords had succeeded in removing the influence of Bothwell over the Queen, but only a few of them had a clear plan of action beyond that. Within four days Mary was taken to her island prison on Loch Leven, with the cries of the Edinburgh mob ringing in her ears. In her wake the fervent Protestant Earl of Glencairn seized the chance – quite illegally – to destroy the furnishings of Mary's private chapel at Holyrood, the symbol of how close to realisation a Catholic revival had come. The prospect of a Catholic Scotland died with the disappearance of its main focus in July 1567; Catholicism continued and even flourished in the provinces, but with little leadership or co-ordination. The General Assembly met in an excited mood within ten days of Mary's capture: the work of Reformation could begin afresh.[35]

Revolution and civil war

This was a revolution in a way that the revolution of 1560 was not. Yet the revolution of 1567 had its oddities too. At least three of the key figures of 1560 were absent. Châtelherault, nominal leader of the Lords of the Congregation in 1559 and still next in line to the throne after Mary's infant son, was not present. Also absent was Moray, who was still in France. And Knox was in England, still enjoying what may be claimed to be the oddest-timed period of sabbatical leave in Scottish history. They had, however, left behind able deputies: George Buchanan, who would take on the role of official apologist of the revolution, was Moderator of the decisive General Assembly of 1567; and Lord Lindsay had no scruples about (literally) forcing the hand of the Queen as she signed the three deeds which ended her rule in favour of her son and granted the regency to Moray.[36]

The Confederate Lords who had confronted Mary at Carberry were by no means a united party of Protestant revolutionaries. Amongst them were a handful of Catholic lords, such as Borthwick and Sempill; professional waverers like the Protestant Bishop of Galloway, who had entered into negotiations with Rome in 1565; and the Earl of Cassillis, who had changed his religion at least three times since 1560. It would have been surprising if men such as these had not been in the Confederacy, for its professed aim, at least before Carberry, was not to dethrone the Queen but to free her and her son from Bothwell's influence. The real revolution – in effect a coup within a coup – took place six weeks after Carberry, when Mary, probably in fear of her life, was forced to abdicate in favour of her son.

Charles James, now restyled James VI, was crowned at Stirling on 29 July 1567. It was a bizarre ceremony that took place, not in the Castle where he had been baptised only seven months before, but a few yards outside it in the parish church of the Holy Rude. The thirteen-month-old infant was crowned and anointed in the style of previous kings of Scots, but he had also to listen to a sermon from Knox, who took his text from the Book of Kings. It was the worst attended coronation in Scottish history – later a spokesman for Mary would claim that only a tenth of the nobility was present. Even the English ambassador – a fervent Protestant – was obliged to boycott the ceremony, for it was the act of an illegal regime that had challenged the sovereignty of the crown and threatened established order. The Elizabethan regime, still in process of establishing its own respectability, could not afford as yet to become entangled with it.

Mary escaped from Loch Leven Castle in May 1568 and for the next five years Scotland would be riven by a civil war, between followers of the young 'godly' prince and supporters of his Catholic mother. It was Mary's cause that was generally judged – both in Scotland and abroad – to be the respectable one. The Queen's party made much of the lack of the 'old blood of the nobility' in the new regime, which was headed by Moray and a council of regency. In retaliation the King's party stressed that this was a war of religion, as in France, and it complained bitterly of the unholy alliance of 'papists' and Protestants 'with no God but gear' among their adversaries. There were a handful of Catholic lords among the King's men, and a wide spectrum of religious opinion among the Queen's. The Marians included extreme Protestants such as the Earl of Rothes, who had approved of the Riccio murder; more moderate men such as Lethington, who was labelled as the 'Michael Wylie' (or Machiavelli) of Scottish politics; and hard-line Catholics such as Seton, the father of Mary's lady-in-waiting. Strange bed-fellows resulted: the Protestant 5th Earl of Huntly and his mostly Catholic family and kindred were loyal Queen's men but the still largely Catholic centre of Aberdeen, often mistakenly thought of as Huntly's pocket burgh, chose this moment to distance itself from its heavy-handed patron and offered its loyalty to the Moray regency.[37]

The issues, as in many civil wars, were not clear-cut. Mary's escape did not spark off an immediate counter-revolution because she had turned to the Hamiltons for aid and had been obliged to play a very Hamilton tune, which involved a sweeping condemnation of those who had opposed her at Carberry (when Châtelherault had been conveniently absent in France). At Langside she had to rely on Hamilton military competence, with disastrous consequences. Her flight into England three days after the battle did more than anything to make the issues unclear and uncertain; support fluctuated with every rumour of her likely return or continuing imprisonment. It was not uncommon for one monarch to hold another captive – Mary described herself as 'arrestée' from early on. There were, however, also unique elements in the situation. As a result, the Elizabethan regime found it difficult to make up its many minds as to how to cope with the presence of the best claimant to be heir-presumptive to the English throne.

For some, this may increasingly have become a war of the Hamilton succession rather than for the restoration of Mary Stewart. The Hamiltons' arch-rivals, the Douglases, were the most loyal of the King's men and the sharpest divide in the war lay between these two rival landed conglomerates. However, the nobles allied to the Hamiltons through marriage had an additional reason for giving them firm support, for it allowed them to harbour secret ambitions to the throne. The minor positions in the line of succession may not matter much in the twentieth century, but they were a key to both status and power in the sixteenth. For others, the main issue in politics was the rule of Moray as regent. The battle at Langside may have consolidated his hold on the regency for a time because of his striking success as a military leader. Compared by an English diplomat to an Old Testament captain of Israel when he took on the regency, he won his spurs against far superior numbers at Langside. Moray gained considerable respect amongst the nobility as a result, but the promised land proved elusive and the next eighteen months would show how difficult it was to construct a stable party of Protestant loyalists, still less to command the natural support which a legitimate monarch could draw upon. His assassination by a Hamilton in January 1570 transformed the nature of the war.

Scotland was without a regent for six months after Moray's death, until Lennox was appointed in July 1570. His death, as Maitland astutely predicted, changed the issues in the war, which were now as much about the 'regiment' of the realm as the succession. The father of the murdered Darnley, however, was not the man to bring about peace and reconciliation. The drift away from the King's party continued until after Lennox was assassinated fourteen months later in a dramatic night raid on a King's party parliament being held at Stirling. He was quickly succeeded by the more conciliatory figure of the Earl of Mar.

In the meantime the war of words had intensified. Each side had its own printer and propaganda machine. Thomas Bassenden printed at least fifteen Marian tracts at his press in Edinburgh,[38] and Robert Lekpreuik, the official printer to the General Assembly, moved from Edinburgh to St Andrews at the same time as Knox, after Marian forces occupied the capital in April 1571. Far more than during the Reformation crisis, both sides appealed to public opinion, both in Scotland and abroad. Each party also tried to lay hands on the instruments of power – the books of parliament and of the law courts – and each held its own parliaments. The fact that no fewer than six rival parliaments were held in the space of ten months after May 1571 is a measure of the dislocation of the political community. In May the Queen's lords held theirs in the accustomed place, the Edinburgh Tolbooth. The King's men held theirs in the Canongate, outside the burgh's walls but technically within its precincts. Greeted by a Marian bombardment from the Castle, what was dubbed the 'creeping parliament' met for little more than ten minutes – but that was long enough for the King's lords who attended it to issue forfeitures against leading Marians, including William Maitland and Gavin Hamilton. The rival parliaments set in motion a pattern of tit-for-tat seizures of lands and goods – a Marian parliament attended by just three nobles issued 200 forfeitures in August 1571 – and random, brutal executions of prisoners that lent a new and unusual bitterness to Scottish politics. A seventy-year-old priest was executed in June 1572 for bearing arms against the King. Thirty houses of King's men who had left Edinburgh were demolished in the early part of 1572 by the notorious Marian 'Captain of the Chimneys'. The violence, dubbed by contemporaries as the 'Douglas Wars', was more severe and more gratuitous than in the crisis of 1559-60 and the damage was worse, some even claimed, than that caused by the 'Rough Wooing'.

After May 1571 the focus of the war settled on Edinburgh, which was split in two in its loyalties. After it was taken by the Queen's lords, it had two town councils and two kirk sessions – the King's men from the burgh set up a complete government-in-exile in its port of Leith, two miles away. John Knox was forced into exile, in the comparative safety of St Andrews; his colleague, John Craig, chose to stay, and after the war would be banished (like Samuel Rutherford sixty years later) to that favourite open prison for dissident clergy – Aberdeenshire. Exactly one-half of the burgh establishment went to Leith, where they could continue trading overseas and nurse their resentments. The other half remained in the burgh, throughout a fifteen-month-long and increasingly bitter siege, called the 'wars between Leith and Edinburgh'. Food prices soared as each side waged a war of attrition, burning the mills and granaries for miles around.[39]

In July 1572 a truce was called and the Leith exiles, who had by now become a militant win-the-war faction amongst the King's men, marched into Edinburgh, in violation of the conditions of the truce, and reclaimed power. Over the next six months a procession of Edinburgh Marians, great and small, were forced to appear before the kirk session, bare-headed and in sackcloth, to confess their sins against their neighbours. They suffered double jeopardy: most also had to pay fines to the King's party which went, characteristically, straight into the pocket of the new regent, Morton. The war was almost over, but two obstacles remained. In February 1573 the major nobles made what amounted to a private deal amongst themselves in the Pacification of Perth – to unravel the feuds, exactions and forfeitures of the past six years. Only the core of the Marians in Edinburgh Castle held out, still hoping for military intervention by the Duke of Alva on behalf of Spain. It would take an English artillery corps and a four-day bombardment to force its inevitable surrender. Morton was ruthless to the last. Maitland, Mary's former secretary, died in suspicious circumstances after the Castle fell. Kirkcaldy of Grange, a distinguished soldier and long-time Protestant, was executed, as were the two Edinburgh goldsmiths who had been minting coin, with the Queen's head on it, in the Castle. One of them, James Mossman, was the owner of the building that is now called –

without irony – the John Knox house in the High Street.

The real turning-point in the war had come probably in September 1571. Until then most of the major nobles had supported Mary, because they still expected her to be freed from her English prison. The discovery in 1571 of a plot on Elizabeth's life organised by an Italian banker, Roberto Ridolfi, compounded the suspicions of the English Queen's counsellors, first roused by the rising of the Catholic northern earls in 1569. By 1572, with the English parliament demanding the Scottish Queen's head, there was little prospect of her return. It was from that point that the moulds of the two rival images of Mary began to set. Her obituary notices were, in a sense, already being composed. The propaganda of the King's party shrewdly grasped the moment and began to portray the young James as the 'rising sun' and Mary as the 'fallen star'. Without prospect of Mary's return, the Queen's cause melted away. Yet this took time and the King's party was in desperate financial straits. Already having raided the episcopal temporalities,[40] it resorted to a new device in March 1572, when a parliament ratified the issue of a coin, called the half merk piece (worth 6s 8d), with the young King's head on it.[41] Its silver content, however, was heavily debased and compared unfavourably with the Marian coinage still being minted in the Castle. It might be thought of as a speculative rights issue in the cause of James VI. Fourteen months later, the investment matured. It was the fall of Edinburgh Castle in May 1573 which finally brought security to the King's men and an end to the reign of Mary Stewart.

The Marian age and its end

Morton had succeeded the Earl of Mar as Regent on 24 November 1572 – the very day of John Knox's death. It was the symbolic end of an era. By 1574 most of the major figures of the Reformation period – Knox, Châtelherault, Archbishop Hamilton (executed in 1571), Moray, and Lennox – were dead or removed from the scene. In France, the picture was the same; the Dukes of Guise and Montmorency and the King of Navarre were all dead by 1568 and the two Guise cardinals by 1578. For Mary, the effect was to leave her almost completely isolated; although only thirty in 1572, she was already the relic of an earlier generation. By now she was forced to rely on the hotheads around her, like John Lesley, Bishop of Ross, or on new recruits to her cause, like the English Catholic, Thomas Morgan, who were usually more Marian and far more inclined to conspiracy than the Queen herself. She would spend another fifteen years in an English prison before she was executed, on the basis of her alleged involvement in the Babington plot, which English *agents provocateurs* had infiltrated. The plot posed no real threat to Elizabeth, but it fitted perfectly the image of a papist threat to the Protestant isle and its Queen. James made a token protest, and demanded compensation. Mary was buried, against her own wishes, at Peterborough and subsequently as part of a rehabilitation programme organised by her son, in Westminster Abbey. Her own preference was to be buried at Rheims, beside her Guise relations. That wish, the detailed bequests made in her will and her correspondence in captivity all point to the likelihood that her greatest interests always lay in the courts and kingdoms of France and Scotland. Her interest in the English succession receded from the time of the Darnley marriage; while never conceded, it was not pursued with any urgency or seriousness after 1565. The real obsession with the English throne lay in the mind of her son.[42]

History tends to show that a nation gets the heroes it needs rather than those it deserves. Often the reign of Mary is personalised as a titanic conflict between the Queen and John Knox. It was hardly ever that. All four of Knox's famous interviews with Mary took place in the first two and a half years after her return; the last came in December 1563. By 1565, although the new Church was still consolidating its position through the plantation of a Protestant ministry in the parishes, Knox's own position in Edinburgh was slipping as the party of radicals brought to power in the capital by the revolution of 1559-60 began to lose control of the town council.[43] Symbols they may have been – Calvinist firebrand and Catholic monarch – but if so, the confrontation needs to be cast in terms contemporaries would have understood: to be set against the formidable persona of Scotland's 'trumpeter of God' is the image of a brilliant Renaissance queen, which reached its peak only in the years 1565-6.

The leading players in Scottish politics were, as ever, the magnates. Knox discovered, to his cost, the price of putting his faith in nobles in 1561 and again in 1565. With most nobles, attitudes to sovereignty and the interest of kin, Knox discovered, counted for more than religious convictions.[44] The concerted assault on the minds of the nobility, which lay behind the cult of honour and culminated in the Renaissance triumph at Stirling in 1566, showed how political attitudes might be changed in the hothouse atmosphere of the court. Images of Diana, Venus, Astrea and an age of gold flooded the court and their impact should not be underestimated. The clash between Knox and Mary had been recast, into terms which favoured the Queen: no longer a simple conflict (if ever it had been) between rival faiths, it was now a confrontation between strict Calvinism and a mature, charismatic Renaissance monarchy.

The scandal of the Bothwell marriage and the revolution of 1567 changed the issues at stake. In the last resort, the events of 1567 had as their underlying cause the memory that Mary, like James II or V, had taken on two of her greatest nobles and eclipsed them. If the heads of the houses of Gordon and Hamilton could fall at the royal whim, who could feel safe in the crisis of 1567? The cult of honour at the court was intended to reassure the nobility, but the fear of an act of oblivion, again rumoured in the spring and early summer of 1567, pulled in the opposite direction. Like other Stewart crises before it, that in 1567 was at bottom a crisis of noble confidence – in the Stewart monarchy. By the summer of 1568, however, that crisis was over, at least for the majority of the magnates who were by then willing to see her return to power. At Langside, Mary put her trust in the Hamiltons and paid the price of their incompetence. Her flight into England compounded that error. Few in Scotland before 1571 could have been confident that she would not return to claim her throne and be acclaimed by the majority of her nobles – despite the calculated campaign of character assassination, including the 'discovery' of the Casket Letters, which had gone on since 1567. The length of the civil war is testimony to the real status of Queen Mary.

There are very few heroes in the final acts of the story of Mary, Queen of Scots. The deciding factor for both Mary and the future of the reformed Church was a civil war, which was conducted with a venom and vindictiveness that was unusual in Scottish history. Both Mary and Knox played largely passive roles in it. The Regent Moray for a brief two years offered a clear and committed path to a godly future. His death brought further confusion and violence. A punitive English raid in 1570 through Clydesdale equalled the devastation wrought during the 1540s. Moray's successor was also assassinated. The Catholic primate of the realm was executed. Homes, crops and mills were burned. The capital was taken and besieged for fifteen months. Foreign powers were courted by both sides to intervene. The Regent who brought the war to an end was a Douglas; he brought pacification rather than peace.

14

THE REIGN OF JAMES VI

O N 29 JULY 1567, FIVE DAYS AFTER HIS MOTHER HAD BEEN FORCIBLY DEPOSED, THE infant Prince of Scotland was crowned. It was an odd ceremony which involved, for only the second time in known Scottish history, a change of name of the monarch. The infant King was crowned, not as Charles James, but as the godly prince James VI (1567-1625). The coronation took place in Stirling, but not in the Chapel Royal where his mother had been crowned in 1542. The venue was the ordinary parish church of the burgh, the Holy Rude. The ceremony underlined some of the tensions which existed in 1567, in both Church and state, for it was an *ad hoc* mixture of new and old. James was inaugurated as well as crowned (as every monarch since David II had been), but some of the more obviously Catholic rites such as anointing were avoided. The crown was placed on his head by the former Catholic Bishop of Orkney, Robert Stewart, and a sermon from the Book of Kings was preached by John Knox. Here was a mixture of broad Protestantism and strict Calvinism.

The King's household had already been established at Stirling Castle and he was kept in its comparative security for most of his childhood, as royal heirs before him including James V and Mary had been. His tutors were the celebrated humanist scholar George Buchanan (who had had charge of the young Lord James Stewart thirty years before) and the younger, though hardly less talented academic, Peter Young; his guardianship rested with the Erskine family, hereditary keepers of the Castle, and (after the death of the Earl who was Regent 1571-2), in effect with the formidable Countess of Mar. What distinguished this royal childhood from many others before it was the fact that possession of the young King was divorced from the reins of power. Morton, who was Regent until 1578 and still the leading figure in government until 1580, paid as little attention to James as he did to most of the great nobles of the realm.

The ascendancy of Morton (1572-80)

The regency of Morton, in many respects, was a turning-point in the sixteenth century. The late 1570s saw the beginnings of a decisive upswing in trade, which pointed to better times ahead; the end of the long slump in exports, which had lasted since the Wars of Independence, brought new levels of prosperity to both merchants and landowners. This was also, however, a decade of severe price inflation; begun by the food shortages provoked by the civil war, it was fuelled by the deliberate depreciation of the coinage by the government. The £ Scots dropped sharply against the English as a result; in 1567 it had stood at 1:5.5, by 1587 it was 1:7.33 and by 1600 it was at 1:12. The regency saw a renewed emphasis on the restoration of law and order, with a flurry of justice ayres in the south-east between 1573 and 1576, but it lacked the arts of patronage to bind the magnates to it. Morton's was the first stable government decisively committed to Protestantism. It was also a regime in new and deep conflict with the reformed Church; anxious to assert royal control over ecclesiastical appointments, it clashed with a new and better-organised generation of ministers headed by Andrew Melville. It was an anger born of mutual disappointment: the close relationship during Moray's regency between a godly church and state had deteriorated after 1571 into a series of controversial appointments of archbishops and bishops which brought sharp criticism of the Regent from both the pulpit and the General Assembly. Morton reacted by increasingly distancing himself from the Assembly.

Morton's was also a government decisively committed to the alliance with England, whose military support had given it final victory in 1573; at the end of the siege of Edinburgh Castle in 1573, Knox's successor as minister of St Giles' had led his congregation in giving thanks to Queen Elizabeth for their deliverance. The Morton government sponsored legislation based on English models on issues as widely separated as ecclesiastical polity and poor relief: the Scottish style of the 1572 Oath of Supremacy closely followed the English version of the same year and the Poor Law Act of 1575 was heavily influenced by the English act of 1572. Yet the victory of 1573 left Anglo-Scottish relations in a curious limbo; there were no permanent ambassadors in either Edinburgh or London, the subsidies promised to Morton failed to materialise and the failure of the Scotland-watchers stationed in Berwick to detect the signs of his growing unpopularity in 1580 would contribute to his fall. The client state which England expected after 1573 slipped out of its sphere of influence by 1578; the complex politics of the period between 1580 and 1582 distanced the two countries and aid given to the short-lived radical Ruthven regime of 1582-3 compromised relations after it fell. The eventual league with England, the Treaty of Berwick concluded in 1586, brought some stability to the relationship, but with closeness also came acrimony. The major problem of the personal reign, which began with the growing role of the King in politics from 1585 onwards, was until 1603 the pursuit of the succession.[1]

The years of James's mature reign were indelibly marked, both by the problems of the period between 1572 and 1584 and by the solutions found for them. At the root of James's difficulties, as with almost every Stewart monarch before him, was finance. Much is sometimes made of the fact that from 1586 James depended on a pension from the English crown. Morton had been promised a pension by the English government in 1573 but never received it. James accepted £4,000 sterling in 1586, seems to have received only £3,000, and between then and 1603 received some £58,000 from Elizabeth. The amount was trifling – less in real terms than Mary's jointure as a Dowager Queen of France in the 1560s.[2] It did not begin to meet the massively rising costs of royal government. The feuing of crown lands by both James IV and V had had the effect of steadily drying up the crown's traditional landed income and forcing increasing resort to other sources of revenue. And the reluctance of James VI to make grants of crown lands forced the largesse always implied in good lordship to take a new form – of pensions. James was a pensioner of Elizabeth; more significant, however, is the fact that increasing numbers of nobles were pensioners of the Scottish crown. The Morton period had shown that the crown neglected patronage at its peril. The cosseting of the nobility put immense strain, however, on the resources of the crown and forced new courses.

Everywhere customary sources of income, both traditional and illicit, were pressed harder upon. The profits made by Morton's government in its manipulation of the silver content of the coinage are unquantifiable. The political effects were akin to the 'black money' of James III; the loudest complaints came from the burghs, and especially from the Edinburgh merchants who had backed Morton in the civil war. In a related incident, four members of the burgh council were imprisoned for five months in 1575 for exporting bullion; the council had not been treated in as cavalier a fashion since the crisis of 1559, but the affair pointed towards the new level of interference in urban government which characterised the personal reign.[3] The government made upwards of £100,000 out of debasements of the coinage between 1583 and 1596. By then, however, protest was more muted; the Mint had become an accustomed part of the revenue-raising machinery of the king's government. The increase in exports brought in more income from customs – £4,494 in 1578 and £5,399 in 1582, but not enough to satisfy the exchequer which sought new means of increasing income. The customs were set in tack (in effect privatised) in 1582, but the return was disappointing and the experiment ended in 1590. In 1597 customs duties were raised sharply, especially on the expanding parts of the export trade such as salmon and coal and a duty on imports was levied for the first time. It had the effect of raising revenues to £11,570 in 1598. Throughout the rest of the reign and especially in the 1610s, the government would repeatedly turn to the growth areas of the economy, such as the export of cloth or the flourishing import-export business in grain to impose taxes on windfall profits.[4]

Although it is usually said that a new resort was made to national taxation after 1581, it was in Morton's regency that the practice first seen in the reigns of James IV and V, was restarted. Four separate taxes totalling £4,666 were levied between 1575 and 1578. Significantly, three of them were for judicial expeditions to the Borders; Morton's justice did not come cheaply. The significance of 1581 was that taxation was raised to new heights; its demand was for £40,000 whereas the largest exaction of the Morton period had been £12,000. By 1588 the scale of tax demands had risen to £100,000, for the King's marriage to Anne of Denmark; the baptism of their first born, Henry, cost a further £100,000 in 1594 – in contrast to the £12,000 levied for James's own baptism in 1566. Diplomatic missions to England brought new levels of expenditure – a tax of 200,000 merks was agreed by parliament in 1597 and a further 100,000 merks in 1601. Yet the 1601 tax was a hard-fought compromise, for in 1600 James had demanded the huge sum of 100,000 crowns (£333,333) in case he had to wage a war of the English succession. The road to London in 1603 was rockier than is often imagined, but it was also paved with Scottish gold. And fiscal demands increased after 1603, to result in what amounted to virtual annual taxation; Edinburgh, for example, paid twenty-two taxes between 1603 and 1625.[5]

The clash of two kingdoms

There were two enduring legacies of the Morton period: a bitter conflict with the Church and an arsenal of weapons to deal with it. The conflicts of the 1560s, so often portrayed as a clash of personality between Queen Mary and John Knox, had had hidden ambiguities: the Kirk was always uncomfortably aware of its economic dependence on the crown and Knox's unrelenting criticism of the Queen made many members of the General Assembly uneasy. In the 1570s the process was rather different: many of the unresolved questions left hanging over from Mary's reign and the civil war period were sucked into a clash of powerful personalities which intensified the acrimony between Church and state.

The leading spokesman of the ministers was Andrew Melville, the son of an Angus laird who, since graduation from St Andrews in 1564, had studied in Paris and taught in Poitiers and Geneva. He returned to Scotland in 1574 to take up the position of Principal of Glasgow University as a scholar with an international reputation rather than as a Calvinist ideologue intent on recasting the mould of the reformed Church. By 1580, when he moved to St Andrews as Principal of St Mary's College, he was the acknowledged 'light and leader' of both the 'schools and Kirk of Scotland'.[6] He played a prominent rather than dominant part in the revision of the programme of the Church in the 1570s. His reputation was formidable, but nonetheless puzzling: the bulk of his writings were in Latin; he left no sermons in print nor a personal manifesto – save for a near-hagiography by his nephew, James – yet he managed something which Knox had never done, to construct a close-knit party of ministers. There was a Melvillian party in the Kirk; there was never a Knoxian party in anything like the same sense. In retrospect, Melville's greatest contribution to the Church was his reorganisation of St Mary's as the major seminary in Scotland for the training of ministers. His work at Glasgow, while impressive in abstract, resulted in only a handful of graduates. St Mary's, designed as an 'anti-seminary' to counter the menace of Jesuit and seminary priests and with a revised curriculum partly based on Glasgow's New Foundation of 1577, quickly became acknowledged as the 'temple' of the new Jerusalem, demanding continuous reform of the Church. It was this academic, who was never a parish minister and held only the office of 'doctor', who, sharp in mind and sharper still in tongue, became a leading figure in the Assembly's protracted negotiations with the regent over church polity from 1575 onwards. He would be the Kirk's chief spokesman for the next thirty years, until an exasperated James VI banished him into exile in France in 1611.

The spectacular confrontations between Melville and James VI are often taken to sum up the irreconcilable stances of Kirk and King; their most famous exchange took place at Falkland Palace in 1596 when Melville declared: 'Thair is twa Kings and twa Kingdomes in Scotland. Thair is Christ Jesus the King, and His kingdom, the Kirk, whase subject King James the Saxt is, and of whase kingdome nocht a king, nor a lord, nor a heid, but a member!'[7] Yet this was a near-parody of the doctrine of the two kingdoms, framed after more than twenty years of confrontation between entrenched positions. The personality clashes of minister with regent or king are similarly a caricature of a much more complex reality. Both Church and state had ambitions to operate in both kingdoms, or at least to redraw the dividing line between them. The Kirk at times since 1580 had thought of demanding direct representation for the General Assembly in parliament – until James gave it in the unwelcome shape of bishops. Yet the crown wanted bishops at least as much for the influence they could provide in the parishes as in parliament or presbytery. The main initial struggle between the two kingdoms lay in the debatable ground of education: commissions had been set up in the 1560s to investigate the universities, but by the Assembly. By the mid-1570s it was Regent Morton who had seized the initiative, establishing rival committees to investigate both schools and universities. The foundation of a new college, at Edinburgh, in the early 1580s saw a bad-tempered tussle between three parties – Kirk, town council and the crown – for control of it and its curriculum. The 'tounis college', eventually established in 1583 as Scotland's fourth university, was the first victory for the new Erastianism and the first serious defeat for the Kirk.[8]

The other main battle-ground lay in church polity. There the affair which cast its shadow over the Morton regency was the Leith settlement of 1571-2. Concluded between a convention of the Kirk and representatives of the privy council amidst the heightened emotions of a civil war which was only beginning to turn in favour of the King's party, the 'settlement' settled little. What happened at Leith were talks about talks. The essential issues were hardly considered: the question of the nature of oversight was shelved; bishops continued, and were to be nominated by the crown, but they were also subject in spiritual matters to the General Assembly. Much ink has been spilt – and wasted – on the subject of whether Knox gave his approval to the bishops enshrined in the settlement. He did, as did most of the Kirk, but the agreement was strictly an interim one.[9] The atmosphere surrounding the issue of oversight was, however, fatally soured by the behaviour of some of the churchmen already appointed, and especially the two kinsmen of Morton – John Douglas, the aged Archbishop of St Andrews, and George Douglas, the loose-living Bishop of Moray. By 1575 explicit criticism of the bench of bishops had begun to surface amongst the more strident voices in the General Assembly: John Durie, one of the Edinburgh ministers but also a late convert (he had been a Benedictine monk until at least 1567), declared his objections 'to the name and office of a bishop'.[10] Yet it seems likely that for most the criticisms were still *ad hominem*. George Douglas had been criticised for sexual conduct not befitting his office, John Douglas for lack of attention to his duties because of his infirmity, and the new Archbishop of St Andrews appointed in 1576, Patrick Adamson, for his energetic embracing of Morton's policy of conformity with England. Alternatively, it was at times the government's insensitive timing of ecclesiastical appointments – as in 1581 with the nomination of Robert Montgomery to Glasgow – which inflamed clerical opinion. It is difficult to make out of this a clear thread of logic which pointed to the renewed embrace of a first principle of the Reformation of 1560, although many historians have spent much effort in doing so. The General Assembly did not declare the office of bishop unscriptural until 1580. There was no headlong rush, despite the all too obvious failings of the bench of bishops, into presbyterianism. The reformers of the 1570s thought in terms of the pressing needs of the Kirk rather than stances on what were as yet fairly abstract principles.

The Kirk faced a threefold crisis in the 1570s: there was a growing crisis of manpower, with many of the pre-Reformation clergy who had filled the posts of readers dying off and as yet not enough young graduates to replace them; the spectre of a Catholic revival, fuelled by a mission directed from the Continent, had begun to haunt its proceedings; and it saw no likelihood of active support from the state for Morton repeatedly refused to consult with the Assembly. It is hardly any wonder that it was desperately concerned to ensure cohesion and direction in its efforts to continue the work of spreading the Gospel. The existing bishops and superintendents, it recognised, were overworked and it repeatedly made appointments of visitors or commissioners to help with the work of oversight. The *Second Book of Discipline*, drawn up in 1578 after two years of work by a series of committees, was both the product of the threefold crisis and an answer to it.

Like the *First Book* of 1560-1, the *Second Book* of 1578 is sometimes given a permanence and status which is at odds with the circumstances of its compilation. Out of date almost from the moment it was approved, it should, like the *First Book*, be seen as a signpost in the Church's developing vision of itself rather than a tablet of stone on which fundamental or immutable principles were written. Its financial claims to the revenues of the old Church were conceived more in hope than in earnest and its view of the relations between Church and state were specifically rebutted by parliament in 1578. The *Second Book* sought to solve the problem of manpower by reducing the number of parishes from over a thousand to about 600, but this too quickly became a dead letter. It did not give birth to a presbyterian system – indeed it has been pointed out that the word 'presbyter' (meaning eldership) occurs only twice in the *Second Book*.[11] What happened was that amidst the frustrations of the failure of its own carefully devised programme of reform and a confused political situation which threatened much but promised little the Kirk cut short its losses.

A revised scheme was drawn up in 1581 in which the Church tried to make the best of its existing assets: thirteen presbyteries were set up, mainly in the Melvillian heartland of the east coast and the Lowlands, 'to be examplars to the rest which may be established thereafter'.[12] Most, in fact, were the reconstruction under a different name with new responsibilities for oversight and discipline of a body which already existed – the exercise, which had been devised after 1560 as an aid to improve the quality and ensure the conformity of the parish ministry. It was the Church's misfortune that these modest beginnings became entangled with the complex feuding which engulfed politics after the fall and execution of Morton in 1581. By 1584 – after the rise and fall of the Ruthven regime of 1582-3 which had been rashly acclaimed by the General Assembly as a 'work of reformation' and the coincidental appearance in print of George Buchanan's *History of Scotland*, the manifesto of the revolution of 1567 – the presbytery had become, in the eyes of those anxious to reassert the authority of the crown, a seditious instrument undermining both state and Church. Like 'puritan', the word presbytery, a 'new erected society of ministers',[13] became something of a smear; its conspiratorial image was at best a half-truth.

The voice that comes through the pages of works such as David Calderwood's monumental *History of the Kirk* is the uncompromising one of Melvillianism. Yet the reformed Church was in reality in two minds on most of the key issues which confronted it in Jacobean Scotland. It was at its most effective and unanimous in its basic mission of spreading the Gospel; beyond that, there was a mixture of opinions or even a lack of interest on questions such as ecclesiastical polity and relations with the state. The General Assembly from the late 1570s onwards was dominated by the 'forward' ministers, who came mostly from Lothian and Fife. Better educated and better paid than most of their colleagues, they were also more conversant with the corridors of power within the Church; they set the agenda for meetings of the General Assembly in the Moderator's privy conference; their rhetorical gifts ensured that they dominated proceedings; and their position in the most prominent pulpits of the land ensured that their views were widely known. The most dramatic example of both the publicity-consciousness of the Melvillian ministers and the new

enthusiasm for Calvinism which was beginning to emerge amongst ordinary folk by
the 1580s came with the return of John Durie to Edinburgh in 1582 after his
expulsion for seditious preaching:

> As he is coming to Edinburgh there met him at the Gallowgreen
> [Grassmarket] 200, but ere he came to the Netherbow their number increased
> to 400, but they were no sooner entered but they increased to 600 or 700, and
> within short space the whole street was replenished even to Saint Geilis Kirk;
> the number was esteemed to be 2,000. At the Netherbow they took up the
> 124 Psalme, 'Now Israel may say'.[14]

For those familiar with the layout of Edinburgh's streets, this may seem a circuitous
route; the point was that it triumphantly retraced the traditional route for formal
royal entries to the capital, such as Queen Mary had made in 1561. Yet the General
Assembly was as yet not at all general. In the absence of full records, it is not known
how many ministers actually attended it but they were almost certainly a small
minority of the total ministry. Even in the frenzied atmosphere of the 1640s, fewer
than one minister in three came to the General Assembly even once; and of those
who did fewer than half ever came a second time.[15]

It was this flaw in the make-up of the Kirk which the Arran regime, brought to
power after the collapse of the Ruthven regime in 1583 and more royalist than the
King himself, ruthlessly exploited in the crisis of 1584-5 and James VI would do the
same, by different means, after 1596. In the parliament of 1584, laws were passed
subjecting all estates, including the Kirk, to the authority of the crown. The
Melvillians objected loudly and more than a score of them fled into exile in England
in protest. The government responded by demanding that the remaining members
of the ministry subscribe articles affirming their attachment to the so-called 'Black
Acts' and condemning the exiles. The subscription crisis was the first time that the
authority of the Melvillians over the Kirk had been shaken. Some of the more
prominent ministers held out; the Edinburgh kirk session was split and those that
refused were called to the King's palace at Falkland to force their hand. The bulk of
the ministry, however, did subscribe, to the dismay of the radicals.

The regime which oversaw the passing of the 'Black Acts' fell at the end of 1585,
yet the legislation remained on the statute book and was reaffirmed in 1596-7. Even
after the 'Golden Act' of 1592 reaffirming the privileges of the Kirk, all ecclesiastical
assemblies – the General Assembly and presbyteries included – met by the implicit
consent of king and parliament. It was this tool which James was able to exploit
after 1596, when he forced the Assembly to meet outside the hothouse climate of
Edinburgh. The Melvillian party resented the influx of ministers from remote parts
which this action encouraged; already in 1596 James Melville, nephew of Andrew,
lampooned the 'drunken Orkney ass' who had then led the subservient rabble from
the north happy to accommodate the crown. The struggle for control of the two
kingdoms was not a simple, clear-cut one between Kirk and King; it was also a battle
for the hearts and minds of the ministry. By 1610 it seemed that the Jacobean
solution had been accepted by a majority within the Church, if with differing
degrees of enthusiasm; 'parliamentary bishops' had been appointed in 1600 and by
1606 bishops had been fully restored to parliament; they were installed as 'constant
moderators' of presbyteries in 1606; and in 1610 the General Assembly approved the
restoring of most of their jurisdictions. The Kirk had shown itself to be caught in

two minds; Morton, Arran and James VI had, by contrast, been single-minded in their determination to force the Kirk to come to terms with living with a godly prince.[16]

The Ruthven raid and royalist reaction

The Morton period had built a log-jam of frustrated expectations, for the nobility as much as for the Kirk. They were released in dramatic fashion shortly after the arrival in September of Esmé Stewart, Sieur d'Aubigné and a nephew of Matthew, 4th Earl of Lennox. The appearance of this thirty-seven-year-old cousin of Darnley created as startling a counter-revolution in politics as had that of Lennox fifteen years before. His immediate preferment at court – in March 1580 he was granted the Earldom of Lennox, which was elevated to a Dukedom in 1581 – caused resentment amongst some nobles but roused expectations amongst others of escaping from the dead hand of the Douglas monopoly of patronage which had prevailed for most of the 1570s. It provoked a frenzied bout of anti-papistry amongst the radical ministers, who suspected Esmé of being a papal agent. To convince them otherwise, James and Esmé subscribed what was in effect the first national covenant – the King's Confession (more usually known afterwards as the Negative Confession) in 1581. Its significance lay far in the future – for it would be incorporated almost verbatim in the National Covenant of 1638 – rather than in the present; it convinced none of the ministers, but it again showed how it was usually the crown which dictated the pace of the dialogue between Church and state. The helplessness of the Melvillians to influence the course of events in 1580-2 made them aware of their vulnerability even in a supposedly Protestant state. They stood by, uncertain and divided, as Morton was accused in a meeting of the privy council in December 1580 of that most flexible of indictments – involvement in the murder of Darnley. By June 1581 Morton was dead – executed with a 'kiss' of the blunt instrument of his own Maiden, a primitive guillotine which he had introduced to Scotland during his regency. The stage was set for a palace coup and a brief alliance between the Melvillian ministers and the disaffected amongst the nobility.

The coup came in August 1582 with the Ruthven raid, which took its name from the ultra-Protestant magnate, Lord Ruthven, Earl of Gowrie. Later these nobles would claim that their action was a repeat of the godly revolution of 1567. The General Assembly clearly thought so, for it endorsed the coup. Yet the rebels were an odd coalition of committed radical Protestants, dissidents with a chequered past, and even some ex-Marians.[17] While the Assembly made haste in 1582 to begin proceedings against a number of bishops, the Ruthven regime itself did little to help the Kirk except to turn a blind eye to its actions. This was not a Protestant regime which, like that in 1567, went hand in hand with the Kirk towards the promised land. It had gained power by the tried and trusted method of seizing the person of the young King; it lost power, in June 1583, by the equally sure means of allowing him to escape. It was hardly surprising that the crown would detect in the events of 1582 a Calvinist conspiracy, yet there are grave doubts as to how real that conspiracy was.

The royalist backlash took a number of forms, but its focus lay in the parliament of May 1584. It met amidst rigorous security: the doors of the Edinburgh Tolbooth were guarded and a number of known Melvillian sympathisers, women as well as men, were forced out of the town during its four-day proceedings. In a flamboyant gesture, some ministers took legal instruments of protest at the Market Cross a few yards away before fleeing into exile in England. They were followed by a smaller rump of nobles. It was symptomatic of the relationship between the two groups of exiles that they set themselves up 300 miles apart – the ministers in London and the nobles in Newcastle. In the meantime the Arran regime ruthlessly exploited the situation. Over the next twelve months ministers were coerced into subscription. In the burghs where a campaign of mass interference with elections had begun in October 1583 – no fewer than seven of the twelve largest burghs of the realm were involved – the advantage was pressed home. It threatened not only the cherished independence of the burghs but also the position of the nobles who were their provosts. In its various ways, the crisis of 1584 was probably as great a threat to aristocratic power as any other incident in the century. In the capital, Arran foisted himself on the council as its provost; the next step, which was without precedent, was for the loyalist town council to nominate the kirk session direct. No repeat performance of a kirk session parading its conscience before the King, as Edinburgh's had done over subscription at Falkland Palace, was to be allowed in the authoritarian climate Arran had created. Arran fell, on the return of the exiled lords in November 1585, but both the climate and the bulk of his administration survived, including the secretary Maitland of Thirlestane (brother of Lethington, Queen Mary's secretary), who was the architect of the subscription scheme.

The personal reign (1585-1603)

When James, now aged nineteen, began to emerge as the predominant factor in politics in 1585, most of the courses he would take until 1603 were already mapped out for him. His had not been a minority of administrative confusion and fast-depreciating royal assets. Despite the tortuous complexity of its politics, clear threads of government – seen by some historians as a *via media* and by others as a new authoritarianism – had already been firmly established.[18] The emergence of a mature king, who, unlike James IV, did not have to serve a period of probation or, unlike James V, have to make the recouping of lost revenues his first priority, permitted what is sometimes called, rather misleadingly, a reassertion of monarchy to gain pace. Nor did his marriage – to Anne of Denmark in 1589 – mark, as with James III, a significant step towards his independence from those around him. The largely anonymous figure of Anne, who was only fourteen at the time of the marriage and made little impact on the very masculine Scottish court, seems out of place in the line of tough-minded spouses of Stewart kings in the fifteenth and sixteenth centuries.

The first crisis of the personal reign came only in 1592, after seven years of almost unreal harmony between King, nobles and ministers. It took the form of the celebrated murder in February 1592 of the 'bonnie Earl of Moray'. The only relationship which the well-known ballad bears to reality is that the Earl was indeed bonnie. The feud between him and the Earl of Huntly was, like most feuds, largely a matter of a local dispute which had been allowed to get seriously out of hand. When Moray's kinsman, the quixotic figure of Francis Stewart, 5th Earl of Bothwell, became involved the feud spilled over into court politics. Bothwell's sensational arrest on a charge of witchcraft along with a coven of North Berwick 'witches' gives the affair an air of supernatural intrigue which it hardly deserves; his escape, the repeated failures of James's government to catch him and his increasingly ostentatious raids on royal palaces – including one on the Palace of Holyroodhouse in July 1593 when the King was trapped in his own inner sanctum, the privy of his own presence chamber – lend it a strong whiff of farce. The persistent demands of Moray's mother for justice – she commissioned a portrait of the corpse, which lay unburied for six years – add an element of the macabre.

Despite its eccentricities, this was a prolonged and major crisis for James's authority, for the Kirk by 1592 had sprung to the defence of the unlikely figures of both Moray and Bothwell, victims, as it saw it, of a papist conspiracy. The fragile understanding between James and the Kirk had broken down and the concessions made in the 'Golden Act' of 1592, which promised less than was apparent at first sight, could not put it back together again.[19] The affair was resolved only through the stupidity of Huntly and Bothwell, who had decided, ironically, to join forces in 1594. A major feud which had threatened to pull apart the carefully constructed coalition of loyalties painstakingly erected by Maitland since 1585 became a rebellion, which was (as always) much easier for the crown to deal with. By early 1595 a chastened Huntly was contained and Bothwell was exiled, never to return. It was the last concerted protest by magnates in James's reign. It had perhaps shown that the system erected by Maitland had stood the test,[20] but it also showed that James was liable to panic in a crisis. This was one of his own making, as was the curious but lesser affair which brought about the killing of the Earl of Gowrie in August 1600. James was perhaps fortunate that noble politics threw up only two crises in his long reign.

Maitland died in 1595 and no replacement as chancellor was made until 1598 when the post was filled by the elderly Montrose. The years that followed are difficult to characterise with any accuracy. They are littered with declarations of James's own intentions – including his manual of kingship, *Basilikon Doron*, written in 1598 – which may give a misleading fixity of purpose to his general desire to be a 'universal king'. After Maitland's death, James declared that 'he would no more use chancellor or other great men in . . . his causes' and he dismissed his treasurer, the Master of Glamis, in the following year. His desire to be his own chief minister was, however, held in check by severe limitations of finance. The crown faced near-bankruptcy: 'All things are come to such confusion . . . that there is not wheat nor bere, silver nor other rent, to serve his Highness sufficiently in bread and drink,' reported the privy council.

The remedy hit upon in 1596 was the appointment of an eight-man commission – the Octavians – to take control of his chaotic finances. Their target was to raise royal income by at least £100,000 a year. Their room for manoeuvre was cramped by the fact that no fewer that five revocations had already been issued, the first as early as 1575 which went back to 1513, and the latest as recently as 1594. Yet their impact was wide-ranging: it was the Octavians who were responsible for the drastic revision of customs rates and the introduction of import duties in 1597; the planning of the largest tax in Scotland's history to date, of 200,000 merks in 1597, came during their period of influence; but they also looked pointedly at the prospects of reviving the crown's traditional sources of income. Crown lands and feudal duties were scrutinised, and so were the possibilities of gaining control of lands in the Lordship

1. From Matthew Paris's map of Britain c. 1250. It shows the barrier of the 'sea of Scotland' and the strategic significance of Stirling Bridge.

2. (Above) David I and his successor, the young Malcolm IV, from Malcolm's charter for Kelso Abbey of 1159.

3. (Left) James II, the first contemporary portrait of a Scottish king, made by Jörg von Ehingen, an Austrian visitor to his court in the 1450s.

4. (*Above*) Columba's *Brecbennach*.

5. (*Right*) The Fetternear Banner, a late fifteenth-century devotion of the Edinburgh merchant guild. It reflects the influence of the Bruges cult of the Holy Blood. (*Above*) A sixteenth-century statue of St Andrew, by then Scotland's sole national saint.

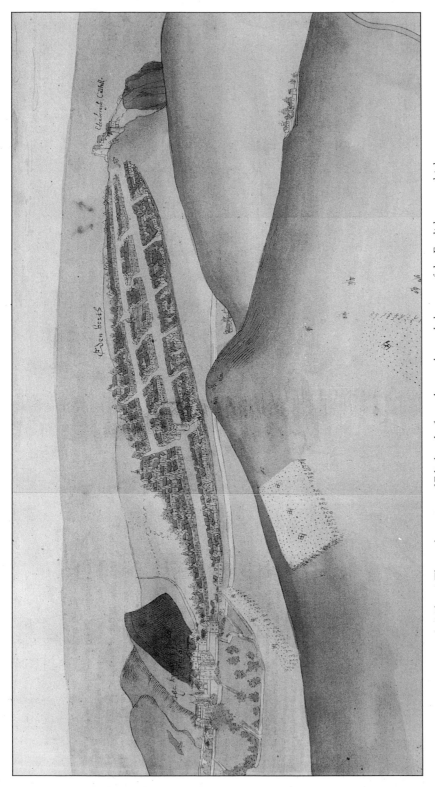

6. (*Above*) The earliest view of Edinburgh, from the north, made by one of the English army which raided the burgh in 1544.

7. (*Below*) A plan of Edinburgh, made in 1773. It incorporates James Craig's plan of 1767 for the New Town, as yet unbuilt.

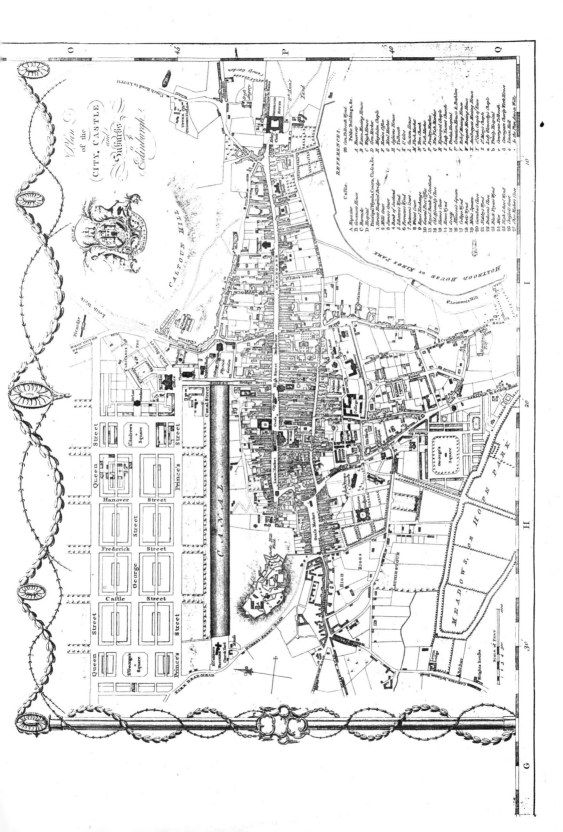

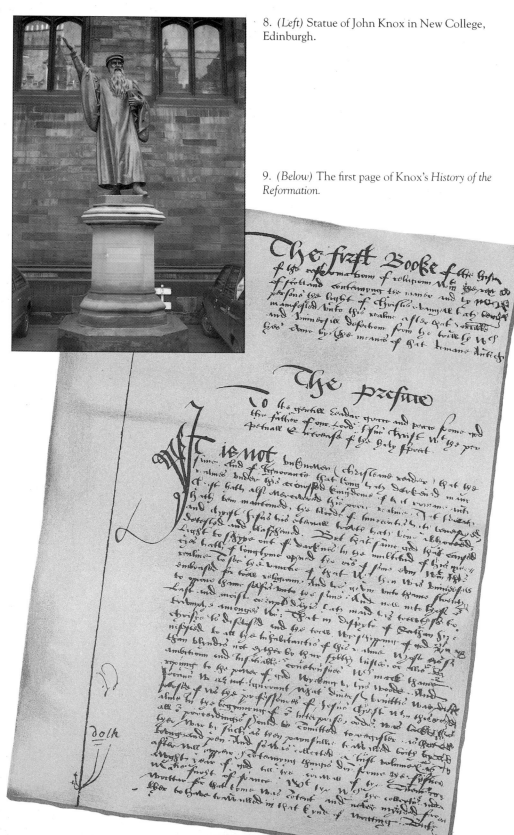

8. *(Left)* Statue of John Knox in New College, Edinburgh.

9. *(Below)* The first page of Knox's *History of the Reformation.*

10. *(Above)* and 11. *(Right)* Albion Street, Aberdeen, before and after the building of a chapel c. 1850.

12. *(Right)* Early twentieth-century banner of the Portobello True Blues, depicting the martyrdom of Patrick Hamilton in 1528.

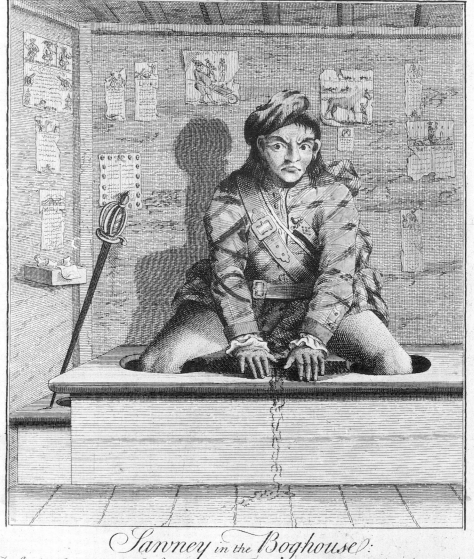

Sawney in the Boghouse:

To London Sawney come, Who, from his Birth, | Then, down each Venthole, thrust his branny Thighs;
Had dropt his Folio Cates on Mother-Earth; | And Squeezing, cry'd — Sawney's a Laird. I tron.
Shewn to a Boghouse, gaz'd with wond'ring Eyes; | Neer did he naatly disemb ange 'till now.

Publish'd June 1st 1745. price 6d.

13. *(Above)* The barbarian Scot. English propaganda during the '45.

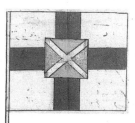
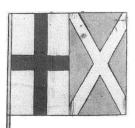

14. *(Left and Right)* Some of the designs for a Union flag, 1603-06

15. (*Above*) A Ross-shire celebration of Queen Victoria's jubilee. The Gaelic banner reads 'Long live the Great Queen of Britain'.

16. (*Right*) Aberdour cabinetmakers, 1902, under an arch of Empire.

17. *(Above)* Some of the 800 Highland mercenaries, here called 'Irishmen', in the army of Gustavus Adolphus of Sweden, at Stettin in 1630.

18. *(Right)* A recruiting poster for the Gordon Highlanders, made in 1870 but used until the First World War.

19a. *(Below)* Soldiers in the 'Black Watch', a British regiment, in 1743, wearing a dark green 'government tartan'.

SIR WALTER SCOTT 1832-1932

RICHARD COEUR DE LION

ROB ROY

JEANIE DEANS

SALADIN

FRIAR TUCK

LUCY ASHTON

EARL OF LEICESTER

DUGALD DALGETTY

THE PALMER

CLAVERHOUSE

AMY ROBSART

HELEN MACGREGOR

THE ASTROLOGER

ISAAC THE JEW

THE TEMPLAR

SOME OF THE CHARACTERS
FROM THE WAVERLEY NOVELS

Sir Walter Scott Centenary
Edinburgh.........1932

(In Waverley Market
21st to 24th September)

McLAGAN & CUMMING, EDINR

19b. *(Above)* A 1932 Scott centenary programme, illustrating characters from the Waverley novels.

20. *(Below)* A Highland Clearance, probably in North Uist in 1895.

21. (*Above*) Blantyre miners and pithead girls, 1898.

22. (*Left*) Postcard of Willie Gallacher, Clydesider, c. 1915. It celebrates his links with the syndicalist Industrial Workers of the World.

23. (*Opposite Above*) A Brechin ploughman, the aristocrat of rural labour.

24. (*Opposite Below*) A fixed-term feeing contract for farm servants and harvesters, 1871.

CONDITIONS OF AGREEMENT

BETWEEN

George Riddell, Farmer, Rink

AND

John Arnott, Steward, Rink

From 26 May 1871, to 26 May 1872.

Cash, £26 Stg	Cow's ~~Keep~~ Milk, or £
Oatmeal, 65 Stones	24 Days' Victuals during Harvest. *with no suppers*
Barley,	Worker's Wage per day in Summer,
Potatoes, 600 yards	Do. do. in Harvest,
Coals ~~at~~ one Ton at 10/	Do. do. in Winter,
	Do. Days' Victuals in Harvest.

Agreed to at *Rink*

On 2nd January 1871

John Riddell

John Arnott

25. *(Above)* Rosyth, Britain's first 'garden city', built for munitions workers in the First World War.

26. *(Below)* Glasgow tenement scene in the 1950s.

28. (*Above*) An unusual domestic scene, East Wemyss, c. 1900.

29. (*Below*) Leith tram conductresses and driver during First World War.

27. (*Above*) Bessie Watson, suffragette, aged 9. The youngest member of the Women's Social and Political Union.

30. *(Above)* Reid's Court. A portrait by Patrick Geddes, pioneer of town planning, of the two classes of children in Edinburgh's Old Town, c. 1910.

31. *(Below)* One of the legends of Scotland's national game – John Thomson, goalkeeper for Glasgow Celtic, c. 1930.

of the Isles. Based in the exchequer and headed by Alexander Seton (the future Earl of Dunfermline), the Octavians had near-draconian powers over both the King's administration and the King himself: James could not spend without the consent of at least five of the eight. Mass redundancies from various branches of the royal household resulted – seventy in January 1596 from the King's household alone; pensions were pruned; economies were suggested so that the celebrations following the birth in 1596 of Princess Elizabeth did not match the huge expenditure on Prince Henry's baptism in 1594. A new realism had entered the finances of the crown.[21]

It did not last. Grumblings from some ministers that many of the Octavians were 'suspected papists' surfaced in the General Assembly in March 1596 and the famous interview between Andrew Melville and James took place in October 1596 against a background of growing criticism of the King's servants and the court. By the end of the year the issue had been settled. The Kirk had over-reached itself by seeking to defend the indefensible – the God-given right of free preaching was stretched to include a sermon by a hot-headed Melvillian, David Black of St Andrews, which was a wild attack on the Queen, her children and even Elizabeth of England. A mysterious riot broke out in Edinburgh in December 1596 while the King and Lords of Session were sitting in the Tolbooth: a papist conspiracy by the Octavians was alleged, but the effect was to give the government the opportunity to dish the Melvillian party. In 1597, in the first of the meetings when the General Assembly moved away from Edinburgh, the Church agreed to restrain excesses from the pulpit. The irony was that the Octavian period of retrenchment hardly lasted a year after the riot. By the end of 1597 the commission was discredited, although most of its members continued to hold individual offices elsewhere in the King's administration. James was free of the accountants in his exchequer, but he depended even more than before on unprecedented, regular taxation and massive credit.

James VI has developed a formidable reputation as an immensely successful King of Scots, both before and after his accession to the English throne in 1603. Such were the differences of expectations that were brought about after his removal to London that separate balance sheets, for 1603 and 1625, need to be made out. By 1603, it has been claimed, he ruled a country which was already 'more peaceful and prosperous than it had been for generations'.[22] That may be taken as common ground amongst most commentators on the personal reign. Yet was it so very different from equivalent points in the reigns of James IV or V? By 1603 James VI had enjoyed eighteen years of personal rule. By 1513, some eighteen years after he had completed his period of probation, James IV had fully restored the confidence of his nobility in the crown, raised the status of the monarchy itself and had begun to increase the resources of the crown quite sharply. By 1542, fourteen years after he escaped from the Douglases, James V had raised crown income still further and exports were at as high a level as at any point since the 1370s. There are analogies in both cases with the reign of James VI, but it is only to be expected that there should be. James would have been a striking failure if he had not managed by 1603 to restore both the prosperity of the country and the status of the crown.

There were three main differences, however, between this reign and previous ones. One was the new world of deficit finance in which the crown was forced to live in the late sixteenth century. Caused as much by the demands for patronage amongst the swelling ranks of the peerage and gentry as by expenditure on the household or price inflation, it resulted in James VI being the first king to make large fiscal demands of the realm in time of peace. The new agents of kingship were the tax collector and the financier, like the Edinburgh lawyer Archibald Primrose, the mastermind of the taxation of the 1580s and 1590s,[23] and 'Jinglin' Geordie', the Edinburgh goldsmith George Heriot. The novel problem of a Protestant Church anxious to stake out its claim in a Protestant state that was still in many respects a feudal realm brought about a new politicisation of many relationships; the contest for power between Church and state reached into most parts of society, including the universities and the parishes. At times the Kirk thought about claiming direct representation for the General Assembly in parliament; James's new bishops blunted that prospect but also opened up a new avenue for royal influence in the parishes, whose administrative roles were expanding. Both the bishop and the justice of the peace were key symbols of Jacobean government. That contest was part of a broader story, which lies at the heart of the manifold changes taking place in Jacobean Scotland – the continuing but accelerating process of the recasting of the relationship between localities and central authority, both in state and Church.

A new order was being imposed on Scottish society in the late sixteenth century, but this was also a society in a state of ferment. By 1610 the two clearest symbols of the independence of local society – the bloodfeud and the bond of manrent – were on the point of disappearing into history.[24] In their place came new and more direct relationships between central government and the localities. Increasingly King or parliament stepped in to settle feuds. The blunt and occasional instrument of the justice ayre continued throughout the sixteenth century but from the 1580s onwards it was complemented by parliamentary commissions set up to implement specific acts – on weights and measures, university reform and much else. The customary authority of sheriffs continued, but it was increasingly subjected to scrutiny by both the central law courts and the privy council.[25] There was undeniably a new quest for order evident in James's long reign. The problem is to identify its origins; was it the product of a new demand in society for greater stability or did it reflect a new authority enjoyed by the crown?

The problem of 'push' and 'pull' factors operates in almost all spheres of government and institutions in the reign. New heights of loyalty were being demanded of subjects by the King – in the quelling of feuds or implementation of statute as much as in an Erastian settlement of church polity. Yet new expectations of kingship were being made of the King by the swelling ranks of nobles and gentry, who all demanded their place in the sun of the King's favour and their proper position in the queue for pensions. The combined effects of feuing, an active land market and a scramble for status and preferment amongst the landed classes, old and new, stretched to the limit the institutions and resources of a feudal realm. New expectations arose, too, of other institutions, such as parliament. Was parliament the meeting place of the different parts of the community of the realm or was it the agent of a central government seeking new ways to impose its authority on the local community? King and parliament cultivated a split personality. Jacobean Scotland was a dual-purpose kingdom: an old feudal realm of regalities and heritable jurisdictions, with its focus in a parliament which was, as James himself said, 'the chief court' of tenants-in-chief of the king, ran side by side with a new, more centralised state structure imposing direct taxation and implementing laws via new avenues of jurisdiction. There was not a take-over of one by the other. The essence of the way Jacobean government worked was as a *modus vivendi*, between new habits of government and old.[26]

Some parts of the political community were less happy with this *modus vivendi* than others. The burghs had formed themselves into the Convention of Royal Burghs in the 1550s and could claim to be the most coherent voice in national politics – it met no less than eighty-seven times between 1600 and 1625. Yet their increasing politicisation was largely forced upon them by the burgeoning demands of the crown and its growing habit of calling conventions of the nobility rather than parliaments – there were forty-nine conventions and only five parliaments between 1588 and 1603.[27] By 1590 the Convention was forced to appoint a permanent political agent to represent its views to parliament and privy council in Edinburgh; by 1613 it needed one in London as well. Individual burghs such as Edinburgh and Aberdeen, never to be outdone in the greasing of palms, also by then had their own agents at court. The day of the political lobbyist had arrived. The lairds had been offered seats in parliament as shire commissioners by an act of 1587 but relatively few took up the offer. More than any other group in society they were uncertain about their status, and in a petition of 1599 demanded a convention of their own, like the burghs.[28]

It was the burgesses and lairds, together with feuars of kirklands, lawyers and other groups on the rise in Jacobean society, who bore the brunt of the new levels of taxation. For the nobles, taxation continued to be firmly divorced from a notion of being linked to ability to pay, still based as it was on the out-dated assessments of the old extent; they paid only their share of the third of taxation which fell on all barons and freeholders. The feuars (lairds and others) who had benefited from the sale of kirklands picked up the bill formerly paid by the pre-Reformation Church, of a half of national taxation; and the burghs paid a sixth. Yet the inequities were further multiplied by random taxation on pensioners and holders of benefices and teinds, as well as more systematic taxation of the growth areas of the economy, such as wadsetting (money lent on the security of an estate) and the export of salmon, grain and coal. The trend towards flagrantly differential taxation came to a climax in the parliament of 1621 in what James himself claimed was 'the greatest taxation that was ever granted in that kingdom', a new tax of 5 per cent on annual rents which, it was hoped, would bring in £230,000 a year. The nobility, by contrast, escaped most of the growing burden of both direct and indirect taxation. Even the new customs rates of 1597 carried exemptions for landowners, who might freely import goods and commodities for their own use. This may still have been *laissez-faire* monarchy, but only a noble would have thought it so.[29]

James's government was random, fussy, and intrusive – like the king himself. It did not, however, bring about a Jacobean revolution in government. The two structures of government continued to cohabit throughout the rest of the reign, and each had its own links with the King and royal policy. The *ménage à trois* in a sense became easier after 1603 with the departure of the King for London. Who were the agents of royal government? The debate as to whether James relied on a new breed drawn mostly from the middling sort – younger sons of peers, lairds, lawyers and prominent burgesses – or on his nobles has been further drawn out by the contradictory evidence of James's own words. One pronouncement, 'choose your servants indifferently out of all quarters. . . . men of known wisdom, honesty and good conscience', seems to be contradicted by another on the next page of *Basilikon Doron*: 'delight to be served with men of the noblest blood that may be had'.[30] Yet James is here describing the different roles of the middling sort and the peerage in his two spheres of government.

It was taxation that was the most intrusive of the many inroads being made into the localities, and there James relied on an efficient but still rudimentary machinery which noticeably depended on the middling sort. The Octavians, in effect a committee based in the Exchequer, had been a mixed bag of professional men, drawn from the upper reaches of the lairdly class and including younger sons of peers. In the traditional places where access to the King was expected, in the court and in parliament (and even more so in conventions), it was the peerage whose voices were loudest and most frequently heard. It was only their general reluctance to accept high office, together with the absence until later in the reign of higher clergy to fill the vacuum, which opened the door to talented administrators such as Maitland, chancellor from 1587 to 1595, and Alexander Seton, chancellor from 1605 until his death in 1622. The humble origins of men such as these can be exaggerated. Both came from prominent families; the Maitlands traced the 'Maitland blude' back to the fourteenth century, and the Setons had commissioned their family history a generation before. Attempts to distinguish between a *noblesse de l'epeé* and a *noblesse de robe* need awareness that the traditional nobility was fast in process of losing its status as a military class – the clinical efficiency of the rapier and the handgun undermined noble status as much as the king's efforts to demilitarise landed society. New emblems of their status were being offered, such as a place in the colourful riding of parliament devised in 1606. If anything marked out the greater nobility from the lesser it was conspicuous consumption – and often, too, the debts which went with it.[31]

In a society as fast-moving and as complex as Jacobean Scotland, new images of kingship were devised to satisfy the ambitions of kingship and the emotional needs of subjects. Like no government before it, that of James VI developed an elaborate propaganda machine that used a variety of channels of communication. One was a Renaissance court, no less distinguished than that of the previous three reigns. Since the 1580s it had begun to assemble the poets of the 'Castalian Band', led by Alexander Montgomerie, who hailed James as the 'Royal Apollo'. Yet the flattery of poets was only part of a new iconography of kingship which gained pace in the 1590s. The printing press published individual acts of parliament and privy council, tracts on kingship and union and officially inspired histories. Various images of James were promoted: Solomon, the wise ruler; Augustus, patron of the arts; Brutus, unifier of Britain; Arthur, recreator of the ancient empire of the legendary King of Britons (and it was even rumoured in 1603 that James intended to change his name to Arthur); Constantine, the Christian Emperor; James as the 'nursing father' of the Church; and David, the leader of a new people of Israel into the promised land of a Calvinist Greater Britain.[32] The campaign, which eclipsed the opposition of the Kirk in the 1590s, was geared towards James's pursuit of the English succession and, after 1603, it gave voice to his idea of a 'perfect union'.

Union and absentee kingship (1603-25)

After 1603 new emblems of a British identity were created: a wave of British histories, seals, flags, and coinage engulfed James's subjects on both sides of the Border. No detail was too small to be overlooked; a new design for the King's Great Seal conjoined not only the English and Scottish arms but also those of Cadwallader and Edward the Confessor, respectively the last undisputed kings of Celtic Britain and Anglo-Saxon England.[33] The elaborate balance struck on the Great Seal was symbolic of the fact that perfect union had at its heart the notion of a genuinely dual monarchy and James was probably, as has been said, the first and last exponent of it ever to sit on the British throne.[34] His efforts to deal with his two principal kingdoms were carefully even-handed, more so than those of any government since: just over four in ten of the appointments in the court at Whitehall went to Scots; one in five of the English privy council were Scots; and eight Scots nobles were installed as Knights of the Garter alongside twelve Englishmen.[35] If politics were about preferment – and most nobles would have thought so – a reasonable number of Scots were made placemen. If politics were about the image of the King's realm, the publicity campaign continued unchecked even after the rejection by the English parliament in 1607 of proposals for a full incorporating union. In his *Apology* written in 1609, James never referred to any of his three kingdoms by name but only to the 'Ile'; his reign, as he saw, had been preordained to bring about the blessed Protestant isle. At least eight attempts were made by the heralds between 1603 and 1606 to harmonise the cross of St Andrew and the English cross of St George. In heraldic terms, this was an attempt to solve the insoluble and convey equal place to two flags when merged into one. The ingenuity of the eventual design cut little ice; it proved highly unpopular, in both Scotland and England, and fell into disuse after 1625.[36] The difficulties in the creation of a new union flag were a symbol of the obstacles in the way of the whole pan-British project.

Yet politics were also about the King himself and his personal management, now not only of his great nobles but also of the new groups in Scottish society which had risen to prominence during his reign. And the greatest factor which the dynastic union had brought about was an absentee monarch. Even his one return visit to his northern kingdom, in 1617, was resolutely opposed by his English privy council, intent on the total 'Englishing' of James I. James was greeted with an uncharacteristic Scots lack of restraint during the eleven-week visit. It was also the first to establish the convention of many royal visits since; rubbish and beggars were cleared from Edinburgh's streets before the King's arrival. Yet there was a serious point about the governing of Scotland which was illustrated during the visit; his intervention in the business of the parliament of 1617 and withdrawal of a bill threatening to bypass the General Assembly in ecclesiastical matters proved the value of a king able to assess opposition for himself.[37]

The practical obstacles in the way of James's vision were formidable. The basic suspicions of the English parliament, especially about the naturalisation of subjects born before and after 1603 and free trade, which it thought would flood the English market with cheap Scottish goods, were never overcome. The hostility of the Scottish parliament was hardly less; in 1607 it daringly voiced its fears of union turning Scotland into 'a conquered and slavish province to be governed by a Viceroy or Deputy'. It had been the example of Brittany which had figured in many minds in the 1550s when offered closer alliance with France; it was the example of Ireland, subdued only in 1601 after more than thirty years of English military conquest, which began to surface in many minds after 1604. The king, as the Scottish parliament said, had promised a 'joyfull marriage and a happie love-knott'; it became ever more obvious as time passed and the King did not return to Scotland, as promised, one year in every three, that the union was, at best, an arranged marriage.[38]

The tangible fruits of union were few. The Borders were converted, at least in name, into the 'Middle Shires' of the realm; a joint Border Commission was established in 1605 to suppress feuds and bring order to the frontier; a mounted police force under the command of Sir William Cranston caught and hanged 104 reivers in its first year. By 1609 the shires were declared to be 'as quiet as any part in any civil kingdom in Christianity' and the Commission was disbanded. The confidence was premature; the new opportunities offered for lawlessness by the increase in cross-Border trade forced renewals of the Commission in 1609, 1618, 1630 and 1635. The other novelty in Border policy – the forced exile in 1606-7 of the most troublesome of the Border families, the Grahams – pointed the way towards similar mass expulsions of four major Highland clans after 1609. Clearance as an instrument of government policy had begun. In terms of lawlessness, Scotland's loss was Ireland's gain; Ireland and the English army in Ireland became the depository for the Grahams.

Comparatively little legislation resulted from the union of 1603. The hostile laws were repealed. Eventually, in 1608, the matter of the *post-nati* was settled, but by a test case (of Robert Colville, a Scots nobleman's son born in Edinburgh after 1603) in the common law courts; all were declared to be 'natural-born subjects within the allegiance of the king of England', able to purchase land and to bring actions before the courts. A licence had been granted for that ubiquitous figure in British history, the London Scot. Yet comparatively few of the Scots who thronged the court at Whitehall in the first dozen years after 1603 were dedicated followers of James's vision of union. By 1620, as a result, the gulf was already opening up between a British king and a nobility which was for the most part still resolutely Scots in its aspirations and habits. A few – but only a few – Scots nobles married into English families,[39] and usually the motive was financial rather than cultural. A British aristocracy did not emerge until the middle of the eighteenth century, but by then it would be North British.

In 1607, in a speech before the English parliament, James uttered his famous claim about the governing of Scotland: 'Here I sit and govern it with my pen, I write and it is done, and by a Clerk of the Council I govern Scotland now, which others could not do by the sword'.[40] The claim, it is usually thought, was well founded, although much of the formation of policy as well as its implementation belonged to James's privy councillors in Edinburgh. Foremost among them were Sir George Hume of Sprott, Earl of Dunbar and Lord Treasurer until 1611; Alexander Seton, Earl of Dunfermline and chancellor between 1611 and 1622; Archbishop Spottiswoode, who joined the council in 1605, and Andrew Knox, Bishop of the Isles, architect of policy towards the Highlands.[41] Yet the timing of the claim was significant. It came just before the final rejection of incorporating union and two years before the major revisions in royal policy towards the Highlands implied in the

Statutes of Iona of 1609; it was amidst the success of the gradual restoration of bishops but eight years before a new, less successful phase in ecclesiastical policy opened in 1615 with what later emerged as the Five Articles of Perth. The three spheres – of union, the extension of law and order to both the Highlands and Borders, and a settlement of the Church – are the major elements in any judgement of James's reign after 1603.[42] Yet it also needs to be remembered that the crown, like Scottish society itself, continued to live on credit, a blind eye turned to the need for retrenchment. Ironically, the house of cards collapsed not on the Stewart monarchy but on the Covenanting regime in rebellion against it in the 1640s.

The court of James VI had little sympathy for Gaeldom. Alexander Montgomerie, the most accomplished of the poets of the Castalian Band, made fun of the Irish legends of the origins of Kings of Scots which had held place as late as the reign of James V: 'How the first Helandman, of God was maid, of a horse turd, in Argyle, it is said'.[43] By the 1590s a counter-culture of British identity had already emerged at the Stewart court, which looked askance at Gaelic culture. After 1603 the natural enemies of union would be lumped together as papists, Irish, Borderers and Highlanders.[44] James, like English observers of Ireland, contrasted two populations of the Highlands in *Basilikon Doron*: '[those] that dwelleth in our mainland, that are barbarous for the most part, and yet mixed with some show of civility; the other, that dwelleth in the Isles, and are utterly barbarous, without any sort or show of civility'.[45] English policy in Ireland between the 1530s and 1570s had oscillated between thinking the Irish could be civilised and finding that they could not, and had to be conquered first. In much the same way, the government of James VI was caught in two minds until c.1608. Before then royal policy had at times resorted to the traditional instruments of lieutenancies granted to the Earls of Argyll and Huntly. Many royal expeditions to the Isles were planned – in 1592, 1596, 1598, 1600 and 1608 – but none materialised.

In the King's place, after 1597, went the adventurers; the Isle of Lewis, base of the MacLeods, was leased to a group of Lowland entrepreneurs headed by the Duke of Lennox. By 1599, however, the enterprise was already in difficulties. In 1605 the adventurers tried and failed again in Lewis, as did a fresh consortium headed by Lord Balmerino in 1607-8. The policy of plantation of the Isles can be traced to the first adventurers' expedition of 1597. Along with colonisation went a barrage of legislation which, in effect, copied the Henrician tactics of the 1540s in Ireland, of surrender and regrant. Charters were demanded by the Edinburgh government as proof of ownership of land; a flourishing cottage industry in the forging of charters grew up and an even more flourishing trade in fake genealogies giving Highland chiefs a link with civilised society.[46]

What had happened between 1587 and 1609 was a history in miniature of the varied English experience in Ireland in the second half of the sixteenth century. By 1609 almost any means – blackmail, kidnapping or legal sharp practice – was legitimate, as part of an official policy to 'bring the Highlands and Isles to civility'. The legislation embodied in the Statutes of Iona of that year unequivocally stigmatised what it called 'Irish' manners, dress and customs; it forced clan chiefs to have their eldest sons or daughters educated on the mainland, safely removed from 'barbarous' influences and taught to 'speak, read and write in English'. The Statutes were subscribed by nine chiefs who had been forcibly abducted for the purpose. The violence of the state went further than that. Plans were already being laid for a largely English expeditionary force to reduce the Isles to obedience. In effect James was planning a conquest of the Isles. The King's privy councillors in Edinburgh found themselves in the role which the Old English (the original settlers of Norman times) had long adopted in Ireland and colonial governors have often used since, of arguing that they were the natural agents of crown policy in Gaeldom.

The Statutes of Iona were a turning-point, but only in terms of the relationship between the King and his council in Edinburgh, which from 1609 onwards took more responsibilities upon itself. The real indictment of James's policy is not that it was ruthless – for its violence arguably only matched that of Highland society – but that it simply did not work. There was no transformation of the Highlands to a new civility. In the Isles, the real change came with forced clearances: the MacLeods were expelled from Lewis by 1616, not by adventurers, but by the rival MacKenzies of Kintail; and the MacDonalds of Kintyre and the Isles and the MacDonalds of Ardnamurchan had fallen victim, along with the Clan Gregor, to the many branches of the Clan Campbell by 1625. It was not a new policy that worked but a very old one, begun by James IV, of using frontier clans with a foot in both Highland and Lowland society as Trojan horses in Gaeldom. The main beneficiaries of it were not the crown but the Campbells, and the spectre of the overmighty house of Argyll would come back to haunt Charles I.[47]

Taken from the viewpoint of 1607 or of 1610, the final step in the restoration of bishops to the Scottish Church, James's ecclesiastical policy had been a signal success. Divisions within the Kirk had been exploited with skill and persistence; the radical presbyterians, with Melville now out of the way, had, it seemed, been reduced to impotence. Yet James wanted more than mere conformity in polity. He believed in his own propaganda, which portrayed him as another Constantine; part of his vision of a unified realm was a common Church, Calvinist in doctrine but Erastian in habits. It would play, he intended, a major role both in a Calvinist Europe and in bringing about a reunited Christendom. There was no room in such a Church for sectional differences on worship or liturgy. The Five Articles – enjoining private baptism, private communion, confirmation by bishops, observance of holy days and kneeling at communion – were rejected by a General Assembly meeting in St Andrews in November 1617, partly implemented by fiat of the privy council two months later, and forced through a second Assembly at Perth in 1618. An even more reluctant parliament meeting in 1621 passed the Articles, but only by eighty-six votes to fifty-nine, despite great pressure put on its more vulnerable members. Opposition had crystallised in some of James's parliaments before, but it was for the most part confined to such traditional areas of disgruntlement as taxation. This was in effect a virtual vote of no confidence in a central plank of the King's policy.

Yet James persisted, and nowhere more strenuously than with the most objectionable of the Articles, on kneeling. Ministers were hounded, at the King's insistence, for years. Members of the privy council were instructed to report on the numbers who took communion in various churches and how they took it; they found a wide variety of postures, including one taken by an Edinburgh minister so convoluted, it was reported, that it was impossible to say with certainty whether he was standing, sitting or kneeling. The magistrates of Edinburgh were forced, ludicrously, to guarantee the compliance of all 12,000 churchgoers in the burgh.[48] The Articles, it has been suggested, were James's 'most serious mistake' during his years of absentee government but they were not 'fatal'.[49] Yet they showed how the King's authority might be defied and how a gap was already beginning to open up between the agents of government in London and Scotland. By 1625 substantial parts of congregations in Edinburgh and Fife had withdrawn from communion. It is difficult to conclude with any certainty that the protracted affair over the Articles threw into jeopardy the whole of the Jacobean Church settlement, so painstakingly constructed in the period up to 1610. Yet it did have the effect of conceding the centre ground in religious affairs to the dissident ministers. The path was already prepared for what Sir James Balfour later conceded to be the capture by the Kirk of 'the conscience of the commonwealth'.[50] Scottish Calvinism entered the reign of Charles I uneasily stretched between the Established Church and the underground conventicle.

Protest movements, such as the one which would reach its climax in 1638, are no respecters of neat historiographical packages. It is difficult to pin with any precision part-responsibility on James VI for the wave of protest which would later engulf Charles I, but it is as difficult to grant him absolution. It needs to be remembered that rebellion is not only a matter of votes in parliament or riots; at bottom it is about the force of ideas. The idea which for centuries had been the most compelling force in politics was the notion of the King of Scots as the main or only guarantor of the independence of the Scottish nation. It was in James's reign that it lost its monopoly status. Gradually over the course of the first three decades of the seventeenth century, two new images which would have huge importance for the future history of Scotland emerged and fused: the Kirk steadily became a metaphor for Scottish identity; and a conviction grew that the maintenance of the 'auld estait' of Scotland was safer in other hands than those of the King of Scots. Foremost amongst the propagandists of these alternative visions were David Hume of Godscroft and John Napier of Merchiston, better known as the inventor of logarithms than as a historian. It was Napier who contested the myth of the good Emperor Constantine and, with it, the notion of a godly prince. It was Hume who first identified the threat to a presbyterian polity as a threat to Scotland itself which would eventually lead to England 'tyrannising' its neighbour.[51]

Judgements of James VI's reign which strictly refuse to look into the future beyond 1625 are no less difficult. The reign ended in severe if temporary economic and social crisis. There were widespread harvest failures in the early 1620s and a fall in trade. In 1623, 500 died of famine out of a population of some 3,000 in Dumfries, and in Perth between ten and twelve died every day between midsummer and Michaelmas, accounting for perhaps a quarter of the inhabitants.[52] It was the very length of the reign, it might be said, that brought stability; yet it was also the length of the reign which was positively alarming to the local community anxious to combat the innovatory strains in government. The later stages of the reign were, it has been argued, a period when the internal frontiers – political and cultural as much as geographical or racial – which had kept Scotland apart were beginning to come down, as part of the process of the growing maturity of the Scottish state.[53] There is a certain truth in the argument but much of it might be put a rather different way. This was a period when many of the familiar landmarks – respect, homage, kinship – which had held a loose feudal kingdom together and staked out the long-accepted relationship between the King and his tenants-in-chief were becoming obscured. It was as a result an age marked by widespread uncertainty. Kingship had seemingly abandoned its key image, of King of Scots, and the crown had adopted a variety of novel expedients, both fiscal and political. The institution of a Register of Sasines in 1617, which had promised a new security to owners of property, can be taken as a symbol of the new security felt by the landowning classes. Yet its formation had been bitterly resisted, by lawyers and localities alike, for quarter of a century; and the appearance of a new swingeing tax on annual rents only four years after its foundation seemed to confirm their worst fears.[54] The new respect within Scottish society for law and order was accompanied by the all too obvious disrespect on the part of the crown for many of the ancient traditions and privileges which had held Scottish society together. Bonds and feuds had been virtually eliminated, but in their place there was a new violence of the state, which could affect burgesses as well as Highlanders or Borderers; the 355 innocent inhabitants of Perth interrogated after the Gowrie plot in 1600 could testify to that. Far from there being a new harmony of understanding between the crown and its subjects, there was, it might well be thought, a fundamental and mutual misunderstanding of the novel roles each had cast for the other in a new, confusing world.

By 1603 James VI had become a highly successful monarch – though perhaps no more or less so than his grandfather and great-grandfather before him. Although a case can be made for his government by pen making him as successful a King of Scots after 1603 as before, it is less certain and some distinctions need to be made. Here was a King of Great Britain whose greatest achievement was to buy time for union, yet the price of this new role was to weaken the unwritten, personal authority of kings of Scots. As James said himself, 'The prerogative is a secret which ryves [tears] with the stretching of it'. Nothing stretched the prerogative more than the King's own conscious attempt to transform the nature of kingship itself; loyalty was owed not to the King as the unifier of the different peoples of Scotland but to him as King of Great Britain, which as yet hardly commanded any affection. Here also after 1603 was a King who was no less an exponent of laissez-faire monarchy than Stewarts before him, but the horizons of politics had widened in this reign more than in any other in Scottish history; the many layers of the middling sort felt the weight of governance but few of the benefits of royal patronage. Kingship, it is sometimes thought, can best be measured by the effectiveness of the points of contact a King maintained with his subjects. In the privy council and in conventions, here was a King who kept closely in touch with his nobles, both old and new. But, with no General Assembly after 1618, no progresses throughout his realm for the last twenty-two years of his reign (except for one brief visit in 1617), and few other opportunities of access, here also was a King who had lost contact with many of his other subjects. James was one of Scotland's most successful feudal kings, but he was also the first failure amongst Stewart absolute monarchs of the seventeenth century.

Part IV
THE CRISIS
OF THE
THREE KINGDOMS

15

The Rise of the Middling Sort

In 1625 Charles I inherited not one kingdom but three; it was a confusing legacy. Each kingdom – England, Ireland and Scotland – had its own expectations of its new monarch, and he himself had something of his father's ambition to forge a British state, embracing the three kingdoms and their three Churches, into a greater, British whole. He was a king in a hurry. Within six weeks of his father's death, Charles, in the tradition of kings of Scots who had reached their majority, issued a revocation. Produced quickly under highly secretive conditions, this highly detailed document proposed to annul all grants of land made by either crown or Church since 1540. It was a startling intervention by the crown, not so much because it went well beyond the King's date of birth – there had been numerous revocations issued by or on behalf of James VI which had predated his minority and one of 1575 when he was only eight went back to 1513 – but more because of its range and ambitious nature. Charles, it has been said, inherited a Scotland which his great-grandfather, James V, would scarcely have recognised.[1] Though still in outline a feudal kingdom, a land of baronies and regalities with its focus in a parliament composed of tenants-in-chief of the crown, the intervening years had seen a profound change in the power and status of both the nobility and the various strands of what was then called the 'middling sort' – the lairds, new feuars and rising professions. As the rancorous and obscure dispute over the revocation dragged on from 1625 until the eve of the revolt of 1637, it seemed that Charles was engaged in an outrageous piece of social engineering, which attempted to rearrange the dynamics of the most dramatic century of social change in Scotland's history. And he did so, it became increasingly clear, as a British monarch rather than as King of Scots.

Nobles, old and new

In 1540 the three most powerful noble houses had been those of Douglas, Hamilton and Gordon: the Douglases had gained control of the young James V in 1528; the Hamiltons, headed by the Earl of Arran, had dominated the royal administration during much of the 1540s; and the 4th Earl of Huntly, who had enjoyed unchallenged sway in three shires of the north-east throughout the minority of Mary, Queen of Scots, had offered a Catholic base to her in 1561. By the early seventeenth century, however, the three most prominent nobles in politics were men of a different stamp: the Earl of Dunbar, who ran the royal administration in Edinburgh for James VI after his departure for London, was the younger son of a laird; his successor, the Earl of Dunfermline, came from a minor noble family and was another younger son; and the Earl of Menteith, the leading figure in Charles's administration until his mysterious fall in 1633, came from an old but obscure family which quickly disappeared into the wasteland of the *Scots Peerage* from whence it had come. They were symbols of a *noblesse de robe* which had conspicuously emerged in the service of the crown since the mid-1580s: in 1585 there had been forty-nine peers, but by 1625 there were ninety-two.

The main agent of the Revocation of 1625 was a lawyer, Sir Thomas Hope of Craighall. Descended from a sixteenth-century Edinburgh burgess family and now a baronet, Hope was a symbol of the spectacular rise to prominence of the lawyers, both in royal service and in landed society. The major beneficiaries of the Revocation, so Charles promised, would be the lairds whom he wished to free 'from all those bonds which may force them to depend upon any other than upon his Majesty'.[2] The bloodfeud and the bond of manrent, emblems of the force of kin and local custom, had all but disappeared since 1600; in their place was offered a new, direct and non-feudal relationship with the crown which threatened to bypass the magnates. Charles's aim, it seemed, was an alliance of new monarchy with the rising and non-feudal elements in landed society and the professions.

Thirteen years later a dramatic demonstration of protest against the rule of Charles I took place. Ironically, all three of these elements – the *noblesse de robe*, lairds and lawyers – took their parts in it with as much enthusiasm as the other sections of Scottish society. The campaign against the Prayer Book had begun in 1637 with a demonstration by an Edinburgh mob, but the notion that the 'Scottish revolution' was a revolt of the ordinary people is as apocryphal as the legend that the first blow was struck by an obscure Edinburgh housewife, Jenny Geddes. The riot in St Giles' in July 1637 was carefully planned by others. The National Covenant was written by members of the two new professions: a Fife minister, Alexander Henderson, and a young Edinburgh advocate, Archibald Johnston of Wariston. Henderson was typical of the rising status of the ministry, whose wealth as measured by their testaments had doubled since 1600; already well enough paid (and in cash) to lend money to lairds in his parish of Leuchars, he would later, when promoted to a charge in the capital, lend to nobles as well. He left the staggering sum of £23,000 when he died in 1647 – as much as the average net estate of peers in the period 1610-37.[3] Wariston came from an Edinburgh merchant family but was also a feuar – twice over. Two of the three nobles immediately connected with the Covenant, Balmerino and Loudoun, were both the second-generation sons of James VI's nobility of service.

The nobles who later emerged as the leaders of the Covenanting movement in 1638 were no Jacobean *arrivistes*: the Earl of Argyll, who would be its guiding hand between 1638 and 1651, was from a noble house promoted by James II but also fond of tracing its genealogy to the tenth century or earlier. And the third of the trio of nobles who oversaw and revised the National Covenant was Rothes, who as an earl and sixth of his line, was hardly a new upstart. He, like Balmerino and Loudoun, had a long history of opposition to the crown, which in his case went back to the Five Articles of Perth of 1618. Rothes, though, was also representative of a class of long-established noble houses barely keeping their heads above a flood of debt in the early seventeenth century. As the Jacobean economic miracle became ever more exposed for the mirage which it was, with trade worsening and one bad harvest following another in the mid-1630s, the aristocratic scramble for pensions and office grew more frantic. Their target was the hated bishops – likened by the ardent royalist Sir James Balfour to the (mythical) counsellors of James III who, like 'mushrooms', prospered in the dark recesses of the royal administration.[4] What this trio of dissident nobles wanted in 1637-8 was office. By 1641, after two expensive military campaigns against Charles and the onset from 1640 of a new system of taxation based on valued rent to pay for them, noble fortunes were still more desperate. Two rumours were then circulating about the 6th Earl of Rothes: that he was about to follow the example of the seventeen other Scots who, since 1603, had found new financial security by marrying into the English peerage and that he had been offered the lucrative position of gentleman of the bedchamber as well as a seat on the English privy council. He died in the same year, near-penniless but with his reputation as a committed Covenanter almost intact.[5]

The revolt against Charles I was led, not by a corps of dissident Calvinist ministers, but by the king's own would-be pensioners. In May 1584 it had been Melvillian ministers who had – in vain – gone to the market cross of Edinburgh to protest against the Black Acts; in February 1638 it was sixteen peers accompanied by Lord Lyon and their lawyer (Wariston) who made the same journey, but to greater effect. Six days later the document now known as the National Covenant was ready. It was in 1638 as often referred to as the 'Noblemen's Covenant' and significantly, it was the nobles and lairds who signed it first, on 28 February; the ministers and burgesses were allowed into Greyfriars Church to subscribe only a day later. Even a revolution – above all a revolution – had to follow the accepted conventions of a still hierarchical society.

The unchallenged role of the nobles in the Covenanting revolution was a reflection of the status which they still enjoyed in seventeenth-century Scotland. The organisation of the movement which emerged in 1637-8 was based on four 'Tables' – of noblemen, barons, burgesses and ministers – but it revolved mostly around a general Table where any number of nobles could sit but only a representative number of the other groups.[6] It was, in a sense, a miniature parliament for there too only the nobles could come – or afford to stay away – as they wished. Their power, despite the concerted encroachments into the local community by James VI, still lay in their own 'countries'. There lords were still expected to maintain a large household and to indulge in conspicuous hospitality, to their kin and to visitors alike. Keeping up appearances was more demanding than ever before as new dictates of fashion, in building and leisure, were added to old-style hospitality as a drain on resources. Some aristocratic pockets – like those of the Hamiltons who began work on a new 'palace' in 1591 and were still busy with its decoration in 1627 – were able to withstand the new demands made of them but others were not; the Earl of Lothian, pursued by creditors, committed suicide in 1624 and the 12th Earl of Crawford died in Edinburgh Castle in 1620, after ten years of protective custody arranged by his own family to prevent his spendthrift habits bringing down his house.[7]

With profligacy and display there still came power: both men and firepower were still based on the noble household and the extended circle of kindred and tenants. In 1638 a muster roll of Campbell of Glenorchy showed that he drew 172 men from five parishes into his regiment, which was one of the three totalling some 5,000 men which were raised by the Earl of Argyll. This was the reason why it was the nobles, despite their lack of military experience, who led six out of every ten of the Covenanting regiments in the two Bishops' Wars of 1639 and 1640-1 from the front – to the dismay of the professional soldiers who had returned with years of experience on the continent in the armies of Gustavus Adolphus, Louis XIII and others. It was only gradually from 1645 onwards, in the Army of the Solemn League which had been sent to England in 1644, that the noble amateur was replaced by – or forced to co-operate with – professional colonels. Part of the conservative backlash of the Engagement of 1647-8 took the form of the return of the aristocrats to arms – the Engager army had as its commander the Duke of Hamilton. The Wars of the Covenant saw the brief – and often disastrous – return of the noble as warlord.[8] The running of the war, except for a few nobles who like Argyll supervised the central organs such as the Committee of Estates, was left (as shall be seen) to others.

The Kirk accepted the natural leadership of the nobility in 1638 in what it considered to be a second Reformation – despite the series of disappointments since 1560 which had told them not to put their faith in godly magistrates. The death in 1588 of the 'ministers' king', the 8th Earl of Angus, had ended the last prospects of an alliance of radical nobles and Melvillian ministers in the reign of James VI. The ministers grew steadily more confident of dealing with errant nobles and even in confronting them with their faults in presbytery and kirk session. The General Assembly in the 1570s devised a new breed of missionary, the uninvited house guest: ministers were sent to knock on the doors of Catholic noble households. Astonishingly, most were allowed in. At times the tactic was less than successful; the Earl of Atholl firmly told his visitor that he preferred a good night's sleep to a theology tutorial, but the persistent badgering of the Kirk resulted in the conversion of the 6th Earl of Huntly – no less than three times. The persuasion of nobility to see the error of their ways usually took place in private, at least for the first two generations after 1560. But increasingly the Kirk dared to call sinning nobles before the church courts. In 1602 the presbytery of Ellon summoned Lady Haddo, another Gordon notable, to answer a charge of adultery. In the tradition of earlier accused such as John Knox, she turned up with a band of supporters including her own minister to attack her accusers as well as to defend herself. The presbytery's verdict was that last refuge of Scots courts, 'not proven' – it might be taken as symptomatic of the Kirk's attitude to the nobility as a whole. It suspected upwards of a third of them of papistry, but it was also aware that a greater threat to its idea of continuing reformation lay in a new Protestant conservatism amongst the nobles which was the product of the long reign of James VI.[9]

By the 1590s the Kirk's criticism had already begun to go beyond the individual conduct of nobles or their failure to act as patrons of reform. Some ministers began to see them as the new Antichrist, blocking further reform of the Church. The Edinburgh minister Robert Bruce, ironically himself the son of a laird who had married a lord's daughter, took the assault on noble privilege a stage further in popular sermons which became some of the bestsellers in print of the 1590s. He distinguished between the true 'spiritual bonds' of grace and faith which held men together and the 'carnal bond of blood or alliance' which constituted the kinship network. It was a startling vision of a new Calvinist future. Bruce predicted that the new 'celestial glue', as he called it, of faith and grace would replace the traditional ties of kin.[10] By the 1630s, after twenty years of intermittent interference in its affairs by that 'nursing father' of the Kirk, James VI and his son, the ministry again turned to the nobles for help. Writing from his internal exile in Aberdeen, the radical minister from the south-west, Samuel Rutherford, who would become the leading theoretician of the Covenanting Kirk, had no doubt of the need of the Kirk for what he called the 'little nursing fathers'. Addressing the Earl of Cassillis in September 1637, six weeks after the riot in St Giles', he was characteristically blunt:

> Ye hold your lands of Christ; your charters are under His seal; and He who hath many crowns upon His head dealeth, cutteth and carveth pieces of this clay heritage to men, at His pleasure . . . Your honourable ancestors, with the hazard of their lives, brought Christ to our land . . . If ye, the nobles, play Christ the slip now, when His back is at the wall, then we may say that the Lord hath casten water upon Scotland's smoking coal.[11]

The nobles were again to be entrusted with the sacred role of leaders of the Reformation; but, it is clear from Rutherford's message, they were being given their last chance.

So it was that at the first General Assembly for twenty years, held at Glasgow in 1638, the nobles – such as Loudoun, Cassillis and the quixotic Montrose – appeared in large numbers in the novel guise of ruling elders 'at a long table in the floor' of Glasgow Cathedral. Above them at the east end of the nave, on either side of the King's commissioner, the Marquis of Hamilton, sat the nobles of the privy council; and in a loft specially reserved for them were the 'young noblemen' such as Lord Fleming and Lord Boyd, who represented only themselves. No meeting of the General Assembly – not even in 1560 or 1567 – had seen the like. For radical ministers such as George Gillespie, disillusionment set in as early as 1641, when he complained of the election of 'disguised and histrionical men puffed up with titles' as ruling elders; for the bulk of the Kirk the process of disenchantment took nearer ten years than three, but the conclusion drawn was no less bitter.[12] By 1648 what had begun as a revolution cast in the clothes of the old order had become a counter-revolution to cast them off: office-holders who had held on to power through eleven confusing years of Covenanting politics were purged; 'malignant' nobles were removed to produce a 'clean army' which had only five earls in it; a parliament with only a small rump of nobles left sitting in it proceeded in 1649 to remove lay patronage in appointment of ministers; and the ruling elder in 1650 was more likely to be a tenant farmer than a lord.[13]

The nobles had gone to war in 1639, it was said at the time, with a Geneva Bible in one saddlebag and a copy of George Buchanan's *History* in the other. Buchanan, the prophet of the Scottish revolution, had assigned the role of correcting the faults of kings to the *populus*, meaning the political nation rather than the people. But the experience of the 1640s, the bitter years of interregnum and the religious strife which followed the Restoration of 1660 cast the nobles in a different light. The seeds were already sown for the deeply embittered atmosphere which would characterise relations between the nobility and many of the ministers throughout the Restoration period. By the 1680s, Alexander Shields, the philosopher of the radical conventiclers and more Buchanan-like than Buchanan himself, would cast doubt on the institution of the lesser magistrate as well as on monarchy:

> There is no title on earth now to the crowns, to families, to persons, but to the people's suffrage. For the institution of magistracy does not make James Stewart a king, no more than John Chamberlain. A man had goods ere ever there was a king; a king was made only to preserve property, therefore he

cannot take it away . . . All these primeval rights that gave rise to societies are equal to both people and peers. The people as well as the peers have a hand in making the king . . . The glory of God and security of religion, the end of all Christian government doth concern all equally.[14]

The revolutionary constitution, designed to give government to the well-born, threatened within half a century of 1638 to give it to all.

Lairds

The revolution of the 1630s and 1640s confirmed the position of the nobles, but it also gave new status to the lairds. In what is one of the most-quoted and misquoted observations in Scottish history, an English agent in 1572 had said:

Methinks I see the noblemen's great credit decay in this country, and the barons, boroughs and such like take more upon them. The ministers and religion increase, and the desire in them to prevent the practices of the papists; the number of able men for service very great and well-furnished in both horse and foot.[15]

Killigrew's comment was more about the increasing role taken by the lairds and the burghs of Edinburgh and Dundee in the King's party in the civil war than the rise of a middling sort in society. The civil war of 1568-73 was the first taste many lairds and burgesses had had of both warfare and national politics. The civil war was a mere apéritif; what was different about the Wars of the Covenant was that they involved the whole of society, noble and non-noble, rural and urban. Regiments were raised by burghs and lairds of modest means as well as by nobles, shires or clans; even the lawyers of the College of Justice raised two regiments, of horse and foot, in 1643-4, as did the ministers, who were each liable for a fully-armed soldier.[16] The Wars of the Covenant brought a whole nation under arms in a way that had never happened before or since, until the twentieth century. Such a war demanded organisation of the machinery of the state as never before. It was the lairds who were the main civil servants of the Revolution.

Somewhere between 200 and 300 lairds signed the supplication of October 1637 demanding that bishops be removed from the privy council and an unknown number of them crowded into Greyfriars Church four months later to subscribe the National Covenant. By June 1638, with commissioners sent from almost every shire, the lairds probably outnumbered all the other Tables put together. A decision was taken to limit their numbers to 600, more than seven times the number of burgh commissioners.[17] At the Glasgow Assembly, the bulk of the 180-odd commissioners sent from sixty-three presbyteries must also have been lairds or barons. That Assembly has often been compared to a meeting of the three estates, but it represented the parliament that would emerge after 1640 rather than the body which already existed. Lairds had come to the Reformation parliament in numbers and to some parliaments before that; they also came with some regularity after 1560 – some eighty-one turned up at a convention in November 1572. The parliament of 1587 had tried to encourage lairds in the guise of shire commissioners but that legislation had had a patchy impact and parliament refused to acknowledge the reality of a fourth estate, which already existed in all but name. So the lairds continued, rather uneasily, as part of an estate which included the nobles as well, although they had their own representation on the Lords of the Articles, a committee which met before parliaments to decide the agenda. In 1599 they petitioned unsuccessfully for their own convention, like that of the royal burghs, and that call was renewed in 1639.[18] It was only in 1640 that they were given full, formal status as a separate estate. By a sleight of hand a parliament of the three estates was preserved; one estate – of the bishops – was abolished and transferred to the lairds. In the process the voting strength of the shire commissoners, which until now had been restricted to one vote per shire, was doubled; each shire was entitled to send two commissioners and both were given a vote. The bishops' loss and the burghs' loss of face – for their voting strength remained the same – was the lairds' gain. Their new status in national affairs was confirmed in 1641 when they were given nine seats on the privy council and the burghs just one.[19]

The real influence of the lairds lay – as is often also said of the nobles – in the local community, whether in the estate or barony court. The crown had long been aware of their potential as part-time local bureaucrats. It had since the 1570s been trying to bring to the surface different layers of the class of landed proprietors as agents of policy at local level; the first attempts were with the poor law legislation of 1575 which talked of 'heidismen' in rural parishes. Increasingly, specific pieces of legislation were given to commissions of parliament to implement at local level. The witchhunters of the 1590s were usually not ministers or kirk elders but lairds acting as commissioners of justiciary or privy council.[20] This process was accelerated dramatically in the late 1630s. The real vehicles of the new-found influence of the lairds lay in the two new units of local government of the Covenanting period, the civil presbytery and the shire committee of war. By early 1639 the Covenanting regime began to set up an administrative machinery which tied the local community more closely to the state than ever before. One of the two commissioners from each shire met others daily in Edinburgh; the second awaited orders in the locality which he passed onwards each week to a commissioner from each presbytery in the shire, and downwards to parish level. By 1640 the locus of power lay in the shire committee, which levied men, raised supplies, collected taxes and loans, and dealt with local dissent.[21]

The men who staffed the new organs of local government were heritors – an old word which had taken on a new meaning and embraced feuars, portioners and many landed groups – for it implied a status based on property rather than feudal superiority.[22] With the new-found status of the heritor went an emphasis on the shire community rather than the network of kin. The shape of the locality had been transformed; its chief voice was now that of the laird in his new guise as heritor. Feudal kingdom and nation state were being welded together. The Restoration period would see a concerted attempt by nobles to expand the role of justices of the peace and other local offices such as the new Commissioner of Supply, but to reduce their independence of central government. As the controversy before the Union of 1707 would show, there was intense political debate at the level of the shire community as well as in parliament. In 1600 politics had operated most effectively in the convention, where the nobles might debate the political issues which concerned them. By 1700 the convention had given way to a much wider representation of the landed community in parliament, but debate had also spilled over into a new forum: the shire community. That was the main reason why Scotland was, some parliamentary managers thought, so unmanageable in the 1690s.

The professions

For the better part of a century before the Revolution of the 1640s lawyers had thronged the adminstration of both local and central government. They were something of an anomaly: largely the product of an urban environment, they were not part of the historic burgh community and not yet liable to burgh taxation. Their rise in the capital after the formal establishment of the Court of Session in 1532 was swift; already in the 1560s the combined wealth of thirty-one lawyers amounted to more than a quarter of that of Edinburgh's 357 merchants. By the 1690s the professions in the capital rivalled the merchants in numbers – there were some 600 and 580 respectively – but the wealth of the 320 lawyers was greater than that of the merchants and craftsmen combined.[23] The seventeenth century saw the spectacular rise of the legal profession. The effects were diverse, for no other group operated in as many spheres of Scottish society – urban and rural, in central administration and in the various spheres of government in the localities.

Usually lawyers took little part in urban politics as such except as town clerks, but their increasing presence accentuated a drift towards more oligarchical burgh government. By the second half of the sixteenth century craftsmen were taking to the courts rather than the streets to settle their grievances; the Edinburgh crafts hired a well-placed advocate, David McGill, to represent their interests in the early 1580s. Conversations between town councils and the king's government were also increasingly being conducted by lawyers during the long reign of James VI. A fast-changing society with an active market in land was also liable to be a litigious one and the increasing centralisation of law in Edinburgh after the erection of the College of Justice there in 1532 had also made justice more costly. A modest Highland chief, John MacLeod of Dunvegan, spent over £3,600 on legal fees in twelve months in 1636-7.[24] With greater organisation as a profession and fatter fees, there came a rise in status, both in town and country. Lawyers were debarred from membership of the Edinburgh town council but not from the kirk session: in 1574 five of the twelve elders were lawyers. It was only natural that lawyers, who recorded both loans and property transactions, were the brokers between town and countryside. And it was they rather than burgh merchants who began to buy country estates. Merchants might often acquire rural property as part of a wadset arrangement in which they held an estate as security for a loan, but it was usually lawyers who wanted the estate as an investment – as much in status as in economic return.

One career will serve to illustrate the phenomenal rise of the legal dynasty. Sir Thomas Hope came to the bar in 1605 and by 1626 he was Lord Advocate, by dint of his work on the Revocation of 1625. His family – he had fourteen children – spread the tentacles of a landed connection far and wide. His sons had interests in manufactories and in leadmines at Crawfordmuir. Hope himself combined the roles of Edinburgh lawyer, servant of the crown and estate manager. By the 1660s and 1670s, Craighall was realising £12,500 a year, mostly in grain and coal, though most of it was being spent on Craighall itself, either in the progressive improvement of the estate or on expensive refurbishment of the house. By the 1690s the family could afford Sir William Bruce as an architect to redesign the house. The Covenanting revolution did not make this ambitious family, but allowed it, like the lairds they were, new outlets for their position in landed society. Hope himself played an elaborate double game after 1638, as part of the King's administration but also an active sympathiser with the rebels and eventually sat as an officer of state in the Covenanting parliament. Three sons, all lawyers, played important roles at the different layers of the regime: his first son, John Lord Craighall, sat on the Committee of Estates, the nerve centre of the revolutionary regime; Sir Thomas Hope of Kerse as Collector General in 1640-1 organised taxation on a new, non-feudal basis; and Sir James Hope of Hopetoun was a shire commissioner for Stirling. All picked up along the way baronetcies as well as knighthoods. The subsequent family tree is an immense and complicated structure, which leads to the commanding heights of all sections of Scottish society in the eighteenth century; it embraces landed society, including the earldom of Hopetoun (created in 1703), all levels of the Scottish bar, and the medical and teaching professions. It was the very model of the rising middle sort.[25]

Seventeenth-century Scottish society witnessed the rise of two professions – lawyers and ministers – and nothing marked it more indelibly. There were a number of similarities about them. Families in each profession tended to intermarry and each developed the hallmarks of a hereditary caste. Sons followed in fathers' footsteps to both the pulpit and the bar. At least 17 per cent of ministers in the Church in the early part of the century had come from the manse and by the 1640s the figure had risen to 27 per cent. Andrew and James Melville were only two of a race of Melvilles in the Kirk; John Row, minister of Perth after the Reformation of 1560, had five surviving sons who all went into the ministry and they in turn fathered six more ministers. In the 1620s dynasties of lawyers were even more common than those of ministers. The Hopes of Craighall were only one of a score or more of major legal families. The proportion of entrants to the bar who had followed their fathers was then a phenomenal 31 per cent. New bonds of kin embraced the new professions – and still do to this day.

The differences between the two professions were more important than their likenesses. There was only a little movement between them. Few lawyers' sons opted for the ministry and fewer still married daughters of the manse; but about one in ten of advocates were ministers' sons. Between the two professions there lay a profound difference: in social origins. There had been some ministers in the first and second generations of the new Church who had come from baronial families – Erskine of Dun was himself a laird and Robert Bruce was the son of another – or from the upper reaches of the urban bourgeoisie, but such connections became rarer as time passed. Sons of nobles were virtually unknown: the kirk could boast just one in its ranks in the 1640s and he was illegitimate. By the 1640s less than one in twenty of the ministry came from the upper reaches of Scottish society, whether landed or urban. The typical minister, if he did not come from the manse, was the son of a modest merchant or craftsman or of a small landed proprietor below the status of a laird. Lawyers, by contrast, were increasingly likely as the seventeenth century went on to come from the landed élite; by the 1670s more than half of all advocates were the sons of lairds or better, and almost one in five of all fathers had a title.[26] The moulds of the two groups which would do more than any other to shape Scottish society in the eighteenth and nineteenth centuries had already set firm in the seventeenth. And each was further preserved by the legislation of the Union of Parliaments in 1707, which guaranteed the status quo.

Within fifty years of the Reformation of 1560, the ministry had built up a formidable *esprit de corps*. Like the lawyers, the ministers stressed their new professional status and clung to the special privileges which set them apart from the rest of society. Only three species escaped taxation in Jacobean Scotland – the poor, the lawyers and some ministers.[27] Their collective self-consciousness was fostered even before their admission to the ministry; the universities continued for most of the seventeenth century to be largely clerical seminaries where bursars had to 'live collegialiter' and remain answerable to their home presbytery. The absence of the laity from presbyteries once they were restored in the late 1580s did much to foster their sense of exclusiveness. The return of the nobles and lairds in 1638 to both presbytery and General Assembly as ruling elders was resented by many ministers. The course of the Covenanting revolution gave the ministers added moral authority but less real influence, both in Church and state. Their capacity to influence events was hampered by the agreement of that Glasgow Assembly of 1638 that they should not hold civil office. The ministers' Table, set up in late 1637, was not replaced when the Covenanting regime reorganised itself in 1640. The boundaries between Church and state, which had been vaguely drawn ever since the earliest days of the reformed Church, were being redrawn after 1638 in favour of the laity.[28]

The ministers, however, also gained immeasurably from the Scottish revolution. The revolt of 1638 completed a process which had been going on since the 1590s of a new emerging vision of Scotland. By the 1630s the state of the Church was widely accepted as a metaphor for the condition of the nation itself. The day of the signing of the National Covenant was hailed by Wariston as 'the marriage day of the kingdom with God'. Scotland was acclaimed as the new Israel, they being 'the only two sworn nations of the Lord'.[29] The identities of Church and state were merged – into a covenanted nation. Even if the ministers did not find office in the Covenanting state, they were secure in their position as its conscience. Every one of the armies of the Covenant went to war under a religious banner – the most common after 1643 proclaimed 'For the Covenant, Religion, the Crown and Kingdom' – and each regiment had a chaplain attached to it.

The twists and turns taken by the Scottish Revolution would bring confusion to the Kirk as well as to other sections of Scottish society. On the major issues thrown up in the 1630s and 1640s the Kirk usually found itself caught in two minds: most of the leading ministers in 1638 had not wanted to abolish bishops outright; and ten years later, on the issue of the Engagement the Assembly came to a decision, but only by a one-vote majority. The course of the Revolution threw into sharp relief different strands of opinion on issues ranging from new forms of worship to problems about the organisation of society on a war footing. By 1650 the Kirk would be split irrevocably into two warring parties of ministers, the Resolutioners and Protesters. The Restoration, which imposed an Erastian settlement on the Church, would strain its fabric still further and the overthrow of James VII in 1689 resulted in the greatest purge the reformed Church had ever experienced – when almost two-thirds of the ministry were removed in the aftermath of what is curiously often called the presbyterian 'settlement' of 1690. The striking fact is that the moral authority of the Church was not damaged more than it actually was by the confused events of the second half of the seventeenth century. The Church of Scotland was split, hopelessly, and beyond repair; but a Calvinist nation was utterly secure.

Seventeenth-century culture

Until the sixteenth century, the focus of culture had been firmly in the royal court. Kings were patrons of historians such as Fordun, Boece and his translator Bellenden, as well as of poets, such as William Dunbar, Alexander Scott and Alexander Montgomerie, or musicians like Robert Carver, Thomas Wood and the Hudsons. These were the essential fashioners of an evermore sophisticated cult of kingship which used the new opportunities afforded by the printing press. The void left by the removal of the royal court after 1603 was not made good by a country house culture. Except in Gaeldom, where the houses of lords and clan chiefs had for long been centres of both culture and schooling and where piping, bardic and medical schools continued, the nobility offered little in the way of literary patronage. A pessimistic view of Scottish culture in the seventeenth century is often taken by literary historians, who can find little popular writing, at least in the form of either comedy or fiction, no popular journalism or theatre and little but the literature of tangled ecclesiastical controversies, political tracts, diaries and letters, all too often of churchmen.[30]

The departure of the court needs to be set against the impact of the printing press, which created a much wider reading public; the anglicisation of Scottish writing, which was already apparent amongst some of the Castalian Band of poets before 1603, must be balanced against the successful reworking of English influences into a distinctively Scottish style; and the agenda for debate needs to be widened beyond the narrow confines of vernacular prose and poetry into the wider world of scholarship, Latin as much as English, music, heraldry and architecture in which the Scottish nobility and the middling sort moved. By 1600 there were already clear signs of a new self-confident literate society existing independent of both the court and the noble household, with its own tastes and demands. The Scottish Renaissance is usually associated with the court – of James IV, V and VI – but by 1600 it had reached a new and wider audience, and in doing so had undergone a change of character. The seventeenth century marked the era of a great literary revival. It produced an intelligentsia, made up largely of the professions and lairds. Its foundations were laid in the institutions which gradually brought organisation to the professions as well as in the private libraries and booksellers' inventories which were the repositories of the new, widespread interest in scholarship.

The most obvious change was in architecture. The half-century between 1490 and 1540, the golden age of Renaissance monarchy, was the period which saw the rebuilding of the royal palaces of Stirling, Holyroodhouse, Linlithgow and Falkland, which were the focal points of a court circle of poets and a cult of honour centred on the tournament or the fête. The half-century after 1590 was the period of a wider Scottish architectural renaissance which saw the part-reconstruction of Crichton Castle and the building of Fyvie Castle, the Argyll Lodging in Stirling and Gladstone's Land in Edinburgh. The elaborate Italianate façade built by the Earl of Bothwell into a fourteenth-century castle at Crichton is a reflection of the influence made on impressionable minds by the Grand Tour and the changing status of the aristocracy. Fyvie Castle in Aberdeenshire is one of the most delightful of many examples of the change from a tower house built for defence to a château built for gracious living and often with formal gardens around them. Like Seton Palace, also built by a French architect for the Earl of Dunfermline, or the castles at Craigievar,

Drum or Inverugie, they were symbols of a new leisured landed class, which embraced not only the old and new nobility but also greater lairds whose income often matched that of peers. In Berwickshire, by 1600, there was a building boom of mock tower houses which reflected the rising wealth of the lairds of the Merse, but on the English side of the Border there were still few signs of architectural renaissance.[31]

Noblemen also built elegant town houses. Two particularly fine examples were both built for royal secretaries: what is now called the Argyll Lodging, an elegant three-storey French-style *hôtel* around a courtyard, was designed for Sir William Alexander, Earl of Stirling, and Acheson House in Canongate, Edinburgh, was built for Sir Archibald Acheson, descendant of an Edinburgh merchant family, in 1633. About half a mile to the west, in the Lawnmarket, the six-storey Gladstone's Land with an arcade at ground level, built about 1600 and acquired by a merchant Thomas Gledstanes in 1617, was the symbol both of the sharply rising population of the capital and of the ability of its merchant establishment to rise above the stench of the street. By 1635, Gledstanes had sold off most of the tenement and lived on the top floor, which would otherwise have fetched £360 per annum in rent; the average rent for the burgh as a whole was £40 and just 200 yards away to the south, amongst the breweries and stables of the Grassmarket, rents fell away to under £10.[32] By the 1690s, the solution for gracious living for the capital's professional classes lay in elegant courtyards such as Milne's Court or the later James's Court, which swept away medieval rigs and the old patterns of urban settlement; they were virtual middle-class suburbs in the centre of a city. Yet in each case – the tenement, the town house and the mock baronial château – foreign influences, French, Italian or Dutch, were moulded into a successful and distinctively Scottish style.

The royal licence for the setting up of the first Scottish printing press by Chepman and Myllar in 1507, which specified 'bukis of our lawis, actis of parliament, chroniclis, mess buiks', made it clear it was a means of promoting both the King's government and the image of kingship. By 1600, despite attempts by both the reformed Church and the crown to keep control of it, the printing press had become an instrument of mass culture of different kinds. There were four general types of book – religious works of various kinds; Latin grammars, the basic curriculum of the grammar school, and vernacular texts, often catechisms and psalm books which were used in the 'English' and 'adventure' schools; histories and chronicles, new and old; and works of vernacular literature. Their popularity can be measured both by the number of editions printed and by the number of copies of them in circulation.[33]

The testament inventory of Henry Charteris, an Edinburgh bookseller who died in 1599, clearly demonstrates the main instruments of evangelisation for the Church: there were 5,400 copies of Calvin's catechism in its simple question and answer format which cost only 2d, designed for use in the 'English' schools which taught children up to the age of about eight; over 3,300 psalm books of various sorts; and 1,000 of the sermons of the Edinburgh minister Robert Rollock. What may seem surprising is the relatively small number of bibles – less than a hundred – but the day of the pocket bible had not yet arrived. By the middle the seventeenth century, it had with a vengeance; James Bryson had 5,000 copies of the New Testament and a further 2,000 copies of a smaller-sized and abridged children's version. By 1716 the widow of the king's printer, Mrs Anderson (Agnes Campbell), had almost 28,000 bibles of various sizes in stock. The same inventory also revealed the growing popularity after about 1660 of various English devotional works, and especially those of Thomas Boston and John Bunyan. The first part of Bunyan's *Pilgrim's Progress*, published in England in 1678, was republished in Scotland in 1680, 1681 and 1683; and in 1717 Mrs Anderson had 618 copies of his *Grace Abounding*.[34] The habits of the middle-class reading public had changed over the course of the century towards a more contemplative brand of Calvinism; but the catechism and the psalms were still the basic primers for ordinary society.

In education the standard grammar remained either that of Donatus or Despauterius over much of the period. Bassenden had over 1,000 copies of Despauterius in stock in 1579, each costing 4d, and Bryson had 4,000 in 1642. Arguments about the breadth of literacy in Scottish society have tended to concentrate either on evidence of the ability to *write*, as measured by the highly imperfect means of the ability to sign one's name,[35] or else on the inexact mathematics of the counting of schools. The number of schools seems to have been seriously underestimated. There were certainly far more pre-Reformation schools than the strictures of the *First Book of Discipline* of 1560 suggest, and the same is true of the two Education Acts of 1633 and 1696. The tactics of ministers and schoolmasters in seeking to paint as black a picture of educational provision as possible also make hazardous the drawing of over-firm conclusions from surveys of schools, such as that of 1627. There were probably at least 700 schools in early seventeenth-century Scotland, spread unevenly over the country's 1,000-odd parishes. The more evidence which is uncovered, the more it seems that the Education Act of 1696 which sought to establish a school in every parish was not a great turning point; over most of central and Lowland Scotland schools were already in place. In Lothian, fifty of the sixty-five parishes had Latin or grammar schools in the 1690s; perhaps only one parish had no school at all. In Fife, fifty of the sixty parishes had a grammar school and probably fifty-seven a parish school.[36]

Little account has been taken in the debate on literacy levels of the presence of schoolbooks in the inventories of booksellers: one Edinburgh printer who specialised in schoolbooks had in 1622 over 1,500 bound Latin books and over 39,000 unbound 'for skoles', mostly grammars or Virgil; he had in addition over 2,300 bound and 42,400 unbound small books in English, which must mostly have been for use in the vernacular schools. The mounting evidence suggests quite widespread provision of a basic education, in reading if not in writing. As far as the grammar schools are concerned, provision was extensive and more sophisticated than might be suspected; Scotland had a virtual national curriculum in the seventeenth century. This was partly due to the use of standard textbooks, but it was also a result of the interest taken by both General Assembly and parliament in what was taught in grammar schools. The General Assembly prescribed the grammar school curriculum – in Latin – in 1583 and parliament legislated for a standard grammar in 1607 and 1612. The grammar school was the first stage towards a career in the professions, but it was also the key to a wider world of scholarship – in Latin – in which much of the achievement of the later Scottish Renaissance was made.[37]

The instinctive reaction of a society in a process of rapid and often bewildering change is to rediscover its links with its past, or to forge new ones. That process took a variety of different forms: never had histories of Scotland been so popular, but there was also a revival from the 1570s onwards of the literary masterpieces of Middle Scots. The Edinburgh lawyer George Bannatyne, who belonged to a family that already had connections both with printers and poets, assembled a huge manuscript collection of medieval Scots verse in the 1560s. The works of Sir David Lindsay, chief poet at the court of James V, were reprinted by the Edinburgh bookseller Henry Charteris in 1568 and in the 1599 inventory of his stock there were 788 copies of it, as well as 554 copies of Henryson's *Testament of Cresseid* and 122 of Blind Harry's late fifteenth-century epic, *The Wallace*. Thomas Bassenden, who had brought out a rival edition of Lindsay's poems in 1574 had 510 copies in 1579 and 300 of the late fifteenth-century romance *Graystiel*. The popularity of such works increased in the seventeenth century – Robert Bryson had 1,150 copies of the complete works of Lindsay in 1646, and at 4s each they were half the price of the Charteris edition. The likely reading public was probably drawn from the ranks of the middling sort, but cheap copies of individual works – such as Charteris's 4d edition of Henryson's *Testament* – hint at a wider popularity for them. And the £388 owed by five chapmen to another Edinburgh bookseller in 1606 suggests that there was already a wide network of demand for the popular literature of the chapbook.

In England there was by 1625 already a cult of a golden age of Elizabeth's reign. In Scotland, there were two sets of myths. Ministers such as David Calderwood looked to the period before 1596 as the golden age of the Kirk, before the interference in it of James VI and the Anglican Church. But there was also in the period of the first British state a wider Scots national consciousness which helps to explain its failure; this was fuelled by works such as *The Wallace* and Barbour's *Brus* and reflected too in a new vogue for both the writing and reading of histories of Scotland. Andrew Melville, who had an alternative career in the 1590s as an unofficial Latin poet laureate, began a verse epic *Gathelus* on the origins and history of the Scots; mercifully only 158 lines ever reached print. His fellow minister John Johnston successfully completed his *Inscriptiones historicae regum Scotorum*, a Latin verse who's who of Scottish kings which began in the fourth century BC. And in 1613 Patrick Gordon of Ruthven composed 8,000 lines of martial epic romance in Scots telling the story of Robert Bruce up to Bannockburn.

The reason given by Gordon for his extraordinary patriotic flurry was the 'recent' loss of King Robert's diary and some 'remarkable tales' he had found, written by a fourteenth-century monk of Melrose. Although those tales were probably apocryphal, there were certainly serious collectors of historical manuscripts at the time; the lawyer Sir Lewis Stewart bought a fifteenth-century copy of *Scotichronicon*, said to have belonged to the Abbey of Coupar Angus, in 1651. It ended up along with a large amount of other manuscripts and printed histories in the impressive collection in the Advocates' Library, which was founded in 1689. The private library of Lauder of Fountainhall amounted to 536 books by the time he was admitted advocate in 1668 at the age of twenty-two; by 1679 he had amassed 992 volumes. The size of his library by his death in 1722 is unknown, but it must by then have far exceeded that of the celebrated Jacobean court poet, Drummond of Hawthornden, who possessed 1,400 books. Like those of the Faculty of Advocates as a whole, Fountainhall's interests were wide-ranging, straddling the classics, modern histories of European countries as well as Scotland or England, and French and English literature. Twenty-seven pages of the 158-page 1692 catalogue of the newly founded Advocates' Library were taken up with historical volumes and a further forty-two pages with non-legal works.[38] It is a striking fact that the most important collections of late medieval Scottish verse *and* of seventeenth-century scholarship were both the work of lawyers.

The search for roots was genealogical and local as well as national. The laird of Glenorchy had a collection of twenty-four pictures of kings and queens of Scotland, but also thirty-four portraits of 'lairds and ladies' drawn from his ancestors as well as a 'grit genealogie bord' painted by the celebrated artist George Jamesone.[39] The later sixteenth century had seen a spate of histories of noble houses: the lawyer Richard Maitland (father of the two royal secretaries, William and John) wrote histories of the families of Seton and Wedderburn and David Hume of Godscroft, a Berwickshire laird, compiled an extensive history of the Douglases which was eventually published in 1644; a history of the otherwise obscure family of the Earls of Sutherland was commissioned in 1615. The fashion extended to burghs too. Edinburgh in 1603 claimed that its roots, like those of the monarchy, went back to 330 BC and a Provost of Aberdeen, Alexander Skene, wrote almost as ambitious a history of that burgh in 1685.

The most visible sign of historic status to contemporaries was in heraldry and Aberdeen also had a coat of arms devised for it in the 1680s. Newly ennobled lairds and lawyers rushed to claim their new-found stake in the community of the realm: Sir Lewis Stewart laid claim to descent from the Wolf of Badenoch by placing the Buchan arms on his seal and edging them in stone at his new mansion at Kirkhill. One of his relations, another Edinburgh lawyer William Stewart, even had his burgess ticket embellished with his arms. The Earl of Dunfermline, the prime example of a family which had won new status through royal office, indulged his taste for heraldry throughout his empire – in his châteaux at Fyvie, Pinkie and Seton, in the parish church of Fyvie and Dunfermline Abbey, and on new arms of the regality of Dunfermline.[40] Status was also for sale. The entrepreneurial Earl of Stirling not only offered tracts of land in New Scotland (modern-day Nova Scotia) in the 1620s and 1630s but also a hereditary baronetcy complete with arms and pendant – all for £2,000. The creation of the Order of the Thistle by James VII in 1687, despite its distinctly Catholic overtones which caused a mob to ransack the Abbey Church at Holyrood in 1688, was re-established by Queen Anne in 1702. The same quest for honour, which had been deprived of the locus of the court for most of the seventeenth century, was what provided a ready audience for translations of continental works of romance and for native works such as the The *Brus*, *Graystiel* or Gavin Douglas's *Palace of Honour*.

The motives that lay behind the cult of honour were twofold. One undoubtedly lay in a scramble for status and the desire of the old nobility to distance itself from such *arrivistes*; their difficulty lay in the fact that there was distinctly more new money than old in seventeenth-century Scotland. There can be little doubt that it was the new arrivals who were both the main cultivators and the reinterpreters of the old order. The other cause, however, had more to do with the status of the nation than of the individuals who made up the political community. The combined effect of new emblems of family status and the literature, both old and new, which celebrated a heroic past was a new patriotism. It fused in the 1630s, with the identification of the Kirk as the symbol of an independent Scotland and the 'auld estait'. The collapse of the quest for the Covenant, the splitting of the Kirk into warring parties after 1650, and the desire of both the nobility and the middling sort to forget their Covenanting past combined to produce a revised ideal after 1660. Once again it found focus in the monarchy, although it was only the brief residence in Edinburgh of James, Duke of York, the future James VII, in the early 1680s which gave it a clear coherence.[41]

In the years between 1679 and 1688, an astonishing number of institutions and offices were founded. The Royal College of Physicians was founded in 1681 and three professors of medicine were appointed at Edinburgh University in 1685; the Order of the Thistle was created in 1687; and the Advocates' Library, planned since 1682, eventually opened in 1689. The offices of Royal Physician, Geographer-royal and Historiographer-royal were all founded between 1680 and 1682. The ideal was aristocratic in tone, but, as before, it glorified the virtuoso, whose intellectual interests ranged across all the arts and sciences.[42] Again, its most enthusiastic converts were the middling sort and, above all, the lawyers. The highlights of the 1680s, however, built on a century of solid if unspectacular achievement. County maps of Scotland, begun by John Adair with the help of a privy council grant in 1682, drew on the work begun in the 1590s of a minister's son, Timothy Pont. Robert Sibbald, physician to Charles II, Geographer of Scotland from 1682, and President of the Royal College of Surgeons, looked back to the intellectual circle of Sir James Balfour of Denmilne in the 1620s and 1630s. The collections of laws published by Stair in 1681 and by Sir George Mackenzie in 1684, which both had the title of *Institutions of the Law of Scotland*, gave a new, philosophical coherence to the work of collecting practicks and digests of laws that had been going on since the 1560s.

The idea that Scotland somehow acquired an intelligentsia between 1660 and 1700 depends on a view of the past which thrives on upheaval and watershed. The one area in which change did outweigh continuity was as yet relatively unimportant: in the universities there had been a large, calculated purge in 1660. That had been done because the universities were still seen primarily as seminaries for the clergy. It was the professions rather than the universities which forced the pace of the seventeenth-century pursuit of the intellect. The political Restoration was marked by the celebrations made by the 'Drunken Parliament' of the end of revolutionary government. There was no dramatic declaration of the birth of a new cultural age in 1660 or after, such as the publicists of the Enlightenment would make in the 1750s. The aim of scholarship was to resolve the clash of change and the old order. 1660, so often seen as a turning-point in many spheres of Scottish history, resulted in only a minor change of direction for the Scottish intellect. Once again, there was a deliberate renewal of links with the past. Learning was again thought of as a patriotic programme. The agents of Caroline culture were the same lairds, lawyers and ministers and often the very same families as before. Far from there being a cultural desert from which Scotland was rescued after 1660, the achievement of the Restoration period was to draw together the threads which linked the long Renaissance of the sixteenth and early seventeenth centuries with the Enlightenment of the eighteenth.

16

REVOLUTION AND WAR

ON 23 JULY 1637, MEMBERS OF CHARLES I'S PRIVY COUNCIL, THE TWO archbishops of Scotland, eight of the bishops and the bulk of the Lords of Session solemnly filed into the High Kirk of St Giles to hear the first service conducted according to the liturgy laid down in the new Prayer Book. As soon as the Dean of St Giles began to read, a riot broke out. A large number of the congregation staged a walk-out and some continued to demonstrate outside; others shouted abuse and at least one hurled a stool as well. The stool missed, but the impact was felt throughout Scotland. It was the first of a series of carefully planned demonstrations against both the new liturgy and bishops. Services in the three other Edinburgh churches were also packed with demonstrators. The hapless ministers retreated in confusion; the Dean himself spent much of the day in the safety of the steeple of St Giles; and the Bishop of Edinburgh fled to the Palace of Holyroodhouse in a borrowed coach which was stoned for most of the way. Within a week the new Prayer Book had been abandoned, but the campaign gathered pace over the next two months as more than sixty petitions and supplications poured into the privy council from kirk sessions and presbyteries in a broad arc from Fife to Dumfriesshire. The internal dissensions within the privy council were increasingly exposed; the bulk of the lay councillors, headed by Traquair, blamed the 'imprudent precipitation' of the bishops, and they, in their turn, tried to pin responsibility for the disturbances on Traquair, who had been notable by his absence on 23 July, for failing to anticipate the troubles. By October, when the King's council moved to Linlithgow for its own safety and virtually abandoned the capital to the dissidents, the battle lines were being drawn up. By November, the 'Supplicants' were beginning to organise themselves into a revolutionary cadre: four 'Tables', representing the nobles, lairds, burgesses and ministers, were set up.[1] Their status was as yet unclear, but in the following February they approved a manifesto – the National Covenant.

Despite appearances, neither the issues nor the actors in this sensational drama were clear-cut. In the Supplication drawn up in October 1637 by the leading dissidents and presented in a new form by Lord Loudoun to the privy council in December, the claim was made that the essence of the issue was 'alteratione of religione'; Rothes in February 1638 asked only that ways be found that the 'incontrollable' bishops, who were blamed for both the Prayer Book and the disaffection between the King and his subjects, 'might be restrained'; but no mention was made of their being dismissed, still less the abolition of their office.[2] Although it had been the interference by the bishops in both central and local government which had galvanised opposition for many, ranging from nobles to the more radical ministers or the urban mob, others – including many ministers – were not so sure that bishops had no place in a reformed Church. The real significance of the Supplication was that it revealed for the first time the aristocratic leaders of the protest movement. Dissident nobles such as Loudoun, Rothes and Balmerino were intent, not so much on protest against the King, but office (and augmented pensions) under him. This was almost the only route which could be taken to resolve the paradox of an opposition movement operating within what was still a one-party state. The bishops were caught in a pincer movement, between their rivals outside the privy council and their enemies within it. What was being staged was the dress rehearsal for the real performance which would take place later, at a General Assembly which met in Glasgow in December 1638.

The manifesto of the revolt bore little trace of revolutionary trappings. The National Covenant – also known as the Noblemen's Covenant – was a document striking for both its length and its dullness. It began with a recitation of the King's or 'Negative' Confession of 1581, a wordy flyting against the evils of papistry, which must have had a popular appeal; its middle sections contained a long list of acts of parliament relating to the Church going back to 1560; it ended with a 'national oath and subscription inviolable', pledging allegiance to both the continuing work of reformation and the authority of the crown.[3] Revolutions are run on slogans, not 5,000-word resolutions, and for ten years or more the cry would be 'For Christ's Crown and Covenant'. It is difficult to imagine that many of the nobles, lairds, ministers and burgesses who signed the Covenant in Greyfriars Church in the capital on 28 February and 1 March 1638, and still less those who had it read out to them over the course of half an hour in churches in all parts of the country over the next few weeks, would have understood what it really meant.

Contained deep within the Covenant, however, were two explosive devices constructed by the two sharpest minds in the Kirk and the Law, Alexander Henderson and Archibald Johnston of Wariston. The first lay within the 1581 harangue against popery's 'manyfold ordoures' and 'wicked hierarchie'; the second, which was subliminally reinforced by the long recitation of parliamentary statute, claimed that changes in the Church had subverted 'our liberties, lawes and estates'.[4] The two planks of the revolution were launched: the removal of bishops because of the alleged 'incompatibilitie betwixt episcopall government and presbyteriall power'[5] and the re-establishment of a free parliament. They depended on two historical myths: a determinedly one-eyed reading of the history of the Kirk since the Reformation of 1560 and historians such as Calderwood and Row rushed into print to secure its foundations; and the right, already established by George Buchanan in his History of Scotland, of the nobles over nineteen centuries to censure their kings. Not for the first time in Scottish history, the course of the future was set by myths of the past.

In late June 1638 Charles acquiesced to the growing demands for a free Assembly – the first since 1618. It met, in Glasgow Cathedral, on 21 November. In the interim, rival strategies were being formed. The King had begun to plan for a military solution, which would crystallise in the summer of 1639; the Covenanters, determined that the Assembly would not be the tame poodle it was in 1610, when it had last met in Glasgow and approved James VI's restoration of episcopacy, made elaborate preparations to pack it. The Glasgow Assembly was unlike any General Assembly before it or since. It sat for fully a month, behind locked doors, with more nobles and lairds present than ever before, including 1560 or 1567. It was called by some the Second Reformation, but there was a vital difference. The Reformation of

1560 had avowedly been a revolt of the provinces; the Revolution of 1637-8 was, by contrast, a self-consciously national revolt – at once difficult for a government to assuage and for the rebels themselves to control. In attendance at Glasgow were not only ministers but also representatives, in the novel guise of ruling elders, of each of Scotland's sixty-three presbyteries, together with forty-seven burgh commissioners. Each commissioner was also accompanied by between four and six lay 'assessors' for moral support, and all noblemen and lairds who had signed the Covenant could also attend in their own right. The packed Cathedral was not so much a debating chamber as a theatre in the round. There could hardly be a debate for the bishops, for once defying the wishes of Charles I, did not turn up; three got perhaps within hearing distance, in the Bishop's Castle, but having experienced the violence of the mob a number of times over the previous sixteen months they ventured no nearer. Archbishop Spottiswoode had left the country in September and resigned as chancellor before the Assembly opened. Left uneasily holding the ring was the King's commissioner, the Marquis of Hamilton.

By 28 November, with the agenda of the Assembly now under the firm control of the joint authors of the Covenant – Wariston was elected its clerk and Henderson its moderator – Hamilton was forced to attempt to dissolve it as it moved inexorably towards the radicals' motion to abolish the office of bishop. Caught between two forces which had already made up their minds, Hamilton was not even spared a dignified exit from this revolutionary cauldron; the key to the door had somehow been mislaid. Little wonder that he exclaimed in a letter to his royal master: 'Next Hell I hate this place'.[6] In his absence, locked in and locked together in each other's embrace for the next ten years, were the Covenanting magnates and ministers. What was now a rebel Assembly meeting in defiance of the express wishes of the King moved on to reject the Five Articles of Perth, the Canons of 1636 and the Prayer Book of 1637 and to abolish episcopacy. It says something for the atmosphere of the Assembly that this was not done by instant acclamation but painstakingly picked over in legalistic fashion over the space of eleven days. Only on 10 December did the Assembly adopt the persona of a show trial; over the next three days eleven bishops were formally tried in their absence, deposed and excommunicated. It was a revolution that drew on the forces of conservatism and legalism so dear to the Scottish psyche – but it was no less a revolution for it. By January 1639 both the Covenanters and the King were openly arming; by February hostilities broke out in the north-east and by the end of March Charles arrived in York, *en route* to crush his rebellious Scottish subjects.

Rule of Charles I (1625-38)

The road to revolution between mid-1637 and late 1638 was the work of a conspiracy which outgrew the expectations of even the most extreme of the conspirators. Wariston had greeted the signing of the National Covenant as 'the glorious marriage day of the Kingdome with God', but by the time of the Glasgow Assembly this insomniac who whispered his revolutionary dreams only to his *Diary* dared to think of extending 'the royal prerogative of King Jesus . . . through all the borders of the earth'. By 1639 dream had become reality: the Scottish Church in its rediscovered perfection would 'be a patterne for uther nations' to imitate; the Scottish apocalypse was first to be found in England, but only as a step towards a greater Calvinist reformation 'to be propagated from Island to Continent'. The idea of a presbyterian international was born.[7]

The revolt of 1638 was also the result of a near-complete breakdown of conciliar government. The Supplicants' campaign had been carefully engineered but its adversaries could hardly have been more maladroit. The first Prayer Book riot in July 1637 is sometimes explained by the time the conspirators were given to hatch their plans; the use of the new Book had been announced from the pulpit a week before. It had also been authorised by a proclamation fully seven months before, in December 1636, and Wariston was then already hard at work on his legal researches. The blunders of the different compartments of the King's government in 1636 and 1637 are not in doubt, but do they explain the unprecedented volume of protest against the new Prayer Book? Scotland, it needs to be remembered, had been bracing itself for twenty years or more. The King had insisted on the use of the Anglican service during his visit in 1633 and in October 1634 its use was again authorised in places such as the Chapel Royal until a new liturgy, 'as neir as can be to this of England', was ready. The activities of the entrepreneurial Earl of Stirling, who had devised a new Psalm Book as yet another means to raise income, had encouraged rumours in 1631 of a new prayer book. Talks on the subject between Scottish bishops and William Laud, then Bishop of London, had begun as early as 1629. But the lack of a set 'form of divin service' had been highlighted as long ago as 1615 and a number of liturgies had been produced during James VI's reign, though none had ever been printed.[8] The length of the road to revolution in 1638-9 is a matter of considerable dispute.

The main steps on the road to revolution seem to be clearly marked. The first was taken by Charles himself, within seven weeks of his father's death in March 1625. His Revocation ensured that this Stewart king enjoyed no honeymoon period. It was seen as a Hydra, whose many heads threatened different things. Initially seeming only to affect grants of crown lands, though going back as far as 1540, it gradually emerged that the Revocation also affected abbey lands, teinds and even heritable jurisdictions – without any limit of time. The whole process of secularisation of church lands over the previous century or more was put in jeopardy. As such, hardly a noble, whether new creation or from an old-established family, would remain unaffected by it. The abbey lands had been the seedcorn of the new nobility of James VI's reign and the 2nd Earl of Dunfermline, son of that king's chancellor, would end up in Covenanter ranks; Montrose, whose estates at Braco had been carved out of the bishopric of Dunblane, was no less representative of older noble families. The potentially devastating effect on the complex class of landowners – superiors, heritors, feuars and lords of erection – who had all benefited from the landed revolution of the previous century might be compared to a sudden collapse in property values. All the tensions inherent within the system became refocused on the King himself. Although the issue seemed to be laid to rest by 1633, the vehicle for implementing the Revocation scheme, the Commission for Surrenders and Teinds, remained in being, a threatening shadow over Scottish politics, until the eve of the riot in July 1637. Even the bishops, potentially the greatest beneficiaries, were unsettled by the Revocation issue; in 1627 they petitioned the king that this land grab, far from helping the Church, might be its 'utter undoing'. Worse still, as critics pointed out, the right of revocation also seemed to extend (in all but the limited matter of feudal tenures) to all of Charles's predecessors as far back as Fergus macErc, first king of Dalriada in 501; so seriously was the prospect taken that the Court of Session acted in 1630 to limit its scope to 1455. The long line of kings of Scots, emblem of Scottish independence, had suddenly turned into a spectre threatening the very basis of property.[9]

The remoteness of the King was exaggerated by his failure to visit his northern kingdom. Rumours circulated of his arrival in both 1626 and in mid-1628, setting in motion elaborate preparations for his coronation. They were renewed late in 1631, but Charles eventually arrived in June 1633, when he also oversaw the first Scottish parliament of his reign. The lapse in time may well have been significant. There had been a severe downturn in the economy after 1627; grain prices were rising and overseas trade was falling at the very time that the fiscal demands of the crown were growing sharply. The burgesses felt the growing burden of taxation most heavily – or were, at least, the loudest in their complaints. Even though Scottish society was still lightly taxed in comparison with many other contemporary states, the comparison which it would naturally draw was with its own past, and the tax increases of James VI paled into insignificance in comparison to those of his son. Edinburgh paid more in tax in the first two years of Charles I's reign than in the last twenty-two years of James's. By the 1630s – faced with the prospect of financing the building of a new parliament house and the conversion of St Giles' into a cathedral at the King's insistence – a revolt of Edinburgh taxpayers, whose numbers had been increased by 50 per cent since 1605 to relieve the burden on the wealthy, must have been predictable. The 'temporary' tax of 1621 on annual rents and interest payments continued; it may have ground the faces of the money-lenders rather than those of the poor, but money markets, in the seventeenth century as much as in the twentieth, worked by an inexplicable chemistry called confidence. By the early 1630s confidence had already begun to dry up and a shortage of credit may have driven many nobles to the brink of bankruptcy or to desperate measures.[10]

Grumblings over higher taxes, anxiety over the economy and fears of the ministers of more interference in the Church were all present in the early 1630s, but the second major step towards 1638 was undoubtedly the parliament of 1633. James VI had arranged discreet surveillance of voting in both parliament and privy council; Charles I sat in parliament on a raised dais openly taking notes himself. It is difficult to guess which specific piece of legislation amongst many seemed the most alarming in 1633 – Sir James Balfour thought that all but three of the thirty-one acts were 'hurtefull to the liberty of the subjecte'. They included the continuation of the new taxes of 1621, but at a higher level of 6 rather than 5 per cent; and an ingenious new fiscal device called the 'two of Ten' milking still further windfall profits from money-lending which, to get accepted, Charles had to promise would never be levied again. It had probably been the first two acts – one ratifying previous legislation on religious matters including the Five Articles, and the other echoing an act of 1609 allowing the king to prescribe clerical dress – which set the tone of suspicion which hung over the whole parliament.[11]

It may be asking too much to look for further clear-cut steps on the road to revolution. Historians disagree and contemporaries were not always clear about either cause or motivation. Sir James Balfour, Lord Lyon, claimed, in what is the most frequently cited quotation about Charles's reign, that the Revocation of 1625 was 'the groundstone of all the mischiefs that followed after'; less often quoted is his opinion of the ecclesiastical acts in the parliament of 1633, for they too were 'the very groundstone' of the coming revolt.[12] The normal identity parade of causes of a revolution – long-term causes set against shorter-term, and identification of the triggers of conflict – is complicated by two factors: the still largely undented reputation of James VI as a highly successful King of Scots and the fact that in the early seventeenth century the stakes are raised and causation complicated. Not simply absentee kingship or 'dual monarchy'[13] is at issue, but the governance of *three* kingdoms.

The wider context helps explain some fears which may otherwise appear exaggerated. It had been in the English parliament of 1629 that fears had first been voiced about a 'crisis of parliaments'; the Irish parliament did meet in the 1630s, but only after high-handed curbs on it.[14] The increasing grip taken on parliamentary elections and procedures in all three of Charles's kingdoms fed on each other, as did the fears of each set of subjects. The unprecedented trial in 1635 of Lord Balmerino, son of a trusted administrator of James VI, which has been called 'Scotland's ship money case',[15] stemmed directly from the loss of points of contact between Charles I and his subjects; his trial and conviction (by a majority of one) of involvement in a petition critical of both royal policy and the proceedings in the 1633 parliament, turned protest into treason. It was no less a show trial than the *cause célèbre* of which it was the harbinger – the ruthless pursuit of William Prynne and other puritan critics of the English Church in 1637. Already there was in prospect not simply a Scottish crisis but a crisis of the three kingdoms.

Was the crisis avoidable? If attention remains focused on Scotland alone, here, some have argued, was essentially a problem of government rather than of religious disaffection, although that existed. Matters had actually improved under the soothing influence of the Earl of Menteith, who had emerged as the King's man of business in Scotland in 1628. The real demoralisation of the privy council set in only after Menteith's rather curious fall from grace in 1633. Archbishop Spottiswoode was appointed chancellor only in 1634 and it was the new treasurer, Traquair, who had the casting vote in Balmerino's trial. Under the stewardship of an elderly cipher (Spottiswoode was seventy) and an abrasive placeman without real influence in Scotland, things rapidly fell apart.[16] The alternative – of a strong man such as Wentworth, who was appointed as Lord Deputy in Ireland in 1632 to put an end to the vacillations of the Irish council since 1625 – was hardly likely to bring about a settlement in Scotland.[17] There was more to the gathering Scottish crisis than an administration of incompetents. The growing presence of bishops on the privy council – rising from six in 1625 to nine in 1637 – became alarming because it coincided with their increasing grip of dioceses taken by a new wave of younger and often gifted men (mostly in their forties) who were profoundly distasteful to radical presbyterians. The situation was clearly reminiscent of the English Church, where a virtual take-over of its key posts by so-called 'Arminians' had been effected between 1628 and 1633. The strength of Arminianism, one contemporary joked, lay in the fact that 'they held all the best bishoprics and deaneries in England'. By 1635 much the the same could be said of Scotland.[18] The new breed of bishops was hard-working – it was, for example, bishops such as Patrick Forbes of Aberdeen and Andrew Boyd of Argyll who were in the front line of the struggle against papistry –

and over-worked. Some of them were also, from at least 1629, in regular contact with Laud. What was in prospect – and what again immeasurably complicated the politics of the 1630s – was a union of the Churches of Charles's three kingdoms. In religion and in other issues as well, the Scottish problem was so difficult to manage because it was in essence a British problem – with tangled roots which went back to 1603.[19]

There were many threads of continuity between the policies of James VI and Charles I. The founding of a Register of Sasines in 1617 bred suspicion of the imminence of yet another of James's revocations and the fears of the landed classes after 1625 had already been aroused by the thirteen-year period allowed in 1617 for the crown to query the legality of existing charters. Charles's taxes were but James's writ larger. A single privy council for the three realms was feared in the 1630s but had first been advocated in 1604. What had haunted the rebels of 1559 had been 'the example of Brittany'; the dissidents of the 1630s had hanging over them the example of Wales, for James had himself said that he hoped that Scotland would 'be as Wales was'. Those fears were sharply aroused in 1630 by the grandiose scheme to erect a fishery company with a monopoly in all British waters. It was at that point that Charles for the first time since 1625 used the style of 'King of Great Britain'.[20]

It was in matters of religion that the continuity of policy was at its closest and where both these Stewart kings were at their most absolute. Prospects of a religious union were an inevitable consequence of the Union of the Crowns. Bancroft had talked of a union of 'one Church and Policie' in a conference with Scottish ministers in 1604; the blueprint for a common liturgy and a transformation of the General Assembly into something resembling the English House of Convocation had been set out in 1615. Charles's notion of himself as supreme head of the Churches in all three of his kingdoms took its lead from his father's many-headed cult of himself as a 'nursing father' of the Church; one of his Scottish bishops had gone as far as to call him 'our great Archbishop'.[21] The last crucial step taken before the Prayer Book of 1637 was the issuing of the Canons of 1636, which was done by 'our prerogative royall and supreme authoritie in causes ecclesiasticall'. It was a direct paraphrase of the standard Jacobean formula of the king's 'right and prerogative in causes ecclesiasticall'.[22] Yet there was more to 1636 than this. The Arminian bishop of London predicted that the Canons would 'make more noise than all the cannons in Edinburgh Castle'; the first impact would be made in Scotland, but it was also intended to be heard in England. The Scottish 1637 Prayer Book, as is well known, was based on an English model; but the Scottish Canons of 1636 also became the precedent for the English Canons of 1640.[23] Over the course of four decades there had been a three-legged progress, uneven but remorseless, towards a British Church. By the later 1630s both its proponents and its enemies were used to thinking in three-dimensional terms. For many Scots ministers, the crucial point may have come in 1633: it was then that the reassuringly Calvinist presence at Canterbury of George Abbot, 'a great friend of Scotland', was replaced by the threatening spectre of Laud.[24]

The longer-term causes of unrest in Scotland lay mostly at the door of the Union of 1603. Intensely personal kingship had given way to absentee monarchy; the 'keystone of the arch of Scottish society', it has been said, was 'loosened' after

1603.[25] Whereas early seventeenth-century English society saw more of the gentry becoming involved in national politics, in Scotland the process was put into reverse; fewer nobles were involved in government than for centuries. There were nobles, such as Montrose, with too much time on their hands and others, such as Loudoun, with too few assets in their pockets; but there were also sectors of a rising middling sort unable to claim a political role in either the local or national community to match their new-found status. Conciliar government was tried after 1603 and eventually found wanting. However manageable Scottish politics may be thought to have been, and however successful individual regimes were at managing, it is nevertheless the case that there was no settled system of management after 1603 – at least five systems bridged the period between Dunbar and Traquair. Ultimately, the Scottish privy council was being asked to operate in an unreal, two-dimensional context. The king and his closest advisers (of whom none was Scots or indeed Old Irish) thought in three-dimensional terms. In the complex vortex of issues which came to a head in 1637, the underlying link was the failure of a three-headed British state and the prospect of a British State Church. The result in 1638 was a nationalist revolt which spoke in the language of religion; but it was also a revolt which had as one of its aims the recasting of the British state.

The Wars of the Three Kingdoms

In the course of 1639 and 1640, the forces of Charles I and his Scottish subjects twice clashed in what has gone down in history as the 'Bishops' Wars' – evidence in itself of the extent to which the Covenanters had won the propaganda initiative. The Wars were a decisive point not only in the history of Scotland but in that of Great Britain. They exposed the hollow shell of Caroline absolute monarchy, which failed to demonstrate *force majeure*; they raised in crisis terms the question of control of the militia. They were the first of three episodes when Charles, in the space of three years between 1639 and 1642, was faced with armed rebellion in each of his kingdoms: what began in Scotland in 1639 led indirectly to the rebellion of Catholic Irish and Old English (the Norman settler class) in Ireland in October 1641, and directly to the outbreak of the Civil War in England in August 1642. And they marked the first of the many interventions by the three kingdoms in each other's affairs over the course of the next twenty years. By early 1642 a Scots army was *en route* to Ulster to protect Protestant settlers there; by early 1644 the Covenanters entered England again, intervening in the English Civil War at the invitation of the English parliament; and by late 1644 an Irish Catholic force would land in Argyll. The Wars of the Three Kingdoms involved the Scots in a war on three fronts.[26]

Like many momentous events in history, the Bishops' Wars were something of an illusion. Most of the real fighting took place not between the forces of King and Covenant but amongst feuding local families, in the north-east and the west; in that sense, they were the first of the Campbell wars of the seventeenth century. The First Bishops' War lasted about five weeks. There had been skirmishing in Inverness-shire as early as February 1639 and the burgh of Aberdeen had been taken and re-taken several times by a Covenanting force under the command of Montrose in a confused preface to the War, but the first serious blood to be spilt was on 10 May in the 'Trot of Turriff', an organised royalist counter-attack.[27] The real campaign, as planned by Charles, never took place. He had planned an elaborate three-pronged assault: he was to lead the main army across the Tweed at Berwick; a naval expedition under the command of Hamilton would, like Hertford in 1544, enter the Forth and land troops there; and an army under Wentworth would cross from Ireland to attack the soft underbelly of the Covenanters in Argyll. None of the components materialised. Hamilton cruised desultorily around the Forth for almost a month, captured one small island, failed to make a landing – perhaps deterred by the threat of his mother, the formidable, pistol-packing Marchioness, to shoot him if he did – and retreated in confusion. The main confrontation, which took place at Duns Law in the Borders on 5 June, was intended by both sides as a battle but ended up as the beginning of peace negotiations, which were concluded in the Treaty of Berwick thirteen days later.

Both sides saw the Treaty as a breathing space rather than a permanent peace. The fragile settlement was broken in a pre-emptive strike by the Covenanters in August 1640. The Second Bishops' War, in effect, lasted ten days. On 20 August 1640, Alexander Leslie led an army across the Tweed, drove an inadequate royal force of 10,000 men back to the River Tyne, defeated it in a short action at Newburn on the 28th and entered the undefended city of Newcastle two days later. Fighting continued in pockets elsewhere – Caerlaverock Castle held out until September and Edinburgh Castle agreed surrender terms in mid-September – but the war was virtually over. The concluding of the peace, which emerged as the Treaty of Ripon on 26 October 1640, took longer than the war itself.

The Bishops' Wars revealed many of the characteristics of what are often called the Wars of the Covenant, which would last until 1651. The leading dissident nobles – such as Loudoun, Eglinton and Rothes – had led regiments into the field in the First Bishops' War; feudal nobles had regained the status of warlords. In each regiment, however, there were also lieutenant-colonels and majors who were professional soldiers with experience abroad; the ensign and two sergeants in each company were also veterans.[28] Montrose had with him in his expedition to the north-east in 1639 a soldier with the Swedish rank of field marshal – Alexander Leslie, who led the assault in August 1640 and would command the Army of the Covenant which invaded England for a second time, in 1644. The differing ethos of the two was highlighted by what amounted to the kidnapping of Huntly by Leslie at a dinner to which he had been invited in April 1639 – this was a war in which the rules of hospitality counted for little.[29] Some of the regiments also took ministers with them as army chaplains in 1639 and 1640 – and eventually over a third of the ministry of the Kirk would serve in one or other of the dozen armies of the Covenant, which were also organised as instruments of a holy war. Yet some were the military arm of local magnates rather than of the Covenant. Many of the regiments of 1639 were raised by the traditional rivals of Gordon power in the north-east – such as the families of Forbes, Fraser and Marischal. Argyll's own regiment in 1639 had at least two ministers attached to it, but the regiment led by his kinsman Glenorchy refused to sign the Covenant.[30] One of the paradoxes of the Wars of the Covenant was that the leading politician of the movement was for much of the 1640s engaged in a private war in his own 'country' of Argyll which had only loose links with national issues. In 1640 Argyll had spent six weeks on a punitive expedition against his personal enemies, which took him to the Braes of Mar,

Atholl, Angus and Rannoch, before he moved, in late August, to secure Dumbarton Castle against a possible invasion force from Ireland. Already unfolded were, in effect, the germs of three wars: a religious struggle for the Covenant; a campaign for a Greater Britain; and a war for the Lordship of the Isles.

For Scotland, the immediate effects of the Bishops' Wars, which marked the triumph of the Covenanters, were twofold. The course of the Wars had seen a shift in the organising machinery of the Covenanting movement and a consolidation of the grip which the nobles had over it; the Tables were replaced in 1640 by a Committee of Estates, which had no place on it for the ministers.[31] The same parliament of 1640 embarked on a virtual constitutional revolution, which Charles ratified when he came to Edinburgh in August 1641. The Estates, which had refused to allow the King to prorogue them in November 1639, had begun in June 1640 to act out the role of a 'free parliament' heralded in the National Covenant: a Triennial Act was passed (eight months before the English Long Parliament did the same), parliament's right to vet nominations to both the privy council and the judiciary was asserted, the Committee of Articles was remodelled and the elaborate cross-election system to parliament set up by James VI in 1612 was dismantled.[32]

This political revolution, for it can hardly be called anything less, did not have the dramatic impeachments and show trials of the King's servants which the English parliament went through in the spring and summer of 1641, if only because there were scarcely any left to impeach; but it was reform root and branch, which showed the way for the English parliament to follow. The extent of Charles's capitulation to the force of events in Scotland in 1641 was symbolised by the noble who presided over the parliament which received the King – it was Balmerino, the rebel sentenced to death in 1635. It could also be measured by the size of the financial settlement to secure withdrawal of the Scots from the north of England – £3,600,000 in the form of 'brotherly assistance' from the English parliament, payable in three instalments. Charles, it has been said, in 1641 had become the kind of king which the moderates had wanted him to be in 1638.[33] The irony was that the Covenanting regime still felt insecure.

There were three reasons for this – one originating in each of Charles's kingdoms. In Scotland, it was by 1640 beginning to be felt – at least in the mind of Montrose – that the revolt had already gone too far. He had tried to organise a conservative reaction, the 'Cumbernauld Bond', while raising an army to fight the King in the Second Bishops' War. It proved abortive, as did his attempts to gather support amongst the regiments occupying Newcastle for opening negotiations with the king. Put under arrest and already on his long road to a Covenanting gallows in 1650, Montrose was the first magnate to show the strain of the irreconcilable principles, calling for defence of both Kirk and King, contained within the National Covenant. It was supremely ironic that the first major Covenanting noble to break ranks was the deviser of what would become the emblems of the Covenanting armies in the 1640s and of militant Protestantism ever since, the blue bonnet ribbons and blue sash for infantry and cavalry, first worn in March 1639. The spectre of civil war in Scotland, which raised itself in 1640, would materialise in 1644.

In Ireland, the outbreak of a rebellion in October 1641 heightened suspicions of Charles's real motives towards Scotland, which since 1639 had always involved an Irish dimension. For Argyll, it raised the prospect of a further heightening of the war in the west between himself and the MacDonalds, both Scots and Irish, which had centred on Kintyre and the islands of Colonsay and Islay in 1639. The dispatch of a Covenanting army to Ulster in early 1642 eventually saved that province from the Irish Catholic Confederacy, but it failed in its primary task of guaranteeing the security of Scotland. In June 1644 an Irish Catholic force, under the command of Alasdair MacColla (a member of the southern branch of the Clan Donald), landed at Ardnamurchan on the west coast; within twelve months it would bring the Covenanting regime to the brink of destruction.

In England, the Irish rebellion had raised in critical terms a vital constitutional issue – who would control the army which put it down? It encouraged English parliamentarians to look to the Scots army rather than a royal one which might be turned against themselves. It also gave further impetus to the logic of events which since early 1640 had pushed the English parliament into closer links with the Covenanters. The wide-ranging negotiations, both official and unofficial, which took place between the Covenanters and commissioners of the English parliament in the course of 1640 and 1641 were a symptom of the mutual frustrations that had built up in these two kingdoms since 1603. The Scots commissioners proposed the economic union based on free trade which had foundered in 1606-7; they demanded that both the King and his heir should visit Scotland periodically, as James VI had promised in 1603; and they suggested a British court, which would guarantee places for representatives from each kingdom but belong to neither. They also suggested, though rather ambiguously, that they sought 'unity in religion and uniformity in church government as a special means for preserving of peace betwixt the two kingdoms'. The dynamic driving all but the extremists among the Covenanters towards religious unity was not a presbyterian imperialism but the quest for security, which was reflected in their other aims; what they wanted was 'a perfect amity and a more neere union than before', which had in the seventeenth century to have a religious dimension to it. What they meant in practice, however, was radical indeed – the abolition of episcopacy in England and Ireland.[34] It was not pressed in 1641, yet it left a legacy of fear of the price of Scottish support which would surface again shortly after the next intervention by the Scots in English politics, which began in 1643-4.

The instinctive reaction of the Covenanters to the English Civil War which broke out in August 1642 was to stay out of it, not least because intervention on either side risked splits within a movement that was always a coalition of overlapping interests. Both the King and the English parliament appealed to the Scots for help before the end of 1642 and the sympathies of the privy council and the General Assembly seemed to point in different directions. It was, however, to the third and premier force in Scottish politics – the Estates – that commissioners from the English parliament appealed in August 1643. Within ten days of their arrival in Edinburgh on 17 August, a draft of the Solemn League and Covenant had emerged. Its aims were far-reaching but suitably vague – the 'firm peace and union' of England and Scotland, the rooting out of popery, the preservation of the religious settlement in Scotland, and the reformation of religion in England and Ireland 'according to the Word of God and the example of the best reformed churches' – a phrase which was in itself an attempt to marry two separate Calvinist traditions. The more practical terms of the alliance were struck three months later, when it was agreed to

273

send a Scottish army of 20,000 men into England. This was the Army of the Covenant which crossed the Border under the command of Alexander Leslie in January 1644 and contributed directly to the defeat of Charles's forces at Marston Moor in July, a battle which transformed the course of the Civil War in the north of England.

By 1644 the Wars of the Covenant had become a War of the Three Kingdoms, fought by the Scots on three fronts, and each carried its threats to Covenanting unity. The simple aims of the Scottish army sent to Ireland in 1642 had by 1644, as in so many Irish wars, become hopelessly confused: internal tensions between new Scots planters and older settlers, both Scots and English, hampered the military effort; and serious defeat for the new Scots at the hands of the Confederate Irish at Benburb in June 1646 virtually ended their contribution to the war in Ireland. The failure of the English parliament to meet its promises to finance the Scots army in Ulster brought an extra dimension to the intensely strained relations between it and the Covenanters in 1646.[35]

The main threat from the Confederate Irish lay, however, in their intervention in Scotland itself in 1644. A modest expeditionary force of less than 2,000 men, led by MacColla, met Montrose, who had only a handful of followers, in the wilds of Atholl in August 1644. Montrose's first campaign, which would inflict six successive defeats on Covenanting armies in the space of thirteen months, was launched. Its first victory came at Tippermuir, near Perth, on 1 September. There it met a strong Covenanting force assembled under a banner with the motto, 'Jesus and no quarter'. The battle itself took less than ten minutes; the rout of the Covenanting army lasted twelve hours, leaving 1,300 dead and 800 captured.[36] The next episode in what Highland bards hailed as Montrose's 'glorious year' was less creditable. The burgh of Perth had been treated with unusual courtesy after Tippermuir but Aberdeen, after a decisive defeat of its Covenanting garrison, was subjected to three days of pillage, rape and murder. It was the first major atrocity of the Wars and it was ironical that it was inflicted on a town that had been circumspect in its political loyalties; it would not be equalled until Monck's brutal taking of Dundee in 1651. From Aberdeen Montrose and MacColla swung north and west, pursued by a Covenanting army commanded by Argyll. From there, despite the snows of winter, they marched south-west into the Campbell heartland as far as Inveraray itself; the 'shaking of MacCailean Mor', Argyll's Gaelic persona, had begun. A string of victories followed – at Inverlochy (2 Feb. 1645), when at least 1,500 Campbells fell; at Auldearn (9 May), near Nairn, which was militarily the most audacious feat of arms but also the bloodiest, with 2,000 Covenanting troops killed, mostly in the rout after the battle ; at Alford (2 July), the first time that Montrose had enjoyed superior numbers; and at Kilsyth (15 Aug.), from which Argyll again escaped, for the third time by water. Argyll had been humiliated in his own Highlands; the Covenanting ministers were incredulous that it was 'the pleasure of our God' to inflict defeat again at the hands of 'a company of the worst men in the earth'.[37] The 'Highland charge', which had first been used in Ulster by MacColla in 1642, had devastated a series of trained and part-professional armies; it would take until 1746 for military technology to find an effective answer to it.

Yet victory revealed the Montrose campaign for what it was: a marriage of convenience temporarily linking a conservative revolt of the far-flung provinces of the kingdom and a loose pan-Celtic alliance held together by hatred of the Campbells. Its inherent paradoxes were exposed in its first moments in Atholl in August 1644, when MacColla and his men from the Irish Catholic Confederacy looked on while Montrose raised his standard 'for the defence and maintenance of the trew Protestant religion' and 'his Majestie's just and sacred authoritie'.[38] By contrast, the Gaelic bard of Keppoch, Iain Lom, who celebrated the campaign as a MacDonald war against Campbells, did not bother to mention Montrose in his account of Inverlochy. As Montrose tried to organise a parliament to translate his gains in Scotland into intervention on the King's side in England, the north-eastern contingent drifted home and MacColla's men left to take up again the more congenial task of killing Campbells. His surprise defeat at Philiphaugh near Selkirk (13 Sept. 1645), at the hands of a Covenanting force which had returned from England under the command of Leslie, brought his greater strategy to an end. But by then the decisive events were taking place in England.

In May 1646 Charles surrendered to the Scottish army at Newark, its headquarters in England. His capture brought the First Civil War to an end, but since Naseby in June 1645 it had reached the stage of a series of mopping-up operations. The Scots quickly withdrew with their prize to Newcastle, where some of the dilemmas posed by the incredible stroke of good fortune that at first made them 'like men that dreame' began to sink in.[39] The King still refused to take the Covenant, which in the version of the Solemn League would have committed him to a presbyterian settlement in all three kingdoms. A return into Scotland with the King risked breathing life into a broader-based royalist movement which Montrose was still striving to construct. Yet security, the Covenanters realised, would come only with a British peace settlement, the terms of which were viewed differently by the three parties involved: the Scots still wanted something like a federal Britain as the natural corollary of religious union; the English parliament, since 1645 increasingly split into two parties, the radical Independents and the more moderate so-called 'Presbyterians', wanted different versions of a separate English peace; and the King, without much in the way of a policy, pursued the tactic of setting his enemies at each other's throats.

For almost nine months Charles remained a hostage of the Scots. After three months, both he and the Covenanters had seen enough of each other to want to part company, but the English parliament was as anxious that he should not be allowed to go to London as he wished. What had seemed the trump card in British politics had become the joker. The eventual solution, arrived at in January 1647 after Charles had by turn rejected peace proposals framed by both parliaments, solved the embarrassment of the King's custodians but did little to advance a British settlement. On 30 January, the Scots army, on receipt of the first instalment of £100,000 sterling agreed with the English parliament to settle its outstanding arrears of pay, marched out of Newcastle; four days later a further £100,000 was handed over. It would be difficult to judge which party to the bargain was more glad to see the Scots leave English soil after their three-year campaign. The King was left in Newcastle – to his fate. A distinction was drawn between the two arrangements and it may have been less wafer-thin in February 1647 than it appeared later in the year or to many historians since. For the King had been left in the hands, not of the radicals but of the Presbyterian moderates who were more favourable towards the

Scots and still commanded ascendancy in the English House of Commons.[40]

What transformed the situation was the King's abduction in June 1647 by a company of soldiers in Fairfax's New Model Army, which the Scots quickly realised was now 'master of all'. Three days after the kidnap, the Earl of Lauderdale protested before a joint meeting of both Houses of Parliament of the new danger to the King from 'Independents, sectaries or even republicans'. The Committee of Estates met twice in emergency session during the next two weeks, but remained undecided on what action to take. In effect the Scots' bluff had been called. Their commissioners in May had warned that any attempted coup by the Independents or the New Model Army would result in military action by the Scots to free their king. The acute dilemma for all shades of political opinion in Scotland in the second half of 1647 was that which faces many governments confronted by the illicit politics of hostage-taking: diplomacy could scarcely begin until the power struggle within the radical party which had carried out the coup was sorted out. The Scots eventually opted for force, and it was their interference in English politics (as the English saw it) which accelerated the shift of power towards the Independents at the expense of the Presbyterians.

It had been an alliance with the Scots that had been the major issue in English parliamentary politics in 1643; it was fear of the Scots which galvanised opinion in the English Commons in 1647. A police action, however, was a drastic step for the Scots to contemplate after nine years of war which had brought punitive taxation, forced quarter and countless thousands of deaths. This was the question that tore apart the efforts to regroup which the Covenanting regime had been making ever since the autumn of 1645. It brought to the surface the underlying conflicts between Church and state and wranglings within both the General Assembly and the Covenanting regime as to what the Wars of the Covenant had been fought for. The supreme irony of the situation was that Charles almost certainly had no desire to be rescued by his Scottish subjects.

Counter-revolution and revolution, 1647-51

By December 1647, after months of clandestine negotiations, a treaty known as the Engagement was concluded between Charles and the more moderate wing of Covenanting opinion; it promised military aid in return for an assortment of promises from Charles including a three-year experimental period of a diluted presbyterian plantation in England and another to 'endeavour a complete union of the kingdoms' according to 'the intentions of his father', but without a firm personal commitment by the King to the Covenant. Personal loyalty to the King or, for some, a commitment to a closer union as the only means of effecting a British peace had superseded the pure milk of the Covenant. The aim – or pious hope – that Charles would take the Covenant, which had for ten years underpinned the unity of the Covenanters, was withdrawn. The result has been called both a counter-revolution and 'the biggest turn-over of opinion in the century'.[41] Such terms may risk over-dramatising what was a pragmatic solution in the longer-term strategy of a search for security which had driven the Covenanters in different tactical directions ever since 1640; the notion of religious union had not been abandoned, but what amounted to a feasibility study had been agreed. The notion of a counter-revolution in 1647-8 risks viewing the Engagement through the narrow prism of the radicals who, after the Engagers' army was destroyed by Oliver Cromwell at Preston (17 Aug. 1648), seized the chance to return with a vengeance to what they saw as the true revolution. To view the Engagers as counter-revolutionaries is to allow the extremists to capture the vocabulary of the Covenanting revolution. What the confused events of 1648-51 would in fact show was how few in Scotland viewed revolutionary politics as ideologues.

The voting patterns in parliament and the General Assembly in 1647-8 over the question of the Engagement give a clear indication of how broad a coalition was the Covenanting revolution. In parliament, where the issue was considered directly, four-fifths of the nobles and more than half the lairds voted for the Engagement; almost half of the burgh commissioners did the same, but they included most of the larger towns, particularly those in the east. In the General Assembly, where the question turned on the choice of a moderator, the pro-Engager candidate lost by a mere four votes.[42] The conclusion to be drawn from 1647-8 was that in a tug of loyalties between expediency and principle the political establishment would give a clear answer whereas the Church was likely to be caught in two minds. It was a cameo of Scottish politics since the Reformation of 1560.

The disagreements in the 1648 Assembly were not solely between ruling elders and ministers. Here it is as well to remember that few of either office regularly attended its meetings. The Assembly, and especially its standing committee called the Commission which had been set up in 1641, were increasingly dominated by the 'busie men', as Robert Baillie, minister and Professor of Divinity at Glasgow, called them. Although they represented only a small fraction of the ministry as a whole, it was the radical ministers who thronged the vital committees of the Kirk. At the same time, there were also increasing strains within the Church, on issues of doctrine and liturgy as well as revolutionary politics. The hallmarks of the new-style radicals of the 1640s were innovations in worship and especially the practice of expounding on Scripture in place of set evening prayers. The conventicle, in effect, was being brought into the open. These new practices were confined largely to the south-west and were the work of ministers from a more rural and appreciably lower social background than the circle which had dominated the Church in 1638. These differences would harden after 1650 in two feuding clerical parties: the Resolutioners and Protesters. The disputes were only partly about the tactics of a continuing reformation. The two parties represented two cultures of neo-Calvinism, and two interpretations of the revolution. One was élitist, accustomed to power and dealing with the nobility and dependent on the leadership of the urban ministers such as Alexander Henderson. The other was rural, provincial and populist, with a strong element within it of social protest, stemming mostly from particular economic grievances felt in the south-west; its archetype was the fire-eating 'Whiggamore' minister from Loudoun, John Nevay. The Kirk had papered over these cracks during ten years of revolution; the events of the next two years, which gave it victory and defeat, would lay them bare.[43]

After the Engagers' heavy defeat at Preston, which left 2,000 dead and almost 9,000 more taken prisoner, power passed by default to what has gone down in presbyterian legend as the regime of the Scottish saints. Covenanters in the 'killing times' of the 1680s would look back on the brief period in power of the Kirk party regime, between the coup staged in September 1648 and the autumn of 1650, as the height of the Second Reformation. The coup had taken the form of a march on Edinburgh by 2,000 'Whiggamores' (as their enemies patronisingly dubbed them) from the radical south-west. The first instinct of a revolutionary regime is a purge and the Kirk party regime was no exception, but it was Cromwell who insisted upon it. The Act of Classes passed by parliament in January 1649 banned both Engagers and outright royalists from all office, whether in the state, local government or the army. In a number of burghs, including Edinburgh and Glasgow, councils which had supported the Engagement were purged in what was a more thorough-going intervention in local politics than any by Stewart kings to date. The idea of continuing reformation had since the 1570s given a dynamic to the Kirk's sense of itself as a missionary church; when translated into revolutionary politics it became the vehicle of a caste of exclusive revolutionary brethren. Purge followed purge in the army throughout the course of 1649, at the insistence of the radical ministers, who maintained that 'The Lord hath shown what he can doe by a few'.[44] The result was that the new Covenanting state relied upon a rump of the godly rather than a nation in arms.

Power also usually brings with it the baggage of compromise, even to the most revolutionary of parties. There were acts passed by the Kirk party regime which showed a strong streak of a social gospel: responsibility for poor relief was passed to kirk sessions which were given a measure of power to force landowners to accept responsibility for their own tenants. Poor relief, however, remained voluntary – unless central government decided to intervene. There was a strong streak of antipathy to the nobility: 1649 was one of the few periods in Scottish history when nobles might be called to public account for adultery. What seemed the most radical action of all, the abolition of lay patronage in the Church in March 1649 contained within it the seeds of compromise: it did not affect ownership of teinds, as the General Assembly had wanted, for that would have jeopardised the support of the lairds. The bitter dispute which broke out between the General Assembly and parliament over patronage revealed how uneasy a coalition the Kirk party regime was. There was a battle between the civil and religious arms of this Covenanted state for the moral high ground; it was reflected in the pursuit of a new spectre threatening the revolution – not papistry, as in 1638, but witchcraft which 'daily increaseth in this land'. Over 350 individual commissions were issued in the summer of 1649, mostly in East Lothian and Berwickshire. This was an action, not of the Assembly, but of the Committee of Estates, anxious to demonstrate its independence of ecclesiastical power. Even the Covenanted regime of 1648-50 could not escape a conflict between Church and state. It was, however, the fundamental issue of the monarchy itself which destroyed it.[45]

On 30 January 1649, a radical minority within the English Independents staged their ultimate coup – the execution of Charles I. It instantly revealed the fragility of the unlikely alliance between two distinctly different strains of zealotry, the presbyterian international of the Kirk party and the religious Independency of Cromwell. But it also demonstrated the differing views of monarchy which had underpinned many of the conflicts between the Covenanters and their English allies throughout the 1640s. Within a few days the Scottish parliament had proclaimed the King's son as Charles II; a month later the English parliament abolished the monarchy. An imprisoned Charles I had proved an effective rallying cry for the innate conservative royalism of the Scots in the summer of 1647; a martyred Charles brought him a popularity in death which he had scarcely ever enjoyed in life.

Charles II seemed briefly to be the king that the Covenanters had longed for ever since 1638. After a series of negotiations, deliberately protracted by him to await the outcome of Montrose's last fruitless campaign, Charles II signed the Covenants while his ship lay at anchor off the mouth of the Spey on 23 June 1650. Montrose's last gamble, launched in the north via the Orkney Islands lasted barely six weeks. Defeated at Carbisdale near Bonar Bridge (27 April) and captured a week later, he was not even given a trial, for sentence had already been passed on him in 1644. The night before his execution, Montrose composed his last piece of verse, bequeathing his soul to God, between visits of Covenanting ministers, intent on prising from him a confession of his sins. On 21 May he dressed as for a wedding, in a richly laced scarlet cloak, white gloves, silk stockings and ribboned shoes. But that did not spare him one last indignity – the hangman's rope rather than the axe.

Within a month of Montrose's execution, Charles was in Scotland, playing the role of a covenanted king. The Army of the Kingdom, under banners with the new motto 'For Religion, King and Kingdome', could do battle with the English republicans – but only after it had undergone the most thorough-going purge yet, for the radical ministers still held sway in the Purging Committee for the army; it accounted for several thousand officers and men.[46] The divisions within the regime were reflected in the fact that Charles was still uncrowned, and under observation day and night. Under siege from Cromwell whose army had crossed the Tweed on 22 July and at odds with itself, the days of the Kirk party regime were numbered. It collapsed shortly after the humiliating defeat inflicted by Cromwell on Leslie's army at Dunbar on 3 September 1650. Despite superior numbers, 4,000 Scots were killed and over 10,000 captured; the flight of Leslie and the remnants of his army to Edinburgh recalled the humiliation inflicted on the Scots at Pinkie in 1547.

The last act in the Wars of the Covenant was quickly played. With no less than four rival armies now in Scotland – the remnants of the official army that survived Dunbar and a radical rump of it in the west, a small royalist army in the north-east and the English invasion force in the Lowlands – events were hectic and the atmosphere tense. The existing splits within the Church became more bitter in the process of finding scapegoats for the defeat at Dunbar: rival resolutions and protests (which gave names to the two parties) greeted the motion of the General Assembly of 14 December 1650 that purges of the army be relaxed. The splits hardened over the general attitude the Church should take to the new and explicitly royalist regime that emerged after Dunbar. Charles was crowned on 1 January 1651 and the Act of Classes repealed in June. The remnants of the Western Army were mopped up by English forces in December 1650. With its attention still largely absorbed in its godly work in Ireland, the Cromwellian army had been slow to consolidate its victory at Dunbar, first trying to secure a pale south of the Forth and Clyde before it ventured north. Its task was eased by a last desperate royalist expedition into England. Four days after a Cromwellian army entered Perth on 2 August 1651, the Scots staged their fourth invasion of England since 1639. It met its inevitable disaster at Worcester on 3 September. The Wars of the Covenant were finally at an end; so was the multifold crisis of the three kingdoms – for the time being.

The price of war

The human cost of almost thirteen years of war is incalculable. A dozen armies of the Covenant had been raised. The people of Scotland had been taxed as never before to pay for them, and many had had free quarter, forced levy or plunder inflicted upon them as well. Part of the price for trying to stop Montrose at Kilsyth in 1645 were the 200 widows of men forcibly recruited in Kirkcaldy days before; these men must have accounted for a third of the adult males in a population of 3,000. Two major burghs had been sacked – Aberdeen by Montrose in 1644 and Dundee by Monck in 1651. At Dundee, it had also been refugees from Edinburgh who were 'stripped unto the sark'. For many merchants, and especially those of the capital who were moneylenders as well, the wars brought financial ruin. The doyen of the Edinburgh merchant establishment and financier of the Covenant, Sir William Dick of Braid, ended his life in a debtors' prison in England in the 1650s. The unique damage inflicted by the 1640s came from the combined effects of war and plague. The outbreak of bubonic plague which hit the east-coast towns in 1645 was the most severe for two centuries. It accounted for two-thirds of the population of Brechin and more than half of that of south Leith. Probably one in five town-dwellers died of it in 1645. Unlike other demographic crises, urban populations did not quickly recover: rents in Edinburgh were reduced by a third in 1651. Some towns, such as Glasgow, escaped both natural disaster and most of the effects of war, but the crisis which affected most east-coast burghs between Edinburgh and Aberdeen was as severe as any since the Wars of Independence. The price paid by ordinary Scots for the Wars of the Covenant is the most difficult to calculate and too often the least considered.[47]

The Revolution which had begun in 1637 under the leadership of the nobles ended with their status uncertain; they had survived an attack from the radicals of the Kirk party regime but after 1651 faced another from a foreign army of occupation anxious to root out the royalist power base. The fate of Argyll was not untypical. His twelve-year reign as the leading politician of the Revolution had been symbolised by the fact that it was he who placed the crown of Scotland on Charles II's head in 1651, but, as with the noble class as a whole, the verdict of history stayed its hand a further ten years, until the Restoration. Cowed by the threat of a Cromwellian invasion of his homeland of Argyll – the very threat which had induced him into national politics in 1639 – he spent the 1650s in unaccustomed obscurity.

What had the Kirk got out of the Covenanting revolution? Bishops had been abolished, the Laudian-style innovations eclipsed, and the moderates within it forced into ever-more radical postures. The Union of 1603, which had in the 1630s seemed so threatening, was recast as 'the greatest blessing that God hath bestowed on this isle . . . next to the Christian faith'.[48] That blessing had proved short-lived. Presbyterianism never found its outlet in England and the excesses of sects and Independents horrified the ministers sent to Westminster in 1644 to negotiate religious union. The protracted musings of the Westminster Assembly eventually yielded a Larger and Shorter Catechism, a Directory of Public Worship, a Form of Church Government and a Confession of Faith. The Westminster Confession of 1647, which survived intact until it was shorn of its worst anti-papist excesses in 1986, remains to this day the basic confessional stance of the Church of Scotland. It is the unlikely product of a revolution which otherwise destroyed the unity of the Scottish reformed Church.

Despite its long-running disputes over polity, the Kirk since 1560 had maintained a broad-based consensus on matters of doctrine and liturgy. By 1651 it was split almost irrevocably into two warring camps. They would spend the bulk of the 1650s replaying the political dilemmas of 1650. Scottish Calvinism had never had an explicit doctrine of resistance against kings, largely because the main obstacles in its path had also been its potential partners – the crown and the magnates. It had only occasionally thought of itself as a suffering Church, most notably during the self-imposed exile of the Melvillian ministers in 1584-5. It had long seen itself as a corrupt Church in need of further reformation, but the expectation of reform had stifled the prospect of secession. By 1651 all three doctrines – resistance, a suffering Church and a secessionist Church of true believers – had begun to emerge and they split Scottish Calvinism asunder. These were the real legacies of the Second Reformation, but another persisted in the minds of those who refused to accept that the Wars of the Covenant were over. Much of Scottish history is fuelled by myths; the most important for many in the second half of the seventeenth century was the cherished myth of the Covenanters that the reformed Church had come in 1648 to 'the top of her perfection and glory' and that in 1650 'her sun went down at noon'.[49]

17

The Making and Unmaking of
the Restoration Regime

IN THE WAKE OF THE CRUSHING DEFEAT AT DUNBAR ON 3 SEPTEMBER 1650, Scotland south of the Forth stood on the brink of anarchy. On the following day, both the town council and kirk sessions of Edinburgh fled the capital, many sailing across to Fife or northwards to Dundee; the ministers retreated into the Castle, their churches being taken over as ammunition stores and stables by the Cromwellian army. By December, when the Castle was surrendered almost without a fight, the national disgrace seemed complete: the Maiden Castle, as it had long been called, was dubbed the 'Prostitute Whore'; some royalists urged the King to abandon Scotland south of the Forth (as well as England and Ireland) to the English and retreat, like Robert Bruce, into the northern heartland. When he was crowned at Scone on 1 January 1651, on a makeshift wooden platform inside the church, Charles II had to subscribe the Covenants again and endure a sermon telling him that he 'hath not absolute power to do what he pleaseth'. His inheritance was a kingdom truncated as it had not been for three and a half centuries.[1]

During the first half of 1651, Cromwell suffered a prolonged illness and, as a result, his campaign temporarily lost its momentum. It was in this period that the relations between Resolutioners and Protesters in the Kirk reached breaking point. At a General Assembly which met at St Andrews and Dundee in July, the majority party attempted to exclude the minority; twenty ministers handed in a protestation and withdrew.[2] The revolution which had begun amidst the orchestrated fervour of the Glasgow Assembly in 1638 had ended in a self-induced partition of the Church. It was a miniature walk-out by comparison with others in the history of the Church of Scotland, but it was a split which was never really healed: rival assemblies and presbyteries contested each other's authority throughout the 1650s, jostled for the favour of the occupying power and despised it when it was given. Each would expect restoration to favour in 1660 and, once disappointed, would find new issues to reopen old wounds. For the moment clerical bickering was overtaken by events. A few days later, Cromwell's army crossed the Forth and inflicted a sharp defeat on a mixed bag of pressed townsmen and Highlanders at Inverkeithing on the 20th; by 2 August it had traversed Fife and captured Perth. With their supply lines to the north now cut and men deserting by the thousand, the King and an army of 13,000 left their base at Stirling, embarking on a desperate gamble. Slipping past the English garrison deployed thinly across the south of Scotland, it set off at a fast pace on the long road to Worcester, where Cromwell finally caught up with it on 3 September. About 2,000 Scots were killed and over 10,000 taken prisoner, including almost all the Scottish leaders. Charles, his legendary luck never more with him than now, escaped to France – the first Stewart pretender 'over the water', in public the symbol of a lost Scottish independence but in private swearing that he would rather be hanged than return to Scotland.

In Scotland, the English campaign, now led by Monck, continued relentlessly.

Stirling surrendered on 14 August and with it the public records of Scotland fell into English hands; the regalia escaped their grasp, buried under a church floor at Kinneff near Dunnottar. The Committee of Estates and the Resolutioner-dominated Commission of the General Assembly, which had been left in joint charge of the running of the country, were taken prisoner at Alyth on the 28th; they ended up in London, along with the captives from Worcester. Dundee was taken by storm on 1 September, with about 1,000 deaths including, it was alleged, some 200 women and children, in the twenty-four hours of pillage that followed.[3] Other burghs surrendered to the inevitable: St Andrews offered £500 sterling as a 'gratuity' to Monck's army and Aberdeen, which staged a banquet for their conquerors, escaped with a fine of £1,000. By the end of 1651, a chain of English garrisons along the east coast stretching from Edinburgh to Orkney had been established; and, with the surrender of the last royalist force, under the command of Balcarres and Huntly in December, active resistance was at an end in the north-east and in the central Highlands. Only the 'pestiferous burden' of the 'wilde Highlanders' in the west remained. The Cromwellian conquest was virtually complete; the peace could begin.[4]

Cromwellian Scotland

The first instinct of the English Commonwealth regime was annexation. Six days after the battle of Worcester, a committee of the Rump parliament was set up to draft a bill declaring 'the right of this Commonwealth to so much of Scotland as is now under [its] forces'. It resulted in a bill 'asserting the right of England to Scotland'. By December, an alternative was devised, bearing in mind 'the good of this island', in which Scotland was to be incorporated into 'the free state and Commonwealth of England'. This was the 'Tender of Union', proclaimed in a bizarre, peculiarly English ceremony at the Edinburgh Mercat Cross on 4 February 1652: eight trumpeters sounded a fanfare, and one of them acted as a town crier 'crying thrie Oyessis'. Three days later, in another symbolic but no less comic ritual, the King's arms were hauled down from the Mercat Cross and ceremonially hanged from the public gallows. Ultimately twenty-nine out of thirty-one shires and forty-four of the fifty-eight royal burghs did assent to the Tender and subscribed the oath that 'Scotland be incorporated into and made one Commonwealth with England'.[5]

This was a kind of union, at least to English eyes; Sir Edwin Sandys, who had wrecked James VI's scheme in the English parliamentary session of 1606-7 in favour of his own notion of a 'perfect union', might well have approved it. The Scottish Estates were swept away along with the monarchy; no institution could meet except with the sanction of the enlarged Westminster parliament. But the bill itself became stuck in the log-jam of acrimony which overtook the Rump; another bill, presented to its successor, the Barebones parliament, in October 1653, fell when it was dissolved. Until 1657, the union rested on an Ordinance of Union passed by the Council of State in April 1654 under the authority of the Instrument of Government. The invitation into this 'happy union' was, however, not to a Great Britain but to the 'Commonwealth of England, Scotland and Ireland'. The central irony of the 1650s is that although Scotland was for the first time offered free trade and governed under distinctively Anglo-Scottish institutions – a separate Council for Scotland was set up in 1657 – it was not as part of an avowedly British union, for that was still seen as an unwelcome reminder of the Stewart monarchy.

The uneasy *ménage à trois* of the three ex-kingdoms can be illustrated by the curious history of the union flag, which had fallen into disuse after 1625. In 1654 it was revived, but again quartered – with 1st and 4th England, 2nd Scotland and an Irish harp (which had, oddly, been devised by Henry VIII) as 3rd. The result smacked too much of political incorporation (which indeed Cromwellian union was) and it was replaced by the Union flag of 1606, with the crosses of St George and St Andrew melded and the Irish harp placed incongruously as an inescutcheon in the centre.[6] In administrative and practical terms, union could hardly have been more rigorous or complete; yet it lacked the essential ingredient of a nation state – symbols through which consent could be expressed.

The army of occupation was never less than 10,000 men. Its grip over the country was built up steadily. By late 1651 passes were needed to move from one part of the country to another. Firearms were restricted, except under licence – Cameron of Lochiel, who could issue licences to his kinsmen recruited large numbers of 'Camerons', for a price. The traditional device of Stewart kings, of making Highland chiefs responsible for the good behaviour of their own clansmen, was used again, but to greater effect than ever before. What made Cromwellian policy more effective was the creation of large garrisons at strategic sites. Citadels were built at Ayr, Perth and Leith, as well as twenty smaller forts as far apart as Orkney and Stornoway, but the most important were the two large strongpoints in the Highlands, at Inverlochy and Inverness. The investment in men and money was enormous: the citadel at Inverness, begun in 1652 and built with stone shipped from as far away as Aberdeen, was still unfinished in 1655, although it had already cost over £50,000 sterling. The 1,000-strong garrison at Inverlochy was in place by 1654; it stood at the centre of a new administrative district of Lochaber which combined three of the remotest and most lawless shires in the country. By 1655 it was boasted that 'a man may ride all over Scotland with £100 in his pocket, which he could not have done these five hundred years'. It was a claim which was exaggerated only slightly: certainly it had taken Cromwell's army to settle the disruption inflicted on the west by the abolition of the Lordship of the Isles 160 years before.[7]

The main weakness of the formidable apparatus of military occupation and civil administration established by the Cromwellian regime was its cost. In the 1630s Charles I's various taxes had cost Scotland about £17,000 sterling per annum. In 1656 the civil list alone cost £25,000. On top of that Scotland had to meet a monthly assessment of £10,000, although its reduction to £6,000 in 1657 was an acknowledgement of the impossible weight of this burden. The total amount of taxation was not less than £90,000 a year, to which should be added the annual revenue from the excise, which in 1659 produced £45,000. It was little wonder that the Scots in the first Restoration parliament happily committed themselves to a mere £40,000 per annum, which left that government always desperately short of cash. It was not enough in the 1650s – there was an annual deficit of £130,000. It was the first time – but not the last – that a London government sought to justify its benevolent treatment of Scotland by pointing to the shortfall between what it raised and what it spent there.[8]

Pacification had come only after a serious royalist revolt in the Highlands in 1653-4, which coincided with the First Dutch War (1652-4). In reality, the revolt was fragmented and riven with internal disputes – like many risings of the 'loyal clans'. It was also afflicted by quarrelling between the Highlanders who made up the bulk of the army and the Lowland officers and nobles in nominal command of men whom they thought no better than 'a pack of thieves and robbers'. The result was a succession of duels: Glengarry, a MacDonald chief, and Sir George Monro, a Lowland officer, quarrelled even over the weapons to use in their duel. The hostility between its leaders – the two Lowland lords, Glencairn and Balcarres, and Middleton, the bluff Lowland soldier officially appointed by Charles who arrived in early 1654, nine months after the outbreak of the revolt – was matched by the marginal and ambivalent support which it attracted amongst many of the clans.[9] It was the story of the 1745 rising before its time. In terms of military tactics, there was no repeat of the 'glorious year' of 1644-5 or of the Highland charge; the royalist tactics were to harry, spoil and burn and by 1655 they were beginning to have a counter-productive effect for Middleton found it difficult to recruit in the Highlands, even when he threatened to 'kill, burn, hang and destroy all before him'. The highlight of the revolt was not the Highland charge but the forced march: Monck's forces, critically short of cavalry, regularly made between twelve and twenty miles a day, complete with baggage train, across difficult terrain. The revolt lasted for sixteen months and eventually collapsed only because of its inner contradictions and the peace made between the Protectorate and the Dutch in April 1654 which, Middleton maintained, 'did strike all dead'.[10]

The Glencairn rising was an important harbinger, not only of the confused loyalties at work in the Highlands and elsewhere in Scotland during the 1650s but also over the next century. It exposed the calculated loyalty of many of the clans to the Stewart monarchy but it also revealed the desperate measures to which many of the nobility and lairds, faced with mounting debts, had been driven by the Cromwellian regime. It also showed a vital difference in the attitudes of the ministers towards the Stewarts: the Protesters condemned the rising and the Resolutioners conducted public prayers for the King throughout it. This was why a company of soldiers broke up the Resolutioner Assembly at Edinburgh in July 1653 and escorted the ministers at gunpoint out of the burgh. It was the only overt interference with the courts of the Church during the occupation; unlike sheriff courts which fell under the order banning all courts deriving from 'Charles Stuart', kirk sessions continued to meet, neither recognised nor sanctioned by the regime. In other respects, the rising was a significant turning-point. Coupled with the arrival in 1655 of an Irish peer, Lord Broghill, as President of the new Council in Scotland, it recast the politics of the Cromwellian Union. Broghill, one of the Protestant 'new English' of the Elizabethan and early Stuart plantations, had long experience of drawing together the natural rulers – a process which had begun in Ireland as early as 1649.[11] The regime would begin to woo back the men of property, or at least the lairds, and the two clerical parties would increasingly vie with each other for the favours of the regime, even to the extent of appointing rival permanent agents in London.

In its first months in power the attitude of the Commonwealth had been clear: to destroy the influence of the nobility who had organised invasions of England in 1648 and 1651 and to promote 'the meaner sort'. At first it had seemed that both planks of the policy might quickly be effected: those nobles not already in exile or languishing in English prisons were deprived of their offices and harried for debt; free elections were re-established in most burghs in 1652. Sheriff courts, with a mixed bag of political opportunists and collaborators appointed as deputes, began to operate again and burgh courts, with their accustomed magistrates, resumed control. Local barony courts and heritable jurisdictions, which had not operated since 1651, were formally abolished in 1657. The Glencairn rising had been a serious check in this process. Burghs elections were suspended in 1653 and not resumed until October 1655. Scots law, with all its overlapping jurisdictions, was a Gordian knot that was not easily unpicked into its different parts. The re-establishment of JPs came only in 1656; it was a further stage in the implementation of justice and one of the first gestures of the regime towards the men of property. The price paid for it was a flood of witchcraft prosecutions, instigated by the new JPs: between 1657 and 1659 there were 102 witchcraft trials – a prelude to the 600 cases which clogged the courts in 1661-2.[12] The Scottish 'gentry' proved reluctant to act out the parts the English regime had cast for them. As for the nobility, it seems doubtful that many of the studied concessions of 1655-9 reached them. The well-known obituary notice written by Baillie:

> Our noble families are almost gone; Lennox hes little in Scotland unsold; Hamilton's estate . . . is sold . . . the Gordons are gone; the Douglases little better; Eglinton and Glencairn on the point of breaking; many of our chief families states are crashing.[13]

was made as late as 1658. It was the reaction of the nobility against their plight which more than any other factor coloured the nature of the Restoration in 1660.

Scotland, under the terms of the Cromwellian Union, had been given thirty seats in the Westminster parliament. The arrangements – for half of the seats went to English army officers – illustrate both the mixture of coercion and consent with which the regime operated in Scotland and the xenophobia which Scots MPs experienced at Westminster. By turn patronised and despised as no better than Jamaica or 'at best' a province, the Scots were largely ignored, except for repeated motions from English members to exclude them.[14] After the death of Oliver Cromwell in 1658 and the rapid eclipse of the administration of his son, Richard, in 1659 the restored Rump parliament briefly considered a bill for a fuller union but ran out of time. When General Monck marched south in the winter of 1659-60 to reconcile the Westminster parliament to a restoration of Charles II, he took with him petitions of the commissioners of shires and burghs to maintain the union, but on better terms for Scotland. The case went virtually unheard and when parliament was dissolved in March 1660, writs for its next meeting did not include Scotland or Ireland. Scotland had regained its independence, but by default and perhaps against the wishes of some sections of Scottish opinion. On 14 May Charles was proclaimed King of all three of his kingdoms in Edinburgh, amidst wild rejoicing; his first proclamation as King of Scots, made three months later, ordered a recall of the Committee of Estates. On 14 May, while artillery rounds were being fired from Edinburgh Castle, one of the cannoneers who had objected to the celebrations was blown up. He was the first casualty of the Restoration settlement.

Restoration (1660-62)

The restoration of the King, his privy council, the Scottish parliament and judiciary and the return of bishops to the Church were the five ingredients of the Restoration. They did not come about simultaneously or quickly, and seldom in a predictable form. From the formal proclamation of the King's return in May 1660, the settlement in all its aspects took twenty-eight months to materialise. The nature of the religious settlement did not crystallise until September 1661 and the restoration of bishops was ratified by the Scottish parliament only in May 1662. Almost its last instalment was an act of idemnity, passed in the following September.

The moving forces behind the settlement are in doubt and dispute. One reason for this is the intricate political intrigue involved in the first uncertain steps taken after the return of Charles. Almost immediately the bizarre two-speed pattern of Caroline politics took shape: the Declaration of Breda, in which Charles handed the contentious matters at stake to an English Convention parliament, had been issued on 4 April 1660; that parliament met on the 25th; it proclaimed him king on 8 May, he arrived in Dover on the 25th and was on London by the 29th, his thirtieth birthday. Breakneck speed then gave way to studied languor. The King spent much of the next two months receiving the congratulations of foreign envoys and local dignitaries and playing out the ancient roles of kingship, which included that of healer of scrofula.

Wedged within these ceremonial rituals of kingship were vital decisions about Scottish politics. In June, the Scottish nobles, invited to the court to advise on the form of an interim government, decided after a day of acrimonious debate to resort to the simplest device – a recall of the Committee of Estates of 1651. Two weeks later, Charles decided on his Scottish ministers.[15] They were a mixed bag: the leaders of the royalist rising of 1653-4, Middleton and Glencairn, were awarded the posts of commissioner to the parliament and chancellor; but there were also others with a Covenanting past, such as Cassillis, the Justice-General, and the Earl of Rothes, appointed Lord President of the Council. The most important office, or so events would prove, was that of Secretary, which was given to Lauderdale, a moderate presbyterian who had spent most of the time since Worcester in a succession of English gaols.[16] The shape of the ministerial team was balanced, representing all opinion in Scotland short of the Protesters, and it probably reflected Charles's own cautious circumspection about his northern kingdom. Yet as the next twelve months would show – and the rest of the reign would echo – the politics of the political jungle would overwhelm this balanced administration and the centre ground, both in religion and civil government.

When it met in Edinburgh on 23 August 1660, the Committee of Estates did little except to arrest some Protester ministers led by James Guthrie who had characteristically assembled at the same time and to ban further such meetings; the Protesters had been removed from the political agenda but little or nothing else was decided. By April 1661, Cassillis had been forced out of office for clinging to his presbyterian principles, while others were fast abandoning theirs amidst a fast-growing royalist reaction; scapegoats for the Covenanting past had been found in the shape of Guthrie and Argyll, who were both executed. The political map had been transformed. If the King had wanted a balanced administration to rule Scotland, by mid-1661 he was presented – to his surprise and delight – with a parliament, privy council and first stage of a settlement which were all a good deal more royalist than he had intended.

Who were leading actors in this notable turn of events? With government conducted on two fronts – in the excitable, cut-throat and often drunken arenas of politics in Edinburgh and in the labyrinth of the royal palace at Whitehall, where policy was made in corners or in rooms with multiple locks to which only the King and a select few had keys – it is difficult to be certain. Histories written years later by contemporary figures, such as those by Clarendon and Gilbert Burnet, lend a rationality to events or give to factions a consistency which few sensed at the time. For his former colleagues and for Covenanting historians ever since, the evil genius of the church settlement was the former Resolutioner minister of Crail, James Sharp, who would be consecrated Archbishop of St Andrews in December 1661; but he, for all his astute skills as a political negotiator, was at best a fellow-traveller.[17]

For many historians, the decision was made not by the Scots but for them, dictated either by the tide of events in England or by the King's militant Anglican adviser, Edward Hyde, Earl of Clarendon.[18] It needs to be remembered, though, that when the first session of the Scottish parliament opened (1 Jan. 1661), the English Convention parliament had recently been dissolved without making any provisions for the settlement of religion there; the actions of the militant Cavalier parliament still lay in the future. The exemption of Scotland from a general indemnity is sometimes seen as one of the arsenal of weapons which Clarendon brought to bear on Scotland to bring it into line with his thinking, but the potentially explosive issue of an indemnity act had been passed to parliament to take its own decision, in Scotland as in England.[19] It was the Scottish parliament which chose to hold it like a gun to its own head and that of presbyterian sympathisers until the settlement was otherwise complete. The bulk of the case for Clarendon's continuing key influence over Scottish affairs after 1662 rests on the role of the new Scottish Council set up at Whitehall, a body swamped by its English members, but it comes largely from his own pen. There can be little doubt that Clarendon believed himself to be the arbiter of Scottish politics, as many English ministers would do in the future; but the Council's role is elusive and it disappeared without trace in 1667.

Attempts have been made, too, to make the hard-drinking ex-soldier, Middleton, the commissioner of the Scottish parliament of 1661, as the architect of a royalist reaction which exceeded even the expectations of Charles II himself.[20] Lauderdale, the secretary, had to spend much of 1660-2 at court in London while Middleton was in Edinburgh, but seems to have been out-manoeuvred in court intrigue and did not favour the religious settlement devised in 1661; by 1663, with Middleton removed from the scene, Lauderdale would grasp the new settlement with all the enthusiasm of a late convert.[21] What remains enigmatic is the role of the restored parliament itself, which would in the course of its two sessions (Jan.- July 1661, May-Sept. 1662) pass over 400 acts.

Middleton came with a set of instructions long on the strategy of the reassertion of the royal prerogative but short on tactics and with nothing to say about religion. The Restoration settlement by 1662 would produce an episcopal formula in all three kingdoms. There was a double irony about this. It was deliberate royal policy to keep the settlement of the three kingdoms apart from each other. The surest way to force the King back on to his travels, it was thought, was the mixed polity which had brought down his father. Sheldon, Archbishop of Canterbury, would play the role of hammer of the dissenters in England and Alexander Burnet, Archbishop of Glasgow, would do the same in Scotland, but no one had been cast for the role of Laud. Each of the three kingdoms, however, showed itself to be of much the same caste of mind and offered similar settlements, each based seemingly on consent. It is likely that the Scottish parliament, usually portrayed as the compliant poodle of the court or as the 'drunken parliament' by presbyterian historians such as Wodrow, was driven by a collective sense of animus and near-hysteria which was easy for Middleton to exploit but difficult to control.

Its tone was set by two events, one planned and the other quite unexpected. On 7 January, on the specific instructions of the king, the remains of Montrose were dug up and his head removed from the spike above the Edinburgh Tolbooth where it had been exhibited since 1650. His state funeral, ordered by the King who had signed the Covenants within days of his death in 1650 and arranged by Middleton who had fought Montrose at Philiphaugh, rewrote the history of the previous twenty years according to a new royalist canon. Every revolution – for this was how contemporaries viewed 1660, as a natural revolution of the spheres to an original state of equilibrium – needs its martyrs. It also needs to find enemies of the revolution. These were obligingly supplied by an event which had happened the day before, in London, where a gathered church of dissenters under the leadership of a cooper, Thomas Venner, had staged a hopeless coup to establish a rule of the saints. It was the cue for a frenzied reaction against 'fanaticks' – in all three kingdoms. Within weeks, as the result of a nationwide scare, more than 5,000 English Quakers were behind bars; and in Edinburgh, amidst rumours of a similar coup, Protesters were banned from the capital – in echoes of 1584. [22]

The act which swiftly followed banning conventicles was part of the reaction of a new establishment faced by the sudden prospect of a return to the abyss from whence it had just come. In such an atmosphere, the decision of the Scottish parliament to call back the Articles to draft its legislation was an act of zeal rather than compliance; it was part of a landslide of royalist sentiment. By the beginning of March, Middleton reported to Hyde that a repeal of all legislation since 1637 was beginning to seem possible – and thus a restoration of bishops. [23] By the time the Rescissory Act was passed on the 28th of that month by a large majority, the tide of royalist feeling had swept further; it cancelled virtually all legislation since 1633. The only surprise was that it did not claim more sacrificial victims – only three were executed. [24] If there was a royalist counter-revolution in the seventeenth century, it took place not in 1647-8 or 1651, when motives were still mixed and events confused, but in the first three months of 1661. Its unexpectedness confounded all those, including the Resolutioner ministers, who had confidently been expecting a restoration of presbyterianism and perhaps of Covenanted politics as well.

The formal decisions which led to an episcopal settlement of the Church were taken at Whitehall in August 1661, with the Scottish parliament in recess. There was again disagreement amongst the King's different sets of advisers: Lauderdale, Hamilton and Crawford-Lindsay, with Sharp in attendance, favoured some sort of presbyterian settlement which was still as yet undefined; but Middleton, Glencairn and Rothes, who seemed to be in closer touch with Scottish opinion and were supported by Hyde, backed what now appeared to be the clearer-cut strategy of the restoration of bishops.[25] The rest of the sequence is not in dispute. By 5 September, the privy council in Edinburgh had received a letter announcing what were termed the King's wishes. On 15 December four Scottish bishops including Sharp were consecrated at Westminster and on 9 January the council banned the meeting of presbyteries and synods without authority of bishops. Legislative sanction was given by the second session of parliament, when it met again in May 1662.

This sequence of events is usually taken to indicate that Whitehall proposed, the privy council disposed and parliament added its rubber-stamp. There is much, however, to suggest that the real sequence began in the Scottish parliament. Along with the Act Rescissory it had agreed to accept the form of church polity 'most suitable to monarchical government' and most conducive to 'the public peace and quiet of the kingdome'.[26] It implied a limitless capacity for loyalty to Stewart ecclesiastical policy but also gave a clear indication of the direction it should take. The King's advisers seized on the hint. They were pragmatic enough to realise that a stable Church settlement might depend on the willingness of the leading Resolutioner ministers to join it. Their first choice as Archbishop of St Andrews was not Sharp but Robert Douglas, who refused it. The bench which gradually emerged was a collection of second-raters and noble clients who lacked the industry of the bishops of the 1630s; its only men of talent were Sharp and Robert Leighton, whose library at Dunblane still testifies to the astonishing range of his scholarship.

When parliament rose on 9 September 1662, much of this still lay in the future. It had intended a stable settlement – and Charles had accepted the formula because it seemed to carry with it a guarantee. Before the end of the year the settlement had begun to list badly – once it had begun to be implemented by the privy council. In October, Middleton and Glencairn, old soldiers to their marrow, had taken the fight to the conventiclers: 200 ministers were expelled from their charges in what looked like an official clearance in the south-west. The bulk of the victims were Protesters, but within a short space the total evicted had reached some 300, almost a third of the total ministry, and so must have included large numbers of Resolutioners as well. South of the Forth/Clyde line, there were probably as many ministers outed as remained; in the far south-west, such as the synod of Galloway where thirty-four of the thirty-seven ministers were removed, the state Church hardly existed on the ground.[27]

Easy labels to describe the Church settlement – whether 'moderate' or 'repressive' – are best avoided. In terms of comparative numbers, there can be no doubt more clergy were ejected in Scotland than in England, where 2,000 or a tenth of the ministry resigned as a result of the Act of Uniformity of 1662.[28] And there was a still greater purge in the Scottish universities. The legislation of 1662 was an attempt to bring peace to a Church which had been at war with itself since 1650 and the next attempt at settlement, after 1690, produced a far larger purge. As shall be seen, the moderation of the Restoration Church is best demonstrated by the fact that the disastrous efforts to harmonise the Churches of the three kingdoms which had marked the period 1614-38 were mostly avoided; it was a distinctively Scottish Church. The repressive character of the Restored Church is best explained in terms of failure; it was a state Church in an insecure state. The government – or its managers in Scotland – had quickly managed to contrive the very situation which the settlement had been designed to avoid: a partitioned Church, with government policy dangerously confusing moderate dissent with Covenanting radicalism.

The reign of Lauderdale (1662-80)

Two spectres haunted the parliaments of 1661-2 and indelibly marked the character of politics throughout the Restoration period. One was the religious 'fanaticks'; the other was bankruptcy. In 1661 the Earl of Traquair, Lord Treasurer in Charles I's privy council of the later 1630s, was to be found begging in the streets of Edinburgh without the means even 'to pay for cobling his bootes'.[29] The climate of James VI's reign had been dominated by a credit boom; that of his grandson was overcast by the debt collector. Parliament and the privy council were teeming with nobles who were technically bankrupt and only a step ahead of their creditors. There had been spectacular bankruptcies of nobles before this,[30] but what was new was the scale of indebtedness and the complex web of loans and debts which enmeshed so many nobles. New too was the fact that Highland chiefs were also, for the first time, caught in this financial morass, caused by two decades of war, forced loans and taxation. Typically, a noble or chief might be evading debt owed to a dozen creditors while pursuing a dozen others at law.[31] The parliament of 1661-2 did its best to serve the interests of its well-born members: it sanctioned a series of personal settlements with leading aristocrats; interest rates were brought down and debtors were allowed to extend or defray what they owed; and the estates of forfeited dissenters went to royalists as compensation. Those best equipped for this elaborate game of financial charades were those who held office or influence.

Not surprisingly, the doyen of both creditors and debtors was the Earl of Argyll, rehabilitated in 1663 despite his father's fall and used by Lauderdale for the rest of the 1660s and 1670s as an old-fashioned royal lieutenant in the Highlands. The debts owed to the Campbell family as a whole were in the region of 1m merks. Clanranald was hopelessly in debt to the Campbells, but the largest single debt owed to Argyll was £100,000, by the chief of the MacLeans; by the 1670s it had risen to £200,000. It was the basis for a full-scale clan war in the 1670s, when Argyll tried to make good his claim to Morvern, Mull and Tiree in lieu of payment. He had behind him both the force of the law (in the convenient figure of Dalrymple of Stair, President of the Court of Session) and government backing.[32] The effects in the Highlands of a society destabilised by debt, with rights to lands and personal obligations both thrown into confusion, were spectacular. They were less dramatic elsewhere, but they created an atmosphere of jobbery and corruption which would last for the rest of the century. Its monuments, and proof of the principle that corruption did usually pay in politics, at least in the seventeenth century, are the splendid houses of Queensberry at Drumlanrig or of Hamilton at Kinneil and Hamilton Palace itself, first planned in 1678.[33]

The period between 1662 and 1682 saw a succession of bewildering changes of policy towards the central problem of dissent. The motives that lay behind the changes are often mysterious, shrouded in the politics of place and intrigue which persisted as the one dynamic of government. Their effects are simply described: they provoked two major risings, in 1666 and 1679, and by the 1680s had induced a growing sense of isolation between the government and significant sections of Scottish opinion. There were sharp differences both within the privy council and the bench of bishops over how to deal with nonconformity. Policy fluctuated wildly between 1666 and 1679, but not because one group of advisers suddenly gained access to the King's ear at the expense of another; it was rather because of the bewildering shifts of ground taken by the two fixtures in Scottish politics – Lauderdale, a virtual viceroy of Scotland, and his partner in the Highlands, Argyll. New political allies were found to launch a new policy and dismissed from favour as its agents once it hit rough water – the classic politics of a one-party state.

This unlikely duo – John Maitland, 2nd Earl of Lauderdale, dubbed 'John Red', the red-haired, hard-drinking descendant of a long line of kings' servants, proficient in both Hebrew and the classics and now elevated to a dukedom, and Archibald Campbell, 9th Earl of a family which had risen on the back of the crown's need for an overmighty subject in the Highlands – both came from convinced presbyterian backgrounds. The latter, Argyll, would contrive in 1685 to follow the family tradition set by his father of dying as Protestant martyrs. Lauderdale had been given unrivalled control, including the office of commissioner to parliament, after a clumsy manoeuvre by Middleton to oust him had backfired in 1663. With the removal of Middleton in 1663 – the expanding English empire offered many graveyards for the hopes of politicians and Middleton was given the governorship of Tangier – and the death of Glencairn in 1664, power rested until 1667 on a triumvirate of Lauderdale, Argyll and Rothes, with Sharp in attendance.

This was the first of four marriages of convenience, each of which had Lauderdale as the main partner and none lasted much more than three years.[34] Rothes and Sharp both fell into disfavour in the aftermath of the rising at Rullion Green in 1666; and Burnet was replaced as Archbishop of Glasgow by Leighton, who advocated comprehension. With a new policy – of reconciliation rather than repression – came new partners, in the shape of the Earl of Tweeddale and Sir Robert Murray, Lauderdale's former agent in Whitehall. The beginnings of another shift in policy – towards limited toleration rather than comprehension which would later surface in the Second Indulgence (Sept. 1672) – activated more changes in 1671, when Lauderdale found a new compliant peer in the genial Earl of Kincardine and a new trusted henchman in his own brother, Charles Maitland. The final shift came in 1674, as part of the discarding of the indulgence policy which had clearly failed; it led to the eclipse of Leighton and the reinstatement of Burnet, who had been nursing new ideas for repression for almost seven years – they included an internment camp for conventiclers in the Northern Isles.[35] More bizarrely, it also led to the promotion of Atholl, a natural supporter of government policy and controller of a growing faction in the council, but also a rival to Argyll's control in the Highlands. Within months Atholl and Argyll were at loggerheads and almost came to a duel.[36]

The irony of the later 1670s – when government policy was becoming increasingly repressive towards conventicles and the Highlands were being swallowed up in a clan war between Campbells and MacLeans – is that the government itself was losing control. Lauderdale was in failing health, culminating in a stroke in 1679; his policy which had always thrived on its very ambiguity was becoming increasingly arbitrary and perhaps even 'inane' long before he formally retired in September 1680.[37] The council was fast becoming strangled in its own web of factions. Lauderdale's growing unpopularity in England had encouraged his political enemies to beat a path, not only to Whitehall but to the door of the English House of Commons; in 1675 the daily procession of Scots was said to be 'like as many porters'.[38] The sudden crisis into which this government was thrown in 1679 by the assassination of the primate, Sharp, revealed that no one was in real control. New purpose and direction – or rival directions – would be offered after 1679 in the shape of two royal interventions in Scottish politics. One was James, Duke of Monmouth, bastard son of Charles II; the other was James, Duke of York, brother of the King and Catholic heir to the throne.

The two risings of 1666 and 1679 were similar in the sense that both were led by smallholders and neither involved a major landholder, still less a magnate.[39] In Covenanting history they are portrayed as steps on the road to the revolution of 1688, which brought an end to twenty-eight years of non-stop persecution. Neither, though, was quite what it seemed. The 'Pentland Rising' – something of a misnomer for it originated in Kirkcudbrightshire in the far south-west – was quite unexpected; Rothes was actually in London assuring Charles of how peaceful the country was when it broke out. The government was particularly fearful of it because there were already links between religious exiles and the Dutch; it was the misfortune of the rebels that the government saw the rising against the background of the second Anglo-Dutch War (1665-7). The flashpoint for the rising was not explicitly religious but had more to do with the heavy-handed soldiery of Sir James Turner's troops who already had a reputation as suppressors of conventicles. The fact that a local fracas swiftly developed into what appeared to be a religious revolt – the insurgents captured Turner at his lodging in Dumfries and also renewed their commitment to the Covenants – seemed to confirm the government's view of the dangerous link between dissent and insurrection. But with never more than 1,000 ill-armed men and with little more in mind than petitioning the privy council in Edinburgh, the rising was never a serious threat. Beaten back from Colinton on the southern outskirts of Edinburgh by the Edinburgh Fencibles, a force of landed vigilantes, the rebels retreated a few miles southwards where they were caught on 28 November at Rullion Green, on the slopes of the Pentland Hills, by a government force under the command of Tam Dalyell of the Binns. Fifty were killed and twenty-one of the eighty taken prisoner were executed; others were banished to Barbados. Almost as soon as the rising was over, Lauderdale's government began to realise how heavy-handed it had been. An inquiry, which briefly threatened Turner,[40] developed into a cover-up and that familiar resort of government failure – resignations. Rothes and Burnet were the obvious candidates for sacrifice.

Conciliation was in the air after 1666, but the form it should take was uncertain. Leighton, who succeeded Burnet at Glasgow, had ambitious but vague schemes for an all-embracing broad church. When Lauderdale was able to establish a more permanent presence in Scotland as a result of his appointment as king's commissioner in 1669, an alternative – usually associated with Sharp – began to emerge, of limited toleration of non-conformity, by licence. The First Indulgence (June 1669) restored forty-two dissident presbyterian ministers to their parishes and a second, in 1672, allowed ninety more to preach outside the Established Church. Although it has been argued that these experiments of 1667-72 had some success, split presbyterian opinion and neutralised the extremists,[41] it is clear that Lauderdale by 1674 had begun to distance himself from yet another failure.

These experiments illustrate two important points about the Restored Church. Lauderdale was able to move so easily from one means of dealing with dissent to another because the restored hierarchy was itself so divided on it. Sharp, Leighton and Burnet all offered different solutions. Burnet was in close touch with Sheldon, Archbishop of Canterbury, but there was no co-ordinated campaign in Charles's three kingdoms. In 1669, as Scotland was moving from one form of conciliation to another, Sheldon was organising the suppression of dissent. In 1674, as the Scots were casting off the indulgence policy and harrying conventiclers again, moderates in England had come to the fore and some nonconformists had expectations of a royal indulgence.[42] Each of the changes in Scotland between 1667 and 1674 were a distinctively Scottish solution to a Scottish problem – and they all failed.

As the 1670s went on, the number of conventicles increased, as did the fears of a renewed campaign of government repression. The problem was worsening – some field conventicles in the south-west now attracted over 10,000 worshippers. With armed men guarding them, they began to look more like armies than gathered churches. House conventicles were growing too – as more moderate presbyterians in the Lowlands and in the larger burghs began to desert the services of the Established Church.[43] The government tried unsuccessfully to force from landowners guarantees of the good behaviour of their tenants. Its most notorious ploy was the 'Highland Host' – an 8,000 strong force assembled in January 1678 to cow the landowners of Ayrshire and the south-west. Much written about it is apocryphal. Only 5,000 of the force were from the Highlands and they came not from the Gaelic heartland of the far west but from the southern and eastern Highlands. It remained in being little more than a month and encountered no active resistance. Only parts of the Host went on the rampage, and they indulged not in murder and rape but simple plunder – horses, shoes and money were favourite items. What the Host did was to suggest to both the government and its opponents a solution to what had long been its problem – a lack of military resources. Fines from dissenters were intended for the pockets of the nobility, not a war chest. The new resort to the military resources of Gaeldom might end the paradox of a repressive regime without the resources to coerce.[44]

On 3 May 1679, James Sharp was brutally murdered in full view of his daughter on Magus Moor, just two miles outside St Andrews. The assassins (like those of Cardinal Beaton in 1546) were almost all local men and their leader was a minor laird, John Balfour of Kinloch, who would later claim to have 'received a call from God' to commit the murder. As in 1666, the link between the first outrage and the mainstream of dissent was tentative: the murderers did not belong to an established gathered church and have been likened to vigilantes.[45] But Sharp became a symbol for both sides. To conventiclers of all shades he was a Judas; to the government the murder of a privy councillor, in itself a capital offence, was but one step away from regicide.

The armed rising which followed in the west was a vital turning-point in the reign. On 1 June, the rebels inflicted a minor but shock defeat on a government force led by John Graham of Claverhouse at Drumclog, a boggy moor to the south-west of Strathaven. They then pitched camp at Bothwell Bridge near Hamilton and over the next three weeks conventiclers flocked to join their ranks and to sow dissension within them. This extraordinary scene, without parallel in Scottish history, bears some resemblance to the debates at Putney amongst different wings of the English Levellers in 1647. Three distinct groups debated the fate of the Covenant and the means of counteracting government policy. The best known – the 'Cameronians' led by a former field preacher Richard Cameron who advocated unrelenting pursuit of the Solemn League – were the most extreme and probably the least important. After the inevitable defeat at Bothwell Bridge (22 July 1679) at the hands of Monmouth, the Cameronians isolated themselves further from the main body of dissent. By July 1680, when Cameron was killed at Airds Moss in Ayrshire, their Sanquhar Declaration (22 June 1680) had disowned 'Charles Stuart that has been reigning or tyrannising as we may say on the throne of Britain'. By 1682 they were reduced to an insignificant remnant without an ordained minister. The second group at Bothwell Bridge, led by John Welsh, represented a broader strand of presbyterian opinion, prepared even to accept the indulged ministers. And the third, led by John Blacader, advocated only the passive resistance of a suffering church; in the 1680s, despite Blacader's imprisonment and death on the Bass Rock, it would mushroom into a wide-ranging network of praying societies.[46] It had been the assassination of Sharp and not government policy which had opened up the splits within the conventiclers. Legend, however, stubbornly clings to the Cameronians.

The Age of James, Duke of York, and James VII (1679-88)

The rising which ended at Bothwell Bridge resulted in sixteen executions and 258 transportations. In the course of the 1680s – dubbed the 'killing time' by Wodrow – about a hundred Covenanters were executed and perhaps eighty more were cut down by troops in the field. It was an unprecedented volume of repression in a country which had until then largely escaped large-scale show trials and martyrdoms. It demonstrated a new sense of purpose in the government, largely the product of the influence of the Duke of York, but it also showed a fatal misreading of the strength of religious extremism. There can hardly be a case in mitigation, but the killing time does need to be put into perspective. Few presbyterians had much sympathy for the extremists who, as they saw it, jeopardised the broad church of dissent. The numbers of martyrs in the 1680s were far less than the number of witches burned in the Restoration period; 300 had died in 1661-2 alone. The numbers punished in England for nonconformity were far greater; over 400 Quakers alone rotted to death in English prisons in the 1680s.[47] The full force of government repression was reserved, not for the Covenanting south-west but for the Highlands during the presbyterian rising attempted by Argyll in 1685: 'All men who joyned . . . are to be killed or disabled ever from fighting again; and burn all houses except honest men's. . . . Let the women and children be transported to remote Isles'.[48] These draconian instructions, watered down by commanders in the field, illustrate that the violence of the Scottish state still operated on two levels; in the Highlands it would be this casual racialism which lay behind the massacre at Glencoe a few years later. The most damning indictment of the killing time is, however, that the government's policy simply did not work.

The 1680s saw a drastic change in the complexion of Scottish politics. The end of Lauderdale's 'system' in 1680 – appropriately almost mid-way between the ages of Dunfermline and Islay, another so-called 'king of Scotland' who developed further the black arts of managing Scottish politics[49] – brought about a new, direct Stewart interest. Like Stewart intruders before him such as Albany and Aubigné, York quickly constructed 'a new mongrel party of his own'.[50] His dislike of a Third Indulgence, issued in June 1679 and easing the harrying of house conventicles, led to its withdrawal in May 1680. His first significant intervention in Scottish politics came, however, in 1681 when he persuaded parliament to pass by a large majority 'extraordinary legislation'[51] enforcing on all office-holders in Church and state an oath of loyalty acknowledging the royal supremacy in all matters temporal and ecclesiastical – in effect, an oath of loyalty to uphold a Protestant Church with a Catholic as its future head. The resilience of loyalty to the Stewarts, the continuing threat of armed insurrection, a fresh flood of pensions and the prospect of bringing down the overmighty Argyll's bloated empire (which parliament had already objected to in 1669) were all reasons for parliament's compliance. York did not stay in Scotland beyond the end of 1681. He left behind him a bitter struggle for power.

The growing repression of the years 1682-5 was played out amidst a ruthless gladiatorial contest within the council. Its first major victim came in 1684 and, predictably, it was Sir George Gordon of Haddo, a laird and lawyer elevated on James's specific advice to the chancellorship but also to a new earldom, of Aberdeen. The fall of Queensberry, elevated to a dukedom in 1684, took longer, but by 1686 the governing of Scotland was firmly in the hands of the two Drummond brothers – the Earl of Perth, the chancellor, and Melfort, secretary of state – both converts to Catholicism. There was thus a clear and unusual fixity of purpose throughout the 1680s, when policy became increasingly co-ordinated through a 'secret committee' of the privy council which reported directly to James in Whitehall. James was master of Scotland well before Charles II died in February 1685 and he succeeded as James VII of Scotland and II of England (1685-9).[52] Yet the awkward question remained, with so many puppets and placemen in positions of power, often as a result of rapid conversions to Catholicism, as to how real the King's authority might be if seriously tested. The longer-term legacy of this skewing of the customary processes of place and profit would be a queue of magnates resentful of their exclusion from politics. They would resurface when their chance came, in 1688-90.

The most dramatic victim of James's recasting of the face of Scottish politics was Argyll. The pretext was the oath attached to the Test Act of 1681, for which Argyll expressed open contempt. By the end of the year, by accident rather than design, the head of the house of Argyll was in exile and the crown was free, for the first time in almost two centuries, to attempt a new policy towards the Highlands and to exploit the widespread hatred of the Campbells amongst the west Highland clans. In 1682 the setting up of a Commission of Highland Justiciary, which contained seventy-five lairds and chiefs rather than magnates, divorced the dispensation of justice from the aggrandisement of Campbell justiciars. Its successes were patchy but by 1684 an impression had been made on the endemic problem of Highland violence. Some of its tactics were reminiscent of the Cromwellian peace of the 1650s: no Highlander carrying a firearm was allowed to travel more than seven miles from his home without a pass; cattle raiding was drastically curbed; and an unsuccessful attempt to reoccupy Inverlochy was made.[53]

In May 1685, Argyll sailed from Amsterdam, landed briefly in Orkney thereby raising the alarm, before raising his standard in Kintyre. His arrival was meant to coincide with Monmouth's landing in the south-west of England and a diversionary rising in Cheshire. Each element quickly floundered. Argyll failed even to raise the bulk of his own kinsmen, but pressed on regardless towards Glasgow, capture and Protestant martyrdom. His collapse was important for it demonstrated both the strengths and weaknesses of James VII's government. This botched Protestant threat to the Stewart monarchy helped the process of appointing Catholics to high office, in both government and army. An anti-Campbell campaign, once unleashed, proved hard to quell and Atholl, who did not control a clan, proved incapable of doing so. By 1688 much of the good work done before 1685 had been undone; the Highlands were as lawless as ever. Once again the greater significance lay in the future – in the double-edged relationship which James VII had forged between himself and the 'loyal clans' of the west Highlands.[54]

The politics of James VII's reign are difficult to assess without an eye on the crisis which suddenly befell him in late 1688, when William of Orange landed at Torbay (5 Nov.) and James took flight (23 Dec.). Yet that was an English crisis, with its roots there, and it is hard to find any trace of the same in Scotland. The Scottish parliament, it is true, had in 1686 refused outright to sanction a general toleration, despite the tempting offer of free trade. Two indulgences issued through the privy council (Feb. and June 1687) granted unlimited toleration to all shades of religious opinion, ranging from presbyterians to Quakers and Catholics. Three privy councillors refused to sign the proclamation and two bishops objected so strongly that they were dismissed. Scotland was still, so far as can be judged, some considerable way from a national rebellion and, ironically, the rate of conversions to Catholicism had slowed rather than quickened in the 1680s. Despite a few spectacular conversions – like that of the Earl of Moray in a vain bid to secure his position against Melfort and of some minor chiefs in the Highlands, such as Coll of Keppoch who returned to the Protestant fold after 1690 – there was no mass capture of offices as in England, where one in five JPs was a Catholic by 1688. All that James had managed to do was to revive the spectre of 'no popery', and his extensive refurbishing of Holyrood as the chapel of the new Order of the Thistle in 1687 gave it a target. Anti-Catholic riots were provoked not by one panic-stricken flight but two.

On 10 December 1688, with rumours of Orange plots and purges swirling about him, the Earl of Perth fled from Edinburgh. He took refuge in Drummond Castle, planning an abortive escape via Lochaber to Ireland, and was captured as he embarked for France. In the highly charged, uncertain atmosphere soldiers guarding Holyrood Abbey fired on some rioters, killing a few. The city guard was called out, but a larger mob stormed the Abbey and sacked it. Its Catholic furnishings were ripped down and the tombs of Stewart kings were desecrated. A crowd of university students burned an effigy of the Pope and took down the heads of Covenanting martyrs hanging above the city gates. The revolution had its mob, but it took the flight of James himself, thirteen days later, to give it real prospect of success.

Restoration society

The Restoration period brings a series of conflicting images. It began with one of the largest witch crazes in Scottish history, but by the later 1670s it was becoming increasingly difficult to secure convictions for witchcraft in the central courts. One of the most sceptical of the judges who by then picked holes in the evidence in witch trials was the Lord Advocate, Sir George Mackenzie, the infamous 'Bluidy Mackenzie' who showed no scruples when pursuing Cameronian rebels. Even in 1662, as a young defence lawyer, Mackenzie had already denounced the 'witch prickers' as 'villainous cheats'.[55] Mackenzie, who in his Institutions of the Law of Scotland (1684) tried to erect the criminal law into a coherent and philosophical system as Stair had already done for civil law in his work of the same title published in 1681, was a typical virtuoso of the Restoration period; his literary works ranged from religious contemplation to a studied defence of royalism, from drama to an attempt at a prose novel, heraldry and history. Mackenzie turned to literary pursuits as a relief from the cares of office. Sir Robert Sibbald, the other charismatic talent of the period who founded the Royal College of Physicians in 1681 and would become the first Professor of Medicine in the University of Edinburgh, turned to science as an antidote to the factionalism of his age:

I saw none could enter to the ministrie without ingadging in factions. I preferred a quiet life, wherein I might not be ingadged in factions of Church or State. I fixed upon the studie of medicine, wherein I thought I might be of no faction and might be useful to my generation.[56]

Sibbald's interests ranged from archaeology and cartography to natural history and botany and it was he who was instrumental in the founding of the botanic garden (now the Royal Botanic Garden) in Edinburgh in 1667. Mackenzie and Sibbald consciously moved in a Jekyll-and-Hyde age, in which political chaos threatened and culture flowered. It was in the 1680s, during and after the brief residence of the Duke of York in Edinburgh, that Restoration culture was given its lasting monuments, such as the Royal College of Physicians, the Advocates' Library, and the Order of the Thistle. Yet the period was also the mustering ground for a century of accumulating scholarship and cultural advance.[57]

The Restoration period laid down a number of important foundations which would last into the nineteenth and even the twentieth centuries: the reorganisation of the Court of Justiciary in 1672 and the widening remit of justices of the peace provided the two pillars of central and local justice until well into the nineteenth century. Legislation on roads, poor relief and education became more detailed and much of it, for good or ill, survived for the better part of 200 years.[58] It was a period when parliament did much to encourage overseas trade and manufactories at home. As a result colonies were established in New Jersey in 1682 and South Carolina in 1684. A chain of soap works, sugar boiling works and woollen manufactories were founded, like the Glasgow Soaperie of 1667, the Easter Sugar works of 1669 and James Armour's serge manufactory set up in 1683 – all of these examples in Glasgow, which has been called the 'boom town' of the later seventeenth century. The same parliament continued the legislation which had since 1606 tied colliers, salters and lead miners ever tighter to their master's whim through the petty tyranny of the local baron court.[59] A wave of minor improvements in the framing of the land – crop rotation, partial enclosure and liming of the soil – was already taking place in parts of the country such as Fife and Lothian, but it was done at the expense of consolidation of farms into larger units, rising rents for tenants and the decline of the 'bonnet laird'.[60] The paradoxes of the age of the improving landlord shine brightly in the figure of Sir John Clerk of Penicuik, whose coal mine at Loanhead made a modest profit of £6,000 a year by the 1720s. As well as making 109 personal covenants with God between 1692 and 1720, Clerk devised individual covenants with each member of his work force, guaranteeing a minumum twelve hours' production a day and four hours' Christian study. Both the employer and the work-force were already in process of having new roles cast for them which would last until the Victorian age.

The internal boundaries which divided Scotland between Highland and Lowland society did not come down but they were being adjusted: the economy of the central and eastern Highlands was becoming more closely tied to adjacent Lowland areas and the rise of cattle mustering points such as Crieff was testimony to this. The heart of Gaeldom, the west Highlands, was probably becoming more rather than less remote. The bridges which existed between the west Highland chiefs and Lowland society were personal; a number visited the court at Whitehall and Cameron of Lochiel was happy enough to be groomed for the part of a 'noble savage' by James. A cult of 'tartanry' at the royal court briefly flowered in the 1680s.[61] Over the next century a gulf of misunderstanding would open up between Gaeldom and central government.

18

UNION

THERE ARE MANY ODD ADJECTIVES USED TO DESCRIBE THE ENGLISH REVOLUTION OF 1688 – including 'glorious', 'respectable' and 'moral' – but few if any to describe the revolution in Scotland beyond the bland and quite misleading term of the 'revolution settlement' of 1689-90. The events in Scotland which followed the flight of James VII to France in December 1688 were confused, drawn-out and often contradictory for all those involved in them, including William of Orange himself. With no revolutionary caucus in being – except for the remnants of the extreme Covenanters who for the moment mattered little – most of the leading players involved in the unfolding drama took time to groom themselves for their parts. There were two distinct oddities about the revolution. No large burgh rallied to the defence of the crown; even Aberdeen, that bastion of loyalty to the Stewarts which had supported James III in 1488 and Charles I in 1638, accepted the proclamation of William (1689-1702) as king in early 1689 without opposition. And, uniquely in a Scottish revolt, almost no major magnates were involved. They either kept to the sidelines, changed sides with a bewildering rapidity – Annandale five times in as many months in the first half of 1689 – or, like the Hamiltons, played the Scottish 'old trick of father knave and son honest'.[1] For a few, Prince William of Orange, son of Charles I's elder daughter Mary and married to James VII's daughter Mary, provided a clear Protestant alternative to the Catholic James. Yet William, as events would show, actually preferred an episcopal solution to a presbyterian. For others, the very nearness of William to the Stewarts provoked what would prove to be a well-founded suspicion that he would be as jealous of his royal prerogative as either Charles II or James had been. The first to declare their loyalty to the new regime were not the critics of the old regime but its agents – such as Dalrymple of Stair, Lord Advocate – who were anxious to retain office and aware that they more than others had to demonstrate their new-found loyalty.

Revolution settlement (1689-90)

The 'settlement' took nineteen months to become a reality; there would be no resolution of the church question until June 1690. The intervening months were scarred by two sets of direct action: shortly after James's flight there began a calculated series of 'rabblings', in which over 200 episcopalian or conformist ministers were forcibly ejected by roving bands of Cameronians; and, beginning in March 1689 but planned months beforehand, there was a full-scale royalist rising in the Highlands led by John Graham of Claverhouse, Viscount Dundee, which for many must have recalled the Montrose years of the 1640s. The revolution settlement was born amidst a political and military crisis; it is hardly to be wondered that it laid the foundations for a profoundly unstable government throughout the 1690s, which lost control of the Highlands, proved unable to manage the Scottish parliament or to curb the excesses of the extreme presbyterians.

Yet the division of Scottish opinion during the forging of the settlement – into 'presbyterian' and 'episcopalian' political stances (the need to add quotation marks to the terms is in itself suggestive) – was also deceptive. There was hardly a magnate who did not change sides more than once during this period. Hamilton, who would emerge as William's commissioner to the Convention parliament of 1689, had been in London in late 1688 and changed his mind three times during the invasion which the English parliament would later decide had never happened – William's 14,000 troops were deemed to have been a personal bodyguard and the revolution retained its respectability. Sir John Campbell of Glenorchy, Earl of Breadalbane, who would take up the role of William's man of business in Scotland from mid-1691, had throughout the spring and summer of 1689 retired to Kilchurn Castle in Argyll hiding behind a cover story of gout and in negotiation with Dundee. The real difference between Hamilton, an episcopalian, deeply conservative figure intent on rebuilding the family's fortunes, and Breadalbane, representative of a presbyterian-inclined dynasty which had twice since 1660 shown itself willing to compromise its ideals to rehabilitate itself, was that they wagered differently on the outcome of Dundee's rising.[2]

In a sense, it was Breadalbane's analysis which was the more acute. Dundee first raised James VII's standard on Dundee Law early in April. On 27 July 1689, Dundee – at the head of what was an almost exclusively Highland rising – inflicted a heavy defeat on a government force under the command of Hugh Mackay of Scourie at Killiecrankie. The battle itself was short, lasting not much more than ten minutes, but murderous. More than 30 per cent of Dundee's force of 2,000 were killed, and probably 60 per cent of Mackay's much bigger army of some 4,000.[3] Killiecrankie, often cast off as inconsequential, in fact potentially opened up the whole of Scotland north of the Tay. The marginal support which it had attracted up to this point, mostly amongst small central or west Highland clans such as the MacDonalds of Glengarry and Keppoch, was typical of Highland risings in their early stages; what victory would normally have done was to tilt the scales in the calculated loyalty of the leading west Highland clans. And it should also have been the signal for Breadalbane to play the Campbell card. What transformed the fate of the rising was the stray bullet which left Dundee himself dead on the battlefield of Killiecrankie.

The predictable, sudden surge of support did materialise after Killiecrankie but Breadalbane's diplomatic bout of gout returned. Nevertheless, it was a Jacobite force of between 3,000 and 5,000 men which met at Dunkeld on 21 August 1689 a much smaller force of about 800, mostly Cameronians described even by a Williamite officer as 'madd men not even to to be governed by master [Alexander] Shields ther oracle'.[4] The battle at Dunkeld took the form of a brief but bloody siege, with no opportunity for the Highland charge which had brought spectacular sucess at Killiecrankie. After four hours of sniping and sorties, the Highlanders withdrew. Both sides claimed a victory which never existed, but it was a turning-point. Under uninspired leadership, the rising lost impetus; it continued, however, to threaten the Edinburgh administration until a final, decisive defeat at Cromdale, near present-day Grantown-on-Spey, on 1 May 1690.

Throughout the thirteen months of the rising, there had also always been a prospect, at least in the minds of the government and the Convention parliament, of a Catholic invasion force from Ireland – as in 1645. Three influences played on the prolonged deliberations of the Scottish parliament throughout this period: its legislation was largely dictated by what had already happened in England; its fears were orchestrated by a Highland rising in Scotland and James's alarmingly successful campaign in Ireland; and its capacity for indecision was manipulated by an expert in the murky underworld of revolution plots and double-dealing, Sir James Montgomerie.

The initial actions of the Convention parliament, shortly after it first met on 14 March 1689, seemed clear-cut and decisive. On the 16th, it received letters from the two rivals for the crown. William's was moderate, conciliatory and carefully composed; James's, scribbled while aboard ship at Brest, was a mixture of threats and vague promises which held out no safeguards for the Protestant faith. By the 18th, with James's support in the Convention dished by the king himself, Dundee had withdrawn. With a rising in the air and the Jacobite Duke of Gordon still in control of Edinburgh Castle, the Convention, now meeting in a highly charged atmosphere behind locked doors and guarded by 1,000 Cameronians, moved quickly. On 4 April, it voted to deprive James of the crown – with only five dissenting. Already the road to revolution taken by the Scottish parliament, seemingly similar and in imitation of the English Convention, had begun to diverge: there was in Scotland no grasping at the convenient fiction of James's abdication but an implication that monarchy had been contractual. It was no coincidence that Buchanan's *De Jure Regni* had enjoyed a renewed popularity in the 1680s.

On 11 and 13 April, those differences of emphasis became explicit with the adoption of two documents, the Claim of Right and the Articles of Grievances. These laid down five key constitutional principles: no Catholic could be monarch or bear office (although no candidates were proscribed by name); the royal prerogative could not override the law; parliament should meet frequently and be able to debate freely, secured by the abolition of the Committee of Articles; the consent of parliament was necessary for the raising of supply (and William would have to wait a further fifteen months to secure it); and episcopacy was condemned as an 'insupportable grievance and trouble to this nation'. It was principle with a healthy dash of pragmatism: a mixture of the English Whig programme of the 1680s, a reworking of the constitution of 1641 which Charles I had agreed to, and a pay-off to the more extreme elements of presbyterian opinion on whom the Convention for the moment depended for its safety. It was at once forward-looking for all its constitutional safeguards would eventually be adopted, but also blinkered by a narrow view of Scotland's past, which asserted that episcopacy had been 'contrary to the inclinations of the generality of the people ever since the Reformation, they having been reformed from Popery by Presbyters'.[5] It is a view closer to myth than history which even the most bigoted presbyterian historian would find difficulty in justifying, but it would be the pretext for the abolition of prelacy by the parliament in the following June and the foundation on which a new-style Church of Scotland would slowly be rebuilt after 1690.

In the view of the Convention, this was the basis on which William was offered the crown of Scotland, which he accepted on 11 May. In William's view, he had done nothing of the sort: the oath taken by William and Mary committed them to maintaining the 'true religion . . . now receaved and preached within the realm of

Scotland' but said nothing about polity; it guaranteed a balance between the 'loveable lawes and constitutiones receaved in this realm' and the 'just priviledges of the Crown' without saying what either consisted of.[6] The rest of the session became a frustrating and increasingly acrimonious stalemate between different interpretations of William's conditional acceptance of the throne and indeed conflicting views of the revolution itself. It was a peculiar situation: the King had been able to appoint ministers in the summer of 1689, but the law courts remained firmly shut because parliament refused to agree to his right to nominate to judicial offices. Although parliament still withheld supply, the new regime had a far larger standing army than either Charles II or James VII, sustained for the moment on its English revenues. A series of acts were passed by the House but refused the royal assent. In the process a distinct opposition point of view had taken place in the 'Club', which at least in theory commanded the support of some seventy-five of the 125 members of the parliament. Strongest amongst the shire members and weakest amongst the peers, it pursued the programme contained within the Claim of Right and Articles of Grievances.[7] In July the government conceded episcopacy but hung on grimly to that other symbol of Stewart authoritarian rule, the Committee of Articles. The proroguing of parliament on 2 August, shortly after news of the disastrous defeat at Killiecrankie reached Edinburgh, completed the rout of the court.

By the time parliament met again, in April 1690, William's main attention was firmly focused on the dangerous situation in Ireland and the need for supply to keep an army in being in Scotland to contain the wilting but still stubborn Jacobite enclaves in the Highlands. His choice of the Earl of Melville as commissioner was more reassuring to presbyterian opinion, but also designed to counteract an elaborate wrecking strategy in which Montgomerie was urging the presbyterians into ever more radical courses, including a return to the church settlement of 1649. The web of Montgomerie plots – alternately wooing 'episcopalian' magnates such as Queensberry and Atholl by promising to prevent the implementation of wholesale presbyterianism and outbidding Melville's natural identity of interests with the presbyterians – seems a good deal more far-fetched now than it must have at the time. He was seeking to polarise two kinds of opposition, the secular and religious, which often were uneasy bedfellows.

What turned the tide in favour of the government was not the news of the victory at Cromdale but the leaking of details of a Jacobite plot in which Montgomerie had been attempting to construct an alliance between a section of the Club and some leading conservative magnates, including Queensberry.[8] Melville astutely chose the panic which resulted as the moment to concede the abolition of the Articles, which was agreed on 8 May. Compromises followed, with an act restoring presbyterian government in the Church passed on 7 June, which was greeted with a grant of supply (for twenty-eight months) on the very same day. A settlement had been reached which met some but far from all of the Club's demands. But further unwelcome elements for the government materialised: on 19 July, the parliament, now freewheeling without the check on it of the Articles, voted to abolish lay patronage in the Church.

The re-establishment of presbyterianism in June 1690 was on the basis of the more moderate position of 1592 rather than 1649, but the Kirk had also been given the right to purge 'all inefficient, negligent scandalous and erroneous ministers'. The abolition of patronage six weeks later and the ruthless implementation of that clause over the second half of 1690 – 182 ministers had been deprived for refusing to say public prayers for William and Mary by November – turned a presbyterian settlement into a militant purge. A presbyterian Church had emerged but without the safeguards both William and the magnates wanted. The lines of Anglo-Scots relations had been decisively redrawn, but the Scots had been given only the means to voice their complaints, not to influence London's decisions over them. For William, the main elements of his prerogative had been preserved, including his right to appoint his own ministers, but the confusions of 1689-90 had already revealed the crown's inability to manage Scottish politics with any consistency. William was – because of and despite the revolution – at once the most distant and the most authoritarian King of Scots in the seventeenth century.

The revolution settlement has a double role to play in Scottish history. It saw a final establishment of a presbyterian Church and most roads to the Union of Parliaments of 1707 either begin in 1689-90 or have a major junction at it. Neither milestone was as final or clear-cut as each is often portrayed. The act of June 1690 restoring presbyterianism was followed in July by the abolition of patronage and the repeal of the Act of Supremacy. But the independence of the Church from the state was no more unqualified after 1690 than it had been after the Act of 1592, and the right of congregations to 'call' a minister was still limited to the nominees of heritors and elders.[9] The common claim that the Church 'by the law established' was after 1690 independent of the state is a caricature of an ambiguous relationship which hovered between a practical Erastianism and a principled stance on a modified two-kingdom doctrine.

What remains unquantifiable is the amount of support presbyterianism or episcopalianism had. The General Assembly which met in November 1690 was not as general as it might have been; only 180 ministers and elders attended, all from south of the Tay. In effect, it was a partition church of southern Scotland which claimed the right to deprive all ministers who fell short of its ideal of full-blown presbyterianism. Two Commissions were set up, for the areas to the north and south of the Tay and a purge set in motion. Over the next twenty-five years it would claim almost two-thirds of the ministry as its victims. A massive retrenchment was needed, for some presbyteries were left with few or no parish ministers; it would take the better part of thirty years to complete. The presbyterian Church, as events would show, was secure. The irony was that its political significance was fast waning. Old-style presbyterian nationalism was dead; the Church had instead become an 'interest' in politics – as the events of 1706-7 would show.

For some, the deposing of the last of the Stewart kings in a dynasty which went back to 1371 was a symbol which summed up the changes taking place in seventeenth-century society and pointing the way forward to the eighteenth. The fact that the (few) rebels in Scotland in 1688-9 relied on the initiatives being taken in England is taken as an indicator of the growing reliance of Scottish parliamentary politics on Whig tactics.[10] For others, however, the revolution pushed the two countries further apart, manufacturing a profound crisis in Anglo-Scottish relations which, it was realised by 1698, had to be resolved by more careful management of Scottish politics by the court – and it was only this improved management of politics which made union feasible.[11] In 1690, union was far from being inevitable. A proposal for a union had been made in 1689 but, despite being adopted by the Convention parliament in its first session, quickly became a dead letter, cast aside by the English Convention parliament. Union became a political issue in England only after the sudden death in 1700 of the eleven-year-old William, Duke of Gloucester, the only surviving child of the heir to the throne, Mary's younger sister Anne; she was then thirty-seven and with seventeen still births or infant deaths already in her obstetric history. The subsequent choice of the house of Hanover as the heirs of William and Mary by the Act of Succession passed by the English parliament in 1701 was the first stage in the crisis which would eventually result in the Treaty of Union of 1706-7. Whether union was inevitable or not, events took a bewildering, meandering course from 1689 onwards which few – in England or Scotland – could have anticipated. It was the caprice of history that made both principled stands and unprincipled manoeuvrings equally vulnerable to changing circumstances. In 1690 incorporating union must have seemed the *least* likely of the many scenarios in an uncertain future. As at other important moments in Scottish history, it was, however, the unthinkable which happened.

The massacre at Glencoe

Like the Caroline regime in 1660, the Williamite government in 1690 had some grandiose schemes for controlling the Highlands, but settled, like many governments before it and since, for the cheapest policy it thought it could get away with. It involved yet another attempt to bind individual chiefs to the government by personal oath; its main agent, predictably, was a Campbell – Breadalbane, anxious to demonstrate his new-found loyalty. Its result was costly indeed – both for the reputation of the Campbells and the authority of the crown in the Highlands. In the early morning of 13 February 1692, a detachment of government soldiers under the command of Captain Robert Campbell of Glenlyon, acting on secret orders which can be traced directly to the Lord Advocate, Dalrymple of Stair, butchered thirty-eight of the small clan of the MacIains or MacDonalds of Glencoe. The massacre had, in fact, been botched. The original scheme had been to bring to bear a huge superiority of firepower: 850 armed men set against 100 men of fighting age and some 500 others, mostly women and children. But the orders, planning a synchronised strike by three separate forces, were over-elaborate and took little account of the problems of a forced march across difficult terrain in appalling weather conditions. The plan to seal off the passes to the north and south was not adhered to and the bulk of the members of the 200 families which inhabited half-a-dozen scattered settlements in Glencoe escaped, although many women and children, some of them allegedly stripped naked by the soldiers, died in the snows. Their houses were plundered and set to the torch along with their barns. Later the clan, which never gave details of the women and children massacred, would claim to have lost 1,500 cows and 500 horses. Amongst those who escaped were two sons of the chief, MacIain himself.[12]

The massacre at Glencoe was neither the first nor the worst atrocity committed by the government in the Highlands in the seventeenth century. There had been a much more savage attack on the Clanranald on the island of Eigg in May 1690 by a naval force under the command of an Ulster naval commodore, Edward Pottinger, as part of a summer of gunboat diplomacy waged against the Inner Isles. The difference was that, in the case of Eigg, there was an effective cover-up and the number of victims is unquantifiable. It was even less justified: the fighting men were absent and, unlike Glencoe, there were rapes as well as murders. Pottinger lay low and doctored his logs; Glenlyon, a hard-drinker even by the exacting standards of the seventeenth-century army, flourished his different sets of orders to any who would listen in the taverns of Edinburgh.[13] The outcome of the Glencoe atrocity, which was seized upon by Jacobite propagandists and political rivals of the administration alike, was the predictable resort of a British government to any serious crisis: an inquiry. The first was inconclusive; the second, published in June 1695, exonerated everyone (including King William who had signed the first order sanctioning the army to 'extirpate' Highland rebels) except Dalrymple and the deputy governor of Fort William. The Scottish parliament immediately voted supply and eventually decided that Glencoe had been an act of murder. The political consequences of the massacre, for both the faction-fighting within the administration and for the wider politics of the Highlands are clear enough: the departure of Dalrymple from office, utterly discredited but still unrepentant, gave the King's government a chance to regroup and reassess its position in Scotland; and it gave a sharp boost to Jacobite sympathies in the western Highlands, if still on the guarded and idiosyncratic terms of the chiefs.[14] Yet its effects were more clear-cut than its origins.

Responsibility for the massacre is difficult to fix with any precision. There should be little surprise about this, for it was the confused product of a government policy towards the Highlands which was double-edged and also the result of a deliberately convoluted chain of command designed to erect a screen between the decision-makers and commanders in the field. Throughout the seventeenth century, government policy towards the Highlands had been an unstable balance between two elements – coercion and consent. In the summer of 1691 the influence of Breadalbane had seemed to push policy towards reconciliation with the chiefs who were still bound in allegiance to James; but the other face of the Williamite government was represented by the formidable presence of Fort William, an earthwork with wooden palisade hurriedly thrown up in July 1690 housing a garrison of 1,200.[15] One of the many paradoxes of the massacre is that it took place as the result of a moderate policy, which could be turned against itself by Breadalbane's rivals within government.

In mid-August 1691, Breadalbane had fixed a deadline for the submission of the chiefs to the government: 1 January 1692. Alasdair MacIain had been one of many chiefs who had waited for formal permission to arrive from James in France releasing him from his bond and allowing him to take a binding oath of loyalty to William. The tragi-comedy of errors that followed – MacIain's mistaken journey to Fort William, whose military commander was unable to accept the oath; his ride sixty miles south to take it before a sheriff at Inveraray; a delay of twenty-four hours when he was arrested en route; and the absence of the sheriff when he arrived – combined to make his submission five days late. In one sense, the delay had been caused by the tortuous decision-making processes of the exiled Jacobite court at St Germain-en-Laye. In another, he was the victim of the intricate politicking of Atholl, intent on destabilising Breadalbane's regime, and of his own kinsman, MacDonald of

Glengarry, who, until late in January, was the intended victim of the government's demonstration of force.[16]

The MacDonalds of Glencoe were an easier target than Glengarry, for any move against him would have entailed a siege of his formidably fortified house. Far from being a natural fortress set amidst impenetrable hills, Glencoe was a virtual death-trap within easy reach of Fort William. The clan had a bad reputation for thieving, even by Highland standards, but the reason Dalrymple of Stair fixed upon Clanranald as a whole was as 'the only popish clan in the kingdom and it will be popular to take severe course with them'.[17] Glengarry would have fitted the bill, as indeed had the MacDonalds on Eigg; not the least of Glencoe's many ironies is that its sept was probably episcopalian.[18] In west Highland history ever since, Glencoe has been assigned as a Campbell atrocity. Although the luckless Glenlyon was a Campbell, most of his troop were not, and he was himself under threat of being treated as a virtual traitor 'not true to King nor Government' if he did not carry out his last, most ruthless set of orders.[19] Amongst his various sets of orders there was a discrepancy that would subsequently prove fatal to the reputation of the Campbells: his immediate superiors had ordered him to move at 7a.m.; he moved at 5a.m., as instructed by Breadalbane. History has usually shuffled Breadalbane's order to the top of Glenlyon's file of orders and drawn its conclusions. The massacre from beginning to end was never quite what it seemed.

The product of a moderate Highland policy which went badly wrong, the massacre was an accurate mirror of the divisions and different lines of communications which existed within William's government and had indeed permeated every Stewart government throughout the century. Breadalbane represented a policy of encouraging civility, co-operation with the chiefs and attaching broken men to established clans; Dalrymple toyed with James VII's different notion of freeing clansmen from the domination of their chiefs but settled in 1692 for James VI's ruthless solution of 'rooting out' the most incorrigible clans, substituting MacDonalds for MacGregors as the symbol of barbarism. The effects of the massacre were complicated but to contemporaries seemed more clear-cut than they really were: the government had lost control of the Highlands; the always fragile balance between an understanding with the chiefs implying their acceptance of the regime and a government presence to enforce it was never more brittle than in the two decades after 1692. The seemingly conspicuous involvement of the Campbells in the massacre made the Clanranald family a hub of Jacobite activity, though now based in Uist rather than Lochaber.[20] And the official inquiry, which dragged on until 1695, again showed a government caught in two minds: political scandals are best covered up either by a whitewash or the sacrifice of a few scapegoats. The government dithered for over three years and eventually settled for both. By 1695, it had also to offer a diversion – which would, ironically, take on a life of its own. Between 1700 and 1702 the Darien affair would become the most contentious issue in Scottish politics.

Darien and the 'seven ill years'

The impetus behind the act of 1695 for a 'Company of Scotland tradeing to Affrica and the Indies' came from the court; the act itself was drafted by the Lord Advocate. Its origins lay with a more general act passed in 1693 'for Encouraging of Foreign

Trade', which extended to trading ventures the privileges already enjoyed by companies engaged in manufactures. Far from being an aberration, it needs to be seen as part of the rising expectations of government in the later seventeenth century; both the privy council and parliament had since the 1660s increasingly intervened directly in agriculture, industry and trade. A commission on manufactures had been established as long ago as 1623, and in 1661 members from each of the estates formed a council of trade empowered to regulate manufactures and found companies. The founding of a fisheries company in 1669, the abortive attempts to negotiate some form of economic union with England in 1668 and 1670, and a series of acts of parliament after 1663 culminating in explicitly protectionist legislation in 1681 'for encouraging Trade and Manufacturies' were all part of an increasingly specific economic policy. By 1681 mercantilism had developed an expansionary arm: it had been the approval by the privy council of a Scottish plantation 'in some place in America' which had led to the attempts to set up colonies in New Jersey in 1682 (which remained in being until 1702) and South Carolina in 1684 (which was destroyed by a Spanish force in 1686).[21] The act of 1695, which gave the new Company of Scotland extensive powers to found colonies and make treaties and promised the backing of the crown, was a sensible measure as well as a diversion from the Glencoe scandal.[22]

By 1697, largely through the single-minded enterprise of William Paterson, a London-based Scot who had made a fortune through trade with the West Indies, the Company had become committed to a high-risk but still secret scheme for the establishment of a colony at Darien, on the narrow isthmus of Panama, which was in Spanish territory. After English investment was withdrawn as a result of pressure put on the crown by the East India Company, the scheme was promoted in Scotland through an astonishing advertising campaign, which appealed to nationalist sentiment and religious xenophobia but also to hard-headed economics:

> This Company . . . is calculat for the general interest of Our Nation . . . Our Nobility and Gentry who are Landed Men will get their rents better paid and raised; out Tenants and Labouring people better employed . . . The Poor will hereby find Work and Food.[23]

The scheme for a national trading enterprise was promoted as a panacea to reinvigorate the whole of the nation's economy; those accustomed to the peddling of economic miracle cures in the twentieth century will more easily understand its appeal and less easily stand in judgement. It had the force of an evangelical appeal – but so would agricultural 'Improvement' in the 1720s. Perhaps a quarter of the total liquid assets of the country were sunk into the enterprise. The investors ranged from Queensberry, the leading courtier of the 1690s, to the Cameronian Alexander Shields, who would be one of the three clergymen who went on the second expedition to Darien; but the core of the investors lay amongst those practised financiers and merchants who had already backed the relaunched cloth manufactory at Newmills and helped found the Bank of Scotland in 1695.[24] The two expeditions to Darien were a disaster. Amongst the first expedition, which set sail in July 1698 fewer than one in four survived the hostile natives and fever-ridden swamps of 'New Caledonia'. A second relief expedition which left in September 1699 was refused provisions in the English colonies in the West Indies and eventually surrendered to Spanish troops in April 1700. The Company of Scotland had collapsed. The impact was more than financial; it would cause a grave political crisis.

The Darien scheme had been promoted amidst a serious economic crisis. The only severe harvest failure between 1660 and 1690 had been in 1674, but a poor harvest in 1695 was followed by a severe failure in the south in 1696, an indifferent harvest in 1697 and a general failure in 1698. The causes of this accumulating crisis were climactic and its economic effects were probably no worse than the much more regular subsistence crises which had marked one year in three in the second half of the sixteenth century, but its social and political impact was much greater. It was the last old-fashioned subsistence crisis,[25] but also the first to be widely publicised and analysed. Perhaps 5 per cent of the population starved to death, though in some localities, like Aberdeenshire, the mortality rate may have exceeded Fletcher of Saltoun's guess that one in five died. Perceptions of the crisis were heightened by the fact that agriculture had since 1660 steadily been improving crop yields to the point that food shortages were rare and grain prices stable. The coincidence of a continental war fought between England and France between 1689 and 1697 (and renewed in 1702) blighting Scotland's shrinking trade was further ammunition for pundits who began to talk in terms of an economic armageddon. In reality, the barrage of economic and social disasters of the 'seven ill years' of the 1690s were no more than a blip in an economy which was in a slow, piecemeal but notably steady state of transition towards more coherent organisation and greater productivity.[26] A series of small-scale improvements over the course of a century or more paved the way for 'Improvement' after 1740. Yet economic forecasters had never before been so conspicuous as in the 1690s, when they played a novel role in politics. It was no coincidence that fifteen of the twenty-five Articles of Union prepared in 1706 were concerned with economics.

The role of economic issues in the debate over the Union of 1706-7 is a highly contentious subject, but there can be little doubt that it was the aftermath of the Darien collapse, exacerbated by other loosely related economic issues, which brought about a political crisis in the last two years of William's reign and put union back on the political agenda. Darien was many things. It was a convenient stick for the Country opposition to use to beat the court. It was flexible for behind the aggrieved pockets of shareholders and the resentments of English double-dealing there lay a deeper issue of sovereignty – the compatibility of the separate imperial crowns of Scotland and England. It was a Trojan horse for other assaults on both the King's ministers and the revolution settlement. By 1702 the scene was set for a confrontation which bore a close resemblance to the later struggle over the Treaty of Union. William twice – in 1700 and 1702 – proposed a more complete union as a means to regain control of Scottish politics. With two exceptions,[27] the line-up of forces for and against the court was much the same in 1702 as 1706; already the strength of the opposition lay amongst the barons and the court's usual majority amongst the burgh members was wavering. Already too, in the 'addresses' designed by the opposition to circumvent the court's natural majority in parliament, there were signs of the extra-parliamentary tactics which the opposition would hold in reserve in 1706.[28] The wide-ranging grievances of the opposition were its great strength in 1702; yet already apparent was the fact that individual grievances could be bought off. The years 1702-3 were a dress-rehearsal for 1706-7, but with one significant difference; the actors and the parts they played were much the same, but the issues would change. *Plus ça change, plus c'est la même chose* – these were characteristics of the restless politics after the revolution.

Union debate (1702-7)

In 1702 perhaps only William and the beleaguered Queensberry administration in Scotland wanted union. Godolphin, Lord Treasurer and the key figure in the English ministry, who would be the architect of the successful Treaty and its passage in 1706-7, was indifferent to it and no group in an almost evenly divided English Commons was conspicuous in its enthusiasm for it. The death of William in March 1702 brought to the throne a genuine rather than a surrogate Stewart monarch, who was more acceptable to some shades of Scottish opinion, but also the first genuine unionist since James VI. This was, however, a very different kind of union, even if it was pursued with a very Stewart-like dogged resolution. Anne, who assured her first parliament that 'I know my heart to be entirely English', had spent only a few months in Scotland in 1681 as a girl of sixteen, had little knowledge of her Scottish subjects – an 'unreasonable' and 'strange people' – and less sympathy. Sir Thomas Craig, apologist for James VI's 'union of love' had talked of a need to bring together the affections of the King's two sets of subjects; Daniel Defoe, an undercover agent working for Anne's English government, would after the deed was done reflect that 'a firmer union of policy with less union of affection has hardly been known in the whole world'.[29] The Union of 1707 was conceived by *raison d'état* and, fittingly, it would produce a union of states rather than a meeting of minds.

It was the accession of Anne (1702-14) which brought to the surface the issue of sovereignty, which had loomed ever since 1701, when the English parliament had without consultation provided for an alternative succession after Anne's death if she (as was now virtually certain) died childless. The issue had different strands to it. The choice of the Lutheran Electress of Hanover, Sophia (who was descended from Elizabeth of Bohemia, a daughter of James VI),[30] excites much puzzlement to modern-day visitors to the wall leading to Linlithgow Palace on which this obscure royal thread is etched in stone. To contemporaries it raised a very clear choice – between the 'Pretender' as Anne called him, proclaimed 'James VIII and III' after his father's death in 1701, and the house of Hanover. The Act of Succession (1701) disputed the right asserted by the Scottish parliament in 1689 to decide the succession; revolution politics had, it seemed, been turned upside down. William's death brought out a further complication. Under the terms of an act of 1696, the Scottish parliament should have been called within twenty days of it. The parliament eventually met in June, after ninety days, during which time the Scottish privy council had by proclamation followed the English parliament into a renewed European war. This was the inflammatory background against which commissioners from both parliaments were nominated – in effect by the court – to negotiate an incorporating union. It was an odd set of negotiations which affected to ignore the key issues in Scottish politics but quickly collapsed at a different obstacle – the issue of compensation. This involved the new burdens of taxation which would affect Scotland in a union and the losses sustained by the Company of Scotland – what would in 1706-7 be encompassed within the ingenious device of the 'Equivalent'.[31] The awkward squad were not the Scots, who were represented only by Queensberry's mostly compliant nominees, but the English Tories.

In 1703 an event of great significance took place – or so it seemed at the time. An election produced a new map of Scottish politics, in which both the court and the Country party were the losers; the Jacobites (who now masqueraded under the name of Cavaliers) made significant gains, and a 'New party', under the leadership of Tweeddale, broke up the old cohesion of the Countrymen. Union, the failed product of the two old parliaments, now seemed further away than ever for in England the Whigs had been driven from office. This was the Scottish parliament which in the course of 1703 wrested control of the House from the court, passed the Act of Security – a specific riposte to the Act of Settlement – by a clear majority of fifty-nine votes in August, and in the Act anent Peace and War took decisive steps to prevent Scotland again being dragged into a foreign war by Anne's successor.

The parliamentary session of 1704 proved to be no less frustrating for Anne, her English ministers and the new Court party in Scotland, temporarily shorn of Queensberry and bolstered by the addition of Tweeddale and his New party. The new configuration of interests served only to push the prospect of union further away from the forefront of Scottish politics: Tweeddale's instructions were limited to gaining supply and securing the regal union by finding means to persuade the parliament to agree to the Hanoverian succession.[32] His failure marked the nadir of the court, reduced to a mere thirty bankable votes. By September 1705 a new ministry, organised by a new broom in the figure of the 2nd Duke of Argyll and a weathered relic of the 1690s in the shape of Queensberry, had managed to focus the Scottish parliament's attention on a scheme for an incorporating union that was little different from that presented in 1702.

The impetus came from England, where a new Whig ministry, galvanised by the events of 1703 into a conviction of the need for some decisive movement to break the deadlock in Anglo-Scottish relations, constructed the Alien Act in February 1705. The act, which threatened to treat all Scots (except those already domiciled in England) as aliens and to ban the main sectors of trade with England (cattle, linen and coal) brought union again to the forefront of politics but only as one possible alternative; the other possibility, which most Whigs privately favoured, remained a treaty. The reaction in Scotland was predictable and furious. Anti-English feeling boiled over on the unfortunate heads of the crew of the English merchant ship, the *Worcester*, which had been seized in the Firth of Forth in August 1704 by agents of the Company of Scotland; what began as a legal action to seize the cargo ended up in a squalid show trial accusing the master and some of the crew of piracy. The execution of Captain Green and two of his crew on 11 April 1705, with the Scottish privy council studiously looking the other way, marked the sordid end to what was otherwise a notably positive phase in Anglo-Scottish relations. By the end of the same month, Argyll, who had until now been carrying out his commissionership from a base in London, had arrived in Edinburgh.

Argyll's arrival signalled both a decisive opting for union rather than a treaty and the jettisoning of the New party, whose priorities were precisely opposite to his own. Cast off in the wilderness between the court and Country parties, Tweeddale and his group of thirty were dubbed the *Squadrone Volante* (Flying Squadron); their support for the court in 1706 would ironically be the factor which carried the union proposals. With Queensberry restored at Argyll's insistence, the ministry was now intent on 'ane entire union'.[33] Parliament's agreement to appoint a commission to negotiate a treaty of union needed one further dramatic development. Late in the evening of 1 September, the Duke of Hamilton, who had adopted the leadership of the Country party almost by default, stood up in the House to move that nomination of the commission should be left to the Queen herself; the ministry rushed through a division, which was carried by four votes. This stunning piece of sharp practice – even by the standards of the house of Hamilton – was what Lockhart of Carnwath dated as 'the commencement of Scotland's ruin'.[34] Hamilton's precise motives are obscure, but there can be little doubt that his action, which dished the Country party in the session of 1705, was the product of graft. The point sometimes made that the bribery of Scottish members was modest – amounting in total to less than £20,000 – and to be expected by the political conventions of the day is debatable, but it applies to the firmness of the court vote in 1706. The collusion of Hamilton in 1705 was a spectacular double-cross which made a Union Treaty possible. The full price paid for it is unknown; it is unlikely that he was content with the honours heaped on him after the Union of an English dukedom, the Orders of Thistle and Garter, and an appointment as ambassador to Paris. The most astonishing aspect of the scandal was that Hamilton kept his position as leader of the Country party and continued to play the popular anti-union card.[35]

The negotiations of the Articles of Union were conducted in an oddly contrived manner. Like rivals in a modern industrial dispute, the two sets of commissioners sat in separate rooms and communicated with each other only in writing. Within ten days of sitting down they had agreed on the outline shape of the Treaty; and within three months a complete set of twenty-five Articles had been agreed. The Treaty was itself a tribute to the extreme care which both ministries had invested in the project. Its passage through both parliaments would be no less carefully monitored. The Scottish parliament opened on 3 October 1706, but the opposition, which embarked on delaying tactics from the outset, succeeded in postponing serious consideration of the first of the Articles for a month. Article I (on the principle of incorporating union) was passed on 4 November by 116 votes to eighty-three, a majority of thirty-three. It was as near as the opposition ever came on a major clause. The majority had been less than the court had expected, and the ministry on the same day brought before the House a bill guaranteeing the presbyterian settlement of the Church, which was passed on 12 November. The Kirk was bought off, like any other interest group; it was a sign that it still had a powerful voice in Scottish life, but that its role in politics was now to sit on the sidelines. On 16 January 1707, the Treaty was ratified, with a majority of forty-three.

Details still remained to be tidied up, including representation in the new British parliament and the distribution of the Equivalent. The allocation of forty-five seats in the Commons on a basis of thirty to the shires and fifteen to the burghs caused numerous protests, but protest turned into outrage when the ministry revealed that the first members in the new parliament would be returned not by means of a fresh election but by nomination – in effect as clients of the ministry itself. The decision to establish a Commission for the Equivalent, answerable to the British parliament, to distribute the £398,085 10s sterling (which included £232,884 5s for reimbursement, with 5 per cent interest, to shareholders in the

Company of Scotland) seems quite proper, but it welched on a deal made with the *Squadrone* that it should oversee the compensation for Darien. Unpaid officers of state and judges, as a result, were given higher priority than aggrieved shareholders, many of whom had to wait years for settlement.

The Treaty received its ratification in the English parliament on 19 March, but only after an expertly guided passage by the court and the Whig Junto working in tandem in which the bill was driven through the all-important committee stage in the Commons at a single sitting. The Scottish parliament was adjourned six days later and formally dissolved by proclamation of the privy council on 28 April. The Treaty's passage through the Scottish parliament had taken ten weeks; it passed both English Houses in less than six. The main difference had not been in parliament, where in each case the opposition had been fragmented and lacking in leadership, but outside. In England, the debate was conducted against a background of popular celebrations; in Scotland, there were riots, protest meetings and petitions from a quarter of the shires and a third of the burghs – all of which were ignored. Later, one of the commissioners, Sir John Clerk, admitted that the Articles had been carried 'contrary to the inclinations of at least three-fourths of the Kingdom'.[36] The fact that the ministry was so keen to avoid elections in 1707 is an important indicator that anti-union feeling was not simply populist. The passage of the Treaty had been a spectacular demonstration of the ability of a determined court party to cajole, persuade and manufacture support for what was, at least in Scotland, an inherently unpopular and novel constitutional device.

Theses of the longer-term 'inevitability' of Union need to take account of the fact that it was only a striking coincidence of short-term political factors which made the passage of a union bill possible. By the autumn of 1705 it was feasible; by October 1706 it was probably inevitable, which was why the opposition resorted to delaying tactics from the outset of the session; but its passage was based on the historical logic only of the moment. In 1702 there had been no support in the English parliament for union; in 1704 circumstances had dictated a succession treaty rather than a union; in 1705 after the Alien Act the odds, in English eyes, still favoured a treaty; by the autumn of 1708, as the toll of the War of the Spanish Succession mounted, the position of the Whigs, architects of the parliamentary coup of 1707 and the war party, was already slipping and it is unlikely that they would have then risked controversial legislation. The passage of the bill took place in the eye of a storm where the unlikely became a *fait accompli*.

Great issues seldom make for great debate. The union debate was something of a disappointment, partly because the court party operated a virtual guillotine. The best-known of the opposition speeches, made by Lord Belhaven on 2 November, was an appeal to opinion outside the House rather than a serious effort to change minds within it; at once colourful and maudlin, it seems more like the speech of a man already condemned than one signalling the beginning of a tough parliamentary campaign. More importantly, whatever was said, the court vote hardly wavered. The breakdown of the first and last votes were significantly similar. With the two other Estates almost evenly split in November, the support of the nobles (consistently more than 2:1 for union) was the most crucial factor.[37] Hidden within the raw statistics are the seven *Squadrone* peers whose votes helped to make the first estate the only one to give a decisive answer in favour of union.[38]

The notable feature of the nobles' voting behaviour is that it hardly wavered before or after consideration of what would have seemed for them the critical Article XXIII, on representation of sixteen Scottish peers in the House of Lords; only three failed to follow party lines in either the first or last votes. Individual noble consciences, pockets and interests can all be scrutinised for most, as landowners, had economic motives pushing them towards union as well as specific inducements. The interests of northern nobles such as Sutherland and Cromartie in the grain trade complemented their support of the court but in other cases motives were more mixed. The economic interests of those, like Wemyss, who were involved in the salt and coal industries, pointed *against* unbridled free trade, but he was a consistent backer of the court.[39] Ultimately the business of individual motivation is a highly uncertain one, for the magnates were conservative politicians who handed from one generation to another the art of conflating private interest and public good. They were the most anglicised section of Scottish society, but this process had been fitful and uneven over the course of the previous century; only two Scots had received English peerages since 1660 – Lauderdale and the 2nd Duke of Argyll. Argyll, the supervisor of 1706-7, had an English mother, wife and title as well as a commission in what was as yet the only truly British institution – the army. But he, as yet, was an exception. The support of the nobles for the Treaty was predictable for it was riddled with concessions to the noble class: their local courts and heritable jurisdictions survived untouched; the intense localism which still underpinned noble power was perpetuated. The new British state seemed to offer old lordship and new patronage yoked together.[40]

The particular interests of the two other estates are not easily categorised. Despite two indisputable facts – by 1700 half of the Scottish export trade was taken up by the English market and exports to England halved between 1700 and 1704[41] – the Convention of Royal Burghs in 1706 was against the Treaty. It was not, however, against what it called 'an honourable and safe Union with England', a federal arrangement which would prevent the built-in English majority in a British parliament from acquiring an unshakeable grip over the Scottish economy. The economic issue was not wholly taken up with the issue of free trade. The narrowest votes in the whole Union debate and the stormiest scenes outside parliament both took place when the details of the 'Explanations' were at issue: what was at stake here were the interests of Scottish *consumers* agitated by the prospects of high taxes on ale, malt and salt.[42] Economic issues, considered as a whole, pointed in different directions and the fact that the burghs' vote was almost evenly split for and against union as a general principle reflected this.

The best-known quotation of the whole prolonged Union debate was made by Roxburgh, a member of the *Squadrone* in November 1705:

The motives will be, Trade with most, Hanover with some, ease and security with others, together with a generall aversion to civill discords, intollerable poverty and the constant oppression of a bad ministry.

Although already in a longer form than that usually offered to examination candidates as a convenient blunt instrument with which to hack their way through the jungle of conflicting motives in 1706-7, what Roxburgh went on to write in what was a private letter to another member of the *Squadrone* was no less significant:

Whatever the inconveniences on't may be, such as quitting a name and a

poor independent sovereignty to Scotland for a small share in a great one, and
degradation to the Scottish nobility . . . yet the risk or rather certainty of the
Prince of Wales, in case of the Union's failing, and the forenamed advantages
in case of its succeeding, have their weight.[43]

What had seemed at first sight to be clear contemporary evidence of the primacy
given by 'most' to free trade turns out to be nothing of the sort.[44] Economic motives,
in Roxburgh's view, were foremost amongst the mixed bag of reasons *for* union; the
single most compelling argument was, however, the one *against* the continuance of
the status quo. Other contemporaries concurred, including Clerk who would later
describe Union as 'the best expedient to preserve the honour and liberties of
Scotland' from the threat of English invasion which would inevitably have resulted
if Union was rejected.[45]

The debate in 1705, in a pamphlet war between Scottish and English
propagandists, was not about economics but about sovereignty: the central theme,
arcane as it may seem to modern-day eyes, was that of imperial crowns and the
various possibilities of federal union.[46] This in turn probably reflected a debate
which had been taking place at various levels ever since the death of William of
Gloucester in 1700. A speech made to the electors of Berwickshire in November
1702 by John Spottiswoode is probably typical of the debate going on in the shire
communities between 1702 and 1707. The core of it was a defence of the imperial
crown of Scotland, which had been 'governed by 112 Kings and Queens of the same
royal blood these 2,000 years and upwards, which no nation under heaven can boast
of'. The specific tactic suggested – of seeking to convert the fourteen-year-old
Prince of Wales while he remained in the pious hands of his mother Maria Beatrice
who was busy counting the miracles needed to groom James VII for canonisation[47] –
was far fetched. Yet the long and widely accepted political tradition which lay
behind the notion of the ancient Scottish constitution should not be so lightly
dismissed. It was, of course, mythology, but no more so than the modern notion of
the House of Commons as 'mother of parliaments' and no less seductive. What was
unique about the situation from 1700 onwards was that it was at bottom a crisis of
the Stewart succession. In that sense, the complicated web of issues for and against
union, often too complex or tangled to result in clear-cut interests, could be refined
into a more straightforward choice. Political management, bribery and sweeteners
all oiled the processes of decision-making, but the need to make a decision at all
depended on the threat of English invasion and English intransigence, which in
1706 rejected all forms of association other than full incorporating union.

Perspectives of union

A political union, no less than a revolution, must have longer-term and medium-
term causes as well as enabling triggers. The delineation of long-term historical
processes is a highly subjective business, even in the seemingly rigorous world of the
economic historian. Over the course of the seventeenth century there was
undoubtedly a drift of trade towards England; it was probably more marked in the
period before 1640 than is usually thought because there were not regular or reliable
customs books for overland trade, but coastal trade did sharply increase after the
1670s. One indicator of the growing importance of this sector of the economy is the
series of efforts made by the Scots to secure some kind of free trade: initiatives came

from them in 1640, 1659, 1668, 1670 and 1689.[48] The fact that there were risks as well as attractions involved in free trade was reflected in the less than clear-cut divisions of the burghs in 1706-7. Some burghs, such as Montrose which was highly dependent on its linen trade, did see the economic issues in clear and stark terms: 'one needs not the gift of prophecy to foretell what shall be the fate of this poor miserable, blinded nation in a few years', it declared.[49] Others, including Edinburgh and Glasgow, were never so sure. As with most other issues, the economic arguments did not point in a single direction. In the 1702-3 negotiations the carrot of free trade probably loomed larger than it did in 1706-7, when the interests of other sectors of the economy came to the surface in the 'Explanations'. And if history had taken a different turning and the vote in the House of Lords in 1713 for dissolving the Union had not fallen (by a mere four votes), a different set of long-term economic explanations, stressing the steady 'improvement' of Scottish agriculture since 1625 rather than the 'underdeveloped' nature of the Scottish economy in 1707, could well be assembled by historians.

In broader terms, the Union of 1707 has been described as the completion of three separate long- or medium-term historical processes:

It marked only a stage, though certainly an important one, in the story of Scotland's absorption into a wider Britain. . . . In a seventeenth-century context, the treaty of 1707 was also only the second half of the Union of 1603, the capstone to a process of constitutional amalgamation. . . . In another sense it was the logical conclusion of 1689, when the nobles of England and Scotland . . . had shown how a British identity of interests could exist outside the personal interests of the monarch.[50]

There is truth and truism in each of these observations, but half-truth as well. The only hint of a broader British identity of interests in 1689 had come from the Scottish parliament which suggested a 'union of parliaments and trade'. The point to realise is that the Scots had offered some such union in 1606 and 1641; 1689 would be the last time they did so. The constitutional safeguards demanded of William in 1689-90 were framed as the Scottish solution to what was perceived as a distinctively Scottish problem and, as a result, the two countries were set on different political courses throughout the 1690s, which meant that they were probably further apart by 1700 than at any point since 1660. The Union of 1707 completed the regal union of 1603 only in a very limited sense. The most determined unionists in both 1603 and 1707, it is true, were the monarchs themselves, but the amalgamation of the two imperial crowns in 1707 was a reflection of how much monarchy itself had changed over the course of the century. The Union of 1603 had been grounded on the royal prerogative; the Treaty of 1706-7 made no mention of the prerogative. Constitutionally, very little was amalgamated in 1707, for the Treaty had scarcely anything to say about the governing of Scotland. That amalgamation would take place, but as part of the creeping frontier of unionism set in train *after* 1707; by May 1708 the hidden agenda had already claimed the scalp of the Scottish privy council.

The absorption of Scotland into a greater Britain had been going on for centuries, but it was a historical process involving a number of different vehicles, each moving at a different pace and sometimes blocking the path of the others. The eventual Union produced the largest free-trade area in eighteenth-century Europe.[51]

It was a truly remarkable achievement, not least because it went against the trends of the later seventeenth century, when tariff barriers rose and the habits of mercantilism became more ingrained. Economic union had (with the brief exception of the period of the Cromwellian union) seemed to be have been growing less rather than more likely as a result; it came about as a result of an abrupt change of direction by English vested interests in 1705. Otherwise, the story of the 150 years before 1707 is not one of absorption but of a series of trial marriages, most of which failed.

Union reflected the areas in which the two countries had grown apart since 1560. As Scots law began to be codified in the later sixteenth century and reshaped as a philosophical entity in the last quarter of the seventeenth, the distinctions between it and English common law grew more marked. The main intellectual influence on Scots lawyers throughout the seventeenth century came not from England but from the Netherlands. But nowhere were the growing differences between the two countries more marked than in religion. Twice the Scots had offered religious amity: in the clauses of the Treaty of Berwick of 1560 and in the Solemn League and Covenant of 1643. Closely allied to this was a genuinely British nationalism, which had been on offer, albeit briefly in 1560, and again in 1606-7 and in the early 1640s when Scots (but not the English) could talk of themselves as 'British subjects'.[52] Neither religious union nor a genuine British nation was being mooted in 1706. The solution offered was a secularised British state. Its full nature was not as yet worked out, nor would it be until after the 1745 rising. Both the novelty and the half-baked appearance of the proto-British state led many in 1707 to believe that they had embarked only on an experiment which might well be reversed. The most inevitable aspect of 1707 was not the fact that it happened; it was rather that the new British state would not remain as the prototype it then was.

19

Union Settlement and Jacobite Risings

THE UNION OF THE TWO PARLIAMENTS CAME FORMALLY INTO BEING ON 1 MAY 1707. Plans to sabotage the passage in January of the final Articles by a resort to extra-parliamentary action had come to nothing; the Duke of Hamilton, leader of the opposition, had again failed to meet his appointment with history, this time owing to a toothache. The words of the Earl of Seafield, chancellor of Scotland, after he signed the engrossed Act of Union are well known: 'There's ane end of ane auld sang', but a new verse of it was already being written. The period of good government Seafield expected to result, with the threat of English military invasion removed and politics now free of the endemic friction between court and opposition which had marked the years since the Convention parliament of 1689-90, had not materialised by 1713, when he proposed a bill in the House of Lords to dissolve the Union.[1] Another of the leading architects of 1707 was the Earl of Mar, who, in 1715, would lead a rising against the new Hanoverian regime – into a morass of indecision and confusion. His nemesis would come at the battle of Sheriffmuir in September 1715, when his much-superior forces were forced into a stalemate by those of the third vital agent of Union in 1707, the Duke of Argyll. Yet Argyll, too, would eventually find only disappointment and disillusionment in the promised land of British politics, becoming a thorn in the side of the London administration for the last dozen years of his life until his death in 1743.

If the years before 1707 were the story of different roads to Union, those after 1707 were for many a conundrum: of how best to seek accommodation within it or an escape route from it. The effect of Union was to muddy the waters of the clear choice which had seemed to exist after 1701 between a Jacobite and a Hanoverian succession. For most, whether amongst the Highland so-called 'loyal clans' or the Lowland nobility, support for one or other was marginal and calculated, a matter of expedient judgement rather than outright principle. The prime difficulty in assessing the strength of support for Jacobitism is that the arithmetic of these calculations fluctuated wildly over the course of the four decades between the first and last of the Jacobite plots, in 1708 and 1745-6.

The security of the Union was threatened even before the new British parliament sat for the first time, in December 1707. Further riots in Glasgow, an abortive rebellion in the Cameronian south-west, a stir in northern Ayrshire and the raising of the Highlanders of the presbyterian Duke of Atholl were all in the air in the spring of 1707.[2] The double game, which would be played out in the court of Versailles and in the minds of Lowland nobles and Highland chiefs over the course of the next forty years, was already in progress: French support was contingent on firm indications of a well-supported rising in Scotland; Scottish commitment depended on specific guarantees of military aid from France. It was a game of poker with its own unusual rules: the higher the opening bid, the less likely was the player to take part in it. Hamilton's opener in 1708, the demand of 15,000 French troops as the price of his support, was as good an indicator of his lack of interest as his later flight to his Lancashire estates to sit out the expected invasion. Yet in 1707 most among the two sets of players were new to this game of blind bids and double-bluff and they may even have believed each other.

On the promise of an army of 25,000 foot and 5,000 horse waiting for it in Scotland, a French squadron set sail from Dunkirk on 6 March 1708, with the Pretender on board. By the 13th it had reached the East Neuk of Fife. There was, however, no landing there or on the coast of the Moray Firth, to where the squadron escaped after encountering the Royal Navy ships of Sir George Byng at the mouth of the Firth of Forth. By the 15th, in the face of high winds and heavy seas, the *enterprise d'Écosse* was abandoned. It was the most short-lived of all the Jacobite plots, but its prospects of success are not wholly to be judged by the luxury of hindsight. Even supporters of the Union admitted that more than three-quarters of the Scottish people disliked it. The arrest of scores of Scottish notables, including a duke and eight earls, after its collapse and their transportation to London 'like hoggs to market' indicated both the breadth of the conspiracy and the extreme nervousness of the London government. The news that a French squadron had slipped out of Dunkirk had been enough to provoke a run on the Bank of England, as the planners of the enterprise had expected. The limits of its ambition were set on the sixty-mile march from the Border to the coal pits of Newcastle rather than the long march to London; the British capital, it was planned, would be frozen into submission rather than assaulted outright.[3] The 1708 plot marked both the beginning of a new Jacobite age and the last prospect of a Jacobite coalition across all the many boundaries which divided post-Union society. The rising in 1715 would be broad-based and involve Lowlands as well as Highlands, but there was no hint then or later of involvement in it by the radical south-west or by committed presbyterian opinion. Already, in its first rising, Jacobitism had shed one of its many skins. By 1745, in its last rising, a different Jacobite configuration would mount the last invasion of England from Scotland and trigger the last Scottish civil war.

'Compleating the Union'

In the Queen's speech to the first session of the new British parliament in December 1707 the intention was already announced of 'rendering the Union more complete', and the phrase 'compleating the Union' was often heard in the remaining circles of power in Edinburgh over the course of the next twenty years.[4] Yet different nuances were meant by London ministers and Edinburgh administrators and lawyers. Ironically, much of the post-Union settlement was unexpected and unpalatable, as much to the ministry in power at Westminster as to various sections of opinion in Scotland. The first casualty of the post-Union settlement was the Scottish privy council, the main instrument of absentee government for the past century. Its abolition was not planned by Godolphin's ministry or Queen Anne, who both wanted it to remain in being, but by the *Squadrone*, who saw it as the instrument of an enlarged court party and successfully appealed to dissidents in the Commons.[5] The effect of its unexpected demise was multifold. Without an agency in Edinburgh to secure the loyalty of individual clan chiefs and without the military arm of the Independent or Highland Companies, which were disbanded in 1717, the Union regime was until the mid-1730s in less control of the Highlands than any government since the late sixteenth century. New channels of communication had to be formed to allow British patronage to pass along them, but until the maturing of a system nurtured by the partnership of Islay, based in London, and his *sous-ministre* Milton in Edinburgh, after 1725, contact was casual, intermittent and unsettled. Without a privy council, the court party under Queensberry which had smoothed the passage of the Act of Union found itself suddenly vulnerable to a new volatility in post-Union politics.

The Union did not bring job security for the holders of the main posts involved in the governing of Scotland. In 1707 there were two Secretaries of State in Scotland; by May 1708 Loudoun had retired and Mar was dismissed early in 1709. At that point a new kind of administration emerged: a new post, of Third Secretary 'for Great Britain' was created, which went to Queensberry, but its powers of patronage were limited since it did not have responsibility for the appointment of officers to the revenue, army or navy; the office itself was fickle, its status shifting with each new incumbent and it would disappear altogether between 1725 and 1742. The Third Secretary was not guaranteed a seat in the new Privy Council of Great Britain, although another courtier, Roxburghe, had been appointed to it in 1708. Real decisions, however, were made not there but in the smaller Cabinet, where Scots were unrepresented and Scottish business usually ignored. Queensberry held the office of Third Secretary until his death in 1711, when it became defunct. Mar, who was far more a creature of the London ministry than the magnate Queensberry, was given the office when it was revived in 1713, but only as Harley's branch manager for Scotland; he lasted barely a year. By September 1714 it was held by a member of the *Squadrone*, Montrose, who was forced out in the growing crisis induced by the Jacobite rising led by his predecessor.

It is a familiar story of unstable one-party states, but it was not the stable British system which the Scottish court party expected and the *Squadrone* feared would result from Union. It emerged because the Union resulted not in a new British politics, which as yet scarcely existed, but in the merging of Scottish politics into English, where they understandably came well down the list of priorities. English attention was focused on Scotland only at occasional points of crisis, such as in 1708, 1713 (when Harley's attempt to take more direct control of Scottish affairs began to break down), 1715 and 1725 (after widespread riots against the new Malt Tax). It was in this confusing kaleidoscope of English party politics before the emergence of Walpole's system after 1721 that the details of the Union settlement were forged.[6]

The 1708 insurrection produced a collective panic at Westminister, which was heightened by the parade of Scottish notables brought to justice in London. Briefly there was talk at Westminster of forcing Highland chiefs into a new obedience to government but that took another forty years and two major Jacobite risings to materialise. The only action taken was the extension into Scotland in 1709 of the more comprehensive English law of treason, which for the first time united the disparate elements of Scottish opinion in the Commons into opposition.[7] The Greenshields case, which in 1711 established a right of appeal in civil cases from the Court of Session in Edinburgh to the House of Lords at Westminster, was the second significant taste for the Scots of the sub-plot written into the crucial Article XIX of the Treaty of Union, which had guaranteed the continuance of Scots law and all Scottish courts, but subject to alterations 'for the better administration of justice as shall be made by the parliament of Great Britain'. This would be the distinctly odd compromise which piecemeal bridged the gap within a British state which lacked a unitary legal system; thus the House of Lords was in the 1830s the deciding forum of the test case over the rights of patronage which would eventually explode in the Disruption of 1843. In 1711, another religious test case – of an episcopalian minister (Greenshields) prosecuted by the presbyterian church courts for using an Anglican prayer book – was settled, but on strict party lines, in the House of Lords. That chamber became the last refuge of the Scottish scoundrel intent on litigation as well as one of the symbols of a largely English system which governed Scotland, as and when necessary, in virtually complete ignorance of it: it was the Lord Chancellor, Erskine, who said in 1806 that 'I know something of the law but of Scotch law I am as ignorant as a native of Mexico'.[8]

The creeping frontier of unionism affected the other Scottish institution which seemed to have had its position guaranteed in 1707 – the Kirk. Presbyterianism had been suspicious of Union and remained so, despite the specific guarantees embodied in the act of 1706. The Greenshields case had on appeal, in effect, invited English Tories to adjudicate on the limits of the discipline of the Church of Scotland. The passing in 1712 of the Toleration Act, which allowed freedom of worship to episcopalians willing to pray for the reigning monarch, was for the Kirk a new kind of indulgence policy, forced on Scotland by a British parliament rather than (as in the 1680s) by an absentee monarch. The third blow to the Kirk – and the third Erastian stab in its back – was the Patronage Act, which came a month later; it was the most grievous for it seemed to reverse the abolition of patronage achieved in 1690. This was, in a sense, the root cause of the series of splits and secessions which afflicted the Church of Scotland over the next 130 years.[9] Ecclesiastical politics was, however, incapable of such an uncomplicated clash of principles: in practice the Act of 1712 was a blow to the rights of kirk sessions and congregations, which were deprived of an active role in the selection of ministers, but it was also a loss inflicted on many heritors who had in 1690 been reserved an important role in local leadership in concert with the session. Effective power had now been passed to noble patrons or to the crown itself, which enjoyed control over a third of the charges in the country. The issue provoked by the 1712 Act was not a starkly simple one of the rights of the 'people' against those of patrons for only the radicals in the Church favoured anything like congregational democracy; it was rather about the breadth of the landed interest which might be expected to work hand in hand with lay elders of kirk sessions and ministers whose power lay in the presbyteries. For most, the issue was not outright principle but working practice.[10]

The consequences of the Patronage Act were considerable. It provoked two major controversies in the Church of Scotland in the 1720s and 1730s – each as obscure as it was bitter. The first arose in 1722, when the General Assembly mounted an inquiry into the beliefs of twelve ministers who had been influenced in their interpretation of the covenant of grace by the re-publication in 1718 of an obscure, highly derivative English work of the 1640s, The Marrow of Modern Divinity. It was an unlikely cause célèbre. The Marrow Brethren (later dubbed the Marrowmen) were never actually tried before the Assembly itself. Nor, when cross-examined by a sub-committee of the Assembly, did they offer much real testimony

321

as to their beliefs; the 'daft praying people', as their opponents slandered them, chose instead to parrot paraphrases of the Westminster Confession and Cathechisms in lieu of answer. It was not so much a dialogue of the deaf as a debate of the dumb. The events of 1722 left a legacy of bitterness which lasted throughout the 1720s as local church courts purged real or imagined Marrow beliefs. The real significance of the controversy was not as a round in the recurrent debate over predestination within the reformed tradition, but as an example of the muddle and fear which characterised the politics of the post-Union Church. The Marrowmen claimed to represent the true reformed tradition, but they belonged to an amorphous Evangelical party which had diverse origins and little real influence. Few in the mainstream of the Assembly had read the book, fewer still had heard the Marrow Brethren preach. Most were nevertheless driven by fear of schism and caught on the horns of a dilemma of their own making; absolving these 'hot brethren' would involve calling doubt on the authority of the Assembly itself, which had in 1720 condemned the book.[11]

The second serious dispute, which came in 1732, was more directly concerned with the issue of Erastianism but it had much the same effect of driving out of the Church (and out of contention) an evangelical splinter group, led by Ebenezer Erskine, minister of Stirling. Erskine's protest was partly about the mechanics of patronage, but it was also about the unscrupulous tactics used by the court interest, largely exercised through the royal commissioner to the General Assembly and a team of influential 'moderate' churchmen. The Church, like other institutions in Scottish society, had by the 1720s become part of one or other of the rival webs of patronage run by the court and the *Squadrone*. It was symptomatic of the victory of the court interest that by mid-century the supporters of patronage would be called 'Moderates'. It is equally revealing of how far the ground of ecclesiastical politics had shifted – and the extent to which radical opinion had been marginalised or forced out – that by then the 'Popular' party would be the faction which favoured the rights, not of congregations, but of heritors and elders. Post-Union ecclesiastical politics, like wider secular politics, was a struggle for respectability rather than principle.[12]

The section of Scottish society which had been firmest in its support for the Union Treaty had been the nobles. Guaranteed sixteen seats in the House of Lords as representative peers, they had expected more under the guise of British peers. The Duke of Hamilton, though he had various honours heaped upon him after 1707, failed in his attempt in 1711 to secure a seat as Duke of Brandon. The obstacles placed in his path were party political rather than principled, but they added another anomaly to a Union which, it seemed, was being drawn up as the politics of the moment dictated.[13] The Union which resulted is hard to describe for its foundations lay deep in the expedience of English party politics, but it was harder still for many to support with any enthusiasm. In 1711, during the peerage controversy, Mar had complained to his master, Harley (by then Earl of Oxford) that although he himself was 'not yet wearrie of the Union', it was difficult to see, how without further concessions 'What Scotsman will not be wearie of the Union, and do all he can to get quit of it'.[14] It was when the government tried in 1713 to extend the duty on malt to Scotland at the English rate (in explicit defiance of the Treaty of 1707) that the first gesture of secession came and, not surprisingly, it was the peers who made it. A motion to dissolve the Union was put before the Lords; the division ended in a tie but when the proxies were counted it failed by four votes.

The benefits of Union

The Lords' motion of 1713, which had been proposed by Seafield, one of the architects of 1707, may have been only a parliamentary gesture,[15] part of the Westminster game of charades, but it is significant that the moment chosen was adjacent to an economic issue. The Union would ultimately succeed on the basis of economics; but initially it almost foundered for the same reasons. Few historians would dispute that tangible economic benefits did not materialise before the 1740s, and even then they came only in specific sectors of the economy, such as linen, coarse woollen cloth and black cattle. Discussion of the long-term effects of Union – whether or not it was instrumental in encouraging a spirit of Scottish enterprise or the extent to which economic growth after 1780 was laid on the foundations of 1707 – needs to be strictly separated from any analysis of a balance-sheet of benefits and losses. That is a largely artificial exercise which is ultimately subjective rather than scientific, and tends to reveal more about the writer's preconceptions than historical evidence. The more economic historians have discovered about the various sectors of the eighteenth-century economy, the more untidy (and plausible) the answers have become: 'Olympian pronouncements' about the economic effects of the Union have gone out of fashion.[16] It will be a brave historian who tries to return to the simpler world when they were in vogue.

The more limited the questions about the economic effects of 1707, the firmer the answers are likely to be. The free trade area which opened up after 1707 brought prosperity only to a few Scots. The most obvious symbol of economic success in post-Union Britain were the Glasgow tobacco lords, who by the 1750s controlled almost half of all Scotland's imports; yet the tobacco trade until the mid-1720s grew not through the new opportunities offered by free trade but through the long-honed skills of Scottish merchants of carrying on an illicit trade evading customs regulations.[17] The enterprising Scot in the 1707 generation was often the smuggler or black marketeer. The worst forecasts of the swamping of Scottish manufactures after 1707 did not happen but such industries found at best only sluggish demand for their products in the new English market, both domestic and colonial. In the most important sector of the Scottish economy, in which eight or nine out of every ten Scots were still employed – in agriculture – the effects of Union were marginal.[18]

The point which impressed itself upon contemporaries was a simpler one: the first years of Union brought new taxes but no new concessions, and it exposed vulnerable industries such as paper-making and woollen cloth manufacture to the chill wind of English competition. In 1711 new duties were imposed on exported linen and salt, in 1713 came the first extension of duties on malt, and in 1715 printed linens were also subjected to duty.[19] The real effects of each of these measures could be and have been debated at length – the linen industry was forced into a shake-out of its practices and quality control which by the 1740s was beginning to yield worthwhile results; the decline in export of salt and an increasing reliance on domestic demand were both patterns which had begun before 1707. A few sectors of the Scottish economy – the export of grain and oatmeal and perhaps too the droving of cattle over the Border, though still from Galloway and Lothian rather than the

Highlands – actually improved sharply in the years immediately following the Union, but this was again at best a continuation of existing trends rather than a new-found prosperity.[20] Union, because of its very unpopularity in Scotland, had in 1706-7 to promise more than it could deliver. The detailed economic concessions in the Articles were designed to assuage special interests, but the focusing of much of the debate in the Scottish parliament on the 'Explanations' was unexpected and it was a harbinger of the more generally felt economic frustrations which for more than a generation after 1707 haunted the Union settlement. Two unflattering images of the post-Union Scot were already born in the mind of London governments – the Scot on the make, usually in London, and the whingeing ingrate, already caricatured by cartoonists as 'Sister Peg' or 'Sorley'. Whether fully justified or not, the disparagement persisted and by the mid-century would reach its mature form. One image was encapsulated in Dr Johson's words of 1763: 'The noblest prospect which a Scotchman ever sees is the high road to England!' The other was given fresh life in a new English patriotism, part of which was a popular song composed in 1745, 'God save the King!'[21]

The first foundations of Union were created not by economic benefits but by political patronage. After 1707 a series of boards or commissions were quickly set up in Edinburgh – the Scottish Court of Exchequer, which administered income and taxes and paid the Civil List; and the Board of Excise and the Board of Customs, which had the task of implementing the new English-style revenue system. Later came the ill-defined Board of Police, set up in 1714 to take over some of the functions of the defunct privy council, and the Commissioners and Trustees for Improving Fisheries and Manufactures in Scotland (usually known as the Board of Trustees), set up in 1727 to encourage economic development.[22] Each of these boards provided the essential lubricant of post-Union politics – jobs.

Until 1725, with a succession of short-lived secretaries, the essential pattern of politics was slow to emerge. From then until 1761 (with a brief interlude in the mid-1740s) the colossus of Scottish politics was Archibald Campbell, Earl of Islay, who succeeded his brother as 3rd Duke of Argyll in 1743. Born in Surrey, educated at Eton (though later at Glasgow University and Utrecht), Islay was a maze of personal contradictions: one-half of a pair of brothers who dominated Scottish politics for almost twenty years although they were hardly on speaking terms; a Scottish politician who developed a reputation as a wily Gael and had ambitious schemes for modernising the Highlands but who did not visit Inveraray for over three decades after 1715; an English politician dependent on his reputation for managing the Scots but able to avoid the 'taint' of being Scotch; the most effective manager of Scottish politics before Henry Dundas but a politician who never held the office of secretary. If Islay was the uncrowned ruler of Scotland who operated from a base in London – the much-quoted description of him by George II in 1746 as 'Vice Roy in Scotland' was not intended as a compliment – his chief executive or *sous-ministre* was Andrew Fletcher, Lord Milton (1692-1766). Milton was the nephew of the anti-Union propagandist of the same name, an advocate who had found employment in the Board of Excise but suddenly rose to prominence under the patronage of Islay – a Lord of Session at the age of thirty-two and Lord Justice Clerk by 1734. Two-thirds of the Scottish bench appointed between 1724 and 1740, like Milton, owed their advancement to Islay. The majority of the Customs

Commissioners were Islay's clients. The tentacles of the Islay/Milton network extended into the old-established institutions such as the Convention of Royal Burghs, the Edinburgh Town Council and the General Assembly as well as into all the new post-Union boards and commissions.[23]

Islay had first been dispatched into Scottish politics to deal with an emergency. The new malt duties of 1713 had not been implemented. Their revival by Walpole in 1725 had brought widepread protest in a number of Scottish towns, a brewers' strike in Edinburgh and a serious riot in Glasgow, where the imposing new house of Daniel Campbell of Shawfield, MP for the Glasgow Burghs, a staunch Unionist and one of the earliest tobacco lords, was attacked and looted.[24] This unlikely crisis was a turning-point in the post-Union governing of Scotland: it brought about the downfall of the *Squadrone*, which was suspected of sympathies with the rioters, the demise of the office of third secretary and the end of the see-sawing politics which had marked the whole period since 1707. Islay, in his capacity as Lord Justice General, was sent to Scotland to make sure that justice was seen to be done and had the Glasgow magistrates brought to trial for dereliction of their duty. Yet it would be an exaggeration to say that Islay after 1725 substituted strong government for weak. What happened was that Walpole's administration abandoned the notion that Scottish ministries should reflect even the limited range of Scottish opinion represented at Westminster.

After 1725 consensus politics, which had produced eighteen years of mixed ministries and a high rate of accidents in ministerial careers, were abandoned in favour of conviction politics, based less on definable political principles as to the governing of Scotland than outright loyalty to the Walpole regime, which rarely had any thoughts about Scotland at all. The emergence of the Board of Trustees, which some historians have seen as the most positive force for economic development in post-Union Scotland, came about as a direct result of the disturbances of 1725.[25] Its foundation in 1727 was symptomatic of the function of management in what was still a highly volatile society: London was interested in Scotland only when it proved troublesome. The function of Islay and Milton as managers was to smooth troubled waters, but otherwise they seldom initiated policy. The difference between the managers who ran Scottish affairs in the 1720s and the privy council which had taken the initiative in making policy during James VI's 'pen government' just a century earlier was symptomatic of how much Scottish politics had become subsumed into English after 1707. Only nine acts relating to Scotland were passed by the London parliament in the period 1727-45 and two of those related to the Board of Trustees. Scotland was run by managers, who were expected to keep Scottish MPs and peers in line in the lobbies and to hold Scotland itself quiet; ministers who would represent Scottish interests at the various levels of government in London were troublesome creatures, as the events of 1707-25 had shown.[26] The balance between these two working principles for the governing of Scotland is one that affects all administrations from 1707 until the 1990s, but seldom has the balance been swung so heavily towards management as in the Islay/Milton years.

The fact that English ministers were so seldom interested in using the power which they had over Scotland and were so reliant on managers as a buffer resulted, the optimists have thought, in 'a state of semi-independence';[27] the Scots at least ran their own branch of the spoils system. Others, more pessimistic, might well conclude from the same evidence that Scotland was, if not quite a provincial colony, certainly a satellite state. What is incontrovertible is that, even after sixteen years of Islay in power, Scottish politics were still unsettled in the 1740s. At the root of the problem was the nature of the Union itself – a quasi-union at best, still afflicted by ambiguities and the vagaries of English party politics. In the election of 1741, there was a substantial shift away from the Walpole administration but it was strongest in what was supposed to have been one of its most reliable fiefdoms. Islay and Milton failed to deliver a pro-Walpole majority amongst the Scottish MPs; before 1741 they had controlled thirty of the forty-five seats, after 1741 they held only nineteen. As a result, the office of secretary returned and Scotland was in 1745 controlled by a *Squadrone* administration headed by Tweeddale. The Islay nexus was restored only in 1746, when it was unable to control the flood of legislative retribution in the aftermath of the last Jacobite rising. A real stability developed probably only in the mid-1750s. A 'compleat' Union settlement was a long time in coming.

The rising of 1715

The death of Queen Anne in August 1714 left Scottish politics in a confusing and self-contradictory state. Just before her death, the fevered struggle for power within the Tory ministry between Oxford and Bolingbroke had provoked Oxford's resignation. Like many other issues, the politics of the succession had been dragged into this struggle; Bolingbroke had been flirting for some time with the prospect of the succession of the Pretender, but Oxford had chosen the summer of 1714 as the moment to play the anti-Jacobite card, devising a proclamation offering a reward of £5,000 for the capture of the Pretender if he landed in Britain. The demise of Oxford threw into jeopardy his 'Scottish system', which operated through the Treasury and the Earl of Mar as Third Secretary.[28] The unexpected appointment by Anne on her death-bed of the Whig politician Shrewsbury to replace Oxford at the Treasury left Mar, the governing of Scotland and Bolingbroke's Jacobite connection (of which Mar had been innocent) each in a separate state of limbo.

The arrival of George I in September was the cue for a revolution in the King's administration, in which Bolingbroke, Oxford and Mar all lost office and face. By mid-1715 Harley was in a political wilderness, Bolingbroke was in France intriguing with Jacobites, and Mar was brooding over his very public snub by George. In Scotland, the administration was put in the hands of a coalition of the *Squadrone* led by Montrose as secretary and the Argyll interest with the Duke as Commander-in-Chief in Scotland; place and profit were carefully shared out between them in both major and minor offices but they remained at each other's throats. Yet there did seem to be activity as well as intrigue. A new Commission of Police was set up in December 1714 and the dissolution of the parliament in January 1715 had been followed by an election in which Mar and his friends had been swamped in the struggle between the *Squadrone* and the Argyll interest, known as the 'Argathelians'. The new secretary had 'delivered' Scotland for the Whigs, to the extent of forty out of the forty-five seats in the Commons. The situation amongst the representative peers was no less decisive; Mar had not even bothered to stand for election.[29]

The crushing victory in the election of 1715 illustrated the near-total eclipse of anything that fell short of a committed Whig position in 'official' politics but it also revealed the yawning gulf between 'British' politics and Scottish opinion. In Inverness, the reading of the proclamation of George as King by a representative of the Sheriff-Depute at the market cross was barracked by the burgh magistrates; official cries of 'God save the King' were drowned out by shouts of 'God damn them and their King'.[30] The extreme nervousness of the Scottish adminstration had been fuelled for over twelve months before the actual rising by rumours of war with France, the imminent landing of the Chevalier and mysterious meetings of clans in the Highlands. In August 1714, when news of Anne's death reached Edinburgh, the Castle garrison took it upon itself to dismantle the bridge, construct a drawbridge and dig a large trench around the eastern part of the walls.[31] It was a symbolic gesture of a beleaguered regime. In August and September 1715, 261 JPs (almost one in five) were dismissed for suspected Jacobite sympathies and 198 new appointments made. If this was a purge it was far from comprehensive, as events would prove; after the rising 77 per cent of the JPs in Kincardine were dismissed, 54 per cent of those in Forfarshire, a half of those in Inverness-shire, and three in ten of those in Aberdeenshire.[32] The extent of the disaffection from the Hanoverian regime in 1714-15 was almost incalculable – for the government at the time as well as for historians since. It suggests a need to look more carefully at the situation in Scotland on the eve of a rebellion which was expected by almost every one and which many thought would succeed.

The reign of Anne had still been a time when, despite the Act of Succession naming the House of Hanover, nothing was guaranteed. Queen Anne had been in touch about the succession with the half-brother she in public stigmatised as the Pretender and some of her ministers had since 1710 been intriguing with Jacobites without her knowledge. The Hanoverian succession when it came about was no less than a revolutionary settlement, in which the issues which had been debated since 1701 were sharpened and to some extent altered as well. The election of 1715 virtually ended any prospect of an outlet for disaffection in the British parliament; the rush of the *Squadrone* and the 'Argathelians' into office skewed the nature of patronage; and the purge of the Commission of the Peace in the autumn of 1715 was a more drastic interference in local politics than in either 1660 or 1688-90. Argyll himself admitted that north of the Forth support for Jacobitism ran at levels of nine to one. Yet there is a point of considerable curiosity about this. Bolingbroke fled to France in March 1715, despairing of ever being able to persuade James out of his Roman Catholicism: 'England', he declared, 'would as soon have a Turk as a Roman Catholic for a King'.[33] By contrast in Scotland, although there were still pious hopes of James's conversion, religion ultimately mattered less than sovereignty. Once again, as in 1641, 1649 and 1685, the Scots in 1715 showed how different their attitude to monarchy was from that of the English.

The '15 rising was a series of contradictions. Its strength lay in the fact that it was a rebellion which did not need the arrival of a Jacobite pretender to spark it off, only the symbolic gesture of a disaffected politician. Mar, stripped of options in London, took ship on a collier for Scotland. Despite landing near Elie in Fife, he chose to travel not to his estates near Alloa but to Braemar in Aberdeenshire. He seems to have had two stratagems in mind. The eighteenth-century equivalent of politicking on the grouse moor was the deer hunt. There confidences might be exchanged and conspiracies launched amidst an innately conservative world of aristocratic privilege, which by then bound together Lowland nobility and a segment of Highland chiefs. It was there, at Braemar, where plans were laid for Mar to raise the banner of the Pretender on the Braes of Mar nine days later, on 6 September 1715; this was a rising of the ruling classes of the north-east Lowlands and the adjacent areas of the Grampian Highlands, bound together by family ties as much as by Jacobite principles or episcopalian sympathies. But simultaneously Mar had also been in touch with the chiefs of the Central Highlands to organise a march on Glasgow; this was far more of a clan rising than that in the north-east, but it hardly got off the ground. By mid-October, the government garrison in Fort William was still intact and the western clans, numbering less than 3,000 men, had advanced only as far as Inveraray, which they failed to take. On 24 October they abandoned the siege in favour of joining Mar's eastern force, then camped at Auchterarder near Perth; the western strategy had already collapsed.[34]

The eastern rising at first made swift progress. Perth was taken by a cavalry raid on 14 September and Inverness, which would hold out for some time in the '45, fell on the same day. By the 20th, James VIII was proclaimed at the Market Cross of Aberdeen. There was little or no resistance to the rising and evidence of considerable popular support in all the burghs north of the Tay. Indeed the level of support for the rising – as distinct from a general but inchoate Jacobitism – was a good deal less qualified in the Lowland society of the north-east than amongst the Highland clans. The '15, like most other potential Highland risings before and after it, needed time to gain ground amongst the clans of the central and western Highlands. The first set-piece victory was always a settler of doubts and consciences; it never came. The stalemate at Sheriffmuir, on 13 November, when only 1,000 troops under Argyll held off almost 4,000 men under Mar, came too late as a battle and was too indecisive a result to translate innate sympathy into actual support. By the time the Pretender arrived, on 22 December at Peterhead, the rising was a spent force. Even his token coronation at Scone went awry. By 4 February, James was aboard ship at Montrose for France.

There are different possible measuring-sticks of the support for Jacobitism in 1715. Few western clans were involved in it. As in the '45, no Highland chief, whether from the western or the eastern Highlands, gave totally unqualified support to it; clans tended to be split within themselves over the level of support to give to the rebellion rather than pitched against each other, for Jacobites or Hanoverians. The heads of the clans of the Great Glen were among the first to submit to the Hanoverian regime once it was learned that the Pretender had cut and run.[35] The '15 was never quite the Highland rising which the government, once it was over, chose to portray it as.

The core of its active support had been in the north-eastern shires of Aberdeen, Forfar, Kincardine and Angus.[36] Its motivation had been a close-knit mixture of traditional residual loyalty to an ancient monarchy and anti-Union feeling, which few as yet saw as other than indistinguishable. Its strength lay in its very inchoateness and the figure of 'Bobbing John' Mar, so often ridiculed, was not unsuited to the paradox of a conservative rebellion; he was typical of many prominent nobles involved in it who had seen their political convictions ebb and flow with the confusing tides of post-Union politics. But the qualities of flexibility and indecision which made Mar the successful politician he was were disastrous in a military leader. The rising of 1715 was one which lost its way, in contrast with those of 1708 and 1745, each of which had a clear – if perhaps a misguided – strategy. Once the pre-emptive strike to take Edinburgh Castle foundered, a mere two days after Mar raised his standard, the '15 began to ape the course of a Highland rising – which it never was. The notion that a common thread of patriarchal culture bound together loyal clans and the cause of the Pretender passes over the more important ties that bound in 1715 – which were common to both Highland and Lowland society.[37] Yet the '15 also showed that a retreat into the heartland of Scotland north of the Tay was no longer, as it had been for centuries, a viable military course of action for an alternative regime.

There were two crucial ironies about the '15. It came, by accident, at a fateful point, for Louis XIV died just five days before Mar began his rebellion. Power for the moment passed to his nephew, the Duke of Orleans, who was as Regent distinctly cooler towards the Jacobite cause; what foreign support there was in 1715 came from Spain, and only in the form of money. Although there were occasional hopes of a renewed French interest in Jacobite schemes during the long domination of French foreign policy between 1726 and 1743 by Cardinal Fleury, it was only after his death in January 1743 that tokenism gave way to the prospect of firm French involvement. The Hanoverian regime had weathered its first crisis by 1720, but a gathering crisis in the 1730s was accelerated by the outbreak of war in 1739. It was fortunate that the first time that a French invasion plan coincided with its own state of weakness came only in 1744.[38]

The other irony was that in 1715 a Jacobite invasion was already in course of preparation in France. Like most Jacobite plots, it was multi-pronged and over-elaborate. The Highlands were included in it, but only as one of two side-shows; the other was in the Borders. The main theatre of activity, where James was to land, was intended to be the south-west of England, but that part of the master plan had been scuppered in September 1715, when it had been exposed by spies. Mar's rising pre-empted the intended conspiracy in the Highlands but his failure to seize either Edinburgh or Glasgow quickly left the branch rebellion on the eastern Border in a no man's land. The English Jacobites of Northumbria linked up with a force under the command of Mackintosh of Borlum which had been sent across the Forth by Mar to outflank Argyll, but they refused to march north, either to threaten Glasgow (as the Scots wanted) or to join forces with Mar himself. Left without a role or a military strategy, the combined force marched west, criss-crossing the border, its English and Scottish arms suspicious of each other. Eventually, lured by the prospect of loot more than by the promise of Jacobite support in Lancashire, it swung south to Preston, where it was encircled and defeated between 12 and 14 November. It was the first and last time English Jacobites materially contributed to a Jacobite rising and the sorry episode showed the extent of the incompatibility of the Scottish and English strains of Jacobitism.

The faces of Jacobitism, 1715-45

The '15 underlined the complex nature of the Jacobite international. Based in St Germain until 1715 when James was exiled from France after the death of Louis

XIV, until 1718 in the unlikely setting Bar-le-Duc, a sleepy provincial town in Lorraine, and after that in Rome, the Jacobite court was an unwieldy colossus made up of the aristocracy of three kingdoms, plotting and counter-plotting against each other as much as against the London regime. It was at once a refugee camp, housing some 2,500 as early as the mid-1690s, a centre of conspicuous consumption swallowing up Louis XIV's subsidy of 50,000 *livres* a month, and a multi-staged theatre in which the fevered imaginations of its various components were given free rein. One government agent reported in 1726 that 'the Irish, Scotch and English seem to have quite different views and ways of thinking, and there are two parties of each Nation, so that I may justly say there are six parties'.[39] Its leitmotiv, it has been said, was paranoia[40], but there were also distinctive national strains of paranoia as well. Almost every prominent figure at the Jacobite court was at one time or another accused of collusion with London. Middleton, who had helped to organise the 1708 invasion attempt, was accused of leaking its plans, even though he sailed with it. Clementina Walkinshaw, the daughter of a Scottish laird and Charles Edward Stewart's mistress in the 1750s, claimed that she was always barred from the use of writing materials because her sister's position as housekeeper to the Hanoverian dowager Princess of Wales cast suspicion on her. Her escape to an Ursuline convent in 1760 was as much a relief to the English Jacobites who suspected her as it was to Clementina herself, who had put up with eight years of intermittent drunken beatings at Charles's hands.[41]

There was some point to all these suspicions. The Jacobite court was riddled with spies and counter-espionage agents had frustrated numerous Jacobite plots in both Scotland and England for more than a decade before the '15. The most spectacular success was yet to come – the part played by an English agent, Dudley Bradstreet, in persuading the Jacobite invasion force to turn back from Derby in December 1745. For the London regime, there were some unwelcome results of the huge wave of propaganda and disinformation which it so assiduously cultivated, especially between 1705 and 1720. Jacobites were seen everywhere. The show-trial of the high Tory clergyman, Henry Sacheverell, in 1710 backfired in Whig faces; intended as a vehicle to mobilise anti-Jacobite populism, it provoked a wave of protest which Whigs interpreted as Jacobite populism. During the Queen's illness in mid-1714, Jacobites were seen if not under the royal bed at least all around it. And the exposure of the Swedish plot of 1717, the most aimless of all Jacobite conspiracies, provoked the government into establishing a large armed camp in Hyde Park. The siege mentality had literally produced a government under siege; the Hanoverian regime had begun to believe its own propaganda.[42]

By the second half of the 1710s, exploitation of the 'British problem' was part of the standard armoury of the European diplomatic scene. Two Swedish ambassadors, based in London and Paris, began a free-lance operation in 1717 whose aims were unclear although there was vague talk of Swedish funding of a 'descent into Scotland'. The plot was discovered before it got beyond the planning stage and from that point it, like French plots of 1722 and 1723, became more important as a propaganda weapon for the London government than as a threat to its security.[43] A Spanish plot, hatched in 1718 by Cardinal Alberoni as part of the retaliation for the defeat of a Spanish fleet at the battle of Cape Passaro, did materialise, or at least part of it did. Again, the second feature in a Jacobite invasion plan became the main one. An invasion fleet of twenty-nine ships, carrying 5,000 Spanish troops and with arms for 30,000 more, set sail from Cadiz early in March 1719 but it was scattered by a violent storm off Corunna a few days later. The invasion of England was over before it could pick up the Pretender at Corunna.

The sideshow – blissfully unaware of the disaster which had overtaken the Duke of Ormonde's fleet – went on. Two frigates, 307 Spanish infantrymen and George Keith, 10th Earl Marischal, reached Stornoway on the Isle of Lewis, where they were joined by two dozen assorted Jacobite exiles including the Marquis of Tullibardine, who had sailed from Le Havre in a small twenty-five tonner. The two forces, tiny as they were, resulted in two commanders with rival strategies and endless disputes in daily councils of war; it was a virtual dress rehearsal for the '45. The plan to march on Inverness never took shape and less than 1,000 from the clans rallied to the cause. Driven from the picturesque Eilean Donan Castle at the head of Loch Alsh by a Royal Navy bombardment and cut off from the sea, the miniature invasion force turned into shooting practice for a battery of mortars hauled west from Inverness. The 1719 rising ended in a minor skirmish in Glenshiel on 9 June. The next day the Spaniards, without food and any sense of where they were, surrendered; by October they were sent home. The scene of the 'battle' is still called, not without irony, *Bealach-na-Spainnteach* (the Spaniards' Pass). The Jacobite leaders all escaped. If the affair had any real effect, it was to introduce a new sense of realism into Jacobite military strategy; as Tullibardine later admitted: 'We came with hardly anything that was really necessary for such an undertaking.'[44] The price of its failure in terms of the damage it inflicted on Jacobite loyalties in Scotland is harder to calculate, but it certainly raised the stakes of foreign support demanded by clan chiefs in any future adventure. A further Spanish-backed plot in 1727 met with a studied scepticism among the chiefs approached.

After 1715 the Hanoverian government faced the problem of the peace. Both punitive measures and reconstruction were muted by hawks in the army and by the Argyll interest in Scotland. The abolition of superiorities was advocated and then shelved. Plans were drawn up for military barracks at Fort Augustus, Inverness and Glenelg but then mothballed. A Disarming Act of 1716 had banned the carrying of weapons in public but not their ownership; the only clans which disarmed were those loyal to the government. A permanent Highland militia was suggested, but the suspicion felt by the government of all things Highland also fell on its own vehicle for mobilising support amongst the loyalist clans; the Highland Companies, whose dark green tartan had already given them the name of The Black Watch, were disbanded in 1717. Estates of Jacobite rebels were declared forfeit and a largely English commission set up to dispose of them. The combined obstacles put up by the impenetrable thicket of Scots law, the inbred conservatism of the Court of Session, the recalcitrance of tenants and the canniness of potential investors frustrated its first efforts. The government finally solved the problem, so it thought, by fostering a private monopoly in the shape of the York Buildings Company, to which rebel estates were sold. Yet this model of Hanoverian enterprise, despite a few choice acquisitions such as the Panmure estates, found most of its purchases unprofitable. By the late 1720s the first Hanoverian land grab was over; most forfeited estates had reverted to the families of their original owners and the government, intent on punishing past disorders, found itself instead fuelling new resentments.[45]

Serious attempts to come to grips with the Highland problem began only in the mid-1720s and they were, ironically, the product of the disturbances which had gripped various Lowland burghs over the malt tax. Although Jacobitism in Scotland never seems to have taken on the populist image which it did at times in England, the Shawfield riots, a limited protest in Scotland's most Whig burgh, were translated in the mind of a still nervous government into a proto-Jacobite rebellion. These disorders of 1725 produced the only two major government initiatives between 1707 and 1747 – the Board of Trustees and the package of measures designed to end the government's chronic weakness in the Highlands. The government already had to hand a blueprint of a new Highland policy in the form of a memorandum drawn up by Simon, Lord Fraser of Lovat in 1724. Drawn up to consolidate his own territorial influence and his reputation as a trusted collaborator of the regime, Lovat, a convicted rapist and former Jacobite agent, painted a vivid portrait of a Celtic society where endemic lawlessness and the patriarchy of the clan system went hand in hand. It was a scenario which told the government what it wanted to hear and which has convinced many historians since.[46]

It was on this basis that General George Wade, an Anglo-Irish soldier with a nose for ferreting out Jacobite sympathisers, was appointed commander in Scotland in 1725. Between 1726 and 1737 Wade organised the building of over 250 miles of military roads deep into the western and central Highlands. In 1725 there were only four isolated government garrisons – at Inverlochy, Ruthven near Kingussie, at Bernera in Glenelg and at Killichiumen, later to become Fort Augustus. Wade's road system was designed to create a *cordon sanitaire* along the line of the Great Glen, reinforced by a naval galley on Loch Ness. It was the Cromwellian system of the 1650s writ large, with arteries linking it to the south, including a road from Perth via Dunkeld to Inverness – a route which the modern A9 road faithfully follows. The point often made that Wade's roads only hastened the southward progress of Charles Edward Stewart's Highlanders in 1745 is a condemnation not of the intricate military system which Wade had erected by 1740 but of its neglect; the strongpoints in the system were not the roads but the garrisons, yet most of them, undermanned and far lower in the government's priorities than the campaigns in Flanders, fell in 1745. Fort Augustus, built between 1727 and 1730 at enormous cost and ironically named after the royal child who would later lead the government army at Culloden, lasted only two days in 1745. Most of the Highland Companies revived after 1725 were by 1743 stationed in England or, like the first battalion of the Royal Scots, in Flanders.

The condition of the Highlands was more complex and less lawless than government policy allowed. The great clan wars had blown themselves out well before even the '15. Lawlessness usually stemmed from broken clans or caterans engaged in freelance cattle reiving rather than from organised clan society. It says much for the confusions into which government policy had fallen that it had found itself promoting the activities of racketeers like Rob Roy MacGregor, ex-Jacobite and cattle dealer turned Campbell client and cattle thief. The fact that he died almost a national hero says much for the limbo into which Scotland had fallen by the 1730s: not yet North British, yet no longer possessed of the clear identity which religious nationalism had given to it in the seventeenth century, Scottish society was culturally adrift amidst a complex of confusing and variously paced changes.

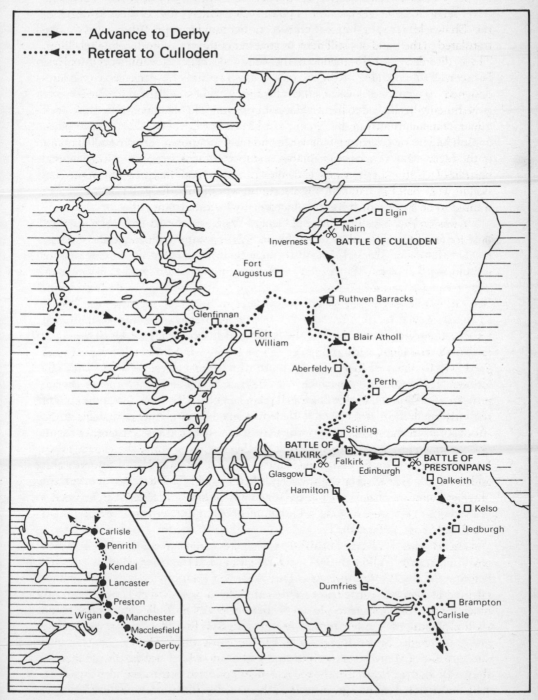

Map 7 *The 1745 Campaign*

Highland society was as much caught up in this complicated clash between continuity and change as any other part of Scotland, even if the clash was taking place at its own distinctive crossroads.

What the government failed to take as a lesson from the '15 was the fact that it had not taken on the familiar seventeenth-century mantle of an anti-Campbell crusade; even the Campbells had been split in their loyalties, with Breadalbane supporting the rising. Highland society was potentially more stable than it had been for a long time; land grabs by one clan at the expense of another were receding – until the government backed adventurers such as Lovat. By the 1740s some clan chiefs, even in the Great Glen, were making signed agreements with each other for their mutual protection and to curb cattle reiving.[47] In another century and a different locale, these might have been called bonds of alliance and historians would have approved of the strength and stability which they lent to local society – a stability which central government was still unable to provide in the early eighteenth century. The real Highland problem in the 1740s already pointed the way towards the future and not to the past; it was, as one rent collector complained in 1744, about the 'extraordinary poverty of the countrie, occasioned by the death of cattle and scarcity of victuale'.[48] The real crisis was not about law and order but about economics; the lack of cash for investment and estate improvement which would scar Highland history for the next century and a half had already become obvious.

The Forty-Five and its aftermath

The rising which broke out after the landing of Prince Charles Edward Stewart at Eriskay in the Outer Isles on 23 July 1745 was, unlike the abortive attempts in 1708 and 1715, a Highland affair from its beginning to its end thirteen months later. Yet, as before, the Scottish expedition was intended only as part of a three-pronged strategy. Its different strands illustrated the inner contradictions within the Jacobite international: Scotland was still the most loyal of the three kingdoms to the Stewarts, yet French attention was more interested in a quick strike across the Channel than the old strategy of using Scotland as the postern gate; Louis XV was willing to toy with an 'enterprise of England',[49] but not a repeat of the 'enterprise d'Écosse' of 1708. The key to the course taken by the '45, of a high-risk march into England, may well have lain in the elaborate plans laid in France for an invasion in early 1744. It was on 9 January 1744 that Charles left Rome in great secrecy, bound for Dunkirk. It was not the Pretender but, unknown to him, his elder son Charles Edward, since 1739 the effective leader of the exile movement, who had been invited by Louis XV to join the French invasion fleet; the father and son would not meet again for twenty-two years. The basis of the enterprise was a pre-emptive strike; it foundered disastrously in a violent storm early in March 1744 when twelve vessels were lost off Dunkirk, seven of them with all hands. Within weeks, France had abandoned the invasion strategy and settled for an official declaration of war, with its major theatre in Flanders. It was, however, Charles's glimpse of the potential of a French invasion of the south coast of England which coloured his plans for an expedition to Scotland and the need for a long march into England.

In a sense, the '45 was a war fought on three fronts: it was a battle for the affections of Charles's Scottish subjects which, at best, he only half won; the advance into England, intended to be sustained by the collection of taxes and rediscovered Jacobite loyalties on its way, was a pyrrhic victory; and it was a feasibility exercise to convince Louis XV's ministers of the prospects of a resuscitated 'enterprise of England'. By November 1745 the campaign to open up a third front seems to have succeeded; large-scale preparations were being made at Dunkirk and Brest; scare stories of French landings swept London almost daily. It was only in January 1746, a month after the retreat of Charles's army from Derby, a mere 127 miles north of London, that the French invasion plan was abandoned. As late as 24 December even Cumberland's pursuit of the retreating Jacobite army was called off at Wigan because of reports of a French landing in the south. In mid-December 1745, before news of Derby reached France, it seemed more likely than not that 'the world's greatest expedition', as Voltaire called it, would set sail.[50] As in 1708, the central feature of the '45 was a foreign invasion – which never happened.

Charles's expedition was financed by a combination of private venture capital largely put up by Aeneas MacDonald, an expatriate Scot with a banking house in Paris, and credit, borrowed on the security of the Sobieski jewels, a legacy from his mother Clementina. It paid for a modest arsenal of twenty field pieces, 3,500 assorted guns, and 2,400 broadswords, which was loaded on two ships berthed at Nantes in June 1745. More than half this arsenal and the hundred marines aboard the *Elisabeth* failed to reach Scotland for it had to turn back after an encounter with an English man-of-war off the Lizard, and only the *Du Teillay* reached Arisaig on 3 August. Earlier in the year Cameron of Lochiel had posited a minimum expeditionary force of 6,000 men; the *Du Teillay* landed only a few more than the Prince and the legendary 'seven men of Moidart'.[51] The hotly disputed point as to whether or not the French government had foreknowledge of the expedition may be a red herring. Although the arrangement by which the *Elisabeth*, a French man-of-war on charter to the Franco-Irish privateer, Antoine Walsh, must have been known to the Secretary to the Navy, the Count of Maurepas, he was only one of six ministers vying for power and their own projects in foreign policy in the Council of State. The necessary fiction that Louis XV did not know of the expedition before it sailed may well have been the case.[52]

On 19 August, the Prince raised his standard at Glenfinnan, fifteen miles west of Fort William. Already some of the patterns of support for the rising had become apparent. The MacDonald chiefs of Glengarry, Morar and Keppoch had rallied, but only with some 500 men; it was only the somewhat unexpected arrival of Cameron of Lochiel with 700 more that made further progress viable. Yet the bulk of the west Highland clans had not turned out. Although Charles had landed in largely Roman Catholic country in Moidart, there was no surge of Catholic support for him. The staunchly Catholic islands of Barra and South Uist took no part in the '45 and nor did Clanranald himself, although some of his clansmen had turned out. Catholic chiefs were as ambiguous and equivocal as the heads of other clans in 1745. When the Prince entered the Great Glen, he was joined by some 800 more clansmen, mostly Glengarry MacDonells and Stewarts from Appin, but it would not be until he reached Perth (on 4 Sept.) that the Prince's force grew much above that of the disastrous '19. The unusual feature of the early stage of the rising was the fact that there was no set-piece battle in the Highlands. A government force under the command of Lieutenant-General Sir John Cope had been dispatched north but, against orders, had veered away from a confrontation in the Great Glen. It was the same force of some 2,000 raw recruits, shipped south from Inverness to the Forth, which would confront the Jacobites at Prestonpans, a few miles east of Edinburgh on 21 September. Prestonpans, rather than attracting more support to the Prince's standard, had scarcely stemmed a rising tide of defections which had been further accelerated by the narrow decision to march south. That was the reason why the Prince was forced to stay in Edinburgh for over a month before he managed to raise the 5,500 men which was the bare minimum needed for an invasion of England.

If marginality was the keynote of support for the Prince in August and September 1745,[53] the same was also the case for the government. Cope had found panic and equivocation but little commitment on his travels. In the capital, a city of some 40,000 inhabitants, 400 men of the Edinburgh Defence Volunteers had mustered on the morning of 15 September; by midday, when they were due to march out of the city to confront the Prince's army, they had shrunk to forty-two.[54] It says much for the strength of his ideological convictions that a young David Hume was one of them. He was an exception amongst both the 'North British' and the Jacobite literati of Edinburgh, whose mental horizons were confined to battles of the books, often ironically about the Stewart past. Hume, it has been said, was the 'most characteristic figure of Great Britain in the 1740s',[55] mid-way between the troubles of the seventeenth century and the turmoil to come at the end of the eighteenth. Yet that in 1745 would have seemed an unlikely judgement, for it is hard to imagine a more unrepresentative figure of Scotland during the '45.

The decision to march south into England had been made by a majority of only one in the Jacobite council of war and the majority of the Highland chiefs involved in the rising were opposed to it.[56] Progress, despite the extreme coolness of Jacobite sympathisers in the north and in Lancashire, was nothing short of phenomenal. By 4 December, only twenty-seven days after crossing the Border, the Jacobite army entered Derby, 127 miles away from London. The fateful decision, taken on the 5th, to retreat northwards was supported by the best military strategist amongst the Jacobites, Lord George Murray, and only one of the chiefs spoke up for Charles's plan to press forward on London. The decision was undoubtedly the correct one from the viewpoint of the military textbook and the alternative still greatly depended on putting blind faith in a French invasion. Much of the information and disinformation available to the Jacobite army pointed towards a tactical retreat, as did much of its experience of the level of active support for it in England.[57] The extreme anxiety of English military commanders who knew that almost nothing lay between the Prince and the capital, the level of Jacobite support in London and the nearness of the French to a decision to press ahead with an invasion of the south coast were all unknown factors, if known to historians who have since made their own judgements. What the retreat certainly did do was to reveal to Hanoverian generals that there was no co-ordinated pincer operation involving a march from the north and an invasion from the south.

The retreat from Derby was orderly and not out of keeping with what has been called 'an outstanding military exploit'.[58] By 20 December, six weeks after the English campaign had begun, the Prince was back in Scotland. The victory at Falkirk, on 17 January, over Cope's successor Hawley, showed that the Jacobite army was still a force to be reckoned with but its failure to storm Stirling Castle underlined its lack of firepower. The defeat at Drummossie Moor, some five miles east of Inverness, on 16 April 1746 has since acquired something of the status of a Flodden. Culloden has become the symbol of the death of an old order as well as the emblem of the calculated brutality of the army of the Duke of Cumberland. Both are to a large extent the product of a remarkable propaganda work, The Lyon in Mourning, a massive collection of the documented genocide of a people which was the life-work of Robert Forbes, an episcopalian minister who later became Bishop of Ross and Caithness; it was probably begun during his imprisonment in Stirling Castle during the '45 and it ended only with his death thirty years later.[59] First published in truncated form in 1835, the Lyon became part of the collective tristesse of a nineteenth-century industrial nation in search of a glamorous past. By the mid-Victorian age the Queen herself could declare, without a trace of irony, that she was herself a Jacobite at heart. And in the 1880s headstones were first erected to identify, somewhat dubiously, the loyal clans which had fallen on Culloden Moor.

The cult of Jacobite nostalgia flies in the face of most of the facts, both about the '45 and about Culloden itself. The battle should not have been fought where or when it was. Charles's men were outnumbered – by 6,000 to 9,000 of Cumberland's force – and were badly positioned so that any advance had to be made uphill, against entrenched mortars, and into the teeth of a biting north-easterly wind. Over 1,000 Highlanders fell, but only three-fifths of the Prince's army had been in the field and the immediate reaction of his commanders was that the battle had not been decisive. This was only Cumberland's first victory (and, as events would prove, also his last); Murray expected to do better in a return contest with Cumberland, and Lochiel was even as late as mid-May planning a summer campaign.[60] Neither defeat at Culloden nor a rout after it had been inevitable. What turned the tables was Charles's own decision to issue a sauve qui peut order.

And so began the five-month clandestine journey of the Prince until he set sail from Borrodale on 19 September – a journey not only into exile but also into mythology for it has added immeasurably to the romantic image of Jacobitism ever since. The story of the zigzag wanderings of the Prince, with a reward of £30,000 put on his head by the Hanoverian government, which threw a huge military and naval cordon across the north-west Highlands and the Outer Isles, was reported in the Scots Magazine throughout the summer of 1746. The story of the 'summer's hunting', as Major General John Campbell, who was in charge of the operation, called it, had already begun to mix fact and fiction: a letter from an anonymous 'officer at Fort Augustus' was published in the Magazine in July, reporting that 'the Pretender has been chased this fortnight past from one island to another, sometimes dressed as a Highlander, sometimes as a woman'. Charles's famous crossing from South Uist to Skye, dressed as 'Betty Burke', the serving-maid of Flora MacDonald, had taken place early in June. By July Flora was in custody, more fêted than villified, and Charles was back on the mainland, picking his way northwards from Moidart into Knoydart. By early September the government had admitted defeat and begun to reduce the scale of the search. The two French frigates which were guided from South Uist, where they first made landfall, to Borrodale were the last of half a dozen various rescue missions which had been sent since late April. The Prince had been protected both by clansmen who had fought for him – most prominently Neil MacEachain, a Uist tacksman who accompanied Flora MacDonald as her 'servant' –

and by others who had remained neutral or ambivalent during the rising. Flora's stepfather, Hugh MacDonald of Armadale, an officer in the Hanoverian Highland militia, had organised the dramatic escape to Skye. Clanranald poets later celebrated the Clan's role in the great escape although their chief had remained studiously detached from the '45 itself and Charles's worst days were those spent in Knoydart, when he feared he would be betrayed by Coll MacDonell of Barrisdale, who was taken in irons in the hold of the same ship as took Charles to France, Le Prince de Conti.[61] The complex loyalties of Charles's last adventure mirrored those of Clan Donald and Highland society as a whole throughout the period of the Jacobite wars.

The '45 has been called a Scottish civil war.[62] The thirty years between the two major Jacobite risings had revealed more clearly the winners and losers from a Union settlement. By 1745, it is true, some sections of Scottish society – most notably the presbyterian clergy, the lawyers and the large southern burghs – were noticeably hostile to Jacobitism. Their support for the Hanoverian regime was often a matter of instinct rather than of active conviction. As in many civil wars, loyalties were in 1745 more ambivalent – on both sides – than the apparently black and white nature of the issues might suggest. If there was a clash within the '45 between a supposedly backward-looking Highland society and a 'progressive', capitalist Lowland economy, it was not a clear-cut one. Cameron of Lochiel, who fought for Charles, was as much a representative of a new capitalist attitude to Highland estate management as was the house of Argyll, ever the mainstay of support for the Hanoverian regime.[63] Since the '15, there had been considerable efforts made in the Highlands by both the Society in Scotland for Propagating Christian Knowledge (SSPCK) and a reorganised Catholic Highland Mission. In a sense, this was a clash of cultures as well as of religions: the SSPCK was determined to 'extirpate the Irish Language' and the Catholic mission made much of its Gaelic roots. The Church of Scotland itself, financed by the 'Royal Bounty', was much more prepared to use Gaelic in the process of evangelising the Highlands and the Highland Mission was rent by internal divisions, ostensibly between Jansenists and anti-Jansenists, but often in reality between Lowlanders and Highlanders.[64] Roman Catholics were no more likely to rise in the '45 than episcopalians, who predominated in a ratio of about seven to three.

Few events in Scottish history have the weight of hindsight hanging so heavily over them as the Jacobite risings. Part of their very attraction is their predestined tragedy. Viewed from another angle, however, what is so startling is the incredible and repeated good luck of the London regime. The news of the scattering of the fleet at Dunkirk in March 1708 was joyously hailed in London as a providential deliverance. The striking regularity of 'Protestant winds', which devastated invasion fleets in March 1719 and March 1744 and treasure ships in January 1716 and April 1746, is testimony to the hazards which might beset any invasion that had to venture across the Channel and North Sea – in the eighteenth century as well as the twentieth. It also shows how each Jacobite invasion came to fruition in mid-winter. What was truly marginal was the narrow gap which separated success from failure, whether in 1708 or 1745.

What was inevitable was the aftermath of the '45. Cumberland's savage orders to harry, burn and kill men, women and children alike in a campaign of mass-reprisal after Culloden was unusual in eighteenth-century warfare but it was no more than a repeat performance of the final Elizabethan conquest of Ireland after 1601, when (as here) the bloodletting came after forty years of frustration and failure in dealing with a Celtic people. It was one more act in the long drama of the consolidation of an English Empire. The Scottish managers, Islay and Milton, were unable to control the legislative programme which resulted between 1746 and 1747. The radical schemes of dismantling Highland society, which had been shelved after 1716 and 1724, were finally given their head. Military tenures were abolished in 1746 and heritable jurisdictions were done away with in 1747. Jacobites' estates were forfeited far more systematically than after 1715 in a programme of legislation which went on between 1746 and 1752. Those incidental symbols of Jacobitism – tartan and bagpipes – were proscribed, except for use by Highland regiments in the British army abroad.[65] Ironically, they would return less than a century later as symbols not of Gaeldom but of Scotland itself.

Part V
THE MOULDING
OF
MODERN SCOTLAND

20

North Britain, Caledonia and Greater Britain

THE UNION OF 1707 LEFT SCOTLAND WITH AN UNCERTAIN FUTURE, BUT ALSO with an ambiguous past. The prospect of the merging of a nation into a different nation state provoked a surge of conflicting thoughts and emotions amongst the different layers of Scottish society. The economic benefits of Union were slow to materialise. The patriotic impulse, which had reached new heights in the pamphlet campaigns over imperial crowns on the eve of the debates of 1706-7 and had plumbed new depths of nostalgia in Lord Belhaven's emotional epitaph to 'our antient Mother Caledonia', made in the last stages of the debates in November 1706, did not die a lingering death after 1707. Instead, it found new forms of expression – in the poetic collections of Allan Ramsay, the Jacobite critique of Whig history and the other publications of the printer, Thomas Ruddiman, and the 'patriotic publishers'.[1] The arguments about the ancient Scottish constitution of George Buchanan were picked over and exposed to ridicule by Jacobite historians. Some pro-Unionists, such as Sir John Clerk of Penicuik, cultivated a different brand of antiquarianism which used the example of Roman conquest to show how a new Caledonia would benefit from exposure to English Augustan civilisation.

The birth of North Britain

Both Belhaven and Clerk were engaged, like many of their contemporaries, on a quest for a new Scottish independence within the framework of a British state.[2] Where they disagreed was on what was worth keeping from Scotland's past. The early seventeenth century had been poised uneasily between an uncritical acceptance of a myth of the origins of kings of Scots and the prospect of an imminent millennium. It had embraced Buchanan, who had rewritten the chronicle of a long line of kings as a morality tale of the faults of princes, and Napier of Merchiston, whose invention of logarithims had been intended to help calculation of the apocalypse, which he had predicted with unerring accuracy as the thirty-eighth year of the century. The early eighteenth century hovered uncertainly between rummaging through the lumber room of Scotland's history for items of value and a celebration of the present as an escape from a troubled past. The new philosophical historians, such as David Hume and William Robertson, saw history as the charting of human development through a number of stages, from barbarity to refinement. By 1770, when Hume proclaimed that: 'This is the historical Age and this is the historical Nation',[3] the Scots had reached politeness and slipped the collar of their past – or so it seemed.

By 1750 most thinking Scots were, as a result, prepared to consider themselves as both British and Scots. In 1755, the first issue of the *Edinburgh Review*, in a confident survey of the course of history since 1688, argued: 'What the Revolution had begun, the Union rendered more compleat'. A comparison of Scotland's history before 1688 with that since the Revolution showed the fruits of the new historical age which stemmed from union with England:

> We may clearly see the superior advantages we now enjoy, and readily discern from what source they flow. The communication of trade has awakened industry; the equal administration of laws produced good manners; and the watchful care of the government, seconded by the public spirit of some individuals, has excited, promoted and encouraged a disposition to every species of improvement in the minds of a people naturally active and intelligent. If countries have their ages with respect to improvement, North Britain may be considered as in a state of early youth, guided and supported by the more mature strength of her kindred country.

The 'Age of Improvement' had already dawned, at least in the collective mind of the Edinburgh literati, and it was an integral part of the birth of a new North Britain – a curiously one-sided concept for the English still invariably thought of themselves as English. Its chief proponents were Adam Smith, Hume and Robertson.

The new age had its absurdities as well as its inspirations. No meeting of Edinburgh's Select Society was as crowded as the one in 1763 addressed by an Irish actor, Thomas Sheridan, on how to eliminate 'Scotticisms' from speech. Authors vied to purge the 'corrupt dialect of English' from their writings, while still claiming to remain patriotic Scots, or North Britons. This was what has since been dubbed 'the paradox of Scottish culture'[4], but the clash usually lay – as yet – within the mind of individuals rather than between rival cultures. No Scot worked harder or agonised longer over his Scotticisms than James Boswell, but he also long harboured plans for a Scottish national dictionary. The major cultural shift between the seventeenth and eighteenth centuries was not a distancing of polite and popular cultures; the *Encyclopaedia Britannica*, first published in three volumes between 1768 and 1771, was one of many efforts made to bridge that gap. The main change was the replacement of Latin by English as a lingua franca.

By the early 1760s, something of a retrenchment had set in, conditioned by what Hume called 'the rage against the Scots' in England. This was in part a by-product of the agitation against the Earl of Bute as a 'northern Machiavel', which resulted in his resignation as the King's first minister in 1763. But in England the 1760s also saw the consolidation of a new populist English nationalism, jingoist, racist and anxious to find as many natural enemies of the English people as it could. John Bull and 'Rule, Britannia!' – both recent inventions and also ironically the work of Scots (of the pamphleteer, John Arbuthnot, and the poet, James Thomson, respectively) – took on added dimensions. The English Empire was being extended – the Seven Years' War (1756-63) was a virtual world war waged from the Elbe to the Americas to protect it – and the Englishman's burden was being invented. A cartoon of 1762 shows a blind John Bull staggering under the weight of his 'Sister Peg', an ugly personification of Scotland, on his back; she is reaching out to grasp a bag of French gold and an olive branch. John Bull was also being found an English heritage; periodical literature of the 1760s traced his descent beyond the Norman Yoke to Saxon times. In the century that Scotland was burying its mythical past, England was happily re-inventing its own.[5] In Scotland, patriotism was less confident, partly because it no longer fed off anti-English feeling. James Boswell might declare that by birth he was a North Briton, but successive issues – a Scots militia, a proposed reduction of the number of judges in the Court of Session, the dangers of a paper currency, highlighted by the collapse of the Ayr Bank in 1772, and reform of the country franchise – came to the surface in the 1760s and 1770s and provoked a distinct sense of unease at the treatment of Scottish politics within the British state.[6]

North British society was caught in an exquisite dilemma as to its own identity. It coincided with the return from London of some of the Scottish aristocracy and a realignment of the network of patronage and politics which had lasted through the long years of the ascendancy of Islay. Parallel to this, there emerged by the 1770s the beginnings of a distaste for the 'manners' of the new thrusting age; a sense of nostalgia had begun to set in, demanding a return to the spirit of the golden years of the 1750s. What is sometimes called the period of 'the growth of political stability' had already begun to give way to an age of anxiety. It was the signal for Henry Dundas to emerge offering a renewed security to the landed classes, claiming as a result to be 'in possession of the Confidence of Scotland'.[7] This was the backdrop for a different version of civic humanism, represented by the consoling sermons of Hugh Blair and the sentimental novels of Henry Mackenzie, promising means of escape from a degenerate age. It worked, but only for a generation. By 1800 North Britain was already defunct. The 'Moderate' clergymen and Enlightened philosophers who were its spokesmen gave way to novelists and essayists, who offered two new identities – a renewed sense of Scottishness and the more complete absorption of Scotland into a British state. The age of Hume gave way to the age of both Sir Walter Scott and a new *Edinburgh Review*.

Age of Improvement?

The whole of the eighteenth century, and sometimes also the period up to 1820, is sometimes described either as the 'Age of the Enlightenment' or the 'Age of Improvement'. One of the ironies of that age is that although there were many improvers, there was comparatively little improvement – until economic circumstances made it profitable in the last two decades of the eighteenth century. There was a rash of improving societies from the 1720s onwards, most notably the Honourable Society of Improvers in the Knowledge of Agriculture in Scotland, founded in Edinburgh in 1723, and the subject was pursued with an almost evangelical zeal, as part of a patriotic programme of national rehabilitation – as North Britain. Only a few improving landlords, such as the well-known cases of Sir Archibald Grant of Monymusk and John Cockburn of Ormiston, practised what so many preached, and usually with little profitable result. 'Improvement' was used by contemporaries in a much wider sense than agricultural reform, but that example is a useful caution against assuming direct causal connections between a seeming new-found political stability, economic growth and intellectual changes. Each of these phenomena underwent setbacks or changed course during the period.[8]

Political stability, hard won in 1746, seemed again at risk in the 1760s and 1770s, but from the insensitivity of the new British politics rather than Jacobitism. This was also the age of an American revolt and an unsuccessful Irish independence movement; it gave little comfort to the new North Britons. The economic benefits of Union, which had begun to emerge only in the 1740s in tangible form, were dampened by overseas war between 1756 and 1763 and the transatlantic trade, the source of the new-found prosperity of the Glasgow tobacco lords, was thrown into jeopardy in 1776. It is possible to link the growth of a polite society to the rock-like stability of British society in the eighteenth century. If, however, Britain – north and south – is seen as a society which, despite underlying economic growth, was deeply riven by many uncertainties, even before the massive strains imposed on it by the French Revolution and the wars which followed, the 'rage for Improvement' takes on a different appearance. It begins to seem less the expression of a confident society than one driven by a restless quest to apply polite 'manners' as a balm to heal its own inner stresses; and no group was more anxious than the landed interest. The inherent values of the literati were those of landed society. Adam Smith and Henry Mackenzie, in their very different ways, both assumed that land rather than trade formed the moral foundation of society. Theirs was a comforting doctrine to what was still a highly aristocratic society, deeply preoccupied with the role of public men and their duties to improve politics, the economy and manners.

Ages of Enlightenment

The swirling ideas of the eighteenth century, which would later be subsumed under the general title of the 'Enlightenment', are difficult to characterise – which is why that description is so useful, and potentially so misleading. There were, more plausibly, at least three stages of development. The first might be seen as the age of Francis Hutcheson (1694-1746), the son of an Ulster presbyterian minister, appointed to the Chair of Moral Philosophy at Glasgow University in 1730. If this was the age of Hutcheson, it was also that of Thomas Ruddiman, Jacobite, printer, co-founder of the first of the literary clubs of the eighteenth century, the Easy Club, and Keeper of the Advocates' Library for thirty years. The rash of clubs, which was a striking feature of Edinburgh society from the 1710s onwards, did not reach Glasgow until the 1740s. There, Hutcheson remained a rather detached figure, not significantly involved even in the Political Economy Club, one of the first and most important of the Glasgow clubs, which aimed to stimulate joint interests between academics and merchants. As for Edinburgh, it remained for Hutcheson *terra incognita*. His chief contribution lay in the minds of the students whom he taught over a period of sixteen years at Glasgow University, and many of them became influential in the new 'Moderate' party within the Church of Scotland which emerged after 1752.[9]

The initial stimulus in Edinburgh had many more strands, and they demonstrate the dangers involved in tracing a single core of 'enlightened' ideas. It is possible to see in the contrast between Ruddiman and the Glasgow printers, the brothers Robert and Andrew Foulis, the differences between 'the old culture of humanist Scotland and a new Enlightenment'.[10] It was the Foulis press, designated official printer to the University of Glasgow in 1743, which printed many of Hutcheson's later works, new editions of the classics and a large number of reprints of English literature. In the charismatic figure of Ruddiman, however, also lay a blend of old and new. His reprint of Gavin Douglas's translation into Scots verse of the *Aeneid* (1710) and his edition of the complete works of Buchanan in Latin (1715) belonged to the tradition of the seventeenth-century renaissance of letters; but he also published the complex texts of Colin MacLaurin (1698-1746), a brilliant mathematician and astronomer, who was appointed at the age of nineteen to a chair at Marischal College, Aberdeen, and was in the van of the application of Isaac

Newton's theories to teaching in the Scottish universities.

Ruddiman espoused the ideal of the virtuoso, which had risen to prominence in the 1680s. It was given new institutional life in clubs such as the Rankenian, founded in Edinburgh in 1716. Its members carried on a correspondence with Bishop Berkeley, whose *Principles of Human Knowledge* (1710) had contained a searing attack on the ideas of John Locke; by the 1730s Edinburgh University students were being set essays on Berkeley's work.[11] In its philosophical mood, the Rankenian Club paved the path for the Moderate ministers of the second half of the century. From 1720, Ruddiman also published one of the first of the new Edinburgh newspapers, the *Caledonian Mercury*. Until the appearance of the *Scots Magazine* in 1739, by which time it had a circulation of 1,400, it was the chief channel of information on topical issues.[12] By the 1730s, the heady world of Edinburgh society, in which lawyers, academics and gentry met, debated and conversed, had laid the foundations, not only for the age of David Hume but for the critique of manners which lay beyond it, in the age of Blair and Mackenzie.

The figure who, more than any other, links the first and second phases of the Enlightenment was David Hume (1711-77), arguably the most influential as well as the best known of all the literati.[13] His main work, the great *Treatise of Human Nature*, was published as early as 1739-40 and was as little read in his own age as in our own; Hume was even driven to the lengths of publishing his own anonymous review of it to bring it to the notice of the reading public. He twice applied for and twice failed to secure university chairs, at Edinburgh and Glasgow, and in 1751 settled for the post of Keeper of the Advocates' Library, where, ironically, he succeeded Ruddiman. He was one of the founder members of the highly prestigious Select Society set up in 1754, but never addressed it. His massive six-volume *History of England*, published between 1754 and 1762, made his fortune as well as his reputation, but it also exaggerated his own feelings of rootlessness; in 1763 he retreated to the literary salons of Paris where his reputation was better acknowledged. By 1767, however, he had succumbed to the Boswell-like nostalgia of Scots exiles elsewhere. He returned to Scotland in 1769, with his reputation lionised in the polite society of the Edinburgh clubs, but paradoxically also as a curiously marginal figure.

Hume's influence is at once the most critical to establish in the eighteenth-century republic of Scottish letters and the most difficult to determine. He was more the *enfant terrible* of the literati than their mentor. To the Moderate ministers who formed an important core of 'enlightened' thought, his cult of scepticism gave him a role akin to that of *agent provocateur*, stimulating the 'common sense' school of philosophers led by Thomas Reid (1710-96), who in 1764 became Professor of Moral Philosophy at Glasgow University. To the wider reading public, Hume was probably best known for his advice to shun Scotticisms; he is alleged to have confessed them rather than sins on his deathbed. Uninterested in the revival in vernacular literature which was beginning to gather pace by the 1770s and impervious to the allure of Macpherson's 'translations' of *Ossian*, first published in 1760-3 but in vogue throughout Europe by the 1770s, his was a determinedly narrow exploration of the human intellect. For posterity, where his fame was greater than in life, his outstanding achievement, revealed in the sub-title of his *Treatise* of 1739 – an 'attempt to introduce the experimental method of reasoning into moral subjects' –

was to link history and philosophy by showing how human behaviour could be studied by empirical method, without recourse to the imaginings of theology. Within a generation of his death, however, history and philosophy would part in the Scottish intellect and go their separate ways.[14]

Hume was succeeded as Keeper of the Advocates' Library by Adam Ferguson (1723-1816), but he, unlike Hume, did acquire a university chair, being appointed Professor of Natural Philosophy at Edinburgh University in 1759. Ferguson, together with another leading Moderate minister, William Robertson (1721-93), who was made Principal of Edinburgh University in 1762, and Adam Smith (1723-90), who first lectured at Edinburgh but was appointed to a chair at Glasgow University in 1751, were the three leading forces in the years of what is sometimes called the 'High Enlightenment'. Each also, however, presents something of a paradox. Smith has rightly been hailed as a thinker who is best understood as a 'practical moralist', offering to a 'modern, commercial society' a carefully worked-out response to issues of great contemporary relevance.[15] The cogency and relevance of Smith's writings to his own times adds, however, a cautionary note to those who would see all-embracing messages in them for the twentieth century. His work spanned a period of fluctuating economic conditions, exaggerated by the depressing effects of the Seven Years' War and the anxieties aroused by the outbreak in 1776 of the revolt in the American colonies. As a result, his most celebrated work, The Wealth of Nations (1776), though hailed by his intellectual friends, found little favour amongst the Glasgow merchants faced by a collapse in the tobacco trade; it was a most uncongenial tract for its times. An infrequent attender of the Select Society, the most important of the clubs of the 1750s, Smith's main impact was probably the effect he had on a generation of students at Glasgow University, most of them candidates for the ministry. Ironically, his own faith seemed more formal than real and his eulogy on Hume at his death provoked an outcry amongst sections of the ministry. Yet in 1764 Smith abandoned his university post to take on the lucrative position of tutor to the young Duke of Buccleuch, which paid him £500 a year and gave him exposure to the leading philosophes in France. After 1766, when he settled in his birthplace of Kirkcaldy on a comfortable pension from Buccleuch to devote himself to his writings, he became a virtual closet philosopher. Like Hume in his later career, Smith had a huge reputation but little influence.[16]

Adam Ferguson, by contrast, remained in tenure of a university chair from 1759, when he was appointed by outrageous jobbery as Professor of Natural Philosophy at Edinburgh University, a subject which he was not qualified to teach; his familiarity with the seedy world of aristocratic patronage earned him the nickname 'Bute's Ferguson'. His move to the chair of Moral Philosophy in 1764 gave a more congenial subject on which to lecture. A more sociable figure than Smith, he was a leading member of both the Select Society and the deviser of the name for the Poker Club, which was formed in 1762 to 'poke up' opinion on the militia issue. The only leading figure in the academic Scottish Enlightenment to have direct links with the Highlands, his first publication was the translation of a sermon he had delivered in 1745 while chaplain to The Black Watch, urging on the regiment the benefits of being North Britons. A new-style jingoism brought him the secretaryship of the commission sent to Philadelphia in 1778 to negotiate with the American rebels and ended any doubts he had previously harboured as to the rightness of the British cause. His most significant work, the *Essay on the History of Civil Society* (1767), reflected the new times which began to emerge in the 1760s; overlain with a veneer of 'moral sentiment', it articulated a deep concern for the social unity of the community. It reflected both the 'rise of sensibility' amongst the Moderate clergy and the new sympathy for the Highlands beginning to surface in some minds after the calculated assaults on clan society after the '45.[17]

If Ferguson was an accurate mirror of changing times, William Robertson has a better claim to be a giant of his age. His first important work, the *History of Scotland* (1759), tackled the thorny reigns of Mary, Queen of Scots and James VI. Although his appointment as Principal of Edinburgh University necessarily followed the well-trodden paths of patronage, his claims as both the outstanding historian of his day and as the candidate of the Moderate party in the Kirk were hard to resist. His three-volume *History of the Reign of Charles V* (1769) gave him a wider stage and his *tour de force*, a two-volume *History of America* (1777), became the standard authority in English until the middle of the nineteenth century.[18] His works, translated into all the main European languages, brought him fame throughout Europe and considerable income, but his lasting achievement was the growth under his principalship of the University of Edinburgh. In the late seventeenth century, it had had some 400 students; by 1789, its numbers were almost 1,100.[19] Some 400 of those students were by then engaged in the study of medicine, and one American student exaggerated only a little when he described it in 1778 as 'the first University in Europe for Medicine'.[20]

If the Select Society and the Poker Club had, together with the *Edinburgh Review*, been the focal points of the central years of Edinburgh's literati, the Mirror Club and its associated journals – the *Mirror* and the *Lounger* – were the symbols of a third and different phase which set in soon after the collapse of the Select Society in 1763. The militia issue lingered into the 1780s as an irritant, and the *Caledonian Mercury*, which came out daily instead of thrice weekly after 1776, increasingly gave itself over to more Scottish content. The first *Edinburgh Review* (1755-6) had had a large component of sermons and the bulk of the contributors were ministers, but the central feature of the 1770s and 1780s were the number of other outlets for the comforting message of Moderatism.[21] The most important Moderate divine of the period was Hugh Blair (1718-1800), Professor of Rhetoric at Edinburgh University from 1759 and the prototype of a new generation of Moderate ministers. His sermons, first published in 1777, have been described as the best-selling work, after Addison's *Spectator*, written in the English language in the eighteenth century. Their attraction to a new, wider reading public, was best summed up by James Boswell, who praised them for their 'comfortable answers'.[22] Published in five volumes and numerous editions between 1777 and 1801, they were the placebo for an increasingly anxious society.

Almost as popular, and now equally obscure, were the novels of Henry Mackenzie, another Moderate minister and the guiding force behind both the Mirror Club and the *Lounger*. His first novel, *The Man of Feeling* (1771), an attack on romantic fiction which went through forty-six editions, established the novel as a new weapon in the armoury of the Kirk.[23] Aimed at both the vulnerable adolescent mind and the female reader, it gained a new and much wider audience for the literati, who had always been an immensely clubbable but inbred male society. The Scottish republic of letters was never more influential. It was ironical that just as it flourished in print as never before, the new strains brought on by the impact of the French Revolution were undermining the closed world of the literati. The Select Society had faded in popularity at the seeming height of its influence, in the early 1760s. A generation later, the Speculative Society, home of most of the later literati, saw attendance at its meetings decline after 1789; the proposal in 1794, supported by Walter Scott and Francis Jeffrey, that the Society be allowed to discuss 'the political topics of the day', split it asunder. Politics had infiltrated the world of the clubs. The new *Edinburgh Review*, founded by Jeffrey and others in 1802 as a mouthpiece of Whig views, confirmed the split.[24] The novel continued and found a new form in Walter Scott; the clubs and journals took up the postures of party politics. The unique atmosphere which for almost a century had stimulated and cosseted the brilliant world of the literati dissolved. It was, as Henry Cockburn, judge, eccentric and spokesman of the Whig ascendancy, later remarked nostalgically and somewhat misleadingly, 'the last purely Scotch age'. The North British option, of a polite society purged of its 'vulgar' Scotticisms yet still distinctively Scottish in both its range of ideas and its common methodology, had gone. A new synthesis, able to accommodate itself to a more uniform British culture, had to be devised.

'Hotbeds of genius'

It was the Edinburgh printer and biographer, William Smellie, who recorded and immortalised a remark made by an English visitor, Mr Amyat, at the height of Edinburgh's reputation as a 'hotbed of genius': 'Here I stand at what is called the Cross of Edinburgh, and can, in a few minutes, take fifty men of genius and learning by the hand'. In Edinburgh there had been indications of a new spirit of the age as early as 1710, when the Assembly Rooms were opened. By 1720, the city had two newspapers. The first circulating library in the country was opened there in 1728. By the 1730s, there were a range of clubs catering for scientific interests as well as literary and agricultural. The Medical Society, founded in 1731, had evolved six years later into the Philosophical Society, which had as its concern 'the study of natural knowledge and the advancement of science'.[25] Plans for a new medical school were hatched by George Drummond in his first term of office as Lord Provost in 1725-6.[26] It was part of a wider vision to revive the city's economic fortunes, which had been badly hit by the abolition of the Scottish parliament and the drain of the landed classes and money from it as a result of the Union of 1707.

Drummond was almost certainly the inspiration for the 'Proposals for carrying on certain Public Works in the City of Edinburgh' devised by Gilbert Elliott (later Lord Minto) in 1752. It was the first explicit vision of a New Town 'to enlarge and beautify the town, by opening new streets to the north and south'. The Nor' Loch, an open sewer, was to be converted into a canal 'with walks and terraces on each side'; it was only in the early nineteenth century that a scheme to turn it into formal gardens was devised. The plan cited the examples of Berlin and Turin, where a beautiful capital city attracted both nobility and trade. 'A capital', it concluded, 'should naturally become the centre of trade and commerce, of learning and the arts, of politeness and refinement of every kind'.[27] In September 1753, the foundation stone for the Royal Exchange, a meeting place for the city's merchants planned by John and Robert Adam, was laid. In 1763, the building of North Bridge across the now drained Nor' Loch began. In 1767, after a competition for designs for a New Town was won by an unknown twenty-two-year-old architect, James Craig, nephew of the poet James Thomson, work on it began. In fact, serious obstacles lay in the way of Drummond's vision. The Royal Exchange was never popular with the city's merchants and was later adapted for use by the Town Council. Part of North Bridge collapsed in 1769, killing five people. Considerable inducements were needed to encourage the reluctant citizens of Edinburgh to invest in the New Town. By the time it neared realisation, the years of Edinburgh as a 'modern Athens' were largely in the past.

The idea of a new town – in Edinburgh and elsewhere – was, nevertheless, of immense significance for the growth of a middle class, which, by the 1820s, would show its new influence in Scottish society. The wide streets, symmetrically ordered in a grid-like pattern, were a visible symbol of a new sense of social order, and the spacious living quarters of the houses bred a new privacy for the family, removed from the workplace. If Blair's sermons and Mackenzie's novels were the stuff of which middle-class morality was made, the New Town was its incubator. Edinburgh's New Town and its programme of public works would become in the space of the next half century a model for other towns to follow. Sir John Sinclair devised an ambitious grid-style plan for Thurso and in Ayr in the early decades of the nineteenth century new streets and a square were laid out in imitation of Edinburgh.[28]

It had been Tobias Smollett in his novel, *Humphrey Clinker*, who first dubbed Edinburgh as a 'hotbed of genius'. But the complex of ideas was not confined to Edinburgh and did not necessarily follow the pattern laid down there. The hub of Glasgow's Enlightenment was its university, where student numbers increased from 400 in 1702 to over 1,200 by 1824.[29] If Francis Hutcheson was the 'father of the Scottish Enlightenment',[30] Adam Smith and Joseph Black, who taught medicine and chemistry there, carried his ideas into various practical fields. Although clubs were late to develop in the city, ambitious plans to break out of the old burgh were devised early, in the 1750s; between then and 1775 a dozen new streets or squares were built, including Buchanan Street and St Enoch's Square.[31] Aberdeen, far from being drowned in conservatism or suffering from Jacobite introspection, showed, even more clearly than in the capital, the fact that the roots of the Enlightenment lay in the century of intellectual vigour which had preceded the Union of 1707. There, although there was less interest in the teaching of medicine or science, the University spawned its own strain of Enlightenment, centred on moral philosophy and political economy. It was there that the thoughts of the 'common sense' school were first formulated by Thomas Reid and later were popularised by James Beattie (1735-83). The main forum for its ideas was the Aberdeen Philosophical Society, founded in 1758. The Gordon Mills Farming Club, formed in the same year, pursued a highly provincialised, and distinctinctly more practical version of agricultural improvement. As in Edinburgh, an architectural competition was launched in 1799 to realise plans to reconstruct the burgh's medieval core. In terms of topographical difficulties to overcome and the scale of the enterprise, the scheme was as ambitious as anything in Edinburgh; the building of the mile-long Union Street belonged to the nineteenth century, but its genesis lay in the cool rationality of civic improvement which had begun in the late eighteenth century.[32]

The circulation of new ideas was not confined to Protestant clergy or to the university towns. Bishop John Geddes and Bishop George Hay, the two leaders of the late eighteenth-century Catholic Mission, drank deep at the well of enlightened manners. Geddes, an archetype of the enlightened man of letters, was a contributor to the *Encyclopaedia Britannica* and a confidant of both Henry Dundas and Lord Buchan, founder of the Society of Antiquaries in 1780. Hay's literary output encompassed philosophy, religion and politics, and his catechisms were reprinted thoughout the English-speaking Catholic world; he was the Catholic Hugh Blair.[33]

By the end of the eighteenth century, almost every sizeable town in the Lowlands had a printing press, and many had a newspaper as well. The first major edition of Robert Burns's work was printed in Kilmarnock, and his printer, John Wilson, produced a range of other titles, including sermons, Milton's *Paradise Lost* and Anson's *Voyage around the World*. He then moved to the county town of Ayr, where since 1762 there had been a 'library society'; in 1777 it had forty-seven members, including merchants, members of the professional classes and local gentry. The minute book of the Ayr Library Society shows the immediate impact of many of the main works of the Enlightenment, which were bought direct from the Edinburgh bookseller, William Creech. In 1776, it acquired Adam Smith's *Wealth of Nations* and Lord Kames's *The Gentleman Farmer* as well as the first volume of Gibbon's *Decline and Fall of the Roman Empire*; all three had been published in that year.[34] As much as Edinburgh's New Town, the growth of a provincial culture in Ayr and elsewhere demonstrated the unmistakable rise of a middle class.

Origins and paradoxes of the Enlightenment

Eighteenth-century Edinburgh is conventionally seen as a metropolis in process of rapid growth, a burgeoning and increasingly sophisticated urban society which by 1755 had a population of 57,000. In 1792 there was one female domestic servant for every eight families.[35] Yet the largest single occupation a century earlier, according to the poll tax of 1691, was female domestic service, which accounted for no less than 34 per cent of all occupations. Edinburgh in the 1690s had already an economy with a highly specialised service sector: there were forty booksellers, printers and bookbinders and no fewer than sixty-five wigmakers.[36] There are grounds for thinking that it was the seventeenth century, by whose end Edinburgh had a population of somewhere between 40,000 and 50,000, that was the century of significant population growth; by contrast, the early part of the eighteenth, it is likely, saw at best modest growth or stagnation. Significant increase came only in the third quarter of the eighteenth century: after twenty years which saw its population increase by some 23 per cent, it had by 1775 about 70,000 inhabitants. And Edinburgh's experience was not unique; Glasgow, Aberdeen and Dundee were all growing at a higher rate, being somewhere between a quarter and a third larger in 1775 than they had been in 1755.[37] The significant increase in a wider middle-class reading public, which can be measured by the number of titles published annually in Scotland, probably came later: there was a slow increase, from 141 a year in the 1750s to 167 in the 1780s, until numbers leapt up to 266 a year in the 1790s. By 1815, however, the number of titles had doubled to 565. The age of the popular novel – and Walter Scott – had arrived.[38]

In both practical civics and in the pursuit of the intellect, it was the later seventeenth century which had first seen Edinburgh's significant advance towards a fashionable, cosmopolitan society. The origins of civic improvement which culminated in James Craig's design of 1767 can be traced to the 1680s, the centrepoint of this period of rising population. Proposals were then mooted, with the encouragement of James VII, for both an expansion of Edinburgh's narrow bounds and a bridge-building programme to improve access to it, but they were overtaken by the crisis of the Revolution of 1689-90. The Loch Bank Estate, on the northern side of the Nor' Loch (where Princes Street and George Street now run), had been acquired by the Council in 1720, with a view to building a residential quarter there, and it was then that the later plans for converting the Loch into a canal were first mooted. The schemes for a new medical school at Edinburgh in the eighteenth century built on three successive attempts of the previous century, in 1617-21, 1630-4 and in the 1650s; they were also linked through the continuing resort of Edinburgh and other Scottish students to the medical school at Leiden. Newton's theories of light and colour were being taught by a number of academics in Edinburgh University from the 1670s onwards. There was a broad-based advance amongst the Scottish universities, and especially those in Edinburgh and Aberdeen, in the study of mathematics, law and some of the physical sciences between the 1670s and the 1720s. The study of the notebooks of students reveals a story of the increasing range and sophistication of teaching in the universities over a long period; it is less dramatic than the pursuit of great men, but it helps explain the force of their impact. Enlightened ideas did not burst upon an unprepared stage in the 1730s; they had been gathering momentum in the universities since at least the 1670s. And the cultivation of manners had a still longer provenance.[39]

In its wider aspects, the roots of the 'Age of Improvement' lay deep in the seventeenth century. Indeed, the Education Act of 1696, far from producing a framework which would eventually lead to a school in every Lowland parish, marked the acknowledgement of what had already largely been achieved over the course of the previous century. The first parliamentary 'improvement' act had been passed in 1649, to make easier the division of commonties. There had been a whole series of minor improvements, including the drainage of fields and the conversion of waste, in the second half of the century; liming of the soil, which was common in Fife and Lothian in the 1620s, can be traced to the 1590s in Orkney.[40] Planned towns or villages can be found in the sixteenth century and were common by the last quarter of the seventeenth. Despite the strictures of Adam Smith, most significant eighteenth-century improvements in roads and bridges and in towns were public works. The Scottish parliament had a long record of intervention in economic enterprises which went back to at least the 1620s. By the 1670s, it was explicitly mercantilist; the activities of the Board of Trustees for Fisheries and Manufactures recalled the earlier attempts of government in the Restoration period to promote economic activity.[41]

The eighteenth century is rightly hailed as the age when Scotland became one of the most important centres of intellectual culture in the western world. It did so, however, not by cutting loose from its past but by building on it. In a figure such as James Tytler (1745-1804), who edited the ten-volume second edition of the Encyclopaedia Britannica single-handed, the popular face of the hotbed of genius is revealed. Tytler – chemist, surgeon, printer, poet, political agitator, hack journalist – also manned the first hot-air balloon ascent in Britain at Edinburgh in 1784; he was the very model of a virtuoso of an enlightened age, but his was also an eclectic mind, little different from those of his forerunners in the Restoration period. Too much reading of the claims of the prophets of a new age has seemed to induce in some historians of the Enlightenment a notion of a watershed whose suddenness was overwhelming. There is little reason to believe that the eighteenth century was not like any other which preceded it: despite appearances, continuity outweighed change.

Another of the products of Enlightenment historiography is the fondness for seeking out things 'modern'. It is an understandable habit, mostly practised by intellectual historians, but it is also usually unhistorical. Historians of Hanoverian England have been warned of the need to view the period in its own terms and not to look for the prototype of a motor car in the outline of a sedan chair.[42] The *philosophes* of the Scottish Enlightenment did view their society from the vantage point of a sedan chair and the privileged world of the clubs. Philosophers may legitimately trace the growth of scepticism to eighteenth-century thinkers such as David Hume. Historians, seeing a society in which bibles and sermons were more popular than at any other period, before or since, should find it harder to view this solely as the 'age of Hume'. Fourteen of the thirty-one articles in the first two issues of the *Edinburgh Review* in 1755 had been taken up with sermons or other religious matters. Nor was it the age of Adam Smith. By the last quarter of the century, the 'pursuit of virtue' (as contemporaries called it) had firmly turned away from the economic to the moral aspect of humankind.

To contemporaries, this was, above all, the age of the Moderate ministers. In some of their concerns, they do seem thoroughly modern: they were involved in opposition to slavery and some shared an early Wordsworth-like enthusiasm for the ideals of the French Revolution. The Moderates were also, however, firmly resolved on the advantages of patronage in the Church and held strictly to a view of society as an ordered hierarchy. The ethos of the Moderates was most characteristically summed up by John Drysdale, a close colleague of Blair, in a sermon 'On the Distinction in Ranks'. In it, Drysdale argued that the relationship between master and servant was inherently natural to society, in both this world and the next.[43] The landed classes, no less than Boswell, would have found comfort in such sermons; some even took notes on them in church. The strength of the Moderate ministers lay in Edinburgh and the General Assembly. Yet, like the other literati, they depended on an intricate web of largely aristocratic patronage to sustain their influence. Both groups were as a result a living paradox. They belonged to a movement which was largely urban in milieu and professional in character, but its values were indelibly those of the landed interest. *Plus ça change, plus c'est la même chose* – or so they hoped. Enlightened ideas were not in pursuit of a Utopian future; they were intended to preserve the status quo and the best values of the age of North Britain.

A new Caledonia?

In 1822, George IV became the first British monarch to see his Scottish kingdom in 171 years. In the last formal visit, of Charles I in 1633, an elaborate tableau depicting Scotland's long line of kings back to Fergus mac Erc had been the centrepiece of his entry into Edinburgh. In 1822, the focal point was the King himself, sensationally dressed in flesh-coloured tights and kilt – a form of dress banned after the '45 and permitted again only in 1782. Like kings of Scots before him, George adopted the clothes of the erstwhile enemies of his dynasty – the Stewart tartan. The impresario of the visit was Sir Walter Scott, who had, so complained one of the few sceptics at the event, 'made us appear a nation of Highlanders'.[44] The cult of tartan, bagpipes and clans – for George had been kitted out as 'Chief of Chiefs' – was a caricature, but it did answer a deeply felt need for some satisfying national identity, which 'North Britishness' had been unable to supply. By 1848, when Queen Victoria acquired Balmoral, reservations had all but disappeared. The Queen proceeded to decorate the newly built house – done in the 'authentic' Scots Baronial style – in a riot of tartans: Hunting Stewart (in green), Dress Stewart (mostly in white) and Balmoral (in grey) were added to the red of Royal Stewart. Lord Rosebery thought its drawing room was the ugliest room in the world, but, as one of a parade of British politicians forced to make the long, late-summer train journey to Deeside for a royal audience, he may have had a jaundiced view of it. Victoria claimed a special affinity with the Scottish people, because of the Stewart blood, 'the family of my ancestors', in her veins. Although it would have taken an expert in haematology to detect it, her larger claim was well founded: the monarchy had discovered a new popularity, which intertwined and camouflaged the conflicting identities of a Scottish nation within a British state. The very 'Scottishness' of Balmoral helped give the monarchy a truly British dimension for the first time.[45]

In 1848, Victoria first attended the Braemar Gathering. Highland gatherings had been held since the Falkirk Tryst, organised by the Highland Society in 1781, and by the 1820s they extended thoughout the country. The stamp of royal approval gave them both respectability and greater popularity, but at the expense of some of the content. The early meetings had been piping competitions and the Highland Society a 'Gaelic Academy'.[46] In 1822 the Society – in origin an Ossianic branch of the Enlightenment dedicated to the preservation of Gaelic language, song and music – was overwhelmed by a flood of queries from aristocrats and Lowland notables as to details of the correct mode of Highland dress. The Society continued, and the founding of a chair of Celtic at Edinburgh University in 1883 – after nearly a century of struggle – was only one of its achievements, but it had also surrendered the popular ground. In Wales, culture and language held together, and produced the *Eisteddfod*. Nothing fostered the radicalism of nineteenth-century Welsh political nationalism more than the fact that 8,500 separate titles were published in Welsh during the period.[47] In Scotland, Gaelic was allowed to wither, and Scottish culture gladly embraced a *Gaedhealtachd* with its linguistic teeth pulled. A new, sanitised vision of Scottishness emerged – in the minds, at least, of Lowlanders and tourists.

Where Scott and monarchy led, others followed. Tartan clothed many of the British aristocracy, opened up a myriad of opportunities for Scottish firms to use it on items ranging from door knobs to biscuit tins, and cloaked the harsh realities of Highland life in the nineteenth century. In 1881, army reforms forced even Scottish Lowland regiments into Highland dress – or a version that passed for it. One of the best-known manifestations of the new Scotland – the modern clan society – came surprisingly late. Clan MacNaughton was founded in 1878 and Clan Mackay was reconstituted in 1888. By the mid-1890s they were, however, in tremendous vogue, to the irritation of one Glasgow newspaper, which complained of the 'innumerable Highland clan societies that are swaggering in tartan, 'painfully acquiring the pronunciation of their respective battle-cries, and searching for chiefs'.[48]

'Tartanry' was substitute history, but a serious search for Scotland's past was again under way. It had been no accident that Scott's first novel, *Waverley*, had been set during the '45 rising. This was history for a mass market. But Scott was also the mentor of the historical clubs, which collectively represented the greatest achievement of any period of Scottish historical scholarship. He founded the Bannatyne Club, the first and greatest of them, which produced 118 separate works between 1823 and 1867. Most are still the standard texts of Scottish history. Its main rival, the Maitland Club, was an extension of the civic pride of the fast-growing city of Glasgow. Other local clubs followed. Their total output in the century was over a thousand works.[49] The intensity of the search for Scotland's history was truly astonishing, but consensus had broken down. Evangelicals such as Thomas McCrie, who wrote well-researched biographies of John Knox and Andrew Melville in the 1810s, looked to the essential truths of the Reformation as a guide to the complexities of the present. It was part of an evangelical counter-Enlightenment, which would flourish amidst the religious diputes of the rest of the century. The break-up of the Established Church in 1843 into two bodies which both claimed to be *the* historic Church produced more writings on both the Reformation and the Covenanters, but it also encouraged different denominations of presbyterians to leapfrog the Middle Ages in a quest for their own roots: the result was a rash of churches named after Columba, often glowering at each other across 'holy corners' in Scotland's towns and cities. Episcopalians, in contrast, revelled in neo-medievalism, and especially in the study of the architecture and liturgy of the medieval Church. This, too, was history with a point to prove. Members of the Oxford movement were dismayed when the greatest of the episcopalian historians, Cosmo Innes, allowed scholarship to outweigh good taste by producing a picture of the medieval Church, warts and all.[50]

The impact of this enormous activity on society as a whole was slight. Scottish history was taught only fitfully in the schools, and hardly at all in the universities before the setting up of chairs of Scottish history at Edinburgh and Glasgow in 1901 and 1913 respectively.[51] Their provenance is instructive. One was founded by a legacy left by Sir William Fraser, an Edinburgh lawyer who had made a lucrative living out of well-researched family histories which pandered to the vanities of the aristocracy. The other was the product of a coalition of interests ranging from Burns Clubs to pan-Celtic enthusiasts; funds were completed by an exhibition of Scottish history, art and industry staged at Kelvingrove, which had an artificial Highland village, 'An Clachan', as its centrepiece.[52] A polite, 'kailyard' vision of the Scottish past became entrenched. Its normal route to the middle-classes lay in publications such as the enormously popular *People's Journal*, which mixed serialised fiction with half-fictitious history of a romantic age before industrialisation. A huge gap had resulted between serious scholarship, practised in the nineteenth century only by the dedicated amateur, and popular history, clothed in prejudice or tartan.

Robert Burns, although honoured in his own land, was not fully lionised until the last years of the century: there were only eight affiliated Burns Clubs in 1885, but 200 by 1911. He was seized upon by some as an antidote to the 'tartan menace' and as the voice of ordinary Scots; in 1858, the centenary of his birth, the *North Briton* appealed to the 'working men of Edinburgh' not to 'give him up to the higher classes'.[53] The real growth of his popularity coincided with the search for a new working-class culture at the end of the nineteenth century. Before then, his reputation – and especially his individuality and libertarian impulses – were celebrated more fulsomely in the Scottish diaspora, made up of emigrants in Canada, New Zealand and Australia. A settler patriotism produced Caledonian societies, Burns Clubs and Highland Gatherings in greater numbers and often earlier than in the homeland. It was in this Greater Scotland overseas that a form of Scottishness – freed from the complexities of living in a nation within a larger nation-state – flourished most.

A Greater Britain
In the course of the nineteenth century the three main institutions which protected Scotland's identity – the Church, education and the law – were all forced on to the retreat. The Church tried to bargain for greater patronage from the British state and ended up in conflict, both with it and with itself. Its distinctive identity retreated into a narrow, legalistic defence of its own privileges; its status slipped from that of a national Church to a minority Establishment. Education underwent profound soul-searching, which began in 1834 with George Lewis's provocatively titled tract *Scotland: a Half-Educated Nation* and lasted through a series of royal commissions which inquired into the workings of the universities. The sense of crisis had been heightened by the introduction of competitive examinations for entry into the Indian civil service in 1852 which were geared to the Oxford and Cambridge system. Scottish-trained candidates did badly; jobs, the basis of the new imperial vision first offered by Dundas in the 1780s, were now more difficult to get. The sense of superiority of Scotland's parochial schools was under threat. Nowhere were Scottish feelings more sensitive, and objections to anglicisation – both real and imagined – louder. Intrusion into Scots law was more subtle but also more substantial. A wave of legislation opened up new areas – in public health, working conditions in factories, the protection of investors – which had not previously been covered, by Scots law or any other. The inexorable process was not so much anglicisation as an assault by the collective British state, which has continued into the late twentieth century.[54]

In 1848 the first railway link to England was completed. In the 1850s, with the journey time between London and Edinburgh or Glasgow reduced from forty-three hours to twelve and the possibility of instant communication opened up by the electric telegraph, the Union was suddenly more complete than ever before. It was no accident that this was also the decade which saw the first concerted 'nationalist' protest, in the shape of the Association for the Vindication of Scottish Rights, formed in 1853. Some of its demands, such as its defence of Scottish heraldry, may give an impression of an eccentric nationalist fringe, but its main rationale was a re-apportionment of the place of Scotland in British politics. Scotland wanted not less union but more – in parliamentary representation and government expenditure –

357

and on a fairer basis. The Association fizzled out by 1855, but it left an agenda which Scottish nationalism has drawn on ever since.[55]

The railways were one symbol of the complex interaction between Scotland and England. Most investors in the longer routes across the Border were English and this has sometimes been taken as symbolic of the control being increasingly exercised over the Scottish economy by England.[56] The traffic was not one-way. The first Scotch Wool Shop opened in Greenock in 1881 and by 1901 there was a chain of 200 branches across Britain. Thomas Lipton, who opened his first grocer's shop in Glasgow's Stobcross Street in 1870, was at the forefront of the British retailing revolution in the late nineteenth century. Much Scottish investment was already by 1850 in the various parts of the Empire and in the USA, where industries and railways attracted Scottish capital.[57]

In both the interplay of ideas and the workings of rival British and Scottish institutions, it is easier to detect mutual influences rather than a simple, overweening process of anglicisation of Scottish society. The Friends of the People imported notions of the long struggle of the English people since the Norman yoke, but some of them also reinterpreted Scottish history in terms of a conquest – by England. The radicals of 1820 talked of Magna Charta, but 'Scots wha hae!' was hummed in the Lancashire cotton mills of the 1830s as a song of liberty.[58] Chartism in Scotland can be seen as an movement imported from England, but it survived after 1838 only in a peculiarly Scottish form – of Chartist churches. In a series of new areas of Victorian Britain – missionary societies, trades unions, friendly societies or even the Boys' Brigade – mutual influences can be detected but usually the Scots preferred to establish their own operations. The stance taken by the president of the newly founded Scottish Trades Union Congress against the British Trades Union Congress in 1897 summed up generations of experience: 'They believed if they wanted anything well done they had to do it themselves'.[59]

Nineteenth-century Scotland was a melting-pot of different, overlapping identities. They might be summed up in the story of three notable banquets. In 1822, in Parliament Hall in Edinburgh, the serried ranks of 300 members of the tartan-bedecked aristocracy celebrated the homecoming of a Hanoverian king with forty-seven toasts, most with their own supporting music, such as *Highland Laddie* and *The Campbells are coming, hurra!*[60] It was a step into a new age of tartanry but it also owed something to the hard-drinking conviviality of the golden age of the eighteenth century, when a head for alcohol was a vital asset of polite manners. Only fourteen years later, 3,383 more sober – and more soberly dressed – members of Glasgow middle classes sat down, in a specially built hall, to the largest banquet ever held in Glasgow. It was to celebrate the guest of honour, Sir Robert Peel, the first British Prime Minister to be elected Rector of Glasgow University; the theme of the occasion was the defence of the British constitution.[61] Bourgeois respectability linked arms with the new British state, which had emerged after the Reform Act of 1832. In 1883, to celebrate the laying of the foundation stone of Glasgow's new Municipal Buildings, located in George Square, another banquet was held – after a day of processions which included dozens of masonic lodges, trades unions, friendly societies and the band of the 93rd Highlanders. It was the celebration of a Greater Glasgow, which now occupied 'first position amongst the industrial cities in the empire' – the claim must have been taken seriously, for it was the Lord Provost of

Edinburgh who made it.[62] The concentric loyalties of Victorian Scotland – a new Scottishness, a new Britishness and a revised sense of local pride – were held together by a phenomenon bigger than all of them – a Greater Britain whose prosperity and stability rested on the Empire.[63]

Cultural loyalties were one matter, but politics was another. The century saw a 'blending' of values and influences into a 'Britannic melting-pot',[64] but politics in Scotland nevertheless remained stubbornly 'Scotch'. The effect of George IV's visit was to let loose a flood of sentiment which closed the gap between Scotland's present and its past, but no nationalist movement of consequence resulted. The AVSR shrank far short of wanting to dissolve the Union and the demand for Home Rule which surfaced in the 1880s was kept firmly within the grasp of the Liberal Party. Peel's visit was part of an attempt to rehabiliate Scottish Toryism after the Reform Act, but he was at a loss to know how to deal with the issue which dominated all others in the later 1830s – the Church question. Although the imperial idea infused local patriotism, it paid poor returns at the ballot box – as the Conservatives, who had groomed themselves in British politics as the 'national' party from the mid-1870s, discovered. In the confusing world of politics, Scottishness, Britishness and even Empire were not assets which could easily be banked. Scottish politics had its own concerns, which operated at two levels. In 'British' politics, it was religious issues – state aid to the Established Church or intrusion into it in the 1830s, the content and control of education in the 1850s and 1860s, and disestablishment intermittently from the 1870s until the 1890s – which mattered most to Scottish voters.[65] In local politics, it was usually civic patriotism which predominated. The control of independent ratepayers over Glasgow's town council was not seriously challenged until 1920, when Labour won a third of the seats; but Labour first gained control of Glasgow from the 'Progressives' only in 1933.

Alternative identities

Glasgow was both the most advanced municipality in Britain and an imperial city. The Glasgow civic state – in which the Corporation ran everything from trams to telephones – was the nineteenth-century 'new town', in which notions of space and order, vital to the middle-class view of the world, were given physical form. Municipalisation was the Victorian version of Improvement – a new philosophy of patriotism, no longer North British but at once civic and imperial. The city was the new reality, to which other, more ephemeral loyalties, both new and old, might stick. For the evangelists it was 'gospel city': the motto, 'Let Glasgow flourish by the preaching of the Word' was the product of its mid-century zeal. For late-Victorian civic reformers, it was the ideal city of the social gospel, a vast working model of Christian enterprise.[66] Civic culture was confident and cosmopolitan – Glasgow was already in the 1880s being likened to a Scottish Chicago. It was the spiritual home of temperance and of friendly societies such as the Rechabites – both imports from the USA. It was the point of embarkation for thousands of emigrants, both to the USA and the Empire, as well as the entry point for huge numbers of immigrants, mostly from Ireland. Sir John A. Macdonald, born in the city in 1815, emigrated to become the first Premier of the Dominion of Canada. A former Governor-General of India, Lord William Bentinck, was invited to represent it in parliament. It hosted

International Exhibitions in 1888 and 1901. The key elements of its economy – ships, marine engines, railway locomotives – thrived on the opportunities afforded it east and south of Suez after the opening of the Canal in 1869.[67] The result was a curious one: Edinburgh remained a capital city without a government, for most functions of government, such as they were, operated from London. Glasgow became an alternative capital, representing not Scotland, but Scotland's place in an imperial Greater Britain.

In the second half of the nineteenth century the big city overtook other spheres of identity. The concentric circles of a 'sense of place' – local community and nationhood – were refashioned to accommodate it. No element was more important in this process than the growth of a 'national game' – football. Scots had played it for centuries. A parliament of James IV had banned it. The first 'internationals' between Scotland and England had been played in the sixteenth century, at the occasional tryst days between wardens from both sides of the Border. In 1568, Mary, Queen of Scots, watched as twenty of her retinue played an English team made up of halberdiers near Carlisle; an (English) observer commented favourably on the superior skills of the Scots, 'the smallness of their ball occasioning fairer playe'.[68] Sir Walter Scott was a passionate follower of the mass scrimmages in some Border towns which passed for football – the game at Jedburgh between 'Uppies' and 'Doonies' of the town survived into the twentieth century. The future, however, belonged to the subtler skills of the 'tanner ba', which was well suited to the back-streets of the cities: by the 1890s, one male in four between the ages of fifteen and thirty belonged to a football club.[69] By then soccer was not only the national sport but *the* working-class game.

The speed of its popular growth was astonishing. Queen's Park Club, founded in 1867, was made up of young businessmen. The spread of the half-day Saturday holiday to the skilled man in the 1870s and to the unskilled in the 1890s transformed football. By the time Celtic was founded in 1887 and began to plan a stadium for 70,000 people, soccer had become the new opium of the masses. A crowd of 40,000 watched them in their first Scottish Cup Final, in 1892. An even bigger stadium, the new Hampden Park – then the largest in the world – was opened in 1903; it accommodated a crowd of 102,000 at the first international gane against England played there. Existing institutions – and especially the churches – tried to accommodate the new mania. Celtic had been founded as a boys' club by a Marist brother and even the Band of Hope ran its own youth teams. But the secularisation of Scottish society, which gathered pace only in the early years of the twentieth century, had much to do with the emergence of an alternative popular culture.

Football became a new focus for the loyalties of the working man – local (and perhaps sectarian), Scottish but, in a sense, British too – for it was both the 'national game' and the British national game.[70] It contained many of the same paradoxes as other, older institutions in Scottish society. The early professional teams were almost all big city teams, like Partick Thistle (1868), Rangers (1872) or Heart of Midlothian (1873) – populist symbols of the rise of the cities to a new pre-eminence in Scottish life. Their grounds were built amidst the new suburban tenements which housed the fast-expanding working classes – such as Hibernian (1875) at Easter Road. They gave fresh outlets to the tensions which had been triggered by large-scale Irish immigration. The 1870s were the decade when

Protestants from Ulster outnumbered all other Irish immigrants and the Orange Order began to expand. Clubs such as Celtic and Hibernian both preserved links with Ireland and set apart the Irish Catholic community from its roots: from 1892 soccer was ostracised as a 'British' game by the Gaelic Athletic Association.

At the outset, the game was explicitly both a British and a Scottish one: Queen's Park affiliated to the English FA, the first international between Scotland and England was played in 1872 at the West of Scotland Cricket Ground in Partick, and a separate Scottish Football Association was formed in 1873. Schism came only in 1886, after a bad foul provoked a riot at an FA cup game between Queen's Park and Preston North End; in the furore which followed Scottish teams were forbidden by the SFA from being members of other national associations. Even after that links persisted. 'Deciding' games between the holders of the Scottish Cup and the FA Cup were common: Hibernian in 1887 and Renton in 1888 claimed the title of 'champions of the world' after they won those matches.[71] Professional players were part of a new mobile workforce, which crossed and recrossed the Border. Most English teams, at least in the north, had at least one Scot; the Preston North End player fouled in that fateful match in 1886 was one of them. Every Scottish international team between 1895 and 1914 had its quota of 'Anglos'. Yet football well before the First World War had become the new focus of Scottish national feeling.[72] Both British and Scottish, together but apart – it was an emblem of the condition of a nation living within a larger nation-state.

21

THE HIGHLAND CONDITION

IN 1787, LESS THAN HALF A CENTURY AFTER CULLODEN, ROBERT BURNS MADE A tour of the Highlands. He was only one of a wave of curious visitors, usually inspired by the 'discovery' made in 1760 by James Macpherson of the works of Ossian. Burns was different only in being as interested in the human landscape of the Highlands as the physical. By 1792, there was an established tourist trail, which took in Loch Lomond, Ben Nevis and Fingal's Cave, set out in a two-volume guide to the Highlands written by an English clergyman, William Gilpin, who had made an alternative career as a propagator of the cult of the picturesque. Armed with Gilpin, visitors such as William and Dorothy Wordsworth were able to substitute a Highland wilderness in place of a 'noble savage'. By the 1820s, tourists also had the works of Walter Scott to inspire them and a four-volume guidebook, *The Highlands and Western Isles of Scotland*, written by John MacCulloch. By the 1830s, the Caledonian coach left Edinburgh for Inverness three times a week, 'crowded with tourists and their baggage, a motley catalogue of guns, fishing rods, pointers, creels and baskets'.[1] In 1842, Prince Albert shot two stags while on a visit to the Marquis of Breadalbane at Drummond Castle. Six years later, Queen Victoria acquired the decaying estate of Balmoral on Deeside. The royal family's identification with the Highlands, first revealed in bizarre form during George IV's visit to Edinburgh in 1822, was established. But the purchase of Balmoral was only one example of a wave of estates bought by Lowland or English incomers for hunting and shooting. Twenty-eight deer forests had been formed by 1839, and a further twenty-six by 1859.[2] Already, however, tourism on a larger scale was under way. The Highlands have some claim to being the venue for the first tourist 'package holiday'; combined tickets for rail and steamboats were being organised by Thomas Cook by mid-century. In 1863 the railway reached Inverness and the Scottish railway companies jointly produced a tourist itinerary. By 1880 trains could be taken to Oban.[3] The Highlands had already largely been recast, in the image of both its tourists and its new landowners.

The beginnings of a new view of the Highlands can be traced to the period soon after the '45, but it was as yet highly equivocal. The two faces of the Enlightenment are never better illustrated than in the ambiguity with which the Edinburgh literati viewed Highland society. The standard North Briton view of a primitive, papist society was part of official government propaganda at the time of the '45. Typical of it was *The Highlander Delineated*, a character assessment published in London in 1745 for the benefit of the English public of the 'ravenous mountaineers', who filled the ranks of the Pretender's army and were notorious for the 'wildness of their Manners'. Few of the leading figures in the Scottish Enlightenment, except for Adam Ferguson, had any direct experience of the Highlands. Their views ranged from David Hume, who despised Gaeldom in all its forms, to fervent Ossianic enthusiasts such as Hugh Blair. The mature cult of a lost Gaelic world, seen in its full mid-Victorian bloom in paintings such as Thomas Faed's *The Last of the Clan* and landscapes of Edwin Landseer such as *The Monarch of the Glen*, belonged to a period when the Highlander had long since been safely tamed; the 'noble savage' could be cultivated with less equivocation now that he belonged to history rather than the present.[4] In the 1750s, however, many Highlanders were neither tamed nor presbyterian, and leading Enlightenment figures such as Lord Kames and the Moderate minister, Dr John Walker, who made an extensive tour of the Western Isles in 1764, saw the civilisation of an alien society as the key to a more secure future.

Both Kames and Walker were Commissioners of the Annexed Estates, the board set up in 1755 to administer some forty Jacobite estates which had been forfeited to the crown after the crushing of the 1745 rising. As the Annexing Act of 1752 made clear, the promotion of the Protestant religion was an integral part of a wide-ranging programme of improvement, which also included the stimulation of 'good government, industry and manufactures'. The Board was at first full of enthusiasm, giving financial assistance to the SSPCK, building prisons at Stonehaven and Inverness, subsidising the manufacture of linen and saltpanning at Brora.[5] Increasingly it fell the way of many other improving landlords whose projects littered the history of the Highlands between 1750 and the 1820s. An absentee landlord which failed to delegate to agents on the spot, the Board lost touch, both with its estates and reality. By the time it was dissolved in 1784, it had left little permanent mark on the Highland economy. Its dissolution also marked the end of official government intervention in the Highlands until the late 1840s. The region was left to its landlords, *laissez-faire* and its own devices.

'Full of hot and furious zeal': religion and revival in the Highlands

The religious condition of the Highlands after the Reformation is something of a puzzle. More ministers and readers were planted there in the 1560s and 1570s, and especially in the dioceses of Dunkeld, Caithness and Ross, than has sometimes been thought and the printing of John Carswell's Gaelic translation of the Genevan Book of Common Order in 1567, the first printed book in Gaelic to appear in either Ireland or Scotland, would have involved a considerable investment of time and skill. The impact of the first generation of the reformed ministry was lessened by the fact that few were Gaelic speakers and Carswell's own influence was limited to the southern part of Argyll, the area controlled by his patron, the Earl of Argyll. In sharp contrast to the efforts of the Protestant churches in both Ireland and Wales, no more books in Gaelic were printed in Scotland until the second half of the seventeenth century. The early Highland ministers lacked the main instruments of evangelism used elsewhere by the Kirk; they had no vernacular catechism before 1653, no psalm book until 1659, and no kirk sessions until well into the seventeenth century. As a result, the first plantation of Protestantism in the Highlands, once outside Campbell territory or the frontier zone close to the Highland line, had shallow roots. The next important step in its history came, ironically, with the appearance of an Irish Gaelic Bible, in the 1690s. By then, there were habitual complaints that there were more Catholic priests than Protestant ministers in the Highlands.[6]

363

Although the SSPCK had been founded by royal charter in 1708 and was by 1715 running twenty-five schools, systematic promotion of Protestantism in the Highlands by the government began only after 1725, when a grant to the General Assembly, known as the Royal Bounty, began to be made on an annual basis. Part of the grant was used to support itinerant ministers, but in 1764 there were still only ten of them, almost the same as the number of Catholic priests in the Highland Mission. In parishes which on average were 400 square miles in area, and with few elders and even fewer boards of heritors on which to rely, the task facing these ministers after a century and a half of neglect was a formidable one, made all the more daunting by the fact that comparatively few spoke Gaelic. More significant to the spread of Protestantism, but more difficult to assess, were the lay catechists, who were the foot soldiers of the Kirk throughout the remainder of the century; no fewer than seventy were appointed between 1725 and 1728, to meet the people 'every Sabbath, to read the Scriptures, and to join with them in psalms and prayers'.[7]

The Established Church spoke to the Highlands with more than one voice, and its message was a confused one. Although there was a substantial overlap between the administration of the SSPCK and the Royal Bounty, their aims were not fully in harmony and they fell out in 1758. The avowed purpose of the SSPCK was to 'wear out' Gaelic and 'learn the people the English tongue'; it spurned the Gaelic catechism and the psalter produced by the Synod of Argyll in the 1650s. The General Assembly was not so consistently dogmatic, requiring that only part of every sermon be in English, and its catechists were Gaelic speakers. By 1754, the SSPCK had reluctantly changed tack, and sanctioned the printing of a Bible in which Gaelic and English text was printed on facing pages. The SSPCK's achievement was striking in terms of statistics: it had 116 schools in 1755 and 149 by 1792, but the bulk of them were crowded into the southern edge of the Highlands or in Moray and Easter Ross, even in 1792; only twenty-two were then located in the Isles. It was not until Gaelic Society schools began to be established after 1811 that a more comprehensive coverage of the Western Highlands and Isles was achieved, or that girls were taught in any significant numbers. The evangelical impact of the SSPCK was fatally hindered by its own cultural dogmatism.[8]

The growing strength of a committed Protestantism in the Highlands in the second half of the eighteenth century is not best measured by the activities of what were still essentially outside agencies. It is better seen in the recurring evidence, from 1740 onwards, of 'awakenings'. First seen in Easter Ross in 1739, this kind of spiritual 'stir among the people' was essentially local, lacking the wide-ranging appeal and publicity of the Cambuslang revival of 1742, but it seems to have attracted much the same age-group; most converts were young adults, aged between twenty and forty.[9] The 'awakened' did not usually indulge in the mass hysteria seen at Cambuslang, but in the Highlands the lack of an established ministry contributed to a pattern of spiritual rebirth, recession and reawakening some years later. It was perhaps the inevitable result of a faith which was forced to live on its nerves, nurtured by the charismatic presence of lay catechists like the 'Men', who combined the roles of modern evangelist and traditional seer. The legacy of the 'Men', combined with the fact that their influence coincided with the remaking of West Highland society into a crofting community after 1770, was long-lasting: they left a tradition of strict Sabbatarianism, handed on to the new parish ministers a role as prophets and leaders of their flock, and forged a popular consciousness in local society which would be reflected in protests against both patronage and Clearances in the nineteenth century.[10]

There was little dissent on the surface of the Established Church in the late eighteenth-century Highlands, but it had already within it the seeds of separation. Paradoxically, a greater social division already existed within the Highland Church than in the Lowlands, which had seen a series of splits and secessions from the 1740s onwards. Moderate ministers represented the landowners, their factors and the wealthier single tenants; increasingly evangelicals spoke for the crofters and cottars. A disruption had already taken place, in all but name, long before 1843. That was why, in Lewis, 98 per cent of parishioners joined the Free Church at the Disruption and in Sutherland the figure was reportedly higher still. The Disruption seemed to offer, for the first time, a Church fully in tune with Highland society. The steady, general drift of the Free Church towards middle-class respectability and the traumatic events of the 1840s and 1850s in the Highlands put this seeming natural alliance under severe strain. It would, however, be the liberalisation of the Free Church's doctrine in the 1890s which provoked secession: the Free Presbyterian Church, formed in 1893, was a new, distinctively Highland homeland for traditional presbyterianism.[11]

The Highlands in the eighteenth century were not a godless society, but one awaiting the opportunity for spiritual rebirth. In 1718, a report to the General Assembly about the state of parishes in Glengairn, on the lower slopes of the Grampians in Deeside, told of 'new converts, full of hot and furious zeal, filling all companies they were amongst with noisy debates'. But these were Catholic converts. Local Protestants, largely Episcopalian in their sympathies whom the Kirk had as yet scarcely reached, were, by contrast, 'cold, careless and generally indifferent'.[12] The evangelisation of the Highlands posed different problems in different areas. In the East and Central Highlands, the main task for the Established Church was how to counter and replace Episcopalianism, which was in a real sense the spiritual arm of Jacobitism. In the Western Highlands and the Isles, it had to choose between evangelising and 'civilising' the people and tried, until the late 1750s, to do both, and with only modest success as a result.

The Catholic Mission to the west was, in contrast, avowedly Gaelic in outlook. It had been fortunate in being able to rely on Irish priests for much of the seventeenth century. A mission of Irish Franciscans in the 1620s and 1630s had, so one of their number claimed, a dramatic impact: Propaganda in Rome received with some scepticism reports that 6,627 had been converted and 3,010 baptised in the course of 1633.[13] The Franciscan mission was, however, confined to the Western Isles between Islay and Skye and parts of the adjacent mainland; it did not reach further north than Glengarry. Jesuits were active in Strathglass from the 1670s, but in too small numbers to be called a mission. There are few physical traces of this 'underground' phase of Highland Catholicism. Even where Catholics were numerous, it was rare to build a church; in Lochaber, two mass stones, used as primitive altars, are its sole monuments.[14] The rebuilding in 1688 of the parish church of St Ninian's at Enzie, in Banff, was highly unusual; it and the seminary founded in 1716 at Scalan, in remote braes of Glenlivet, provided a base for Scottish Catholicism in the north-east during the eighteenth century.

Matters improved only slowly after the appointment of Thomas Nicolson as the first Vicar Apostolic over a separate Scottish Mission in 1694. A long campaign for a separate Highland Mission eventually bore fruit in 1732, when separate Highland and Lowland Districts were formed. The size of the Highland Mission was modest: it was staffed by a dozen priests or less until the 1760s; by the 1770s there were an average of fifteen and, by the 1790s, twenty. No fewer than six attempts were made between 1732 and 1828 to found a separate Highland seminary to train local boys; each limped from one financial crisis to another. Unsuccessful attempts were made to have the Lowland District seminary, transferred in 1799 to the more accessible Aquhorties, near Inverurie in Aberdeenshire, turned into an institution for the whole of the Scottish Mission, but it was not until Blairs College opened its doors in 1829 that Highland boys had a secure place of training. Even then the atmosphere at Blairs was for long hostile to young seminarians from Gaeldom.[15]

The strengths of Highland Catholicism belied the numbers of its clergy. All of its priests in the eighteenth-century, except for two from Ireland, were native Gaelic speakers. It was no accident that its first five bishops were all related to clan chiefs. Over three-quarters of its seminarians were MacDonalds or MacEachans. Despite its small numbers, the Highland Mission was rent by internal divisions. Accusations of Jansenism and drunkenness, which were all the more damaging because each had a grain of truth, were thrown at Hugh MacDonald, the first Highland Vicar-Apostolic, and his supporters by a disappointed rival. The fact that the vendetta was conducted by a Campbell, a most unusual convert from an otherwise vehemently Protestant family, added to the bitterness of a dispute which seriously rent the Highland Mission for a generation.[16]

Catholicism nevertheless held its ground, despite the efforts of the SSPCK and the General Assembly, which were both supported by the London government. It did so because its real props were Catholic landowners and heritors. On Barra, there were only forty Protestants and more than 1,000 Catholics in 1760. On South Uist, a minister reported in 1720 that although he had soldiered for forty years, he had never had more than eighteen attend his services; by 1764, matters had improved, but there were, according to the Moderate minister, Dr John Walker, who visited the island in that year, only 160 Protestants amidst 1,400 Catholics.[17] The common link was a Catholic laird. The influence of Clanranald, stretching far into Moidart, Knoydart and Lochaber, was the most important in the Western Highlands and the Isles. The patronage of landowners preserved Catholic enclaves, but also protected Catholic minorities in parishes like Boleskine, where their numbers remained relatively unchanged for much of the eighteenth century. In parishes such as Snizort and Sleat, where there were committed Protestant lairds, Catholicism was, by contrast, noticeably absent.[18]

By the last three decades of the century, however, some Catholic patrons were beginning to desert their faith. One example, on South Uist, was the opening of a Protestant school in 1770 by MacDonald of Boisdale. The desertion of many of its local patrons resulted in a rather different kind of Church. By 1799, the chief patron of Scottish Catholicism was none other than the government, which, concerned by the flood of Highland Catholics overseas and no longer obsessed by the spectre of Jacobitism, had secretly endowed the Aquhorties seminary. This was done at a time when the government was also encouraging the foundation of Irish Catholic colleges at Carlow and Maynooth, but there may have been other, distinctively Scottish factors at work to produce government pensions for the clergy of the Scottish Mission. The twin leaders of the Mission, Bishops Hay and Geddes, had a long connection with Dundas, and the government was already concerned to find ways to stem the flood of Highland Catholics overseas. It was out of gratitude as well as a deep political conservatism that Scottish priests and seminarians conscientiously prayed for 'our Sovereign King George'.[19]

Scottish Catholicism was at its crossroads. In 1764, it had been estimated that there were 13,166 Catholics in the Highlands; perhaps a quarter of them had emigrated by 1790. In 1792, Catholics in Glasgow could be counted in their hundreds. By 1827, when the Scottish Mission was again remodelled, with three Districts – Western, Eastern and Northern – it was estimated that the Western Vicariate, which stretched from Morar in the north to Galloway in the south-west, had 70,000 Catholics, but the vast bulk of them were concentrated in Glasgow and Lanarkshire, and only 4,000 spoke Gaelic. In the Highlands, there were more priests, but hardly any had a permanent abode; there were few chapels and very limited funds.[20] By then, Catholicism in the Highlands had been decisively overtaken by a much more dynamic Protestant mission. The causes of the decay of the Highland Mission lay, however, largely within the Catholic Church itself: in its underfunding and the lack of status accorded to it throughout the eighteenth century, both by Rome and its better-off neighbour, the Lowland District.

The debate on the Clearances

There are few issues in Scottish history which rouse such deep feelings as the Clearances and fewer still in which there is such a profound collision of evidence. Oral history, folk memory, Gaelic poetry, sensational newspaper reports and the evidence given before the Napier Commission in 1883 of the happenings which had taken place one or two generations before are all the stuff of the clearing times. Estate records, learned editorials of pro-landlord newspapers such as the *Inverness Courier* or the *Scotsman*, which was fond of blasts against 'Celtic laziness', demographic statistics showing a growing population on the land and the analysis of seemingly inexorable economic factors by some modern historians have all contributed to a defence of landlords. In one view, the logic of Clearance had an inexorable and gathering momentum, because the basic problem was population growth and pressure on the land: the population of the Highlands rose from 115,000 in 1755 to 154,000 in 1801 and to 201,000 by 1831. Congestion on the land inevitably led to the clearance of it.[21] In another, the 'Highland problem' was the creation of the landlords, who encouraged a new structure of small holdings in the period between 1770 and 1810, picked up the new profits to be made from kelp or sheep, and cleared the land when economic trends turned against them.[22]

Debate has, inevitably, often focused on the most notorious *cause célèbre* in the popular mind, the clearances which took place on the huge estate of the Countess of Sutherland in three phases between 1807 and 1821; the number of families involved is difficult to quantify with precision, but some 700 were removed from their farms between 1819 and 1821. The principal estate factor, Patrick Sellar, was acquitted in a High Court trial held at Inverness of the charge of arson, stemming from an eviction in Strathnaver during which some of the houses caught fire. He remained,

THE MOULDING OF MODERN SCOTLAND

however, convicted at the bar of Highland folk memory. He has since, on the whole, been defended by most modern economic historians, who have seen no other answer to the problem of growing population on the Sutherland estates. The Sutherland clearances are, however, the wrong case to debate for there were a number of aspects to them which were untypical. Population pressure was not always so unambiguously a factor in favour of clearance. Few Highland landlords of the period had the resources of the Countess of Sutherland, bolstered by her marriage to a wealthy English landowner. Few 'improving' landlords or factors had before the 1840s the same depth of conviction as Sellar, who was convinced as early as 1813 that, in order for the estate to become economically viable, the land had to be completely cleared, if necessary by emigration to North America.[23] And the classic cases of Clearance came, not in the straths of Sutherland over a fourteen-year period, but some forty years later in the rather different economy of the Western Highlands and Isles, and over a much shorter space of time.

At stake too, it is sometimes argued, was a clash of two cultures, Highland and Lowland, which had fundamentally different understandings of the nature of the land.[24] Those who lived on the land were deeply attached to it, convinced by the 'traditional' notion of *duthchas* that they held it in heritable trusteeship. In contrast, landed proprietors, who since the later seventeenth century had become increasingly exposed to the cosmopolitan (and expensive) world of British landed society, had begun, like Lowland landowners, increasingly to view their estates as commercial enterprises; lordship, which viewed the land as a source of manpower, began to give way to a more 'modern' view which saw it as a resource to be exploited for productivity and profit.

Although there is a basic truth in this antithesis, there are three important complications which need to be noted. Few landowners were as thoroughly 'modern' in their thinking as this black and white formula might suggest. Most were happy, at least until the 1820s, to encourage population growth, and not wholly as productive manpower; Sir John MacDonald of Sleat admitted in 1763 that he could not help rejoicing 'in the flourishing condition of the country when it overflows with people'.[25] Old notions of lordship were hard to shed completely. One of the most important changes which took place in the history of the period was a shift in the minds of improving landlords. Sir John Sinclair, the compiler of the *Old Statistical Account* and the very model of an ambitious improver, brought a range of agricultural changes including the abolition of runrig and the enclosing of wastes to bear on his estates in Caithness in the 1790s, in the belief that productivity could be doubled 'without diminishing the numbers of the people'. By the 1820s, he had changed his mind and had begun to preach the dangers of overpopulation and the need to encourage migration to the towns.[26]

The case for the defence of clearing landlords needs to take account of two facts. Many backed the wrong option between 1770 and 1820 and may have made matters worse, both for themselves and their tenants. As a result, there was a clearance of Highland landlords in the early nineteenth century. By the 1830s, the composition of the class of Highland landowners had undergone a profound change; for the first time it had admitted a wave of outsiders, both from the Lowlands and England.[27] The fact that these new landlords were often absentee as well as incomers exacerbated the gulf of misunderstanding which overtook landlord and tenant in the crisis years of the 1840s and 1850s. Some of the most unsympathetic estates were those where bankruptcy had resulted in their being taken over by trust funds, where the obligation was narrowly interpreted as the commercial running of the estate. Such estates were the rural equivalent of the complex structure of trust and bonds which lay behind much speculative urban building and allowed respectable people of moderate means to distance themselves from the slum tenements in which they invested.[28] The clearance of whole communities in Ardnamurchan in 1850, which saw many forced to emigrate and others 'removed down to narrow and small places by the shore' with no land or only 'a cow's grass', was carried out by the agent of a trust fund.

The 'traditional' view of the land was not based solely on immemorial custom. It had been deeply reinforced in the second half of the eighteenth century by large-scale grants on some estates of leases in return for service in the British army. Somewhere between 40,000 and 75,000 Highlanders were recruited into twenty-four regiments of the line and twenty-six of fencibles during the period between 1756 and 1815. This was, in a sense, a new form of a very old relationship, of military service, which had always involved tenure of land. It also often had the effect of going against economic sense, by subdividing already small holdings, but landowners had been attracted by the prospect of cash grants from the state in return for becoming recruiting sergeants for the British army.[29]

The third point to note is the most important. The 'Highlands' as such did not exist. For almost any purpose in Scottish history it is necessary to distinguish between Eastern, Central and Western Highlands as well as between the mainland and the Western Isles. Allegiance to the Jacobite cause varied significantly in the different parts of the Highlands. The eighteenth-century Church discovered that its Highland 'problem' was very different in the east and the west. Like the Lowlands, the Highlands were a collection of intensely local societies and sweeping generalisations are difficult to sustain, even those made by dispassionate economic historians. The seemingly unassailable case that the root of the Highland 'problem' lay in its rapid population growth begins to crumble when individual areas of the Highlands are looked at more closely. In the north-eastern part of the Highlands, some 60 per cent of parishes experienced falls in their population in the second half of the eighteenth century and growth of only 7 per cent in the first four decades of the nineteenth. In central and eastern Inverness-shire and Easter Ross, migration to the Lowlands successfully compensated for the difficulties in the local economy. In the Western Highlands, the real rate of population growth, it has been pointed out, was 'comparatively modest', in most years between 1801 and 1841 being lower than that in Scotland as a whole.[30]

Macro-economic analyses have their place in the story of the Clearances, but each set of evictions had its distinctive history, its own pattern of cause and effect. The Clearances from the Western Highlands and the Isles were generally later, brusquer and more traumatic in their effects than those which took place elsewhere; the steam packet waiting at the jetty ready to transport evicted families across the Atlantic (as at Barra in 1850) was the symbol of these Clearances. Yet the impact each clearance made depended largely on the previous history of the area. It was the districts which had since 1770 come to be most dependent on the potato which suffered most in the famine of the late 1840s.[31] It was the estates which had invested most in kelp, cattle or sheep which were worst affected by the drop in the prices of each in the decade after 1810 and were the most vulnerable. On some estates, as many as 10,000 families were turned by estate owners to the highly labour-intensive process of collecting and processing kelp.[32] Once kelp prices dropped, they were the natural victims of the next crisis. The press discovered Clearances on a national scale only in the 1840s. Although the short-term trigger was then the widespread failure of the potato crop, the Clearances were still, as they had always been, essentially local tragedies.

The first phase: improvement or prelude to Clearance?

Highland society was far from being unresponsive to change in the eighteenth century. The first signs of a new commercial attitude to Highland estates, similar to that which had gradually overtaken Lowland landowners in the course of the seventeenth century, is usually taken to be the practice of Dukes of Argyll from the 1710s onwards to offer the tacks (leases) of farms and townships at open auction to the highest bidder. This exposure of Highland society to the pressures of the market was, however, more gradual than might be supposed. The first auctions were confined to Campbell holdings in Kintyre, and spread only after 1737 to Argyll's other holdings. In Kintyre, enjoying the nearby stimulus of Campbeltown, the result was the early emergence of a new class of tenant farmers. On Argyll's estates in the pastoral areas of Mull and Morvern, the pattern of smallholdings persisted and at least a third of farms remained in the hands of tenants who had the name of Campbell. It was a muddled pattern of change, but by 1800, when only one in five of the old Campbell tacksmen were left amongst the ranks of the officials who ran the Duke's estates, it was near-complete. The traditional township or *baile*, the basic unit of settlement, had given way to a dual economy, characterised by larger single-tenant farms and individual smallholdings, which were usually located near the coast and shared common pasture. Less striking were the various efforts made to promote industry; most of the projects, which included a spinning factory at Inveraray and an iron furnace on Loch Fyne, were short-lived.[33]

The practice on Argyll's estates, though earlier than elsewhere, was typical of the changes which, with local variations, affected much of Highland society in the second half of the eighteenth century. It was an age of confident expansion and improvement, in the Highlands as much as in the Lowlands. The price of black cattle was rising faster than general agricultural prices after 1740; new opportunities for profit without a large outlay of capital came from kelp, which increased fivefold in price between 1760 and 1790 and often brought landlords more income than rents; and wool prices reached unprecedented levels after 1800. Highland society was not a dinosaur, unable to adjust to new conditions. On the contrary, it showed itself highly adaptable. One in five of the planned villages built in the century after 1750 were located in the Highlands. Larger single-tenant farms were established and the making of the crofting community was complete by 1820.[34]

A drastic change in the pattern of settlement had been effected in the course of three quarters of a century; joint tenancies had given way to the crofting townships which are now thought to be characteristic of society in the Western Highlands and the Isles. But in Easter Ross and the eastern parts of Inverness-shire, the same period had seen the emergence of large farms, as it had in the Lowlands. Three out of every five of the planned villages were situated at the eastern or southern edge of the Highlands.[35] The course of the period between 1750 and 1820 had seen the Highlands respond with marked thoroughness to the pressures which brought economic and social change; but the different parts of the Highlands had responded in quite different ways. It was in the west and the Isles, where kelp made large demands on labour, that a class of crofters and cottars emerged. It was there that many landowners were worried by the prospect of depopulation rather than overpopulation and persuaded the government to pass the Passenger Vessels Act of 1803 to stem the flow of emigration. It was from the east that surplus labour had been most attracted into migration, to jobs in the Lowlands.

By 1820, however, a number of the props which sustained the new crofting community were crumbling. Kelp prices fell steadily but slowly after 1810, but the bottom fell out of the market in 1827. Prices at Liverpool, the main marketing centre, dropped from £9 a ton in 1823 to £3 13s 4d in 1828. There was, over the same period, a slump in cattle prices, which fell from £6 a beast in 1810 to £3 10s by the early 1830s. Wool prices fell, from £2 2s a ton in 1818 to 10s 6d in 1823, as did those for sheep, though less drastically.[36] The bubble of expansion of the West Highland economy had burst. By 1827, when – significantly – restrictions on passenger ships were removed, landowners were beginning to rethink the basics of the economy of their estates. The flow of emigrants began to quicken in the 1830s. A government report of 1841 concluded that the West Highlands now suffered from overpopulation, on the huge scale of between 45,000 and 60,000 people.[37] The Highland 'problem', which was in essence a West Highland phenomenon, had materialised.

The second phase: famine and Clearances

By the 1830s, the bulk of the society of crofters and cottars in the West Highlands and the Isles depended on the potato for at least three quarters of their diet. There were partial failures of the potato crop in 1836 and 1837. They provided a glimpse of the prospect of mass starvation which overtook Highland society in 1846. A reporter from the *Inverness Courier*, sent to Skye, Knoydart and Kintail at the end of August 1846, reported that the smell of rotting potatoes filled the whole districts he had visited. On Skye, only a fifth of the crop was harvested and one minister accurately predicted a 'winter of starvation'. By the end of the year, it was estimated, probably accurately, that three-quarters of the whole population of the north-west Highlands and the Outer Isles had no food left. The Revd Norman MacLeod, a highly respected Church of Scotland minister who had testified before the Select Committee on the Highlands in 1841, talked in apocalyptic terms: 1846, he claimed, was 'the most momentous calamity in the condition of the Highlands that has occurred for a century – that has taken place since 1746'.[38]

A demographic disaster, such as had overtaken Irish rural society when the potato crop had failed in 1845, was averted in the West Highlands, but more by chance than as the result of direct intervention. With a few honourable exceptions, both landlords and the government waited throughout the autumn and early winter of 1846 for the other to begin a programme of concentrated relief. Two naval frigates were sent to Tobermory and Portree to act as meal depots, but it was a sign of the extraordinary confusion which the potato crisis had caused at the heart of the *laissez-faire* principles of Peel's government that throughout the winter it was the price of meal rather than its distribution which caused agonising at the Treasury. As at Paisley in 1841, the government was more impressed by the evils which wholesale public relief would engender, 'tending . . . to an entire disorganisation of society', according to Sir Charles Trevelyan, Assistant Secretary at the Treasury, rather than the benefits it would bring to victims of the famine.[39] Fortunately, it was rescued from the horns of its dilemma by private charity, which was co-ordinated from January 1847 under an umbrella organisation with the long-winded title of the Central Board of Management of the Fund for the Relief of the Destitute Inhabitants of the Highlands. Its emergency programme in the spring and early summer of 1847 averted a human tragedy of immense proportions. It had been formed originally only for a single season, but the continuing effects of the crop failure of 1846 in the harvest of the following year forced it to remain in being, and gradually it took on the worst features of mid-Victorian philanthropy. At once autocratic and bureaucratic, the Board became a gradgrind employer, paying rock-bottom wages in kind in return for hard labour on a programme of public works, including road building.[40]

The Board's programme, which had been heavily influenced from behind the scenes by the government, was a surrogate form of able-bodied poor law. As time went on, landowners became increasingly anxious that the private charity which financed the 'meal roads' might be replaced by 'the terror of the poor rates'.[41] That prospect explains much of the highly-charged atmosphere which prevailed in 1849. But the terms of the debate were different from those during the Sutherland clearances, which had begun some forty years before. The case for Clearance had moved from dispossession to depopulation. It was urged not only by landowners and their agents but even by newspapers which had usually been sympathetic to the plight of crofters. The debate was conducted on a national level, but the instances of wholesale clearance were largely confined to the Inner and Outer Isles and the remoter parts of the mainland, including Ardnamurchan and Knoydart. Within those crofting areas, however, more than four inhabitants out of every ten were evicted in the decade after 1846.[42] It was, by any measure, Clearance on a huge scale.

The famine Clearances were carried through with a mixture of brutality and conspicuous philanthropy. The bulk of the 16,000 people who emigrated to North America or Australia between 1847 and 1856 had their passages paid, either by public subscription, the government or, more usually, by their own landlords. One of the most notorious of alien Highland landlords was John Gordon of Cluny, whose dispossessed, starving and largely monoglot Gaelic-speaking Barra tenants shocked the Edinburgh public by turning up at the door of St Giles' in December 1850, provoking another thundering editorial from the *Scotsman*, this time deploring the burden placed by rogue landlords on Edinburgh's poor rate. Petitions to parliament in 1851, however, indicated that 3,000 of Gordon's various tenants wanted to emigrate, and he, at considerable expense, helped no fewer than 1,700 to take ship to Canada and Australia from his South Uist estates in 1851 alone.[43]

The Clearances of these years were intended as a final solution. The Duke of Argyll later wrote of a policy designed to ensure the 'survival of the fittest' and the elimination of the 'very lowest class' of crofters and cottars.[44] There are various standards by which such Clearance landlords might be judged, particularly if it is borne in mind that the crofting community had been of their own – or their predecessors' – making. To take the case only on the landlords' own terms, Clearance on such a scale might be justified if the ends, of creating a more viable crofting community, were achieved. Like previous economic solutions, mass Clearance had, however, very mixed success. In some islands, such as Barra and Lewis, forcible depopulation had a paradoxical effect; both had a larger population in 1901 than in 1841, before their clearances. The decade of human misery had been for very little. The recovery which began to set in during the 1860s and 1870s came, not from calculated pieces of social engineering, but wider movements of prices, which encouraged a revival in cattle and a growth of fishing, as well as better job opportunities for those prepared to migrate for a season to jobs in the Lowlands.

Migrants, emigrants and protesters
Highlanders had been migrating to the Lowlands in numbers since at least the seventeenth century. They helped fill the ranks of the miniature army of carters and sledders who carried goods between Edinburgh and its port of Leith, but it is likely that most were attracted to seasonal employment in Glasgow, where 'Highland boys' were working in 1649, or its satellite towns such as Greenock. By the 1790s, almost three in ten of Greenock's population had been born in the Highlands and regular Gaelic services were held there. In 1836, a census made by the minister of the Gaelic congregation in Glasgow established that there were 22,000 Highlanders in the city, but this was almost certainly an underestimate because of the seasonal nature of the search for work.[45] The first migrants, it is likely, were the young and single, both male and female, and, increasingly after the formation of the crofting community, male heads of the poorest households amongst the crofters and cottars.[46] Migration performed different functions for the two Highland societies. In the farming areas of Easter Ross and eastern Inverness-shire, it was an outlet which allowed the land to be radically reorganised on a more commercial basis. In the peasant society of the Western Highlands and the Isles, it was a safety valve for crofters and cottars who always, at best, lived close to the margin of subsistence.

Migration depended, however, on the availability of work. Most temporary migrants in the early years of the nineteenth century were probably employed on Lowland farms during the harvest. It was fortunate that the worst years of famine coincided with the expansion of job opportunities, especially in railway construction. On many of the railways built in the 1840s, such as the line between Edinburgh and Berwick, the Highland navvy was as common as the Irish. It is unlikely that Highlanders followed the Irish in such numbers into the cotton mills of Lanarkshire and Glasgow, but there were plenty of other jobs for them, often labouring for men and domestic service for girls. As job opportunities in Glasgow and nearby towns grew in the third quarter of the nineteenth century, the transition from seasonal migration to permanent settlement became more common.[47]

Emigration also began early. There were a number of instances of small-scale emigration to the American colonies, and especially to North Carolina, from the 1730s onwards. These were usually close-knit groups of kinsmen, led by tacksmen, who may have been making a protest against their own displacement in Highland society during the improvement years. This first phase of emigration is difficult to quantify, but by the 1770s there was, according to Dr Johnson, 'an epidemical fury of emigration', fed by a 'general discontent'. Harvest failure and famine in 1771-2 and 1782 increased the flow of emigrants, especially from Sutherland, and may also have created a new kind of emigrant, for there were reports in 1772 of 'a sort of madness among the common people', directed at both landlords and tacksmen. By the 1790s, there was a tussle for the minds of prospective emigrants: itinerant agents advertised in newspapers and recruited at church doors; landlords fumed and petitioned the government. The numbers who left in these years are impossible to quantify, but many contemporaries made guesses. It is not unlikely that at least 20,000 left in the 1760s, some 30,000 in the 1770s and another 20,000 in the twenty years before the restrictions enforced by the Passenger Act in 1803.[48]

This was, in the words of one historian, 'the people's clearance', a conscious protest by sections of Highland society in order to preserve their traditional way of life.[49] They took with them, in the period between 1780 and 1820 usually to the Maritime provinces of Canada, the values and the close-knit texture of the local society from whence they came. Between 1815 and 1838, 22,000 Scots arrived in Nova Scotia but by the 1840s conditions there were almost as bad as at home. In the 1850s, the bulk of a rather different kind of emigrant, victims of the famine and wholesale Clearance, went either to Ontario, where the economy was in process of recovery, or to Australia, where the gold rush was by then in full flow. In Canada especially, the mass shipment of whole communities helped to preserve a consciousness, both of the distinctive society from which they came and a folk memory of the Clearances which had brought them to where they were. In Australia, which was to a far greater extent the resort of the single Highlander or emigrants from the eastern Lowlands, the sense of an expatriate community was consequently much slighter.[50]

Emigration is a revealing commentary on many aspects of the condition of the Scottish working classes in the nineteenth century. Like the early emigrants from the Highlands, there were skilled artisans from the Lowlands who took ship, usually to Canada or the USA, in search of better prospects, and their experience is testimony to the extraordinary lure which the Empire played on Victorian working-class consciousness as much as on conditions at home. Emigrants from the north-east were likely to be small farmers or farm servants, pushed by the harsh pressures of the soil, climate and landlordism and pulled by land-hunger; their destination was usually Upper Canada, where land was still cheap and plentiful.[51] Other cases, difficult to quantify statistically but sometimes revealed in the history of individual families, underline the remarkable mobility of some sections of the working classes. Countless Highland families may have followed the example of that of Anne Beaton Boggie, a native of Stromness in Orkney married to a handloom weaver, who was forced to go 'on the tramp' for labouring work, moving from Tranent to Pollokshaws, Old Monkland, Edinburgh and Airdrie before the family left for America in 1856. There, it was as rootless as in industrial Scotland, passing through Illinois, Nebraska and Iowa before settling in Utah.[52] There were many routes to the emigration ships, and the experience of the Highlanders cleared off their land directly into a packet, as at Barra or South Uist in 1850-1, though it imprinted itself on mid-Victorian public opinion, was not the most common one.

For many, but not for all, emigration was a form of protest. There were others.

More than fifty individual acts of protest have been traced in the years between 1792, which came to be known as the 'year of the sheep', and the Crofters' Wars of the 1880s.[53] They remained, however, hopeless gestures – inchoate, largely leaderless and apolitical – of local communities against landlords who had the law on their side and the forces of law and order in reserve. Women – and men dressed as women – took a prominent role in what were essentially acts of defiance. The most violent of the demonstrations were often those which involved patronage disputes or, in the uncertain years immediately following the Disruption of 1843, when landlords tried to deny access to what they saw as a breakaway church which seemed to 'bid defiance to the powers that be'. By the 1860s, however, the Free Church had largely lost its radical image and the agitations seemed to have died away.[54]

'Crofters' Wars', Napier Commission and aftermath

By the mid-1850s, the major Clearances were over. The impression which they had made on the popular consciousness of Highland society and a lingering sense of insecurity combined with poor harvests in 1881 and 1882 and a contraction of job opportunities for migrants to the Lowlands to produce six years of agitation between 1882 and 1888, which came to be known as the 'Crofters' Wars'. The wars began in April 1882 with what newspapers promptly dubbed the 'Battle of the Braes', part of the 140,000 acre estate of Lord MacDonald in Skye, some eight miles south of Portree. There, the attempt by a sheriff's officer, backed by a force of fifty Glasgow policemen, to arrest crofters who had resisted the earlier serving of notices of eviction was met by a barrage of sticks and stones. The protest, in which women were prominent, resembled earlier demonstrations against evictions which had marked Highland history throughout the nineteenth century in all but three respects: it was more violent than usual, it attracted immediate national attention and it quickly led to a co-ordinated campaign which linked strong feelings in the Highlands with sympathisers beyond.

There was one further, vital difference. The early 1880s were years of bitter rural unrest, in Ireland and Wales as well as Scotland. Landlords were especially nervous of the 'Irish disease' and an application to the Highlands of the remedy that had been devised for it, the Irish Land Act of 1881. That Act, which has been described as 'less of an economic policy than a political stroke', was Gladstone's solution to a mass movement which did not scruple to use rent strikes, mutilation of animals and the threat of intimidation. The government had, in 1881, passed extensive coercive measures alongside the Land Act. It is against the background of the renewed agitation by the Irish Land League that the government's reaction to the sudden wave of violent protest which broke out in the Highlands in 1882 must be seen. In February 1883, the government set up a commission, under the chairmanship of Lord Napier, an ex-Indian civil servant, 'to inquire into the condition of the crofters and cottars in the Highlands and Islands of Scotland'. The Commission, which was greeted with intense suspicion by the newly formed Highland Land Law Reform Association, set up its work with a notable show of industry. In the course of a five-month tour of the Highlands, it held seventy-one meetings in sixty-one places and heard evidence, often made in Gaelic, from 800 witnesses. It first public meeting, held in May 1883, was, significantly, at Braes. Rather than dampening agitation, as the government hoped, the proceedings inflamed it; in the course of 1883 an unwonted element of co-operation emerged, linking local protest with a national lobby, which had offices in London and Edinburgh. By the end of 1884 the HLLRA, popularly known as the Land League, for it had been loosely modelled on the Irish Land League, claimed to have 160 local branches and 15,000 members.[55]

The findings of the Napier Commission were published in April 1884, but failed to put an end to the campaign of Irish-style rent strikes and land raids, which by then was spreading across the north-west Highlands. Its proposals, which combined security of tenure for larger crofts with the phasing out of smallholdings of less than six acres, were carefully balanced, though unquestionably disposed towards the crofters' case; they satisfied few, and especially disappointed the landless cottars who made up a large part of the Land League's organisation. The decision of the Land League to form a Crofters' Party to contest Highland seats at the next general election brought a quite new form of pressure to bear on the government, which was alarmingly reminiscent of the links forged between the Irish Land League, the Fenians and the Irish Parliamentary Party. The election of four MPs, who arrived at Westminster in January 1886, produced a promise in the Queen's Speech of a bill for 'mitigating the distressed condition of the poorer classes' in the Highlands.

The eventual Crofters' Holdings Act of 1886, the only major piece of legislation produced by Gladstone's short-lived third administration, did not live up to that claim. Based on the Irish Land Act of 1881, it was grounded on the 'three Fs' – fixity of tenure, free sale and fair rent – but, like the Irish Act, it had nothing to offer the landless. In retrospect, the Crofters Act was a major turning-point in the attitude of the British government to the Highlands.[56] At the time, it produced more disturbances, of a sharper kind, which again echoed the threat of rural anarchy in Ireland, where rent strikes had restarted in 1886. Sheep farms and deer forests were systematically raided, especially on Lewis. Under the charismatic leadership of John Murdoch, links between the Land League and its Irish sympathisers were strengthened; many branches passed resolutions in support of Home Rule for Ireland. Michael Davitt, the Catholic founder of the Irish Land League, was even invited to stand as parliamentary candidate for Skye in 1887. Wide though Davitt's horizons ran, they did not, however, extend to more than a brief visit to presbyterian Skye.[57] The spectre of a widening pan-Celtic campaign, linking land reform to political demands for Home Rule in both Ireland and Scotland, loomed large in the late 1880s, but it died away as quickly as it had arisen.

It took a series of further pieces of legislation, most notably the setting up by a Conservative government of a Congested Districts Board in 1897, which made some more land available to the crofting community, to complete the settlement of the Highland question begun in the Crofters Act of 1886. The land settlement question was not fully addressed until after the First World War, when soldiers returned from the front with a renewed determination to exact from the government the promise made to volunteers in recruitment propaganda that they would be granted land. The 1920s, as a result, saw renewed, bitter agitation, especially on Lewis, where war heroes launched land raids and occupied farms owned by the new proprietor, Lord Leverhulme, a soap millionaire who had acquired the island in 1918.[58] The outcome there was unsatisfactory, as was much of the wider settlement of the crofting question as it emerged, piecemeal, in the decades after 1886, even if most who wanted land were able to acquire it by the 1920s. Critics of the Act of 1886 have argued that it produced an over-protected crofting class and the result was to increase rather than stem the outflow of migrants and emigrants; the population of the crofting counties dropped from 180,000 in 1881 to 120,000 in 1931. But this is to take a simple view of the causes of depopulation. Both before the Clearances and after them, the basic health of the Western Highlands and Islands depended, not on the inherent productivity of crofts, but on the wider Highland economy and the availability of seasonal work in the Lowlands. The crofting legislation did not produce a dependent economy; it confirmed one which already existed.

A CENTURY OF MUDDLE AND CHANGE

SCOTLAND IN THE 1740S WAS A SOCIETY POISED ON THE BRINK OF DRAMATIC change. To contemporaries, however, it could hardly have seemed so. Other than in the Highlands, where the government had been stung by its own failings quickly to quell the '45 into a programme of calculated social engineering, Scotland did not seem set for a drastic transformation, either of its economy or the shape of its society. Its population was stagnant, probably still trying to recover from the losses sustained during the hard years of the 1690s, when somewhere between 5 and 15 per cent of the Scottish people had died of starvation or disease. In some areas, the losses sustained may have been still higher; probably one person in four died in Aberdeenshire.[1] Even Edinburgh and Glasgow, whose populations had continued to increase throughout the second half of the seventeenth century, had, it is likely, not grown appreciably in the half-century since the 1690s. The economic benefits of Union had as yet scarcely materialised. Stagnation had been the by-word for many of the country's industries, including coal and the manufacture of woollen cloth. The Union had brought considerable economic risks as well as opportunities and the risks of exposure to English manufactures still outweighed the benefits.

Improvement, trade and industry before 1780

The outlook was not totally black. Long-term improvements, especially in certain areas of agriculture, had been in train since the third quarter of the seventeenth century, if not before. In prosperous farming areas of the south-east such as Roxburghshire and Berwickshire, the amount of arable land set in runrig had steadily been reduced ever since 1660. This was why, in many of the reports of the *Old Statistical Account* compiled in the 1790s, runrig was but a distant memory. In counties like these, as well as in parts of Aberdeenshire, Angus and Midlothian, there had also already occurred a decisive shift away from farms held in multiple tenancy.[2] The later eighteenth century would see the wholesale disappearance of the Lowland sub-tenant as the commercialised estate or new consolidated farm, run by a single tenant, emerged; but this was also part of a longer, drawn-out process, which greatly eased its social effects. The 'Clearances' are part of Highland history, but not of Lowland, despite the fact that a whole class of cottars and sub-tenants disappeared from much of Lowland society in the century after 1750.[3]

All of these patterns were set in train well before the 'rage of Improvement' had first become fashionable in the 1720s or clubs such as the Society of Improvers in the Knowledge of Agriculture had elevated agricultural improvement to the status of a patriotic duty. Early 'Improvers', such as John Cockburn of Ormiston in East Lothian or Archibald Grant of Monymusk in Aberdeenshire, were few and far between before the 1780s, for the simple reason that Improvement was not usually profitable. Cockburn over-extended himself and by 1748 was forced to sell up. Grant of Monymusk was something of an exception, probably because his estate already had a history of heavy investment before his father acquired it in 1713. The road towards the enlargement of the size of farms, which called for the elimination of sub-tenants, would be the groundstone for calculated attempts to increase agricultural yields in the last quarter of the eighteenth century. It, too, began at least a century earlier than the so-called 'Age of Improvement'.

Although the years after 1750 saw better evidence of the zeal of improving landlords in the rapid growth of planned villages – two were founded in the 1740s, fifteen in the 1750s and no less than forty-five in the 1760s – that phenomenon, too, had its antecedents in Restoration Scotland, which had seen a sharp increase in the creation of rural burghs of barony and licensed market centres. The first 'planned village', in the sense of a deliberate plan being drawn up, was the much earlier burgh of barony of Edzell, founded in 1588, and further 'planned' in 1839; it is unlikely that the map which happens to survive from 1588 was unique. Most of the wave of new villages developed before 1770 were probably an extension of settlements which already existed.[4] Many were developed as centres of rural industry, usually in woollen cloth or linen. But the location of textile villages was much the same in the eighteenth century as it had been in the seventeenth, linked to the same major towns; Aberdeen in the 1680s was the central point of an elaborate system of 'putting out', by which stockings were knitted and rough plaiding woven in its hinterland before being finished in the town; and hosiery was still the major rural industry of Aberdeenshire in the 1790s. Linen production was concentrated largely in arable areas, which had been the focus of the growth of burghs of barony in the Restoration period.[5] Almost all of the significant improvements in rural society in the first three quarters of the eighteenth century – whether in farming methods or domestic industry – had a platform of previous development.

General improvement did not take place on a widespread scale before the 1770s or 1780s and the typical improvers were not conspicuous landowners, who often limited improvement of their estates to the area immediately adjacent to their mansion or to a 'model' farm, but single tenants, the beneficiaries of a century or more of changing practices in land tenure, who were encouraged by the rise in agricultural prices and intent on limited but concentrated improvement for a specific purpose. Agriculture was undoubtedly the most important bottleneck which had to be passed through before general economic growth could establish itself. But far from providing the best case of a 'revolution', where there was a sudden and dramatic transformation of habits of work and investment, agricultural development is the most persuasive example of long-term patterns of change. Primitive mechanisation came slowly, over the course of the half-century after 1790. Threshing machines were gradually introduced to replace flails, machine fanners began to be used and a more efficient two-horse plough (called Small's plough) replaced the old model that needed a team of oxen. The sickle, often used by women, gave way in the early years of the nineteenth century to the scythe, which needed a man's strength to use it. Productivity rose, but it was as much the result of more efficient use of horsepower and manpower as of new machines. The rise was steep: by 1840, an acre of barley, oats or wheat was produced by only half the labour used in 1760. Agriculture, striving to meet the demands for food of a rising population, nevertheless, was still a labour-intensive industry. Substantial shedding of labour came only after a series of technological innovations in the three decades after 1860, which saw the introduction of steam threshing, steam ploughing and machine reaping.[6]

This was change, too, which varied greatly in different sectors of agriculture and proceeded at quite different paces in various parts of the country. Far from creating a typical farm or a single pattern of husbandry, agricultural change in the eighteenth century and for much of the first half of the nineteenth provincialised rural society as never before. In the arable south-east Lowlands, such as in East Lothian or Berwickshire, the farm was becoming a compact block of land of between 200 and 600 acres, where rotation of crops was practised and formerly scattered buildings of the ferm toun were being grouped together into more compact units to house the labour force. It was worked by farm servants, hired for six or twelve months at a time at hiring markets or feeing fairs, the married among them paid mostly in kind and the single, both male and female, paid partly in cash; they were joined in the busy season by day labourers, who were paid in cash. The physical organisation of such a farm was new, but its hiring practices provided a link with the past. The farm servant was a landless labourer, but the fact that farming still depended on large numbers of manual workers gave this class security, at least when in work. A hire brought a temporary home as well as a job; failure meant a long wait until the next fair and little choice but to look elsewhere for work. Jobs for married males were limited, unless they were ploughmen (called 'hinds' in the Lothians), the aristocrats of rural labour, and a single man in his twenties was likely to be a rootless migrant, finding work, in town or countryside, where he could. This new rural society was confined, however, in most of its aspects, to the Lowlands; it was remote from the smaller farm in the Mearns or Moray, which was worked by a bothy of labourers, a semi-permanent but independent-minded workforce, who slept, cooked and ate in an outhouse or 'bothy'. The ferm toun by 1830 had given way to the consolidated farm, but only in the Lowlands.[7]

In a few sectors, such as the black cattle trade, the tobacco trade with the American colonies and in the linen industry, limited but distinct advances had been made between 1707 and 1750. Although general agricultural prices had remained flat, there had been some rise in the price of black cattle, even if much of the fourfold rise in the century to 1794 was concentrated in the period after 1740. Before the Union, a maximum of perhaps 30,000 cattle a year were driven across the Border into England; by 1750, 80,000 head followed the same route and by 1800 the number had risen to 100,000. The bulk of the early trade was concentrated in Galloway, and increasingly after 1750 it was located in the Highlands.[8] The fastest-growing sector of the economy in the 1740s was, however, probably the tobacco trade carried on between the Clyde and Chesapeake. That trade had been going on for more than three-quarters of a century, even if illegally (under English law) until 1707. By 1741, Glasgow's merchants were importing 8 million lb of tobacco; by 1745 the figure stood at 13 million; in 1755 it was a little over 15 million, and it peaked in 1771 at the phenomenal total of 47.3 million – accounting for 36 per cent of the value of all imports into Scotland.[9]

In each of these cases, however, the economic impact was limited. Each undoubtedly benefited some Scots but had at best only a marginal effect on the general Scottish economy. The sale of cattle helped sustain the increasingly more expensive lifestyle of the Highland landed classes, now more used to the delights of

London society than those of Edinburgh; and the huge profits to be made from tobacco brought landed estates as well as town mansions within the scope of the bulging pockets of Glasgow's tobacco lords. The practice of rearing cattle on Highland estates but fattening them on lusher pastures in England continued and prevented the cattle trade becoming a platform for wider agricultural advance. The store system which developed after 1730 alongside the tobacco trade, by which payment was made partly in kind rather than cash, did stimulate the development of a range of manufactories in and around Glasgow, which had already been evident before 1707. But these consumer goods – pots, pans, spades, leather goods and the like – were often of low quality and payment lagged so much behind supply that manufacturing was a highly risky business; they were not the stuff of which agricultural or industrial revolutions were made. There can be no doubt that both these sectors contributed in a general and indirect way to the atmosphere which would sustain wider economic growth in the later part of the eighteenth century.[10] But the tobacco lords were not proto-industrialists and Highland cattle breeders were amongst those landowners least imbued with the spirit of 'Improvement'.

The third area which saw early advance was the linen industry, which has been claimed to represent one of the most impressive developments of eighteenth-century Scotland. In 1728, 2.2 million yards of linen cloth had been produced; by 1730 output had increased by a half, by 1750 it had reached 7.6 million yards, and by 1775 it peaked at 12.1 million yards. Hidden within these figures, however, are slumps for much of the decades between 1734 and 1744 and between 1763 and 1772.[11] Linen, with a sixfold increase in output over a period of fifty years, can be taken as the measuring-stick of an age marked by growth that was at once impressive and unstable. Although its advance was less than spectacular, it was more significant than the trade in either tobacco or cattle. By the 1730s, linen had already supplanted woollen cloth as Scotland's biggest manufacturing industry and it remained so until the 1790s, when it was overtaken by the spectacular rise of a rather different industry – cotton. Linen was a domestic, cottage industry, which was never organised on factory lines. The numbers it employed were, however, large. Conservative estimates suggest that as many as 100,000 hands were involved in it. Of these, it is likely that four out of every five were women, who spun the flax, while the men operated the looms.[12]

Although the linen industry was based in rural areas rather than in towns or their suburbs, its links with farming were less direct than they might have been. Despite efforts by the Board of Trustees to encourage its cultivation, most flax was imported, and there were few cases where flax was grown, spun and woven in the same household or farm. One incidental result was probably an improved standard of living for many employed on the land and it may have tempted some to abandon the ritual, fixed-term hiring of the farm servant. It also gave men and women labour skills which could be used elsewhere. In both its organisation and the modest demands it made on capital, linen belonged to the old economy; but its workforce, already partly divorced from the land, was able to make the jump from cottage industry to the more mechanised world of cotton.

What these sectors had in common was the demand each made on the provision of extended credit. The founding of the Royal Bank of Scotland in 1727 had resulted in the rapid extension of a cash credit system needed in the cattle trade, where there were comparatively few overheads but there was a need for extended credit. The British Linen Company, chartered in 1746, had originally been intended to limit itself to the mercantile sector of the industry but quickly extended its activities to provide cash credits for widely dispersed weavers and spinners; it was an industrial bank in all but name long before it took on the title of the British Linen Bank. By 1761, Glasgow had three banks – the Ship Bank and the Glasgow Arms Bank, both founded in 1752, and the Thistle Bank, established nine years later. Banking provided for the short-term needs of the tobacco trade, like port and freight charges, rather than long-term capital; the connection between the growth of the tobacco trade and the rise of banking was, at best, indirect. The demands of the tobacco merchants were only one of many which can explain the fifteen-fold increase in the number of banknotes in circulation between 1744 and 1772. As never before, Scottish society ran on credit. The number of banks multiplied at an astonishing rate – no fewer than six separate banks were founded in Perth in 1763. Commentators such as David Hume and Adam Smith warned of the dangers of inflation and over-issue, and were vindicated by successive financial crises, in 1762 and 1772, when the Ayr Bank crashed spectacularly; the Glasgow Arms Bank followed suit in 1793.[13] The precocious history of Scotland's banks in the second half of the eighteenth century is an integral part of the story of sustained economic growth in which there were many components but no leading sector. It also reveals a picture of a free market economy which lurched dangerously between boom and crash. When linen prices began to fall steeply after the peak of 1771, fears were expressed of another Darien disaster. Well before the slump of the 1820s and the urban crises of the 1840s, the pattern of general growth but recurrent crisis in some sectors of the economy had claimed many victims.

Much of the success of Scotland's trade and industry in the third quarter of the eighteenth century depended on cheaper costs. The trade with Chesapeake thrived on low operating costs; ships, refitting charges and labour were all cheaper on Clydeside than in London or Bristol. Elsewhere in the economy, the story was the same. Wages were much lower than in England, both in new trades and old. In the printing trade, whose expansion can be measured by the fact that Edinburgh had four printing houses in 1740 and twenty-seven by the 1770s, skilled men were at a premium, but wage rates were markedly below those of London. In bookbinding, Edinburgh journeymen claimed in 1811 that their average wage of 16s was almost half the rate paid in London. In tailoring, another trade where there was a marked increase in earnings in the last quarter of the century, wage rates were still pegged at half those of London or less.[14] This lesson from what was still a pre-industrial society was well learned by employers; for it would be repeated in the new world of heavy industry in the mid-nineteenth century and after.

The age of cotton

In the period up to the 1780s, advance was broad-based, links with the past were often prominent, and there were no obvious or dramatic turning-points. The linen industry had been fuelled by the provision of credit and a plentiful supply of cheap labour. The cotton industry, on the face of it, seems to mark a new departure. Precise statistics for the output of cotton are elusive; others have to make do, but whichever ones are used the impression is startling. The first cotton spinning mill was built at Penicuik in 1778. By 1787 there were nineteen mills in Scotland, and by 1795 there were ninety-five. By 1839, there were 192, and ninety-eight of them were located in Glasgow. Imports of raw cotton into the Clyde went up from 137,000 lb in 1775 to over 11 million lb in 1812 – an eighty-fold increase. There was a sevenfold increase in capital invested in the industry between 1790 and 1840.[15] This dramatic rise of a new industry was not suddenly triggered by the introduction of mechanised production; steam-powered machines were not put into operation before 1792 and, when they were, factory owners experienced severe difficulties in recruiting labour. The initial stimulus probably came – not for the last time in the history of Scotland's industrial revolution – quite by chance, in a sudden, unexpected drop in the cost of raw materials; the price of raw cotton from the West Indies happened to fall sharply at the same time as prices of raw flax were rising.[16]

The essential pre-condition for both the age of cotton and the age of linen and woollen cloth production which preceded it was an ample supply of cheap labour. Population growth during the eighteenth century, though modest, had been significant; the population of Scotland increased probably by some 600,000 over the course of the century, although its net rate of growth in 1750 was less than a third of what it would be a century later.[17] The first census of Scotland's population, compiled in 1755 by Alexander Webster, minister of the Tolbooth parish in Edinburgh, revealed a total of 1,265,400. By 1775, it is likely that the population had risen to 1,398,250, an increase of 10.5 per cent. Calculations comparing Webster's figures for 1755 with population returns made by the General Assembly in 1748 show rates of population growth of more than 5 per cent in Lothian, Tweeddale, Angus and the Mearns and in Glasgow, Ayrshire and Dumfriesshire over the course of the intervening years. If population increase and a surplus of available labour were the vital stimuli towards economic growth, the marked differences in rates of population growth – with rates of only 2 per cent common in Fife, the north-east and the Highlands over this seven-year period, and outright falls of population of up to 8 per cent traceable in some Aberdeenshire parishes and the southern Uplands – underline the very uneven frontier between the old economy and the new. The fastest rates of growth, as much as three times the average, were undoubtedly in some of the towns; Aberdeen, Dundee and Glasgow all grew by a third or more between 1755 and 1775 and Paisley, a textile town, more than doubled its population, though at 9,300 it was still only one-seventh of its size in 1841.[18]

With the exception of Paisley, this was general urban growth, which had little to do with even primitive industrialisation. This was still the world of the craftsman rather than the factory operative, but urban growth had already brought with it changes in the workplace. Hours were shorter, perhaps an average for the journeyman of ten or twelve hours a day rather than the fifteen he would have worked in 1700, but workshops were larger and the social distinctions between master and journeyman or apprentice had been replaced by a more absolute division between employer and wage earner.[19] Weaving was in origin an urban craft but in the sixteenth century weavers had often moved to the suburbs or rural hinterland to secure lower operating costs. In the second half of the eighteenth century, the handloom weaver was the fastest increasing trade in Scottish towns. By the 1830s, however, two-thirds of all handloom weavers were still based in villages or at the edges of towns. The age of cotton had not entirely taken the shape of a decisive drift towards an urbanised workforce. Nor had there been a wholesale move into mechanisation. Productivity was doubled by the introduction of the flying shuttle in the 1770s, but as late as the 1830s there were more handlooms in operation than power looms. Like the age of linen and woollen cloth before it, which had seen an extension of the system of putting out part of the textile processes to rural industry, the half-century after 1780 had brought town and country closer together.

The result was a muddled world, which was not usually seen by contemporaries in the stark terms – of industrialisation and urbanisation progressing hand in hand – with which the twentieth century tends to characterise it. When a contemporary such as Thomas Chalmers envisaged a return to a rural economy as a remedy for the problems of the 1820s he was not entirely engaging in the fantasy of a golden age which had never existed. The rise of the iron industry still lay in the future, as did much of the technology which marked the second phase of industrialisation; coal and blackband ironstone, the essential fuels of the iron industry, had yet to fall sufficiently in price to open the door to a second industrial revolution. Chalmers and his contemporaries had to contend with a rather different industrial revolution, which was fuelled largely by plentiful supplies of cheap labour – women and children, migrants from the Highlands and immigrants from Ireland – but also constrained by access to water power. Urbanisation was part of that process, but also largely incidental to it. For those who might see into the future, the collapse of the cotton industry, which came about with startling speed after 1838, was more predictable than the rise of heavy industry, to the accompaniment of much more rapid urbanisation than ever before.[20]

The coming of cotton brought new-style regimentation in the alien world of the factory for the spinners of yarn. It was an easily learned skill, practised in a hostile environment where heat and dust threatened tuberculosis, even though conditions in the cotton mills were generally better than in the flax mills where the risk of bronchitis and pneumonia was endemic to the damp atmosphere. It was a trade for the young: almost two out of every three of both the male and female workforce were under twenty-one, and only one man in four was over thirty. The factory was only one aspect of the novelty of the cotton industry; the other was the breadth of its employment. It used cheap labour from wherever it might get it: unskilled migrants from the Highlands or Ireland, skilled handloom weavers who had emigrated from Ulster when their trade hit difficulties there in the 1790s, and the semi-skilled rural workforce trained in the linen industry. Cotton brought with it increased demand for the handloom weaver, who still worked in his own home; as a result, by 1800 50,000 of the 60,000 weavers were involved in the cotton industry, a phenomenal shift from a position where, only ten years before, it had employed less than 10,000.[21]

If the history of the textile industry is taken as a whole rather than that of cotton alone, it can be seen that it was the century after 1740 which marked a transitional stage in industrial development. The huge increase in production depended on the old workplace of the home or the larger workshop or weaving shed which emerged steadily after c.1740 as well as on the new world of the factory. Especially in broadloom carpet weaving, large workshops might have anything between twenty and seventy looms. Even in the 1830s, looms were still located in rural villages as well as in specialist textile towns such as Paisley and in the larger cities. Even in Glasgow, where cotton mills had been located only at the pace of the gradual application of steam power within the industry, it was estimated by Cleland in 1831 that less than a third of the 36,000 employed in textile manufacture worked in factories. And the enclosed environment of the cotton mill was less dramatic a watershed, for at least part of its workforce, than is sometimes supposed. That fact was due largely to the successful opposition put up by trades committees, such as the Spinners' Association, in the 1820s and 1830s to the unbridled introduction of new technology on to the factory floor by mill owners. Although the issues were usually not about general conditions of work but the maintenance of differentials between skilled and unskilled, they helped maintain an aristocracy of labour set apart from the rest of the workforce.[22]

The power of the cotton spinners was broken in the strike of 1837 and the nakedly political trial which followed it. Although the most serious charges, of murder and conspiracy, against leading members of the Association were found not proven, the heavy sentences imposed by Sheriff Archibald Alison, of seven years' transportation, for trivial and technical offences such as picketing had the effect of removing the main barrier against technological change within the industry. New enlarged machines, bringing inevitable unemployment in their wake, were quickly introduced. It was a turning-point in the history of Scottish trade unionism. For a generation, the grievances of industrial society sought new, political outlets, such as in Chartism. Tainted by the brush of the 'disorderly' with which the establishment had tarred them, Scottish unions went on to the defensive, turning to local co-operative societies, temperance leagues and pressure groups for factory regulation or other social reforms. When they emerged again on the national stage, in the 1860s and 1870s, unions took pains to cloak themselves in a new *petit bourgeois* respectability, which had the philosophy of thrift and self-help at its core.

For the factory owners, 1837 was a pyrrhic victory; their new unfettered control of a low-paid workforce induced more emphasis on the mass production of cheap, less specialised goods. By the mid-1840s, the strategy already showed signs of failing. By 1857, the industry was on the brink of collapse.[23] Cotton had 'led' the first phase of the industrial revolution, encouraging a broad-based climate of expansion in the textile industry and outside it up until the 1830s; but it had also led itself into a blind alley of its own making. The history of the cotton industry, whose fall was as startling to contemporaries as was the collapse of the Scottish shipbuilding industry in the 1920s, is a strong caveat to be entered against the notion of the inevitability of progress from one phase of the industrial revolution to another. Economic growth was, by its very nature, limited, not expansive. The next phase, of an economy based in a complex of heavy industry and sustained by cheaper coal and blackband ironstone, first needed an 'energy revolution' to launch it. The transition from the age of cotton to the High Victorian period of heavy industry was hazardous and took time. Thomas Chalmers was genuinely frightened in the 1820s by the appalling vision of a new industrial society. By the early 1840s, others were alarmed by a rather different prospect: of mass unemployment and what would now be called a 'post-industrial society'. History proved them wrong, but it was a close-run thing.

Politics, reform and revolution

In the second half of the eighteenth century Scotland was a society that was fundamentally stable but obsessed by its own instability. In reality, the grip of the landed interest was tightening. The great landowners owned half of all agrarian wealth in 1770, and many of them were growing greater still.[24] Their control over the electoral system was tightening too, because the voting qualification depended on who held the superiority of the land as well as those who owned it. The restoration of patronage in 1712 was only one of a number of developments which gave landowners – both greater and lesser – widening spheres of influence over local society. Heritors had responsibilities to provide not only a minister, parish church and manse, but also had, in practice, to make increasing provision for relief of the poor and education in the parish schools; so had the greater landowners, if they chose to exercise their powers. The commercialisation of estates, which was proceeding apace for most of the century after 1760, was the passport to London society and the Grand Tour and the basis for the many great houses of the period, such as Culzean Castle and Dalkeith Palace.

Conspicuous spending in all of these forms had the same effect. The great landowners were increasingly remote from their fellow Scots, both on their own estates and in society as a whole, but their political position remained intact, cocooned by an elaborate apparatus of wealth, privilege and law.[25] It was never so candidly revealed as by the Justice-Clerk, Lord Braxfield, who at the trial of Thomas Muir in 1793, declared that 'A Government in every country should be just like a Corporation, and in this country, it is made up of the landed interest, which alone has a right to be represented'. Concessions would be made by the landed interest in this period, but only after thirty years of sustained crisis brought on by the French Wars and the chronic social and political instability which followed them. When the concessions were made, in the 'Great' Reform Act of 1832, they were, in the view of those who made them, the minimal required to assuage the most powerful groups amongst the unenfranchised and to ensure that power remained in the same hands as before. The consequences of the First Reform Act were born of miscalculation and muddle as much as a calculated extension of the franchise to the 'respectable' classes.

In 1788, the thirty county members in the post-Union parliament were elected by a mere 2,662 voters. The average county had between forty and sixty freeholders on its roll, the average burgh had rather less. The county of Bute had twelve entitled to vote, eight of them belonging to the family of Lord Bute; Ayr had most on its roll, with 205, though only eighty of them were individual voters. The electorate in the royal burghs was smaller still; Edinburgh, the only burgh to be individually represented by an MP, had thirty-three voters. Although the burghs were the most indefensible part of the electoral system, their ingrained corruption was also one of the major obstacles in the way of reform; 'it would', according to Henry Dundas, 'be easier to reform Hell'. Little effort was spared, however, to find new means to secure the interests of party. Increasingly from the 1760s onwards, jobs were on offer in the various departments of the British state and Empire; more than half the officer corps of the British army was made up of Scots or Irish, and Scots were the most prominent element in the administration of India.[26] In the 1770s, the device of fictional 'parchment' barons was exploited to swamp, where needed, real voters. In the 1780s, steps were taken to tighten the grip which Islay had already established over the General Assembly in the 1740s; patronage was made available not only to the Moderate party but to the Evangelicals, who affected to despise it. In the closed mind of this narrow electorate, deep-felt grievances such as vails – the tips expected by servants in the country houses, which, it has been argued, was the most serious issue in politics in 1760 – could figure as highly as issues of 'national' importance, such as the long dispute over a Scottish militia or the reduction of the number of judges in the Court of Session.[27] This was the ambiguous world in which Henry Dundas operated for thirty years after 1775, with greater success than any political manager before or after him.

Dundas, the son of a minor landowner but also connected to the Edinburgh legal establishment, in one sense only continued where his predecessors as managers had left off, but in another he was a new phenomenon – not a grandee such as Islay or the Argyll man of business, as Lord Milton had been, but a loyal agent of the landed interest as a whole. His career seems to have been launched on the promise of limited electoral reform; his success was to reconcile the grievances of the county freeholders about absentee proprietors and the creation of fictitious votes and the fears of the old nobility about loss of their influence. Dundas managed to convince peers including Buccleuch and Argyll into a new 'patriotism', akin to the aims of the civic virtue preached by Enlightenment literati; Argyll in 1775 founded a woollen cloth manufactory at Inveraray and Buccleuch was hailed as a 'great chief' in the *Caledonian Mercury* for his public works. Dundas himself practised as well as preached the doctrine of civic virtue: he found the finance to complete the building of the Forth/Clyde Canal in 1784 and sponsored a series of parliamentary acts to enable the continuing improvement of Edinburgh, including the building of the University, designed by Robert Adam and now called 'Old College'.[28]

Dundas's reputation as 'Harry the ninth, uncrowned King of Scotland', the supreme manipulator of a corrupt electoral system, is an over-simplification of the politics of the time. The government did not always get its way in elections, which tended to be decided in the constituencies rather than London or Edinburgh. A number of seats repeatedly changed hands, as one electioneering device was countered by another. Appointments were the essential lubricant of the political system, but they did not directly buy allegiance. The building up of an interest rested ultimately on the ability of a politician to make and keep his friends.[29] The subtleties inherent in patronage and management make his success in electoral politics more mixed than raw statistics might suggest, but also more formidable. In the election of 1780, forty-one government supporters were returned out of forty-five seats and Dundas personally controlled twelve of them; by 1784 the web of his personal connection extended over twenty-two MPs; and in 1796 government supporters won all but one of the Scottish seats. More significant than mere numbers was the discipline Dundas managed to exert over his interest. Again, party loyalty was not automatic. The dilemma of MPs, as one carefully explained in 1783, was that they were expected to be 'independent men and men of influence at the same time'.[30] Political management was an art of polite persuasion rather than a science of weighing votes in the whips' office. Dundas's skill was never better illustrated than in 1780 when a motion, at the height of the unpopularity of George III (1760-1806), that 'the influence of the Crown has increased, is increasing, and ought to be diminished' was passed in the Commons by 233 votes to 215. The English managers had failed, but in Dundas's province only seven of the forty-five Scots MPs had supported it. This was the dependable buttress of support which, through the many troubles of the next two decades, Dundas gave to the regime of William Pitt the Younger after he came to power in 1783. It is small wonder that he has been called 'the father of the Tory party' in Scotland,[31] although that was a description which he never used of himself. Modern Conservatism, however, has been reluctant to adopt him as one of its eldest statesmen.

Dundas bestrode Scotland in the last two decades of the eighteenth century. He unified the landed interest. He had contacts with the Mirror Club and the new wave of Enlightenment thought popularised by Moderate clergy such as Henry Mackenzie. The Moderate clergy ruled the General Assembly, but not without difficulty, and Dundas never went so far as to turn them into the Dundas interest at prayer. In 1793, much against advice, he promoted 'fanaticks and demagogues' from the Evangelical party and Moderates to royal chaplaincies in equal numbers. The careful ambiguity of his relations with the two parties in the Church prevented an open split on the pro- and anti-establishment lines which would eventually convulse it in the 1830s and early 1840s and end in the Disruption. It also ensured that all shades of clerical opinion within the Assembly, which had in 1776 been tempted to support the American colonists, were quick to back the side of order in 1792, when the first enthusiasm for the French Revolution and the ideas of Tom Paine spread across the country with alarming speed.[32]

Dundas was, however, more than the 'satrap' of a Scottish province within the British state, however subtly he managed it. If, as Lord Advocate, he was a surrogate Secretary of State for Scotland (a post abolished after the '45), he was also, as a leading member of the Board of Control after it was set up in 1784, a virtual Secretary of State for India.[33] In Scotland, Dundas was the patronage broker for jobs in the universities and the Church. In the British state and the wider Empire, as Treasurer of the Navy from 1782 and President of the Board of Control after 1793, he was the main provider of career opportunities for the sons of the landed classes. Dundas was the vital element in the 'compleating of the Union', which had exercised post-1707 administrations throughout the century.

The British state of the late eighteenth century, however, was a quite different construct from that of 1707 or even 1745. Despite the fact that it had almost collapsed from within during the '45, had been lucky to survive intact a virtual world war between 1756 and 1763, and had been shaken by successful colonial revolt in 1776, it underwent a quite unexpected metamorphosis after 1784, when the door of opportunity to a new Empire, in India, first opened. India became, in the words of Sir Walter Scott, the 'corn chest for Scotland'. The French wars brought a huge expansion of the army and navy after 1793. The Irish and Scots were the first and the largest contingent to enjoy this new, larger network of state patronage.[34] It was predominantly jobs and jobbery which lured Scots into the wider patriotism of an imperial mission. The new patriotism, linking self-interest, a measure of Scottish sentiment and Empire, was far stronger in its appeal than the North British ideal which it replaced. It was Dundas's most lasting achievement.

In 1792, the most serious challenge to the established order to date took place. It was provoked by the refusal of the House of Commons in April 1792 even to set up a committee of inquiry to investigate the manifold corruptions of the electoral system in the burghs. Effigies of Dundas were burned in Aberdeen, Brechin and Dundee, and in Edinburgh the King's birthday was followed by three nights of rioting, on 4-6 June.[35] In an effort to stem the wave of handbills and placards which accompanied these disturbances, the government in May had issued a proclamation against the circulation of seditious literature; its main target was, however, the second part of Thomas Paine's The Rights of Man, which had appeared three months earlier. The proclamation gave the agitation a new focus; sales of the book mushroomed. A rash of new political clubs followed, taking as their model the Edinburgh Society of the Friends of the People, which was formed in late July. By the end of 1792, virtually every town south of Aberdeen had its own parliamentary reform society, as did many villages throughout Lowland Scotland. The excited atmosphere, in which newspapers sprang up almost weekly, was heightened by the remarkable success of the French revolutionary armies in the summer of 1792.[36]

Before the end of 1792, the campaign already showed signs of slipping out of the control of the coalition of middle-class merchants and lawyers and respectable shopkeepers and skilled artisans who made up the Friends of the People. Trees of liberty, the symbol of radical democracy, were planted, not only in the major towns but in places as unlikely as Auchtermuchty and Fochabers.[37] The burgh reformers, already in two minds as to whether to join an agitation for more general parliamentary reform, were subjected to the full weight of establishment propaganda directed against the 'levelling spirit'. Rival loyalist associations, dedicated to the defence of the constitution and intent on branding the Friends as dangerous Jacobins, sprang up, many probably 'planted' by the government. By early 1793, most burgh reformers and conventional parliamentary reformers had begun to make their dash for respectability; attendance at meetings of the Friends slumped and subscriptions went unpaid. Undeterred, Thomas Muir, a young Edinburgh advocate who was the son of a Glasgow merchant of modest means, used the first national convention of the Scottish Friends of the People in December 1792 to present an address from the Dublin Society of United Irishmen. The Friends unwittingly took on the unlikely role of revolutionaries which the government had cast for them.[38]

Muir was arrested, released on bail and set off on a quixotic mission to London and France. He returned, via Dublin, to face his trial, which by then was a foregone conclusion. Given an exemplary sentence of fourteen years' transportation to Botany Bay, Muir became a political martyr to many nineteenth- and twentieth-century working-class radicals, but the fact that he made the long voyage to Australia not in the hold but in a cabin which he paid for illustrated the distance between the man and the martyr. The short, turbulent history of the associations of Friends of the People, in search of wider representation in frequent parliaments, was, despite appearances, that of reformers of a fairly conventional cast of mind. They had become entangled, in the heady atmosphere of 1792-3, with a wider, uncoordinated campaign of protest, which was itself, however, far from being revolutionary in aims or tactics.[39]

The most radical ideas in the 1790s stemmed from the United Scotsmen, a shadowy organisation modelled on the United Irishmen and drawn probably from tradesmen and skilled craftsmen in the eastern Lowlands. Although it has been claimed that they were planning an insurrection in 1797,[40] their activities were probably exaggerated by becoming linked, at least in the mind of the authorities, with a wave of popular but conventional protest against the passing of a Militia Act in July 1797. Despite another show trial, of a Dundee weaver called George Mealmaker, the United Scotsmen never remotely threatened the regime, but they did help consolidate the sense of outrage and fear amongst the propertied classes.[41] The tangled history of middle-class parliamentary and burgh reform, popular protest and quasi-revolutionary societies demonstrated, not a popular front, but the uncoordinated nature of radicalism in the 1790s. Middle-class motivation was primarily and narrowly political. Most popular agitation was either economic in origin or bound up in single-issue politics; meal rioters and militia mobs might protest but there was no fusion of economic distress and political action until after the end of the Napoleonic Wars in 1815.

The disturbances of the 1790s had taken place during the third of three decades during which most of the working classes, in both town and countryside, had experienced a real, if modest increase in their standard of living.[42] Although these had been years of economic crisis for some groups, especially in 1782-3, 1792-3 and 1799-1800, the system of poor relief was still being operated flexibly enough, in most parishes, to embrace the able-bodied unemployed. The years after 1800 saw much more prolonged and acute distress, which coincided with a much stricter attitude being adopted in the implementation of the Poor Law.[43] The wages of a number of groups, including the handloom weavers, began to fall sharply after 1813, and the pressure was felt particularly in the west of Scotland. The pace of the drift off the land into the cotton mills of Glasgow and Lanarkshire was quickening, as were the signs of acute urban distress.[44]

The results were twofold: there was a much closer link than before between economic distress and political action and there was also a much sharper sense of class consciousness – perhaps for the first time in Scottish history. According to Alexander Richmond, government informer and *agent provocateur*:

The minds of the people were completely inflamed. A line of demarcation was drawn between the different ranks of society, and rooted antipathy and a ferocious spirit of retaliation was engendered in the minds of the labouring classes.[45]

In 1816 and 1817, there were mass political meetings rather than protesting mobs; one, held at Thrushgrove, just outside the Glasgow city boundary, in October 1816 attracted between 30,000 and 40,000. Strikes – by colliers and cotton spinners – followed. With the first wave of mass arrests and trials for sedition, in 1817, any last link between working-class protest and the parliamentary reform movement evaporated.

The upshot was predictable. Amidst a wave of government panic which attacked peaceful protest (at 'Peterloo' in Manchester in August 1819) and armed conspiracy (at Cato Street, in London, in February 1820) alike, conspiracies were seen everywhere; Walter Scott managed to detect a 50,000 strong rising in the unlikely habitat of Northumberland. Conveniently, not one but two 'rebellions' materialised in Scotland early in April 1820. The first, organised by three Parkhead weavers, issued a proclamation establishing a Provisional Government of Scotland; it coincided with a strike in Glasgow's cotton mills, but only a few weavers took up arms. Better known is the hapless march made by a small band of weavers and others from Glasgow Green to Falkirk to seize the Carron Iron Works; it ended when they were mown down by a cavalry charge at Bonnymuir. The 'Radical War' had lasted five days. Three were executed, sixteen transported to Australia, but the authorities drew back from a campaign of mass trials once juries showed signs of an unwillingness to convict.

The War had a paradoxical effect. It gave added momentum to industrial unrest in the 1820s, a decade which has been singled out as one in which a new working-class identity was first forged.[46] That agitation often had an uncurrent of violence about it, but the prospect of 'physical force' reform had died in April 1820. Even Chartism, when it cast its spell over sections of the Scottish working classes in the decade after 1838, was overwhelmingly of the moral force variety. By the 1820s, the middle classes had also developed a distinct sense of their own identity, which had been lacking in the 1790s.[47] Freed from the fear of revolution by the swift collapse of the Radical War, the middle classes could turn again to the lure of electoral reform.

Reform eventually came, more by accident than grand design, in 1832. It was the product of a Whig administration, brought to power by the internal splits within the Tory administration responsible for the passing of Roman Catholic Emancipation in 1829. That measure was deeply unpopular in Scotland and it forced the resignation of Robert Dundas, 2nd Viscount Melville, whose demise brought about the end of a system of political management which had scarcely changed since his father's fall from grace in 1805. The Dundas regime continued, a huge political machine run on traditional lines, seemingly oblivious to the growing ferment around it in the 1820s. A new radical press was emerging, which sharpened the tone of political debate; the *Aberdeen Chronicle* had been founded in 1806, the *Scotsman* was established in Edinburgh in 1817, and the new *Edinburgh Review*, which had first appeared in 1802, took on sharper political teeth after 1808. Whig politics came out of its self-imposed *purdah*. In December 1820, they held their first public meeting for almost three decades in Edinburgh. Petitions for burgh reform poured into the Commons, where they were studiously ignored. It was the increasing disarray within the ministries of Lord Liverpool and his successor, Canning, which forced Catholic Emancipation to the forefront of Westminster politics; it gave the administration, now under the leadership of Wellington, some respite, but only for two more troubled years. In November 1830, the Wellington government fell and a Whig administration, under Earl Grey, succeeded it.

The architects of the Reform Act (Scotland) of 1832, which accompanied a separate and more carefully drafted Reform Bill for England and Wales, were Francis Jeffrey and the Solicitor-General, Henry Cockburn. It was Cockburn's millennium and his own commentary on the Bill has an unmistakably apocalyptic ring to it; Scotland, he claimed, was being given 'a political constitution for the first time'.[48] In at least one sense, he was correct: the Act increased an electorate which numbered 4,239 in 1820 to 65,000; before 1832 only one in 125 adult males could vote, whereas after 1832 the vote was held by one in eight. Yet, in comparison with the franchise in England and Wales, the Scottish electorate remained narrow, both before and after 1832; there, reform had improved the position from one in eight to one in five. It was one of the reasons why British politics in Scotland remained distinctively 'Scotch', with their own agenda and ethos. The growth of urban Scotland was given striking, if belated, recognition by a series of measures: there was an increase of burgh representation, from fifteen seats to twenty-two; 'parliamentary burgh' status was granted to fast-growing towns such as Paisley and Greenock which were not royal burghs; Aberdeen, Dundee and Perth were given their own MP for the first time, and Edinburgh and Glasgow each acquired two members. In most of its other respects, however, the Act introduced 'as many evils as it cured'.[49] Fictitious votes were given a fresh lease of life in the counties. Without the security of a secret ballot, tenants, it was complained in 1835, were driven to the polls by landowners like 'a herd of vassals'. Within a short space, the Reform Act was being described as a charter of slavery rather than enfranchisement. Although the effects of the new £10 householder franchise were more decisive in the burghs, where a Whig ascendancy was guaranteed until the Reform Act of 1886, and a good deal more radical than in England or Wales, this was more by accident than design. The Act had been designed to conserve property by enfranchising only the respectable. It was a classic illustration of the muddle which marked parliamentary legislation in the two vital decades of the 1830s and 1840s.

'A new order of things':
Scotland in the 1830s and 1840s

The Scottish Royal Commission on the Poor Law, when it reported in 1844, was forced to admit that in many areas of the country the rise of manufacturing and coalmining had created 'a new order of things'. The Commission, nevertheless, managed to close its eyes to the new order by stoutly maintaining that the existing Poor Law was 'not inadequate' to deal with social distress.[50] In a society still hidebound by legalism and different local interpretations of a statute that originated in 1575, that conclusion was not surprising, and it was probably still true of most rural parishes and small towns. In the second and third decades of the nineteenth century, however, with waves of migrants as well as immigrants on the move and the population of Glasgow increasing at the rate of 5,000 a year, the system of poor relief, which required at least three years' residence in a parish to establish qualification, had already all but collapsed in the larger towns. The very concentration of the problem, in towns such as Paisley, which had increased fivefold since 1800, made the impression of the seismic nature of the shift all the more sharply etched in the mind of the authorities. The first major urban crisis of the 'new order of things' came in 1841-2, when almost a quarter of the 60,000 population of Paisley were living on charity and the corporation, crippled by the ramshackle assessment in the town which was based on only half the real property, was forced into bankruptcy.[51] For the panic-stricken magistrates, it was the first glimpse, in miniature, of the 'shock' city, which Frederick Engels would see in the back-to-back slums of Salford in the 1840s and would, in Edinburgh and Glasgow, motivate Poor Law reformers such as W.P. Alison and public health campaigners such as Edwin Chadwick alike. The realities of a free market economy dependent on a plentiful supply of cheap labour could no longer be ignored.

Urban crisis resulting from industrial depression, first seen in Paisley in 1841, was a commentary, not only on the Scottish Poor Law but on 'reform' of it made in the 1820s. The first alterations to the system had come in 1819, when new legal 'clarifications' had been made, seeking to exclude the adult able-bodied unemployed. By 1825, amidst the vociferous campaigning of Thomas Chalmers against relief which was anything other than voluntary, a series of legal judgements were made which rewrote the history of the Scottish Poor Law. The most important of the reworkings was a disablement rule, which interpreted the phrase 'not able to work for their living' as meaning only the disabled, not the unemployed.[52] Chalmers was a High Tory, but most of the bright legal minds at work on the limitation of the Poor Law were Whig. The eventual reform, which set up a new Poor Law in 1845, was no panacea for the problem of mass unemployment which had first surfaced in 1841. It was another, typical piece of legislative muddle – clever but blinkered, seemingly forward-thinking but in reality rooted in the obscurantism of the 1820s. Responsibility for administration was shifted from the Church to the state, a change made inevitable by the huge scale of the Disruption which struck the Church of Scotland in 1843. It was, however, a good deal less than the replacement of the localist Scottish parish by the collectivist British state. The fact that the basic unit of the system remained the parish and the nature of the transfer of authority, from kirk session to a parochial board made up of session elders as well as heritors and others, blurred the change. A central Board of Supervision exercised only loose oversight. Outdoor relief continued, as did largely voluntary assessment; only 420 parishes were assessed in the famine year of 1846. The familiar legalism of the old system was absorbed into the bureaucracy of the new. The amount of relief actually dispensed probably increased only marginally. The real difference was that, although the system was still a local rather than a national one, debate of its workings now went on in a wider forum.[53]

In the 1820s and for much of the 1830s, there was much talk of reform – of schooling and church extension as well as the Poor Law – amongst the propertied and middle classes, but it was reform cast in the straitjacket of self-help. Chalmers set up an experiment in St John's parish in Glasgow to prove that the poor could be adequately sustained by voluntary contributions; but this parish, though largely working class, was hardly, as Chalmers claimed, the poorest in Glasgow. Its boundaries had been carefully drawn so as to exclude the worst districts such as the Saltmarket.[54] Like Chalmers's, most of the social experiments of the period were largely self-deceiving or self-serving. In 1836 George Lewis, minister of St David's parish in Dundee, published a pamphlet, *Scotland: a Half-Educated Nation*, which created another crisis of conscience; it lasted until the Education Act of 1872 but was oddly off the point. A survey made in 1818 had already shown that the real problem was poor school attendance in the new industrial and urban areas, prompted by low wage rates, which forced families of unskilled workers to put children out to work to supplement their income. Chalmers would lead a campaign in the 1830s demanding greater state aid for schools, but what was at stake, so far as the Established Church was concerned, was another branch of the programme of church extension. Churches had to be built in the new urban areas to reach the unchurched poor; town schools, which already existed but lay outwith the control of the Church, had to be taken over.[55]

The programme to collect funds to build new, inner-city churches began only in the 1830s, by which time it was already too late. By 1830, 29 per cent of the population of Scotland were presbyterian dissenters. In Glasgow, in 1835-6, the figure was no less than 40 per cent and in Edinburgh it was 42 per cent.[56] In the major cities, the Established Church of Scotland was, in effect, a minority church before the Disruption of 1843. The root of the problem was not, as yet, irreligion but an evangelical fervour amongst the working classes which dissent was better able to satisfy than the Established Church; to dissenters in the 1830s, Glasgow was called 'Gospel City'.[57] The Free Church, despite a largely middle-class leadership, would do better after 1843, but only briefly.

Scotland in the 1840s had a dual economy, which mirrored a deeply divided society. In reality, the crucible of change was highly concentrated, in certain kinds of towns and in a limited number of industries. In numerical terms, Scotland was still largely a rural society, with two-thirds of its people living on the land and dependent on it. The processes of industrialisation and urbanisation were only beginning to link up. Fundamental decisions were made in the 1840s, with effects which lasted for much of the rest of the century, but they were done in a curiously off-hand way. Religious issues still managed to raise more sound and fury than social and economic problems. Reform was debated in the language of the propertied classes; the resultant reforms were often divorced from a reality which it took successive parliamentary commissions and inquiries the better part of three decades to grasp. The new industrial society, ever more concentrated and fast-growing, moved faster than the conscience of Victorian Scotland. The 1840s brought a new Poor Law which contrived to detach itself from the basic problem of poverty. The 1850s would bring improvements in sanitation in the worst of the cities. Yet relief for the new industrial masses would come less from calculated reform than from a general improvement in the standard of living. That took longer still.

The making of the Scottish working classes

The long-term nature of the changes in industry, especially in parts of the textile trades, had produced a distinct, skilled working class; by the 1820s, it has been claimed, it had developed a consciousness akin to a working-class identity.[58] The extreme short-term fluctuations in demand, which had marked the whole period from the 1790s until the 1820s, had helped provoke a series of disturbances among the less skilled, who were more vulnerable to the vagaries of low wages. The events of 1817 to 1820 had briefly seemed to bring together these two strands; the largest group indicted at the treason trials of 1820 had been weavers, but they were in the company of a motley collection, which included five nailers, four shoemakers, two tailors and smiths and a bookbinder.[59] The Radical War also divorced the skilled working-class from the middle-class involvement which had been so characteristic of the agitation of the early 1790s.

The leadership of this new consciousness lay in the skilled crafts, who were, however, the worst hit by the slump of the late 1820s. The introduction of the Neilson hot blast furnace in 1828 was the harbinger of a new kind of industrialisation. Heavy industry, based in iron and engineering, was no longer dependent on water power or existing craft skills and no longer based in the characteristic mix of new factory, old workshop and home, which had been the location of the dramatic expansion of textiles in the period since 1780. By the second half of the 1830s, this fledgeling working-class consciousness would disappear and different sections of the working classes would find their own salvation. The most politically aware was still the skilled artisan, better paid and fed than the rest of the workforce, his wife able to afford to avoid the workplace and his children able to attend schooling; he would find his place in the milieu of the friendly or temperance society and the masonic lodge or in the bosom of presbyterian dissent, often in the Free Church after 1843 – the spokesman of an industrial society but largely uninterested in the central issues which confronted it.[60]

The new, largely Irish, immigrant workforce, which flooded into the new factories and the mines in the 1830s and 1840s – perhaps 60-70 per cent of the colliers in Lanarkshire were Irish by the 1840s – is usually, by contrast, seen as a largely docile enclave, divorced from radical movements in both politics and the workplace. The new emergent Catholic community was, however, an amorphous body, at war with itself. Scottish priests were intensely apprehensive, both of absorbing waves of often unchurched Catholic Irish and of importing O'Connellite radicalism. The 'new Scots' built up, as early as the 1820s and 1830s, different reactions to the different worlds – of workplace, Catholic community and wider radical politics – in which they lived. There are cases of Irish cotton spinners involved in the Short Hours Movement in the 1830s; the wave of Catholic O'Connell associations emerging even before O'Connell's visit to Scotland in 1835 shows the forging of a distinctive immigrant community; and the involvement in the 1840s of Catholic Irish immigrants in a range of quasi-political causes ranging from Chartism to temperance movements, both in the teeth of opposition from the priesthood, demonstrates a wider political consciousness which belies the notion of a compliant force of migrant workers.[61] Again, however, the dawn of a second industrial age, combined with fears unleashed both by news of a grant made by the government to the Roman Catholic seminary at Maynooth in Ireland and the Great Famine of 1845 resulted in a new, more sharply etched Protestant sectarianism; it brought any prospect of a wider working-class consciousness which would embrace all the working classes, new and old, native and immigrant, to a premature end. As a result, the Catholic community by 1850 was retreating into its laager – though it was not as deeply entrenched as was the conspicuously separatist Irish community in English cities and it did not remain there for as long as is sometimes thought.[62]

About a quarter of Irish immigrants in the nineteenth century, it is usually thought, were Protestant. Definitions of the Protestant Irish are as problematic as those of their Catholic counterparts. Much immigration was still seasonal or temporary, and those kinds of migrants were, like the predominantly Catholic Irish navvies working on the construction of railways like the Caledonian line in the 1840s, likely to be labourers, also employed on transport or on public works in or around Glasgow.[63] Amongst the settlers, it is probable that there was a bulge of Protestant Irish in the first decades of the century: the census of Glasgow in 1831 made by James Cleland revealed 35,554 Irish out of a total population of 202,426, but only 19,333 were listed as Catholics. The immigration of Protestant Irish was coagulated rather than evenly dispersed; it was concentrated into certain areas and attracted by specific job opportunities, especially in the textile trades. Even if the proportion of Protestants to Catholics amongst immigrants in Glasgow was as high as 45 to 55 in 1831, in some parts of the city it was higher still. In the weaving area of Calton and Mile End, Protestants probably outnumbered Catholics by three to two in 1831. There and in weaving centres such as Ayr and Maybole, they congregated in significant numbers.[64]

Like the Catholic Irish, these Protestant immigrants operated in different, but interconnected worlds. Their concentration in the weaving trades suggests that government suspicions that refugee Ulster weavers were involved in some of the agitations of the years 1817-20 may have been well-founded; some of the early contacts forged between the Society of United Irishmen, founded in 1791, and the United Scotsmen may have survived the collapse of the rebellion of 1798. They also erected their own cultural apparatus. The Orange movement had grown up in Armagh in 1795, as a protective umbrella for Ulster Protestantism. The first Orange lodge set up in Scotland was in the weaving town of Maybole, about 1800. By the 1830s, Orangeism had established itself amongst immigrant communities in both the south-west and in Glasgow, which had twelve lodges in 1835. Distinctively working-class and still largely Ulster Irish, Orangeism in the 1830s may have already begun to tap into the deeply rooted Covenanter tradition in the south-west, but it also experienced extreme suspicion from the clergy of both the Established Church of Scotland and the Free Church after 1843. Divorced as well from militant native Protestant organisations such as the West of Scotland Protestant Association, it remained a largely self-sufficient entity, until it was reinforced by a new wave of Protestant immigration in the decades after the 1850s. Then, by contrast, the immigrants went no longer into weaving areas or only into the mines of Lanarkshire, but into skilled engineering jobs in the shipyards of Govan and iron foundries such as that of Baird's at Coatbridge, which recruited by placing advertisements in Belfast newspapers. In the process, the Ulster Protestants came out of the inner urban slums or the railway labour camp, into specifically Protestant areas such as Govan or towns like Larkhall. The history of both the Irish communities would be markedly different in the second phase of industrialisation.[65]

The growing friction between the two sets of Irish immigrants, which was especially marked in coalmining, compromised their own involvement in trade unionism. It combined with many other factors to keep separate the many strands of working-class consciousness in Victorian Scotland. The crucial second quarter of the nineteenth century witnessed not so much the birth of a uniform Scottish working class as the making of the distinctive strains which set apart the various working classes for a long time to come. The middle classes, by contrast, largely enfranchised in 1832, turned, after the repeal of the Corn Laws in 1846, to good works. Philanthropy could take the form of founding poor hospitals, supporting 'ragged schools' like those of Thomas Guthrie or orphanages like those of William Quarrier. It could also turn the middle classes, by now well advanced in the process of finding a new sense of security in their own suburbs, into Sunday missionaries to working-class slum areas. The zeal of the missionary visitor, who might start at six o'clock on a Sunday morning, knocking on doors in the east end of Glasgow to keep the ranks of bible classes filled, was a formidable symbol of the self-confidence of the middle classes in the middle of the nineteenth century.[66] With state intervention largely staved off, Chartism seen off and trade unionism inward-looking, God was placed firmly in a middle-class heaven.

23

VICTORIAN SCOTLAND

IN THE AFTERNOON OF 18 MAY 1843, THE MARQUIS OF BUTE, LORD HIGH Commissioner to the General Assembly, arrived at St Andrew's Church, in George Street, Edinburgh. Its public galleries were already filled to capacity and by then the street outside was filled with a crowd which numbered thousands. Inside, the retiring Moderator, David Welsh, suddenly departed from procedure after the opening prayer to read out 'amid the breathless stillness' a long statement of protest. After laying it before the Commissioner, he walked out into the street, followed by Thomas Chalmers, the undisputed leader of the Evangelical party within the Church since 1831. According to Henry Cockburn, 123 ministers and seventy elders filed out behind them. Outside, they were joined by tens of other ministers from recently erected chapels of ease who had not the right, as *quoad sacra* rather than parish clergy, to attend the General Assembly. The press of the crowd forced them to walk in procession, three or four abreast and strung out over quarter of a mile, the short distance down Hanover Street to Canonmills, where 3,000 spectators crowded into Tanfield Hall, a recently converted gas works. There, 470 ministers signed a 'Deed of Demission', separating themselves from the 'ecclesiastical Establishment in Scotland'. The Disruption, the most momentous event in nineteenth-century Scottish history, had split the established Church of Scotland in two.[1]

Of the 1,195 ministers in the Church, 454 entered the Free Church. They were joined by some 40 per cent of the total membership and a rather higher percentage of the eldership. 408 teachers in parish and private schools followed, dismissed for holding Free Church principles. The impetus of the new Church in the mid-1840s was truly astonishing. Within a year, 470 new churches were said to have been built. By 1847, it claimed to have 730. They were financed by a huge drive of private subscriptions, which raised about £1 million over that period, enough also to pay the stipends of the ministers who had abandoned salary and manse as well as their established charges in 1843. By May 1847 it was claimed that over 44,000 children were being taught in Free Church schools, with 513 teachers being paid direct from a central Educational Fund. By 1850, New College, a seminary which had begun life in rented rooms in George Street in late 1843, was built on a commanding site at the head of the Mound, obliterating from view from Princes Street all but the spire of the new Tolbooth Church, begun before 1843 and intended as the venue for the General Assembly. The structure of an alternative national Church, able to train its own ministers, run its own schools and support itself, was complete. It was the greatest single achievement of Victorian philanthropy, and testimony to the centrality in Scottish life which religion still commanded.[2]

The impact made by the Disruption was a shattering blow to the Established Church, but it varied across the country. In the northern Synod of Ross, almost 76 per cent of ministers 'went out' and in parts of the Western Isles, such as Lewis, more than nine in every ten in congregations joined them. In the Borders, the figure was much lower, sinking to 19 per cent of ministers in the synod of Dumfries. The secession was at its greatest in the Highlands, but at its weakest in the countryside of the Lowlands and the Borders. It was conspicuously successful in the large cities – in Glasgow twenty-five out of thirty-four left, in Edinburgh twenty-four out of thirty-five, in Dundee nine out of fourteen, and in Aberdeen all fifteen – but it had a far less devastating impact in many of the new growing industrial towns or in mining areas. Amongst the ministers themelves, it captured only one in four of the older generation, to which Chalmers, born in 1780, himself belonged. In contrast, over half of those ordained since 1830 had joined it, and they were joined by a further young 192 probationers. The Free Church was, in that sense, almost a repeat of the Melvillian protest of the 1570s – a mission dominated by its younger men, and especially by those who had been ordained as part of the campaign of church extension of the 1830s.[3]

The Disruption was a turning-point in Scottish history, for it signalled the end of the 'parish state'.[4] Schooling, poor relief and moral discipline had all been organised through the medium of the parish since the Reformation, and much of the legislation on which it was based also went back to the sixteenth or seventeenth centuries. The spectacular break-up of the Established Church ended its monopoly powers in such areas. New agencies – like the parochial boards set up after 1845 to deal with poor relief – had to be found, although the unit of administration remained the parish. In education, a complicated picture resulted. The Church lost its legal powers over parochial schools only in 1861, but in the late 1860s a government commission could find only one Free Church member teaching in these schools in the whole of the Lowlands. When a national system emerged with the Education Act of 1872, it was notionally based on the newly created Scotch Education Department but power effectively rested at local level, with elected school boards.[5] The new, 'non-denominational' schools were run by bodies which mirrored the balance between the various denominations. By then, the Church of Scotland had regained its nerve and some of its position, enabling it to become the loudest voice on school boards. In the schools themselves, as a result, there was little change, before or after 1872, in the nature of religious education. The new jurisdictions claimed by a collectivist British state were offset by the power which continued to be held at local level, in a recast parish which still reflected the moral authority of the presbyterian churches.[6] It was a delicate and shifting mechanism, but it acknowledged the strong position which religion still commanded in Scottish consciousness. The parish state lived on, in different guises.

To many politicians at Westminster, the Disruption was incomprehensible, the work of fanatical zealots. From a longer perspective, it may seem to be a curious diversion from the cares of a society caught up in a quickening process of industrial change. It came during what otherwise seems a lull in history. The cotton spinners' strike of 1837 was past, and trade unionism was in retreat. Chartism had peaked in its appeal in 1838 and quickly evaporated. The first urban subsistence crisis, at Paisley in 1841-2, was over and the Famine, which would bring social crisis and a fresh wave of Clearances to the Highlands, lay some way off in the future. But this was also the age of quickening religious revivals. Chartism lived on, in the shape of a score of Chartist churches, usually in industrial towns such as Paisley or Alloa but also in Glasgow, which had five separate congregations.[7] The Disruption saw Scottish society at a crossroads. Religion still pervaded every corner of its being. The 1840s saw the collapse of the Established Church, and the 1850s and 1860s witnessed the crumbling of the Free Church as an alternative establishment. Much of the story of the rest of the century can be told as the search for alternatives – in presbyterian dissent, in a surrogate culture which was usually no less religious in tone, or in the new worlds of the friendly society and the Co-operative movement. Many took comfort not from 'national' churches but from the local society in which they lived.

Schism, reunion and dissent

The Disruption came at the end of the 'Ten Years' Conflict', when the struggle between rival Moderate and Evangelical parties within the Church had come to a head. That struggle might be traced to the 1780s and the principles which were involved in it to the Patronage Act of 1712, which had restored to patrons the right of nomination removed from them in 1690. Almost annually after the Act of 1712, the Church had made its protests, but it was over one of the many ambiguities inherent within the system, the right to appoint where a patron made no effort to present a candidate, that the first of a series of secessions took place in 1733. It was on a small scale, consisting of only four clergymen led by Ebenezer Erskine, minister of Stirling, and for seven years an odd situation lingered, in which the Seceders, as they were popularly called, denounced the Church in ever-more strident terms but continued to be paid their official stipends and to preach from their own pulpits.

In 1740, the ministers of the Associate Presbytery, as they termed themselves, were finally deposed, but by then the Church had become something of a temporary refuge for a variety of different kinds of dissent. From 1733 onwards, they had been swamped by petitions from praying or 'correspondence' societies asking for preaching. Their links with the remnants of Covenanting groups were celebrated by the renewal of the Solemn League and Covenant at its centenary, in 1743. These were years of religious revivals, seen at both Kilsyth and Cambuslang in 1742, but the Seceders had an ambiguous relationship with them. Themselves more prone to millenarianism and strict Calvinist days of fast, they condemned the feverish atmosphere of the Cambuslang 'wark' as inspired by the devil. George Whitefield, the apostle of English Methodism, was invited to help them and then condemned as a 'wild enthusiast'. The Seceders were the most important of the dissenters of the eighteenth century, not least because their position seemed to point towards a new, fragmented world of dissenting congregations but they actually belonged firmly in the Covenanting past. They were, as a result, both a haven for more refugees from patronage disputes and a disruptive force within the increasingly complex diaspora of presbyterian dissent.[8]

By 1747, the Seceders had split over the question of the taking of a Burgess Oath, which had been introduced into Edinburgh, Glasgow and Perth at the time of the '45 as an anti-Catholic measure. By 1747 an 'Anti-Burgher' sect had established itself, under the leadership of 'Pope' Andrew Gibb, and excommunicated the original 'Burgher' element, still led by Erskine. The cause of the dispute, though seemingly arcane, was another aspect of the same central, but increasingly complicated issue of the nature of an Established Church, for the oath implied recognition of it. The origins of the next major secession also stemmed from patronage, but its adherents were temperamentally far removed from the Seceders. In 1761, the Relief Church, offering 'relief of Christians oppressed in their Christian privileges' was formed. Evangelical in doctrine but much more liberal in its attitude to membership than either branch of the Seceders, who maintained that they alone 'were the Lord's people', the Relief Church was a dissenting body which avoided the rancour of schism. Its suggestion that its members were still in full communion with the Established Church unerringly pointed towards a wider presbyterian fellowship, but it was a prospect which alarmed both parties within the Established Church.[9]

The question of what constituted an Established Church was not a simple or fixed matter. It took a number of forms, and they evolved in direct response to the fast-changing society of the early nineteenth century. It was not a simple, once-for-all decision, to be settled either by 'coming out' or staying in. In the 1790s, this moving frontier began to question the historical status of presbyterianism itself. This was the New Light controversy, in which the 'Auld Lichts' held firmly to the cause of the Covenants, whereas the 'New Lichts', more concerned with personal salvation, did not see them as literally binding. Although to the modern mind this was an obscure controversy, it was fundamental to the very nature of both personal faith and the position of Church and state.

During the first four decades of the nineteenth century a battle for the soul of presbyterianism was taking place in both the Established and the Dissenting Churches. The chief weapon of evangelicals everywhere was a strict version of its own past. Monumental biographies of John Knox and Andrew Melville were written by Thomas McCrie in 1811 and 1819 and it was no accident that they were reprinted in the 1840s, which also saw the first full-scale edition of Knox's works. Between 1799 and 1806 the New Light controversy split both the Burghers and the Anti-Burghers. In time, a variant of it would also underlie the furious dispute within the Established Church in the 1830s. More schisms also, paradoxically, had within them the seeds of reunion. In 1820, the two 'New Licht' bodies came together in the United Secession Church, which claimed 361 congregations and a following of 261,000. In 1847, they were joined by the Relief Church to form the United Presbyterian Church, which had, according to the religious census of 1851, 518 congregations and one in five of all churchgoers in Scotland.[10]

The statistics of 1851 are hazardous to use, but they do reveal the important, but largely hidden story of the growth of presbyterian dissent in the century before 1843. It is, in outline, a tangled tale of schisms and further splits, but its complexity is a reflection, not only of the capacity of the Scottish presbyterian mind to split theological hairs, but of the different potential audiences in Scottish society which dissent seemed better equipped to reach. No one was more aware of the danger of dissent than Thomas Chalmers. The history of the Disruption can too easily be told in terms of a struggle between two parties within the Established Church. Each was, however, aware of a growing third force, making a powerful claim on the presbyterian conscience.[11] The 'Ten Years' Conflict' was not only about the intrusion by the state in church matters. It was also about a race to reach the unchurched, by a programme of church building, in which the Established Church expected support from the state. 'We are not Voluntaries' (dissenters), declared Chalmers in 1843, but 'advocates for a national recognition and national support of religion'.[12] The stance of the Evangelicals was at once anti-Erastian and étatiste.

The steps on the road to secession in 1843 are well known, but they carry about them a sense of inevitability which was not wholly apparent, either to the rival parties in the Church or to the government. In 1834, the year that the General Assembly acquired a decisive Evangelical majority, the Veto Act represented a pre-emptive strike by it, claiming that congregations had a right to veto a patron's choice of an 'intruded' minister. The test case, at Auchterarder, was, like many test cases, not as clear-cut as might have been wished: the candidate, Robert Young, proved to be a diligent pastor, despite the handicap of being the nephew of the Earl of Kinnoul's factor. It dragged on for five years, being eventually passed from the Court of Session to the House of Lords for resolution in 1839. The test case had not hit its intended target but had, shotgun-like, hit many others. It had grown into a British constitutional question, which made a happy solution all the less likely. The seemingly simple issue of the veto versus the 'call' had widened into more complex questions of non-intrusion and the spiritual independence of the Church. Here, neither side had a water-tight case, but the Evangelicals took a determinedly narrow view, based on history and legal precedent, in the Claim of Right, passed by the Assembly in 1842. The dispute galvanised not only the Evangelicals but the Moderates as well. And within the Evangelicals the impetus had gradually passed to young zealots who made up the 'Wild party'. In 1834, Chalmers had been confident of state support for Extension. By 1840, when he rebuffed a despairing attempt by Lord Aberdeen to find a compromise legislative formula, he had alienated most of the key members of both the Whig and Tory parties.[13]

The actual Disruption was a miscalculation – by both parties in the Assembly and by the government, which did not believe it would come to that. The Moderates had been confident that, at the crux, little more than 200 ministers would secede. Chalmers, with a party strength of over 700 ministers behind him, expected many more than 454 to come out. Chalmers himself embodied a host of contradictions. More than any other minister in the Church, he had concerned himself, from 1819 onwards, with a crusade amongst the unchurched poor, but his influence was limited to the upper and middle classes. He had in the mid-1830s been largely responsible for defending the Church from the threat of disestablishment, yet he was, more than any other single figure, responsible for destabilising it. Ruggedly Scots in speech and temperament, he was also, unique amongst Scottish churchmen of his age, a 'British phenomenon', well known on the English lecture circuit. Yet, however good Chalmers's London contacts were, the Disruption was allowed to happen because neither the Evangelicals nor Peel's government really understood each other's position.[14]

Chalmers died in 1847, while the Free Church was still in its heady years of reconstruction of an alternative national church. Already, however, it had begun to reveal internal tensions. In its initial years, local Free Church ministers held services anywhere they could, including barns, gravel pits, makeshift boats and at least one disused public house; but they were also often offered temporary facilities by dissenting churches. The Free Church, according to Chalmers, was intended as a national establishment, committed to the goal of a Christian commonwealth. But it was a child of the age of religious revivals as well as a product of the 'Ten Years' Agitation'. Its Evangelicals drew inspiration from events like the 'awakening' at

Kilsyth in 1839 as well as feeding on a growing animus against the state. It had the inspiration of a local, gathered church and the ambition to be a national and highly centralised organisation. After 1847 the Free Church moved away from Chalmers's vision of a Christian commonwealth.[15] Inevitably, the drive to establish itself began to wane. Its working-class members grew tired of its incessant demands for contributions, however small. The sneer of the Established Church – 'Money! money! money! with the Free Church is everything' – had some substance to it. By the 1860s, the Free Church was as thoroughly middle-class, in both its eldership and ethos, as the Established Church, although there is room for wondering, on the basis of an analysis of elders in Aberdeen, whether it was *petit* rather than *haut bourgeois*.[16] Only in the Highlands, where Clearances in the years after 1846 and the Crofters' Wars in the 1880s provided a vehicle for religion with a more sympathetic face, did the Free Church break out of the embrace of respectable middle-class morality.

Religion in the Victorian age

The stunning success of the Free Church in galvanising the middle classes but losing touch with large sections of the working classes should not necessarily be taken as a paradigm of the mid-Victorian age. The secularisation of society, often (probably mistakenly) taken as one of the best indicators of the approach of a 'modern' age, was not the inevitable accompaniment of the rapid urbanisation of society. The nineteenth century, which saw a mobile, often rootless workforce, redrawn divisions between skilled, semi-skilled and unskilled, as well as a physical gulf opening up between them and the middle classes, posed a series of challenges, not only for the Established Church but for all churches. There was not one but three points of crisis: the first came in the 1820s when the Church of Scotland realised that its church-building programme had begun to lag far behind the growth of an increasingly mobile working population; the 1860s saw the emergence of a new but often alienated class of skilled working men; and in the 1890s the middle classes began to move to their own suburbs.[17]

The Established Church had already by the 1790s begun to try to make separate provision for the working classes. In Edinburgh, separate evening services were held for servants and the 'common people'. But low pew rents – subsidised by the town council in Glasgow at 2s 6d per annum – were already beginning to disappear and poorer sections of the working classes, especially in the large cities, were being priced out. The advent of a new tradition of 'Sunday best' clothes, traceable to about 1800, may have alienated many. Pew rents were lower in the dissenting churches and some of them seem to have had a distinct appeal in the 1830s and 1840s to specific groups of workers: the Secession Church had within it tradesmen, handloom weavers and spinners. By mid-century, it was clear that both the Established and the Free Churches had made better headway amongst the skilled working class than the unskilled, but the dissenting churches were doing better still. In four dissenting congregations in Glasgow, analysed between 1845 and 1865, the skilled outnumbered the unskilled by four to one.[18] In terms of membership, two separate patterns were taking root amongst most presbyterian churches: as more of the working classes dropped away, at best into a notional, 'rites of passage' membership, the pews were increasingly filled by the douce, sober-minded families of skilled, but highly mobile artisans; the prevailing ethos, of thrift, self-help and sobriety, was shared by them and the middle-class members of congregations, but it was the latter who provided the leadership. Each denomination and each individual congregation had its own subtle variations, but the general trend was unmistakable.

Various means were used to reach out to the unchurched poor. Sunday schools, first devised by town councils in the 1780s, were used by all denominations. By the 1830s and 1840s, they had widened into a barrage of mission schools and ragged schools, Bible societies and improvement classes, which were usually open to Protestants of all denominations.[19] The beginnings of the formidable temperance movement can be traced to 1828-9, when it was imported from North America to Maryhill and Greenock. By 1850, it was also an integral part of the missionary assault on the urban working classes. By the 1870s, a new-style revivalism, inspired by the work of American evangelists such as Dwight Moody and Ira Sankey, which combined comfort with joy, infused working-class presbyterianism. Integral to it were hymns of praise and the harmonium, a development which caused profound heart-wrenching to the orthodox Calvinism of the Church of Scotland, which had already had internal wranglings in the 1860s over church music. Before the end of the century, however, the failure of self-help to alleviate the condition of the poor and changing facts of geography had combined to undermine many of these agencies. The Church of Scotland acknowledged that it had to do more for the 'lapsed masses' than 'shower upon them tracts and good advices', but its zealous missionaries were already losing interest.[20] In 1850, less than a mile separated the worst slums of Glasgow, such as the Bridgegate, from new middle-class areas like Blythswood Square; the Sunday middle-class assault on the homes of the poor was then the central prop of the mission to the inner cities. In Edinburgh and Glasgow, the middle classes by 1890 were beginning to move to new suburbs, such as Morningside and Jordanhill, and to form their own distinctive culture *in situ* – the women's guild, young men's societies and a rather different brand of Sunday school.

Where the conventional churches flagged, others stepped in. By 1890, the Baptists had more Sunday schools than churches, and taught over 10,000 children; by 1914 the figure had risen to almost 20,000 – which equalled their total membership. New-style, full-time missionaries emerged. The Band of Hope, with only seven branches in 1871, had 570 in 1887, and 700 by 1908. An alternative, distinctively working-class culture began to emerge, which had both a religious and a secular face. The *Glasgow Echo*, a rank-and-file newspaper produced by locked-out printers in 1893, was typical: church notices appeared in it alongside reports of friendly societies, trade unions and individual trades, and, inevitably, sports. New kinds of temperance organisations, like the Rechabites and the Independent Order of Good Templars, imported in 1869 from the USA, began to gain in popularity. An upsurge in the Orange Order began in the early 1870s, and within twenty years it had 15,000 members in Glasgow. Freemasonry gained ground amongst skilled artisans; by 1911 there were forty lodges in Glasgow. There were many new homes for working-class culture and religion. With some, sectarianism or job protection combined with evangelicalism. All had in common some combination of moral work ethic and facilities for leisure pursuits; the Band of Hope offered football as well as salvation. The orthodox churches were forced to compete along the same lines, but usually with much less success.[21]

By 1900, a society had emerged which was profoundly different from a century before. A Protestant working-class culture, which could be either evangelical or quasi-religious in tone, had emerged. The secularisation of society, which still lay largely in the future, would affect it as much as the churches. The middle classes were secure in their possession of the morality and eldership of the Established and Free Churches, but had also carved a deep niche on the mentality of the mainstream presbyterian dissent. Their different layers were still perhaps distributed unevenly amongst the various branches of the presbyterian diaspora, but the social foundations of the Union of 1929, which would reunite the bulk of dissenters within the body of the Church of Scotland, were already beginning to fall into place. The landed classes had gone elsewhere. Many took refuge in the Scottish Episcopal Church, consoled perhaps by its steady process of anglicisation, which began with the adoption of the Thirty-Nine Articles in 1804 and culminated with the part-adoption of the Church of England's communion service in 1863. Others became converts to Roman Catholicism. There, despite the overwhelmingly working-class complexion of the Church, they took charge of the Catholic revival. Religion had diversified, like society itself.

The Roman Catholic Church had its own distinctive problems. Its growth, fuelled almost exclusively by immigration from Ireland, was too rapid for the Church to keep pace in the 1830s and 1840s. By 1840, Glasgow probably had a Catholic population of 40,000, but only two churches and four priests to cater for it; the Church itself thought that only three in ten attended mass regularly in the 1830s.[22] By the 1850s, however, the nature of the Irish Catholic community had begun to change. Settlers began to outweigh temporary migrants, and probably the proportion of transient single males within it had begun to fall. Gradually, a programme of church building and increased numbers of clergy began to catch up with the earlier surge of immigrants. But the Church remained conspicuously divided: the Western and Eastern Districts each had its own policy and priesthood: the former resorted to the temporary secondment of Irish priests, but outside Dundee the Eastern District had few Irish clergy, turning instead to the Low Countries for extra priests. By 1859 Glasgow had seven new chapels, but in Dundee the growth period for building was not until the 1860s, when the number of both churches and schools doubled.[23]

In other respects, the Catholic Church faced many of the same problems as other churches and found similar solutions. It devised its own system of pew rents, either by 'doorpence' payable at mass or by a systematic collection, made at every home, of a weekly contribution from all adults. This was remarkably similar to Chalmers's attempt to collect at least a penny a week from all church members; the difference was that, unlike Chalmers's scheme, it succeeded, quickly paying off the large building debt in Glasgow. Alongside new churches came a wide-ranging programme, involving temperance societies, co-operative and savings societies, and self-help organisations such as the St Vincent de Paul Society, which encouraged much the same combination of thrift, work and sobriety as characterised Protestant bodies of the same period. A Catholic Total Abstinence Society, begun in the west of Scotland in 1839, may have had initial links with Irish Chartism, but by the mid-1840s Catholic temperance societies were, remarkably, making common cause with Protestant organisations, holding joint processions. Both sets of links aroused profound suspicion amongst the clergy, but by the 1850s temperance had become respectable, grounded in quasi-bourgeois activities like the soirée.[24]

Temperance briefly acted as a bridge between the largely Irish Catholic community and Protestant society beyond, but otherwise Catholicism evolved its own distinctive culture. The import from Ireland in the 1850s of new devotions and devotional aids, like the *Via Crucis* and the Sacred Heart, helped keep an Irish stamp on what was otherwise evolving as a distinctive community in its own right. Glasgow's Irish Catholic community was far less a separate enclave than its equivalent in major English cities.[25] The relationship with Ireland was an ambiguous one. Even Celtic Football Club, founded by a Marist brother in 1887, faced both ways. The first sod of earth at Celtic Park was dug in 1892 by none other than Michael Davitt, but that same year also marked the condemnation by the Gaelic Athletic Association of soccer as a 'foreign sport'.[26] Catholic society is often described as a 'dependency culture', but the ethos of the self-enclosed social world which the Church created, helping its members 'live upright and well-ordered lives', was little different from that of other churches in the period.[27] The real difference may rather lie in the fact that it was an organised church which was the main vehicle for self-help rather than outside agencies. Not only was the membership of the Catholic Church more heavily drawn from the unskilled working classes than any other Victorian church, it also, for both good and ill, kept a tighter discipline on its flock.

In one sense, there was a close-knit Catholic community, held more harmoniously together after the restoration of the hierarchy in 1878. In another, there was not. In social terms, the structure of the Catholic community varied almost as much as that of the rest of the workforce. In Glasgow, Catholics were concentrated in slums like the Saltmarket, Cowcaddens and Maryhill, but they were also dispersed across the city; although most filled the ranks of the unskilled, they were not concentrated to a great extent in any particular occupations. In Dundee, by contrast, a far larger proportion of Irish immigrants were concentrated in the Catholic ghetto of Lochee, and in 1850 half the labour force in the linen industry was Irish-born.[28] The concentration of the Irish workforce in the textile industry throughout the nineteenth century, together with the fact that women outnumbered men there by two to one, made for a quite different, far closer-knit enclave. In Glasgow, Catholics were to be found from the 1870s onwards involved in trade union organisation of the casual and sweated trades. In Dundee, so dominated by the textile industry, they stayed away, even as late as 1906.[29]

An Industrial Revolution?

The picture of the Established Church, still in 1800 the most important single institution in Scottish society, spluttering fitfully into hectic activity, obsessed by the details of traditional regulations – whether the Poor Law or Sabbatarianism – which were supposed to control society, splitting into competing branches and losing ground, suggests a dramatic wider revolution overtaking society, linking the eighteenth century to the modern age. The sheer scale of that change, spread over almost a century and a half, persuaded historians of a past generation to find a single term to explain it all – the 'Industrial Revolution'.

Historians of Scotland, although at pains to point out that both the shape and the pace of economic change was different there from that in England, have generally accepted the term, and an older generation gloried in it. 'Clyde-built' became the symbol of the intense pride of a new, skilled working class. For historians, the Industrial Revolution became the celebration of an heroic age: the story of a century or more of sustained economic growth (in Scotland between the 1780s and 1914), an unprecedented growth of population, a sequence of brilliant inventions (with gratifyingly many of them the work of Scots), and a huge increase in capital investment.[30] Like any good story, it had its heroes and villains, who could be varied to suit the inclinations of author or reader. Men of genius, such as Joseph Black, James Watt and William Thomson, Lord Kelvin, had their inventions turned to profit at each stage of industrialisation, in the iron industry, railways or shipbuilding. The profitmakers – or profiteers – were giants of Victorian industry. Six Scots made the league table of the top forty nineteenth-century British multi-millionaires, including the ironfounder William Baird, the Paisley sewing-thread magnates, Peter and James Coats, and Charles Tennant, owner of the huge St Rollox chemicals works. All six had in common the fact that the new urban landscape of Glasgow or its environs was their Elysian fields.[31] Alternative heroes – and alternative villains as well – were to be found in the story of 'Red Clydeside', which was for long taken as the slogan (as distinct from the reality) of the new late-Victorian industrial society, despite the fact that it was generally slow to organise into effective trade unionism.

The idea of an Industrial Revolution gave drama and meaning to a long period of bewildering change. It also gave order to it. Reinterpreted to suit the Scottish experience, historians were able to point to different, successive phases of economic and industrial development.[32] The period 1750-80 was usually seen as an 'early industrial phase' or, if the model of W. W. Rostow was used, as the 'prelude to self-sustained growth';[33] the half-century after 1780 was the 'age of cotton', when 'cotton led' with the iron industry (unlike England) still in its infancy; the years between 1830 and 1870 were the 'age of iron', marking a second 'take-off' into sustained economic growth and a new society; and a 'late industrial phase', between c. 1870 and 1914, was seen by some as the 'age of shipbuilding' and by others in terms of the emergence, not of a new leading sector, but of an interdependent complex of heavy industry. The terminology and the precise dating of the various phases might vary but, common to all who used it, the Industrial Revolution was an idea that helped convey a huge phenomenon which was 'unitary, progressive and integrated' – a revolutionary, but ordered evolution.[34]

There are two sets of objections to this view of the Industrial Revolution. One is the result of applying to it the standard test used in other fields of Scottish history – of localism. The picture which emerges is of not one but many industrial revolutions in different parts of Scotland, each proceeding at its own pace and with its individual characteristics.[35] Shipbuilding was confined largely to the Clyde, as was the classic complex of heavy industry. There was not one Scottish coal industry but two, in the eastern and western coalfields, which served quite different kinds of markets. Dundee expanded in the nineteenth century, not (like Glasgow) by diversifying out of textiles into other industries, but by massively increasing its textile output. Aberdeen, fuelled by a rather different kind of migration from the Irish influx into Dundee, nevertheless experienced similar population growth but its industry moved in a quite different direction, after its textiles collapsed in mid-century. Others have decribed three or four motors of economic change, centred in either a trio or a quartet of industrial regional complexes, each with a major city at its core – Glasgow, Edinburgh and Dundee and perhaps also Aberdeen – and with its own distinctive features.[36] There have also been some who, preferring to stress continuity rather than change, have come close to suggesting that Aberdeen, despite its population growth, did not experience an Industrial Revolution at all.[37] The differences reflect the fact that the expectations of Industrial Revolution are as variable as the term is flexible.

The second set of doubts concerns the notion of successive phases and the connection between them. The 1820s, as has been seen, was an age of uncertainty, filled with the objections of skilled workers to the new factory age, which had as yet only half arrived. The victory of the factory owners over the cotton spinners in the strike of 1837 was the prelude to a new age of more complete mechanisation of the industry, which promptly fell on hard times. The sudden surge of iron output over the same period is undoubted. Scotland had twenty-seven iron furnaces in 1830, seventy in 1840, 143 in 1850 and it reached a peak of 171 in 1860. But if put in terms of the workforce, the statistics of change are less striking. In 1831, the largest single occupation in the country was handloom weaving, with a massive army of 78,000 workers; Glasgow alone had over 15,000, some 15 per cent of the workforce, with a further 10,000 cotton spinners and steam-loom weavers.[38] Despite the fall-off in the textiles industry and the disappearance of a whole class of handloom weavers, it was not until the census of 1871 that the percentage of the workforce employed, not only in iron, but in all heavy industry in what is now Strathclyde region, exceeded that in textiles. In Scotland as a whole, heavy industry overtook textiles only in 1891.[39]

This was again a muddled age of change, which saw the drawn-out decline of one kind of workforce and the slow but steady rise of another. There was no carry-over of labour skills or capital investment from the 'age of cotton' to an 'age of iron', as there had been from the linen or woollen industries into cotton two generations before. For the thousands who worked in the various sections of the textile industry, the difference in the years after 1840 lay in more and more work being concentrated in a factory environment, such as the giant Camperdown jute works built at Lochee in Dundee in the 1860s, a higher proportion of it drawing on cheaper female labour, and an increasing chance of either long stretches of unemployment or broken time. Almost seven out of every ten in textiles were female in 1839. The gradual decay of the industry was probably the main reason for a drop in the proportion of women in the overall workforce, but that change again belonged to the 1860s, when the percentage fell from 37 to 32 per cent, rather than the 1830s.[40] The iron industry, by contrast, pointed the way towards a new kind of workforce, located entirely in the factory rather than the mixed world of textile production, and overwhelmingly male. The 1830s was the culmination of the first phase of industrialisation, which had seen the skilled worker put under greater pressure and eventually eclipsed. By the 1850s, a quite different kind of industrialisation was gaining momentum. In it, increase in output went hand in hand with specialisation and the development of specific skills. By the 1880s, especially in engineering and shipbuilding, the age of the semi-skilled worker was dawning. The result was that, in Glasgow, by the end of the century, three-quarters of the male workforce was either skilled or semi-skilled.

It was a man's world, but it belonged, above all, to the skilled trades associated with the new industries which had emerged since 1850. It symbol was not the cloth cap of the labourer but the blue suits and bowler hats which skilled engineers wore at weekends to set themselves apart.[41]

If the nature of the workforce was one sign of the new industrial society, the other lay in a novel form of increased output. Increase in productivity could happen without revolutionary changes taking place in mechanisation. On Lowland farms, 50 per cent gains were made in arable yields in the early part of the century by better management of horse and manpower; extensive mechanisation took place only in the 1870s. To increase output, textiles had drawn on massive extra numbers of workers and on water power as well as steam. In the coal industry, there was substantial increases in output long before steam engines and underground haulage revolutionised work at the coalface in the 1870s. For coal, the bottleneck had been a plentiful supply of cheap labour, which was provided by Irish immigrants from the 1830s onwards, and the creation of an efficient distribution network, which came with railways like the Monkland & Kirkintilloch, opened in 1826. The rapid growth of the iron industry called for a very different kind of development – the increased use of mechanical energy derived from coal. Scotland had had an iron industry since the founding of the Carron Iron Works at Falkirk in 1759, and small foundries had also been set up in the Highlands, but the ore used was mostly imported from England and the fuel used was usually charcoal. The Carron works had developed a coke-smelting technique, but it was largely for specialised work in fine casting for guns. It was the combined effect of the discovery of black-band ironstone, available locally at low cost and in plentiful supply, and the application of Neilson's hot blast process, patented in 1828, which reduced by two and a half tons the amount of coal needed to produce a ton of iron, which constituted the 'energy revolution' – a genuine revolution, which lay at the heart of the new industrial society of the second half of the nineteenth century.[42]

The speed of the Scottish iron industry's expansion in the late 1830s came from the double but chance discovery of new-found cheaper, local minerals and lower costs of production. Between 1830 and 1844 output increased from 40,000 tons a year to 412,000; the fact that a tenfold increase in output came from a fourfold expansion in the number of furnaces over the same period testified to the new technological efficiency of production methods. It represented an increased share of British output from 5 to 25 per cent.[43] The iron industry stood at a mid-way stage in industrial development and it pointed in different directions. By 1850, its output accounted for 90 per cent of all British exports – an early indicator of the marked characteristic of Scottish heavy industry in the future, a heavy dependence on overseas markets. The new world of the huge industrial complex had arrived. In 1847, a reporter described the huge Vulcan Foundry near the Broomielaw, which covered several acres and employed 1,400 men, as a 'triumph of talent and enterprise'; each man 'seems perfectly master of his department'.[44]

This was, however, a foundry producing malleable iron, which accounted for only 14 per cent of all Scottish production at best. The Scottish iron industry, unlike its counterpart in England, did not markedly diversify into the more complex industrial processes involved in the production of malleable or wrought iron. There was, as a result, little connection between it and the rise of a steel industry, which came late, in the 1870s, and remained oddly disconnected from other branches of metal-making. Most of the Scottish iron industry remained in pig, which demanded only limited labour skills; it was content to mass-produce pots, pans and the thousands of implements needed by a consumer society. It was, in that sense, more like the cotton industry than its companions in heavy industry: a producer of low-cost, basic items.[45] It had risen on the basis of lower costs. Once reserves of cheap domestic iron ore began to run out in the 1870s, it began to lose its competitive edge. The bubble did not burst, but it did slip steadily away in the last quarter of the century.

There was a clearer connection between the branch of the industry in malleable iron and the growing complex of heavy industry, characterised by the production of high-quality, usually costly goods, which demanded specialised skills of the workforce. The Vulcan works were owned by Robert Napier & Sons, whose yard in Govan was the first to start production of large passenger iron ships, in the 1840s. As late as 1835, when it produced just 5 per cent of Britain's total tonnage, the Clyde had not been a significant centre of shipbuilding. It was a new industry, whose workers had to accumulate quite new skills. There was, however, no clear-cut or sudden move from wooden construction to the iron ship, for various reasons. Lloyd's of London proved reluctant to insure the new iron ships until 1855; iron ships were generally more expensive to produce until c.1850; and wood continued to be used well into the 1860s in hulls of composite construction, like that of the famous clipper, the *Cutty Sark*, launched at Dumbarton in 1869. Cost was also the prohibitive factor in making an early transition from the iron ship to steel hulls; as late as 1879 only 18,000 tons of steel-built shipping was launched on the Clyde, some 10 per cent of all tonnage. The same muddled transition took place in methods of propulsion. Both running costs and costs of production fluctuated wildly in the middle years of the century, with the result that Clyde yards shifted rapidly from sail to steam and back again between the 1840s and the mid-1880s; sail made up 45 per cent of all shipping launched in 1868, but 5 per cent in 1871, 45 per cent in 1877 but 6 per cent in 1879. The stop-go pattern was brought to an end only by the adoption of a more efficient steam turbine engine in the 1880s. There was, as a result, a rapid switch into steel-hulled construction: its share of 10 per cent of tonnage in 1879 rose to 97 per cent by 1889.[46]

Shipbuilding has variously been called the barometer and the chief growth point of the Scottish economy in the three decades before the First World War. Its tonnage increased over sixfold between 1880 and 1914, by which time it commanded a 35 per cent share of all British output. The industry occupied a strategic position, using a high proportion of steel produced in Scotland, but it was dependent on an unusual pattern of demand. Unlike engineering or even marine engineering, it relied on a few customers, many of them fickle, and none more so than the Admiralty.[47] If shipbuilding had taken on the mantle of chief determinant of the progress of the Scottish economy by the end of the century, it was by its very nature more narrowly based than either of its predecessors, iron or textiles, which had been industries based on cheap production for a mass market. The markets for cotton had faltered in the 1830s without damage being done to the sectors of the economy outside textiles; the slow tailing-off of demand for cheap iron products also had limited impact; but a sudden drop in orders for shipping had a much wider and quicker adverse effect on the other sectors of heavy industry. For the shipyard worker, highly specialised skills learned in the yard were of little use outside it. In lean times, employers resorted to a variety of methods to press down on wage rates, including increasing the numbers of semi-skilled and apprentices. The class bitterness bred on Clydeside in the years after 1900 had much to do with the peculiar pressures which the shape of the industry made on both employers and the workforce in the shipyards.[48]

All sectors of heavy industry were critically dependent on coal and railways. Each of these two industries was, however, highly individual. The increasing links which had begun in the 1830s to tie the output of the western coalfield closely to the iron industry began to loosen in the 1860s, when demand in its overseas markets, in North America and Ireland, was also beginning to dip. One of the two props of its increased output, the availability of plentiful cheap labour, also began to meet difficulties in the 1870s, when miners were attracted into better-paid jobs in the USA and a wave of mass strikes hit the industry. These were, especially in the Lanarkshire coalfield, a gesture of despair rather than militancy; wage cuts had to be swallowed, but the legacy was a new, better-organised trade unionism which was unusual in Scottish industry. The confrontation between employers and the workforce took place against a background in which thinner, more difficult seams had to be worked and costs were rising. The plentiful supply of cheap coal, which had been vital to the accelerating industries of the mid-Victorian age, was almost at an end.[49]

Railways, probably the single most dramatic development of the nineteenth century, had unexpected effects. Their origins lay, like canals, as the vital lifelines conveying vast quantities of mineral deposits to factory or furnace. Wagonways and tramways had existed since the early seventeenth century: a two-mile wagonway linked the coal mines at Tranent with the port of Cockenzie in 1722, and by the 1820s more than ninety miles of track existed. The Monkland & Kirkintilloch Railway, opened in 1826, heralded the age of the steam locomotive, but it was seen as fitting into the existing system of communications rather than replacing it; the line took coal from the Monklands field only to the nearest waterway, the Forth/Clyde Canal. By the late 1830s, an impressive network of railways had cropped up, including lines linking Dundee with Arbroath and Glasgow with Paisley and Ayr, but they were all for bulk transport and only two were more than twenty miles in length.[50] The opening of the line between Edinburgh and Glasgow in 1842, intended for passenger traffic, was far more successful than even its investors had hoped. By 1845, the great 'mania' of railway development had begun. The race to reach England was under way between the two rival trunk railways: the North British east-coast route reached Berwick by 1846 but passengers had still to be conveyed by omnibus across the river to Tweedmouth; the Caledonian opened a west-coast route via Carlisle in 1848. Suddenly the journey time between London and Edinburgh or Glasgow had been reduced from forty-three hours to seventeen; by the 1880s fierce competition had reduced it to eight hours.

The role of the railways in Victorian Scotland is elusive. They were not significant consumers of Scottish coal, iron or steel; the bulk of iron rails and most rolling stock were imported and Scottish industry was slow to produce steel rails. Investment in railways was untypical of that in the rest of Scottish industry. Much of it was private and came from English investors; in the Edinburgh to Berwick line they outnumbered Scots by three to one. The contribution made by railways – and it has been argued that they were a central feature of the Scottish economy – was indirect and emerged only in the late 1840s. In practical terms, an incorporating union took on new effect once the distance between London and Scotland was cut, in real terms, by three-quarters.[51] Within Scotland, the railways transformed costs, encouraged economic growth and brought together the expanding urban network. Perishable goods could be transported long distances, migrants became more mobile. In one sense, the railways forged a single Scottish economy, as never before. In another, they encouraged the growth of specialisation in different regions: they underlay the extension of Dundee's textile industry into jute, the expansion of woollen knitting in Hawick, tweed in Selkirk, and carpets in Kilmarnock.[52] The very special case of the railways, a new kind of linking mechanism between the various parts of the Scottish economy, demonstrates that after 1850 industrialisation was no longer – if it ever had been – a matter of one industry acting as a 'leading sector', pulling others along in its wake. It was the essential ingredient of a very different form of economy, interdependent and complex as well as industrial. A new kind of society was its offspring.

The rise of the cities

The nineteenth century was the age, not simply of urban society, but of the large city. In 1800, 17 per cent of Scotland's people lived in towns of more than 10,000 inhabitants; by 1850 the figure had risen to 32 per cent, and by 1900 to 50 per cent. The equivalent figures for towns of 5,000 inhabitants or more – 21, 36 and 58 per cent respectively – demonstrate that one of the main features of urban life in the nineteenth century was the sheer size of towns. The other was the stunning rate of their growth. A number of towns had been growing quickly before the 1820s: they included not only old-established burghs like Edinburgh, Glasgow or Dundee, but virtual new towns such as Greenock, which grew from 2,000 in 1700 to over 27,000 by 1830 and Paisley, under 7,000 in 1750 but over 47,000 in 1820. The half-century after 1830 saw a different kind of urbanisation. Most towns increased in size, sharing in the overall increase in population growth; by 1900 there were seventy-five burghs which has a population of 5,000 or more. Few new towns sprung up. There were no cases in Scotland of a Manchester-like mushrooming of an area which suddenly drew together a previously unlinked rural hinterland; urbanisation usually took place within the structure and culture which already regulated burgh society. Life in the mid-Victorian city was far from tranquil, but it was not afflicted by the violent anarchy which could overtake settlements clustered near mines or iron works, such as Blantyre and Old or New Monkland. There, violence, strikes and industrial intimidation – by both employers and by fellow-workers – added extra hazards to life. In Edinburgh there was one public house for every 150 inhabitants; in shanty towns like these, there was likely to be one for every eighty or so.[53]

The most striking change lay in the massive, rapid consolidation of the existing large centres of population. By 1850, one Scot in five lived in one of the big four cities – Glasgow, Edinburgh, Dundee or Aberdeen; in 1900, it was one in every three. The Scottish experience was overwhelmed by the great cities. The scale and pace of population growth is hard to grasp, especially in the case of Glasgow. There, the increase before 1820 had been startling: 43,000 in 1780 became 84,000 by 1800 and 147,000 by 1820 – a net increase of more than a third in most decades. By 1841, its population was 255,000, 396,000 in 1861, 511,000 in 1881 and 762,000 by 1901 – but by 1870 this was achieved amidst new circumstances, of a falling birth rate and far lower levels of migration and immmigration. Put simply, there were less incomers in the second half of the century, but more Glaswegians lived longer. The continuing growth of the city after 1840 posed massive problems for public health, housing and its infrastructure. Some of these problems were solved, others were not. Glasgow was, nevertheless, a very different city in 1900 from what it had been in 1840.[54]

In 1840, Glasgow was still a textile town. Cleland's analysis of 1819 found over 12,000 handloom weavers, who made up by far the largest single occupation, and in some parts of the city, such as Calton and Anderston, they made up over 40 per cent of the workforce. At least a quarter of the workforce, so Cleland estimated, was made up of casual labourers, forced to find work where they could. One in five of the population was Irish-born, though if their children are taken into account, the true figure was probably closer to one in three. In some parts of the inner city around the Tron, six out of every ten inhabitants were outsiders, coming from outwith the city or Lanarkshire. It was into the central parishes, where land was at its most expensive and housing at its cheapest and therefore its most overcrowded, that this new workforce, unskilled or alien, poured. The number of persons per dwelling rose rapidly, from 4.4 in 1819 to 5.2 in 1841. But this was an average, and in St John's, Chalmers's old parish, the figure in 1841 was 5.9. Sanitation was often, literally, non-existent. The inevitable result was a high incidence of disease, and especially those which were water-borne like cholera or directly related to over-crowding like typhus, and rocketing mortality rates. There were three major outbreaks of typhus between 1817 and 1837, and 3,000 of the 10,000 who died in the first major outbreak of cholera, in 1832, lived in in Glasgow. It was a primitive city, which was on the brink of being overwhelmed by a social crisis on an unprecedented scale.[55]

By 1900, Glasgow was a skilled man's city. The proportion of unskilled in the male workforce had fallen steeply, especially after 1870, to the point where it made up less than a third. The numbers in the female workforce had fallen in relative terms. The waves of Irish immigration had stabilised and then fallen, in both absolute and relative terms, since the 1870s. The population of inner city parishes fell, from the 1870s onwards, as skilled or semi-skilled artisans moved out to new suburban communities like Partick and Govan, which were close to the booming shipyards and engineering works and demanded higher rents. Those who stayed were often the new immigrants, Irish, unskilled and low-paid – an underclass rather than representative of the working classes as a whole. The first steps taken towards an ordered urban society had come in the area of public health, in the period between 1855 and 1875. In 1859, fresh water reached the city from Loch Katrine. In 1862, the Glasgow Police Act was used to authorise the setting up of a sanitary department and in 1863 a Medical Officer of Health was appointed. The problem of cholera quickly faded, with Glasgow suffering only fifty-three out of some 400 deaths in the epidemic of 1865-6, but it took until the 1880s to bring typhus under control. Infant mortality rates dropped by a quarter in the period between 1870 and 1908. But overall statistics disguise the likelihood that the gulf between the destitute and those enjoying the average standard of living was widening.[56]

The second phase took the form of a calculated programme of civic improvement, following the 1866 Improvement Act. Gas was municipalised in 1867 and electricity in 1891; trams were taken over in 1894 and telephones in 1890. This was municipal government run by ratepayers for the benefit of ratepayers; it was imbued with the spirit of civic patriotism rather than socialism. It was only after 1894 that party politics began to intrude; by 1900 a left-wing alliance had ten of the seventy-five seats on Glasgow town council. The motives were always laudable; the methods were often authoritarian. The system of 'ticketing' houses, by fixing a metal plate to the door of all houses of less than three rooms which limited the number of occupants permitted, was one arm of a drive against overcrowded housing. The knock on the door in the night by the police was frequent – 55,000 in one year, with less than one in seven found breaking the law. Another means was the clearance of whole areas of slum dwellings. Between 1871 and 1874, over 15,000 houses were demolished by the Improvement Trust, but it began to finance house building only in the late 1880s and even then at a slow rate. By 1900, Glasgow's major problem lay in the area where it was slowest to municipalise – housing. The Corporation in 1902 employed over 10 per cent of the city's workforce, but it owned only 2,488 houses.[57]

In housing, the picture was very different from the steady improvement of amenities elsewhere in the city. Most new housing built in the last decades of the century was still of only one or two rooms, and in 1901 seven out of ten Glaswegians lived in such dwellings. The new stone tenement blocks were better built than the old slums, but their facilities were still rudimentary. Compared with English cities, space was more cramped and rents were higher. The road to housing improvement in Glasgow was a much longer one, though a start was made, as a deliberate act of policy, after 1902. By 1914, 2,199 houses had been built by the Trust, which was then landlord to about 2 per cent of the population. It was a modest start, but it set a precedent which would become more important in the 1920s and 1930s. It came about, not as the result of creeping municipalisation, but as a reluctant response to the growing failure of private enterprise in the rented housing sector. It is unwise to see the growth of the late-Victorian cities in simple terms of the rise of a 'nanny' civic state; at issue was also a real crisis for private enterprise.[58]

The stunning rise of Glasgow to 'second city of the Empire' made it both unique and typical of other Scottish larger towns. There, the problems posed by urbanisation had been at their worst, and the sheer scale of them had forced solutions to be found earlier than in most other towns. In sanitation, Edinburgh (which had appointed the first Medical Officer of Health in 1862) and Glasgow clearly led the way. In contrast, Dundee, which had only five water closets for a population of 92,000 in 1861, with three of those in hotels, municipalised its water only in 1869, but did not achieve an adequate supply until 1875.[59] Glasgow's civic housing record was modest, even after 1890, but it accounted for 63 per cent of all local authority housing in Scotland between then and 1914.[60] The worst slums, in the old city centre, had had been cleared, not least by the need to build railway termini, like St Enoch's. The problem which remained was not one of slum areas but of lower-quality tenement housing which stood side by side with better. A report in 1905 by the Dundee Social Union made the point well. It compared two neighbouring tenement blocks. In one, there were six WCs for 429 people, almost all the flats were one-roomed and the average rent was £4 11s a year. A typical family comprised an unskilled mason's labourer, his wife and eldest son, aged fourteen, who both worked in a mill, two younger daughters and the wife's mother – in one room measuring 12ft by 10ft. In the other, a three-storey tenement, there were two WCs for twelve flats, which were all two-roomed, and the average rent was £6 8s. In a typical family here, the man had steady semi-skilled employment in an iron store, his wife did not go out to work, his eldest son had just won a bursary to secondary school, and two younger children were also still at school.[61] If this tenant belonged to a friendly or savings society and perhaps a lodge, was a member of a temperance union and still voted Liberal, if his wife had worked before marriage but not after, devoting most of the next fifteen years to the exhausting drudgery of keeping a 'respectable' home, and if the children attended not one but several Sunday schools, one after another on the Sabbath, the contrast would be complete. Self-help as late as 1905 was still expected to help more than either civic improvement or the state.

The effect of Westminster legislation was patchy in most areas of social welfare until the very end of the century or beyond. The 1866 Sanitary Act, drawn up largely to force English local authorities to improve provision, proved unworkable in Scotland. Local solutions came first, sanctioned by the Burgh Police Act of 1862, which allowed individual communities to establish and enforce their own by-laws. Many, however, chose to turn a blind eye – and nose – even to flagrant nuisances. It was only with the Public Health Act of 1897 and the increasing supervisory role taken on by the Board of Supervision for the Relief of the Poor after it was reconstituted as a Local Government Board in 1894 that any systematic effort was made to improve the patchwork of public health. By then, sanitation was a post-urban problem. The worst cases were in small communities – the habits of the population of Dysart were discovered to be 'disgusting', Cockenzie's domestic water supply was 'dangerous' and Kirkintilloch was 'repulsive' – but there were also sizeable burghs, such as douce Ayr and St Andrews, where local authorities had to be bullied into taking basic measures. Housing, however, remained the least effective area of the Board's activities until the eve of the First World War.[62] The building of low-rent homes for the poor was the last item on the agenda of both civic patriotism and the British state.

Politics, political identities and trade unionism
To its architect, Henry Cockburn, the 1832 Reform Act had provided Scotland with 'a constitution at last', by which he meant a Whig electorate. For William Gladstone, it marked the 'political birth' of Scotland, by which he meant the happy subordination of its institutions to the discipline of British parliamentary representative government.[63] Yet 1832 did not produce either a predictable electorate or a settled pattern of Scottish politics. In retrospect, Scotland voted solidly Liberal: every general election between 1832 and 1918, with the exception of 1900, saw that party with a majority of Scottish seats. Some burghs, ranging from Elgin and Arbroath in the north-east to Dumfries District in the south-west, returned an unbroken train of Liberal MPs up until 1914. In reality, the cataclysmic events of the 1840s – and none more so than the Disruption – widened the political

agenda, tempted the churches into politics as never before and pushed Whig managers into a frenzy of anxiety which lasted until the mid-1850s. Most ministers of the Church of Scotland remained staunchly Tory – 1,221 out of 1,228 voted Conservative in 1868 – but it had to wait for the revival of Tory fortunes to recover much effective say in party politics.[64]

There was no automatic rendering up unto Caesar by seceders or dissenters what the Whigs had expected would be theirs by right, as authors of the Reform Act. The Free Church, its ego badly bruised by the events which had led to 1843 and claiming that 'what the country wants is neither Whigs nor Tories', bid to become a third force in politics but found it difficult to convert evangelical fervour into votes. The effect of the Disruption had been to let loose into Scottish politics a series of emotive issues which excited the new middle-class voters, detached Scottish from British politics and perplexed Westminster governments. Education, temperance and disestablishment – rather than the Corn Laws, Protection and the retreat from 'centralisation' which resulted in the dismemberment of Edwin Chadwick's Board of Health for England and Wales in 1858 – were the issues which vied for first place in Scottish politics. Bemused British politicians, even those with good Scottish credentials such as Lord Aberdeen, despaired: 'This education issue', he complained in 1854, 'is likely to become a real torment, as indeed everything Scottish is'. By the 1870s, it was the tangled thicket of disestablishment which dominated politics in Scotland and perplexed party managers in London. The Liberal leader, Lord Hartington, appealed for 'a safe sentence or two on Scottish Church matters' to use in his speeches on a Scottish tour in 1877.[65] The 'new liberalism' of social welfare which by 1900 had begun to galvanise the Liberal Party in England and Wales fell on stony soil north of the Border. Up until the eve of 1914, Scottish politics stubbornly retained its own idiosyncrasies – posing a dilemma for each of the British parties to solve. Even the new Liberal Unionists, who emerged in the mid-1880s as an important third force in both British and Scottish politics, complained that 'Scotland gives us more trouble than the rest of the United Kingdom put together'.[66]

To Sir Walter Scott, parliamentary reform would 'destroy and undermine until nothing of what makes Scotland Scotland shall remain'.[67] Some of his fears were realised. Until 1868, when it acquired seven more seats, Scotland had only fifty-three MPs out of 658, whereas its population entitled it to nearer ninety; twelve more were added by 1885. At Westminster, Scottish issues were, as far as possible, decently kept out of sight: debates were relegated to the small hours, Scottish MPs were encouraged to reach 'an understanding on Scotch questions' to hurry business through.[68] Much legislation was, in consequence, either badly drafted or bore the heavy imprint of English precedent, whether suitable or not; the Education Act of 1872, the cornerstone of Scottish education until 1918, had, astonishingly, nothing to say about religious education until a clause was added to it at the last possible moment. The Scottish Grand Committee, which emerged out of this informal caucus in 1894, was attacked as 'revolutionary' by some English MPs and dissolved when a Conservative government came to power in 1895; it became a permanent fixture only after 1907.[69]

Even the major steps forward in recognition of a Scottish dimension – the creation of a Scotch Education Department in 1872 and of a Secretary for Scotland in 1885 – were not quite what they seemed. The new Department was a single room, with the sign SCOTLAND on the door, within the Department of Education for England and Wales, and the new Scottish Office, located at Dover House in London, had only a token presence in Edinburgh. The Secretary did not command a place in the Cabinet until 1892 and the office did not become a full Secretaryship of State until 1926. The management of Scottish legislation, which had largely continued in the hands of the Lord Advocate after 1832, mostly stayed there because most early Secretaries were peers. The first Secretary, the Duke of Richmond and Gordon, privately thought it 'quite unnecessary'. He took to heart the advice of his prime minister on his new responsibilities: 'It really is a matter where the effulgence of two Dukedoms and the best salmon river in Scotland will go a long way'.[70] The Duke lasted only a short time in office, but the principle survived him. The Secretary's work was largely ceremonial and an ability to stir up apathy was one of the main talents it demanded.

Politics and government in Victorian Scotland were a unique blend of deference and native idiosyncrasies, a half-way house on the way to a uniform British political system. Even after the Reform Acts of 1868 and 1884, there was not a homogeneous British electorate. The 1868 Act gave Scotland an electorate of 230,606, but the franchise was still hedged about with residential qualifications peculiar to Scotland. Their effect was significant: in Glasgow, the electorate notionally went up from 18,000 to 47,000, but the rule that non-payment of rates disqualified voters disenfranchised two-thirds of Irish householders there. In 1884, its electorate increased to 560,580, but that represented only three out of every five adult males whereas in England and Wales two out of every three had gained the vote. In practice, the unskilled and much of the Irish community remained unenfranchised until 1918.[71] With the flamboyant exception of 'Don Roberto' – R.B. Cunninghame Graham, landowner, Argentinian rancher, married to a Chilean poetess and Liberal MP for North-West Lanarkshire, 1866-92, who was imprisoned for 'illegal assembly' at an unemployment demonstration in Trafalagar Square in 1887 – most Scots returned in Scottish seats for the two main parties were undistinguished; the five Crofters Party MPs elected in 1885 were stars in a dull firmament. Its most distinguished MPs were leading figures in Liberalism – such as Asquith who sat for East Fife, James Bryce who represented South Aberdeen for over twenty years but visited his constituency only one or twice a year, or Gladstone himself, who used Midlothian as the venue for the relaunch of his political career in 1879 – who had been found safe seats in Scotland and took almost no part in Scottish politics. The constituencies they represented were content to bathe in their reflected glory. Both local associations and the electorate were astonishingly compliant. In 1888, when Keir Hardie, a talented firebrand with well-established mining connections, stood in the Mid-Lanark by-election as an independent who claimed that he was the real Liberal – his campaign address claimed a vote for him was 'a vote for Gladstone, Parnell and YOU' – he was heckled by miners in Wishaw and managed just 617 votes, 8.3 per cent of the poll. Mid-Lanark returned instead a Welsh barrister who lived in Wiltshire – the Liberal candidate.[72] The most compelling voice representing Scottish interests, though less often than their own, was that of the Scottish peers in the Lords, such as the Duke of Argyll. A number of them – Aberdeen, Buccleuch and Dalhousie – held high office, but largely because they had managed the metamorphosis into British politicians with a characteristically easy grace which

Scotland itself had only half achieved.[73]

The day-to-day business of the governing of Scotland had, however, developed its own characteristics, if largely by accident. A number of Scottish Boards had been set up to deal with matters such as the promotion of fisheries and industry. They were not government departments as such, but agencies operating under the nominal control of the Home Secretary and, after 1885, for the most part, of the Secretary for Scotland. The most important of these was the Board of Supervision. The Secretary's control over it extended to receiving an annual report. To some extent, these Boards developed a life of their own, which necessarily took a different route from administration in England and Wales, where such bodies had largely disappeared by the third quarter of the century. The growing professional expertise of these Boards was, however, matched by the benevolent paternalism which ran them. Control of the Board of Supervision rested with a chairman and a select band of full-time members who were usually landowners, educated at English public schools and remote from the problems of industrial Scotland. It was, at best, government by lairds.[74]

Scotland after 1832 was akin to something like a one-party state. The Tory Party, disadvantaged by the First Reform Act and left in disarray after internal splits over both the Disruption and the repeal of the Corn Laws, took far longer to recover in Scotland than elsewhere. There was no radical nationalist movement in Scotland, even in the excited years of the mid-1880s when both Ireland and Wales honed to a new perfection their own unique rhythms of radical politics. The Liberals in election after election won a comfortable majority of the Scottish seats until 1886, when a splinter group of more conservative-minded Liberal Unionists, alarmed by the prospect of Irish Home Rule, took sixteen of the fifty-seven Liberal seats gained at the previous election. By 1900, the Liberal vote had shrunk to 50.2 per cent, which resulted in a failure, for the first time since 1832, to capture a majority of Scottish seats, with only thirty-four to twenty-one for the Conservatives and seventeen for the Liberal Unionists. By 1906, however, its vote had risen to 56.4 per cent, giving it fifty-eight seats with the Conservatives reduced to eight and the Liberal Unionists to a rump of four. Despite the fact that Scottish Liberalism had been hesitant to embrace the 'new liberalism', which had been instrumental in the restoration of Liberal fortunes elsewhere in 1906, its dominance seemed to be as complete as ever when war began in 1914.

Like many grand coalitions, Victorian Liberalism contained within it a bewildering and self-contradictory mixture of different factions and pressure groups. It thrived on high principle, moral indignation and the philosophy of the self-made man. It was bound together by a common detestation of the 'land laws', by which was meant the collective privileges of the landed aristocracy. Its sense of solidarity waxed and waned in time with the great causes – of free trade, reform, temperance, disestablishment and imperial politics; it was never more enthusiastic than during the Midlothian campaign, when Gladstone appealed to issues such as 'the sanctity of life in the hill villages of Afghanistan'.[75] History now belonged, so the veteran reformer, John Bright, claimed in a speech made to Glasgow University students in 1883, not to 'emperors and kings' but the 'intelligence and morality amongst the people'.[76] Yet this was a party which contained within it Whig landowners such as the Duke of Argyll and a compliant, distinctly unthrifty Irish vote as well as middle-class radicals and the skilled working classes. It was always a broad church and therein lay its strength. It was also an incubator for the breeding of various political cultures, which would eventually destroy it.

The Indian summer of Liberalism came in 1884 and nothing symbolised the breadth of Liberalism better than the huge procession of 64,000 which paraded to Glasgow Green to protest against the obstructions put in the way of the Third Reform Act by the Tory House of Lords; there it was greeted by further 200,000 people. Countless portraits of Gladstone were carried, alongside Chartist flags, banners of the reform campaigns of 1832 and 1866-8 and working models of craft unions. 'No Surrender' Orange banners mixed, incongruously, with others celebrating Catholic Emancipation in 1829. Trades councils, craft unions and friendly societies – the three most important formulators of working-class opinion in late-Victorian Scotland – were all represented in force. Workers in the tobacco trade carried the motto, 'Tobacco and the Lords are all equal – they are all weeds'; the Amalgamated Carpenters and Joiners marched behind an 1868 flag, 'You have chiselled us long enough'; and nine branches of the Potters carried a pottery kiln with the inscription, 'We'll fire them up'.[77] By 1886, however, Irish Home Rule had begun to drain off some middle-class support towards Liberal Unionism and working-class Orange elements towards Conservatism. The land question in the Highlands was taken over by the Crofters' Party in 1885 and the foundation of the Scottish Labour Party after the Mid-Lanark election of 1886 offered the first of many surrogate homes for the socialistic conscience. But this was drift – in many directions – rather than a series of outright schisms. It is difficult to detect a long march towards either socialism or Conservatism before 1914, when Liberals held fifty-eight of the seventy-two Scottish seats. Liberalism was by then again on the defensive, but only as a result of another Irish crisis, in Ulster.

If Scottish Liberals thrived by the exploitation of high principles – 'its platforms were also pulpits' complained John Buchan[78] – the Conservatives desperately pursued almost any principle that might help to revive their fortunes. An appeal to Protestant sentiment was the basis on which an urban Tory vote was built up: the party used the revival of the Orange Order in the 1870s, issues such as religious instruction in schools, and fears kindled by both the declaration of papal infallibility and the revival of the Scottish Catholic hierarchy in 1878.[79] The main root of the Conservative revival lay, however, in the shock-waves caused by Gladstone's commitment to Irish Home Rule in 1886, although there was no sudden merger with the Liberal Unionists. It was not until 1895 that they sat on the same benches at Westminster and formal merger, into a Scottish Unionist Party, came only in 1912. Like the Liberals, Scottish Conservatives were a coalition, with different warring factions based in Edinburgh and Glasgow. They were also a British party which found itself obliged to devise a distinctive Scottish political programme. Its official stance – 'Unionism in matters Imperial and Trade Unionism in matters industrial' – had greater appeal amongst the small businessmen who were typical Liberal Unionists than the working men to whom it was addressed. Despite its claims in the 1880s that it was the party which had done most for the wage-earning classes, it found it difficult to shake off the mantle of being, in the words of a report made for it in 1885, the 'creed for lairds and law agents'.[80] Conservatism made better progress in Scotland as the party of Protestantism and the Union rather than as the vehicle of either a new social radicalism or Imperialism.

The Conservatives were the first to take party organisation seriously. A Scottish National Constitutional Association was formed in 1867 and a National Union of Scottish Conservative Associations in 1882. Gladstone's Midlothian campaign had been a barnstorming but brief affair, and it was Tory politicians who made mass meetings a regular feature of politics in the 1880s. By the 1890s, considerable efforts were being made to reach working-class voters. Full-time constituency agents appeared in almost half the Scottish constituencies, working-men's clubs were set up, lantern lectures organised, the Dunbartonshire Association set up a cycling task force to distribute leaflets throughout the shire and Central Office offered the 'services of a Working-man Speaker', complete with a van.[81] The shape of both Conservative politics and party organisation was undergoing a transformation in the 1890s – but the electorate had yet to recognise it. Their sweeping victory at the general election of 1900, which brought them twenty-one Scottish seats, was in Scotland largely the result of temporary Liberal disarray over a 'khaki' election, called amidst the Boer War. The decisive defeat suffered in 1906, when they were reduced to only eight Scottish seats, forced the Conservatives into another reappraisal. It had not produced any results by 1910, when the Conservatives' recovery in the rest of Britain was not matched in Scotland. For the Liberals, the land issue had been given a fresh lease of life and Home Rule had acquired a new respectability as part of a programme of 'Home Rule all round', which might be offered to different parts of the Empire as well as Scotland and Ireland. The combination was potent enough to keep at bay both Unionism and a vigorous challenge from the left.

The fact that religion – in its various forms – was etched more sharply on the working-class psyche than the politics of industrial society affected all the parties, but none more so than Labour. Until at least 1890 the most important expressions of opinion of the Scottish working classes were not trade unions but trades councils, friendly societies and the Co-operative movement. Beatrice Webb was told by her secretary in 1893 that: 'In Glasgow there are a hundred trade unions but very little trade unionism'.[82] Only a quarter of workers on Clydeside were then members of a trade union. Those who were belonged mostly to small, conservative craft unions, which were the preserve of the skilled man: the engineers in the Clyde Workers' Committee, according to the veteran socialist Harry McShane, came to mass meetings with their rolled umbrellas.[83] The twin processes of the period between 1890 and 1914 – the growth of a skilled urban workforce and the casualisation of the unskilled – dampened militancy where unions existed and made general unions more difficult to organise. The most militant groups, such as the miners, were the most fragmented. Although there was a four-month strike of the 70,000-strong workforce in 1894, only one miner in ten belonged to a union; and they were dispersed through eight separate unions.[84]

A gap also existed between trade unionism and socialist politics. Although a separate Scottish Trades Union Congress was formed in 1896, its affiliated unions covered only a half of all trade unionists in Scotland. By the 1890s trades councils, first formed in Edinburgh and Glasgow in the late 1850s and for long loyal supporters of the Liberal consensus, were beginning to find new forms of political expression in bodies such as the STUC, but the Co-operative movement was still staunchly

Liberal in 1914. In retrospect, it can be seen that a battle had already been joined for the loyalties of the working man. But before the First World War, the diverse attractions of freemasonry, friendly societies – such as the Rechabites which had 27,000 members in Lanarkshire alone in 1910 – and the Orange Order were more than holding their own against the growing appeal of organised labour.[85]

If there were many unions but little trade unionism, there were also several 'labour parties' but only a muted, organised socialist voice. The Scottish Labour Party was founded in 1888, as a direct result of the coalition which had backed Keir Hardie's campaign at Mid-Lanark. It was neither particularly working-class in composition nor socialist in outlook. It espoused every species of land reform known to Liberal man, a reflection of the fact that most of its members came from somewhere in the great Liberal consensus. Its first president was Cunninghame Graham, embarking on the second stage of an eccentric but brilliant political career. Hardie himself had been an organiser for the Good Templars before he became an agent for the Lanarkshire Miners' Union, and was an apostle of both the temperance and Co-operative movements.[86] The diverse roots of so many of the leading figures in labour politics, together with the reluctance of Scottish Liberals to strike 'Lib-Lab' pacts help explain the pattern of ceaseless activity. Two sorts of organisation – the gathered church and the sect – resulted, which underlined the paradox of Labour politics in the period up to 1914. It was a movement, not with too few causes but too many.

The most important of the umbrella organisations, in which different stances on issues were acknowledged but did not divide, was undoubtedly the Independent Labour Party, founded in Bradford in 1893 and merged with the SLP a year later. It was a coalition like the SLP, but this time more socialist than socialistic, even though it also embraced favourite Liberal themes such as temperance, anti-landlordism and 'Home Rule all round'; it became the linchpin of a new, growing labour alliance which was beginning to emerge after 1900. The sects, led by such restless socialist consciences as those of James Connolly (born in Edinburgh in 1868) and John Maclean, formed breakaway groups, which regularly re-formed and realigned with others. These politics was byzantine in complexity, insignificant so far as the ballot box was concerned and still patchy in their effects on working-class agitation. A trade depression in 1908, which saw unemployment in Clydeside shipbuilding soar to over 28 per cent, provoked a new militancy amongst skilled men, in which at least one of the sects – the Marxist Social Democratic Federation – became involved, but it subsided in a spectacular economic recovery after 1909.[87]

Support for the ILP is difficult to gauge with much precision. Its membership in 1900 amounted to some 1,250, a high proportion of the British total of 9,000. Yet most of its twenty-two Scottish branches were based in cities or larger towns, and only three were in mining districts. In 1895, it put up eight candidates, compared with just thirty in England and Wales; but in 1900 none stood in Scotland. No Labour candidate was returned for a Scottish seat before 1906, whereas two had succeeded south of the Border as early as 1892. The Labour vote in Scotland fluctuated wildly: it stood at 5.1 per cent in the election of January 1910 but fell back to 3.6 per cent eleven months later. There were signs, however, of a change of direction after 1910, by which time ILP Scottish membership had probably risen to 5,000 and was more prominent in the coalfields, which accounted for fifty of its 125 branches.[88] Socialism was beginning to take on a more populist appeal, but it had still a long way to go before it fully joined forces with the unions. Secular politics was emerging, but class politics was still in its infancy.

24

A New Society?

THE OUTBREAK OF WAR IN AUGUST 1914 PROVOKED AN IMMEDIATE AND widespread response in Scotland. Harry McShane, a shop steward in the Amalgamated Society of Engineers (ASE), later talked in his memoirs of a 'terrible war fever', in which so many men rushed to enlist that there were not enough uniforms to go round and 'daft middle-class women with white feathers' cajoled the reluctant.[1] With some idiosyncratic exceptions – such as the revolutionary socialist, John Maclean, who was in Tarbert on holiday when war was declared and spent a night drawing the slogan 'Grey is a liar' on walls – there were few voices which spoke up against the war. Only two of the seventeen Labour Party representatives on Glasgow Corporation argued against it in public. Pulpits of all denominations supported the war. For the Church of Scotland minister of Paisley, Walter Mursell, 'Belgium is Christ for us today' and the clarion call of a righteous war was widely echoed. For the Roman Catholic Archbishop of Glasgow, John Maguire, the war brought a new lease of life. This virtual recluse, who had languished on a sick-bed since 1910, became an enthusiastic 'recruiting sergeant' in both sermons and pastorals, not having scruples to point out the influence German theologians had had on much contemporary presbyterian thought. For many, the war restored a much-needed sense of unity to the nation, linking, in the words of W.P. Paterson, Professor of Divinity at Edinburgh University, the aristocrats usually in August to be found on the grouse moors and the working-class 'slouching spectators of the football spectacle'.[2]

More than one miner in four joined up in the first year of the war, but this was no higher than in industrial Scotland as a whole. Height restrictions, which would have kept out many of what Christopher Harvie has called the 'wee hard men', were waived. 'Pals' battalions', such as those of the Highland Light Infantry which recruited mainly from Glasgow's slums, were formed almost overnight from particular localities or the workplace: another battalion in the same regiment was entirely made up, in the space of sixteen hours, of the employees of Glasgow Corporation tramways. In other cases, it was fear of unemployment, which resulted in 36 per cent of miners in the vulnerable Lothian coalfield enlisting, or pressure from employers such as the Earl of Weymss, who threatened to dismiss any employee on his estates between the ages of eighteen and thirty who did not volunteer. With Scottish regiments comprising twenty-two of the 157 battalions which made up the British Expeditionary Force, no part of the British Empire reacted more patriotically and few parts suffered more heavily. No official overall death roll of Scots was ever issued, but it is likely that Scotland lost nearer 110,000 dead than 75,000, a fifth rather than an eighth of the total of 573,000 for the four nations. In Glasgow, the 18,000 dead accounted for some 10 per cent of all adult males, but in many country districts, where the Territorials had been popular before the war, the impact was twice as great.[3] The longer-term effects are incalculable.

Although most who died – twelve in every thirteen – were privates in the infantry and the majority were aged between twenty and forty, the shape of the post-war generation may have been more severely affected by the number of middle-class recruits who did not return: they included one in six of the graduates of Glasgow University who went to war and one in seven of those from Edinburgh University. The failure of Scottish industry in the 1920s and early 1930s has been interpreted as largely the product of a weakness of management.[4] It is perhaps the lost generation which lies at the root of it.

In 1913 the unemployment rate in Scotland stood at only 1.8 per cent, whereas in London it was 8.7 per cent. By 1923, the positions had been reversed, with 14.3 per cent out of work in Scotland compared with 11.6 per cent in the United Kingdom as a whole. It was, however, a different kind of unemployment from the short, irregular lay-offs which had marked the years before 1914; it was long-term and affected the skilled more than the unskilled. Edwin Muir, who had spent most of his teenage years in Glasgow after an idyllic childhood in Orkney, left the city in 1919; he returned in 1934 to find an uncanny 'silence of a dead town' in the shipbuilding areas and thousands of workmen for whom 'life now is a long and dreary Sunday'.[5] The war had brought about a major shift in the balance within Great Britain between north and south; unemployment rates in the north-east of England were marginally worse than in Scotland until the early 1930s. Wage rates in Scotland, which had slowly been catching up with those in England over the two decades prior to 1914, began to slip back. Although the standard of living, at least for those in work, was improving in the Scotland of the 1920s, it was not keeping pace with the level of improvement in the south of England.[6] The theme of a rich south and poorer north, which dominates much of Britain's social history for the rest of the twentieth century, was a product of the First World War.

In other respects, however, the war may have acted as a brake on social change rather than an accelerator of it. The years immediately before 1914 had seen a narrowing of the wage gap between skilled and unskilled workers and the beginnings of 'industrial unionism', in which all grades of workers, men and women, were organised in one union.[7] The huge demand for labour in wartime manufacturing produced pressures which varied from one industry to another. Although in engineering there are indications that differentials continued to reduce, it seems that elsewhere, and especially in the shipyards and the mines, bonuses and the adoption of piece rates meant that the gap in earnings between skilled and unskilled persisted and even widened.[8] Militancy was confined largely to the skilled craft unions, although it was conducted there in an odd mixture of new socialist ideas and old Victorian habits.

The war brought into employment thousands of women – the 'clippies' on Glasgow's trams with their distinctive Black Watch tartan uniforms were among the most visible of the new female workforce – but it did not keep them in work after 1918. Most were put to work on jobs – such as the filling of shells with high explosive – which came to a natural end in 1918. In 1914 over two million women in Britain already worked outside the home; the war brought a further million into the workplace, mostly in the munitions industry, although less than one in four – despite the outcry over 'dilution' of male labour – were doing men's work. By 1921, however, there were slightly fewer women going out to work, some 34 per cent, than there had been in 1911. In Britain, there was a decided shift after 1918 with women moving out of domestic service into clerical jobs or the service sector. In Scotland, although there was a similar decline in domestic service – the disappearance of a maid's bedroom in post-1918 houses in middle-class suburbs of Edinburgh is as good a guide to the trend as any – the long-term decline in the inter-war years of the textile and jute industries, which was its other major employer of female labour, probably resulted in an actual decline in numbers of women at work. The trend was not reversed until the 1950s.[9] If the war was a crucible, producing a heightened working-class consciousness, a new involvement of women in the national effort and a new relationship between organised labour and the state, it also reproduced some of the old moulds which had distinguished pre-1914 society. The paradoxes which resulted, when coupled with the fact that wartime boom had turned by 1921 into post-war slump, dominated the inter-war years.

War, protest and 'Red Clydeside'

The First World War is so often seen as a watershed in the development of Scottish society and its economy that the complex, bewildering events of both 1914-18 and its immediate aftermath are easily compacted into a colourful, compelling drama. 'Total war', in which industrial production had to be raised to new heights to meet demand for munitions, produced a series of issues – 'dilution' of skilled work by unskilled or female labour, sharply rising rents, and conscription from 1916 onwards – each of which provoked unrest. The legend of 'Red Clydeside' was born of the efforts made, both by a small band of socialist enthusiasts and by a panicky wartime coalition government, to link together different episodes – industrial disputes, rent strikes and demonstrations – into a revolutionary conspiracy. The first major outbreak was a strike in February 1915 amongst engineering workers, provoked by the paying of much higher rates of pay to American workers brought in by the hawkish industrialist, William Weir, managing director of G. & J. Weir Pumps of Cathcart; they demanded twopence an hour more – an unprecedented increase. The dispute lasted two weeks before a compromise was reached. Agreement was concluded with the government rather than the employers, and it involved a pact, the 'Treasury Agreements', for the conduct of wartime industrial relations. The issue of 'dilution' affected the munitions industry rather than the whole of Clydeside; it was confined mostly to the engineering workshops, which were the hitherto unchallenged preserve of the time-served craftsmen of the conservative ASE, rather than the shipyards, which were scarcely touched by it; and the issue took over a year to emerge fully, for it was only in April 1916 that a strike broke out at the giant Parkhead Forge. It found little sympathy elsewhere, even in the other factories in which shop stewards of the Clyde Labour Withholding Committee, an activist wing of the ASE later renamed the Clyde Workers' Committee (CWC), were prominent. There was no general strike of the skilled engineers, still less one of the unskilled in the industry. The dispute at Parkhead was quickly nipped in the bud by the arrest of ten of the CWC's leaders. It says much for the 'revolutionary' nature of the strike that it was organised by a body which carefully avoided the word 'strike' in its title, and that its leaders were not imprisoned but deported – to Edinburgh.[10]

The first year of the war brought 20,000 munitions workers into the Glasgow area, concentrated in Govan, Parkhead and Clydebank. Empty flats were quickly filled, overcrowding became endemic as families took in lodgers unable to find even a 'single end'. With the building of new housing brought to a halt by the war and demand vastly exceeding supply, rents rose steeply; rises of 23 per cent were recorded in Fairfield and Govan. The first rent strike took place in May 1915, in south Govan; within six months some 25,000 tenants were withholding their rent. Standardised defiant placards, with the words 'Rent Strike. We are not Removing', appeared in windows; factors were set upon by women and pelted with rubbish and flour in ritual rites of violence which were reminiscent of the demonstrations against bailiffs during the Clearances in the Highlands; mass protests were held when tenants answered summonses to appear in small debt courts. The rent strike of 1915, which ended with the agreement of the government to a state-imposed freeze on house rents, was the most startling display of militant action in the period. It was the only issue successfully to link industrial and political protest: trades councils, the Co-operative movement and the ILP were all involved in it; munitions workers demonstrated alongside clerical workers. The Act which it forced the government to concede four weeks later was a turning-point in British social history. The militancy of the rent strike wrung a major concession, which goes some way towards explaining the relative stability and lack of protest of society – in both Scotland and Britain as a whole – on social issues after 1915.[11]

When workers in the Govan shipyards downed tools in November 1915 to join the thousands of demonstrators outside the court where rent defaulters were appearing it was hailed by the ILP as the greatest event in the history of the Clyde workers.[12] The claim was misleading: the rent strike succeeded where industrial disputes failed, for it combined patriotism – prominent among the placards at such demonstrations were slogans such as 'We are fighting landlord Huns' – with the pent-up animus of the peace movement, and it built upon the issue of poor housing which had been the most telling factor in the ILP's rising popularity in the years immediately before 1914. Two additional elements gave the movement a unique cutting edge. One was the notable role taken in it by women, who became its shock troops; more radical than the ILP, which preferred the tactic of a token strike in the shipyards to a total walk-out, it was they who seized the initiative and co-ordinated the November demonstration.[13] The other was the overlapping roles played by unconventional institutions such as local tenants' associations and the Women's Housing Association, which did not conform to the inbred stereotypes of conventional political or industrial democracy. As in other issues, it was the skilled workers who took the lead, for south Govan, where the strike had started, was a better-off area, but it was the unique mixture of interests making up the housing campaign which gave it its staying power. The different wings of the Clydesiders, it has been said, 'worked, politicised, socialised and talked endlessly with each other'.[14] But there was no other issue where they found such a waiting public.

The *annus mirabilis* of 1919, when the Red Flag was brandished during a demonstration of more than 100,000 in George Square in Glasgow, and the government sent in troops and tanks to quash what the Scottish Secretary, Robert Munro, described as a 'Bolshevist rising', coincided with more industrial unrest. The Forty Hours' Strike of January 1919, however, was the first serious dispute for almost three years, and again it was centred on the craft unions. The issue of the length of the working week was closely tied to the after-effects of 'dilution' and the desire of skilled workers to maintain employment by sharing out what work there was. The demand for a forty-hour week was a sign of the internal divisions within the ASE, whose executive had negotiated one of forty-seven hours and hailed it as 'one of the greatest triumphs of British Trade Unionism';[15] it was also a compromise, stopping far short of the thirty hours demanded by some CWC shop stewards. As in 1916, the arrest of its leaders – including Emmanuel Shinwell, chairman of Glasgow Trades Council and William Gallacher, former chairman of the CWC – removed what teeth the dispute had. According to Sir Basil Thomson, head of Special Branch and keen to detect a Bolshevik amidst every disturbance, the plan of the strike leaders was 'to use the Clyde as the touchstone of a general strike' and to seize the Municipal Buildings in George Square. Efforts to spread the strike beyond Glasgow proved desultory; only in Belfast was there any response. Seventeen years later, Gallacher, by then an orthodox Communist, lamented the lost opportunity: 'A rising was expected. A rising should have taken place. The workers were ready and able to effect it; *the leadership had never thought of it*'.[16] This retrospective prognosis has etched a deep impression of the combustibility of 'Red Clydeside'. A lost revolution has since become the talisman of a Left trying to retrace its own footsteps.

The 'riot' in George Square was not planned, and it happened when most of the strike leaders were engaged in negotiations inside the City Chambers. It began with a baton charge by the police to try to clear a way for tramcars at one side of the Square; it continued up a sidestreet with a 'hurricane of blows which fell indiscriminately' on strikers and curious bystanders alike; the words are from the account in the highly conservative *Glasgow Herald*. Gallacher's horrified reaction at the time was to urge the crowd to disperse. If a general strike was the plan, the issue of the length of the working week was the wrong one – wage rates were much closer to the hearts of groups such as the railwaymen, who struck later in the same year – and this was the wrong union to organise it, for friction still existed between skilled and unskilled workers and the national executive of the ASE refused to support it. Two other key unions held aloof – the Scottish Horse and Motormen's Association and the Municipal Employees' Association, which organised the tramwaymen whose path the police tried to clear in George Square. A drift back to work began on the Monday following the 'riot' of 'Bloody Friday'; within a further week the strike was officially abandoned. It had lasted sixteen days. The swift collapse of the strike may, however, be misleading. The CWC had found most support, not in the engineering factories where its own shop stewards held influence, but in the railway workshops of Cowlairs and Springburn and in some of the shipyards. Although the 'Strike Bulletin' was efficiently distributed by a fleet of bicycles, it was an idiosyncratic document, which recalled earlier agitation of 1908 and referred to a mass strike in Bombay as its parallels. This was a strike for the craft aristocracy of the CWC rather than the rank and file.[17] The rent strike of 1915 – which had galvanised an instinctively *laissez-faire* government into intervention in the market-place, presaged a new social dimension for official policy in the inter-war years and brought about a quiet social revolution – was a greater landmark than the revolution that never was in 1919.

There is a curious lack of connection between the chief events in the history of 'Red Clydeside' and its leading apostle. John Maclean, the Govan schoolmaster, socialist and relentless opponent of the war, who was appointed by Lenin in 1918 as the first Soviet consul for Scotland, was singled out by the authorities as the most dangerous of the Clydesiders; he was arrested six times between 1916 and 1923. Maclean was an omni-present figure but one without real influence.[18] Throughout the war and after he kept up a punishing schedule of meetings at factory gates and on street corners; his first arrest took place at what he had established as his regular speaking platform – opposite the main recruiting office in Glasgow. His description of the war as 'this murder business' was deemed to be 'language likely to cause a breach of the peace', but it provided the excuse for the Govan School Board to dismiss him. Yet Maclean was a member of a party, the British Socialist Party, which was deeply divided on the issue of the war. So was the CWC, the prickly but ultra-respectable craft aristocrats in their 'blue suits and bowler hats'. Although Maclean was allowed to address its meetings, the CWC was far too conservative and divided a body to adopt the stratagem which he began to urge from late 1915 onwards – a political strike as a means to end the war.[19] His involvement in the rent strike campaign came late and from the sidelines. In 1919, he had hopes for a revival of the 'triple alliance' of miners, railwaymen and transport workers, which had been interrupted by the outbreak of war in 1914. He expected the stimulus towards a general strike to come from the miners and significantly he spent most of the period of the Forty Hours' Strike on a speaking tour in England.[20] Maclean was the nagging conscience of the Left; always a charismatic orator rather than a leader, he had a following but lacked an organisation. The fact that he joined and left so many parties of the Left without influencing them meant that he lacked the typical baggage of political sectarianism; it makes the claim that he was 'the outstanding British Marxist'[21] the simpler to establish. The one party which he was instrumental in forming – the short-lived Scottish Workers' Republican Party, founded in February 1923, nine months before his death – has been dismissed as 'claymore communism', both by the Labour Party which it threatened and by orthodox Marxist canons which were in the early 1920s moving towards a British theatre of operations. The man described by Hugh MacDiarmid as 'the greatest leader the working class of Scotland have yet had'[22] remains an enigma, not only the symbol of a revolution that never was but also the awkward reminder of a lost Scottish Left.

Maclean was the chief exhibit in a Pantheon of Red Clydeside which was built up after his death. Like him, most of the Clydesiders – a term which came to be associated with the group of largely ILP members returned as Labour MPs in 1922 – were not drawn from the ranks of unskilled workers. Maclean's own leaflets always carried the description 'John Maclean MA', a reference to the part-time degree in Political Economy which he was awarded by Glasgow University in 1904. Like him, many of the 'Clydesiders' were schoolmasters – as were six of the ten Glasgow Labour MPs elected in 1922 – or journalists or skilled workers. They still carried much of the values of late Victorian society and the broad church of Liberalism from whence many had come. More than six in ten of those active in the Labour movement between the two wars were total abstainers; their heated debates were usually conducted over endless cups of tea.[23] Although Harry McShane claimed that most of the Clydesiders were 'free thinkers', the service of dedication in St Andrew's Hall in Glasgow after the 1922 election victories in Glasgow when the crowd sang the traditional Calvinist battle hymn, the 124th Psalm 'Had not the

Lord been on our side', reflected a deeply felt if denominationally vague presbyterianism.

Did the new Labour leadership distance itself from the values of the working classes as it became an establishment in the inter-war years?[24] There had long been a strong streak of the *petit bourgeois* as well as the craft aristocracy about the various labour parties which had dotted the Scottish political landscape since the 1880s. Those values persisted. The efforts of the ILP before 1914 to organise Socialist Rambling Clubs or ILP Cycle Scouts belonged to an era in which political parties and the churches alike had to offer healthy outdoor activity as well as ideology. Amidst the new temptations of the 1920s – the socialist weekly *Forward!* was particularly scathing about jazz, dance halls and cinemas – the puritanical streak in the Labour movement strengthened. At the heart of Labour politics was a deeply conservative attitude to society and family life. As a result, the role of women, despite their prominence in the rent strike of 1915, remained typecast, in 'the home struggling to make ends meet'.[25] Other factors would conspire to keep them there.

A new politics?

Two factors transformed politics. The signing of the Anglo-Irish Treaty in 1922 removed the Irish issue – in its double aspect of north and south – from the centre stage of politics, where it had been since the 1880s; it allowed a new system of British politics to emerge.[26] The Representation of the People Act of 1918 added women above the age of thirty to the electoral register and increased the number of males entitled to vote by fully a half. The Scottish electorate rose from 779,012 at the 1910 election to 2,205,383. The effects in Scotland, where a lower proportion of adult males had been eligible to vote before 1918 than in England and Wales, were commensurately greater. A predominantly working-class electorate was now a reality, and greatly feared by the old parties, but neither the war nor the confusing party politics which marked its aftermath brought automatic gains for Labour.

The immediate beneficiaries were the Unionists, whose seven seats gained in 1910 increased to thirty-two in the 'khaki' election of 1918. The Liberal Party remained a potent, but mysterious force in Scottish politics: its real strength was disguised by its internal rifts and the pacts with which it became entangled. The four Liberal Unionists returned in the December 1910 election had united with the Conservatives in 1912 to form the Scottish Unionist Association. In the 'coupon' election of 1918, where Liberals were torn between loyalty to Lloyd George and Asquith, only eight candidates who stood without the coupon were returned. The breach between the Asquithians and the National Liberals remained unhealed in 1922, but it was still a separation rather than a divorce. The National Liberals were more fervently wooed by the Unionists in Scotland than they were by the Conservatives elsewhere in Britain, but there was a good deal of shadow boxing about their prickly relations with Asquith's faction: in the 1922 election, although the two Liberal parties fielded a total of eighty-one candidates, they confronted each other only in eighteen Scottish seats. The total 'Liberal' vote was 39 per cent, more than that for either the Unionists or Labour. It was ironic that in 1923 the Liberals, now reunited by the threat to free trade, suffered a collapse in their share of the vote, down to 28 per cent, but they did win twenty-three seats, almost half as many again as the Unionists.[27] In Labour politics, the latter stages of the war had seen a sharp rise in membership of the ILP, but this development had proved less easy to translate into national electoral gains than it had in municipal politics, where it gained forty-four of the 111 seats in the Glasgow municipal elections of 1920. Labour did not gain a majority of Scottish parliamentary seats until 1945, although it came close in both 1923 (with thirty-four) and 1929 (with thirty-six). Even so, Glasgow town council was not captured by Labour until 1933.[28]

The chequered fortunes of the three main parties demonstrated the extent to which class politics had advanced. The agitation after 1915 and the strikes of 1919 had done at least as much to provoke a middle-class consciousness as they had to forge a working-class identity. An anti-Bolshevik panic swept through Glasgow's bourgeoisie: organisations such as the Middle Classes Union and the People's League set up an extensive network of branches; and in 1919 students volunteered as blackleg labour to break the railwaymen's strike.[29] The industrial unrest of 1919 failed to produce a general strike but the General Strike, when it came (rather unexpectedly to the trade unions) in 1926, was more than matched by the new militancy of the middle classes: one worker in nine struck, but the government had 25,000 volunteers in Scotland alone, more than it could use as blackleg labour.[30]

Freed from the complications of the Irish issue in British politics, the Unionists by 1922 had detached themselves from the Orange Order; that specific appeal to the working-class Protestant voter was abandoned in favour of a new concentration on the middle-class vote. Unionist working-class candidates, who had been a feature of Scottish politics since the 1890s, virtually disappeared, except in a few hostile constituencies. The *People's Politics*, a populist propaganda paper, was revived in 1919, described by the Party as of 'immense value' – usually the kiss of death in Conservative politics – in 1920, and was abandoned in 1921. The thrust of the new Tory politics was towards women, young people and farming interests. A women's organiser was appointed in 1920 and Lady Edith Baxter took on a self-appointed role touring Scotland to address village hall meetings which warned women of the horrors of Bolshevism. The Junior Imperial League was revived and the Young Unionists founded to cater for those under sixteen. The Unionists' capture of the rural vote – against a background of the growth of trade unionism amongst farm workers and fears of Labour's agricultural policy – was confirmed by their gain of twenty-two county seats from the Liberals in 1924. The Unionists, paradoxically, were the first to carve out a distinctive, new niche for themselves in post-war politics. A new Britishness, shorn of the embarrassments of Ireland, and an avowedly class stance were their hallmarks.[31]

The war had divided the Labour movement, not least over the peace issue. It had survived, more or less intact, largely as a result of the increasing grip gained over it by the ILP, whose membership in Scotland had tripled in 1917-18. Other developments helped it. The Co-operative movement, already in 1911 rather bigger than that in England, saw a 30 per cent increase in numbers by 1918, by which time it was well along the path towards explicit support for Labour.[32] Labour, too, had benefited from the sharp increase in membership of trade unions, which doubled in Britain between 1914 and 1920. Equally important was the consolidation of organised labour: although there were no fewer than 227 unions in Scotland, eight out of every ten men by 1920 belonged to a core of thirty-six and these were more prepared than before to affiliate to Labour.[33] But there was a price to be paid for greater liaison with the unions, which had acquired new status during the war by negotiating directly with government. This did not make them eager partners in Labour politics; they were wary of risky political ventures. Nothing characterised the Labour Party in Scotland more than the gulf between its new Clydeside radicals and the ingrained conservatism of the MPs sponsored by the mining unions: the long-serving MP for West Fife, the ex-miner William Adamson, was caricatured by Beatrice Webb as 'a typical British proletarian in body and mind, with an instinctive suspicion of all intellectuals or enthusiasts . . . He has neither wit, fervour nor intellect'. Adamson summed himself up better in a casual aside made in 1924, when he was the minority Labour government's Scottish Secretary: 'You must remember I'm only a miner. You'll be surprised to find what a Tory I am.'[34] The better-known Clydesiders such as Jimmy Maxton brought the passion; men such as William Adamson provided the ballast.

Although Labour was a more cohesive movement in 1918 than it had been in 1910 not all portents pointed in its favour. The election of 1918, fought before the new Reform Act had been able to take full effect, had returned seven Labour MPs from Scotland, but only two of them belonged to the ILP. There was a shift of support towards Labour, but it was as yet more noticeable in urban and industrial areas outside Glasgow, where its only success had been in Govan.[35] Party workers interpreted the result as a protest against Toryism rather than a vote for socialism; Labour was as anxious as the Unionists about a Liberal revival. Amidst a slump in the shipyards and rapidly rising unemployment, at 16 per cent in 1920 and 25 per cent in 1921, the new props of the Labour movement seemed in jeopardy. 'Destitution, hunger and unemployment are not aids to the Labour cause,' complained Patrick Dollan, chairman of the Glasgow ILP in late 1921. The party's organisation was wilting: membership of the ILP halved in Glasgow in 1921 and numbers in the ten largest unions fell by more than a third between 1920 and 1922. Labour, despite its successes in the municipal elections of 1920, held only a third of the seats on Glasgow Corporation: for the beleaguered Dollan, 'all the talk of Glasgow being the Petrograd of Britain was a great deal of moonshine'.[36]

The gain of twenty-nine MPs in the general election of 1922, with no fewer than ten of Glasgow's fifteen seats falling to Labour, was all the more notable for being so unexpected. In retrospect, it is possible to see that Labour's gains closely corresponded to the twenty-three seats where the Catholic working-class comprised more than one in five of the voters, but the inevitability of the transfer of Catholic Irish loyalties from Liberalism to Labour after the treaty of 1921, which had given a measure of self-government to the Irish Free State, was not so obvious to contemporaries. The bargain struck in 1922 can be made to seem explicit: Catholic votes were traded in return for Labour support for Catholic sectional interests and especially for the continuation of separate Catholic schools.[37] It assumes an ability of Irish Catholic organisations such as the Catholic Union to deliver not only the old Catholic vote but also the newly enfranchised one, and to do so not on single issues (as it had done before) but in the broad panoply of politics. Put simply, the question – which is still unresolved – is whether Catholics voted *en bloc* as an enclave or as part of a broader feeling amongst the working classes, Catholic and non-Catholic, that Labour best represented their interests.[38] The ILP, whose paper *Forward!* had boasted that it was not read in the slums, had long been pre-eminently the party of the skilled working class; the Irish were overwhelmingly unskilled. The size of the gulf between them was indicated in the evidence given by the President of Edinburgh Trades Council to the Royal Commission on Housing in Scotland in 1917, when he admitted that he usually did 'not come into communication' with 'the Irish element, labourers and what not'.[39] It takes two to make an embrace and the reservations on each side need to be remembered.

The main bridges between the Catholic community and the Labour movement were forged by two Labour politicians who came from an Irish Catholic background – Patrick Dollan, who has been described as the 'party machine man *par excellence*',[40] and John Wheatley, Clydeside MP and later Minister of Health in the first Labour government. They were exceptional figures in more ways than one: Dollan had been an agnostic since 1911 and Wheatley, a year later, had to witness seeing himself being burnt in effigy during an attack on his home in Shettleston by a Catholic mob whipped up by a local priest. It is a double irony that the victorious Glasgow MPs, who left for Westminster in 1922 amidst the strains of the 124th Psalm, owed much of their success to Dollan, a lapsed Catholic who otherwise eschewed Westminster politics in favour of richer rewards in municipal politics. He was one of the earliest examples of the characteristic divide in Scottish Labour politics between Westminster politicians and the careerists who ran the local party machines; his reward was a knighthood in 1941.[41]

John Wheatley was memorably described by King George V in his diary in 1924: 'Received Mr Wheatley. . . . He is an extreme socialist and comes from Glasgow. I had a very interesting conversation with him'.[42] Born in Ireland, brought up in the bleak poverty of a single-room cottage without water or sanitation near Ballieston in the north Lanarkshire coalfield, Wheatley worked in the mines for eleven years before setting himself up in a small business. His first experience of politics was in the United Irish League, a vehicle for mobilising the Irish vote behind the Liberals, but by 1912 he was a Labour councillor on Glasgow Corporation. Although he had grown up with Dollan, their journeys to socialism took significantly different paths, not least in their Catholicism, for throughout his life Wheatley remained devout. He saw the 1922 election result as marking only the beginning of a new relationship between Labour and the Catholic Irish community. No one did more to cement the growing bond between the two. But less expectedly, no one did more to turn the Labour movement in Scotland into a British milieu. In 1915 Labour was the party of Home Rule and housing. By 1924 its first priorities were housing and jobs, but each was to be remedied in a British context. Of the three legs on which it stood in 1915, local action and a commitment to Scottish Home Rule were far more important than a British socialist agenda. After 1924 the balance of the movement began to swing away from a decidedly Scottish stance. Its distinctiveness lay in its municipal politics; its direction was firmly towards a British Labour Party. For good or ill – and much might be said for both – much of the responsibility for this shift, which remained decisive until at least the 1970s, lay with Wheatley.[43] The greatest monument to the success of his strategy was the Housing Act of 1924, which found a formula for subsidising the building of local authority housing; it has been described as the single most significant achievement of the short-lived first Labour government.[44] The most telling criticism of Scottish Labour's drift into British politics was the largely grey character of its MPs after the mid-1930s; few parliaments produced the formidable or unpredictable array of talent of the 'class of 22' – of such as Wheatley, Maxton, Johnston, Kirkwood and Shinwell.

The most decisive factor in 1922 was the fact that in twenty-two of the twenty-nine seats it won, Labour was confronted by a split middle-class vote. It amassed 32 per cent of the popular vote and won twenty-nine seats; the Unionists and the 'Coalition Liberals' gained 43 per cent between them and twenty-seven seats; the Liberals had over 21 per cent and sixteen seats. In 1931, Labour again gained 32 per cent of the vote – and won only seven seats, because of the collapsed Liberal vote. Inter-war politics were a complex, shifting world, but one in which clear, largely unchanging threads of support persisted amongst the voters. Labour's share of the vote between 1922 and 1935 remained somewhere between 32 and 42 per cent; Unionist support between 1924 and 1935 remained steady at between 36 and 42 per cent, save in the exceptional circumstances of 1931, when voters' support for a National Government gave them 49 per cent of the poll. The wild card, which greatly complicated politics, was the Liberal vote, which was presented with different 'Liberal' options in every election between 1918 and 1929 except 1923.[45]

The strange, lingering death of the once great phenomenon of Scottish Liberalism has still satisfactorily to be explained. Its nemesis can variously be placed: in 1924, when the Liberals' support for the minority Labour government cost them dearly in the middle-class vote, Asquith was bundled out of a Scottish seat for a second time and the party in Scotland was reduced to a rump of eight MPs; in 1929, although it slightly increased its share of the poll and gained a further five seats, its performance was distinctly inferior to that in England; or in 1935, when desertions to the National Government left it in disarray and with only three Scottish seats.[46] The issue of the Liberals is central to the puzzle of Scottish politics in the inter-war years. Historians sympathetic to the Labour and Unionist parties have claimed each as the 'natural' party enjoying a bed-rock of Scottish support. For Labour, it could be said that it was temporary but severe internal dissensions, which led to a virtual collapse over the issue of support for Ramsay MacDonald's National Government in 1931 and the disaffiliation of the ILP in 1932, which brought about its crisis. It recovered, though a shadow of its former charismatic self, only after a largely two-party system had taken hold in 1935. Creative arithmetic – counting various strands of Liberal coalition partners as intrinsic Conservatives – can lead to a radically different conclusion: that by the mid-1930s Unionists had managed to construct a formidable right-wing natural majority.[47] Yet the Unionist share of the vote in 1935 was 42 per cent, less than half a point more than Labour's; it was the distribution of the vote and rogue element of National Liberal support which put clear water between the two main parties.

The continuing ability of Liberalism – in its various disguises – to attract Scottish voters, despite its own organisational disorders and with little new in the way of policy except a growing nostalgia for the pre-1914 world, blunted the new politics of class. Its adoption of Keynesian economics in the 'Yellow Book' of 1926, *Britain's Industrial Future*, charted a new and distinctive alternative route out of the slump, but did little for it at the ballot box.[48] The roots of almost all the significant figures in Scottish politics in the inter-war years – ranging from John Wheatley on the Left to Walter Elliot, Conservative Secretary of State for Scotland from 1936 to 1938 – lay somewhere in the broad church of Liberalism. The organisation of the

'Young Scots', an important but unofficial Liberal pressure group in the pre-1914 period, crumbled during the war; its members were to be found on various shores of the 1920s, and especially those of nationalism. As ever, Liberalism wrote its own rules. The hopeless split at the election of 1935 led to reorganisation of the Scottish Liberal Federation in 1937. This was, however, a different kind of Scottish party from that of Labour or the Unionists, where the Scottish element was only a branch subject to the oversight of the British party. The SLF was independent of the Liberal Party elsewhere, with its own chairman and rationale.[49] Its actual support at the ballot box, however, made it paradoxically a party of the Scottish periphery rather than of Scotland as a whole.

A new Union?

In 1918 Labour fought the election in Scotland on two distinctively Scottish planks: 'The Self-Determination of the Scottish People' and 'The Complete Restoration of the Land of Scotland to the Scottish People'. Both were testimony to the powerful influence of the old Liberal programme, as was Labour's pact with the Highland Land League. But Home Rule, shorn of both the Irish dimension which had given it much of its cutting edge and a real prospect of success in the form of 'Home Rule all round', became increasingly incompatible with the drift of the parties towards the new British politics. The Labour Party did not quickly abandon its commitment to Home Rule, but after the failure of Ramsay MacDonald's minority government to give its full support to a Government of Scotland Bill in 1924 the issue became increasingly conspicuous by its obscure placement on Labour Party conference agendas. As the paradox of a Home Rule party intent on making its way in British politics deepened, the chief standard bearer of devolved government became the Scottish Home Rule Association, nominally a non-party organisation which had been revived in 1918. The STUC, which had consistently supported Home Rule since its inception in 1897, began to lose interest in it after 1926 and the failure of the General Strike. Here the dilemma posed by the post-war slump was acute: rising unemployment and falling union membership forced Scottish trade unionists to rely more heavily on national collective wage bargaining and federal, British unions. By 1923 three out of every five trade unionists in Scotland belonged to a British organisation. The demands made by the unions of central government increased, as did expectations of the Union.[50]

Labour was not alone. In the 1920s all three major parties, for their own particular reasons, became more firmly thirled to British politics. The politics of 'semi-independence',[51] which had marked the period up until 1832, were long gone but so was the Victorian equipoise, in which loyalties to both a reawakened sense of Scottish nationhood and the Empire had kept the British state at arm's length. Economic pressures, which resulted in the sudden take-over of five Scottish railway companies and most of the banks by English capital in 1919-20, pushed in the same direction, as would the long slump after 1920. Yet the Scottish electorate resolutely refused to follow English electoral trends.

This was the background for the emergence in the 1920s of Scotland's first explicitly nationalist party. Its gestation period was drawn-out and complicated. In the 1920s federalists vied with fundamentalists; all-embracing pressure groups like the SHRA, which organised the two unsuccessful bills of 1924 and 1927, competed with exclusive sects such as the Scottish National League, founded in 1920, which aimed at separation rather than devolution and flayed the SHRA for being the poodle of the Labour Party; Celticists, who looked to a union of Celtic peoples and some who saw the Irish troubles of 1921-2 as another English colonial war, confronted imperialists who saw Home Rule as the best guarantee of the continuing benefits of Empire. Each conflict disguised another: there was a basic division between Home Rulers, whose roots lay in the late Victorian period, and nationalists, who were especially alarmed by what they saw as a tide of anglicisation of Scottish culture; there was a never-ending debate about strategy, whether the movement's ends were better served by applying pressure on existing parties or making a direct appeal to the electorate; and, with Ireland removed from the agenda of British politics, the issue of self-government was a mirror image of sharply differing attitudes to Empire.[52] To add to the heady brew, the intellectuals of the 'Scottish Literary Renaissance' (a phrase of MacDiarmid's first used in the *Scottish Chapbook* of February 1923) were happy to play the role of *enfants terribles*, pouring scorn on the pragmatists and brandishing their inevitable expulsions as a badge of ideological pride. The atmosphere of nationalist politics was dynamic, vituperative, portentous and endlessly garrulous. Usually these debates, unlike those of the sober-minded radicals of the ILP, were lubricated by whisky or beer rather than tea.

The National Party of Scotland was founded in May 1928, a glittering coalition of irreconcilable talents. Its first president was R.B. Cunninghame Graham, as omnipresent a figure in inter-war nationalist politics as he had been in pre-war labour parties. Its chairman and secretary, respectively Roland Muirhead, a wealthy businessman, and John MacCormick, a lawyer and former Glasgow student activist, both had come from the ILP. The formula devised to hold together the refugees from the ILP and SHRA on the one side and radicals from the SNL such as Tom Gibson or MacDiarmid (whose argumentative instincts, recorded in lines such as 'I'll ha'e nae hauf-way hoose, but aye be whaur/ Extremes meet', were given a new sphere of operations) was Delphic-like: the new party committed itself to 'independence within the British group of nations'.[53]

Returns at the ballot box proved meagre: in the 1929 general election MacCormick and Muirhead received a total of 3,000 votes, less than 5 per cent of the vote in each constituency. Already the paradox of nationalist politics had begun to take shape. Set against dismal returns in elections – five candidates in the 1931 election polled a total of 20,000 votes, with two lost deposits and a best showing of only 14 per cent of the vote in one of the seats[54] – there were in the early 1930s signs of a widening interest in some nationalist aims: the novelist, Compton Mackenzie, was elected rector of Glasgow University in 1931; and a poll organised by the *Scottish Daily Express* in 1932 found 113,000 in favour of some form of self-government and less than 5,000 opposed.[55] With the new interest came a fresh, but classic dilemma. In 1932 a break-away group from the Cathcart Unionist Association formed the Scottish Party: its members, such as the Duke of Montrose, firmly belonged to the establishment, its views were right-wing and imperialist, and its spoiling tactics were revealed in a by-election in East Fife in early 1933, when the NPS candidate, Eric Linklater, was baited over his party's policy on Empire and came bottom of the poll. MacCormick, faced with the prospect of a bruising fight between rival nationalist parties, chose the road of comprehension: the two parties amalgamated in April 1934 to form the Scottish National Party. Two prices had to be paid: the vagueness in NPS aims became a studied ambiguity in the programme of the SNP; the inevitable purges, including MacDiarmid, rid the party of its most troublesome luminaries but gave it an anti-intellectual image which it found hard to shed.[56]

The years between 1939 and 1945 brought many of the underlying differences into the open. With a falling membership – down from 10,000 in 1934 to less than 2,000 in 1939 – activists within the Party in 1937 staked a claim for its conscience on the twin issues of conscription and neutrality in a future war; it was no more than a gesture of fringe politics. MacCormick's plans for a renewed all-party approach in the form of a National Convention, interrupted by the outbreak of war in 1939, were revived by him in 1942, when the SNP was abandoned to its radical, pacifist wing.[57] MacCormick and much of the membership set up the Scottish Union, soon renamed the Scottish Convention and dedicated to the cause of building a broad consensus for Home Rule. The ironical result was that the two bodies for a time did better apart. The SNP, not having scruples about breaching the gentlemen's agreement made amongst the major parties, put a candidate up at a by-election at Kirkcaldy in 1944 and took 42 per cent of the vote; in April 1945 another by-election, at Motherwell, brought its first parliamentary seat, held by Dr Robert McIntyre. Six weeks later, now shorn of its monopoly of the anti-government vote, it lost the seat at the general election. The SNP, with a membership which stayed stubbornly at the 4,000 mark, retreated to regroup; it took them twenty years.[58] In the first years after 1945, the balance within the nationalist movement would swing decisively towards MacCormick's pressure-group politics.

The 1920s and 1930s saw a series of concessions offered by Westminster to Scotland; each seemed to grant a measure of devolution but in reality made its embrace all the tighter. In 1926 the full status of a Secretary of State was granted to the Scottish Secretary. The first holder of the restyled office was Sir John Gilmour, Unionist MP for Pollok, who by 1929 had reorganised the old administrative boards and staffed them with Whitehall career civil servants. The overhauled Scottish Office, still based in London, was more efficient but also more remote and probably more authoritarian. It could not last. By 1934 more and more elements were being transferred, piecemeal, from London to Edinburgh. An inquiry set up in 1936 produced a tidier solution: the new departments and the surviving boards were recast into four departments – Agriculture & Fisheries, Education, Health and Home – and moved to the fortress-like structure of St Andrew's House in Edinburgh, built on the site of the old Calton Gaol.[59] Until both the internal processes and the personnel of the new-style Scottish Office have been scrutinised by historians, two impressions are possible: that this was another Dublin Castle or that it allowed a unique measure of autonomy to the conduct of Scottish government – although the same could have been said of Dublin Castle before 1922.[60]

The bonds of a new Union, routed through St Andrew's House, were shaped less by the reforms of 1936-9 than by the way the adminstration was run by two distinguished Secretaries of State, Walter Elliot, who held the office between 1936 and 1938, and Tom Johnston, who was appointed by the National Government in 1941.[61] Elliot was an unusual creature in Scottish Unionism – a thinker, whose book *Toryism and the Twentieth Century* (1927) sketched the outlines of a new corporate

435

state; he was the architect of both the Local Government Act of 1929, which swept away the powers of parish councils in favour of larger units, and of the administrative reforms of the mid-1930s. Johnston, the first editor of *Forward!*, a pioneer of Scottish labour history with his book *A History of the Working Classes in Scotland* (1920) and a devout Home Ruler who in 1935 had been one of the founders of the Saltire Society, was an unlikely agent of Westminster government. Yet the two had much in common. Both had been members of the Fabian group at Glasgow University before 1914. Each had a special interest in housing, not surprisingly so with Johnston, whose mentor had been Wheatley; Elliot's foundation of the Scottish Special Housing Association in 1937 was more surprising for it was a victory for a view which was explicitly connected with the Scottish Office and long opposed by most of his own party, the application of preferential subsidies which departed from the so-called 'Goschen formula', based on a pro-rata apportioning of finance according to levels of population.[62] Both believed in a strong, but benevolent centralist state, and preferred doing business with like-minded men behind closed doors. The distance between what have variously been called the 'Unionist experiment' and 'informal Home Rule'[63] was not great, at least in social policy; it reflected the growing consensus in British politics of the 1930s about the need to close the gap between 'inner' and 'outer' Britain.[64] The vital difference between them lay in the sphere of economic intervention. Both were decent-minded men, appalled by the social consequences of the slump and anxious to remedy its worst aspects, especially in housing. Elliot, like most of his generation in the inter-wear years, clung to the pre-1914 nostrum that it was not the business of government to accept responsibility for the economy or to interfere in the marketplace. Despite appearances, his was not a policy of regional industrial development a decade before its time. Johnston, in contrast, was willing to countenance a planned economy, although he was able to use the 'people's war' to launch it.[65]

The Second World War began with news of the U-boat sinking of the transatlantic liner *Athenia* off the Outer Isles and the naval base at Rosyth in the Forth was raided by German bombers before the end of September 1939. The grim realities of the Blitz were brought home by two devastating nights in March 1941, when Clydebank was subjected to a raid by 200 bombers; 1,200 died and only eight houses out of a total of 12,000 in the burgh were left untouched. Although the town was eventually rebuilt, in a series of scattered housing schemes, the close-knit tenement community clustered around the shipyards never recovered.[66] The authorities had learned a painful lesson, so when Greenock was attacked in the following May almost the whole population was evacuated, to avoid a second raid – which never came. Although Scotland's other cities knuckled down to the strange routine of nightlife in Anderson bomb shelters, they otherwise largely escaped the traumas experienced in the Midlands and south-east of England. War production largely involved screwing up Scotland's heavy industries to something like old-time production levels. The shipyards hummed with an activity unmatched since the First World War, with five ships a week being launched on the Clyde in 1943.

The problems faced by Tom Johnston in mobilising Scotland were considerably less than during the First World War: there was considerable muted criticism of the running of the war, but few strikes; the spectre of Scottish nationalism – a 'sort of

Sinn Fein movement' as he liked to call it – was skilfully used by Johnston to cajole Churchill's National Government. He gave a Scottish dimension to the new wave of collectivism which was already running through Whitehall. A Scottish Council for Industry – what Johnston called his 'industrial parliament' – was set up in 1942, representing employers, trade unions, the banks and other interests. Its function was less to mobilise the war effort than to persuade Whitehall to locate more of the expanding war industry in Scotland. The founding of the North of Scotland Hydro-Electric Board in 1943 was a major innovation in public ownership, but it was backed by the Council of State, a vetting body made up of all the ex-Secretaries of State for Scotland. The roots of much of the post-war administration of Scotland are to be found in the Johnston years: an emergency hospital scheme for war workers was a precursor of the National Health Service set up in 1948; the separate Scottish Tourist Board founded in 1945 was a forerunner of later autonomous quasi-governmental organisations; the Scottish Office was given part responsibility for the Forestry Commission. A considered judgement is made the more difficult because of Johnston's journalistic talents; he wrote his own headlines, both before and after his period in office. His claim that 'we had got Scotland's wishes and opinions respected and listened to as they had not been respected or listened to since the Union'[67] has not yet been seriously disputed. It was centralisation without tears, devolution without anxieties. The intricate mechanisms of the new Union were a solution for a collectivist age.

Scottish Society in the 1930s and after

In 1929 the Church of Scotland and the bulk of the United Free Church reunited. It was a momentous but not unexpected landmark, virtually bringing the long Disruption to an end; only three small rumps – in the UFC, the Free Presbyterian Church (1893) and the Free Church (1903) – remained detached. It completed a reunion process under way since 1908 but interrupted by the First World War. The result, a 'National Church' accorded a degree of 'state protection' rather than an Established one, was an adroitly drawn compromise which satisfied theology but left many questions unanswered. The two Churches in 1919 had launched a National Mission of Rededication, an ecclesiastical 'new deal' intended to give an avowedly presbyterian direction to the process of post-war reconstruction. By 1929, with levels of unemployment stubbornly settled at over 12 per cent and about to lurch higher, the Church had already begun to look with nostalgia to the mid-Victorian ideals of personal salvation and individual self-help. Thomas Chalmers's idea of a Christian commonwealth, however, had slipped away in the decade after the Disruption of 1843; no amount of speeches from the floor of the Assembly on a 'Protestant nation' could bring it back. The General Assembly, it is often said, reflected Scottish opinion – though, with a largely middle-class eldership and a conservative-minded ministry, some parts were better represented than others – but it can hardly be said to have led it.[68] Despite the striking success of the 1929 reunion in bringing together more than 90 per cent of Scotland's presbyterians, the Church of Scotland was undergoing a crisis of identity: it was nervous of the new weapons in the armoury of the forces of secularism and lashed out at cinemas, ice rinks and even ice-cream parlours; it was apprehensive of the new working-class consciousness which had emerged during the First World War; and it was resentful of the status given to both

Roman Catholicism and separate Catholic schools by the Education Act of 1918. The election of 1922, which seemed to reflect a pact made between a newly militant Labour Party and the Catholic Irish vote in the West of Scotland, confirmed its worst fears. The result was a campaign urging a stop put on the immigration into Scotland of an 'inferior' and 'alien race' which lasted until 1938.[69] It proved futile, confirmed the limited influence the Church now had on government and failed, despite a flurry of sectarianism in other parts of Scottish society in the 1920s and 1930s, to harness to the Church a populist strain of Protestantism which still thrived. The false turnings taken by the Church of Scotland in the inter-war years go a long way towards explaining the new directions it took after 1945 – to the dismay of some of its fundamentalists.

By 1900 the focus of Scottish identity – in lieu of both a national political forum and a single Church which embraced the bulk of the Scottish people – had already shifted to new, local institutions which commanded loyalty. Foremost among them was the town hall, the centrepiece of municipalisation. It was a double loyalty. 'I belong tae Glesca', ran the song, but equally important was its next line: 'and Glesca' belongs tae me'. The inter-war years brought massive unemployment, a severe blow to the self-confident world of the skilled man's workplace and a huge crisis in the area where the municipality had done least for the working classes – in housing. The growth of the cities – the central phenomenon of nineteenth-century Scotland – ground almost to a halt. In 1911, a fraction under 40 per cent of Scots lived in towns of 50,000 inhabitants or more; in 1951 the figure was only just over 42 per cent. Glasgow's 'growth' over the same period, from 784,000 to 1,089,000, stemmed largely from the inclusion of Govan and Partick within the city after 1912; in reality its population was virtually static, as were those of Aberdeen and Dundee. It was Edinburgh, whose population increased by a sixth between 1911 and 1951 to 467,000, that was the only major city to maintain anything like a momentum of growth.[70] This was the age of emigration and de-urbanisation. The face of urban Scotland was transformed in the inter-war years. Its symbol was the new-style tenement or cottage in 'garden suburbs', such as Hamiltonhill and Possil.

The Royal Commission on Housing in Scotland of 1917 had recommended in unusually strong terms a massive house-building programme after the war designed to sweep away the enormous disparity in levels of overcrowding between Scotland and the rest of the United Kingdom. Setting its face against the traditional multi-storey tenement, it had preferred the English-style cottage or flatted villa, but also allowed for a novel style of tenement, of no more than three storeys. It and the Addison Act which followed in 1919 represented a major turning-point in the shape of urban settlement.[71] But the actual achievement was a mixed one. 213,000 council houses were built in Scotland between 1919 and 1939, compared with 104,000 in the private sector. In 1911 almost exactly half the Scottish population lived in one- or two-roomed dwellings; by 1951 the figure had been cut, but only by half, such was the scale of the problem. The ideal of the 1919 Act, that council houses 'should serve as a model for building by private enterprise in the future', was realised only until the economic crisis of the mid-1920s; the ironical effect was that the first homes built could be afforded, not by the poorest housed, but by skilled workers, who were paid perhaps £5 a week and were able to afford rents of £20 or £30 per annum. It was all a far cry from Wheatley's ideal of *Eight Pound Cottages for*

Glasgow Citizens made in 1914.[72] In the 1930s low rents became the main priority. The results were more tenements, a return to building two-roomed houses or new, cheaper materials and methods of construction, including concrete blocks, steel frames and flat roofs. Another innovation, the cavity wall, which the test of time has treated more kindly, was treated with great suspicion: one critic – an Englishman – argued that 'a Scottish worker coming home full of whisky' would fall straight through it.[73] The new breed of municipal architects, who had no experience of public housing on any scale before 1919, deserve considerable credit for the means by which they worked with very limited resources. What they did, however, was to create sprawling, one-class dormitory suburbs on the edge of towns, where land was cheaper; the inevitable product was what a Glasgow councillor in 1941 called a 'nation of bus-catchers and strap-hangers'.[74] Or half a nation – for these remote housing estates, with minimal shops or amenities, isolated women who stayed at home in a way which their slum dwellings never had. The backlash against the housing of the 1930s was felt after the Second World War: new towns were built rather than new suburbs and the sprawling garden suburb gave way to the more compact, new-style tenement – the multi-storey tower block.[75]

The symbol of the new standards of living for the middle classes was a different kind of suburb, aligned in long, neat ribbons. The bungalow provided modern amenities – including metal windows, separate kitchenette and (critically) a garage – for relatively low cost. It was the visible sign of a new 'property-owning democracy', a phrase first coined by Noel Skelton, Unionist MP for Perth and East Perthshire in 1931.[76] Bungalows cost between £300 to £800, but they and other housing had come within the purchasing power of the lower middle classes and skilled artisans as a result of a 20 per cent drop in building costs between 1925 and 1933 and a fall in interest rates from 6 to 4.5 per cent; at the same time real wages, for those in work, were rising. This brought the weekly cost of a mortgage for an average three-bedroom house down from 12s a week to 7s 8d, and builders used a variety of incentives, including free removals and legal expenses, to lure prospective buyers. Subtle differences in the appearance and amenity of a bungalow – its facing, a verandah or a dormer bedroom – preserved the vital distinctions within the complex army which made up the middle classes. The fashion was also – like the 'new towns' of the late eighteenth century before it – the mark of a renewed, physical divide between middle and working classes.[77]

If the inter-war years saw a quiet revolution in urban Scotland, they did no less in the Highlands. The depression witnessed a sharp drop in levels of employment in most of the furthest-flung rural areas, including Shetland, which lost one in six of its inhabitants in the 1920s, and Ross and Cromarty, where the population fell by 12 per cent. The effect of the nineteenth-century Famine and Clearances had been to leave the Highlands as a dependent economy; crofting was viable only if supplemented by seasonal work in the Lowlands. That essential prop all but disappeared in the lean years of the 1920s and 1930s. The result was a new Clearance: between 1911 and 1951 the number of men in work in agriculture in the Highlands almost halved and the population of the Western Isles dropped by 28 per cent. It was a fall which was sharper than any during the nineteenth century and, unlike then, there was no recovery to previous levels of population.[78] By 1939 the shape of life in both the Scottish city and the Highlands had been transformed.

By 1936 the Scottish Renaissance, an astonishing outburst of creative talent, self-propagandising, emotion and vituperation, was all but over. Its effects are still reverberating over half a century later. More immediate in its impact was a new popular culture. In 1928, the height of the era of silent pictures, a town such as Paisley, with a population of some 86,000, had eight cinemas; even the smallest of the Fife burghs, such as Crail, Earlsferry and Pittenweem, each had one picture house. Glasgow had ninety-six, and by 1938 it had 114. More Glaswegians went to the cinema more regularly than anywhere else in Britain, or indeed anywhere except Chicago; it is likely that, as elsewhere, the most avid cinemagoers were young, working-class and, more often than not, female rather than male. Scots were also avid readers of newspapers. In Britain as a whole, newspapers were taking on a new importance as moulders of popular opinion: in 1900 daily newspapers were read by one adult in six, but by 1920 the figure was one in two. Scotland, to a far greater extent than in England, had a national press, even though much of it was increasingly English-owned; unlike England, a few newspapers commanded a huge share of the Scottish readership.[79] The papers themselves were avowedly national – not least because of the habit of Scotsmen to read them from the back to the front. Football, given a new glamour by the growth of the sporting pages in more avowedly popular newspapers and the appearance of newsreels in the cinema, still kept the Scottish working-class male in its vice-like grip; it also provided an outlet for the heightened sectarian feelings which marked the 1920s. The combined effect of these vital organs of popular culture was to keep at bay English influences. 'Americanisation' was a greater threat than anglicisation. In 1926 only one film in twenty was British-made, and even the quota restrictions introduced in 1933 raised the figure only to one in five.

In one sense the story of the inter-war years was of the increasing intrusion made by the British state into the ordinary lives of those who lived in Scotland. It is difficult to believe that the re-allocation of administrative functions to St Andrew's House effected a revolution in government. In 1937 Walter Elliot privately recognised the 'dissatisfaction and uneasiness amongst moderate and reasonable people of every view and rank'.[80] A few wanted independence; more still hankered after some form of Home Rule; others wanted not less Union but more – in the economy. It was a state of semi-Union. It was Scotland's culture rather than the new 'Scottish' institutions of government which maintained a distinct national identity. And low culture played a greater role than high in keeping it so.

25

A Nobler Prospect?

IN 1918 LESS THAN ONE SERVICEMAN IN FOUR HAD VOTED IN THE ELECTION WHICH
followed the war. In 1945, six in ten did, voting by proxy or special air post. The
result was hailed as a triumph for the Labour Party and the dawn of a new era. The
two myths were important, but were, in retrospect, half-truths. Labour gained a
little less than half the total vote; there was only a 12 per cent swing from the
position at the last election, nine long years before. In Scotland the *Glasgow Herald*
confessed to 'stupefied surprise', but the swing there had actually been two points
below that average and less than in any other part of the United Kingdom; it
resulted in thirty-seven seats, the same total as Labour had had in 1929. The bulk of
Scottish Labour MPs were trade union-sponsored members, more so than the 30 per
cent in the Party as a whole: the brilliant years of Maxton and Wheatley had gone
and a duller reality had set in. These were unpromising agents of the 'British
revolution' which had been heralded. Tom Johnston retired from party politics to
chair the Hydro-Electric Board and other creations of his period in office; the new
Secretary of State was his former parliamentary private secretary, Joseph Westwood,
who was dismissed after only two lacklustre years in office. His successors
distinguished themselves only in their hostility to what they called 'nationalistic'
discontent in Scotland: Arthur Woodburn, who held office until 1950 and had
supported Home Rule in the past, railed against it; Hector McNeil, an ex-journalist
who had come from the Foreign Office and enjoyed office only for eighteen months
until the general election of 1951, was uninterested in continuing the administrative
devolution which had marked the years since 1941.[1] For ordinary people, experience
of the new lesser Britain did not take long to establish itself: the bitterly cold winter
which followed the end of the war brought food shortages, power black-outs and two
million unemployed. The worst levels of unemployment of the pre-war years did not
return but the pattern of the 1930s, when Scotland's unemployment had been
consistently higher than the UK average, did.

Scotland had been less drastically affected by the war itself than many other
parts of Britain. Wartime production had been concentrated in the traditional parts
of the Scottish economy. By 1945 one in four of the male workforce was employed
in heavy industry, a figure not equalled since 1911; by 1951 it had fallen back, even
in the west of Scotland, to one in seven. In other areas of manufacturing, workers
travelled south rather than orders coming north; the SNP briefly benefited from a
flurry of public anxiety about innocent Scots girls being exposed to the 'moral
dangers' of working in the English Midlands. Much factory space in Scotland was
used for storage rather than production. The war brought little in the way of new
industries, which remained concentrated in the south, and that fact would strike
home after 1945. The post-war years would bring a surge of demand, especially for
ships, but by 1957-8, when the numbers of unemployed in Scotland suddenly
doubled, the death knell of much of old heavy industry, which had failed to

diversify or reinvest, was beginning to ring. Its suffering was drawn-out, and the final wound was not inflicted until 1971, when Upper Clyde Shipbuilders, a consortium of the yards on Clydeside thrown together by a Labour government in 1966, was taken into receivership. Like the First World War, the Second had had the effect of straitjacketing Scotland in its old economy.[2]

'Internal independence'?

In 1950, a week before the general election, Winston Churchill made an astonishing speech in the Usher Hall, Edinburgh. In it he decried Scotland's experience over the previous decade as the onward march towards the 'serfdom of socialism' in breach of what had been 'contemplated in the Act of Union' of 1707, carefully ignoring the fact that much of the progress had been made during his own time as wartime Prime Minister. He offered, as an alternative, fresh 'guarantees of national security and internal independence', including a Royal Commission to review 'the whole situation between Scotland and England' and a second representative in the Cabinet, to protect its interests; Scotland, as in a hockey match, was offered two umpires, one operating in each sphere of the Scoto-British arena. Labour won the subsequent election and the undertakings were quietly forgotten, like many others made by each of the two main parties in post-1945 politics.

The speech did not herald a new debate over Scotland's position within the United Kingdom, for the 1950s were marked by a benign neglect of all such awkward constitutional questions, by both Conservatives and Labour. It did, however, highlight the dilemmas and logical absurdities of semi-Union. In 1937, the Secretary of State had brought to Edinburgh some hundred civil servants; by the early 1970s he had an army of 10,000, housed in St Andrew's House and overspilling elsewhere. Here was a virtual prime minister, backed by his own civil service and a miniature cabinet in the shape of under-secretaries, who also enjoyed large-scale patronage in the appointment of some 5,000 nominees to quasi-governmental bodies such as the Scottish Arts Council and the Royal Commission on the Ancient and Historical Monuments of Scotland. It gave to secretaries of state (of both main parties) and to the Scottish Office a powerful incentive to maintain the status quo – an odd term to describe the restless, creeping frontier of administrative devolution. Tom Johnston's legacy – or was it Walter Elliot's? – was a state within a state, the apparatus of a Scottish state within a British one. It was little understood by the Scottish electorate, who had no need to do so as long as it delivered what it promised in economic planning. When the economy worsened, the first instinct of St Andrew's House was to add extra strands to the Gordian knot – such as the new controls over regional planning introduced during the period of the Labour government of 1964-70 – not to unravel it, still less to cut it. The introduction of a Highlands & Islands Development Board, in 1965, described at the time by the Conservatives as 'undiluted Marxism', became part of the collectivist consensus. It survived, virtually intact, until the early 1970s.

For more than twenty years after 1945, Scotland was a virtual two-party state. In every election between 1950 and 1959 Labour polled between 46 and 49 per cent of the Scottish vote; the Unionists and their allies gained between 45 and 50 per cent. Scotland, which, because of its class structure, should have shown a more decisive tilt towards Labour, remained broadly in line with the patterns set by British politics.[3] The lack of a third force in politics – other parties took only 3 per cent of the vote in 1955 – which had been such a characteristic of Scottish politics between 1918 and 1935, left a curious consensus between the two main parties, each content to leave Scotland in its condition of semi-Union. The SNP languished, with a membership of little more than 2,000 throughout the 1950s; it did not contest a single by-election between 1952 and 1960. The main challenge, in the form of the Covenant campaign organised by John MacCormick, stubbornly refused to translate itself into electoral gains. Its appeal, however, was considerable. The device of a new national covenant, demanding a Scottish parliament within the framework of the United Kingdom, attracted over 400,000 signatures within three months of its launch in October 1949, and would eventually claim over two million. It was striking testimony to the underlying strength of a powerful 'middle opinion' in Scotland, in favour of Home Rule rather than independence, but reluctant to make it the central issue in politics. After two elections, in 1950 and 1951, in which it failed to make an impact and despite the colourful episode in 1950 when the Stone of Destiny was briefly 'liberated' from Westminster Abbey, the campaign ran out of options; rather than evaporating, the opinion which lay behind it went underground, awaiting a political vehicle able to give it new direction.

The new Conservative government of 1951 set up the Balfour Commission to inquire into Scottish affairs, but removed Home Rule from its remit and forgot Churchill's promises of 1950; it took over the view that most roads should lead to St Andrew's House. The main issue in politics was not a matter of the principle of 'controls', but a pragmatic one as to their number. Its reward in the 1955 election was thirty-six seats and a fraction over half the poll; it was the all-time apex of Unionist fortunes in Scotland. The Labour Party, which had endorsed Home Rule in 1941, 1945 and 1947, rejected it outright in 1958; the process of its becoming a British party, begun in the mid-1920s, was complete. Its party organisation in Scotland was almost non-existent: in 1962 it had five full-time agents and an income of £760.[4] The 1959 election, in which the Conservative government's slogan, 'You've never had it so good', did not strike the same chord in Scotland as in the more prosperous south, left an ambiguous result: Labour won seven more seats than the Unionists, but on a smaller share of the vote. Third parties, however, could command the support of no more than 6 per cent of the Scottish electorate.

The general election of 1964 brought two new factors into play. The years since 1959 had seen rising levels of unemployment, despite the bringing of prestige projects to Scotland, such as motor plants at Linwood and Bathgate and a steel strip mill at Ravenscraig. The gap between a richer south and poorer north was widening, and Labour began to present itself as the truly Scottish party which would bring more jobs, through greater direction of industry and more powers delegated to the Scottish Office. By chance, the fact that the Labour government under Harold Wilson elected in 1964 with a slender overall majority depended on its forty-three Scottish MPs gave to the new Scottish Secretary, the gruff, autocratic William Ross, a lever not enjoyed by any of his predecessors since Tom Johnston. The fact that he pushed the Labour vote up to 49.9 per cent in the election of 1966, its highest ever to date, underlined the appeal of his *National Plan* for Scotland, published in 1965; it and its brainchild, the new Scottish Development

Department, implemented planning on a far more rigorous basis than in any of the English regions. The whole of Scotland, except for Edinburgh, was made a 'development area'.

Many of the results of Labour government between 1964 and 1970 were noteworthy: new towns were founded at Livingston in 1966 and Irvine in 1969; between 1964 and 1967 universities were established at Strathclyde, Heriot-Watt in Edinburgh, and Dundee by giving existing institutions a new status and a completely new campus was built at Stirling; a network of social services was created almost out of nothing through the Social Work (Scotland) Act of 1967. The Plan, however, had been based on the assumption of continuous economic growth of almost 4 per cent per annum. By 1967, with the government in drastic economic difficulty and forced to introduce a series of deflationary measures, the Plan already had begun to lose its way. A beleaguered government, under fire from its own MPs and beset by a series of strikes, began to lose its nerve with the onset of a series of stunning reverses at by-elections. One of the most notable was the loss of Pollok to the Conservatives in March 1967; the result made headlines, however, less for the Conservative victory in a seat which had voted that way before than for the fact that the SNP had emerged from the wilderness to claim 28 per cent of the vote. At another by-election in November of the same year, a Labour majority at Hamilton of 16,000 was overturned by Mrs Winifred Ewing of the SNP. In the following May, at the local elections, the nationalist vote reached 30 per cent. Two-party politics were at an end. The Scottish card, which Labour had played to produce its majorities in 1964 and 1966, had been trumped.

The rise and fall of Scottish politics

Two unmistakable trends marked out Scottish politics from 1966 onwards. One was the growing discomfiture of the Conservatives (who had relegated their old name, Unionist, to secondary status in 1965). In every election from 1959 onwards until 1974, their share of the vote fell; the party which had a majority of Scottish seats in 1955 had only sixteen at the end of 1974. In each of those elections Labour did better in Scotland than elsewhere in the United Kingdom – which had not been the case between 1945 and 1955. A distinctively Scottish pattern of political loyalties seemed to be emerging, but only slowly. Scotland, which had not been the natural Labour fiefdom now sometimes imagined, gradually lost patience with a party whose Scottish image was, paradoxically, less forward-looking in the 1950s and early 1960s than it had been in the 1930s. Influence seemed to rest with its lairds on the grouse moor rather than its businessmen in the real world,[5] a view confirmed by the sudden descent of the 14th Earl of Home from the House of Lords to claim the seat of Kinross and West Perth and take on the leadership of the Party in 1963. But the slow slippage of the Unionist vote was overtaken by another factor which transformed its significance. From 1945 until 1966, third parties had never taken more than 7 per cent of the popular vote at general elections. By the election of October 1974 they claimed almost 39 per cent and the Conservatives were beaten into third place, five points behind the SNP (although they still won more seats, sixteen to SNP's eleven).

The dawn of a new era in Scottish politics was not without its difficulties. The SNP local councillors elected in 1967 were inexperienced and many proved incompetent. With a membership which had shot up from 4,000 to almost 100,000 in the space of two years, the Party was unable to maintain discipline within its own ranks. Its electoral momentum faltered. By the next council elections, in May 1969, its vote had fallen by a half, to 20 per cent, and in the 1970 general election it managed 11 per cent, giving it only one seat, in the Western Isles. Both main parties, however, had had a severe fright and were intent on drawing up lines of defence.

In 1968, the Conservative leader, Edward Heath, came to the Scottish party conference, to make his Declaration of Perth, which bound it to respond to Scottish feeling by finding a mechanism for devolution. He consigned his Party to eleven years of internal squabbling over the issue. Different sections of the Party gave various answers to the question; others, including Sir Alec Douglas-Home, who in 1968 had been charged with the task of providing a solution, still affected in 1979 not to have the answer. Conservative sensitivities were sharpened by the fact that when they were voted back into power in 1970, they had only 23 MPs in Scotland and 38 per cent of the vote; Gordon Campbell, their Secretary of State for Scotland, was the first to hold the office since 1895 without a majority, either of Scottish seats or the popular vote.

Labour held out longer against devolution, despite suffering another staggering by-election reverse, this time in its heartland at Govan, where a 16,000 majority was set aside by Mrs Margo MacDonald of the SNP in 1973. The fact that the Royal Commission on the Constitution set up by the Labour government headed by Harold Wilson in 1968 to review the devolution question took five years to report rather than three gave time for the forces of inertia within the Party to regroup; in 1973 the Scottish Secretary of the Party, Peter Allison, was able to claim that Labour was the only party intent on maintaining the status quo – against devolutionists, federalists and separatists. If Labour's conversion came late on the road to Damascus, it was probably all the more decisive for it. The Kilbrandon Report, which came out in October 1973, agreed on the need for change but its members disagreed on the form devolution should take. That internal disagreement offered an escape hatch to the Conservatives, who had blown hot but more usually cold on the question in its various aspects since 1968. Labour found its recommendation that the office of Secretary of State be swept away with devolution particularly unpalatable. It went into the general election of February 1974 still opposed to devolution, and emerged as a minority government. By the time of a second election, seven months later, it had a policy committing it to a Scottish assembly, but it was a conversion, rather like Mr Heath's Declaration of 1968, which involved obedience to instructions from London rather than repentance in the grass roots in Scotland for past errors.

Victory for Labour in a second general election in 1974, which also saw 30 per cent of the vote and eleven seats going to the SNP, sharpened its dilemma, for again a Labour government with a wafer-thin majority depended on its phalanx of Scottish seats to stay in power; in the debate over the Queen's Speech the Prime Minister, Harold Wilson, promised a White Paper and Bill on devolution. The dice were cast, but the gamble provoked non-stop dissension inside the Party, both in Scotland and in the Cabinet itself. The White Paper, which took more than a year to materialise, was a compromise document, which preserved the vice-regal powers of the Secretary of State, kept Scotland's seventy-one seats (and the advantage which Labour had enjoyed in Scotland since 1959), and gave the Assembly a mixed bag of responsibilities without real power, either over the limits of its authority or finance.[6] It provoked a serious split: in January 1976 two MPs left the Party to form the Scottish Labour Party, a deliberate evocation of the name of the party founded by Keir Hardie in 1888. Led by Jim Sillars, who, ironically, had been a late convert to devolution, the SLP was a short-lived distraction which helped to convince the bulk of the Labour Party that there was no turning back from the road to devolution, even though the first Bill had been talked out in February 1977.

The atmosphere in the 1970s was confused, fearful and without real precedent in either Scottish or British politics. The discovery by British Petroleum of the first major oilfield in the North Sea, in the Forties Field, in November 1970 offered a new direction for the Scottish economy; UCS, taken into receivership in June 1971, found a new lease of life when it was taken over by the Marathon Engineering Company of Texas to build oil rigs. Yet the Forties Field did not start production until September 1975, and the political consequences of the new industry took time to sink in. It was not until September 1972 that the SNP – somewhat reluctantly and tentatively – launched its emotive campaign, 'It's Scotland's Oil'.[7] It was followed in 1973 by a war in the Middle East and a sharp rise in the world price of oil. Although the SNP had not been the first to try to exploit oil as a political resource – some of Labour's devolutionists had been quicker off the mark – it did prove better suited as a vehicle to exploit it. It gave to nationalism the opportunity to cut free from a lesser Britain; the alternative was neatly encapsulated in another SNP slogan, 'England Expects . . . Scotland's Oil'. Britain, it was said by Dean Acheson, a former American secretary of state, in 1962, had after 1945 lost an Empire but failed to find a role. The same point applied with added force to Scotland, which had been so dependent on the Empire for both its economy and its sense of belonging within the British state. Oil offered Scots the prospect of escape from their dependency on the new, lesser Britain.

The consequences were far-reaching. The oil industry began to court the SNP. London journalists began to take the shuttle north to see for themselves the new Scottish politics. Although there was no second Scottish Renaissance to match the cultural achievements of the 1920s and early 1930s, there was a sustained rise in political and historical writing and a genuine ferment of the Scottish intellect. 'British' histories, in which English historians had relegated Scotland and Wales to the Celtic fringes, were suddenly exposed as insular and outdated.[8] SNP support seemed to stem from a widening of interest amongst sections of the public which were new to active party politics.[9] It also appeared, though perhaps more to those who wished it so, to break out of the class politics which had increasingly gripped Scottish politics since 1959.

The preparations for the introduction of a second Bill into the Commons, in November 1977, coincided with the peaking of support for the SNP, at 36 per cent of the electorate; but its difficult passage through the Committee stage came after that peak had passed. Critics, on the government benches as much as elsewhere in the House, were more vocal than its supporters; a unique attachment requiring that 40 per cent of the whole electorate would have to vote 'Yes' for the advisory referendum to take effect was proposed by George Cunningham, an expatriate Scot who represented an English constituency. It was accepted, ironically, on Burns Night 1978, and against the wishes of more than 80 per cent of Scottish MPs. The referendum campaign lasted much longer than the usual length of time taken up by a general election and it became increasingly entangled with the issues of the 'winter of discontent', when a series of strikes brought a number of essential services to a halt. Labour refused, in its own words, to 'soil its hands' by running a joint 'Yes' campaign with the SNP. The 'No' campaign, though no better co-ordinated, was better funded. Two weeks before the vote, Lord Home (who had been restored to the Lords by a life peerage in 1974) cast fresh doubt upon the waters by defining a 'No' vote as one for a better Assembly, with tax-raising powers and proportional representation, which might materialise in the future. The plot began to resemble a Victorian melodrama, with Lord Home cast in the unlikely role of the saviour of real Home Rule.

On 1 March 1979 Scotland and Wales voted in their separate referenda. In one sense, the result in Scotland was as confused as the campaign before it. 32.9 per cent voted 'Yes' and 30.8 per cent 'No', in a 63.9 per cent poll. The leading popular daily newspaper, the *Daily Record*, led the next day with the headline, 'A Nation Divided'. Amongst the regions, Strathclyde, Central and Fife had voted in favour, as had Lothian and Highland, though in their cases only narrowly; Borders, Grampian, Orkney and Shetland had voted against, and in Tayside barely 1,000 votes separated the two sides. Yet, in conventional electoral terms, the result translated into a 52 per cent 'Yes' vote. The arguments about the status of the result were academic amidst the gathering crisis which enveloped the Labour government. The final irony lay in the fact that it was the SNP which was ultimately responsible for the vote of no confidence which brought the Labour government led by James Callaghan down, by a single vote.

The results of the referendum are often carelessly misrepresented. In the distinctive climate of British politics, where narrowly elected candidates are fond of the saying that a majority of one is good enough, the issue can hardly be said to have been defeated. It was only the unique condition attached to the question, of an overall 40 per cent majority, which brought it down. Under the same terms, the Scottish people could be said to have voted aginst EEC membership in the referendum of 1971. The question before the electorate, it also needs to be emphasised, was not devolution but the Scotland Act of 1978. The Act had become, to a considerable extent, a party issue and, as such, detached from the broader question of devolution.[10] Devolution, despite the reverse suffered in 1979, did not as a result go away. The mistake of the next government was to assume that it had.

The return of British politics?
The election of a Conservative government, with Mrs Thatcher as Prime Minister, in May 1979 came after an election which lacked a Scottish dimension. After it, Mrs Thatcher was quick to brush aside any notion of a commitment of the Conservatives to review the question of devolution. Yet the pattern of a distinctive Scottish political process stubbornly refused to go away. The long-term drift of support away from the Conservatives continued; they had in 1979 only twenty-two

MPs, on the basis of a popular vote of 31 per cent. The increasing gap in patterns of voting in England and Scotland widened further than ever before: the Conservatives won by 10.5 per cent over Labour in England but lost by 10.5 per cent in Scotland. These two trends continued in the elections of 1983 and 1987. The 1983 result gave the Conservatives their greatest election victory for half a century in Britain as a whole, but their share of the vote dropped by 3 per cent in Scotland and resulted in twenty-one seats. The 1987 election, another comfortable Conservative victory in Britain as a whole, was a disaster for the Party in Scotland, where it was reduced to 24 per cent of the poll and a rump of ten MPs, less than at any time since 1910. Although political commentators could again contentedly write their histories of the period without a single reference to either Scotland or Wales in their indexes,[11] the Thatcher government had failed to grasp the opportunity to recast a new, wider *British* politics, which drew on the experiences of the period since 1968. To many Scots, it seemed like a little Englander administration.

With the SNP reduced from eleven seats to two and 17 per cent of the poll, nationalism seemed to have shot its bolt. Yet the very imbalance of power within Scottish politics became the largest threat to the Union. It left a beleaguered Conservative Secretary of State, George Younger, shorn of the fig leaf of a Scottish mandate to a greater extent than any of his predecessors. The historic dual role of the Scottish Secretary drastically altered: the mantle of representing Scottish interests at Westminster was cast off in favour of the exclusive role of London's viceroy in Scotland. The main confrontation came over the forcing of local authorities into the financial disciplines decided by the government, which was fortunate in the early 1980s to have a convenient 'loony left' high-spending council, Lothian Regional Council, to use as a stalking horse. By 1983, with a marked shift towards the centre ground in Labour local politics evident, scapegoats, however, became less easy to find and 'reasonable' levels of expenditure imposed on them from London became harder to justify. Malcolm Rifkind, Younger's successor, pressed on regardless.

The government's solution was the Community Charge, a substitute for local rates; it was designed not only to appeal to its own natural voters but also to force accountability on local authorities, which would now be confronted by the electoral consequences of excessive spending. Devised by right-wing ideologues of the Adam Smith Institute, many of whom had found a born-again, radical Conservatism while students at St Andrews University, the Community Charge, which was introduced into Scotland a year before it became operative in England and Wales, became the focal point of Thatcherite politics in the later 1980s. It was an instructive episode. Unpopular from the moment it was introduced, the Poll Tax, as it was commonly dubbed, provoked a widespread campaign of non-payment throughout Scotland. The opprobrium for its collection fell, not on allegedly spendthrift councils, but on the government which had devised it. These warning signals were ignored. The tax was duly introduced into England and Wales, where it lasted less than eighteen months before a new ministerial team, produced by a 'palace coup' against Mrs Thatcher in the autumn of 1990, quickly declared it to be 'unworkable'. This bruising experience seemed to demonstrate that, in many respects, Scottish society was not so very different from English. It revealed a government which had become accustomed to turning a deaf ear to all Scottish opinion save for that of its own activists. As with the rent strike of 1915 with which it shared a striking number of characteristics, the anti-Poll Tax agitation showed that a British government was still vulnerable to a vigorous one-issue campaign which cut across class divisions. The reluctance of the Labour establishment to give full backing to the campaign revealed the Party's nervousness of adopting Scottish issues, but the support given to it by the SNP also showed that such single issues brought only limited political returns. It was a classic example of the ambiguous, dual politics of the Union – of a unitary state which was still not fully unified.

The Thatcherite era, which for a time seemed to presage an eternal Conservative majority in the British parliament and an ever-widening fissure within the fabric of the Union, concentrated many sophisticated Scottish minds on whether there was life in devolution after the referendum of 1979. The result in 1988 was *A Claim of Right for Scotland*, a carefully cast demand designed to appeal to a wide variety of opinion above and beyond party for 'the constitutional rights Scotland expects within the United Kingdom'.[12] It gave birth to the Scottish Constitutional Convention, a cross-party body intent on presenting detailed proposals for a Scottish Assembly which would enjoy wide support. The Conservative government ignored the initiative and the SNP, wary of again bringing to the surface the latent divide between devolution and independence within its own support, spurned it, although some prominent individuals among its membership endorsed it. The general election of April 1992, however, confounded many expectations, including those of a 'Tory free' Scotland and a government committed to Home Rule. It saw the re-election of a Conservative government and a minor recovery in its vote in Scotland, with a gain of two seats there. Hailed by Scottish Conservatives as the first step on their road to recovery and the beginning of a new chapter in Scotland's history, the result in 1992, however, differed little in practice from that in 1987. A prospect at least as likely as a Tory recovery is a new anti-Unionist coalition, broader based and more resilient than in the 1970s and 1980s. The 'end of history' is not yet in sight.

Despite 1992, the auguries for change seem better than those for stasis. The future governing of Scotland, after a decade of confrontation which stretched the very fabric of the Union thinner than ever before, is still uncertain. Home Rule has been debated for over a century. Every decade since the 1920s has seen some adjustment in the nature of Scotland's government within the Union; the 'status quo' is a much-misrepresented term. Yet history bears a second message. In 1974 all parties were committed to some form of devolution; in 1992 the parties representing fifty-eight of Scotland's seventy-two MPs are again. Yet, with the exception of the Liberal nexus, where added venerability has come to Home Rule with age, every party has turned a somersault over a major constitutional issue in the quarter of a century since 1966. History, to which too many turn for answers, is ambivalent. The unknown new factor after 1992 is Europe and the workings of its new 'single market'; the prospects which might result range from an even more centralist Unionism to a new-style 'federalism' all round as well as the SNP's declared aim of 'Independence in Europe'. Yet if Scotland manages twice in the 1990s to evade some form of Home Rule it will be a remarkable escape story. As Oscar Wilde said of the death of Little Nell, the historian would then need a heart of stone not to laugh.

Notes and References

Introduction

1 R. Mitchison, *A History of Scotland* (London, 1970; 2nd edn., 1982).
2 *The New History of Scotland*, 8 vols. (London, 1981-4); People and Society in Scotland, 3 vols. (1988-91).
3 M. Fry, *Patronage and Principle: a Political History of Modern Scotland* (Aberdeen, 1987), 18.
4 D. Cannadine, 'British history: past, present – and future?', *Past and Present* cxvi (1987), 183.
5 T. Nairn, *The Break-Up of Britain* (2nd edn., London, 1977), 139. Cf C. Beveridge and R. Turnbull, *The Eclipse of Scottish Culture* (1989), 51-61.
6 R.F. Foster, *Modern Ireland, 1600-1972* (London, 1988).
7 H. Kearney, *The British Isles* (Cambridge, 1989), 106-48.
8 A.D. Gibb, *Scotland in Eclipse* (London, 1930), 187. See R.J. Finlay, '"For or against?": Scottish nationalists and the British Empire, 1919-39', *SHR* lxxi (1992).
9 *Atlas*, 95-6. J.G. Duncan, 'Trade and traders: some links between Sweden and the ports of Montrose and Arbroath, 1742-1830', *Northern Scotland*, vii (1986), 23-37.
10 E. McGrath, 'Local heroes: the Scottish humanist Parnassus for Charles I', in E. Chaney and P. Mack (eds.), *England and the Continental Renaissance: Essays in Honour of J.B. Trapp* (London, 1990), 257-70.
11 R. Lyall, 'Scottish students and masters at the Universities of Cologne and Louvain in the 15th century', *IR* xxxvi (1985), 55-73.
12 J. Durkan, 'The French connection in the 16th and early 17th centuries', in T.C. Smout (ed.), *Scotland and Europe, 1200-1850* (1986), 19-44.

I Early Scotland

I The Land and its People before AD 400

1 The account of Agricola's campaigns was written by his son-in-law, the historian Tacitus, at the end of the 1st century AD to show how the whole of Britain had been conquered and then 'immediately lost'; see *Agricola*, 29, 3-4.
2 For the location of Mons Graupius, cf A.R. Burn, 'In search of a battlefield: Agricola's last battle', *PSAS* lxxxvii (1953), 127-33 (Pass of Grange); J.K.S. St Joseph, 'The camp at Durno and Mons Graupius', *Britannia*, ix (1978), 271-88, and L. Keppie, *Scotland's Roman Remains* (1986), 10-11 (both Durno); and G. Maxwell, *A Battle Lost: Romans and Caledonians at Mons Graupius* (1990), 120-1 (Monboddo). The word 'Grampian' derives from a setting error in the text of Tacitus' biography of Agricola when it was printed in the 1470s, but 'Graupius' was still in use as late as 1633, when it figured in one of the tableaux erected for the entry of Charles I into Edinburgh.
3 W. Hanson and G. Maxwell, *Rome's North West Frontier: the Antonine Wall* (2nd edn., 1986), 70-71, 196-7; G.D. Thomas, 'Excavations at the Roman civil settlement at Inveresk, 1976-7', *PSAS* cxviii (1988), 139-79.
4 I.B. Ralston, *Foul Hordes: the Picts in the North-East and their Background* (Aberdeen, 1984), 11.
5 A.A.M. Duncan, *Scotland: the Making of the Kingdom* (1975), 84.
6 *Atlas*, 106-07, 114-15; also 13, 451n5, below.
7 A.P. Smyth, *Warlords and Holy Men: Scotland AD 80-1000* (London, 1984), 53-5.
8 L. Alcock, Rhind Lectures 1988-9, in *PSAS* cxviii (1988), 327-34.
9 *Early Maps of Scotland to 1850* (1973), 3-5; *Atlas*, 164.
10 Keppie, *Roman Remains*, 160-3.
11 Hanson and Maxwell, *North-West Frontier*, 59-74.
12 Keppie, *Roman Remains*, 38.
13 D. Breeze, 'Why did the Romans fail to conquer Scotland?', *PSAS* cxviii (1988), 20.
14 Thomas, 'Excavations at Inveresk', 160-3.
15 Duncan, *Scotland*, 30-3.
16 See 28-30, below.

17 C. Thomas, *Christianity in Roman Britain to AD 500* (London, 1981), 285.
18 Smyth, *Scotland*, 36.

2 The Making of the Kingdom of Fortriu

1 Duncan, *Scotland*, 41-78.
2 D.P. Kirby, 'Bede and the Pictish church', *IR* xxiv (1973), 23; M.O. Anderson, *Kings and Kingship in Early Scotland* (2nd edn., 1980), 79-84.
3 Smyth, *Scotland*, 64-7.
4 See *Atlas*, 114-15, for the distribution of the three classes of Pictish standing stones.
5 The symbolic meaning of the symbols, almost invariably animal, on early (Class I) Pictish stones is unclear, but it is not unexpected in a hunter's art. Some argue that the more sophisticated art on later Pictish stones shares a common provenance with that in illuminated Gospel books, such as those of Kells and Lindisfarne. Still more controversial are the finer worked cross-slabs: these were, it is sometimes argued, unique in form. Those called Class II stones have an interlaced cross carved in relief on one side and on the other intricate iconography, often of battle scenes (such as on the Aberlemno stone), and perhaps sometimes portraying marriage alliances between different Pictish lineages. In the third phase of Pictish sculpture, found in Class III stones, the enigmatic symbolism has been replaced by thoroughly Christian images, which (like the depiction of Daniel in the lions' den at Meigle) are more easily understood by modern eyes. See I. Henderson, 'Pictish art and the Book of Kells', in D. Whitelock *et al.* (eds.), *Ireland in Early Medieval Europe* (Cambridge, 1982), 79-80, and idem, 'The problem of the Picts', in G. Menzies (ed.), *Who are the Scots?* (London, 1972), 63-5.
6 The terminology used to describe the art which produced such illuminated manuscripts is also highly controversial. 'Insular' is perhaps preferable to 'Hiberno-Saxon', but 'Celtic' is both less technical and more understandable.
7 Duncan, *Scotland*, esp. 79-116.
8 The word *Picti* may also have been a Latin form of the Picts' own name: W.J. Watson, *History of the Celtic Place-Names of Scotland* (1926), 67-8.
9 See H.M. Chadwick, *Early Scotland: the Picts, the Scots and the Welsh of Southern Scotland* (Cambridge, 1949), 38-49; F.T. Wainwright (ed.), *The Problem of the Picts* (1955), 46-8.
10 *Cataibh*, the Gaelic name for Sutherland, is clearly linked to 'Cait'.
11 Notably by Smyth, *Scotland*, 52ff.
12 J. Bannerman, *Studies in the History of Dalriada* (1974), 130-56.
13 Wainwright (ed.), *Problem of the Picts*, 25.
14 Bannerman, *Dalriada*, 154.
15 It was not until the reign of James V that a King of Scots made a circumnavigation of his kingdom and it was only then that there was drawn a map of the Scottish coastline; it was so great a state secret that the English diplomatic service of Henry VIII arranged for its theft. In terms of sea power, what medieval king before James IV could boast of an effective navy?
16 P. King, 'The barbarian kingdoms', in J.H. Burns (ed.), *Cambridge History of Medieval Political Thought* (Cambridge, 1988), 133, 137-53.
17 The idea of Pictish matrilineal succession was attacked in Smyth, *Scotland*, esp. 57-66. A carefully argued defence is contained in D.H. Sellar, 'Warlords, holy men and matrilineal succession', *IR* xxxvi (1985), 29-43. By it, a 'king's title to rule stemmed from his descent from a matriline or matrilines, with typically, nephew succeeding mother's brother'. The debate underlines how complex succession to high office could be as well as the meagreness of the information on which elaborate conjectures have to be drawn.
18 Practices of king-making amongst barbarian peoples were diverse; neither the Franks nor Vandals, for example, confined election to kingship from within the ruling dynasty. King, 'Barbarian kingdoms', 137, 151n.
19 The evidence of Irish kingship has been complicated by a recent revision of the role of both the *derbfine* ('certain kindred'), which comprised the descendants in the male line of a common great-grandfather and used to be considered to define a virtual law of succession, and the *rigdamna* (literally, 'the makings of a king'), who was formerly thought to be an eligible prince of the blood royal. In theory, any male descendant was eligible to succeed but in practice succession, it is now accepted, was pragmatic, depending largely on the prevailing balance of power amongst different segments of the *derbfine*. The *rígdamna* or *tànaise* ('the expected one') was likely to be the head of the most powerful segment of the dynasty. Usually a dynasty consisted of only two or three such segments, thus producing a pattern of cousin succeeding cousin, each having been the son of a former king. D. Ó Corráin, 'Irish regnal succession: a reappraisal', *Studia Hibernica*, xi (1971), 7-39.

20 D. Ó Corráin, *Ireland before the Normans* (Dublin, 1972), 28-32.
21 J. Bannerman, 'The Scots of Dalriada', in Menzies (ed.), *Who are the Scots?*, 69-72.
22 Ibid., 75-6.
23 M.O. Anderson, 'Dalriada and the creation of the kingdom of the Scots', in Whitelock (ed), *Ireland*, 118.
24 See Smyth, *Scotland*, 69; Chadwick, *Early Scotland*, 42-3.
25 The prominence given to Kenneth mac Alpin, with whom some modern lists of kings of Scots begin, derives largely from king-lists which were not contemporary but belonged to the medieval period.
26 See 36, 42, 44-5, below.
27 W.F. Skene, *Celtic Scotland* (2nd edn., 1886-90), i, 286-91; cf. Smyth, *Scotland*, 79-80.
28 Ibid., 65.
29 Ibid., 67, 83.
30 Ibid., 54, 57.
31 Skene, *Celtic Scotland*, i, 334.
32 A.O. Anderson (ed.), *Early Sources of Scottish History, AD 500 to 1286*, (London, 1922), i, 268.
33 Burns (ed.), *Early Medieval Political Thought*, 137.
34 Ibid., 165-7.
35 Ibid., 146-7; Kirby, 'Bede and the Pictish church', 17-18.
36 Curiously, the first King Constantine still remains without a number even in modern histories, just as chroniclers of the 12th and 13th centuries, intent on embellishing the history of the mac Alpin dynasty, left him. He deserves a better place in the making of the kingdom, as does the dynasty of Fortriu.
37 Cf S. Reynolds, *Kingdoms and Communities in Western Europe, 900-1300* (Oxford, 1984), 250, 256-61.

3 Apostles of the Scots, Picts and Britons

1 Donald III Ban had first been buried at Dunkeld and his remains were moved to Iona *c*.1099. Smyth, *Scotland*, 189; Duncan, *Scotland*, 127-8. For a critical view of Iona's status as a burial place of kings, see E.J. Cowan, 'The Scottish Chronicle in the Poppleton Manuscript', *IR* xxxii (1981), 6-7.
2 B. Colgrave and R.A.B. Mynors (eds.), *Bede's Ecclesiastical History of the English People*, (Oxford, 1969), iii, 4. For Patrick's letter to Coroticus, see J.F. Kenney, *The Sources for the Early History of Ireland: Ecclesiastical* (Dublin, 1979), 165-9.
3 Bede, *History*, v, 9.
4 *Early Sources* i, 365, 445; see also 42, 453n16, below.
5 Cf. Thomas, *Christianity*, 319; Duncan, *Scotland*, 34.
6 A. Macquarrie, 'The date of St Ninian's mission: a reappraisal', *RSCHS* xxiii (1987), 1-25, at 12; J. MacQueen (ed.), *St Nynia* (2nd edn., 1990).
7 G.W.S. Barrow, 'The childhood of early Christianity', *Scottish Studies* (1983), 1-15.
8 See C. Thomas, *The Early Christian Archaeology of North Britain* (London and Glasgow, 1971), 58. There was, however, a vogue in the 12th century of dedications to Ninian which can lay false trails in the search for his early influence. I am grateful to Dr David Brown for this point.
9 A. Macquarrie, 'The career of Saint Kentigern of Glasgow: *Vitae, Lectiones* and glimpses of fact', *IR* xxxvii (1986), 3-24.
10 D. Kirby, 'Bede and the Pictish church', *IR* xxiv (1973), 17.
11 It is important in gaining an understanding of Scottish religion to realise that the analogy of Protestantism with a primitive and pure early Christianity was made at regular intervals after 1560, and not least in the highly charged atmosphere of the Disruption crisis in the 1840s. George Buchanan, turning a blind eye to St Andrew and his status as Scotland's national saint, was the first to claim the *Céli Dé* as Protestants before their time, and the mid-19th century saw sharp competition between the Church of Scotland and the Free Church to emphasise their links with Columba; the result can still be seen in the names of local churches in many parts of the country.
12 M. Herbert, *Iona, Kells and Derry* (Oxford, 1989), 11, 31-2.
13 Duncan, *Scotland*, 67; also Thomas, *Early Christian Archaeology*, 30-1.
14 Herbert, *Iona*, 70; Smyth, *Scotland*, 185-6.
15 Ibid., 84; Herbert, *Iona*, 141-2.
16 Smyth, *Scotland*, 24-8.
17 Ibid., 107-10.
18 Ibid., 136-7.
19 Herbert, *Iona*, 47-8.

20 See Burns (ed.), *History of Medieval Political Thought*, 165-6, 243, for the cult of Constantine.
21 I. Henderson, 'Pictish art and the Book of Kells', in Whitelock (ed.), *Ireland in Early Medieval Europe*, 95-7; Smyth, *Scotland*, 125-6.
22 Thomas, *Early Christian Archaeology*, 156-7; D. McRoberts (ed.), *The Medieval Church of St Andrews* (Glasgow, 1976), 2-3.
23 It is uncertain which Pictish king named Óengus founded a church at Kilrimont. Both Óengus son of Fergus (729-61) and Óengus (820-34) are possible candidates.
24 I.B. Cowan, 'The post-Columban church'. *RSCHS* xviii (1974), 245-60; G. Donaldson, 'Bishops sees before the reign of David I', in *Scottish Church History* (1985), 11-24.
25 Cowan, 'Post-Columban church', 254.

4 The mac Alpin Kings and Alba

1 See 25, above. In Ireland, where *natio*, a notion of a community wider than the tribe, had emerged at least as early as the 9th century, the development of kingship and the growth of a national self-consciousness fed off each other – as they did in Scotland. See D. Ó Corráin, 'Nationality and kingship in pre-Norman Ireland', in T.W. Moody (ed.), *Nationality and the Pursuit of National Independence* (Belfast, 1978), 1-35.
2 *Atlas*, 26.
3 Duncan, *Scotland*, 1.
4 Cf Mitchison, *Scotland*, 2.
5 See Smyth, *Scotland*, 181, 184-5.
6 Forteviot, palace of kings of Picts and Scots before the time of Kenneth mac Alpin, was sited in Perthshire, at the junction of the River Earn and the Water of May.
7 This is based on Regnal List I, in Anderson, *Kingship*, 282-3, 196.
8 Anderson, 'Dalriada', 118.
9 See 24-5, above.
10 Smyth, *Scotland*, 190. Cf D.H. Sellar, 'The origins and ancestry of Somerled', *SHR* xlv (1966), 123-42.
11 I am grateful to Dr John Bannerman for this point.
12 Anderson, 'Dalriada', 118.
13 Anderson, *Kingship*, 198-9.
14 See 38, above.
15 *Melrose Chronicle*, 7, 17; Anderson, *Kingship*, 213; idem, 'Dalriada', 122.
16 There is no contemporary account of Kenneth's or Donald's promulgation of a new code of laws. All law codes, in contemporary Continental Europe as much as in England or Pictland, were a mixture of old and new. As with the *Lex Salica*, which is attributable more to Frankish kings before him than to Charlemagne himself, what was more important than the content of a law code was the act of its promulgation. Most 'new' codes were restatements of the obvious and the familiar, a reformulation of old custom and practice. What such a new code did was to reassure a people of their own distinctive identity, especially if they were subject to a new and non-native king. It also gave extra authority to the ruler as a law-giving king, for had not Moses been such? P. Wormald, 'Lex Scripta and Verbum Regis: legislation and Germanic kingship from Euric and Cnut' in P.H. Sawyer and I.N. Woods (eds.), *Early Medieval Kingship* (private pub., 1977), 108-09; Burns (ed.), *History of Medieval Political Thought*, 138-9.
17 See Duncan, *Scotland*, 114-16, for rites of inauguration of kings.
18 The exception to mac Alpin succession in the male line was Eochaid (878-89), who succeeded through his mother, a daughter of Kenneth mac Alpin who had married Rhun, King of Strathclyde.
19 The acid test of a system of primogeniture is succession by a minor. Even the Canmore dynasty experienced difficulty in such circumstances in the 12th century.
20 See Ó Corráin, 'Irish regnal succession', 36. Although Duncan seems to have succeeded through the female line in 1034, as a grandson of Malcolm II, it is likely that he also claimed descent in a male line from a previous king of Scots.
21 The phrase belongs to somewhere in the period 1214-49. The chronicler would thus have seen the problem of disorder in Moray become intertwined with a crisis of rival segments in which the descendants of Duncan II would dispute the succession to the Canmore line of kings. Duncan, *Scotland*, 95, 113-14; Smyth, *Scotland*, 223-4; Skene, *Celtic Scotland*, i, 365-70, 380-3.
22 Crisis in the north would, however, flare up again in the 12th century. See 85-7, below.
23 Tanistry was the system of kin-based regnal succession. See 451, n19, above, and the entry in D.S. Thomson (ed.), *The Companion to Gaelic Scotland* (London, 1983), 285.
24 Smyth, *Scotland*, 222, 229.

25 *Early Sources*, i, 268.
26 Smyth, *Scotland*, 215; Skene, *Celtic Scotland*, i, 347-8.
27 Smyth, *Scotland*, 192.
28 See ibid., 199-208, for a detailed discussion of this complex period.
29 *Early Sources*, i, 426.
30 Ibid., i, 430. It is not certain that Constantine II was at the battlefield of Brunanburh. Only the *Anglo Saxon Chronicle* claims so. See *Scottish Annals from English Chroniclers*, ed. A.O. Anderson (London, 1908), 71, 72.
31 *Early Sources*, i, 449-50.
32 See Smyth, *Scotland*, 199-200, for a realistic analysis of what Anglo-Saxon chroniclers claimed as the 'submission' of Constantine and his allies to the King of Wessex.
33 Skene, *Celtic Scotland*, i, 374-5.
34 *Early Sources*, i, 528; cf Skene, *Celtic Scotland*, i, 386, 390; *Atlas*, 21.
35 Duncan, *Scotland*, 94; Skene, *Celtic Scotland*, i, 372.
36 *Early Sources*, i, 572.
37 Skene, *Celtic Scotland*, iii, 52-60.
38 *Early Sources*, i, 407, 446, 480; Skene, *Celtic Scotland*, iii, 55-6; Duncan, *Scotland*, 111; *Atlas*, 20-21.
39 Skene, *Celtic Scotland*, i, 380.
40 *Atlas*, 20-1.
41 Ó Corráin, *Ireland before the Normans*, 168; idem, 'Irish regnal succession', 37.
42 *Early Sources*, i, 572. I am grateful to Dr David Brown for his advice on these points.
43 *Early Sources*, i, 573-4.
44 Smyth, *Scotland*, 226.
45 Skene, *Celtic Scotland*, i, 400-3.
46 See ibid., i, 413.

II Medieval Scotland

5 Peoples of the Kingdom

1 *Scottish Annals*, 181, 202.
2 G.W.S. Barrow, *The Anglo-Norman Era in Scottish History* (Oxford, 1980), 153-5; Duncan, *Scotland*, 116; G.W.S. Barrow, *David I of Scotland (1124-1153): the Balance of New and Old* (Stenton Lecture, 1984), 11.
3 J.W.M. Bannerman, 'The Scots language and the kin-based society', in D.S. Thomson (ed.), *Gaelic and Scots in Harmony* (Glasgow, 1990), 1-19.
4 A. Grant, 'Scotland's "Celtic fringe" in the late Middle Ages: the MacDonald Lords of the Isles and the kingdom of Scotland', in R.R. Davies (ed.), *The British Isles, 1100-1500* (1988), 119.
5 Cited in Barrow, *Era*, 139-41; also Bannerman, 'Scots language'.
6 A. Small, 'Dark Age Scotland', in G. Whittington and I.D. Whyte (eds.), *An Historical Geography of Scotland* (London, 1983), 36.
7 See *Atlas*, 3-5, 106, 109.
8 G.W.S. Barrow, *The Kingdom of the Scots: Government, Church and Society from the Eleventh to the Fourteenth Century* (London, 1973), 278; Small, 'Dark Age Scotland', 26, 38.
9 Duncan, *Scotland*, 314-15.
10 G.W.S. Barrow, *Kingship and Unity: Scotland 1000-1306* (London, 1981), 2; A. Grant, *Independence and Nationhood: Scotland 1306-1469* (London, 1984), 72.
11 A. Ritchie, 'Excavation of Pictish and Viking-Age farmsteads at Buckquoy, Orkney', *PSAS* cviii (1977), 174-227.
12 See Grant, *Scotland*, 63.
13 Ibid., *Scotland*, 69; D, Metcalf (ed.), *Coinage in Medieval Scotland* (Brit. Arch. Reports, xlv (1977)), 85-102.
14 See Barrow, *Scotland*, 43-5.
15 Idem, 'Badenoch and Strathspey, 1130-1312: secular and political', *Northern Scotland*, viii (1988), 2.
16 Bannerman, 'Scots language', 8-9.
17 Barrow, *Scotland*, 20.
18 K.J. Stringer, *Earl David of Huntingdon, 1151-1219: a Study in Anglo-Scottish History* (1985), 62, 66; G.S. Pryde, *The Burghs of Scotland: A Critical List* (Glasgow, 1965), no. 30.
19 Stringer, *Earl David*, 76-7; Barrow, *Kingdom of Scots*, 337-61; idem, *Era*, 17-18.
20 See list of charters for knight service in Barrow, *Kingdom of Scots*, 311-14.
21 See G.G. Simpson and B. Webster, 'Charter evidence and the distribution of mottes in Scotland', in

K.J. Stringer (ed.), *Essays on the Nobility of Medieval Scotland* (1985), 6; a list of mottes is given in ibid., 14-21.

22 Barrow, 'Badenoch and Strathspey', 2-4.

23 Barrow, *Era*, 84-90; J.W.M. Bannerman, 'MacDuff of Fife'.

24 R.R. Davies, 'Kings, lords and liberties in the March of Wales, 1066-1272', *Trans. Royal Hist. Soc.* (5th series), xxix (1979), 52.

25 R. Frame, *English Lordship in Ireland, 1318-1361* (Oxford, 1982), esp. chs 1, 2.

26 Barrow, *Era*, 91-2, 100.

27 Grant, *Scotland*, 64-5.

28 Duncan, *Scotland*, 328-9, 410.

29 The word husbandman is derived from *hus*, meaning a house or holding, and *bond*, a cultivator.

30 *Registrum Honoris de Morton* (Bann. Club, 1853), i, pp. xlvii-lxxvi; Grant, *Scotland*, 61-8. 88.

31 F.W. Maitland, *Memoranda de Parliamento 1305* (London, 1893), 230.

32 Barrow, *Kingdom of Scots*, 262-3.

33 Ibid., 262; R.A. Dodghson, *Land and Society in Early Scotland* (Oxford, 1981), 92, 157-62.

34 R.A. Dodghson, 'Medieval rural Scotland', in Whittington and Whyte (eds.), *Historical Geography*, 60-3.

35 Duncan, *Scotland*, 470.

36 See Pryde, *Burghs*, 3-10.

37 Barrow, *Scotland*, 93, 97.

38 Duncan, *Scotland*, 489.

39 Ibid., 515; D. Ditchburn, 'Trade with northern Europe, 1297-1540', in M. Lynch, M. Spearman and G. Stell (eds.), *The Scottish Medieval Town* (1988), 162, 164.

40 E. Ewan, *Townlife in Fourteenth-Century Scotland* (1990), 77.

41 N. Shead, 'Glasgow: an ecclesiastical burgh', in Lynch (ed.), *Medieval Town*, 123.

42 M. Spearman, 'Workshops, materials and debris: evidence of early industries', in ibid., 139; Duncan, *Scotland*, 491, 500-1.

43 Ibid., 429-30; Grant, *Scotland*, 62.

44 W. Stevenson, 'The monastic presence: Berwick in the 12th and 13th centuries', in Lynch (ed.), *Medieval Town*, 99-115.

45 Ewan, *Townlife*, 16-18; G. Stell, 'Urban buildings', in Lynch (ed.), *Medieval Town*, 60-80, and M. Spearman, 'The medieval townscape of Perth', in ibid., esp. 46-55. A useful diagram of burgage rigs is in A. Gibb, *Glasgow; the Making of a City* (London, 1983), 24.

46 Lynch, *Medieval Town*, 7.

47 J.W.M. Bannerman, 'The Lordship of the Isles', in J.M. Brown (ed.), *Scottish Society in the Fifteenth Century* (London, 1977), 238; J. Dunbar, 'The medieval architecture of the Scottish Highlands', in L. MacLean (ed.), *The Middle Ages in the Highlands* (Inverness, 1981), 57-9.

48 Efforts were made to plant burghs of barony at Inveraray and Kilmun in Argyll in 1474 and 1490. For a fuller list of markets, see *Geographical Colls.* (SHS, 1906-08), i, pp. xviii-xix; iii, pp. xxii-xxiii; also Pryde, *Burghs*, 11ff.

49 Lynch, *Medieval Town*, 271.

50 Bannerman, 'Lordship of the Isles', 220; Skene, *Celtic Scotland*, iii, 318.

51 *Highland Papers*, ii (SHS, 1916), 121-3; Barrow, *Era*, 138-40.

52 T.C. Smout, *A History of the Scottish People* (London, 1969), 47.

53 Duncan, *Scotland*, 128.

54 W.D.H. Sellar, 'The origins and ancestry of Somerled', *SHR* xlv (1966), 123-42; Barrow, *Kingdom of Scots*, 377-9.

55 Bannerman, 'Lordship of the Isles', 237-8.

56 John of Fordun, *Chronica Gentis Scotorum*, ed. W.F. Skene (1871-2), i, 24. There are a number of possible variations in the translation of this key passage; see Grant, 'Celtic fringe', 119.

57 D. Murison, 'Linguistic relationships in medieval Scotland', in G.W.S. Barrow (ed.), *The Scottish Tradition: Essays in Honour of Ronald Gordon Cant* (1974), 75, 81.

58 *Scottish Verse from the Book of the Dean of Lismore*, ed. W.J. Watson (Scottish Gaelic Texts Society, 1937), 161.

59 Grant, *Scotland*, 207-9; I.F. Grant, *The Social and Economic Development of Scotland before 1603* (1930), 481-3.

60 Ibid., 502-3; R.W. Munro, 'The clan system; fact or fiction?', in McLean (ed.), *Middle Ages in the Highlands*, 125.

61 G.W.S. Barrow, 'The sources for the history of the Highlands in the Middle Ages', in ibid., 18; Grant, *Social and Economic Development*, 501.

62 Ibid., 496.

63 Ibid., 510-11.

64 The phrase 'clan system', it has been pointed out, is an invention barely a century old: see Munro, 'Clan system', 117.
65 Duncan, *Scotland*, 464; Lynch, *Medieval Town*, 5-7.
66 See the useful abstract of customs statistics for 1327-1469 in Grant, *Scotland*, 236-7; *Atlas II* analyses customs data 1327-1599.
67 Grant, *Scotland*, 77.
68 A. Stevenson, 'Trade with the south, 1070-1513', in Lynch, *Medieval Town*, 180-206; also ibid., 4.
69 M. Lynch, 'Towns and townspeople in 15th-century Scotland', in J.A.F. Thomson (ed.), *Towns and Townspeople in the Fifteenth Century* (Gloucester, 1988), 175-7.
70 *Early Sources*, ii, 224, 587.
71 Grant, *Scotland*, 73-5.
72 See below, 171.
73 Dodghson, *Land and Society*, 17; Grant, *Scotland*, 75-9.
74 Ibid., 85-6; Lynch, 'Towns and townspeople', 184-6; see below, 181-3, 252-5.
75 Grant, *Scotland*, 80-1, 240.
76 Smout, *History*, 42.

6 The macMalcolm Dynasty

1 W.E. Kapelle, *The Norman Conquest of the North: the Region and its Transformation, 1000-1135* (London, 1979), 48.
2 The date of Earl Thorfinn's death is uncertain: both 1057 and 1065 are possible. Cf above, 50, and Barrow, *Scotland*, 27.
3 Although there were attempts by later chroniclers to cast doubt on the legitimacy of Duncan, it was ironically the very strength of the claim of a son of the marriage of Malcolm III and Ingibjorg which threatened chaos after 1093.
4 Donald, another son of Malcolm and Ingibjorg, died before 1085. There is no reason to suppose, as sometimes suggested, that Malcolm disposed of her in some way.
5 Kapelle, *Norman Conquest*, 93, 123-4.
6 *Scottish Annals*, 95.
7 Kapelle, *Norman Conquest*, 135, 147; R.L.G. Ritchie, *The Normans in Scotland* (1954), 50-1.
8 Kapelle, *Norman Conquest*, 150.
9 *Early Sources*, ii, 59-88.
10 A cult which refers to David as son of Margaret rather than of Malcolm, as custom demanded, was the product of the 13th century.
11 *Scottish Annals*, 118.
12 An alternative explanation, based on the near-contemporary *Anglo-Saxon Chronicle*, would date the expeditionary force as having been formed within a month of Malcolm III's death, in November 1093. The suggestion would extend Duncan II's reign to almost twelve months (Nov./Dec. 1093 – Nov. 1094) rather than six: see Kapelle, *Norman Conquest*, 154; *Scottish Annals*, 118.
13 Ritchie, *Normans*, 63, 60-1.
14 Duncan, *Scotland*, 125-6; Kapelle, *Norman Conquest*, 156-7, 192. Donald Ban III was the last King of Scots to be buried on Iona.
15 Chroniclers would later labour hard to rewrite the dynastic facts of 1093; the 13th-century *Chronicle of Melrose*, for example, portrays both Donald III and Duncan II as usurpers, displacing the rightful heirs, all sons of Margaret. The rewriting of history is usually the sign of a new confidence of the establishment, and so it was here. Succession by primogeniture happened only by accident and through later creative genealogy.
16 *Scottish Annals*, 118, 128.
17 Cf Kapelle, *Norman Conquest*, 153; Barrow, *Scotland*, 196.
18 One example of the still-dynamic nature of Gaelic culture is the likelihood that the early 12th century saw 'the beginning of the process that produced the style and surname *mac* in Scotland'. By 1128, for example, *macDuib* (or macDuff) had become a surname: Bannerman, 'MacDuff of Fife'.
19 See Barrow, *David I of Scotland*.
20 Ritchie, *Normans*, 96; Duncan, *Scotland*, 126-7; *Scottish Annals*, 128. The exact boundary between the jurisdictions of kings of Scots and Norway, fixed in 1098 as 'all the islands that lie to the west of Scotland separated by water navigable by a ship with the rudder set', was nebulous. The story in more than one saga that Magnus Bareleg claimed Kintyre by the device of being pulled in a skiff across its narrow neck (of no more than two miles at Tarbert) may not be apocryphal. It need not be supposed to mean that any kind of practical Norwegian control of Kintyre resulted between then and the Treaty of Perth in 1266: *Early Sources*, ii, 112-13.

21 Duncan, *Scotland*, 128; Ritchie, *Normans*, 164.
22 The dates of birth of a number of the children of Malcolm Canmore and Margaret are uncertain. David's birth is sometimes given as 1080 but is more likely to have been *c.*1084, although it has been argued that his participation in the campaign of 1097 makes him likely to have been born nearer 1080 than 1084: cf A.H. Dunbar, *Scottish Kings* (2nd edn., 1906), 58; Duncan, *Scotland*, 134n. Edgar, it is usually agreed, was born *c.*1074 and Alexander *c.*1077.
23 K.R. Potter (ed.),*Gesta Stephani* (Oxford, 1976), 55.
24 Ritchie, *Normans*, 409.
25 Kapelle, *Norman Conquest*, 202-3.
26 Ibid., 213.
27 Barrow, *David I of Scotland*, 7-8; idem, *Scotland*, 32.
28 Barrow, *David I of Scotland*, 11.
29 Pryde, *Burghs*, 3-9.
30 S. Cruden, *Scottish Medieval Churches* (1986), 79; Barrow, *Kingdom of Scots*, 189-211; I.B. Cowan and D.E. Easson, *Medieval Religious Houses: Scotland* (1976), 66-82, 100-4.
31 Cruden, *Churches*, 68, 77.
32 Duncan, *Scotland*, 135.
33 A 13th-century statute decreed that the nave of parish kirks be built by the parishioners, and the chancel by the rector himself: *Statutes of the Scottish Church, 1225-1559* (SHS, 1907), 10.
34 *Atlas*, 39-40.
35 Ibid., 35-7; G. Donaldson, 'Bishops' sees before the reign of David I', in *Scottish Church History*, 11-23.
36 *Atlas*, 30, 129; cf Duncan, *Scotland*, 169.
37 The classic conjunction of near-simultaneous foundation of burgh and castle is more easily found in the reign of William I – as at Ayr and Inverurie – rather than in that of David I.
38 M. Chibnall, *Anglo-Norman England, 1066-1166* (Oxford, 1986), 54.
39 Bannerman, 'Macduff of Fife'.
40 Barrow, *David I of Scotland*, 5.
41 Barrow, *Era*, 153-5. Arguments as to the authenticity of a diploma of Duncan II, dated 1094 and carrying within it the earliest example of the phrase 'rex Scotie', go on; the advantage currently seems to rest with the sceptics.
42 The allegation that Malcolm 'the Maiden' had an illegitimate son depends on a single entry in the *Kelso Liber*, which contradicts other contemporary sources. The likeliest explanation is that the scribe, in describing Inverlethan Church where 'my son's body rested the first night after his death' made a slip, intending instead to refer to Henry, Earl of Huntingdon, Malcolm's father. I am grateful to Professor G.W.S. Barrow for this point. Cf Dunbar, *Scottish Kings*, 74.
43 G. Donaldson, *Scottish Kings* (London, 1967), 16.
44 Ritchie, *Normans*, 400-1.
45 Barrow, *Scotland*, 48.
46 Ferteth, one of the rebellious earls of 1160, was connected to the royal house by marriage: Dunbar, *Scottish Kings*, 68.
47 A list of royal castles to 1249 is given in Stringer (ed.), *Nobility*, 22-4.
48 Stringer, *Earl David*, 31-2.
49 Duncan, *Scotland*, 178, 187-8, 204-5.
50 Chibnall, *Anglo-Norman England*, 51.
51 Walter of Coventry, *Memoriale*, ed. Stubbs, ii, 206; see also Barrow, *Kingdom of Scots*, 285.
52 Barrow, *Scotland*, 153, 149.
53 Although the basic line of the Anglo-Scottish border was settled in 1237, the problem of the 'Debateable lands' was not solved until 1551.
54 Duncan, *Scotland*, 554-8.
55 D.E.R. Watt, 'The minority of Alexander III of Scotland', *Trans. Royal Hist. Soc.* (5th series), xxxi (1971), 1-23.
56 This view of the reign depends heavily on A. Young, 'Noble families and political factions in the reign of Alexander III', in N. Reid (ed.), *Scotland in the Reign of Alexander III* (1990), 1-30.
57 N. Reid, 'Alexander III: the historiography of a myth', in ibid., 186-94.
58 N. Mayhew, 'Alexander III – a silver age?' in, ibid., 60-2, 66.
59 E.J. Cowan, 'Norwegian sunset – Scottish dawn: Hakon IV and Alexander III', in ibid., 116; Duncan, *Scotland*, 578-80; *Early Sources*, ii, 605-6.
60 R.I. Lustig, 'The Treaty of Perth: a re-examination', *SHR* lviii (1979), 35-57.
61 Barrow, *Scotland*, 49.
62 Ibid., 121; Cowan, 'Hakon IV and Alexander III', 126.
63 Stringer, *Earl David*, 54, 211.

64 Davies, 'British history', 15-16.
65 Duncan, *Scotland*, 188; Young, 'Noble families', 8-16.

7 The Medieval Church

1 M. Ash, 'The Church in the reign of Alexander III', in Reid (ed.), *Alexander III*, 31-3, 47. The first formal coronation involving the full rite of anointing was that of David II in 1331. Although still conducted in the open air as a largely secular ceremony, the 1249 inauguration may have had extra elements suggesting crown, mantle and sceptre: Duncan, *Scotland*, 554-7.
2 *Early Sources*, i, 599; M.O. Anderson, 'The Celtic Church in Kinrimund', *IR* xxv (1974), 69-70; W.F. Skene (ed.), *Chronicles of the Picts: Chronicles of the Scots* (1867), 151.
3 R.G. Cant, 'The building of St Andrews Cathedral', *IR* xxv (1974), 77. The eventual structure of St Andrews Cathedral, when finished during the period of Bishop William Malvoisin (1202-38), was 357ft long; Glasgow was 285ft, Dunfermline 268ft and Elgin 263ft.
4 The attraction of the legend of St Andrew to the Pictish king, Constantine, may have been the version which claimed that his bones were taken to Constantinople in the reign of Constantine the Great. *Early Sources*, i, 407-8; Smyth, *Warlords*, 187; D. McRoberts, '"The glorious house of St Andrew"', *IR* xxv (1974), 129.
5 *Scottish Annals*, 116; McRoberts, 'Glorious house of St Andrew', 130.
6 *Chron. Picts-Scots*, 183-93; Ash, 'Church', 47-8; McRoberts, 'Glorious house of St Andrew', 143-4. By 1350 the saltire began to appear on the coinage. In 1385 parliament ordered that every man in the Scots army wear a white cross of St Andrew.
7 Barrow, *Scotland*, 90. The custom of the new religious houses of appointing a historiographer also encouraged a cult of both national and local saints.
8 D. McRoberts, 'The Scottish Church and nationalism in the 15th century', *IR* xix (1968), 8-10; J. Galbraith, 'The Middle Ages', in D. Forrester and D. Murray (eds.), *Studies in the History of Worship in Scotland* (1984), 21-6. The *Aberdeen Breviary* was also notable for its emphasis on elaborate musical settings.
9 Galbraith, 'Middle Ages', 20. By the 15th century, the most popular pilgrimage centres were Tain (St Duthac) and Whithorn (Ninian). Both were regularly visited by James IV, although mistresses conveniently placed at Darnaway and in Ayrshire also laid claim to his attentions.
10 Fothad II (c.1059-93) was the first of his line to be called 'chief bishop of Scotland' (*ardescop Alban*), according to his obit in the *Annals of Ulster*; this Gaelic title was acknowledged by an Augustinian canon writing between 1144 and 1153, who said that bishops of St Andrews were called *Summi Archiepiscopi Scotorum*. He is to be distinguished from an earlier bishop of St Andrews, Fothad I, who died c.963: *Chron Picts-Scots*, 190.
11 M. Ash, 'David Bernham, bishop of St Andrews, 1239-1253', *IR* xxv (1974), 3-14.
12 There were some important exceptions to the increasingly Scottish complexion of the later 13th-century Church. One such was Bishop John Cheam of Glasgow, who was appointed in 1259 in acrimonious circumstances. He was, however, followed after 1268 by a line of Scots.
13 There were over thirty houses of Augustinian canons already established in England by the time the first Scottish priory, at Scone, was founded c.1120: Cowan and Easson, *Religious Houses*, 88.
14 Cruden, *Scottish Medieval Churches*, 63.
15 W. Stevenson, 'The monastic presence in Scottish burghs in the 12th and 13th centuries', *SHR* lx (1981), 97-118.
16 It was ironically the closeness of the religious houses to the crown which ultimately sealed their fate. The Prior of the abbey at St Andrews at the Reformation was James Stewart, better known as the Earl of Moray, illegitimate half-brother of Mary, Queen of Scots. Under his guidance more than twenty of the canons joined the reformed ministry after 1560. More generally, the vital change in the status of many religious houses came in the 15th or early 16th centuries with the provision of a secular cleric as their head. More than half of the monasteries were controlled at some point in the 16th century by a bishop. It was the vacuum left after Flodden which produced a new kind of intruder – the secular commendator, often under-age and related either to the royal house or a noble family. M. Dilworth, 'The commendator system in Scotland', *IR* xxxvii (1986), 51-72.
17 Ash, 'Church', 35; Cowan and Easson, *Religious Houses*, 107-39.
18 I.B. Cowan, 'Some aspects of the appropriation of parish churches in medieval Scotland', *RSCHS* xiii (1959), 203-22; J. Durkan, 'Chaplains in late medieval Scotland', *RSCHS* xx (1979), 91-103; Grant, *Scotland*, 99. A 13th-century statute of the Scottish province tried to enforce a maximum stipend for chaplains of £5 per annum, 'although for some time past by reason of the exceptional dearness of provisions another usage has obtained'. Vicars-pensioner were allowed 10 merks, a sum doubled to 20 or 24 merks in 1549, but few then received it in practice. In the 16th century, despite

sharp price inflation, the average stipend for vicars-pensioner, curates and chaplains was probably not much above the figure set in the 13th. *Statutes of Scottish Church*, 11-12, 53-4, 112.

19 Ibid., 9-10.

20 G.W.S. Barrow, *Robert Bruce and the Scottish Identity* (Saltire Soc., 1984), 3; M. Lynch, 'Queen Mary's triumph', *SHR* lxix (1990), 16.

21 Duncan, *Scotland*, 284-90.

22 Barrow, *Scotland*, 152.

23 Barrow, 'The clergy in the War of Independence', in *Kingdom of the Scots*, 233-54.

24 New holders of greater benefices had to pay to the papacy 'common services' amounting to a third of their assessed income. Holders of lesser benefices had to pay 'annates' amounting to a half of their first year's income to a papal collector. Nicholson, *Scotland*, 151-2.

25 J. Dowden, *The Bishops of Scotland* (Glasgow, 1912), 287-8; Nicholson, *Scotland*, 192-3.

26 Ibid., 245-6; *Calendar of Papal Letters to Scotland of Benedict XIII of Avignon, 1394-1419* (SHS, 1976), esp. pp. xix-xxii.

27 Nicholson, *Scotland*, 294-7.

28 J.H. Burns, 'Scottish churchmen and the Council of Basle', *IR* xiii (1962), 3-53, 157-89.

29 Nicholson, *Scotland*, 461-4.

30 Ibid., 459; L.J. Macfarlane, *William Elphinstone and the Kingdom of Scotland, 1431-1514* (Aberdeen, 1985), esp. chs. 1-2.

31 J.A.F. Thomson, 'Innocent VIII and the Scottish Church', *IR* xix (1968), 23-31; I.B. Cowan, 'Patronage, provision and reservation: pre-Reformation appointments to Scottish benefices', in I.B. Cowan and D. Shaw (eds.), *The Renaissance and Reformation in Scotland: Essays in Honour of Gordon Donaldson* (1983), 75-92.

32 The text of Hawthornden's account of the entry is printed in L.E. Kastner (ed.), *The Poetical Works of William Drummond of Hawthornden* (STS, 1913). I am grateful to John A.F. Martin for access to his unpublished dissertation, 'A study of the entertainments for the state entry of Charles I: Edinburgh, 15 June 1633'. See also McGrath, 'Local heroes: the Scottish humanist Parnassus for Charles I', 256-70.

33 See 257-61, below.

34 McRoberts, 'Scottish Church and nationalism', 11; D.E.R. Watt, 'Scottish university men of the 13th and 14th centuries', in Smout (ed.), *Scotland and Europe*, 1; Cowan and Easson, *Religious Houses*, 231-4; J. Durkan, 'Education: the laying of fresh foundations', in J. MacQueen (ed.), *Humanism in Renaissance Scotland* (1990), 150-9; J. Durkan, 'William Turnbull, Bishop of Glasgow', *IR* ii (1951), 5-61.

35 Watt, 'Scottish university men', 12-13.

36 Durkan, 'Education', 123-4.

37 Macfarlane, *Elphinstone*, 423; J. Robertson, 'The development of the law', in Brown (ed.), *Scottish Society*, 136-52.

38 L.J. Macfarlane, 'The primacy of the Scottish Church, 1472-1521', *IR* xx (1969), 117-18; Thomson, 'Innocent VIII', 30; N. Macdougall, *James IV* (1989), 211-14.

39 Cowan and Easson, *Religious Houses*, 213-30; Cruden, *Medieval Churches*, 187-94; I.B. Cowan, 'Church and society', in Brown (ed.), *Scottish Society*, 115-19.

40 G. Donaldson, *Faith of the Scots* (London, 1990), 49.

41 D. McRoberts, 'The rosary in Scotland', *IR* xxiii (1972), 81-6.

42 These three devotional poems survive in the collection Arundel MS 285, which was included along with others in *Devotional Pieces in Verse and Prose*, ed. J.A.W. Bennett (STS, 1955). Cf Donaldson, *Faith of the Scots*, 62, who claims that 'clerical eyebrows must have been raised by lines such as these'. The various parts of the Church tended to favour different devotions. Usually, however, the cult of the Virgin Mary was linked to (and subsumed within) the overarching devotion of the Passion, as it was in the *Contemplacioun*.

43 A.A. MacDonald, 'Catholic devotion into Protestant lyric: the case of the *Contemplacioun of Synnaris*', *IR* xxxv (1984), esp. 65-7, shows how this poem was altered, with references to the Virgin Mary pruned and treatment of the doctrine of penance rearranged, when it reappeared in the 1560s in the Bannatyne Manuscript in a fit state to pass a censorship committee of the Protestant Church.

44 J. Durkan, 'The Observant Franciscan province in Scotland', *IR* xxxv (1984), 51-7; Cowan and Easson, *Religious Houses*, 129-33; W. Moir Bryce, *The Scottish Grey Friars* (1909), i, 92. In 1467 the Scottish province of the Observant Chapter was erected, a forerunner of separate Scottish provinces for the Dominicans (1481) and the original Franciscans (1483). The Charterhouse had been transferred from the English province to that of Geneva in 1460.

45 Macfarlane, *Elphinstone*, 220, 226, 242, 256, 269, 349, 356, 379.

46 D. McRoberts, *The Heraldic Ceiling of St Machar's Cathedral, Aberdeen* (Friends of St Machar's Cathedral, Occasional Papers, no. 2, 1976).

47 C. Burns, 'Papal gifts to Scottish monarchs: the Golden Rose and Blessed Sword', *IR* xx (1969), 172-3.

8 **The Wars of Scotland**

1 The rediscoverers of the Declaration of Arbroath were the royalist and episcopalian scholars, Sir James Balfour of Denmilne and Archbishop Spottiswoode. The document, despite its hint of the election of Robert Bruce, was neglected by George Buchanan in his *History* published in 1582 and by Covenanting thinkers in the 17th century. See G.G. Simpson, 'The Declaration of Arbroath revitalised', *SHR* lvi (1977), 11-33.

2 *Liber Pluscardensis*, ed. F.J.H. Skene (1877-80), ii, 170.

3 R.R. Davies, *Domination and Conquest: The Experience of Ireland, Scotland and Wales, 1100-1300* (Cambridge, 1990), 16-18, stresses the 'alternative ecclesiastical culture', based on an 'English model', imposed on the three Celtic churches. Cf 94-101, above, which sees a distinctively Scottish *ecclesia Scoticana* which absorbed both continental and English influences.

4 The chronicler of Hailes Abbey, cited in Barrow, *Robert Bruce and Scottish Identity*, 7.

5 For the significance of Edward's notion, made explicit by 1305, of Scotland as a 'land' (*terre*), like Ireland or Wales, rather than a kingdom, see Davies, *Domination and Conquest*, 126-8, and R. Frame, *The Political Development of the British Isles, 1100-1400* (Oxford, 1990), 142.

6 *The Chronicle of Walter of Guisborough* (Camden Soc., lxxxix, 1957), 281.

7 G.W.S. Barrow, *Robert Bruce and the Community of the Realm of Scotland* (3rd edn., 1988), 73; Davies, *Domination and Conquest*, 125-6.

8 Frame, *British Isles*, 168.

9 J. Bain (ed.), *Calendar of Documents relating to Scotland* (1881-8), ii, no. 1926; Frame, *British Isles*, 140.

10 The Lanercost chronicler put the pregnancy down as counterfeit. It is much more likely that it was genuine; see Barrow, *Robert Bruce*, 15-16. It has been speculated that Yolande suffered a miscarriage, probably in August 1286: A.A.M. Duncan, 'The community of the realm of Scotland and Robert Bruce', *SHR* xlv (1966), 187-8.

11 The terms of the Treaty of Birgham provide an instructive contrast to those of the eventual Union of the Crowns in 1603. Separate parliaments and legal systems would have continued; the only taxation and military service to be imposed would be after existing Scottish custom; 'the rights, liberties and customs' of the Scottish kingdom were guaranteed as inviolable 'in all things and in all ways . . . for all time'; and although the monarch would be expected to reside mostly in England a royal representative would be based in Scotland. It did not attempt a 'perfect union', as James VI did, and failed to secure. The fact that there was, in a sense, a ready-made 'British' aristocracy in the 13th century, owning land on both sides of the Anglo-Scottish border, as there was not in the 17th, might have made the process of a union settlement less painful than it would later prove to be.

12 Seen in retrospect, there were already in 1290 some straws in the wind showing the less acceptable face of Edward I. The seizure of Man in June 1290 and the appointment of Anthony Bek, Bishop of Durham, as lieutenant in Scotland prior to the marriage of Margaret and Edward showed both the typical resort to force and the characteristic legal mind of Edward I: Barrow, *Robert Bruce*, 28-9.

13 E.L.G. Stones and G.G. Simpson (eds.), *Edward I and the Throne of Scotland, 1290-1296*, 2 vols. (Oxford, 1978), i, 11-21. The background and connections of the three generations of Bruces shows the difficulties inherent in any attempt to generalise about the 'pro-English' or 'pro-Scottish' interests of the nobility in the 13th century. Each generation of this one family – Robert 'the Noble' and Competitor (d. 1295), his son Robert (d. 1304), and his son Robert, Earl of Carrick and eventual King of Scots – might be cast in a different camp. The one most closely attached to the government of Edward I was Robert II, who held office as governor of Carlisle in 1297 when his son, against his wishes, joined the insurgents.

14 Strictly, Edward I did not act as an arbiter of the Great Cause, but adjudicated in his own court: Stones and Simpson, *Edward I*, i, 21-2.

15 Ibid., i, 188; Barrow, *Robert Bruce*, 41, 49.

16 G.G. Simpson, 'Why was John Balliol called "Toom Tabard"?', *SHR* xlvii (1968), 196-9. Cf A.M. Mackenzie, *Robert Bruce, King of Scots* (London, 1934), pt. 2, 'The War of the Empty Jacket'. Edward I was fond of such rituals of humiliation. The defenders of Stirling Castle in 1304 were similarly forced to parade with a rope about their necks after their surrender – the symbol of treason inflicted on those below the rank of knight.

17 A.A.M. Duncan, 'The early parliaments of Scotland', *SHR* xlv (1966), 36-47; Nicholson, *Scotland*, 44-5.

18 *Rotuli Scotiae*, i, 11.

19 A. Tuck, *Crown and Nobility, 1272-1461: Political Conflict in Late Medieval England* (Oxford, 1986),

30-1; E.L.G. Stones (ed.), *Anglo-Scottish Relations, 1174-1328* (Oxford, 1965), 65.

20 It was ironical that it was Edward I's own refusal to appear before the court of Philip IV at Paris in January 1294 to answer to a claim for restitution after a naval incident off the coast of Brittany, and his being held in contempt and forfeiture of the Duchy of Aquitaine (Gascony), which provoked war with France. The parallel with the Balliol case was close. Tuck, *Crown and Nobility*, 31-2.

21 Barrow, *Robert Bruce*, 63-4.

22 Ibid, 129, 112.

23 M. Prestwich, *War, Politics and Finance under Edward I* (London, 1972), 93-4; G.W.S. Barrow, 'The army of Alexander III's Scotland', in Reid (ed.), *Alexander III*, 132-47.

24 Davies, *Domination and Conquest*, 126; see eg. Stones, *Anglo-Scottish Relations*, 214-17, 254-5.

25 Quoted in Barrow, *Robert Bruce*, 61.

26 J. Stevenson (ed.), *Documents Illustrative of Scottish History, 1286-1306* (1870), ii, 31, 163-4.

27 M. Prestwich, 'Colonial Scotland: the English in Scotland under Edward I', in R.A. Mason (ed.), *Scotland and England, 1286-1815* (1987), 7.

28 E. Barron, *The Scottish War of Independence: a Critical Study* (2nd edn., 1934), 21; Barrow, *Robert Bruce*, 90-93.

29 Barron, *War of Independence*, first published in 1914, exhaustively set out the widespread nature of the 1297 revolt; see esp. chs. iv-vii.

30 *Documents Illustrative of Sir William Wallace, His Life and Times* (Maitland Club, 1841), no. xv.

31 Barrow, *Robert Bruce*, 100; Prestwich, *War, Politics and Finance*, 109.

32 Ibid., 66, 73; idem, 'Colonial Scotland', 6-17.

33 *Chronicon de Lanercost* (Bann. Club, 1839), 217; Barrow, *Robert Bruce*, 215-16.

34 Prestwich, *War, Politics and Finance*, 47, 53-4, 94, 98.

35 Barrow, *Bruce and Scottish Identity*, 3.

36 Barrow, *Robert Bruce*, 104, 109, 114-15. It has been suggested in N. Reid, 'The kingless kingdom: the Scottish guardianships of 1286-1306', *SHR* lxi (1982), 112-13, that Comyn held office as an 'under-Guardian' in 1301-02, with Soules as senior.

37 Duncan, 'Bruce and the community of the realm', 194-8.

38 Barrow, *Robert Bruce*, 140-1.

39 M. Ash, 'William Lamberton, Bishop of St Andrews, 1297-1328', in G.W.S. Barrow (ed.), *The Scottish Tradition: Essays in Honour of R.G. Cant* (1974), 48.

40 Barrow, *Robert Bruce*, 166-71.

41 Ibid., 184-5; see Stones, *Anglo-Scottish Relations*, 280-7.

42 N. Denholm-Young (ed.), *Vita Edwardi Secundi* (London, 1957), 48.

43 *Cal. Docs. Scot.*, ii, no. 1923.

44 Tuck, *Crown and Nobility*, 59; Barrow, *Robert Bruce*, 71.

45 Ibid., 204-9; Tuck, *Crown and Nobility*, 68.

46 *Vita*, 54.

47 Barrow, *Robert Bruce*, 230.

48 Different views are offered in A.A.M. Duncan, 'The Scots invasion of Ireland, 1315', in Davies (ed.), *British Isles*, esp. 103-4, and J.F. Lydon, 'The Bruce invasion of Ireland', *Historical Studies*, iv (1963), 111-25.

49 *Vita*, 54, 71.

50 Tuck, *Crown and Nobility*, 73-4; N. Fryde, *The Tyranny and Fall of Edward II, 1321-1326* (Cambridge, 1979), 122-3.

51 A.A.M. Duncan (ed.), *The Acts of Robert I, King of Scots*, (1988), 291ff.

52 Ash, 'William Lamberton', 54.

53 Bernard, a monk and Abbot of the Tironensian house at Kilwinning, was appointed Abbot of Arbroath, another Tironensian abbey, sometime between 1301 and 1303. The identification 'of Linton', first made in the 18th century from a stray reference in the Ragman Roll, is spurious. See Duncan, *Acts of Robert I*, 3, 198-203.

54 Recent research has made authorship of the Declaration of Arbroath problematic rather than certain. The case for a clerk in Bernard of Arbroath's writing-office is put in Duncan, *Acts of Robert I*, 165-6; that for Kinninmonth, a member of the Lamberton circle, in Barrow, *Robert Bruce*, 165-6.

55 David II was the first Scottish monarch to receive the full rights of anointing, at what may properly be called a coronation, in 1331.

56 Ditchburn, 'Trade with northern Europe', 162-4; Stevenson, 'Trade with the south', 181.

57 W.C. Dickinson and A.A.M. Duncan, *Scotland from the Earliest Times to 1603* (3rd edn., Oxford, 1977), 186ff; Ewan, *Townlife*, 147-8.

58 In 1319 Aberdeen was granted feu-ferm tenure, transferring all the king's revenues in the burgh except the great customs to the community in return for a fixed annual fee or 'feu'. Edinburgh was similarly treated in 1329. By the end of the 14th century, most royal burghs had been granted this

privilege, which gave them an important measure of fiscal independence.

59 Barrow, *Robert Bruce*, 292.

60 W.D.H. Sellar, 'The common law of Scotland and the common law of England', in Davies (ed), *British Isles*, 91-2.

61 Duncan, *Acts of Robert I*, 48-52; Barrow, *Robert Bruce*, 286-9.

62 Ibid., 270-81.

63 Grant, *Scotland*, 128.

64 Ibid., 26-8.

65 Tuck, *Crown and Nobility*, 96-7; A. Goodman, *A History of England from Edward II to James I* (London, 1977), 164-6.

66 R. Nicholson, *Edward III and the Scots, 1327-1335* (Oxford, 1965), 105-6.

67 Quoted in Tuck, *Crown and Nobility*, 107.

68 Nicholson, *Edward III*, 75-99.

69 Ibid., 126-7, 134-8.

70 G.W.S. Barrow, 'The aftermath of war: Scotland and England in the late 13th and early 14th centuries', *Trans. Royal Hist. Soc.*, xxviii (1978), 122-5. The general significance of *vastatio*, a war of economic attrition, is discussed in Davies, *Domination and Conquest*, 40.

71 J. Campbell, 'England, Scotland and the Hundred Years War in the 14th century', in J.R. Hale *et al.* (eds.), *Europe in the Late Middle Ages* (London, 1965), 186.

72 Ibid., 196-201; Grant, *Scotland*, 22-4.

9 The Making of the Stewart Dynasty

1 Walter Bower, *Scotichronicon*, ed. D.E.R. Watt (Aberdeen, 1987-), viii, 63. See 71-2, above, for a discussion of the effects of the eight outbreaks of plague between 1349 and 1455.

2 Grant, *Scotland*, 79-80, 236-7; *Atlas II* tabulates the revenue from customs 1327-1599.

3 J. Wormald, 'The house of Stewart', *History Today*, xxxiv (Oct., 1984); reprinted in J. Wormald (ed.), *Scotland Revisited* (London, 1991).

4 A. Grant, 'Crown and nobility in later medieval Britain', in R. Mason (ed.), *Scotland and England* (1987), 43; idem, *Scotland*, 123, 127-30, 191.

5 Ibid., 123; Dunbar, *Scottish Kings*, 166-9.

6 Campbell, 'Hundred Years War', 201-16; Grant, *Scotland*, 40-5.

7 Frame, *British Isles*, 168, 195-6.

8 Robert the Steward (later Robert II) was heir-presumptive from 1318 until the birth of David II in 1325; he again became heir-presumptive on the death of his grandfather, Robert I, in 1329.

9 The title, Duke of Rothesay, first conferred on David, Earl of Carrick, in 1398, has ever since then been conferred on the royal male heir to the throne.

10 The term was first used in Brown (Wormald), *Scottish Society*; see esp. 33-51.

11 Nicholson, *Scotland*, 140; B. Webster, 'David II and the government of 14th-century Scotland', *Trans. Royal Hist. Soc.*, xvi (1966), 119-20.

12 Ibid., 120-1; R. Nicholson, 'David II, the historians and the chroniclers', *SHR* xlv (1966), esp. 59-61.

13 Nicholson, *Scotland*, 170-2.

14 Ibid., 177.

15 Grant, *Scotland*, 177.

16 Nicholson, *Scotland*, 182-3.

17 Donaldson, *Scottish Kings*, 36-7.

18 Nicholson, *Scotland*, 186-7; Grant, *Scotland*, 123.

19 Brown, *Scottish Society*, 47; Donaldson, *Scottish Kings*, 37-8, 40.

20 Jean Froissart, *Chronicles*, trans. W.P. Ker (London, 1902), iv, 48-9.

21 Nicholson, *Scotland*, 187-8; Grant, *Scotland*, 178.

22 Nicholson, *Scotland*, 203; A. Goodman, 'The Anglo-Scottish marches in the 15th century: a frontier society?', in Mason (ed.), *Scotland and England*, 22.

23 *The Acts of David II, King of Scots*, ed. B. Webster (1982).

24 Grant, *Scotland*, 180.

25 *Chron. Fordun*, i, 24; ii, 38; see above, 67-9.

26 The siege at Dumbarton could, alternatively, had been in 1395-6: see Bower *Scotichronicon*, viii, 5, 150. For Robert III's children, see *Exch. Rolls*, iv, pp. clxxiii-clxxv.

27 It is worth noting that Bower's account of the encounter at Perth between two Highland clans in 1396 is wedged between references to two conventional tournaments; see *Scotichronicon*, viii, 7-11.

28 Frame, *British Isles*, 126-7; Grant, *Scotland*, 214-15.

29 See 167-8, below.
30 Grant, *Scotland*, 184-5.
31 A total of seventy-two nobles or their sons were held at one time or another to guarantee payment of James I's ransom. A third of the first batch of twenty-seven died in English captivity; most of them were held for periods between two and five years, but Malise, Earl of Menteith, was kept for twenty-six. At least a third of the last batch of hostages, exchanged for their compatriots in 1432, were detained until the 1440s. E.W.M. Balfour-Melville, *James I, King of Scots, 1406-1437* (London, 1936), 293-5.
32 Nicholson, *Scotland*, 254.
33 Cf. *Exch. Rolls*, iv, p. lvii; also Nicholson, *Scotland*, 255.
34 Grant, 'Celtic fringe', 127.
35 Nicholson, *Scotland*, 281-324,
36 A.A.M. Duncan, *James I, King of Scots, 1424-1437* (Glasgow, 2nd edn., 1984), 6-7.
37 Bower, *Scotichronicon*, viii, 245.
38 Duncan, *James I*, 8; Nicholson, *Scotland*, 287.
39 Bower's account of James I, though flattering, is confined to generalities and the early part of the reign. For Sylvius's, see Balfour-Melville, *James I*, 236.
40 Duncan, *James I*, 10, 20.
41 Nicholson, *Scotland*, 314-17.
42 Ibid., 284; Grant, *Scotland*, 188.
43 The same image, of the arm of a lady-in-waiting barring a door, was preferred by some later portrait painters to convey the horror of the murder of David Riccio at Holyrood in 1566, although there was no evidence for it then.
44 C. McGladdery, *James II*, (1990), 10-12.
45 Ibid., 14; Grant, *Scotland*, 123, 191-2.
46 The marriage between Annabella, youngest daughter of James I, and Louis, Count of Geneva, though arranged in 1444, never materialised. It was broken off in 1456 and she subsequently married George, Lord Gordon, 2nd Earl of Huntly. Cf. Dunbar, *Scottish Kings*, 192.
47 Cf. the interpretations of the resilience of Douglas power in Grant, *Scotland*, 193-5, and McGladdery, *James II*, 75-89.
48 Nicholson, *Scotland*, 355.
49 The 'Auchinleck Chronicle', reproduced in McGladdery, *James II*, 165.
50 Nicholson, *Scotland*, 360.
51 A.I. Dunlop, *The Life and Times of James Kennedy* (1950), 382.
52 Ibid., 284, 385-6; G. Stell, 'Architecture: the changing needs of society', in Brown, *Scottish Society*, 153-9.
53 Nicholson, *Scotland*, 369-73; McGladdery, *James II*, 154-5.
54 Ibid., 70, 89.
55 Nicholson, *Scotland*, 378-80; Brown, *Scottish Society*, 37.
56 J. Wormald, 'Taming the magnates', in Stringer (ed.), *Nobility*, 276; Nicholson, *Scotland*, 364.

10 Late Medieval Kingship: James III, IV and V

1 N. Macdougall, *James IV* (1989), 51.
2 Macfarlane, *Elphinstone*, 22.
3 J. Wormald, *Court, Kirk and Community: Scotland, 1470-1625* (London, 1981), 12-13.
4 N. Macdougall, *James III: a Political Study* (1982), 305-08; Macfarlane, *Elphinstone*, 182-4.
5 Cf R.L. Mackie, *King James IV of Scotland* (1958), 201; N. Macdougall, 'The kingship of James IV of Scotland', *History Today* (Nov., 1984), 34.
6 J. Wormald, *Mary Queen of Scots: a Study in Failure* (London, 1988), 32; Donaldson, *Scottish Kings*, 163-4.
7 Wormald, *Scotland*, 13.
8 Macfarlane, *Elphinstone*, 405; Nicholson, *Scotland*, ch. 17.
9 Macdougall, *James III*, 301.
10 Hector Boece, *Aberdonensium Episcoporum Vitae* (Bann. Club, 1825), 52; Macdougall, *James IV*, 53.
11 Nicholson, *Scotland*, 557.
12 Ibid., 558.
13 Ibid., 408; MacDougall, *James III*, 78, 91.
14 N. Macdougall, 'Bishop James Kennedy of St Andrews: a reassessment of his political career', in N. Macdougall (ed.), *Church, Politics and Society: Scotland 1408-1929* (1983), 53-67.
15 Macdougall, *James III*, 70-85; Nicholson, *Scotland*, 420-1.

16 Donaldson, *Scottish Kings*, 111; Macdougall, *James III*, 130-33..
17 Ibid., 177-82.
18 *APS*, ii, 210-11.
19 Macdougall, *James IV*, 81, 86.
20 Ibid., 171, 175.
21 *APS*, ii, 240.
22 The phrase comes from Sir David Lindsay's poem, 'Testament and Complaynt of Our Soverane Lordis Papyngo'.
23 Macfarlane, *Elphinstone*, 183.
24 Macdougall, *James IV*, 117-28, 140.
25 Ibid., 233-7; Macdougall, 'Kingship', 36.
26 Mackie, *James IV*, 114-16; Nicholson, *Scotland*, 577.
27 Macdougall, *James IV*, 117-28, 271.
28 Ibid., 138-9, 273-6; Mackie, *James IV*, 251-80; Nicholson, *Scotland*, 604-5.
29 W.K. Emond, 'The minority of King James V, 1513-1528' (St Andrews University Ph.D., 1988), appendix A, has the most accurate Flodden death roll.
30 Macfarlane, *Elphinstone*, 427.
31 Cf. Wormald, *Scotland*, 7.
32 See Macfarlane, *Elphinstone*, 428.
33 The most detailed account of the politics of the minority is in Emond, 'Minority of James V'.
34 M.N. Baudouin-Matuszek, 'Henri II et les expéditions françaises en Ecosse', *Bibliothèque de l'Ecole des chartes*, cxlv (1987), 343.
35 W.S. Reid, 'Clerical taxation: the Scottish alternative to dissolution of the monasteries', *Catholic Historical Review*, xxxv (1948); Macdougall, *James IV*, 204.
36 John Lesley, *History of Scotland* (Bann. Club, 1830), 155; see also A.L. Murray, 'The revenues of the bishopric of Moray in 1538', *IR* xix (1968), 45-8.
37 Macdougall, *James IV*, 147; M. Lynch (ed.), *Early Modern Town in Scotland* (London, 1987) (hereafter Lynch, *EMTS*), 72-3. Cf. Wormald, *Scotland*, 15-16, where there is said to be 'little taxation' before the 1580s.
38 F.D. Bardgett, *Scotland Reformed: the Reformation in Angus and the Mearns* (1989), 12-13.
39 R.K. Hannay and D. Hay (eds.), *Letters of James V* (1954), 271.
40 Macdougall, *James IV*, 280n; G. Donaldson, *Scotland: James V to James VII* (1965), 60.
41 Macdougall, *James IV*, 306.
42 Bardgett, *Scotland Reformed*, 10-12, 26.
43 Wormald, *Scotland*, 14-26; Wormald, *Mary*, 34.
44 Macdougall, *James IV*, 63, 137-9; Lynch, *EMTS*, 73.
45 Grant, *Scotland*, 196.
46 Ibid., 195-6; J. Wormald, 'Taming the magnates?', in Stringer (ed.), *Nobility*, 275-6.
47 Macdougall, 'Kingship', 36.
48 Dunbar, *Scottish Kings*, 219.
49 B.E. Crawford, 'William Sinclair, Earl of Orkney and his family: a study in the politics of survival', in Stringer (ed.), *Nobility*, 239.
50 J. & R.W. Munro (eds.), *Acts of the Lord of the Isles, 1336-1493* (SHS, 1986), 126; J. Wormald, *Lords and Men in Scotland: Bonds of Manrent, 1442-1603* (1985), 328.
51 Crawford, 'William Sinclair', 241, 243.
52 K.A. Steer and J.W.M. Bannerman, *Late Medieval Monumental Sculpture in the West Highlands* (1977), 201-13; Grant, *Scotland*, 127, 129; Grant, 'Celtic fringe', 118-34; Macdougall, *James IV*, 175.
53 J. MacInnes, 'Gaelic poetry and historical tradition', in Maclean (ed.), *Middle Ages in the Highlands*, 149.
54 Steer and Bannerman, *Sculpture*, 211.
55 Wormald, *Scotland*, 10.

III THE LONG SIXTEENTH CENTURY

11 Rich and Poor in the Reformation Century

1 J. de Vries, *European Urbanisation, 1500-1800* (London, 1984), 255-7; M. Lynch, *Edinburgh and the Reformation* (1981), 9-14.
2 M. Lynch, 'Whatever happened to the medieval burgh?', *SESH* iv (1984), 7.
3 P. Hume Brown, *Early Travellers in Scotland* (1891), 93.

4 S.G.E. Lythe, *The Economy of Scotland in its European Setting, 1550-1625* (1960), chs. 5, 6; Ditchburn, 'Trade with northern Europe', 167; *Atlas*, 211, 213.
5 C. Whatley, *The Salt Industry and its Trade in Fife and Tayside, 1570-1850* (Abertay Hist. Soc., 1984), 26; J. Brown, 'Merchant princes and mercantile investment in early 17th-century Scotland', in Lynch, EMTS, 130-1.
6 The customs returns in £ Scots for exports for the years 1538-41 (on average), 1544, 1550 and 1553 were: Haddington £124, 44, 1, 12; Dundee £378, 148, 65 and 239; nationally £5476, 672, 1852, 3215. *Exch. Rolls*, vols. xvii, xviii; I. Guy, 'The Scottish export trade, 1460-1599', in Smout (ed.), *Scotland and Europe*, 62-81.
7 Lynch (ed.), *Medieval Town*, 268-9.
8 Ibid., 268-75.
9 Ibid., 281; Lynch, 'Whatever happened', 7-8.
10 E.P.D. Torrie, *Medieval Dundee* (Abertay Hist. Soc., 1990), 59, 105-07; *Historical Works of Sir James Balfour* (1824-5), iv, 315-16.
11 Lynch (ed.), *Medieval Town*, 54-5, 263; *Chronicle of Perth* (Maitland Club, 1831), 4-26; M. Lynch, 'Continuity and change in urban society, 1500-1700', in R.A. Houston and I.D. Whyte, *Scottish Society 1500-1880* (Cambridge, 1989), 102.
12 *Edin. Recs.*, i, 97; *Exch. Rolls.*, vols. xi, xxiii.
13 Lynch, 'Continuity', 108-10; H. Dingwall, 'The social and economic structure of Edinburgh in the late 17th century' (Edinburgh Ph.D., 1989), 619-21; I.D. Whyte, 'The occupational structure of Scottish burghs in the late 17th century', in Lynch, EMTS, 236.
14 G. Marshall, *Presbyteries and Profits: Calvinism and the Development of Capitalism in Scotland, 1560-1707* (Oxford, 1980), 284ff.
15 Whatley, *Salt Industry*, 24, 26-7.
16 C. Wilson and G. Parker, *An Introduction to the Sources of European Economic History, 1500-1880* (London, 1977), 147-8, 125; a fuller analysis of the 1614 survey is in *Atlas II*.
17 Lythe, *Economy*, 49-51; Whatley, *Salt Industry*, 26-9; T.C. Smout, *Scottish Trade on the Eve of Union, 1660-1707* (1963), 219-32.
18 M. Meikle, 'Lairds and gentlemen: a study of the landed families of the eastern Anglo-Scottish borders, 1540-1603' (Edinburgh Ph.D., 1989), 431-9; J. Brown, 'The social, political and economic influences of the Edinburgh merchant élite, 1600-38' (Edinburgh Ph.D., 1985), 160.
19 Ibid., 114-24.
20 I.D. Whyte, *Agriculture and Society in Seventeenth Century Scotland* (1979), 259.
21 Wormald, *Scotland*, 40.
22 *Ayrshire and Wigtonshire Arch. Assoc.*, iv (1884), 17-25; M. Sanderson, 'Some aspects of the church in Scottish society in the era of the Reformation', RSCHS xvii (1970), esp. 81-8.
23 Nicholson, *Scotland*, 570-1; G. Donaldson, *Scotland*, 56.
24 M. Sanderson, 'The feuing of Strathisla', *Northern Scotland*, ii (1974-5), 1-11.
25 M. Sanderson, *Scottish Rural Society in the Sixteenth Century* (1982), 77.
26 Houston and Whyte, *Scottish Society*, 16.
27 W.H. Makey, *The Church of the Covenant, 1637-1651* (1979), 6.
28 Ibid., 3; Lythe, *Economy*, 113-14.
29 A, Gibson and T.C. Smout, 'Scottish food and Scottish history, 1500-1800', in Houston and Whyte (eds.), *Scottish Society*, 73.
30 The idea of the commonweal was new, originating in the 1520s. Its best-known manifestation was the figure of John the Commonweal in Sir David Lindsay's *Ane Satyre of the Thrie Estatis*, first performed in 1540. See R.A. Mason, 'Covenant and commonweal: the language of politics in Reformation Scotland', in Macdougall (ed.), *Church, Politics and Society*, 108.
31 See 257-62, below.
32 C. Larner, *Enemies of God: the Witch-Hunt in Scotland* (London, 1981), 61, 84-7.

12 Roads to Reformation

1 See e.g. J. Kirk, *Patterns of Reform: Continuity and Change in the Reformation Kirk* (1989), p. xv; J. Scotland, *History of Scottish Education* (London, 1969), i, 43-4; J.D. Mackie, *A History of Scotland* (London, 1978), 157-8.
2 J. Durkan, 'Education: the laying of fresh foundations', 126-30.
3 W.C. Dickinson (ed.), *John Knox's History of the Reformation in Scotland* 2 vols. (1949), i, 6.
4 Knox, *History*, i, 8-11; M. Sanderson, *Cardinal of Scotland: David Beaton, c.1494-1546* (1986), 207.
5 I.B. Cowan, *The Scottish Reformation* (London, 1982), 103-4, 113; Macdougall, *James IV*, 105-7.
6 Sanderson, *Cardinal*, 88, 275.

7 Knox, *History*, i, 60, ; Sanderson, *Cardinal*, 211-19.
8 Donaldson, *Faith of the Scots*, 62, 66-9; *History of the Kirk of Scotland by Mr David Calderwood*, 8 vols. (Wodrow Soc., 1842-9), i, 141-3.
9 G. Donaldson, *All the Queen's Men: Power and Politics in Mary Stewart's Scotland* (London, 1983), 9, 11, 22.
10 Sanderson, *Cardinal*, 189, 270-84.
11 *Wodrow Misc.* (1844), 54; Bardgett, *Scotland Reformed*, 36, 72; Kirk, *Patterns*, 152: 'the diffusion of Protestantism in society . . . depended on a network of communications'.
12 D. Laing (ed.), *Works of John Knox*, 6 vols. (1846-64), vi, 78; Lynch, *Edinburgh*, 76, 97, 86.
13 Ibid., 38, 83-5; Bardgett, *Scotland Reformed*, 52-3; Kirk, *Patterns*, 13.
14 Bardgett, *Scotland Reformed*, 42-4.
15 Ibid., 45; Donaldson, *Faith of the Scots*, 12; *Wodrow Misc.*, 54.
16 Lynch, *EMTS*, 42, 48-50.
17 G. Donaldson (ed.), *Scottish Historical Documents* (1970), 116-17.
18 John Lesley, *Historie of Scotland* (STS, 1888-95), ii, 383.
19 M. Lynch (ed.), *Mary Stewart: Queen in Three Kingdoms* (Oxford, 1988), 8-9, 105-06; D. McRoberts (ed.), *Essays on the Scottish Reformation* (Glasgow, 1962), 473-6; *Papal Negotiations with Mary Queen of Scots* (SHS, 1901), 525-30.
20 G. Donaldson, *The Scottish Reformation* (1960), 3, 6.
21 Dilworth, 'Commendator system', *IR* xxxvii (1986), 51-72.
22 Cowan, *Reformation*, 38-9, 44.
23 Ibid., 64-5, 103-4; Sanderson, 'Aspects', 88-9.
24 Donaldson, *Reformation*, 35; McRoberts (ed.), *Essays*, 352, 357.
25 Knox, *History*, i, 55; George Buchanan, *History of Scotland*, trans. J. Aikman (1827-30), ii, 301; D.H. Fleming, *The Reformation in Scotland* (London, 1910), 45.
26 McRoberts (ed.), *Essays*, 51.
27 Sanderson, *Cardinal*, 223-8.
28 Donaldson, *Reformation*, 34; McRoberts (ed.), *Essays*, 214, 285-6.
29 See e.g., M. Lee, *Great Britain's Solomon: James VI and I in his Three Kingdoms* (Chicago, 1990), 18-22. An exception, however, is Kirk, *Patterns*, pp. xv-xvi.
30 *CSP Scot.*, i, no. 516.
31 *Mary of Lorraine Corresp.* (SHS, 1927), 429.
32 J. Dawson, 'Two kingdoms or three?', in Mason (ed.), *Scotland and England*, 119.
33 J. Goodare, 'Parliament and society in Scotland, 1560-1603', (Edinburgh Univ. Ph.D., 1989), 480: other acts recorded elsewhere included a ratification of the right of the lairds to be present.
34 Macdougall, *James IV*, 17-18.
35 J.K. Cameron (ed.), *The First Book of Discipline* (1972), 9-14; M. Lynch, 'Calvinism in Scotland, 1559-1638', in M. Prestwich (ed.), *International Calvinism, 1541-1715* (Oxford, 1985), 228-9.
36 Kirk, *Patterns*, 130; Cowan, *Reformation*, 159, 162, 170.
37 Ibid., 173; Kirk, *Patterns*, 305, 332.
38 D.E. Meek and J. Kirk, 'John Carswell, superintendent of Argyll: a reassessment, *RSCHS* xix (1975), 1-22; Lynch, 'Calvinism', 242.
39 *Wodrow Misc.*, 396; Lynch, 'Calvinism', 247-9.
40 *Thirds of Benefices* (SHS, 1949), 150.
41 *First Book*, 105, 115; *BUK*, i, 109, 369
42 Ibid., i, 3, 13, 25.
43 Knox, *History*, ii, 29.
44 *BUK*, i, 94-5, 106-7, 121.
45 Cf. Donaldson, *Queen's Men*, 31-47.
46 Lynch, *Edinburgh*, 192; Lynch, 'Calvinism', 244, 248-9. The Church held the power of excommunication, but banishment rested with the civil magistrate: cf. Kirk, *Patterns*, 273.
47 M. Lee, *James Stewart, Earl of Moray* (New York, 1953), 219; Lynch, 'Calvinism', 244-5.
48 In September 1571, while Mar was Regent, the privy council appointed ministers as Archbishops of St Andrews and Glasgow without consulting the Kirk. They were nicknamed 'tulchans', after the stuffed calf-skin put beside a cow to induce her to give milk. The King's party took the opportunity to raid the revenues of the two sees. See 229, below.
49 *Wodrow Misc.*, 289.

13 The Reign of Mary, Queen of Scots

1 Sanderson, *Cardinal*, 155.
2 Ibid., 162, 165-6.
3 APS, ii, 415; Knox, *History*, i, 45; Lynch, *Edinburgh*, 82.
4 Sanderson, *Cardinal*, 173.
5 Steer and Bannerman, *Sculpture*, 212-13.
6 M.H. Merriman, 'The assured Scots: Scottish collaborators with England during the Rough Wooing', *SHR* xlvii (1968), 10-34.
7 Cf ibid., 33-4, and Donaldson, *Queen's Men*, 22-4.
8 *Exch. Rolls.*, vols. xvii, xviii.
9 Donaldson, *Queen's Men*, 21.
10 M. H. Merriman, 'Mary, Queen of France', in Lynch (ed.), *Mary Stewart*, 39; Baudouin-Matuszek, 'Henri II', 366.
11 Merriman, 'Queen of France', 39-40.
12 Donaldson, *Queen's Men*, 160.
13 M. Verschuur, 'Merchants and craftsmen in 16th-century Perth', in Lynch, *EMTS*, 45-8; also ibid., 60-1.
14 Knox, *History*, i, 322.
15 Donaldson, *Queen's Men*, 31-47.
16 I am grateful to Mark Loughlin for this point.
17 *SHR* ii (1905), 157-62.
18 M. Greengrass, 'Mary, Dowager Queen of France', in Lynch (ed.), *Mary Stewart*, 172-80; also ibid., 11.
19 I.B. Cowan, *Mary, Queen of Scots* (Saltire Soc., 1987), 8-9; *Papal Negotiations with Mary, Queen of Scots* (SHS, 1901), 94.
20 Cf Donaldson, *Scotland*, 110-13; Wormald, *Mary Queen of Scots*, 127.
21 Ibid., 129-47.
22 Donaldson, *Queen's Men*, 56, 77; Lynch, *Mary Stewart*, 9-10.
23 *Atlas*, 198-9. Fuller details are given in E. Furgol, 'The progresses of Mary, Queen of Scots, 1542-8 and 1561-8', *PSAS* cxvii (1987), 219-31.
24 Donaldson, *Scotland*, 113.
25 J. Goodare, 'Queen Mary's Catholic interlude', in Lynch (ed.), *Mary Stewart*, 157-9.
26 A.A. MacDonald, 'The Bannatyne Manuscript: a Marian anthology', *IR* xxxvii (1986), 36-47.
27 Lynch (ed.), *Mary Stewart*, 15-17.
28 *Cal. State Papers, Scot.*, ii, no. 168.
29 Lynch (ed.), *Mary Stewart*, 14, 164.
30 Ibid., 17-18, 165-6; Donaldson, *Queen's Men*, 79; Lynch, *Edinburgh*, 114-18.
31 J. Small, 'Queen Mary at Jedburgh in 1566', *PSAS* iii (1881), 210-33, at 228.
32 M. Lynch, 'Queen Mary's triumph: the baptismal celebrations at Stirling in December 1566', *SHR* lxix (1990), 1-21.
33 Patrick Adamson (later Archbishop of St Andrews), *Serenissimi ac Nobilissimi . . . Mariae Reginae* (Paris, 1566). The poem shows that Adamson was at the opposite end of the spectrum from Knox in his attitude to Mary, but also shows the extent of disagreement within the Church over the Queen. I am grateful to Mrs Evelyn Stalker for a translation of it.
34 Lynch, 'Mary's triumph', 17-20.
35 See 200, above.
36 D.H. Fleming, *Mary Queen of Scots* (London, 1897), 168-9, 474.
37 Donaldson, *Queen's Men*, 83-116; Lynch, *Edinburgh*, 146, 204; Lynch, *EMTS*, 84.
38 Lynch, *Edinburgh*, 316.
39 Ibid., 131-48.
40 See 201, above.
41 The act, which exists only in manuscript, is given in full in Goodare, 'Parliament', 486-7.
42 Lee, *Solomon*, 65.
43 Lynch, *Edinburgh*, 117, 183-4.
44 Donaldson, *Queen's Men*, 117, 149.

14 The Reign of James VI

1 Lee, *Solomon*, 113-14, 313.
2 K. Brown, 'The price of friendship: the "well affected" and English economic clientage in Scotland

before 1603', in Mason (ed.), *Scotland and England*, 154; Goodare, 'Parliament', 188.

3 Lynch, *Edinburgh*, 154.

4 Wormald, *Scotland*, 166; *Exch. Rolls*, vols. xx-xxiii; Lynch, *EMTS*, 73.

5 The taxes are listed in J. Goodare, 'Parliamentary taxation in Scotland, 1560-1603', *SHR* lxviii (1989), 48-52. Also Wormald, *Scotland*, 161; Lynch, *EMTS*, 73.

6 John Spottiswoode, *History of the Church of Scotland*, 3 vols. (Spot. Soc., 1847-51), ii, 308-9.

7 Melville, *Diary*, 370-1.

8 W.R. Foster, *The Church before the Covenants* (1975), 15; Goodare, 'Parliament', 123-4; M. Lynch, 'The origins of Edinburgh's "toun college"', *IR* xxxiii (1982), 3-14.

9 Cowan, *Scottish Reformation*, 122-3.

10 Calderwood, *History*, iii, 347; M. Dilworth, 'Monks and ministers after 1560', *RSCHS* xviii (1974), 216-20.

11 J. Kirk (ed.), *The Second Book of Discipline* (1980), 102.

12 *BUK*, ii, 469-70; 482ff.

13 *Historie of King James the Sext* (Bann. Club, 1825), 186-7.

14 Calderwood, *History*, viii, 226.

15 Lynch, 'Calvinism', 250-3; D. Stevenson, 'The General Assembly and the Commission of the Kirk', 1638-51', *RSCHS* xix (1975), 63, 75-9.

16 Goodare, 'Parliament', 17; Melville, *Diary*, 440; M. Lee, 'James VI and the revival of episcopacy in Scotland, 1596-1600', *Church History*, xliii (1974), 50-64.

17 Donaldson, *Queen's Men*, 140-3.

18 Cf Donaldson, *Scotland*, 181; Lynch, *EMTS*, 58.

19 Lee, *Solomon*, 74-6.

20 Ibid., 76-7.

21 Ibid., 77, 134-6; *Reg. Privy. Co.*, v, 254-8, 757-61; Goodare, 'Parliament', 161, 168, 178, 186, 459-60.

22 Lee, *Solomon*, 105. Cf also R. Mitchison, *Lordship to Patronage: Scotland 1603-1745* (London, 1983), 21.

23 Goodare, 'Parliamentary taxation', 37.

24 Wormald, *Lords and Men*, 157-67; K. Brown, *Bloodfeud in Scotland, 1573-1625* (1986), 268-72.

25 Ibid., 217-18; Goodare, 'Parliament', 22, 29, 111.

26 The substance of the argument here, though phrased somewhat differently, depends on the important insights in the work of Julian Goodare; see 'Parliament', esp. chs. 1, 2.

27 A list of parliaments and conventions 1560-1603 is given in Goodare, 'Parliament', appendix 1.

28 Goodare, 'Parliament', 37, 62; Lynch, *EMTS*, 65-6.

29 Goodare, 'Parliamentary taxation', 45-7; D. Stevenson, 'The burghs and the Scottish Revolution', in Lynch, *EMTS*, 176; also ibid., 70, 73.

30 J. Craigie (ed.), *Basilikon Doron of King James VI* (STS, 1944-50), i, 115, 117. See J. M. Brown (Wormald), 'Scottish politics 1567-1625', in A.R. Smith (ed.), *The Reign of James VI and I* (London, 1973), 22-39.

31 K. Brown, 'Noble indebtedness in Scotland between the Reformation and the revolution', *Bull. Inst. Hist. Research*, lxii (1989), 260-75.

32 Lee, *Solomon*, 153; A.H. Williamson, *Scottish National Consciousness in the Age of James VI* (1979), 39-44; B. Galloway, *The Union of England and Scotland, 1603-1608* (1986), 33-4.

33 Ibid., 16, 82, 166.

34 J. Wormald, 'The first King of Britain', in L. Smith (ed.), *The Making of Britain: The Age of Expansion* (London, 1986), 45; also Galloway, *Union*, 172.

35 K. Brown, 'Playing second fiddle? The nobility and the regal union' (Assoc. Scot. Hist. Studs., 1989), 17, 19.

36 Galloway, *Union*, 182-4.

37 M. Lee, *Government by Pen: Scotland under James VI and I* (Chicago, 1980), 163-70. A protest letter from fifty-five mostly moderate ministers is printed in *Original Letters relating to Ecclesiastical Affairs of Scotland* (Bann. Club, 1851), ii, 501-4.

38 *Reg. Privy Co.*, vii, 536.

39 Brown, 'Playing second fiddle', 27.

40 C.H. McIlwain (ed.), *Political Works of James I* (Cambridge, Mass., 1918), 301.

41 Lee, *Government by Pen*, 39-42.

42 See ibid., 218.

43 *Poems of Alexander Montgomerie* (STS, 1887), 280-1.

44 E.g., *The Jacobean Union* (SHS, 1985), p. xlviii.

45 *Basilikon Doron*, 71.

46 D. Gregory, *A History of the Western Highlands and Isles to 1625* (2nd edn., 1881), 261-70, 278-82,

290-3, 315-16, 319; Lee, *Solomon*, 213-17; Wormald, *Scotland*, 164-5.
47 *Scot. Hist. Docs..*, 171-5; Lee, *Solomon*, 215-18; D. Stevenson, *Alasdair MacColla and the Highland Problem in the Seventeenth Century* (1980), 27-31.
48 *Orig. Letters*, ii, 670ff; Calderwood, *History*, vii, 547; Makey, *Church*, 157-8; Lynch, *EMTS*, 71.
49 Lee, *Solomon*, 179, 181. It is also argued in D. Stevenson, *The Scottish Revolution 1637-1644* (Newton Abbot, 1973), 24, that 'little attempt' was made to enforce the Articles and that James had 'the sense to turn back'. The significance and scale of the dissent is analysed differently in Donaldson, *Scotland*, 210-11.
50 *Historical Works of Sir James Balfour* (1824-5), iii, 426-7.
51 Williamson, *National Consciousness*, 21-30, 89.
52 M. Flinn (ed.), *Scottish Population History* (Cambridge, 1977), 115-17; *Chronicle of Perth* (Maitland Club, 1831), 24.
53 G. Donaldson, 'James VI and vanishing frontiers', in G. Menzies (ed.), *The Scottish Nation* (London, 1972), 112-14.
54 Goodare, 'Parliament', 112; Lynch, *EMTS*, 73, 176.

IV THE CRISIS OF THE THREE KINGDOMS

15 The Rise of the Middling Sort

1 Makey, *Church*, 1-2.
2 G.W.T. Omond, *The Lord Advocates of Scotland* (1883), ii, 102; *Reg. Privy Co.*, 1625-7, 230-32.
3 Foster, *Church before the Covenants*, 167; Makey, *Church*, 106; Brown, 'Aristocratic finances', 51.
4 Balfour, *Works*, i, 205-6.
5 Stevenson, *Scottish Revolution*, 224; Brown, 'Aristocratic finances', 68.
6 D. Stevenson (ed.), *The Government of Scotland under the Covenanters, 1637-1651* (SHS, 1982), pp. xiv-xvii.
7 R. Marshall, *The Days of Duchess Anne* (London, 1973); Brown, 'Noble indebtedness', 260, 271-2.
8 *The Black Book of Taymouth* (Bann. Club, 1855), 398; E.M. Furgol, *A Regimental History of the Covenanting Armies, 1639-1651* (1990), 4-5, 41.
9 Foster, *Church*, ch.5; K. Brown, 'In search of the godly magistrate in Reformation Scotland', *J. of Ecc. Hist.*, xl (1989), 579-81; Lynch, 'Calvinism', 246-7.
10 *Sermons of Robert Bruce* (Wodrow Soc., 1843), 66, 154.
11 *Letters of Samuel Rutherford*, ed. A.A. Bonar (1891), 519-21.
12 *Letters of Robert Baillie* (Bann. Club, 1841-2), i, 123-4; Makey, *Church*, 131.
13 Rutherford, *Letters*, 650; Furgol, *Regimental History*, 296ff; D. Stevenson, *Revolution and Counter-Revolution in Scotland, 1644-1651* (London, 1977), 133-9; Makey, *Church*, 136.
14 Alexander Shields, *A Hind let loose* (Utrecht, 1687).
15 Partly cited in *CSP, Foreign, Eliz.*, 23 Nov 1572.
16 Furgol, *Regimental History*, 124, 126, 170.
17 Stevenson, *Government*, p. xvii.
18 Goodare, 'Parliament', 62; Stevenson, *Scottish Revolution*, 139, 219-20. I am grateful to Julian Goodare for advice on these points.
19 Stevenson, *Government*, pp. xxii-xxiii; xxviii.
20 Goodare, 'Parliament', 149; Larner, *Enemies of God*, 35-7.
21 Stevenson, *Government*, pp. xviii, xxvi-xxvii; Makey, *Church*, 23, 56-7.
22 *Ibid.*, 11; Mitchison, *Lordship to Patronage*, 67.
23 Lynch, *Edinburgh*, 373-7; Dingwall, 'Edinburgh', 380, 428.
24 Brown, 'Aristocratic finances', 65.
25 M. Sanderson, *Mary Stewart's People* (1987), 22-33; J. di Folco, 'The Hopes of Craighall and land investment in the 17th century', in T.M. Devine (ed.), *Lairds and Improvement* (1978), 1-10; Stevenson, *Scottish Revolution*, 366n; Stevenson, *Government*, 58, 193, 104. G. Seton (ed.), *Memoirs of Alexander Seton, Earl of Dunfermline* (1882), appendix ii, prints the Hope family tree.
26 Makey, *Church*, 94-105; I. Rae, 'The origins of the Advocates' Library', in P. Cadell and A. Matheson (eds.), *For the Encouragement of Learning* (1989), 3-8.
27 Ministers were variously paid. Those who had inherited benefices paid tax, like other benefice-holders. Those paid by other means generally escaped taxation. Goodare, 'Parliamentary taxation', 31-2.
28 Lynch, 'Calvinism', 251-3; R. Mitchison, 'The social impact of the clergy of the reformed Kirk of Scotland', *Scotia*, vi (1982), 1-13.
29 *Diary of Sir Archibald Johnston of Wariston, 1632-1639* (SHS, 1911), 321-2.

30 See e.g. R. Jack (ed.), *The History of Scottish Literature*, i (Aberdeen, 1988), 183-4.
31 C. McKean, *The Architecture of the Scottish Renaissance* (1990). *Memoirs of Seton*, 171-2; Meikle, 'Lairds and gentlemen', 267-9.
32 W.H. Makey, 'Edinburgh in mid-17th century', in Lynch, *EMTS*, 206-7.
33 H.G. Aldis (ed.), *A List of Books printed in Scotland before 1700* (1970) lists books year by year; thirty booksellers' inventories dating between 1579 and 1717 are printed in *Bann. Misc.*, ii, 191-296.
34 For details of Mrs Anderson, the printer, see *Reg. Privy Co.* (3rd series), vii, 257. I am indebted to Julian Goodare for this reference.
35 See R.A. Houston, *Scottish Literacy and the Scottish Identity* (Cambridge, 1985).
36 J. Durkan, 'Education: the laying of fresh foundations', 129-30; D. Withrington, 'Lists of schoolmasters teaching Latin, 1690', *SHS Misc.*, x (1965), 119-42.
37 MacQueen, *Humanism*, 180; Rae, 'Advocates' Library', 15.
38 Jack (ed.), *Scottish Literature*, 37; J. M. Sanderson, 'Two Stewarts of the sixteenth century', *The Stewarts*, xvii (1984), 38; Rae, 'Advocates' Library', 11, 13, 25.
39 *Black Book of Taymouth*, 350.
40 Sanderson, 'Two Stewarts', 25; *Memoirs of Seton*, 174.
41 H. Ouston, 'York in Edinburgh: James VII and the patronage of learning in Scotland, 1679-1688', in J. Dwyer, R. Mason and A. Murdoch (eds.), *New Perspectives on the Politics and Culture of Early Modern Scotland* (1982), esp. 133-7.
42 Donaldson, *Scotland*, 394-5; H. Meikle, *Some Aspects of Later Seventeenth Century Scotland* (Glasgow, 1947); A. Hook (ed.), *History of Scottish Literature*, ii (Aberdeen, 1987), 12-14.

16 Revolution and War

1 See 249-53, above, for a social analysis of the Tables.
2 Balfour, *Works*, ii, 240-46; John Leslie, Earl of Rothes, *Proceedings concerning the Affairs of the Kirk of Scotland* (Bann. Club, 1830), 56.
3 Both are conveniently printed in *Scot. Hist. Docs.*, 150-3, 194-201.
4 See R. Mason, *The Glasgow Assembly 1638* (Glasgow Cathedral Lecture Series, 1988), 9; Donaldson, *Scotland*, 313-14.
5 The phrase used in the Glasgow Assembly in the motion to abolish episcopacy: *Records of the Kirk of Scotland*, ed. A. Peterkin (1838), 168.
6 Quoted in Stevenson, *Scottish Revolution*, 122.
7 *Diary of Sir Archibald Johnston of Wariston, 1632-1639* (SHS, 1911), 322, 347-8, 401.
8 Rutherford, *Letters*, 60; *Orig. Letters*, i, 445; D.G. Mullan, *Episcopacy in Scotland, 1560-1638* (1986), 175-7.
9 Balfour, *Works*, ii, 156; A.I. Macinnes, *Charles I and the Making of the Covenanting Movement, 1625-1641* (1991), 56-72.
10 Stevenson, *Scottish Revolution*, 51; Stevenson, 'Burghs and the Scottish Revolution', in Lynch, *EMTS*, 176-7.
11 Ibid., 177; Balfour, *Works*, ii, 200.
12 Ibid., ii, 128, 199; cf M. Lee, *The Road to Revolution: Scotland under Charles I, 1625-37* (Chicago, 1985), 68-9.
13 Wormald, 'First king of Britain', 45.
14 Quoted in C. Russell, *The Crisis of Parliaments: English History, 1509-1660* (London, 1971), 299; Foster, *Modern Ireland*, 57.
15 Lee, *Road to Revolution*, 160.
16 Ibid., chs. 3, 5, and pp. 241-2.
17 It was striking that it was the Scots who pressed hardest in 1641 for Strafford's execution: C. Russell, 'The British problem and the English Civil War', *History*, lxxii (1987), 407-08.
18 Quoted in N.Tyacke, *Anti-Calvinists: The Rise of English Arminianism, c.1590-1640* (1987), 247; Mullan, *Episcopacy*, 175.
19 Ibid., 170; Russell, 'British problem', esp. 395-401.
20 B.P. Levack, *The Formation of the British State: England, Scotland and the Union, 1603-1707* (Oxford, 1987), 34, 61; Lee, *Road to Revolution*, 105.
21 Russell, 'British problem', 401; *Orig. Letters*, i, 295.
22 Calderwood, *History*, vii, 335; Mullan, *Episcopacy*, 174, 335.
23 Baillie, *Letters*, i, 439; Tyacke, *Anti-Calvinists*, 238-43; Levack, *British State*, 127.
24 John Row, *History of the Kirk of Scotland* (Wodrow Soc., 1842), 368. But radicals, like Calderwood, had identified the Archbishop of Canterbury as a 'vice-pope' under an absolutist prince as early as 1621: see Mullan, *Episcopacy*, 161.

25 Stevenson, *Scottish Revolution*, 16.
26 Cf Russell, 'British problem', 397.
27 Stevenson, *Scottish Revolution*, 147.
28 Furgol, *Regimental History*, 2.
29 E.J.Cowan, *Montrose: For Covenant and King* (London, 1977), 73.
30 Furgol, *Regimental History*, 16.
31 See 256, above.
32 W. Ferguson, *Scotland's Relations with England: a Survey to 1707* (1977), 118.
33 Makey, *Church*, 57.
34 Ibid., 64-5; *Orig. Letters*, i, 305-6; Stevenson, *Scottish Revolution*, 221.
35 D. Stevenson, *Scottish Covenanters and Irish Confederates: Scottish-Irish Relations in the Mid-Seventeenth Century* (Belfast, 1981), 233-8.
36 Cowan, *Montrose*, 160.
37 Baillie, *Letters*, ii, 304, 313-14.
38 M. Napier (ed.), *Memorials of Montrose and his Times* (Maitland Club, 1850), ii, 146-7.
39 Quoted in R. Ashton, *The English Civil War: Conservatism and Revolution, 1603-1649* (London, 1978), 253.
40 Ibid., 289-90.
41 D. Stevenson, *Revolution and Counter-Revolution*, 120; Donaldson, *Scotland*, 337.
42 Baillie, *Letters*, iii, 35; Makey, *Church*, 73-4.
43 Ibid., 91, 104, 177-8; D. Stevenson, 'The radical party in the kirk, 1637-45', *J. Ecc. Hist.*, xxv (1974), 150-5.
44 Stevenson, *Revolution and Counter-Revolution*, 151; Stevenson, 'Burghs', 185-6.
45 Stevenson, *Revolution and Counter-Revolution*, 139-44; Makey, *Church*, 78-80; Larner, *Enemies of God*, 74.
46 Stevenson, *Revolution and Counter-Revolution*, 175.
47 Stevenson, 'Burghs', 181, 182; also ibid., 18; Flinn, *Scottish Population History*, 133-49.
48 Wariston, *Diary*, 410.
49 James Kirkton, *Secret and True History of the Church of Scotland*, ed. C.K. Sharpe (1817), 2.

17 The Making and Unmaking of the Restoration Regime

1 L.M. Smith, 'Scotland and Cromwell: a study in early modern government' (Oxford D.Phil., 1979), 23-4; Stevenson, *Revolution and Counter-Revolution*, 195-6, 197.
2 W.L. Mathieson, *Politics and Religion* 2 vols. (Glasgow, 1902), ii, 136-8.
3 Balfour, *Works*, iv, 315.
4 *Scotland and the Commonwealth, 1651-53* (SHS, 1895), 10, 14, 343-4; F.D. Dow, *Cromwellian Scotland* (1979), 18.
5 *The Cromwellian Union, 1651-52* (SHS, 1902), pp. xvii, 178; J. Nicoll, *A Diary of Public Transactions* (Bann. Club, 1836), 79-81.
6 Galloway, *Union*, 85. I am grateful to Charles Burnett, Dingwall Pursuivant of Arms, for advice on these points. The inescutcheon containing the Irish harp in the revised Cromwellian union flag showed greater ambiguity still as to its position in the Commonwealth.
7 *Scotland and the Protectorate, 1654-59* (SHS, 1899), pp. xxxviii-li; Smith, 'Scotland', 2.
8 Ibid., 251; *Protectorate*, pp. lv-lvi.
9 Ibid., 89; Stevenson, *MacColla*, 273; Dow, *Scotland*, 87-98.
10 *Protectorate*, pp. xxvi, 201n; *Commonwealth*, 361.
11 I. Roots (ed.), *Into Another Mould: Aspects of the Interregnum* (London, 1981), 16-17; Dow, *Scotland*, 165-94.
12 Dow, *Scotland*, 162-4; Smith, 'Scotland', 181-2, 216; Larner, *Enemies of God*, 75-6.
13 Baillie, *Letters*, iii, 387.
14 Dow, *Scotland*, 237-40; Roots, *Aspects*, 11.
15 R. Hutton, *Charles II* (Oxford, 1989), 136; J. Buckroyd, *Church and State in Scotland, 1660-1681* (1980), 26.
16 Dow, *Scotland*, 269.
17 Buckroyd, *Church and State*, 22-40.
18 Ferguson, *Scotland's Relations*, 144, 147-8.
19 Hutton, *Charles II*, 141.
20 Ibid., 160-61, 179.
21 Buckroyd, *Church and State*, 41-56.
22 Nicoll, *Diary*, 319-20; Hutton, *Charles II*, 162-3.

23 Ibid., 161.
24 Wariston would follow, after extradition from France, in July 1663.
25 Cf Hutton, *Charles II*, 179, 487n; Buckroyd, *Church and State*, 39-40.
26 APS, vii, 87-8.
27 I.B. Cowan, *The Scottish Covenanters, 1660-1688* (1976), 50-2.
28 Hutton, *Charles II*, 183; cf. Donaldson, *Scotland*, 366.
29 *Chronicles of the Frasers* (SHS, 1905), 476.
30 See 249, above.
31 P. Hopkins, *Glencoe and the End of the Highland War* (1986), 27.
32 Ibid., 41, 46; Stevenson, *MacColla*, 280.
33 Marshall, *Duchess Anne*, 189-91.
34 See Hutton, *Charles II*, 205-6, 246, 309, 322, 349.
35 Ibid., 227. The site for a new state prison to house Covenanters was the Bass Rock, an island only a mile in circumference rising 350 feet out of the sea, off North Berwick. The deciding factor was probably the financial stake Lauderdale held in it: A. Lang, *Sir George Mackenzie of Rosehaugh* (London, 1909), 101.
36 Hopkins, *Glencoe*, 61; Hutton, *Charles II*, 322.
37 Hopkins, *Glencoe*, 39; Ferguson, *Scotland's Relations*, 157-8.
38 Quoted in Hutton, *Charles II*, 349.
39 Mitchison, *Lordship to Patronage*, 73-4.
40 J.K. Hewison, *The Covenanters* 2 vols. (Glasgow, 1913), ii, 218.
41 Donaldson, *Scotland*, 369.
42 Hutton, *Charles II*, 267, 274, 326.
43 Cowan, *Covenanters*, 82-7.
44 Hopkins, *Glencoe*, 62-3; Stevenson, *MacColla*, 284-5.
45 J. Buckroyd, *The Life of James Sharp, 1618-1679* (1987), 106-9.
46 Cowan, *Covenanters*, 97-8; Hewison, *Covenanters*, ii, 343.
47 Larner, *Enemies of God*, 76; Hutton, *Charles II*, 457.
48 James, Duke of Atholl, *Chronicles of the Atholl and Tulibardine Families* 5 vols. (1908), i, 219-20.
49 W. Ferguson, *Scotland: 1689 to the Present* (1968), 143.
50 Quoted in Hutton, *Charles II*, 387.
51 Ferguson, *Scotland's Relations*, 160.
52 Ibid., 161-2; Hutton, *Charles II*, 430-1.
53 Hopkins, *Glencoe*, 92-4; Stevenson, *MacColla*, 291.
54 Ibid., 293; Hopkins, *Glencoe*, 95.
55 A. Lang, *Sir George Mackenzie* (1909), 45.
56 Meikle, *Later Seventeenth Century Scotland*, 29.
57 Ouston, 'York in Edinburgh', 133-7; see also 257-62, above.
58 Donaldson, *Scotland*, 400.
59 Smout, *History*, 179-81.
60 Houston and Whyte (eds.), *Scottish Society*, 18.
61 Stevenson, *MacColla*, 294-5.

18 Union

1 B. Lenman, *The Jacobite Risings in Britain, 1689-1746* (London, 1980), 42; Hopkins, *Glencoe*, 122, 124.
2 Ibid., 123-4; Lenman, *Jacobite Risings*, 37.
3 Hopkins, *Glencoe*, 157-60.
4 Quoted in ibid., 184. The 'oracle' was Alexander Shields, Cameronian propagandist and author of *A Hind let loose* (1687); see 251-2, above.
5 The texts of both are printed in *Source Book*, iii, 200-08.
6 Ibid., iii, 208-9.
7 J. Halliday, 'The Club and the Revolution in Scotland, 1689-90', SHR xlv (1966), 143-59.
8 Hopkins, *Glencoe*, 208-9, 220-21; P. Riley, *King William and the Scottish Politicians* (1979), 39-41.
9 Cowan, *Scottish Covenanters*, 137-40.
10 T.C. Smout, 'The road to union', in G. Holmes (ed.), *Britain after the Glorious Revolution, 1689-1714* (London, 1969), 176-96.
11 Ferguson, *Scotland's Relations*, 244.
12 Hopkins, *Glencoe*, 337.
13 Ibid., 234-5.

14 Riley, *King William*, 96; B. Lenman, *The Jacobite Clans of the Great Glen, 1650-1784* (London, 1984), 55.

15 The rebuilding in stone of Fort William, on the foundations of the Cromwellian fortification of Inverlochy, began in 1698. Unlike Fort Augustus and Fort George, it withstood Jacobite siege in 1745.

16 Lenman, *Jacobite Clans*, 53-4; Hopkins, *Glencoe*, 489, 491.

17 *Papers illustrative of the Political Condition of the Highlands of Scotland, 1689-1696* (Maitland Club, 1845), 53.

18 Ferguson, *Scotland*, 22.

19 Hopkins, *Glencoe*, 335; J. Prebble, *Glencoe: the Story of the Massacre* (London, 1966), 227-8.

20 Hopkins, *Glencoe*, 493.

21 Marshall, *Presbyteries and Profits*, 130-9; *Source Book*, iii, 338.

22 Riley, *King William*, 97-8.

23 *A Letter from a Gentleman in the Country to his Friend at Edinburgh* (Edinburgh, 1696), 11.

24 Marshall, *Presbyteries and Profits*, 201-4.

25 Mitchison, *Lordship to Patronage*, 109-10.

26 T.M. Devine, 'The Union of 1707 and Scottish development', *SESH* v (1985), 25-7.

27 The exceptions were the Jacobite 'Cavaliers', who returned in numbers in the election of 1703 to swell the ranks of the opposition, and the 'New party', later to be called the *Squadrone Volante*, usually a semi-detached element of the court.

28 Riley, *King William*, 134; P.W.J. Riley, *The Union of England and Scotland* (Manchester, 1978), 282-4.

29 Daniel Defoe, *Union and No Union* (London, 1713), 4.

30 Sophia's son, George, would eventually succeed in 1714 despite fifty-eight better claimants, even if many were female. All, of course, were Catholics.

31 C.A. Whatley, 'Economic causes and consequences of the Union of 1707: a survey', *SHR* lxviii (1989), 154; Ferguson, *Scotland's Relations*, 202.

32 Ibid., 217.

33 *Letters relating to Scotland . . . by 1st Earl of Seafield* (SHS, 1915), 84-5.

34 George Lockhart of Carnwath, *Memoirs* (London, 1817), 172.

35 Lenman, *Jacobite Risings*, 82-3; P.H. Scott, *1707: The Union of Scotland and England* (1979), 35-8.

36 'Sir John Clerk's observations on the present circumstances in Scotland, 1730', *SHS Misc.*, x (1965), 192.

37 The figures in the first vote, on 4 Nov. 1706, and the last on 16 Jan. 1707, to ratify the Treaty (in brackets), were as follows. Approvers – 46 (42) Nobles; 37 (38) Barons; 33 (30) Burghs. Noes – 21 (19) Nobles; 33 (30) Barons; 29 (20) Burghs.

38 Individual and party voting patterns are given in Riley, *Union*, 326-36.

39 Whatley, 'Causes and consequences', 159-60.

40 Cf the general argument in Mitchison, *Lordship to Patronage*, esp. 136, 162-3, 175

41 Smout, *Scottish Trade*, 238, 255.

42 Whatley, 'Causes and consequences', 160-2.

43 *Correspondence of George Baillie of Jerviswood, 1702-1708* (Bann. Club, 1842), 138. Cf the passages cited in Whatley, 'Causes and consequences', 153; Riley, *Union*, 216; and the fuller extract in Scott, *1707*, 27.

44 Roxburgh was *wrong* in thinking that the burghs would be 'all for it'. Only nineteen votes were cast against the main Article (IV) on free trade, but on the general principle of the Union the burghs were evenly split. Edinburgh's two members voted in different directions and Glasgow's one voted against, despite being a member of the Court party: Riley, *Union*, 331-4.

45 'Clerk's observations', 191.

46 W. Ferguson, 'Imperial crowns: a neglected facet of the background to the Treaty of Union of 1707', *SHR* liii (1974), 22-44.

47 Lenman, *Jacobite Clans*, 68.

48 For the union negotiations of 1668 and 1670, see *Cromwellian Union*, 187-224, and Ferguson, *Scotland's Relations*, 154-6.

49 T.C. Smout, 'The burgh of Montrose and the Union of 1707 – a document', *SHR* lxvi (1987), 184.

50 Smout, *History*, 215.

51 Levack, *British State*, 138.

52 E.J. Cowan, 'The union of the crowns and the crisis of the constitution in 17th century Scotland', in S. Dyrvik (ed.), *The Satellite State in the 17th and 18th Centuries* (Bergen, 1979), 131.

19 Union Settlement and Jacobite Risings

1 Cf Riley, *Union*, 317.
2 J.S. Gibson, *Playing the Scottish Card: the Franco-Jacobite Invasion of 1708* (1988), 81-90.
3 Ibid., 93-131.
4 P.W.J. Riley, *The English Ministers and Scotland, 1707-1727* (London, 1964), 92; R. Mitchison, 'The government and the Highlands, 1707-1745', in N.T. Phillipson and R. Mitchison (eds.), *Scotland in the Age of Improvement* (1970), 27.
5 Riley, *English Ministers*, 92-5.
6 Ibid., 29, 117-18; J.S. Shaw, *The Management of Scottish Society, 1707-1764* (1983), 42, 48; A. Murdoch, *The People Above: Politics and Administration in Mid-Eighteenth Century Scotland* (1980), 4-5, 29; J. Simpson, 'Who steered the gravy train, 1707-1766?', in Phillipson and Mitchison (eds.), *Age of Improvement*, 50-2.
7 Riley, *English Ministers*, 103, 119-20.
8 Murdoch, *People Above*, 29; A. Murray, 'Administration and the law', in T.I. Rae (ed.), *The Union of 1707: its Impact on Scotland* (Glasgow, 1974), 44-6, 47.
9 Lenman, *Jacobite Risings*, 103.
10 Shaw, *Management*, 99; R. Sher and A. Murdoch, 'Patronage and principle in the Church of Scotland, 1750-1800', in Macdougall (ed.), *Church, Politics and Society*, 205, 214.
11 D.C. Lachman, *The Marrow Controversy, 1718-1723* (1988), esp. ch. 3.
12 Shaw, *Management*, 99-100, 105; Sher and Murdoch, 'Patronage', 208; Ferguson, *Scotland*, 122-4.
13 The point was not settled until 1782, when the decision was reversed.
14 *HMC Mar and Kellie* (London, 1904), i, 490.
15 Riley, *English Ministers*, 243.
16 Whatley, 'Causes and consequences', 181.
17 J.M. Price, 'Glasgow, the tobacco trade and the Scottish customs, 1707-1730', *SHR* lxii (1984), 1-36.
18 Devine, 'Union of 1707', 26.
19 A. Durie, *The Scottish Linen Industry in the Eighteenth Century* (1979), 9-11.
20 C. Whatley, *Salt Industry*, 30-32; Durie, *Linen Industry*, 11; Devine, 'Union of 1707', 29; Whatley, 'Causes and consequences', 174, 169.
21 See below, 344.
22 Murdoch, *People Above*, 15-22.
23 Simpson, 'Gravy train', 65; Shaw, *Management*, 43-4, 67.
24 Lenman, *Jacobite Risings*, 206-10.
25 Shaw, *Management*, 126-8.
26 See Murdoch, *People Above*, 6-7.
27 Ibid., 27.
28 Riley, *English Ministers*, 230-55.
29 Ibid., 253-62.
30 See G. Menary, *The Life and Letters of Duncan Forbes of Culloden* (London, 1936), 21.
31 K.A. Moody-Stuart, 'Lieutenant-Colonel James Stewart: a Jacobite Lieutenant-Governor of Edinburgh Castle', *SHR* xxi (1923), 12.
32 E.K. Carmichael, 'Jacobitism in the Scottish Commission of the Peace, 1707-1760', *SHR* lviii (1979), 60-1.
33 Quoted in Riley, *English Ministers*, 155.
34 Lenman, *Jacobite Risings*, 134-6; idem, *Jacobite Clans*, 82-4.
35 Ibid., 87; F. McLynn, *The Jacobites* (London, 1985), 65-8.
36 Lenman, *Jacobite Risings*, 129-38, 150.
37 See ibid., 128-30.
38 Mclynn, *Jacobites*, 31-3.
39 Quoted in E. Gregg, 'The politics of paranoia', in E. Cruickshanks and J. Black (eds.), *The Jacobite Challenge* (1988), 43.
40 Ibid., 42.
41 Ibid., 51; McLynn, *Jacobites*, 201-3.
42 M. Steele, 'Anti-Jacobite pamphleteering, 1701-1720', *SHR* lx (1981), 151-4.
43 Lenman, *Jacobite Risings*, 186-8.
44 *The Jacobite Attempt of 1719* (SHS, 1895), 269-73.
45 Lenman, *Jacobite Clans*, 89; Mitchison, 'Government and Highlands', 31-4; Lenman, *Jacobite Risings*, 177-9.
46 See eg Mitchison, 'Government and Highlands', 32-4.
47 Lenman, *Jacobite Clans*, 73, 107, 171.

48 Quoted in ibid., 152.
49 F. McLynn, *France and the Jacobite Rising of 1745* (1981), 97.
50 Ibid., 24, 129, also chs. 5-7.
51 McLynn, *France*, 29, 31-2.
52 Cf ibid., 2, 32-4; Lenman, *Jacobite Risings*, 242-3.
53 Ibid., 246.
54 J. Gilhooley, 'The Edinburgh Local Defence Volunteers of 1745', *Edinburgh History Magazine*, i (1989), 4-7.
55 McLynn, *Jacobites*, 122.
56 F. McLynn, *The Jacobite Army in England, 1745* (1983), 8-13.
57 Ibid., 126, 130-1.
58 Ibid., 197.
59 See Introduction to *The Lyon in Mourning*, 3 vols. (SHS, 1895-6), i, pp. xi-xxii.
60 McLynn, *Jacobites*, 118; Lenman, *Jacobite Clans*, 162.
61 J.S. Gibson, '"The summer's hunting": the historiography of Charles Edward's escape', in L. Scott-Moncrieff (ed.), *The '45: To Gather an Image Whole* (1988), 140-55.
62 Ferguson, *Scotland*, 153.
63 Lenman, *Jacobite Risings*, 245-6; see E. Cregeen, 'The changing role of the house of Argyll', in Phillipson and Mitchison (eds.), *Age of Improvement*, 5-23.
64 Even the Catholic Mission did not escape pro- and anti-Argyll factions. Their existing quarrels were sharpened by the ambition for office of Colin Campbell, a convert and kinsman of the Duke of Argyll. See below, 366.
65 Ferguson, *Scotland*, 154-6; A. Smith, *Jacobite Estates of the Forty-Five* (1982), 1-18.

V THE MOULDING OF MODERN SCOTLAND

20 North Britain, Caledonia and Greater Britain

1 I. Ross and S. Scobie, 'Patriotic publishing as a response to the Union', in Rae (ed.), *Union of 1707*, 94-119.
2 I.G. Brown, 'Modern Rome and ancient Caledonia: the Union and the politics of Scottish culture', in Hook (ed.), *History of Scottish Literature*, 33-48; J. Robertson, *The Scottish Enlightenment and the Militia Issue* (1985), 44-6.
3 J.Y.T. Greig (ed.), *The Letters of David Hume* (Oxford, 1932), ii, 230.
4 See D. Daiches, *The Paradox of Scottish Culture: the Eighteenth Century Experience* (London, 1964); cf. A. Murdoch and R.B. Sher, 'Literary and learned culture', in T.M. Devine and R. Mitchison (eds.), *People and Society in Scotland, vol. i, 1760-1830* (1988), 127-42.
5 G. Newman, *The Rise of English Nationalism, 1740-1830* (London, 1987), 48, 116-18; H.M. Atherton, *Political Prints in the Age of Hogarth* (Oxford, 1974), 84-5, 216.
6 Robertson, *Militia Issue*, esp. 159-99; N.T. Phillipson, 'Scottish public opinion and the Union in the age of the Association', in Phillipson and Mitchison (eds.), *Age of Improvement*, 125-47; J. Dwyer and A. Murdoch, 'Paradigms and politics: manners, morals and the rise of Henry Dundas, 1770-84', in Dwyer (ed.), *New Perspectives*, 230-7.
7 Dwyer and Murdoch, 'Rise of Dundas', 214. Cf J.H. Plumb, *The Growth of Political Stability in England, 1675-1725* (London, 1967).
8 T.C. Smout, 'Where had the Scottish economy got to by the third quarter of the 18th century?' (hereafter '1776'), in I. Hont and M. Ignatieff (eds.), *Wealth and Virtue: The Shaping of Political Economy in the Scottish Enlightenment* (Cambridge, 1982), 45-72.
9 R.F Teichgraeber, 'Politics and Morals in the Scottish Enlightenment' (University of Brandeis Ph.D., 1978), 47-8, 80-134; T.D. Campbell, 'Francis Hutcheson: "father" of the Scottish Enlightenment', in R.H. Campbell and A.S. Skinner (eds.), *The Origins and Nature of the Scottish Enlightenment* (1982), 167-85.
10 D. Duncan, *Thomas Ruddiman* (1965), 85.
11 J. Rendall, *The Origins of the Scottish Enlightenment* (London, 1978), 22-4; D. Duncan, 'Scholarship and politeness in the early eighteenth century', in Hook (ed.), *History of Scottish Literature*, 58-60.
12 W.J. Couper, *The Edinburgh Periodical Press* (Stirling, 1908), 45.
13 See N.T. Phillipson, *Hume* (London, 1989).
14 For Hume, see also D. Daiches, P. & J. Jones (eds.), *A Hotbed of Genius: The Scottish Enlightenment, 1730-1790* (1986), 43-67; Teichgraeber, 'Scottish Enlightenment', 135-83.
15 N.T. Phillipson, 'Adam Smith as a civic moralist', in Hont and Ignatieff (eds.), *Wealth and Virtue*, 179-203.

16 For an introduction to the thought of Adam Smith, see esp. Daiches (ed.), *Hotbed of Genius*, 69-91; Rendall, *Scottish Enlightenment*, 176-205.

17 For Adam Ferguson, Teichgraeber, 'Scottish Enlightenment', 230-62, is useful on the social nature of man; see also B. Lenman, *Integration, Enlightenment and Industrialization: Scotland 1746-1832* (London, 1981), 30-1, 63-4.

18 For William Robertson as historian, see Rendall, *Scottish Enlightenment*, 123-47.

19 A. Grant, *Story of the University of Edinburgh* (London, 1884), ii, 200.

20 Quoted in Rendall, *Scottish Enlightenment*, 226.

21 J. Dwyer, *Virtuous Discourse: Sensibility and Community in Late Eighteenth-Century Scotland* (1987), 10-37.

22 R.M. Schmitz, *Hugh Blair* (New York, 1948), 1, 53-4.

23 Dwyer, *Virtuous Discourse*, 141-67.

24 Ibid., 190-92; *History of the Speculative Society of Edinburgh* (1845), 29.

25 See Rendall, *Scottish Enlightenment*, 64-5.

26 A.C. Chitnis, 'Provost Drummond and the origins of Edinburgh medicine'. in Campbell and Skinner (eds.), *Scottish Enlightenment*, 86-97.

27 A.J. Youngson, *The Making of Classical Edinburgh* (1966), 1-17.

28 S. Nenadic, 'The rise of the urban middle class', *People and Society*, i, 121; T. Markus (ed.), *Order and Space in Society* (1982).

29 A.C. Chitnis, *The Scottish Enlightenment: A Social History* (London, 1976), 134.

30 Campbell, 'Francis Hutcheson', 167.

31 Gibb, *Glasgow*, 69-78.

32 For Aberdeen, see J.J. Carter and J.H. Pittock (eds.), *Aberdeen and the Enlightenment* (Aberdeen, 1987), esp. 95-179, 207-10.

33 M. Goldie, 'The Scottish Catholic Enlightenment', *J. of British Studs.*, xxx (1991), 20-62.

34 J. Strawhorn, 'Ayrshire and the Enlightenment', in G. Cruickshank (ed.), *A Sense of Place: Studies in Scottish Local History* (1988), 188-201.

35 Nenadic, 'Urban middle class', 112.

36 Dingwall, 'Edinburgh', ch.5; Whyte, 'Occupational structure of Scottish burghs', 237.

37 Smout, '1776', 56, 67.

38 Murdoch and Sher, 'Literary and learned culture', 195.

39 M.K. Meade, 'Plans of the New Town of Edinburgh', *Architectural History*, xiv (1971), 40. Chitnis, 'Origins of Edinburgh medicine', 87-8; C.M. Shepherd, 'Newtonianism in Scottish universities in the 17th century', 65-85, and R.G. Cant, 'Origins of the Enlightenment in Scotland: the universities', 42-64, all in Campbell and Skinner (eds.), *Scottish Enlightenment*.

40 Whyte, *Agriculture and Society* .

41 R.H. Campbell, 'The Enlightenment and the economy', in Campbell and Skinner (eds.), *Scottish Enlightenment*, 17-20; Smout, '1776', 45-9.

42 J.C.D. Clark, *Revolution and Rebellion: State and Society in England in the Seventeenth and Eighteenth Centuries* (Cambridge, 1986), 102.

43 I.D.L. Clark, 'From Protest to reaction: the Moderate regime in the Church of Scotland, 1752-1805', in Phillipson and Mitchison (eds.), *Age of Improvement*, 200-24; Dwyer, *Virtuous Discourse*, 22.

44 J. Prebble, *The King's Jaunt: George IV in Scotland, 1822* (London, 1988), 269.

45 K. Robbins, *Nineteenth-Century Britain. England, Scotland and Wales: The Making of a Nation* (Oxford, 1988), 172.

46 R. Black, 'The Gaelic Academy: the cultural commitment of the Highland Society of Scotland', *Scottish Gaelic Studs.*, xiv (1966), 1-38.

47 G. Williams, 'Wales – the cultural bases of nineteenth and twentieth century nationalism', in R. Mitchison (ed.), *The Roots of Nationalism* (1980), 121-2.

48 There were earlier clan organisations, usually founded for charitable purposes, such as Clan Buchanan (1725), but most clan societies were formed after 1888. See R.W. Munro, *Highland Clans and Tartans* (London, 1977), 116, for a roll of clan societies; also idem, 'Claims to clanship', *Story of Scotland*, xxxviii (Glasgow, 1988), 1048.

49 M. Ash, *The Strange Death of Scottish History* (1980), 59-86.

50 Ibid, 131.

51 B. P. Lenman, 'The teaching of Scottish history in the Scottish universities', *SHR*, lii (1973), 176.

52 Ibid, 177.

53 C. Harvie and G. Walker, 'Community and culture', in W.H. Fraser and R.J. Morris (eds.), *People and Society in Scotland, vol. ii, 1830-1914*, 355.

54 R. Mitchison, '19th century Scottish nationalism: the cultural background', in idem (ed.), *Roots of Nationalism*, 136-7.

55 Ferguson, *Scotland*, 320-2.
56 B. Lenman, *An Economic History of Modern Scotland* (London, 1977), 168.
57 Robbins, *Britain*, 128; N. Morgan, 'Enterprise and industry' *History Today*, xl (May, 1990), 39.
58 T.C. Smout, 'Problems of nationalism, identity and Improvement in later 18th-century Scotland', in T.M. Devine (ed.), *Improvement and Enlightenment* (1989), 11-12; J.D. Brims, 'The Scottish "Jacobins", Scottish nationalism and British union', in Mason (ed.), *Scotland and England*, 247-65.
59 Cited in W.H. Fraser, 'Trades councils in the Labour movement in 19th century Scotland', in I. MacDougall (ed.), *Essays in Scottish Labour History* (1978), 23.
60 Prebble, *King's Jaunt*, 312-20.
61 Robbins, *Britain*, 100.
62 R.J. Morris, 'Urbanisation and Scotland', *People and Society*, ii, 98.
63 Cf Smout, 'Problems of nationalism', 2-7, on 'concentric loyalties'.
64 Cf Robbins, *Britain*, 3-5; Kearney, *British Isles*, 149-73.
65 I.G.C. Hutchison, *A Political History of Scotland, 1832-1924* (1986).
66 B. Aspinwall, 'The Scottish religious identity in the Atlantic world, 1880-1914', *Studs. in Church History*, xviii (1982), 505-18.
67 K. Robbins, 'The imperial city', *History Today*, xl (May, 1990), 48-54.
68 CSP Scot., iii, no.703 (14 June 1568). Queen Mary had fled into England four weeks before this football 'international'. I am grateful to Mark Loughlin for drawing my attention to this reference.
69 N.L. Tranter, 'Popular sport and the Industrial Revolution in Scotland', *International J. of the History of Sport*, iv (1987).
70 W.H. Fraser, 'Developments in leisure', *People and Society*, ii, 256.
71 K. McCarra, 'Football kicks off', *Story of Scotland* vi (1988), 158-62.
72 C. Harvie, *Scotland and Nationalism* (London, 1977), 37; Robbins, *Britain*, 166.

21 The Highland Condition

1 C.W.J. Withers, *Gaelic Scotland: the Transformation of a Culture Region* (London, 1988), 65-72; T.C. Smout, 'Tours in the Scottish Highlands from the 18th to the 20th centuries', *Northern Scotland*, v (1983), 99-121; *Inverness Courier*, 13 July 1836.
2 W. Orr, *Deer Forests, Landlords and Crofters* (1982), 28, 168-80.
3 J.B. Simmons, 'Railways, hotels and tourism in Great Britain, 1839-1914', *J. of Contemporary History*, xix (1984), 206-12; Robbins, *Britain*, 23-4.
4 Withers, *Gaelic Scotland*, 66, 70.
5 Smith, *Jacobite Estates*.
6 J. Kirk, 'The kirk and the Highlands at the Reformation', *Northern Scotland*, vii (1986), 1-22; Meek and Kirk, 'John Carswell', 1-22; J. MacInnes, *The Evangelical Movement in the Highlands of Scotland, 1668-1800* (Aberdeen, 1951), 62, 66.
7 Ibid., 202; M. Mackay (ed.), *The Rev Dr John Walker's Report on the Hebrides of 1764 and 1771* (1980), 20-1.
8 Withers, *Gaelic Scotland*, 127-32, 135, 150.
9 MacInnes, *Evangelical Movement*, 154-66. Cf T.C. Smout, 'Born again at Cambuslang: new evidence on popular religion and literacy in 18th-century Scotland', *Past and Present*, xcvii (1982), 114-27; A. Fawcett, *The Cambuslang Revival* (London, 1977).
10 MacInnes, *Evangelical Movement*, 211-20.
11 C. Brown, *The Social History of Religion in Scotland since 1730* (London, 1987), 120, 125.
12 N.M. Wilby, 'The "encreasce of popery" in the Highlands, 1714-47', *IR* xvii (1966), 97.
13 C. Giblin, *Irish Franciscan Mission to Scotland* (Dublin, 1964), pp. xii, 149.
14 A.S. MacWilliam, 'A Highland mission: Strathglass, 1671-1777', *IR* xxiv (1973), 75-102; A. MacDonnell and D. McRoberts, 'The mass stones of Lochaber', *IR* xvii (1966), 71-81; P. Anson, *Underground Catholicism in Scotland* (Montrose, 1970).
15 F. Forbes and W.J. Anderson, 'Clergy lists of the Highland District, 1732-1828', *IR* xvii (1966), 129-84; C. Johnson, *Developments in the Roman Catholic Church in Scotland, 1789-1829* (1983), 71-8, 231-5.
16 Ibid., 42; J.F. MacMillan, 'Jansenists and anti-Jansenists in 18th-century Scotland', *IR* xxxix (1988), 12-45.
17 *Walker's Report*, 18, 73.
18 M. McHugh, 'The religious condition of the Highlands and Islands in the mid-18th century', *IR* xxxv (1984), 12-21.
19 Johnson, *Catholic Church*, 1, 46, 119-29; Goldie, 'Scottish Catholic Enlightenment', 58-61.
20 Ibid., 2, 248.

21 See M. Gray, *The Highland Economy, 1750-1850* (1957), 57-66; also Smout, *History*, 351-60.
22 J. Hunter, *The Making of the Crofting Community* (1976), esp. 15-33.
23 E. Richards, *A History of the Highland Clearances* 2 vols. (London, 1985), ii, 220-3.
24 T.C.Smout, *A Century of the Scottish People, 1830-1950* (London, 1986), 68; R. Mitchison, 'The Highland Clearances', *SESH* i (1981), 15-17.
25 Richards, *Clearances*, ii, 197.
26 Ibid., ii, 25-31.
27 T.M. Devine, 'The emergence of the new élite in the Western Highlands and Islands, 1800-60', in idem (ed.), *Improvement and Enlightenment*, 109-10.
28 T.M. Devine, *The Great Highland Famine* (1988), 185; Smout, *Century*, 38-9.
29 A.I. Macinnes, 'Scottish Gaeldom: the first phase of Clearance', *People and Society*, i, 83; Devine, *Famine*, 10.
30 Ibid., 1-4, 21.
31 Ibid., 12-18.
32 Hunter, *Crofting Community*, 17.
33 E. Cregeen, 'The changing role of the house of Argyll in the Scottish Highlands', in Phillipson and Mitchison (eds.), *Age of Improvement*, 5-23.
34 Macinnes, 'Scottish Gaeldom', 72-82; Hunter, *Crofting Community*, 16, 21-2, 29.
35 Devine, *Famine*, 1; D.G. Lockhart, 'The planned villages', in M.L. Parry and T.R. Slater, *The Making of the Scottish Countryside* (London, 1980), 249-70.
36 Hunter, *Crofting Community*, 35; Devine, *Famine*, 15; Richards, *Clearances*, ii, 485.
37 Ibid., ii, 250.
38 Hunter, *Crofting Community*, 53-4; *Extracts from the Letters to Rev Dr McLeod regarding the Famine and Destitution in the Highlands of Scotland* (Glasgow, 1847), 71.
39 Hunter, *Crofting Community*, 56-60.
40 Ibid., 63-72.
41 Devine, *Famine*, 189.
42 Ibid., 176-7.
43 Cf E. Richards, *Clearances*, i, 402-18; ii, 254; and Hunter, *Crofting Community*, 82.
44 Duke of Argyll, *Crofts and Farms in the Hebrides* (Edinburgh, 1883); see Devine, *Famine*, 234, 239.
45 R.D. Lobban, 'The Migration of Highlanders into Lowland Scotland, c.1750-1890, with special reference to Greenock' (Edinburgh Univ. Ph.D., 1969); Richards, *Clearances*, i, 237.
46 Devine, *Famine*, 149.
47 Ibid., 150-65.
48 J.M. Bumsted, *The People's Clearance: Highland Emigration to British North America, 1770-1815* (1982), 55-82; Richards, *Clearances*, i, 183-7, 194.
49 Bumsted, *People's Clearance*.
50 I. Levitt and T.C. Smout, *The State of the Scottish Working Class in 1843* (1979), 236-49.
51 Ibid., 249. M. Harper, *Emigration from North East Scotland*, 2 vols. (Aberdeen, 1998); see esp. vol. 1, *Willing Exiles*.
52 F.S. Buchanan (ed.), *A Good Time Coming: Mormon Letters to Scotland* (Salt Lake City, 1988).
53 Richards, *Clearances*, ii, 301-50.
54 Brown, *Religion in Scotland*, 125; Hunter, *Crofting Community*, 103-6.
55 Ibid., 131-45; I.F. Grigor, *Mightier than a Lord; The Highland Crofters' Struggle for Land* (Stornoway, 1979), 60, 94; Foster, *Modern Ireland*, 405-6, 412-13.
56 Hunter, *Crofting Community*, 178-9.
57 J. Hunter (ed.), *For the People's Cause: From the Writings of John Murdoch* (1986), 38; Foster, *Modern Ireland*, 413.
58 L. Leneman, *Fit for Heroes? Land Settlement in Scotland after World War I* (Aberdeen, 1989), esp. 117-33; Smout, *Century*, 75-6.

22 A Century of Muddle and Change

1 Flinn (ed.), *Population History* , 181; R.E. Tyson, 'The population of Aberdeenshire, 1696-1755', *Northern Scotland*, vi (1985), 113-31.
2 R.A. Dodghson, 'The removal of runrig in Roxburghshire and Berwickshire, 1680-1768', *Scottish Studies*, xvi (1972), 121-7; B.M.W. Third, 'Changing landscape and social structure in the Scottish Lowlands as revealed in 18th-century estate plans', *Scot. Geog. Mag.*, lxxi (1955), 83-93.
3 T.M. Devine, 'Social responses to agrarian "Improvement": the Highland and Lowland clearances in Scotland', in Houston and Whyte (eds.), *Scottish Society*, 148-68.
4 Smout, '1776', 68; G. Whittington, 'Agriculture and society in Lowland Scotland, 1750-1870', in

Whittington and Whyte (eds.), *Historical Geography*, 157-8. For Edzell, see Bardgett, *Scotland Reformed*, 152.

5 I.D. Whyte, 'Proto-industrialisation in Scotland', in P. Hudson (ed.), *Regions and Industries: a Perspective on the Industrial Revolution in Britain* (Cambridge, 1989), esp. 229-39.

6 R.H. Campbell, 'The industrial revolution: a revision article', *SHR* xlvi (1967), 44-6; T.M. Devine (ed.), *Farm Servants and Labour in Lowland Scotland, 1770-1914* (1984), 41-4.

7 Ibid., 3,6, 29-35; M. Gray, 'The social impact of agrarian change in the rural Lowlands', *People and Society*, i, 53-69.

8 R.H. Campbell, *Scotland since 1707: the Rise of an Industrial Society* (2nd edn., 1985), 34-6; Lenman, *Economic History*, 87-9.

9 T.M. Devine, *The Tobacco Lords* (1975), 73, 108; Campbell, *Scotland*, 39-43.

10 Devine, 'Union of 1707', 31-7.

11 A.J. Durie, *Linen Industry*, 22-31, 65-7.

12 Ibid., 55; Smout, '1776', 64.

13 S.G. Checkland, *Scottish Banking: A History 1695-1973* (Glasgow, 1975), 91-135; Campbell, *Scotland*, 57-63.

14 W.H. Fraser, *Conflict and Class: Scottish Workers, 1700-1838* (1988), 29-31, 35.

15 Lenman, *Economic History*, 119-20; S.G.E. Lythe and J. Butt, *An Economic History of Scotland, 1100-1939* (Glasgow, 1975), 187-8.

16 Campbell, 'Industrial revolution', 49.

17 Lythe and Butt, *Economic History*, 87-9.

18 R. Mitchison, 'Webster revisited: an examination of the 1755 census of Scotland', in Devine (ed.), *Improvement and Enlightenment*, 75-6; Smout, '1776', 56, 67.

19 Fraser, *Conflict and Class*, 30, 34-5.

20 For the element of unexpected growth in England, fuelled by an 'energy revolution', see E.A. Wrigley, *Continuity, Chance and Change: the Character of the Industrial Revolution in England* (Cambridge, 1988), 19, 67, 73-9.

21 Smout, *History*, 414; Fraser, *Conflict and Class*, 32.

22 T. Dickson (ed.), *Scottish Capitalism* (London, 1980), 185; Fraser, *Conflict and Class*, 153-4.

23 Campbell, *Scotland*, 88-91.

24 L.R. Timperley, 'The pattern of landholding in 18th-century Scotland', in Parry and Slater (eds.), *Making of Scottish Countryside*, 137-54.

25 R.H. Campbell, 'The landed classes', *People and Society*, i, 91-108.

26 R.B. McDowell, 'Ireland in the 18th-century British Empire', *Historical Studies*, ix (1974), 61-2. The Scottish soldier, however, was not as prominent in the 19th-century army. By 1830 the percentage of Scots in the British army had dropped to 13.5 per cent (still higher than the 10 per cent of Scots in the British population); by 1870 it was only 8 per cent. Some of the Highland regiments had more non-Scots than Scots in them. The Scottish vogue was not for the Army but the Volunteers. See H.J. Hanham, 'Religion and nationality in the mid-Victorian army', in M.R.D. Foot (ed.), *War and Society* (London, 1973), 160-72.

27 R. Mitchison, 'Patriotism and national identity in 18th-century Scotland', *Historical Studies*, xiii (1978), 90-1.

28 Dwyer and Murdoch, 'Rise of Dundas', 220, 237-43.

29 Sunter, *Patronage and Politics*, 2, 233-5.

30 Quoted in ibid., 4.

31 M. Fry, *Patronage and Principle*, 18.

32 Dwyer and Murdoch, 'Rise of Dundas', 220-30; Clark, 'Moderate regime', 213, 220-2.

33 Lenman, *Scotland*, 80.

34 Ibid., 80-4.

35 K.J. Logue, *Popular Disturbances in Scotland, 1780-1815* (1979), 133-43.

36 J. Brims, 'From reformers to Jacobins: the Scottish Association of the Friends of the People', in T.M. Devine (ed.), *Conflict and Stability in Scottish Society, 1700-1850* (1990), 31-50.

37 Logue, *Popular Disturbances*, 148-53.

38 Brims, 'Friends of the People', 45-7.

39 C.A. Whatley, 'How tame were the Scottish Lowlanders during the 18th century?', in Devine (ed.), *Conflict and Stability*, 23-4.

40 P. Berresford Ellis and S. MacA'Ghobhainn, *The Scottish Insurrection of 1820* (London, 1970), 77.

41 Logue, *Popular Disturbances*, 110-15.

42 J.H. Treble, 'The standard of living of the working class', *People and Society*, i, 188-226.

43 R. Mitchison, 'Scotland, 1750-1850', in F.M.L. Thompson (ed.), *The Cambridge Social History of Britain, 1750-1950*, vol. i (1990), 172-5, 177-9; R.A. Cage, *The Scottish Poor Law, 1745-1845* (1981), 34, 41-2.

44 Fraser, *Conflict and Class*, 100-3, 166-7.
45 A.B. Richmond, *Narrative of the Condition of the Manufacturing Population* (London, 1824), 54.
46 Fraser, *Conflict and Class*, 169.
47 Nenadic, 'Urban middle classes', 118-24.
48 Lenman, *Scotland*, 162-4.
49 W. Ferguson, 'The Reform Act (Scotland) of 1832: intention and effect', *SHR* xlv (1966), 105-14; Robbins, *Britain*, 99.
50 *Report of the Royal Commission on the Poor Law (Scotland)*, 1844, vol. 20, xvi, lxi. See Levitt and Smout, *Scottish Working-Class in 1843*, 161, 173-4.
51 Ibid., 156-9.
52 R. Mitchison, 'The creation of the disablement rule in the Scottish Poor Law', in T.C. Smout (ed.), *The Search for Wealth and Stability: Essays in Economic and Social History presented to M.W. Flinn* (London, 1979), 199-217; idem, 'Scotland, 1750-1850', 199, 205-7.
53 Ferguson, *Scotland*, 313; Levitt and Smout, *Scottish Working-Class in 1843*, 184.
54 S.J. Brown, *Thomas Chalmers* (Oxford, 1982), 129-30.
55 D.J. Withrington, 'Schooling, literacy and society', *People and Society*, i, 163-87.
56 Brown, *Religion in Scotland*, 31, 61.
57 Ibid., 141.
58 Fraser, *Conflict and Class*, 169-70.
59 Ibid., 111.
60 Ibid., 168-9; Smout, *Century*, 89-92.
61 J.F. McCaffrey, 'Irish issues in the 19th and 20th century: radicalism in a Scottish context', in T.M. Devine (ed.), *Irish Immigrants and Scottish Society in the Nineteenth and Twentieth Centuries* (1991), 123-5.
62 J.F. McCaffrey, 'Irish immigrants and radical movements in the West of Scotland in the early 19th century', *IR* xxxix (1988), 46-60. Cf Foster, *Modern Ireland*, 347-8, 369.
63 J.E. Handley, *The Navvy in Scotland* (Cork, 1970), 35.
64 G. Walker, 'The Protestant Irish in Scotland', in Devine (ed.), *Irish Immigrants*, 49-50.
65 Ibid., 51-3; A.B. Campbell, *The Lanarkshire Miners* (1979), 179-201.
66 Smout, *Century*, 51; Brown, *Religion in Scotland*, 143-6.

23 Victorian Scotland

1 A.L. Drummond and J. Bulloch, *The Scottish Church, 1688-1843* (1973), 246-8.
2 Brown, *Chalmers*, 338-44.
3 Ibid., 335; Drummond and Bulloch, *Scottish Church*, 249-50.
4 Brown, *Religion in Scotland*, 135.
5 Ferguson, *Scotland*, 313-17.
6 Hutchison, *Political History*, 83; Brown, *Religion in Scotland*, 198-200.
7 A. Wilson, *The Chartist Movement in Scotland* (Manchester, 1970), 138-50.
8 Ferguson, *Scotland*, 121-5; Drummond and Bulloch, *Scottish Church*, 41-4, 53.
9 Ibid., 80-81; Brown, *Religion in Scotland*, 36-7.
10 Drummond and Bulloch, *Scottish Church*, 150-51; Ferguson, 228-9; J. McKerrow, *History of the Secession Church* (Glasgow, 1841), ii, 541-3. For a revealing table of churchgoers by denomination in 1835/6 and 1851, see Brown, *Religion in Scotland*, 61: the Free Church claimed 22% and the Church of Scotland 22% in Glasgow in 1851; in Edinburgh the equivalent figures were 33% for the Free Church, a startling 16% for the Established Church, and 27% for the United Presbyterian.
11 G.I.T. Machin, *Politics and the Churches in Great Britain, 1832-1868* (Oxford, 1977), 116-18.
12 W. Hanna, *Memoirs of Dr Chalmers* 4 vols. (1849-52), iv, 348-9.
13 Brown, *Chalmers*, 301-03; Fry, *Patronage and Principle*, 50; Machin, *Politics and the Churches*, 126-30.
14 Brown, *Chalmers*, 336; Robbins, *Britain*, 71.
15 Brown, *Chalmers*, 347, 350-79.
16 A.A. MacLaren, *Religion and Social Class: The Disruption Years in Aberdeen* (London, 1974).
17 This section is dependent on the pioneering work in Brown, *Religion in Scotland*, esp. 135-68.
18 P. Hillis, 'Presbyterianism and social class in mid-19th century Glasgow', *J. Ecc. Hist.*, xxxii (1981), 47-64.
19 P. Hillis, 'Education and evangelisation: presbyterian missions in mid-nineteenth century Glasgow', *SHR* lxvi (1987), 46-62.
20 *Non-Churchgoing and the Housing of the Poor* (1888), cited in A.C. Cheyne, *The Transforming of the Kirk* (1983), 135.
21 D.W. Bebbington (ed.), *The Baptists in Scotland: a History* (Glasgow, 1988), 62; J.M. Smith,

'Commonsense thought and working class consciousness: some aspects of the Glasgow and Liverpool Labour Movements in the early years of the twentieth century' (Edinburgh Ph.D., 1980), 180, 182.

22 W. Sloan, 'Religious affiliation and the immigrant experience', in Devine (ed.), *Irish Immigrants*, 69.

23 C. Johnson, 'Scottish secular clergy, 1830-1878', *IR* xl (1989), 24-68, 106-52; W.M. Walker, *Juteopolis: Dundee and its Textile Workers, 1885-1923* (1979), 128.

24 McCaffrey, 'Irish immigrants', 51-4.

25 Robbins, 'Religion and identity in modern British history'. *Studies in Church History*, xviii (1982), 473-4, 484.

26 T. Gallagher, 'The Catholic Irish in Scotland: in search of identity', in Devine (ed.), *Irish Immigrants*, 26.

27 S. Gilley, 'The Roman Catholic Church and the 19th-century Irish diaspora', *J. Ecc. Hist.*, xxxv (1984), 198.

28 Smith, 'Commonsense thought', 164-6; Collins, 'Origins of Irish Immigration', in Devine (ed.), *Irish Immigrants*, 9.

29 J.F. McCaffrey, 'Irish issues in the 19th and 20th century', 125; Walker, *Juteopolis*, 144.

30 See D. Cannadine, 'The present and the past in the English industrial revolution', *Past and Present*, ciii (1984), 131-72.

31 W.D. Rubinstein, 'The Victorian middle classes: wealth, occupation and geography', *Econ. Hist. Rev.*, xxx (1970), 614-18.

32 See e.g., G. Gordon, 'Industrial development, c.1750-1980', in Whittington and Whyte (eds.), *Historical Geography*, 166-81.

33 W.W. Rostow, *The Stages of Economic Growth* (London, 1960).

34 Wrigley, *Continuity, Chance and Change*, 132.

35 Lenman, *Economic History*, 182-91.

36 T.C. Smout, 'Scotland, 1850-1950', in Thompson (ed.), *Cambridge Social History*, i, 212-16; O. & S. Checkland, *Industry and Ethos: Scotland, 1832-1914* (2nd edn., 1989), 35-50.

37 T. Donnelly, 'Shipbuilding in Aberdeen, 1750-1914', *Northern Scotland*, iv (1980), 23-42.

38 Lythe and Butt, *Economic History*, 192-4; James Cleland, *Enumeration of the Inhabitants of the City of Glasgow, 1831* (Glasgow, 1832).

39 Smout, 'Scotland, 1850-1950', 211, 214-15.

40 E. Gordon, 'Women's spheres', *People and Society*, ii, 209.

41 Smout, 'Scotland, 1850-1950', 213; R.J. Morris, 'Urbanisation and Scotland', *People and Society*, ii, 76; H. McShane and J. Smith, *No Mean Fighter* (London, 1978), 42.

42 Wrigley, *Continuity, Chance and Change*, 73-9.

43 Lythe and Butt, *Economic History*, 192-4.

44 S. Berry and H. Whyte (eds.), *Glasgow Observed* (1987), 82-4.

45 R.H. Campbell, *The Rise and Fall of Scottish Industry, 1707-1939* (1980), 19, 21.

46 Lenman, *Economic History*, 178-80; Campbell, *Rise and Fall*, 121.

47 Ibid., 61-8.

48 J.H. Treble, 'The occupied male labour force', *People and Society*, ii, 184-6; Smout, 'Scotland, 1850-1950', 220.

49 Campbell, *Lanarkshire Miners*, 299-301; Campbell, *Rise and Fall*, 101-10.

50 C.J.A. Robertson, *The Origins of the Scottish Railway System, 1722-1844* (1983).

51 W. Vamplew, 'Railways and the Scottish transport system in the 19th century', *J. of Transport History*, i (1972), 133-45; Robbins, *Britain*, 25-7.

52 Morris, 'Urbanisation in Scotland', 80-83.

53 Ibid., 91; T.M. Devine, 'Urbanisation', *People and Society*, i, 27-52.

54 Gibb, *Glasgow*, 105, 124.

55 Ibid., 104-10; Devine, 'Urbanisation', 41, 47-8; Berry and Whyte, (eds.), *Glasgow Observed*, 86.

56 Gibb, *Glasgow*, 124-36.

57 I.H. Adams, *The Making of Urban Scotland* (London, 1978), 160-62; S. Damer, 'State, class and housing: Glasgow, 1885-1919', in J. Melling (ed.), *Housing, Social Policy and the State* (London, 1980), 73-112.

58 Adams, *Urban Scotland*, 166-7; J. Butt, 'Working class housing in Glasgow, 1851-1914', in S.D. Chapman (ed.), *The History of Working Class Housing* (Newton Abbot, 1971), 60-3.

59 Adams, *Urban Scotland*, 136.

60 Ibid., 167.

61 See A. Hogg, *Scotland: The Rise of the Cities, 1694-1905* (London, 1973), no. 61.

62 I. Levitt (ed.), *Government and Social Conditions in Scotland, 1845-1919* (SHS, 1988), pp. xi-xii, xxxiv-xxxv, 177, 208, 217.

63 W.E. Gladstone to Sir John Cowan, 17 March 1894, cited in J. Morley, *Life of Gladstone*, 2 vols. (London, 1908), ii, 582.

64 J.G. Kellas, *Modern Scotland* (2nd edn., London, 1980), 53.
65 See Hutchison, *Political History*, 59, 60, 143.
66 Cited in Robbins, *Britain*, 104.
67 J.G. Lockhart, *Life of Sir Walter Scott*, 2 vols. (1836-8), ii, 299.
68 J.B. Balfour, ex-Lord Advocate, in the Commons on 3 Aug 1866; cited in Kellas, *Modern Scotland*, 123.
69 Ibid., 123-4.
70 H.J. Hanham, 'The creation of the Scottish Office, 1881-7', *Juridical Review*, x (1965), 209.
71 Hutchison, *Political History*, 132; Smout, 'Scotland, 1850-1950', 229; Robbins, *Britain*, 103.
72 K.O. Morgan, *Keir Hardie* (London, 1975), 25-9.
73 Harvie, *Scotland and Nationalism*, 35-6; Robbins, *Britain*, 101.
74 Levitt (ed.), *Social Conditions*, pp. xl-xli.
75 Speech at Dalkeith, 26 Nov 1879, cited in Fry, *Patronage and Principle*, 93.
76 Speech in Glasgow, 22 March 1883, cited in Smith, 'Commonsense thought', 101.
77 Ibid., 202-20.
78 J. Buchan, *Memory Hold-the-Door* (London, 1940), 146, cited in Fry, *Patronage and Principle*, 129-30.
79 Hutchison, *Political History*, 120-5.
80 See ibid, 200, 206.
81 Ibid., 194, 198; Robbins, *Britain*, 104.
82 Cited in Smith, 'Commonsense thought', 177.
83 McShane, *No Mean Fighter*, 74.
84 Morgan, *Keir Hardie*, 42.
85 C. Harvie, 'Before the breakthrough, 1888-1922', in I. Donnachie, C. Harvie and I.S. Wood (eds.), *Forward! Labour Politics in Scotland, 1888-1988* (1989), 12-13; Smith, 'Commonsense thought', 175.
86 Morgan, *Keir Hardie*, 4-12, 33.
87 Ibid., 62-8; Harvie, 'Before the breakthrough', 14.
88 Ibid., 13-16; Hutchison, *Political History*, 183.

24 A New Society?

1 McShane and Smith, *No Mean Fighter*, 62.
2 P.C. Matheson, 'Scottish war sermons, 1914-19', *RSCHS* xvii (1971), 203-13; J. Darragh, 'The Apostolic Visitations of Scotland, 1912 and 1917', *IR* xli (1990), 7, 60n.
3 C. Harvie, *No Gods and Precious Few Heroes: Scotland 1914-1980* (London, 1981), 10-15, 24; Ian Hay, *The First Hundred Thousand* (London, 1915).
4 Campbell, *Rise and Fall of Scottish Industry*, 164-82.
5 Edwin Muir, *Scottish Journey* (London, 1935).
6 Smout, *Century*, 112-18; idem, 'Scotland, 1850-1950', 224-6.
7 Smith, 'Commonsense thought', 412-13.
8 A. Reid, 'World War I and the working class in Britain', in A. Marwick (ed.), *Total War and Social Change* (London, 1988), 20-1.
9 Ibid., 18; Smout, 'Scotland, 1850-1950', 222.
10 B.J. Ripley and J. McHugh, *John Maclean* (Manchester, 1989), 81-5.
11 J. Melling, 'Clydeside housing and the evolution of state rent control', in idem (ed.), *Housing, Social Policy and the State*, 147-51; idem, 'Clydeside rent struggles and Labour politics, 1900-39', in R. Rodger (ed.), *Scottish Housing in the Twentieth Century* (Leicester, 1989), 65-72; Smith, 'Commonsense thought', 469-79; M.J. Daunton, 'Housing', in Thompson (ed.), *Cambridge Social History*, ii, 247-8.
12 Patrick Dollan in *Labour Leader*, 25 Nov. 1915.
13 Smith, 'Commonsense thought', 478.
14 Damer, 'State, class and housing', 105.
15 Cited in I. McLean, 'Red Clydeside, 1915-1919', in R. Quinnalt and J. Stevenson (eds.), *Popular Protest and Public Order* (London, 1974), 29.
16 W. Gallacher, *Revolt on the Clyde* (London, 1936), 234.
17 Smith, 'Commonsense thought', 568-74; McLean, 'Red Clydeside', 215-42; see also idem, *The Legend of Red Clydeside* (1983), 111-39.
18 For John Maclean, see esp. Ripley and McHugh, *John Maclean*; D. Howell, *A Lost Left* (Manchester, 1986), 158-225; and W. Knox (ed.), *Scottish Labour Leaders, 1918-39: a Biographical Dictionary* (1984), 179-92.
19 Ripley and McHugh, *John Maclean*, 79-85.
20 Howell, *Lost Left*, 196, 313n; see N. Milton (ed.), *John Maclean: the Seeds of Revolution* (London,

1978), 156, for Maclean's expectations of the miners in 1919.
21 Ripley and McHugh, *John Maclean*, 169.
22 Hugh MacDiarmid, *The Company I've Kept* (London, 1966), 125.
23 Harvie, 'Before the breakthrough, 1886-1922', 28; Knox (ed.) *Labour Leaders*, 22-6.
24 See Harvie, *Scotland*, 86, 114-15.
25 McShane and Smith, *No Mean Fighter*, 34.
26 K. Robbins, *The Eclipse of a Great Power: Modern Britain, 1870-1975* (London, 1983), 218-22; Kearney, *British Isles*, 196-8.
27 Hutchison, *Political History*, 277, 321-6; T. Wilson, *The Downfall of the Liberal Party, 1914-1935* (London, 1968), 281-4.
28 See the useful table of election statistics in Harvie, *Scotland*, 90.
29 Smith, 'Commonsense thought', 574.
30 I. MacDougall, 'Some aspects of the 1926 General Strike in Scotland', in idem (ed.), *Essays in Scottish Labour History* (1978), 170-206; J. Harris, 'Society and the state in twentieth-century Britain', in Thompson (ed.), *Cambridge Social History*, iii, 82.
31 Hutchison, *Political History*, 317-24.
32 Harvie, 'Before the breakthrough', 24; idem, *Scotland*, 30.
33 Hutchison, *Political History*, 285-6.
34 M.I. Cole (ed.), *Beatrice Webb's Diaries, 1912-1924* (London, 1952), 142; Adamson quoted in I.S. Wood, 'Hope deferred: Labour in Scotland in the 1920s', in Donnachie, (ed.), *Forward!*, 45.
35 Hutchison, *Political History*, 283.
36 Dollan quoted in Harvie, 'Before the breakthrough', 28, and Hutchison, *Political History*, 278.
37 Smout, *Century*, 270.
38 J.F. McCaffrey, 'Irish issues in the nineteenth and twentieth century: radicalism in a Scottish context?', in Devine (ed.), *Irish Immigrants*, 120-1, 129-35.
39 I.S. Wood, 'John Wheatley, the Irish and the Labour movement in Scotland', 78.
40 Smout, *Century*, 274.
41 R.K. Middlemas, *The Clydesiders* (London, 1965), 100-02; Knox (ed.), *Labour Leaders*, 92 9.
42 H. Nicholson, *King George the Fifth* (London, 1952), 389.
43 Howell, *Lost Left*, 254.
44 Ibid, 258; see also Melling, 'Clydeside rent struggles', 76.
45 Harvie, *Scotland*, 89-92.
46 Cf the different dating of the Liberals' fall in Hutchison, *Political History*, 327-8; Ferguson, *Scotland*, 369-70; Harvie, *Scotland*, 92; Fry, *Patronage and Principle*, 147-8, 178. See also Wilson, *Downfall*, 324-36.
47 Ibid., 183-7.
48 R. Skidelsky, *Politicians and the Slump* (London, 1970), 67-73.
49 Kellas, *Modern Scotland*, 134.
50 M. Keating and D. Bleiman, *Labour and Scottish Nationalism* (London, 1979), 92-101.
51 Harvie, *Scotland and Nationalism*, 62, 67.
52 A. Marwick, 'Scottish nationalism since 1918', in K. Miller (ed.), *Memoirs of a Modern Scotland* (London, 1970), 13-33; Finlay, 'Scottish nationalism and the British Empire'.
53 *Scots Independent* (July 1928) has the full NPS programmme.
54 R.J. Finlay, 'The Origins and Development of Scottish Nationalism, 1919-1945' (Edinburgh Ph.D., 1991), 114-15.
55 K. Webb, *The Growth of Nationalism in Scotland* (Glasgow, 1977), 47.
56 Finlay, 'Scottish nationalism'; Harvie, *Scotland and Nationalism*, 156.
57 H.J. Hanham, *Scottish Nationalism* (London, 1969), 167-9.
58 Finlay, 'Origins and Development', 306.
59 Fry, *Patronage and Principle*, 144, 185-7; Ferguson, *Scotland*, 376-7.
60 Cf Harvie, *Scotland and Nationalism*, 51-2; Kellas, *Modern Scotland*, 98-100.
61 Cf Fry, *Patronage and Principle*, 184-92; Ferguson, *Scotland*, 383-5.
62 R. Rodger and H. Al-Qaddo, 'The Scottish Special Housing Association and the implementation of housing policy, 1937-87', in Rodger (ed.), *Scottish Housing*, 186-7.
63 Fry, *Patronage and Principle*, 174; Harvie, *Scotland and Nationalism*, 55.
64 Kearney, *British Isles*, 203.
65 R.H. Campbell, 'The economic case for nationalism: Scotland', in Mitchison (ed.), *Roots of Nationalism*, 146-51.
66 B. Kay, 'The Clydebank Blitz', in idem (ed.), *Odyssey: the Second Collection* (1982), 1-11
67 T. Johnston, *Memories* (London, 1952), 169.
68 See Brown, *Religion in Scotland*, 219; W. Storrar, *Scottish Identity: a Christian Vision* (1990), 70, 202-3.

69 Ibid., 218-20; S.J. Brown, '"Outside the Covenant": the Scottish presbyterian churches and Irish immigration, 1922-38', *IR* xlii (1991).
70 Smout, 'Scotland, 1850-1950', 244-6; Gibb, *Glasgow*, 154.
71 M. Horsey, *Tenements and Towers: Glasgow Working-Class Housing, 1890-1990* (1990), 11-22; Adams, *Urban Scotland*, 170-2.
72 Ibid., 170-6; Smout, 'Scotland, 1850-1950', 253-4.
73 N.J. Morgan, 'Innovations in municipal house-building in Glasgow in the inter-war years', in Rodger (ed.), *Scottish Housing*, 125-54.
74 Baillie Jean Mann, quoted in Adams, *Urban Scotland*, 209.
75 Horsey, *Tenements and Towers*, 45-59.
76 N. Skelton, *Constructive Conservatism* (London, 1931), 24; see Fry, *Patronage and Principle*, 289.
77 Daunton, 'Housing', 243; C. McKean, *The Scottish Thirties: an Architectural Introduction* (1987).
78 Smout, 'Scotland, 1850-1950', 224, 258-60.
79 H. Cunningham, 'Leisure and culture', in Thompson (ed.), *Cambridge Social History*, ii, 312; Harvie, *Scotland*, 122-4.
80 Scottish Office memorandum, 18 Dec. 1937; cited in Campbell, 'Economic case for nationalism', 151.

25 A Nobler Prospect?

1 C. Harvie, 'The recovery of Scottish Labour', in Donnachie (ed.), *Forward!*, 78-80.
2 Heavy industry accounted for 16.5% of the employed population in 1931 and 15.7% in 1951; by 1971 it was 10.5%. Smout, 'Scotland, 1850-1950', 211.
3 W.L. Miller, *The End of British Politics? Scots and English Political Behaviour in the Seventies* (Oxford, 1981), 130-1, 217-28.
4 F. Wood, 'Scottish Labour in government and opposition, 1964-79', in Donnachie (ed.), *Forward!*, 102.
5 Fry, *Patronage and Principle*, 232.
6 Harvie, *Scotland and Nationalism*, 268-9.
7 Miller, *British Politics*, 59-60.
8 See e.g. H. Hopkins, *The New Look: a Social History of the Forties and Fifties in Britain* (London, 1963), which has one reference to Wales and two to Scotland in 490pp. The same point was made in Robbins, *Eclipse of a Great Power*, 77-8, in 1983. Since then, however, the English 'British' history has returned; see n11, below.
9 Harvie, *Scotland*, 148.
10 Miller, *British Politics*, 252-3.
11 E.g. P. Riddell, *The Thatcher Decade: How Britain has changed during the 1980s* (Oxford, 1989), which has a chapter 'The two nations', meaning rich and poor, but no mention of the other nations which make up the United Kingdom.
12 Also printed in O.D. Edwards (ed.), *A Claim of Right for Scotland* (1989).

Bibliography

The Bibliography includes all secondary works, including books, articles and pieces in collected essays, which have been cited more than once in the Notes and References. In the case of works which are cited only once in the Notes, a full reference is given there. Printed primary sources other than important source collections are generally not included. Place of publication is given, unless it was Edinburgh.

Adams, I.H., *The Making of Urban Scotland* (London, 1978)

Anderson, M.O., 'Dalriada and the creation of the kingdom of the Scots', in Whitelock *et al.* (eds.), *Ireland*

Anderson, M.O., *Kings and Kingship in Early Scotland* (2nd edn., 1980)

Ash, M., 'The Church in the reign of Alexander III', in Reid (ed.), *Alexander III*

Ash, M., 'William Lamberton, bishop of St Andrews, 1297-1328', in Barrow (ed.), *Scottish Tradition*

Ash, M., *The Strange Death of Scottish History* (1980)

Balfour-Melville, E.W.M., *James I, King of Scots, 1406-1437* (London, 1936)

Bannerman, J.W.M., 'The Lordship of the Isles', in Brown (ed.), *Scottish Society*

Bannerman, J.W.M., 'The Scots language and the kin-based society', in D.S. Thomson (ed.), *Gaelic and Scots in Harmony* (Glasgow, 1990)

Bannerman, J.W.M., *Studies in the History of Dalriada* (1974)

Bardgett, F.D., *Scotland Reformed: the Reformation in Angus and the Mearns* (1989)

Barron, E., *The Scottish War of Independence: a Critical Study* (2nd edn., 1934)

Barrow, G.W.S., *The Anglo-Norman Era in Scottish History* (Oxford, 1980)

Barrow, G.W.S., 'Badenoch and Strathspey, 1130-1312', *Northern Scotland*, viii (1988), 1-16; ix (1989), 1-16

Barrow, G.W.S., *David I of Scotland (1124-1153): the Balance of New and Old* (Stenton Lecture, 1984)

Barrow, G.W.S., *The Kingdom of the Scots: Government, Church and Society from the Eleventh to the Fourteenth Century* (London, 1973)

Barrow, G.W.S., *Kingship and Unity: Scotland 1000-1306* (London, 1981)

Barrow, G.W.S., *Robert Bruce and the Community of the Realm of Scotland* (3rd edn., 1988)

Barrow, G.W.S., *Robert Bruce and the Scottish Identity* (Saltire Soc., 1984)

Barrow, G.W.S. (ed.), *The Scottish Tradition: Essays in Honour of Ronald Gordon Cant* (1974)

Baudouin-Matiszek, M.N., 'Henri II et les expéditions françaises en Ecosse', *Bibliothèque de l'Ecole des chartes*, cxlv (1987), 339-82

Berry, S. and Whyte, H. (eds.), *Glasgow Observed* (1987)

Brims, J., 'From reformers to Jacobins: the Scottish Association of the Friends of the People', in Devine (ed.), *Conflict and Stability*

Brown, C., *The Social History of Scottish Religion since 1730* (London, 1987)

Brown J. (ed.), *Scottish Society in the Fifteenth Century* (London, 1977)

Brown, J., 'The social, political and economic influences of the Edinburgh merchant elite, 1600-38' (Edinburgh Ph.D., 1985)

Brown, K., 'Aristocratic finances and the origins of the Scottish Revolution', *Eng. Hist. Rev.*, civ (1989), 43-87

Brown, K., *Bloodfeud in Scotland, 1573-1625* (1986)

Brown, K., 'Noble indebtedness in Scotland between the Reformation and the revolution', *Hist. Research*, lxii (1989), 260-75

Brown, K., 'Playing second fiddle? The nobility and the regal union' (Assoc. Scot. Hist. Studs., 1989)

Brown, S.J., *Thomas Chalmers* (Oxford, 1982)

Buckroyd, J., *Church and State in Scotland, 1660-1681* (1980)

Bumsted, J.M., *The People's Clearance: Highland Emigration to British North America, 1770-1815* (1982)

Burns, J.H. (ed.), *Cambridge History of Medieval Political Thought*, vol. i (Cambridge, 1988)

Campbell, A.B., *The Lanarkshire Miners* (1979)

Campbell, J., 'England, Scotland and the Hundred Years War in the 14th century', in J.R. Hale *et al.* (eds.), *Europe in the Late Middle Ages* (London, 1965)

Campbell, R.H., 'The industrial revolution: a revision article', *SHR* xlvi (1967), 37-55
Campbell, R.H., *The Rise and Fall of Scottish Industry, 1707-1939* (1980)
Campbell, R.H., *Scotland since 1707: the Rise of an Industrial Society* (2nd edn., 1985)
Campbell, R.H. and Skinner, A.S. (eds.), *The Origins and Nature of the Scottish Enlightenment* (1982)
Campbell, T.D., 'Francis Hutcheson: "father" of the Scottish Enlightenment', in Campbell and Skinner (eds.), *Scottish Enlightenment*
Chadwick, H.M., *Early Scotland: the Picts, the Scots and the Welsh of Southern Scotland* (Cambridge, 1949)
Chadwick, S. & O., *Industry and Ethos: Scotland 1832-1914* (2nd edn., 1990)
Chibnall, M., *Anglo-Norman England, 1066-1166* (Oxford, 1986)
Chitnis, A.C., 'Provost Drummond and the origins of Edinburgh medicine'. in Campbell and Skinner (eds.), *Scottish Enlightenment*
Chitnis, A.C., *The Scottish Enlightenment: A Social History* (London, 1976)
Clark, I.D., 'From protest to reaction: the Moderate regime in the Church of Scotland, 1752-1805', in Phillipson and Mitchison (eds.), *Age of Improvement*
Cowan, E.J., *Montrose: For Covenant and King* (London, 1977)
Cowan, E.J., 'Norwegian sunset – Scottish dawn: Hakon IV and Alexander III', in Reid (ed.), *Alexander III*
Cowan, I.B., 'The post-Columban church', *RSCHS* xviii (1974), 245-60
Cowan, I.B., *The Scottish Covenanters* (London, 1976)
Cowan, I.B., *The Scottish Reformation* (London, 1982)
Cowan, I.B. and Easson, D.E. (eds.), *Medieval Religious Houses: Scotland* (1976)
Cowan, I.B. and Shaw, D. (eds.), *The Renaissance and Reformation in Scotland: Essays in Honour of Gordon Donaldson* (1983)
Crawford, B.E., *Scandinavian Scotland: Scotland in the Early Middle Ages* (Leicester, 1987)
Crawford, B.E., 'William Sinclair, earl of Orkney and his family: a study in the politics of survival', in Stringer (ed.), *Nobility*
Cregeen, E., 'The changing role of the house of Argyll', in Phillipson and Mitchison (eds.), *Age of Improvement*
Cruden, S., *Scottish Medieval Churches* (1986)
Daiches, D. (ed.), *A Companion to Scottish Culture* (London, 1981)
Daiches, D. and Jones, P. & J. (eds.), *A Hotbed of Genius: the Scottish Enlightenment, 1730-90* (1986)
Damer, D., 'State, class and housing: Glasgow, 1885-1919', in Melling (ed.), *Housing*
Daunton, M.J., 'Housing', in Thompson (ed.), *Cambridge Social History*, vol. ii
Davies, R.R. (ed.), *The British Isles, 1100-1500* (1988)
Davies, R.R., *Domination and Conquest: The Experience of Ireland, Scotland and Wales, 1100-1300* (Cambridge, 1990)
Devine, T.M. (ed.), *Conflict and Stability in Scottish Society, 1700-1850* (1990)
Devine, T.M. (ed.), *Farm Servants and Labour in Lowland Scotland, 1770-1914* (1984)
Devine, T.M., *The Great Highland Famine* (1988)
Devine, T.M. (ed.), *Improvement and Enlightenment* (1989)
Devine, T.M. (ed.), *Irish Immigrants and Scottish Society in the Nineteenth and Twentieth Centuries* (1991)
Devine, T.M., 'The Union of 1707 and Scottish development', *SESH* v (1985), 23-40
Devine, T.M., 'Urbanisation', in Devine and Mitchison (eds.), *People and Society*, vol. i
Devine, T.M. and Mitchison, R. (eds.), *People and Society in Scotland*, vol. i (1760-1830) (1988)
Dickinson, W.C. and Duncan, A.A.M., *Scotland from the Earliest Times to 1603* (3rd edn., Oxford, 1977)
Dilworth, D., 'The commendator system in Scotland', *IR* xxxvii (1986), 51-72
Dingwall, H., 'The social and economic structure of Edinburgh in the late 17th century' (Edinburgh Ph.D., 1989)
Ditchburn, D., 'Trade with northern Europe, 1297-1540', in Lynch *et al.* (eds.), *Medieval Town*
Dodgshon, R.A., *Land and Society in Early Scotland* (Oxford, 1981)
Donaldson, G., *All the Queen's Men: Power and Politics in Mary Stewart's Scotland* (London, 1983)
Donaldson, G., *Faith of the Scots* (London, 1990)
Donaldson, G., *Scotland: James V to James VII* (1965)
Donaldson, G., *Scottish Church History* (1985)
Donaldson, G., *Scottish Kings* (London, 1967)
Donaldson, G., *The Scottish Reformation* (Cambridge, 1960)
Donnachie, I., Harvie, C. and Wood, I.S. (eds.), *Forward! Labour Politics in Scotland, 1888-1988* (1989)
Dow, F.D., *Cromwellian Scotland* (1979)
Dowden, J., *The Bishops of Scotland* (Glasgow, 1912)
Drummond, A.L. and Bulloch, J., *The Scottish Church, 1688-1843* (1973)
Dunbar, A.H., *Scottish Kings* (2nd edn., 1906)

Duncan, A.A.M. (ed.), *The Acts of Robert I, King of Scots* (1988)

Duncan, A.A.M., 'The community of the realm of Scotland and Robert Bruce', *SHR* xlv (1966)

Duncan, A.A.M., *James I, King of Scots, 1424-1437* (Glasgow, 2nd edn., 1984)

Duncan, A.A.M., *Scotland: the Making of the Kingdom* (1975)

Durie, A., *The Scottish Linen Industry in the Eighteenth Century* (1979)

Durkan, J., 'Education: the laying of fresh foundations', in MacQueen (ed.), *Humanism*

Dwyer, J., *Virtuous Discourse: Sensibility and Community in Late Eighteenth-Century Scotland* (1987)

Dwyer, J. and Murdoch, A., 'Paradigms and politics: manners, morals and the rise of Henry Dundas, 1770-84', in Dwyer *et al.* (eds.), *New Perspectives*

Dwyer, J., Mason, R.A. and Murdoch, A. (eds.), *New Perspectives on the Politics and Culture of Early Modern Scotland* (1982)

Early Sources of Scottish History, AD 500 to 1286, ed. A.O. Anderson (2 vols., London, 1922)

Emond, W.K. 'The minority of King James V, 1513-1528' (St Andrews University Ph.D., 1988)

Ewan, E., *Townlife in Fourteenth-Century Scotland* (1990)

Ferguson, W., *Scotland: 1689 to the Present* (1968)

Ferguson, W., *Scotland's Relations with England: a Survey to 1707* (1977)

Finlay, R.J., '"For or against?"; Scottish nationalists and the British Empire, 1919-39', *SHR* lxxi (1992)

Finlay, R.J., 'The Origins and Development of Scottish Nationalism, 1919-1945' (Edinburgh Ph.D., 1991)

The First Book of Discipline, ed. J.K. Cameron (1972)

Fleming, D.H., *Mary Queen of Scots* (London, 1897)

Flinn, M. (ed.), *Scottish Population History* (Cambridge, 1977)

Forrester, D. and Murray, D. (eds.), *Studies in the History of Worship in Scotland* (1984)

Foster, R.F., *Modern Ireland, 1600-1972* (London, 1988)

Foster, W.R., *The Church before the Covenants* (1975)

Frame, R., *The Political Development of the British Isles, 1100-1400* (Oxford, 1990)

Fraser, W.H., *Conflict and Class: Scottish Workers, 1700-1838* (1988)

Fraser, W.H. and Morris, R.J. (eds.), *People and Society in Scotland*, vol. ii (1830-1914) (1990)

Fry, M., *Patronage and Principle: a Political History of Modern Scotland* (Aberdeen, 1987)

Furgol, E.M., *A Regimental History of the Covenanting Armies, 1639-1651* (1990)

Galbraith, J., 'The Middle Ages', in Forrester and Murray (eds.), *Worship*

Galloway, B., *The Union of England and Scotland, 1603-1608* (1986)

Gibb, A., *Glasgow: the Making of a City* (London, 1983)

Goldie, M., 'The Scottish Catholic Enlightenment', *J. British Studs.*, xxx (1991), 20-62.

Goodare, J., 'Parliament and society in Scotland, 1560-1603', (Edinburgh Univ. Ph.D., 1989)

Goodare, J., 'Parliamentary taxation in Scotland, 1560-1603', *SHR* lxviii (1989), 23-52

Grant, A., *Independence and Nationhood: Scotland 1306-1469* (London, 1984)

Grant, A., 'Scotland's "Celtic fringe" in the late Middle Ages: the MacDonald Lords of the Isles and the kingdom of Scotland', in Davies (ed.), *British Isles*

Grant, I.F., *The Social and Economic Development of Scotland before 1603* (1930)

Gray, M., *The Highland Economy, 1750-1850* (1957)

Hanham, H J., *Scottish Nationalism* (London, 1969)

Hanson, W. and Maxwell, G., *Rome's North-West Frontier: the Antonine Wall* (2nd edn., 1986)

Harvie, C., 'Before the breakthrough, 1888-1922', in Donnachie *et al.* (eds.), *Forward!*

Harvie, C., *No Gods and Precious Few Heroes: Scotland 1914-1980* (London, 1981)

Harvie, C., *Scotland and Nationalism* (London, 1977)

Henderson, I., 'Pictish art and the Book of Kells', in Whitelock *et al.* (eds.), *Ireland*

Henderson, I., *The Picts* (London, 1967)

Herbert, M., *Iona, Kells and Derry* (Oxford, 1989)

Hewison, J.K., *The Covenanters*, 2 vols. (Glasgow, 1913)

Hook A. (ed.), *History of Scottish Literature*, vol. ii (Aberdeen, 1987)

Hopkins, P., *Glencoe and the End of the Highland War* (1986)

Horsey, M., *Tenements and Towers: Glasgow Working-Class Housing, 1890-1990* (1990)

Houston, R.A. and Whyte, I.D. (eds.), *Scottish Society, 1500-1800* (Cambridge, 1989)

Howell, D., *A Lost Left: Three Studies in Socialism and Nationalism* (London, 1986)

Hunter, J., *The Making of the Crofting Community* (1976)

Hutchison, I.G.C., *A Political History of Scotland, 1832-1924* (1986)

Hutton, R., *Charles II* (Oxford, 1989)

Jack, R. (ed.), *The History of Scottish Literature*, vol. i (Aberdeen, 1988)

Johnson, C., *Developments in the Roman Catholic Church in Scotland, 1789-1829* (1983)

Kapelle, W.E., *The Norman Conquest of the North: the Region and its Transformation, 1000-1135* (London, 1979)

Kearney, H., *The British Isles* (Cambridge, 1989)
Kellas, J.G., *Modern Scotland* (2nd edn., London, 1980)
Keppie, L., *Scotland's Roman Remains* (1986)
Kirby, D.P., 'Bede and the Pictish church', *IR* xxiv (1973), 6-25
Kirk, J., *Patterns of Reform: Continuity and Change in the Reformation Kirk* (1989)
Knox, W., (ed.), *Scottish Labour Leaders, 1918-39: a Biographical Dictionary* (1984)
Lang, A., *Sir George Mackenzie of Rosehaugh* (London, 1909)
Larner, C., *Enemies of God: the Witch-Hunt in Scotland* (London, 1981)
Lee, M., *Government by Pen: Scotland under James VI and I* (Chicago, 1980)
Lee, M., *Great Britain's Solomon: James VI and I in his Three Kingdoms* (Chicago, 1990)
Lee, M., *The Road to Revolution: Scotland under Charles I, 1625-37* (Chicago, 1985)
Lenman, B., *An Economic History of Modern Scotland* (London, 1977)
Lenman, B., *Integration, Enlightenment and Industrialization: Scotland 1746-1832* (London, 1981)
Lenman, B., *The Jacobite Clans of the Great Glen, 1650-1784* (London, 1984)
Lenman, B., *The Jacobite Risings in Britain, 1689-1746* (London, 1980)
Levack, B.P., *The Formation of the British State: England, Scotland and the Union, 1603-1707* (Oxford, 1987)
Levitt. I. (ed.), *Government and Social Conditions in Scotland, 1845-1919* (SHS, 1988)
Levitt, I. and Smout, T.C. (eds.), *The State of the Scottish Working Class in 1843* (1979)
Logue, K.J., *Popular Disturbances in Scotland, 1780-1815* (1979)
Lynch, M., 'Calvinism in Scotland, 1559-1638', in M. Prestwich (ed.), *International Calvinism, 1541-1715* (Oxford, 1985)
Lynch, M., 'Continuity and change in urban society, 1500-1700', in Houston and Whyte (eds.), *Scottish Society*
Lynch, M. (ed.), *The Early Modern Town in Scotland* (London, 1987)
Lynch, M., *Edinburgh and the Reformation* (1981)
Lynch, M. (ed.), *Mary Stewart: Queen in Three Kingdoms* (Oxford, 1988)
Lynch, M., 'Queen Mary's triumph', *SHR* lxix (1990), 1-21.
Lynch, M., 'Towns and townspeople in 15th century Scotland', in J.A.F. Thomson (ed.), *Towns and Townspeople in the Fifteenth Century* (Gloucester, 1988)
Lynch, M., 'Whatever happened to the medieval burgh?', *SESH* iv (1984), 5-20
Lynch, M., Spearman, R.M. and Stell, G. (eds.), *The Scottish Medieval Town* (1988)
Lythe, S.G.E., *The Economy of Scotland in its European Setting, 1550-1625* (1960)
Lythe, S.G.E. and Butt, J., *An Economic History of Scotland, 1100-1939* (Glasgow, 1975)
McCaffrey, J.F., 'Irish issues in the 19th and 20th century: radicalism in a Scottish context', in Devine (ed.), *Irish Immigrants*
McCaffrey, J.F., 'Irish immigrants and radical movements in the West of Scotland in the early 19th century', *IR* xxxix (1988), 46-60
Macdougall, I. (ed.), *Essays in Scottish Labour History* (1978)
Macdougall, N. (ed.), *Church, Politics and Society: Scotland 1408-1929* (1983)
Macdougall, N., *James III: a Political Study* (1982)
Macdougall, N., *James IV* (1989)
Macdougall, N., 'The kingship of James IV of Scotland', *History Today* (Nov., 1984), 30-6
Macfarlane, L.J., *William Elphinstone and the Kingdom of Scotland, 1431-1514* (Aberdeen, 1985)
McGladdery, C., *James II* (1990)
McGrath, E., 'Local heroes: the Scottish humanist Parnassus for Charles I', in E. Chaney and P. Mack (eds.), *England and the Continental Renaissance: Essays in Honour of J.B. Trapp* (London, 1990)
Machin, G.I.T., *Politics and the Churches in Great Britain, 1832-1868* (Oxford, 1977)
Macinnes, A.I., *Charles I and the Making of the Covenanting Movement, 1625-41* (1991)
Macinnes, A.I., 'Scottish Gaeldom: the first phase of Clearance', in Devine and Mitchison (eds.), *People and Society*
Macinnes, J., *The Evangelical Movement in the Highlands of Scotland, 1668-1800* (Aberdeen, 1951)
Mackay, M. (ed.), *The Rev Dr John Walker's Report on the Hebrides of 1764 and 1771* (1980)
Mackie, R.L., *King James IV of Scotland* (1958)
MacLean, I., *The Legend of Red Clydeside* (1983)
McLean, I., 'Red Clydeside, 1915-1919', in R. Quinnalt and J. Stevenson (eds.), *Popular Protest and Public Order* (London, 1974)
MacLean, L. (ed.), *The Middle Ages in the Highlands* (Inverness, 1981)
McLynn, F., *France and the Jacobite Rising of 1745* (1981)
McLynn, F., *The Jacobite Army in England, 1745* (1983)
McLynn, F., *The Jacobites* (London, 1985)
McNeill, P.G.B. and Nicholson, R. (eds.), *An Historical Atlas of Scotland, c.400-c.1600* (St Andrews,

1975)

McNeill, P.G.B. (ed.), *An Atlas of Scottish History to 1707* (1993)

MacQueen, J. (ed.), *Humanism in Renaissance Scotland* (1990)

McRoberts, D. (ed.), *Essays on the Scottish Reformation*, (Glasgow, 1962)

McRoberts, D. (ed.), *The Medieval Church of St Andrews* (Glasgow, 1976)

McRoberts, D., 'The Scottish Church and nationalism in the 15th century', *IR* xix (1968), 3-14

McShane, H. and Smith, J., *No Mean Fighter* (London, 1978)

Makey, W.H., *The Church of the Covenant, 1637-1651: Revolution and Social Change in Scotland* (1979)

Marshall, G., *Presbyteries and Profits: Calvinism and the Development of Capitalism in Scotland, 1560-1707* (Oxford, 1980)

Marshall, R., *The Days of Duchess Anne* (London, 1973)

Mason, R.A. (ed.), *Scotland and England, 1286-1815* (1987)

Maxwell, G., *Rome's North-West Frontier: the Antonine Wall* (2nd edn., 1986)

Meek, D.E. and Kirk, J., 'John Carswell', superintendent of Argyll: a reassessment', *RSCHS* xix (1975), 1-22

Meikle, H., *Some Aspects of Later Seventeenth Century Scotland* (Glasgow, 1947)

Meikle, M., 'Lairds and gentlemen: a study of the landed families of the eastern Anglo-Scottish borders, 1540-1603' (Edinburgh Ph.D., 1989)

Melling, J., (ed.), *Housing, Social Policy and the State* (London, 1980)

Menzies, G. (ed.), *Who are the Scots?* (London, 1971)

Merriman, M.H., 'Mary, Queen of France', in Lynch (ed.), *Mary Stewart*

Middlemas, R.K., *The Clydesiders* (London, 1965)

Miller, W.L., *The End of British Politics? Scots and English Political Behaviour in the Seventies* (Oxford, 1981)

Mitchison, R., 'The government and the Highlands, 1707-1745', in Phillipson and Mitchison (eds.), *Age of Improvement*

Mitchison, R., 'The Highland Clearances', *SESH* i (1981), 4-24

Mitchison, R., *A History of Scotland* (2nd edn., London, 1982)

Mitchison, R., *Lordship to Patronage: Scotland 1625-1746* (London, 1983)

Mitchison, R. (ed.), *The Roots of Nationalism* (1980)

Mitchison, R., 'Scotland, 1750-1850', in Thompson (ed.), *Cambridge Social History*, vol. i

Mitchison, R. (ed.), *Why Scottish History Matters* (Saltire Soc., 1991)

Morgan, K.O., *Keir Hardie* (London, 1975)

Mullan, D.G., *Episcopacy in Scotland, 1560-1638* (1986)

Munro, R.W., 'The clan system; fact or fiction?', in MacLean (ed.), *Middle Ages in Highlands*

Munro, R.W., *Highland Clans and Tartans* (London, 1977)

Murdoch, A., *The People Above: Politics and Administration in Mid-Eighteenth Century Scotland* (1980)

Murison, D., 'Linguistic relationships in medieval Scotland', in Barrow (ed.), *Scottish Tradition*

Nenadic, S., 'The rise of the urban middle class', in Fraser and Morris (eds.), *People and Society*

Nicholson, R., *Edward III and the Scots, 1327-1335* (Oxford, 1965)

Nicholson, R., *Scotland: The Later Middle Ages* (1974)

Ó Corrain, D., *Ireland before the Normans* (Dublin, 1972)

Ó Corrain, D., 'Irish regnal succession: a reappraisal', *Studia Hibernica*, xi (1971), 7-39.

Ouston, H., 'York in Edinburgh: James VII and the patronage of learning in Scotland, 1679-1688', in Dwyer *et al.* (eds.), *New Perspectives*

Parry, M.L. and Slater, T.R. (eds.), *The Making of the Scottish Countryside* (London, 1980)

Phillipson, N.T. and Mitchison, R. (eds.), *Scotland in the Age of Improvement* (1970)

Prebble, J., *The King's Jaunt: George IV in Scotland, 1822* (London, 1988)

Prestwich, M., *War, Politics and Finance under Edward I* (London, 1972)

Pryde, G.S., *The Burghs of Scotland: A Critical List* (Glasgow, 1965)

Rae, T.I., 'The origins of the Advocates' Library', in P. Cadell and A. Matheson (eds.), *For the Encouragement of Learning* (1989)

Rae, T.I. (ed.), *The Union of 1707: its Impact on Scotland* (1974)

Reid, N. (ed.), *Scotland in the Reign of Alexander III* (1990)

Rendall, J. *The Origins of the Scottish Enlightenment* (London, 1978)

Reynolds, S., *Kingdoms and Communities in Western Europe, 900-1300* (Oxford, 1984)

Richards, E., *A History of the Highland Clearances*, 2 vols. (London, 1982, 1985)

Riley, P.W.J., *The English Ministers and Scotland, 1707-1727* (London, 1964)

Riley, P.W.J., *King William and the Scottish Politicians* (1979)

Riley, P.W.J., *The Union of England and Scotland* (Manchester, 1978)

Ripley, B.J. and McHugh, J., *John Maclean* (Manchester, 1989)

Robbins, K., *The Eclipse of a Great Power: Modern Britain, 1870-1975* (London, 1983)

Robbins, K., *Nineteenth-Century Britain. England, Scotland and Wales: the Making of a Nation* (Oxford, 1988)

Robertson, J., *The Scottish Enlightenment and the Militia Issue* (1985)

Rodger, R. (ed.), *Scottish Housing in the Twentieth Century* (Leicester, 1989)

Roots, I. (ed.), *Into Another Mould: Aspects of the Interregnum* (London, 1981)

Russell, C., 'The British problem and the English Civil War', *History*, lxxii (1987), 395-415

Sanderson, J.M., 'Two Stewarts of the sixteenth century', *The Stewarts*, xvii (1984), 25-46

Sanderson, M., *Cardinal of Scotland: David Beaton c.1494-1546* (1986)

Sanderson, M., *Scottish Rural Society in the Sixteenth Century* (1982)

Sanderson, M., 'Some aspects of the church in Scottish society in the era of the Reformation', *RSCHS* xvii (1970), 81-98

Scott, P.H., *1707: The Union of Scotland and England* (1979)

Scottish Annals from English Chroniclers, ed. A.O. Anderson (London, 1908)

Scottish Historical Documents, ed. G. Donaldson (1970)

The Second Book of Discipline, ed. J. Kirk (1980)

Sellar, W.D.H., 'The origins and ancestry of Somerled', *SHR* xlv (1966), 123-42

Shaw, J.S., *The Management of Scottish Society, 1707-1764* (1983)

Simpson, J., 'Who steered the gravy train, 1707-1766?', in Phillipson and Mitchison (eds.), *Age of Improvement*

Skene, W.F., *Celtic Scotland*, 3 vols. (1886-90)

Small, A., 'Dark Age Scotland', in Whittington and Whyte (eds.), *Historical Geography*

Smith, A., *Jacobite Estates of the Forty-Five* (1982)

Smith, J.M., 'Commonsense thought and working class consciousness: some aspects of the Glasgow and Liverpool Labour Movements in the early years of the twentieth century' (Edinburgh Ph.D., 1980)

Smith, L.M., 'Scotland and Cromwell: a study in early modern government' (Oxford D.Phil., 1979)

Smout, T.C., *A Century of the Scottish People, 1830-1950* (London, 1986)

Smout, T.C., *A History of the Scottish People, 1560-1830* (London, 1969)

Smout, T.C., 'Problems of nationalism, identity and Improvement in later 18th-century Scotland', in Devine (ed.), *Improvement and Enlightenment*

Smout, T.C., 'The road to union', in G. Holmes (ed.), *Britain after the Glorious Revolution, 1689-1714* (London, 1969)

Smout, T.C., 'Scotland, 1750-1850', in Thompson (ed.), *Cambridge Social History*, vol. i

Smout, T.C. (ed.), *Scotland and Europe, 1200-1850* (1986)

Smout, T.C., *Scottish Trade on the Eve of Union, 1660-1707* (1963)

Smout, T.C. (ed.), *The Search for Wealth and Stability: Essays in Economic and Social History presented to M.W. Flinn* (London, 1979)

Smout, T.C., 'Where had the Scottish economy got to by the third quarter of the 18th century?', in I. Hont and M. Ignatieff (eds.), *Wealth and Virtue: The Shaping of Political Economy in the Scottish Enlightenment* (Cambridge, 1982)

Smyth, A., *Warlords and Holy Men: Scotland AD 80-1000* (London, 1984)

A Source Book of Scottish History, ed. W.C. Dickinson, G. Donaldson and I.A. Milne, 3 vols. (2nd edn., 1958-61)

Steer, K.A. and Bannerman, J.W.M., *Late Medieval Monumental Sculpture in the West Highlands* (1977)

Stevenson, A., 'Trade with the south, 1070-1513', in Lynch et al. (eds.), *Medieval Town*

Stevenson, D., *Alasdair MacColla and the Highland Problem in the Seventeenth Century* (1980)

Stevenson, D., 'The burghs and the Scottish Revolution', in Lynch (ed.), *Early Modern Town*

Stevenson, D. (ed.), *The Government of Scotland under the Covenanters, 1637-1651* (SHS, 1982)

Stevenson, D., *Revolution and Counter-Revolution in Scotland, 1644-1651* (London, 1977)

Stevenson, D., *The Scottish Revolution, 1637-44* (Newton Abbot, 1973)

Stones, E.L.G. (ed.), *Anglo-Scottish Relations, 1174-1328* (Oxford, 1965)

Stones, E.L.G. and Simpson, G.G. (eds.), *Edward I and the Throne of Scotland, 1290-1296*, 2 vols. (Oxford, 1978)

Stringer, K.J., *Earl David of Huntingdon, 1151-1219: a Study in Anglo-Scottish History* (1985)

Stringer, K.J. (ed.), *Essays on the Nobility of Medieval Scotland* (1985)

The Sunday Mail Story of Scotland, 52 issues, (Glasgow, 1988)

Sunter, R.M., *Patronage and Politics in Scotland, 1707-1832* (1986)

Teichgraeber, R.F., 'Politics and Morals in the Scottish Enlightenment' (University of Brandeis Ph.D., 1978)

Thomas, C., *Christianity in Roman Britain to AD 500* (London, 1981)

Thomas, C., *The Early Christian Archaeology of North Britain* (London, 1971)

Thomas, G.D., 'Excavations at the Roman civil settlement at Inveresk, 1976-7', *PSAS* cxviii (1988), 139-79

Thompson, F.M.L. (ed.), *The Cambridge Social History of Britain, 1750-1950*, 3 vols. (1990)

Thomson, D.S. (ed.), *The Companion to Gaelic Scotland* (London, 1983)

Thomson, J.A.F., 'Innocent VIII and the Scottish Church', *IR* xix (1968), 23-31

Torrie, E.P.D., *Medieval Dundee* (Abertay Hist. Soc., 1990)

Tuck, A., *Crown and Nobility, 1272-1461: Political Conflict in Late Medieval England* (Oxford, 1986)

Vita Edwardi Secundi, ed. N. Denholm-Young (London, 1957)

Wainwright, F.T. (ed.), *The Problem of the Picts* (1955)

Walker, W.M., *Juteopolis: Dundee and its Textile Workers, 1885-1923* (1979)

Watson, W.J., *History of the Celtic Place-Names of Scotland* (1926)

Watt, D.E.R., 'Scottish university men of the 13th and 14th centuries', in Smout (ed.), *Scotland and Europe*

Webb, K., *The Growth of Nationalism in Scotland* (Glasgow, 1977)

Whatley, C.A., 'Economic causes and consequences of the Union of 1707: a survey', *SHR* lxviii (1989), 150-81

Whatley, C.A., *The Salt Industry and its Trade in Fife and Tayside, 1570-1850* (Abertay Hist. Soc., 1984)

Whitelock, D. *et al.* (eds.), *Ireland in Early Medieval Europe* (Cambridge, 1982)

Whittington, G. and Whyte, I.D. (eds.), *An Historical Geography of Scotland* (London, 1983)

Whyte, I.D., *Agriculture and Society in Seventeenth Century Scotland* (1979)

Whyte, I.D., 'The occupational structure of Scottish burghs in the late 17th century', in Lynch (ed.), *Early Modern Town*

Williamson, A.H., *Scottish National Consciousness in the Age of James VI* (1979)

Wilson, T., *The Downfall of the Liberal Party, 1914-1935* (London, 1968)

Withers, C.W.J., *Gaelic Scotland: the Transformation of a Culture Region* (London, 1988)

Wodrow Miscellany (Wodrow Soc., 1844)

Wood, I.S., 'John Wheatley, the Irish and the Labour movement in Scotland', *IR* xxxi (1980), 71-85

Wormald, J., *Court, Kirk and Community: Scotland, 1470-1625* (London, 1981)

Wormald, J., 'The first king of Britain', in L. Smith (ed.), *The Making of Britain: The Age of Expansion* (London, 1986)

Wormald, J., *Lords and Men in Scotland: Bonds of Manrent, 1442-1603* (1985)

Wormald, J., *Mary Queen of Scots: a Study in Failure* (London, 1988)

Wormald, J. (ed.), *Scotland Revisited* (London, 1991)

Wormald, J., 'Taming the magnates', in Stringer (ed.), *Nobility*

Young, A., 'Noble families and political factions in the reign of Alexander III', in Reid (ed.), *Alexander III*

Youngson, A.J., *The Making of Classical Edinburgh* (1966)

KINGS OF SCOTS 843 - 1286

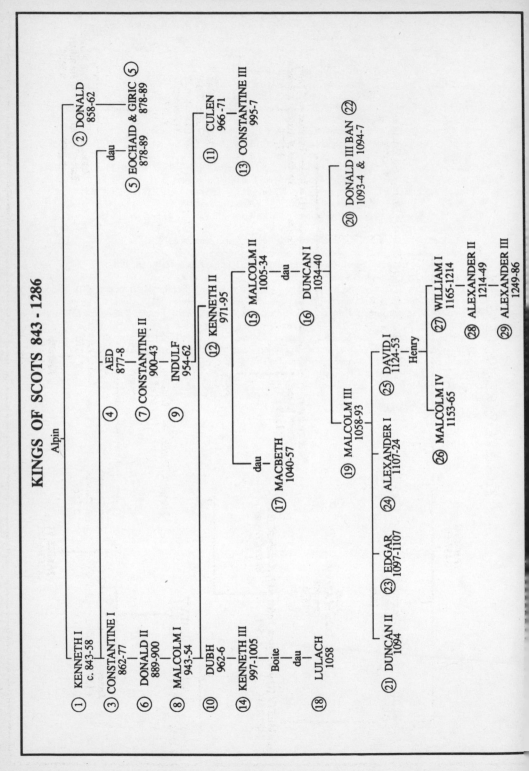

Alpin

① KENNETH I c. 843-58
② DONALD 858-62

③ CONSTANTINE I 862-77
④ AED 877-8
dau
⑤ EOCHAID & GIRIC 878-89 ⑤

⑥ DONALD II 889-900
⑦ CONSTANTINE II 900-43

⑧ MALCOLM I 943-54
⑨ INDULF 954-62

⑩ DUBH 962-6
⑪ CULEN 966-71

⑫ KENNETH II 971-95
⑬ CONSTANTINE III 995-7

⑭ KENNETH III 997-1005
⑮ MALCOLM II 1005-34

Boite
dau
⑯ DUNCAN I 1034-40

⑰ MACBETH 1040-57
dau

⑱ LULACH 1058
⑲ MALCOLM III 1058-93
⑳ DONALD III BAN 1093-4 & 1094-7

㉑ DUNCAN II 1094
㉓ EDGAR 1097-1107
㉔ ALEXANDER I 1107-24
㉕ DAVID I 1124-53

Henry

㉖ MALCOLM IV 1153-65
㉗ WILLIAM I 1165-1214

㉘ ALEXANDER II 1214-49
㉙ ALEXANDER III 1249-86

492

THE STEWART SUCCESSION

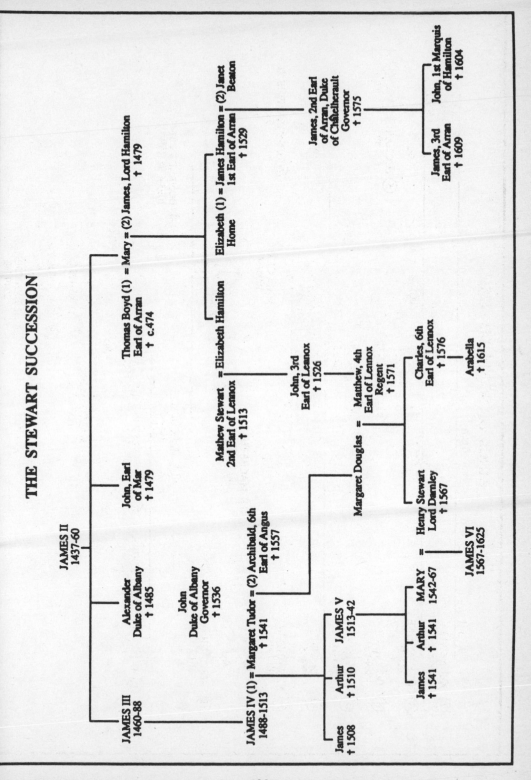

Index